Fodor's 2003

W9-CNS-083

Paris

The Guide
for All Budgets

Completely
Updated

Where to Stay, Eat,
and Explore

On and Off
the Beaten Path

When to Go,
What to Pack

Maps, Travel Tips,
and Web Sites

Fodor's Travel Publications • New York, Toronto, London, Sydney, Auckland
www.fodors.com

Fodor's Paris 2003

EDITOR: Robert I. C. Fisher

Editorial Contributors: Simon Hewitt, Rosa Jackson, Nicola Keegan, Christopher Mooney

Editorial Production: Tom Holton

Maps: David Lindroth, *cartographer;* Bob Blake and Rebecca Baer, *map editors*

Design: Fabrizio La Rocca, *creative director;* Guido Caroti, *art director;* Jolie Novak, *senior picture editor;* Melanie Marin, *photo editor*

Cover Design: Pentagram

Production/Manufacturing: Angela L. McLean

Cover Photograph: Robert Holmes/Corbis (Right Bank book stall)

Copyright

ISBN 1-4000-1037-3

ISSN 0149-1288

Important Tip

Although all prices, opening times, and other details in this book are based on information supplied to us at press time, changes occur all the time in the travel world, and Fodor's cannot accept responsibility for facts that become outdated or for inadvertent errors or omissions. So **always confirm information when it matters,** especially if you're making a detour to visit a specific place.

Special Sales

Fodor's Travel Publications are available at special discounts for bulk purchases for sales promotions or premiums. Special editions, including personalized covers, excerpts of existing guides, and corporate imprints, can be created in large quantities for special needs. For more information, contact your local bookseller or write to Special Markets, Fodor's Travel Publications, 280 Park Avenue, New York, NY 10017. Inquiries from Canada should be directed to your local Canadian bookseller or sent to Random House of Canada, Ltd., Marketing Department, 2775 Matheson Boulevard East, Mississauga, Ontario L4W 4P7. Inquiries from the United Kingdom should be sent to Fodor's Travel Publications, 20 Vauxhall Bridge Road, London SW1V 2SA, England.

CONTENTS

Maps and Plans

ON THE ROAD WITH FODOR'S

A TRIP TAKES YOU OUT OF YOURSELF. Concerns of life at home completely disappear, driven away by more immediate thoughts—about, say, what marvels will beguile the next day, or where you'll have dinner. That's where Fodor's comes in. We make sure that you know all your options, so that you don't miss something that's around the next bend just because you didn't know it was there. Mindful that the best memories of your trip might have nothing to do with what you came to Paris to see, we guide you to sights large and small all over town. You might set out to conquer the Louvre, but back at home you find yourself unable to forget shuddering through a tour of Paris's immortal Catacombs or the night you karaoked your heart out to Edith Piaf's "La Vie en Rose." With Fodor's team of endearingly picky know-it-alls at your side, serendipitous discoveries are never far away.

Simon Hewitt headed to Paris straight from studying French and art history at Oxford. It was a return to base: His grandmother was French, as are his wife and daughter. He moved to Versailles a few years ago to gain a different perspective on life in and around the French capital. When not contemplating the Sun King's bicep-flexing Baroque, his thoughts often turn to cricket—he is captain of the French national team.

Nicola Keegan was born in Ireland and raised in Iowa. But after spending one year at the Sorbonne, she knew Paris was going to be her home forever. Now famous for crossing the city on foot even in the worst storms, and her uncanny knowledge of where to purchase absolute necessities from truffle oil to that perfect pair of gold-hued boots, she brings all her hard earned "savoir faire" to the Shopping and Sports chapters, as well as the Smart Travel Tips section.

Nancy Coons has lived in France for many years and has written many books for Fodor's, including *Provence and the Côte d'Azur, Escape to Provence,* and *Escape to the Riviera.*

Robert I. C. Fisher, New York City–based editor of *Fodor's Paris 2003,* succeeded in getting one foot in the caviar when he was sent to the French capital to write up the Hôtel Lambert—the noted Ile St-Louis residence of Baron and Baroness Guy de Rothschild—for the April 1988 issue of *Town & Country.* He still fondly recalls a pre-dawn hike up to the Sacré-Coeur to catch the sun come up over Paris.

Rosa Jackson's love affair with French pastries began at age four, when she spent her first year in Paris before returning to the Canadian north. Early experiments with eclairs and croissants led her to enroll in the Paris Cordon Bleu, where she learned that even great chefs make mistakes. A food writer for the past ten years and a Parisian since 1995, Rosa has eaten in hundreds of Paris restaurants—and always has room for dessert.

Christopher Mooney originally came to Paris to study French philosophy, smoke Gîtanes cigarettes, and hang out in cafés. Twelve years later he's still there, but his taste for Gallic thought and tobacco has given way to an unslakeable thirst for fine Burgundy vintages. For this edition, this passionate writer (his pet computer often doubles as an additional pillow when he's traveling on the road to update *Fodor's France*) devoted his efforts to finding the best Parisian hotels and also added his special brand of wit and charm to the What's Where section in Chapter 1.

Don't Forget to Write

Your experiences—positive and negative—matter to us. We follow up on all suggestions. Contact the Paris editor at editors@fodors.com or c/o Fodor's, 280 Park Avenue, New York, NY 10017. Have a fabulous trip!

Karen Cure
Editorial Director

Paris with Arrondissements

Paris Métro

ESSENTIAL INFORMATION

Half the fun of traveling is looking forward to your trip—but when you look forward, don't just daydream. Making plans and finding out about your destination might sound like serious work, but it means you won't squander valuable holiday-time organizing everyday minutiae once you've arrived. You won't lose spontaneity by planning ahead either, because you'll hit the ground a bit less of a tourist and a bit more streetwise, freeing up your time to explore the aspects of Paris that drew you here in the first place. The information in this chapter will give you helpful pointers on many of the questions that arise when planning your trip. In addition, the organizations listed in this section will supplement the information in this guidebook.

ADDRESSES

Addresses in Paris are fairly straightforward: There is the number, the street name and, often, the location in one of Paris's 20 arrondissements (districts); for instance, Paris 75010 or, simply, the last two digits, 10ᵉ, each of which indicates that the address is in the 10th. Due to its large size, the 16ᵉ arrondissement has two numbers assigned to it: 75016 and 75116. For the layout of Paris's arrondissements, consult the map at the end of this section. They are laid out in a spiral, beginning from the area around the Louvre (1ᵉʳ arrondissement), then moving clockwise through the Marais, the Quartier Latin, St-Germain, and then out from the city center to the outskirts until it reaches Menilmontant/Père-Lachaise (20ᵉ arrondissement). Occasionally you may see an address with a number plus *bis*—for instance, 20 bis rue Vavin. This indicates that 20 bis is the next entrance or door down from 20 rue Vavin. Please note that in France, you enter a building on the ground floor, or *rez-de-chausée* (RC or 0),

and go up one floor to the first floor, or *premier étage*. General address terms used in this book to keep in mind are: *av.* (abbreviation for avenue); *bd.* (abbreviation for boulevard); *carrefour* (crossway); *cours* (promenade); *passage* (passageway); *quai* (quay/wharf/pier); *rue* (street); *sq.* (abbreviation for square).

AIR TRAVEL

TO AND FROM PARIS

As one of the premier destinations in the world, Paris is serviced by a great many international carriers and a surprisingly large number of U.S.-based airlines. **Air France** is the French flag carrier and offers numerous flights (often several per day) between Paris's Charles de Gaulle airport and New York City's JFK airport; Newark, New Jersey; Washington, D.C.'s Reagan airport; as well as the cities of Miami, Chicago, Houston, San Francisco, Los Angeles, Toronto, Montréal, and Mexico City. American-based carriers are usually less expensive but offer, on the whole, fewer nonstop direct flights. **Delta Airlines** is a popular U.S.–France carrier; its departures to Paris leave from Atlanta, Cincinnati, and New York City's JFK, while Delta's regional flights link airports through the southeast United States and the Midwest with its main international hub in Atlanta. Travelers in the northeast and southwest of the United States often use **Continental Airlines,** whose nonstop Paris flights generally depart from Newark and Houston; in peak season, they often offer daily departures. Another popular carrier is **United Airlines,** with nonstop flights to Paris from Chicago; Washington, D.C.; and San Francisco. **American Airlines** also offers daily nonstop flights to Paris's Orly airport from numerous cities, including New York City's JFK, Boston, Miami, Chicago, and Dallas/Fort Worth. **Northwest** offers a daily departure to Paris from its hub in Detroit; connections from Seattle, Minneapolis, and numerous other airports link up to Detroit. In Canada, Air France and **Air Canada** are the leading choices for departures from Toronto and Montréal; in peak season, departures are often on a daily basis. From London, Air France, **British Airways,** and **British Midland** are the leading carriers, with up to 15 flights daily in peak season. In addition, direct routes link Manchester, Edinburgh, and Southampton with Paris. Considering the expense of this short flight, however, more and more travelers are using train transport via the Eurostar Express through the Channel Tunnel. Options are more limited for travelers to Paris from Australia and New Zealand, who usually wind up taking British Airways and **Qantas** flights to London, then connections to Paris.

BOOKING

When you book **look for nonstop flights** and **remember that "direct" flights stop at least once.** Try to avoid connecting flights, which require a change of plane. For more booking tips and to check prices and make on-line flight reservations, log on to www.fodors.com.

CARRIERS

➤ MAJOR AIRLINES: **Air Canada** (☎ 800/776–3000 in the U.S. and Canada). **Air France** (☎ 800/237–2747 in the U.S.; 08–02–80–28–02 in France, WEB www.airfrance.com). **American Airlines** (☎ 800/433–7300 in the U.S.; 01–69–32–73–07 in France, WEB www.aa.com). **British Airways** (☎ 800/247–9297 in the U.S.; 0345/222111 in the U.K.; 08–25–82–54–00 in France, WEB www.britishairways.com). **Continental** (☎ 800/231–0856 in the U.S.; 01–42–99–09–09 in France, WEB www.continental.com). **Delta** (☎ 800/241–4141 in the U.S.; 08–00–35–40–80 in France, WEB www.delta.com). **Northwest** (☎ 800/225–2525 in the U.S.; 01–42–66–90–00 in France, WEB www.klm.com). **Qantas** (☎ 800/227–4500 in the U.S.; 08–03–84–68–46 in France, WEB www.qantas.com). **United** (☎ 800/538–2929 in the U.S.; 08–

01–72–72–72 in France, WEB www.unitedairlines.com). **US Airways** (☎ 800/428–4322 in the U.S.; 08–20–30–49–23 in France, WEB www.usairways.com).

➤ TRAVEL BETWEEN THE U.K. AND FRANCE: **Air France** (☎ 020/8742–6600 in the U.K.; 08–02–80–28–02 in France, WEB www.airfrance.com). **British Airways** (☎ 0345/222–111 in the U.K.; 08–02–80–29–02 in France, WEB www.britishairways.com). **British Midland** (☎ 020/8754–7321; 0345/554–554 in the U.K.; 01–48–62–55–65 in France, WEB www.british-midland.com).

➤ TRAVEL WITHIN FRANCE: **Air France** (☎ 800/237–2747 in the U.S.; 08–02–80–28–02 in France, WEB www.airfrance.com). **Air Liberté** (☎ 08–03–80–58–05, WEB www.air-liberte.fr).

CHECK-IN AND BOARDING

You can save on air travel within Europe if you plan on traveling to and from Paris aboard Air France. If you **sign up for Air France's Euro Flyer program,** you can buy between three and nine flight coupons, valid on the airline's flights to more than 100 European cities. At $120 each (April–October) and $99 each (November–March), these coupons are a good deal, and the fine print still allows you plenty of freedom.

Most carriers require you to check in two hours before your scheduled departure time for domestic flights and 2½ to 3 hours before international flights. Always **ask your carrier about its check-in policy.**

On the assumption that not everyone with a ticket will show up, airlines routinely overbook their flights. However, when everyone does show up, airlines ask for volunteers to give up their seats. In return, these volunteers usually get a certificate for a free flight and are rebooked on the next flight out. If there are not enough volunteers, the airline must choose who will be denied boarding. The first to get bumped are passengers who checked in late and those flying on discounted tickets, so **get to the gate and check in as early as possible,** especially during peak periods.

Always **bring a government-issued photo ID to the airport;** a passport is best. You may be asked to show it before you are allowed to check in.

CUTTING COSTS

The least expensive airfares to Paris must usually be purchased in advance and are nonrefundable. It's smart to **call a number of airlines, and when you are quoted a good price, book it on the spot**—the same fare may not be available even the very next day. Always **check different routings** and look into using different airports. Travel agents, especially low-fare specialists, can be helpful.

Consolidators are another good source. They buy tickets for scheduled international flights at reduced rates from the airlines, then sell them at prices that beat the airlines' own best fares, usually without restrictions. Sometimes you can even get your money back if you need to return the ticket. Carefully read the fine print detailing penalties for changes and cancellations, and **confirm your consolidator reservation with the airline.**

When you **fly as a courier,** you trade your checked-luggage space for a ticket deeply subsidized by a courier service. There are restrictions on when you can book and how long you can stay.

➤ CONSOLIDATORS: **Cheap Tickets** (☎ 800/377–1000, WEB www. cheaptickets.com). **Discount Airline Ticket Service** (☎ 800/576–1600). **Unitravel** (☎ 800/325–2222, WEB www.unitravel.com). **Up & Away Travel** (☎ 212/889–2345, WEB www.upandaway.com). **World Travel Network** (☎ 800/409–6753).

➤ COURIERS: **Air Courier Association** (✉ 15000 W. 6th Ave., Suite 203, Golden, CO 80401, ☎ 800/282–1202, WEB www.aircourier.org). **International Association of Air Travel Couriers** (✉ 220 S. Dixie Hwy. No. 3, Box 1349, Lake Worth, FL 33460, ☎ 561/582–8320, FAX 561/582–1581, WEB www.courier.org).

ENJOYING THE FLIGHT

For more legroom, **request an emergency-aisle seat.** Don't sit in the row in front of the emergency aisle or in front of a bulkhead, where seats may not recline. If you have dietary concerns, **ask for special meals when booking your flight.** These can be vegetarian, for example, or low-cholesterol, or kosher. On long flights, try to maintain a normal routine, to help fight jet lag. At night, **get some sleep.** By day, **eat light meals, drink water** (not alcohol), and **move around the cabin** to stretch your legs. For additional jet-lag tips consult *Fodor's FYI: Travel Fit & Healthy* (available at bookstores everywhere).

FLYING TIMES

Flying time to Paris is 7 hours from New York, 9½ hours from Chicago, and 11 hours from Los Angeles. Flying time from the United Kingdom to Paris is 1½ hours.

HOW TO COMPLAIN

If your baggage goes astray or your flight goes awry, complain right away. Most carriers require that you **file a claim immediately.**

➤ AIRLINE COMPLAINTS: U.S. Department of Transportation **Aviation Consumer Protection Division** (✉ C-75, Room 4107, Washington, DC 20590, ☎ 202/366–2220, WEB www.dot.gov/airconsumer). **Federal Aviation Administration Consumer Hotline** (☎ 800/322–7873).

AIRPORTS AND TRANSFERS

The major airports are Charles de Gaulle (also known as Roissy), 26 km (16 mi) northeast of Paris, and Orly, 16 km (10 mi) south of Paris. It doesn't really matter which one you fly into; both are easily accessible to Paris, though Roissy is the only one with a TGV (high-speed train) station. **Whether you take a car or bus to travel from Paris to the airport on your departure, always allot an extra half hour (at least) due to the often horrendous traffic tie-ups within the airports proper** (especially in peak seasons and at peak hours): once you arrive at the airports, you'll often need to take the inter-airport buses to shuttle you from one terminal to another and if this bus is held up due to traffic congestion (often the case), a serious case of nail-biting will result.

➤ AIRPORT INFORMATION: **Charles de Gaulle/Roissy** (☎ 01–48–62–22–80 in English, WEB www.adp.com). Orly (☎ 01–49–75–15–15, WEB www.adp.com).

AIRPORT TRANSFERS

Charles de Gaulle/Roissy: From the Charles de Gaulle airport, **the least expensive way to get into Paris is on the RER-B line,** the suburban express train. Each terminal has an exit where the free RER shuttle bus (a white and yellow bus with the letters ADP in gray) will pass every 7–15 minutes to take you on the short ride to the nearby RER station: Terminal 2A (exit A8), Terminal 2C (exit C8), Terminal 2B (exit B6), Terminal 2D (exit D6), Terminal 2F (exit 2.08). Trains to central Paris (Les Halles, St-Michel, Luxembourg) depart every 15 minutes. The fare (including métro connection) is €7.62, and journey time is about 30 minutes. Note that you will have to carry your luggage down to the train tracks, and trains will be crowded if you are traveling during rush hour.

You don't need to have flown Air France to take their comfortable shuttle service to the city. Line one goes from the airport to Charles de Gaulle Etoile and Porte Maillot from 5:45 AM to 11 PM. It leaves every 12 minutes and costs €10 which you can pay on board. Passengers arriving in Terminal 1 need to take exit 34; Terminal 2A and 2C, exit 5; Terminal 2B and 2D, exit 6, Terminal 2F, exit 0.07. Line Four goes to Montparnasse and the Gare de Lyon from 7 AM to 9 PM. Buses run every 30 minutes and cost €11.50. Passengers arriving in Terminal 1 need to look for exit 34, Terminal 2A and 2C need to take either exit 2 or 2C, Terminal 2B and 2D exit 2 or 2B, and Terminal 2F exit 0.07.

Another option is to **take Roissybus, operated by the Paris Transit Authority,** which runs between Charles de Gaulle and the Opéra every 20 minutes from 5:45 AM to 11 PM; the cost is €8.08. Note that you have to hail the bus that you want—it will not stop automatically—and that rush-hour traffic can make for a slow ride.

For a comfortable, hassle-free arrival in Paris, you can **arrange a ride with Paris Airports Service or Airport Shuttle,** and a bilingual chauffeur will be waiting with a minivan to drive you directly to your destination. Rates are set so there are no unpleasant surprises due to poor traffic conditions. Rates are nominal—approximately €19 for one person and €13 per person for two or more people traveling together, and can be prepaid by credit card. It is best to call, fax, or e-mail your request at least 24 hours in advance, noting your flight number, expected time of arrival, and your destination address in Paris.

Taxis are your least desirable mode of transportation into the city. If you are traveling at peak tourist times, you may have to stand in a very long line with a lot of other disgruntled European travelers (most of whom smoke). Journey times, and as a consequence, prices, are therefore unpredictable. At best, the journey takes 30 minutes but it can take as long as one hour. The average fare falls between €30 and €45. You can ask for a quote before getting into the taxi, but it is almost certain that your driver (grumpy) will respond with a shrug. There is also a €.90 supplement per piece of luggage. Please note that drivers can no longer refuse to take a fourth person; it's the law.

Orly: From the Orly airport, **the most economical way to get into Paris is to take the RER-C or Orlyrail line;** catch the free shuttle bus from the terminal to the train station. Trains to Paris leave every 15 minutes. Passengers arriving in either the South or West Terminal need to use exit G. The fare is €5.20, and journey time is about 35 minutes. Another option is to **take the monorail service, Orlyval,** which runs between the Antony RER-B station and Orly airport every four to eight minutes. The fare to downtown Paris is €8.70.

You can also **take an Air France bus** from Orly to Les Invalides on the Left Bank and Montparnasse; these run every 12 minutes from 6 AM to 11:30 PM (you need not have flown on Air France to use this service). The fare is

€7.50, and journey time is between 30 and 45 minutes, depending on traffic. The Paris Transit Authority's **Orlybus is yet another option**; buses leave every 15 minutes for the Denfert-Rochereau métro station; the cost is €5.65.

With advance reservations **Paris Airports Services or Airport Shuttle can pick you up at Orly** and drive you directly to your destination. If possible make your reservations at least 24 hours in advance; MasterCard and Visa are accepted and the operators speak English. The fare for one person traveling alone is €16.80 or €13 per person with two or more people traveling together. At best, **taxis take around 25 minutes from Orly to downtown Paris;** the fare falls between €15.25 and €30.55.

➤ TAXIS AND SHUTTLES: **Air France Bus** (☎ 01–41–56–89–00 recorded information in English, WEB www. cars-airfrance.com). **Airport Shuttle** (☎ 01–30–11–11–90; 888/426–2705 toll free from the U.S., FAX 01–30–11–11–99, WEB www.airportshuttle.fr). **Paris Airports Services** (☎ 08–21–80–08–01, FAX 01–49–62–78–79, WEB www.parisairportservice.com).

DUTY-FREE SHOPPING

Duty-free shopping is no longer possible when you are traveling within the European Union; you will benefit from duty-free prices only when you are leaving European territory.

BOAT AND FERRY TRAVEL

Linking France and the United Kingdom, a boat or ferry trip across the Channel can range from a mere 40 minutes (via hovercraft) to 90 minutes (via ferryboat). Trip length also depends on your departure point: popular routes link Boulogne and Folkestone, Dieppe and Newhaven, Le Havre and Portsmouth, and, the most booked passage, Calais and Dover. Driving distances from the French ports to Paris are as follows: from Calais, 290 km (180 mi); from Boulogne, 243 km (151 mi); from Dieppe, 193 km (120 mi); from Dunkerque, 257 km (160 mi). The fastest routes to Paris from each port are via N43, A26, and A1 from Calais and the Channel Tunnel; via N1 from Boulogne; via N15 from Le Havre; via D915 and N1 from Dieppe; and via A25 and A1 from Dunkerque.

➤ DOVER–CALAIS: **Hoverspeed** (✉ International Hoverport, Marine Parade, Dover CT17 9TG, ☎ 01304/240241, WEB www.hoverspeed.com) operates up to 15 crossings a day by Hovercraft and catamaran. The crossings take 35 minutes (Hovercraft) or 95 minutes (catamaran).

P&O European Ferries (✉ Channel House, Channel View Rd., Dover, Kent CT17 9TJ, ☎ 020/8575–8555, WEB www.poportsmouth.com) has up to 25 sailings a day; the crossing takes about 75 minutes. **Seafrance** (✉ 23 rue Louis-le-grand, 75002 Paris, ☎ 01–44–94–40–40, WEB www. seafrance.net) operates up to 15 sailings a day; the crossing takes about 90 minutes.

➤ FOLKESTONE–BOULOGNE: **Hoverspeed** is the sole operator on this route, with ten 35-minute crossings a day.

➤ NEWHAVEN–DIEPPE: **Seafrance** has as many as four sailings a day, and the crossing takes four hours.

➤ PORTSMOUTH–LE HAVRE: **P&O European Ferries** has up to three sailings a day, and the crossing takes 5½ hours by day, 7½ by night.

FARES AND SCHEDULES

Schedules and tickets are available at any travel agency throughout France or via the Internet. Travel agencies accept traveler's checks, major credit cards, and cash. Fares vary, but a round-trip from Dover to Calais completed within five days costs €36.65 for one person, €221.40 for two adults plus a car. The price doubles if the visit exceeds five days.

BUS TRAVEL AROUND PARIS

Bus travel in Paris has always had the reputation of catering to that very small population of people who actually have the time to sit in the bus and read a good book as it snails its way through impossible Parisian traffic. All that changed in 2002 when special protected bus lanes were created throughout Paris—over 41 km

(25 mi) of them in every arrondissement except the 13ᵉ. Travel time has been cut, on the average, by a whopping 50%; for example, a trip from Saint-Michel to the place de la Concorde now takes 9 minutes instead of the usual 25. This, of course is to discourage the stubborn Parisian population from taking their cars to work and creating impossible congestion in the city, but it can benefit you too: **Buses are a scenic, convenient, and efficient way to see the city** and the new ones are equipped with air-conditioning—something to think about on one of those sweltering August days.

Paris buses are green and white; route number and destination are marked in front, and major stopping places along the sides. The brown bus shelters, topped by red-and-yellow circular signs, contain timetables and route maps; note that buses must be hailed at these larger bus shelters, as they service multiple lines and routes. Smaller stops are designated simply by a pole bearing bus numbers.

Of Paris's 250 bus routes, three main lines circle the *grands boulevards* and are known as the *petite ceinture* (small belt). These constitute bus numbers PC 1, PC 2, and PC 3, which run in a continuous circle covering the major *portes,* or entryways, into the city center. More than 200 other bus routes run throughout Paris, reaching virtually every nook and cranny of the city. During weekdays and Saturday, buses run every five minutes (as opposed to the 15- to 20-minute wait on Sunday and national holidays). One ticket will take you anywhere within the city; once you get off at any point, that ticket is no longer viable. Bus transport is ideal for the elderly, women with children (easy access with strollers), and anyone who likes to take the scenic route. Needless to say, seats are more difficult to find during rush hours.

A map of the bus system is on the flip side of every métro map, in all métro stations, and at all bus stops. Maps are also found in each bus. A recorded message announces the name of the next stop. To get off, press the red

button located on all the silver poles that run the length of the bus and the *arrêt demandé* (stop requested) light directly behind the driver will light up. Use the rear door to exit.

The Balabus, a public orange-and-white bus that runs between May and September, gives an interesting 50-minute tour around the major sights. You can use your Paris-Visite, Carte Orange, or Mobilis pass, or one to three bus tickets depending on how far you ride. The route runs from La Défense to the Gare de Lyon.

FARES AND SCHEDULES

Regular buses accept métro tickets, or you can buy a single ticket on board (exact change appreciated) for €1.30. If you have individual tickets, you should **be prepared to punch your ticket in the red-and-gray machines located at the entrance of the bus.** You need to show (but not punch) weekly, monthly, and Paris-Visite/Mobilis tickets to the driver. Bus tickets can be bought on board buses, in the métro, or in any bar/tabac store sporting one of the lime-green métro symbols above its street sign.

Most routes operate from 7 AM to 8:30 PM (or 20h30 to the French); some continue to midnight. After 8:30 PM you must either take the métro or one of the 18 "Noctambus" lines (which are indicated by a brown owl symbol at bus stops). These bus lines operate hourly (1:30 AM–5:30 AM) between Châtelet and various nearby suburbs; they can be stopped by hailing them at any point on their route. Paris-Visite/Mobilis passes are accepted on the Noctambus. A regular ticket costs €2.30 and allows for one transfer.

➤ BUS INFORMATION: **RATP** (✉ Pl. de la Madeleine, 75008; 53 bis quai des Grands Augustins, 75006 Paris, ☎ 08–36–68–41–14, 🆆🅴🅱 www.ratp.com).

BUS TRAVEL TO AND FROM PARIS

The excellent national train service in France means that long-distance bus service in the country is practically nonexistent; **regional buses are found where train service is spotty.** Local bus information to the rare rural areas where trains do not have access can be obtained from the SNCF.

The largest international operator is Eurolines France, whose main terminal is in the Parisian suburb of Bagnolet (a half-hour métro ride from central Paris, at the end of métro line 3). Eurolines runs international routes to over 1,500 cities in Europe.

FARES AND SCHEDULES

It is possible to take a bus (via ferry) to Paris from the United Kingdom; just be aware that what you save in money will almost certainly cost you in time—the bus trip takes about seven hours as opposed to the three it takes on the Eurostar train line (Gare du Nord–Victoria Station). In general, the price of a round-trip bus ticket is 50% less than that of a plane and 25% less than a train ticket, so if you have the time and the energy, this is a good way to cut the cost of travel. Eurolines also offers a 15-day (€150), 30-day (€215), or 60-day (€270) pass if you're planning on doing the grand European tour. Ask about one of the "circle tours" which depart from Paris, for example, via London, Amsterdam, then back to Paris again). Eurolines operates a service from London's Victoria Coach Station, via the Dover–Calais ferry, to Paris's Porte de Bagnolet. There is a 9 AM departure that arrives in Paris at 4 PM, a 2 PM departure that arrives at 9 PM, and the overnight trip from 9:30 PM, which arrives in Paris at 7 AM. Fares are £60 round-trip (under-25 youth pass £56), £35 one-way. Other Eurolines routes include the following: Amsterdam (7 hours, €70); Barcelona (15 hours, €160); and Berlin (10 hours, €145). There are also international-only arrival-departures from Avignon, Bordeaux, Lille, Lyon, Toulouse, and Tours. Hoverspeed offers up to four daily departures from London's Victoria Coach Station. Fares are £60 round-trip, £38 one-way.

➤ BUS INFORMATION: **Eurolines** (✉ 28 av. Général-de-Gaulle, Bagnolet, ☎ 08–36–69–52–52 in France; 020/7730–3499 in the U.K., WEB www. eurolines.fr). **Hoverspeed** (✉ International Hoverport, Marine Parade,

Dover CT17 9TG, ☎ 01304/240241, WEB www.hoverspeed.com). **Paris Vision** (✉ 1 rue d'Auber, 75009 Paris, ☎ 01–47–42–27–40). **SNCF** (✉ 88 rue St-Lazare, 75009 Paris, ☎ 08–36–35–35–39 in English).

BUSINESS HOURS

BANKS AND OFFICES

On **weekdays, banks are open** generally 9:30 AM–4:30 or 5 PM (note that the Banque de France closes at 3:30), and some banks are also open on Saturday 9–5 as well. In general, government offices and businesses are open 9–5.

GAS STATIONS

Gas stations in the city are generally open 7:30 AM–8 PM, though those near the city's *portes* (or principal entranceways) near the *péripherique* (beltway) are open 24 hours a day.

MUSEUMS AND SIGHTS

Most **museums are closed one day a week**—usually either Monday or Tuesday—and on national holidays. Generally, museums and national monuments are open from 10 AM to 5 or 6 PM. A few close for lunch (noon–2) and are open Sunday only in the afternoon. Many of the large museums have one *nocturne* (night-time) opening per week, when they are open until 9:30 or 10 PM. The Louvre is closed on Tuesday and stays open late on Wednesday until 9:45 PM. The Centre Pompidou is closed on Tuesday and has late opening hours daily until 10 PM. The Musée d'Orsay is closed on Monday and stays open until 9:30 PM on Thursday. All national museums are free to the public the first Sunday of every month.

PHARMACIES

Pharmacies are generally open Monday–Saturday 8:30 AM–8 PM. Nearby pharmacies that stay open late, or for 24 hours, or on Sunday, are listed on the door.

SHOPS

Generally, **large shops are open from 9:30 or 10 AM to 7 or 8 PM** and remain open through lunchtime. Many of the large department stores stay open until 10 PM on Wednesday or Thursday. Smaller shops and many supermarkets often open earlier (8 AM) but take a lengthy lunch break (1 PM–3 PM) and generally close around 8 PM; small food shops are often open Sunday mornings, 9 AM–1 PM. There is always a small corner grocery store that stays open late, usually until 11 PM, if you're in a bind for basic necessities like diapers, bread, cheese, and fruit (and perhaps the unnecessary bottle of chilled champagne or the disposable plastic rain hat, circa 1950). Note that prices are substantially higher in such outlets than in the larger supermarkets. Most shops close all day Sunday, except in the Marais (where shops that stand side by side on rue des Francs Bourgeois, from antiques dealers to chic little designers, jewelry to home decoration, open their doors to welcome hordes of Sunday browsers); the Bastille, the Latin Quarter, and the Ile de la Cité also have shops that open on Sunday.

CAMERAS AND PHOTOGRAPHY

If you need to get your camera repaired, your best bet is to go to one of the FNAC stores in Paris. Note that it might take some time for the camera to be fixed. The *Kodak Guide to Shooting Great Travel Pictures* (available at bookstores everywhere) is loaded with tips.

➤ CAMERA REPAIR AND PHOTO DEVELOPING: **FNAC** (⊠ 26–30 av. des Ternes, 17ᵉ; in the Forum des Halles, 1–7 rue Pierre-Lescot, 1ᵉʳ; 136 rue St-Lazare, 9ᵉ; 157 rue du Faubourg St-Antoine, 11ᵉ).

➤ PHOTO HELP: **Kodak Information Center** (☎ 800/242–2424).

EQUIPMENT PRECAUTIONS

Don't pack film and equipment in checked luggage, where it is much more susceptible to damage. X-ray machines used to view checked luggage are becoming more powerful and therefore are much more likely to ruin your film. Always **keep film and tape out of the sun.** Carry an extra supply of batteries, and **be prepared to turn on your camera or camcorder** to prove to security personnel that the device is real. Always **ask for hand inspection**

of film, which can become clouded after repeated exposure to airport X-ray machines, and **keep videotapes away from metal detectors.**

FILM AND DEVELOPING

The easiest place to get film developed and printed is at one of the various FNAC stores around the city. Keep in mind that it is expensive to have film developed and printed in Paris—around $20 per 36-exposure roll.

VIDEOS

Video systems are not the same all over the world. The United States, for instance, uses NTSC and France uses SECAM. Other European countries, including the United Kingdom, use PAL. This means that you probably won't be able to play videotapes from the United States in France. You should also **bring extra blank videotapes with you from home** for your camcorder as you may not be able to find compatible tapes in France.

CAR RENTAL

Rates in Paris begin at approximately $70 a day and $200 a week for an economy car with air-conditioning, manual transmission, and unlimited mileage. This does not include tax on car rentals, which is 20.6% or, if you are picking one up at the airport, the airport tax. To save money, **make reservations before you go;** you can generally get a much better deal. Note that driving in Paris is best avoided, and parking is very difficult to find. You're better off renting a car only when you want to take excursions out of the city.

Renting a car through a local French agency has a number of disadvantages, the biggest being price, as they simply cannot compete with the larger international companies. These giants combine bilingual service, the security of name recognition, extensive services (such as 24-hour hot lines), and fully automatic vehicles. SNAC, a France-based agency, can be useful if you are interested in luxury cars (convertible BMWs) or large family vans (Renault Espace, for example).

➤ MAJOR AGENCIES: **Alamo** (☎ 800/522–9696; 020/8759–6200 in the

U.K., WEB www.alamo.fr). **Avis**
(☎ 800/331–1084; 800/879–2847 in
Canada; 02/9353–9000 in Australia;
09/525–1982 in New Zealand; 0870/
606–0100 in the U.K., WEB www.avis.
fr). **Budget** (☎ 800/527–0700; 0870/
607–5000 in the U.K. through affili-
ate Europcar, WEB www.budget.fr).
Dollar (☎ 800/800–6000; 0124/
622–0111 in the U.K. through affili-
ate Sixt Kenning; 02/9223–1444 in
Australia, WEB www.dollar.com).
Hertz (☎ 800/654–3001; 800/263–
0600 in Canada; 020/8897–2072 in
the U.K.; 02/9669–2444 in Australia;
09/256–8690 in New Zealand,
WEB www.hertz.com). **National Car
Rental** (☎ 800/227–7368; 020/8680–
4800 in the U.K. where it is known as
National Europe). **SNAC** (☎ 01–44–
05–33–99).

CUTTING COSTS

To get the best deal, **book through a
travel agent, who will shop around.**
Note that the big international agencies, like Hertz and Avis, offer better
prices to clients who make their
reservations from their home countries; prices quoted in France are
usually higher. If you need to rent a
car while in France, it even pays to
call home and have a friend take care
of it for you from there.

Do **look into wholesalers,** companies
that do not own fleets but rent in
bulk from those that do and often
offer better rates than traditional car-
rental operations. Payment must be
made before you leave home.

➤ WHOLESALERS: **Auto Europe**
(☎ 207/842–2000 or 800/223–5555,
FAX 800/235–6321, WEB www.
autoeurope.com). **DER Travel Services** (✉ 9501 W. Devon Ave., Rose-
mont, IL 60018, ☎ 800/782–2424,
FAX 800/282–7474 information; 800/
860–9944 brochures, WEB www.
dertravel.com). **Europe by Car** (☎
212/581–3040 or 800/223–1516, FAX
212/246–1458, WEB www.europebycar.
com). **Kemwel Holiday Autos** (☎
800/678–0678, FAX 914/825–3160,
WEB www.kemwel.com).

INSURANCE

When driving a rented car you are
generally responsible for any damage
to or loss of the vehicle. Before you

rent, see what coverage your personal
auto-insurance policy and credit cards
provide.

Before you buy collision coverage,
check your existing policies—you
may already be covered. However,
collision policies that car-rental companies sell for European rentals
usually do not include stolen-vehicle
coverage.

REQUIREMENTS AND
RESTRICTIONS

In France, you drive on the right and
**yield to drivers coming from streets to
the right.** However, this rule does not
necessarily apply at roundabouts,
where you should watch out for just
about everyone. You must **wear your
seat belt,** and children under 12 may
not travel in the front seat. Speed
limits are 130 kph (80 mph) on
expressways (*autoroutes*), 110 kph
(70 mph) on divided highways (*routes
nationales*), 90 kph (55 mph) on
other roads (*routes*), 50 kph (30 mph)
in cities and towns (*villes et villages*).

In France **your own driver's license is
acceptable.** An International Driver's
Permit is not necessary unless you are
planning on a long-term stay; you can
get one from the American or Canadian Automobile Association, and, in
the United Kingdom, from the Automobile Association or Royal Automobile Club. You must be 18 years
old to drive, but there is no top age
limit for those whose faculties are
intact. To rent a car you must be 21
or older and have a major credit card,
though you are charged a €16.80 per
day supplement if you're under 25.

SURCHARGES

Before you pick up a car in one city
and leave it in another, **ask about
drop-off charges or one-way service
fees,** which can be substantial. Note,
too, that some rental agencies charge
extra if you return the car before the
time specified in your contract. To
avoid a hefty refueling fee, **fill the
tank just before you turn in the car,**
but be aware that gas stations near
the rental outlet may overcharge.

CAR TRAVEL

France's roads are classified into five
types, numbered and prefixed *A*

(*autoroute*), N (*route nationale*),
D (*route départmentale*), C, or V.
Roads marked A (*autoroutes*) are
expressways. There are excellent links
between Paris and most French cities.
When trying to get around Ile-de-
France, it is often difficult to avoid
Paris—just **try to steer clear of the
rush hours** (7–9:30 AM and 4:30–7:30
PM). A *péage* (toll) must be paid on
most expressways: the rate varies but
can be steep. Certain booths allow
you to pay with your credit card.

There are two major rings that run
parallel to each other and encircle
Paris: the *périférique intérieur,* the
inside ring also known as the *grands
boulevards* (not to be confused with
the major avenue layout in the center
of Paris's Right Bank) and the
périférique extérieur, the outside
ring, which is a major highway and
from which *portes* (gates) connect
Paris to the major highways of
France. The names of these highways
function on the same principal as the
métro, with the final destination as
the determining point in the direction you must take.

Heading north, look for Porte de la
Chapelle (direction Lille and Charles
de Gaulle airport); east, for Porte de
Bagnolet (direction Metz and Nancy);
south, for Porte d'Orléans (direction
Lyon and Bordeaux); and west, for
Porte d'Auteuil (direction Rouen and
Chartres) or Porte de St-Cloud.

EMERGENCY SERVICES

If your car breaks down on an expressway, pull your car as far off the
road as possible, set your emergency
indicators, and, if possible, put the
emergency triangle located in the
trunk of your car at least 30 yards
behind your car to warn oncoming
traffic; then **go to a roadside emergency telephone.** These phones put
you in direct contact with the police,
automatically indicating your exact
location, and are available every 3 km
(2 mi). If you have a breakdown
anywhere else, find the nearest garage
or contact the police. There are also
24-hour assistance hot lines valid
throughout France (available through
rental agencies and supplied to you
when you rent the car), but do not

hesitate in calling the police in case of
any roadside emergency, for they are
quick and reliable and the phone call
is free. There are special phones just
for this purpose on all highways—just
pick up the phone and dial 17.

➤ CONTACTS: **Police** (☎ 17). **Club
Automobile de l'Ile de France** (☎ 01–
40–55–43–00) is for members only.

FROM THE U.K.

Motorists from the United Kingdom
have a choice of either the Channel
Tunnel or the ferry services when
traveling to the continent. Reservations are essential at peak times and a
good idea at any time, especially
when going via the Chunnel. Cars
don't drive in the Chunnel but are
loaded onto trains.

GASOLINE

Gas is expensive and prices vary
enormously; anything from €1 to
€1.40 per liter. Credit cards are
accepted in every gas station. There
are very few self-service gas stations
in Paris.

PARKING

Finding parking in Paris is very difficult. Meters and ticket machines (pay
and display) are common: make sure
you **have a supply of €1.50 coins.** If
you're planning on spending a lot of
time in Paris with a car, **it might be a
good idea to buy a parking card**
(*carte de stationnement*) for €15.25
or €30.55 at any café sporting the
red TABAC sign. This card works like a
credit card in the parking meters,
allowing you to avoid the inconve-
nience of finding exact change. After
depositing enough money (or using
your parking card) in the ticket machine, you will receive a receipt; **be
sure to display the receipt on the
inside window of the vehicle,** the
dashboard on the passenger side
being best. Note that in August,
parking is free in certain residential
areas. However, **only parking meters
with a dense yellow circle on them
indicate free parking in August; if you
do not see the circle, pay up.** Parking
tickets are expensive and there is no
shortage of the blue-uniformed parking police. Parking lots, indicated by
a blue sign with a white *P*, are usually

underground and are generally expensive (due to the 24-hour surveillance systems).

RULES OF THE ROAD

A native quirk that takes some getting used to is the famous *priorité à droite* law that states that all drivers must yield to any vehicle coming from the right—to be safe, slow down at *all* crosswalks and make sure no one is coming from the right.

Some important traffic terms and signs to note: *Sortie* (Exit); *Sens Unique* (One Way); *Stationnement Interdite* (No Parking); *Cul de Sac* (Dead End). Blue rectangular signs indicate a highway; triangles carry illustrations of a particular traffic hazard; speed limits are indicated in a circle with the maximum speed encircled in red.

THE CHANNEL TUNNEL

Short of flying, taking the "Chunnel" is the fastest way to cross the English Channel: 35 minutes from Folkestone to Calais, 60 minutes from motorway to motorway, or 3 hours from London's Waterloo Station to Paris's Gare du Nord.

➤ CAR TRANSPORT: **Le Shuttle** (☎ 0870/535–3535 in the U.K.).

➤ PASSENGER SERVICE: In the United Kingdom: **Eurostar** (☎ 0870/518–6186, WEB www.eurostarplanet.com). **InterCity Europe** (☎ 0870/584–8848 for credit-card bookings). In the United States: **BritRail Travel** (☎ 800/677–8585). **Rail Europe** (☎ 800/942–4866).

CHILDREN IN PARIS

If you are renting a car, don't forget to **arrange for a child's car seat** when you reserve. For general advice about traveling with children, check out the family travel tips in the Family Travel section of www.fodors.com and consult *Fodor's FYI: Travel with Your Baby* (available in bookstores everywhere).

BABY-SITTING

Agencies can provide English-speaking baby-sitters with just a few hours' notice. The hourly rate is approximately €5.35 (three-hour minimum) plus an agency fee of €9.25.

➤ AGENCIES: **Ababa** (⌧ 8 av. du Maine, 15ᵉ, ☎ 01–45–49–46–46). **Allo Maman Poule** (⌧ 7 Villa Murat, 16ᵉ, ☎ 01–45–20–96–96). **Baby-Sitting Service** (⌧ 18 rue Tronchet, 8ᵉ, ☎ 01–46–37–51–24).

FLYING

Experts agree that it's a good idea to use safety seats aloft for children weighing less than 40 pounds. Airlines set their own policies: U.S. carriers usually require that the child be ticketed, even if he or she is young enough to ride free, since the seats must be strapped into regular seats. Do **check your airline's policy about using safety seats during takeoff and landing.** And since safety seats are not allowed everywhere in the plane, get your seat assignments early.

When reserving, **request children's meals or a freestanding bassinet** if you need them. But note that bulkhead seats, where you must sit to use the bassinet, may lack an overhead bin or storage space on the floor.

FOOD

The best restaurants in Paris do not welcome small children; except for the traditional family Sunday-noon dinner, fine dining is considered an adult pastime. With kids, **you're best off taking them to more casual bistros, brasseries, and cafés**; these also offer the flexible mealtimes that children often require. Stick with the familiar when you are ordering; an omelet with fries, a sausage with whipped potatoes, or a ham-and-cheese sandwich are comforting for jet-lagged tummies. Do not expect child-friendly amenities like high chairs, coloring books, a smoke-free atmosphere, or even an indulgent waiter, for that matter. Other restaurant options include one of the many Chinese restaurants that serve favorites such as grilled chicken, shrimp, or spring rolls or one of the American restaurants on the Champs-Élysées or near Les Halles. If it is sunny you can always buy a fresh roasted chicken (have it cut up), some cherry tomatoes, and raspberry tarts and have a picnic in the Luxembourg or Tuileries Gardens. Remember though—if you (or they) get desperate, Paris has its share of McDonald's, Pizza Huts, and other fast-food restaurants.

LODGING

Most hotels in Paris allow children under a certain age to stay in their parents' room at no extra charge, but others charge for them as extra adults; be sure to **find out the cutoff age for children's discounts.**

The Novotel chain allows up to two children under 15 to stay free in their parents' room, and many properties have playgrounds. Sofitel hotels offer a free second room for children during July and August and over the Christmas period.

➤ BEST CHOICES: **Novotel** (☎ 800/221–4542 international reservations). **Sofitel** (☎ 800/221–4542 international reservations).

SIGHTS AND ATTRACTIONS

Paris has plenty of diversions for the young (noted by a 😊 duck icon in the margin throughout this book), and **almost all museums and movie theaters offer discounted rates** to children. *Le Pariscope* and *L'Officiel des Spectacles* are two weekly publications that have sections in English about entertainment for children. The **CIDJ,** the Centre d'Information et de Documentation pour la Jeunesse (Center for Information and Documentation for Young People), also has information about activities and events for youngsters in Paris. *Fodor's Around Paris with Kids* (available in bookstores everywhere) can help you plan your days together.

SUPPLIES AND EQUIPMENT

Supermarkets carry several major brands of diapers (*couches à jeter*), universally referred to as Pampers (pronounced "pawm-paires"). Junior sizes are hard to come by, as the French toilet-train early. Baby formula is available in grocery stores or pharmacies. There are two types of formula: *lait premier age,* for infants 0–4 months, and *lait deuxième age,* for 4 months or older. French formulas come in powder form and need to be mixed with a pure, low-mineral-content bottled water like Evian or Volvic (the French *never* mix baby formula with tap water). American formulas do not exist in France. If you're looking for treats for your little ones, some items to keep in mind are *coloriage* (coloring books); *crayons de couleur* (crayons); *pâte à modeler* (modeling clay); and *feutres* (markers).

COMPUTERS ON THE ROAD

If you use a major Internet provider, getting on-line in Paris shouldn't be difficult. Call your Internet provider to get the local access number in Paris. Many hotels have business services with Internet access and even in-room modem lines. You will, however, need an adapter for your computer for the European-style plugs. If you're traveling with a laptop, carry a spare battery and adapter. Never plug your computer into any socket before asking about surge protection. IBM sells a pen-size modem tester that plugs into a telephone jack to check if the line is safe to use.

➤ ACCESS NUMBERS IN PARIS: **AOL** (☎ 01–41–45–81–00). **Compuserve** (☎ 08–03–00–60–00, 08–03–00–80–00, or 08–03–00–90–00).

➤ INTERNET CAFÉS: **Café Orbital** (✉ 17 rue de Médicis, 6ᵉ, Latin Quarter, ☎ 01–43–25–76–77). **Cybercafé** (✉ 72–74 passage de Choiseul, 2ᵉ, Opéra/Grands Boulevards, ☎ 01–47–03–36–12, WEB www.cari.com, métro Opéra). **Cybercafé de Paris** (✉ 15 rue des Halles, 1ᵉʳ, Beaubourg/Les Halles, ☎ 01–42–21–11–11). **EasyEverything** (✉ 37 bd. Sébastopol, 1ᵉʳ, Beaubourg/Les Halles, ☎ 01–40–41–09–10). **Les Jardins de l'Internet Cybercafé** (✉ 79 bd. St-Michel, 4ᵉ, Latin Quarter, ☎ 01–44–07–22–20, WEB www.jardin-internet.net, métro Cluny La Sorbonne). **Web Bar** (✉ 32 rue de Picardie, 3ᵉ, République, ☎ 01–42–72–66–55, WEB www.webbar.fr, métro République).

➤ INTERNET PROVIDER IN ENGLISH: **Almanet** (✉ 8 rue Dupont des Loges, 2ᵉ, ☎ 01–44–18–70–70, WEB www.alma-net.net).

CONCIERGES

Concierges, found in many hotels, can help you with theater tickets and dinner reservations: a good one with connections may be able to get you seats for a hot show or prime-time dinner reservations at the restaurant of the moment. You can also turn to your hotel's concierge for help with travel arrangements, sightseeing plans, services ranging from aroma-therapy to zipper repair, and emergencies. Always, **always tip** a concierge who has been of assistance.

CONSUMER PROTECTION

Whenever shopping or buying travel services in Paris, **pay with a major credit card,** if possible, so you can cancel payment or get reimbursed if there's a problem. If you're doing business with a particular company for the first time, **contact your local Better Business Bureau and the attorney general's offices** in your state and (for U.S. businesses) the company's home state as well. Have any complaints been filed? Finally, if you're buying a package or tour, always **consider travel insurance** that includes default coverage.

➤ BBBs: **Council of Better Business Bureaus** (✉ 4200 Wilson Blvd., Suite 800, Arlington, VA 22203, ☎ 703/276–0100, FAX 703/525–8277, WEB www.bbb.org).

CUSTOMS AND DUTIES

When shopping, **keep receipts** for all purchases. Upon reentering the country, **be ready to show customs officials what you've bought.** If you feel a duty is incorrect or object to the way your clearance was handled, note the inspector's badge number and ask to see a supervisor. If the problem isn't resolved, write to the appropriate authorities, beginning with the port director at your point of entry.

IN AUSTRALIA

Australian residents who are 18 or older may bring home $A400 worth of souvenirs and gifts (including jewelry), 250 cigarettes or 250 grams of tobacco, and 1,125 ml of alcohol (including wine, beer, and spirits). Residents under 18 may bring back $A200 worth of goods. Prohibited items include meat products. Seeds, plants, and fruits need to be declared upon arrival.

➤ INFORMATION: **Australian Customs Service** (Regional Director, ✉ Box 8,

Sydney, NSW 2001, Australia, ☎ 02/9213–2000; FAX 02/9213–4043; WEB www.customs.gov.au).

IN CANADA

Canadian residents who have been out of Canada for at least seven days may bring home C$500 worth of goods duty-free. If you've been away fewer than seven days but more than 48 hours, the duty-free allowance drops to C$200; if your trip lasts 24–48 hours, the allowance is C$50. You may not pool allowances with family members. Goods claimed under the C$500 exemption may follow you by mail; those claimed under the lesser exemptions must accompany you. Alcohol and tobacco products may be included in the seven-day and 48-hour exemptions but not in the 24-hour exemption. If you meet the age requirements of the province or territory through which you reenter Canada, you may bring in, duty-free, 1.14 liters (40 imperial ounces) of wine or liquor *or* 24 12-ounce cans or bottles of beer or ale. If you are 16 or older you may bring in, duty-free, 200 cigarettes and 50 cigars. Check ahead of time with Revenue Canada or the Department of Agriculture for policies regarding meat products, seeds, plants, and fruits.

You may send an unlimited number of gifts worth up to C$60 each duty-free to Canada. Label the package UNSOLICITED GIFT—VALUE UNDER $60. Alcohol and tobacco are excluded.

➤ INFORMATION: **Canada Customs and Revenue Agency** (✉ 2265 St. Laurent Blvd. S, Ottawa, Ontario K1G 4K3, ☎ 204/983–3500, 800/461–9999, WEB www.ccra-adrc.gc.ca/).

IN FRANCE

If you're coming from outside the European Union (EU), you may import duty free: (1) 200 cigarettes or 100 cigarillos or 50 cigars or 250 grams of tobacco (twice that if you live outside Europe); (2) 2 liters of wine and, in addition, (a) 1 liter of alcohol over 22% volume (most spirits) or (b) 2 liters of alcohol under 22% volume (fortified or sparkling wine) or (c) 2 more liters of table wine; (3) 50 ml of perfume and 250 ml of toilet water; (4) 200 grams of coffee, 100 grams of tea; and (5) other goods to the value of €46 (€15.3 for those under 15).

If you're arriving from an EU country, you may be required to declare all goods and prove that anything over the standard limit is for personal consumption. But there is no limit or customs tariff imposed on goods carried within the EU.

Any amount of euros or foreign currency may be brought into France, but foreign currencies converted into euros may be reconverted into a foreign currency only up to the equivalent of €769.

➤ INFORMATION: **Direction des Douanes** (✉ 16 rue Yves Toudic, 10ᵉ, ☎ 01–40–40–39–00).

IN NEW ZEALAND

Homeward-bound residents 17 or older may bring back $700 worth of souvenirs and gifts. Your duty-free allowance also includes 4.5 liters of wine or beer; one 1,125-ml bottle of spirits; and either 200 cigarettes, 250 grams of tobacco, 50 cigars, or a combination of the three up to 250 grams. Prohibited items include meat products, seeds, plants, and fruits.

➤ INFORMATION: **New Zealand Customs** (Head office: ✉ The Customhouse, 17–21 Whitmore St., Box 2218, Wellington, ☎ 09/300–5399, WEB www.customs.govt.nz.

IN THE U.K.

If you are a U.K. resident and your journey was wholly within the European Union (EU), you won't have to pass through customs when you return to the United Kingdom. If you plan to bring back large quantities of alcohol or tobacco, check EU limits beforehand. In most cases, if you bring back more than 200 cigars, 800 cigarettes, 10 liters of spirits, and/or 90 liters of wine, you have to declare the goods upon return. From countries outside the EU, you may bring home, duty-free, 200 cigarettes or 50 cigars; 1 liter of spirits or 2 liters of fortified or sparkling wine or liqueurs; 2 liters of still table wine; 60 ml of perfume; 250 ml of toilet water; plus £136 worth of other goods, including gifts and souvenirs. If returning from outside the EU, prohibited items include meat products, seeds, plants, and fruits.

➤ INFORMATION: **HM Customs and Excise** (✉ Portcullis House, 21 Cowbridge Rd. E, Cardiff CF11 9SS, ☎ 029/2038–6423, WEB www.hmce.gov.uk).

IN THE U.S.

U.S. residents who have been out of the country for at least 48 hours may bring home, for personal use, $400 worth of foreign goods duty-free, as long as they haven't used the $400 allowance or any part of it in the past 30 days. This exemption may include 1 liter of alcohol (for travelers 21 and older), 200 cigarettes, and 100 non-Cuban cigars. Family members from the same household who are traveling together may pool their $400 personal exemptions. For fewer than 48 hours, the duty-free allowance drops to $200, which may include 50 cigarettes, 10 non-Cuban cigars, and 150 milliliters of alcohol (or perfume containing alcohol). The $200 allowance cannot be combined with other individuals' exemptions, and if you exceed it, the full value of all the goods will be taxed. Antiques, which the U.S. Customs Service defines as objects more than 100 years old, enter duty-free, as do original works of art done entirely by hand, including paintings, drawings, and sculptures.

You may also mail or ship packages home duty-free: up to $200 worth of goods for personal use, with a limit of one parcel per addressee per day (except alcohol or tobacco products or perfume worth more than $5); label the package PERSONAL USE and attach a list of its contents and their retail value. Do not label the package UNSOLICITED GIFT or your duty-free exemption will drop to $100. Mailed items do not affect your duty-free allowance on your return.

➤ INFORMATION: **U.S. Customs Service** (✉ 1300 Pennsylvania Ave. NW, Washington, DC 20229; WEB www.customs.gov; inquiries ☎ 202/354–1000; complaints c/o ✉ 1300 Pennsylvania Ave. NW, Room 5.4D, Washington, DC 20229; registration of equipment c/o ✉ Resource Management, ☎ 202/927–0540).

DINING

For information on mealtimes, reservations, what to wear, and specific restaurants, *see* Chapter 3. The restaurants listed are the cream of the crop in each price category.

DISABILITIES
AND ACCESSIBILITY

Although the city of Paris is doing much to ensure that public facilities accommodate people with mobility difficulties, it still has a long way to go. Some sidewalks now have low curbs, and many arrondissements have public rest rooms and telephone boxes that are accessible to travelers using wheelchairs.

➤ LOCAL RESOURCES: **Association des Paralysés de France** (✉ 17 bd. Auguste-Blanqui, 75013 Paris, ☎ 01–44–16–83–83) is a very helpful organization. **Comité Nationale Français de Liaison pour la Réadaptation des Handicapés** (✉ 236 bis rue de Tolbiac, 75013 Paris, ☎ 01–53–80–66–66) publishes an extensive guide in English entitled "Paris for Everyone" that costs €9.20 and has in-depth information on hotels, transportation, and interesting, accessible activities in the capital.

RESERVATIONS

When discussing accessibility with an operator or reservations agent, **ask hard questions.** Are there any stairs, inside *or* out? Are there grab bars next to the toilet *and* in the shower/tub? How wide is the doorway to the room? To the bathroom? For the most extensive facilities meeting the latest legal specifications, **opt for newer accommodations.**

TRANSPORTATION

The Paris métro is a labyrinth of winding stairs, malfunctioning doors, and hordes of scurrying Parisians, all of which make it a less than ideal mode of transport for travelers with disabilities. In addition, very few métro and RER stations are wheelchair-accessible with the exception of the new, fully automated line Météor. For those with walking difficulties, all stairs have handrails, and nearly two-thirds of the stations have at least one escalator. Avoid peak hours between 8 and 9 AM and 6 and 7 PM. Bus lines Nos. 38, 62, 68, and 91 are wheelchair-accessible, but note that you will be more comfortable traveling with someone who can help you. For information about accessibility, **get the RER and métro access guide,** available at most stations and from the Paris Transit Authority. The SNCF has special accommodations in the first-class departments of trains that are reserved exclusively for people using wheelchairs (and are available for the second-class price). **It is essential to reserve special train tickets in advance—this not only assures a comfortable seat but guarantees assistance at the station.** Taxi drivers are required by law to assist travelers with disabilities in and out of their vehicles.

The Airhop shuttle company runs adapted vehicles to and from the airports; Orly–Paris costs €27.50 and Charles de Gaulle–Paris costs €38.15; this service is available weekdays only. Reservations (in French) must be made in advance. Note that you must pay €2.40 for every 15 minutes there is a delay.

➤ LOCAL RESOURCES: **Airhop** (☎ 01–41–29–01–29). **G.I.H.P.** (✉ 98 rue de la Porte Jaune, 92210 St-Cloud, ☎ 01–41–83–15–15). **Paris Transit Authority** (RATP; (✉ 54 quai de la Rapée, 75599, Cedex 12, ☎ 08–36–68–77–14, WEB www.ratp.com).

➤ COMPLAINTS: **Aviation Consumer Protection Division** for airline-related problems. **Civil Rights Office** (✉ U.S. Department of Transportation, Departmental Office of Civil Rights, S-30, 400 7th St. SW, Room 10215, Washington, DC 20590, ☎ 202/366–4648, FAX 202/366–3571, WEB www. dot.gov/ost/docr/index.htm) for problems with surface transportation. **Disability Rights Section** (✉ NYAV, U.S. Department of Justice, Civil Rights Division, 950 Pennsylvania Ave. NW, Washington, DC 20530; ☎ ADA information line 202/514–0301, 800/514–0301, 202/514–0383 TTY, 800/514–0383 TTY, WEB www. usdoj.gov/crt/ada/adahom1.htm).

TRAVEL AGENCIES

In the United States, the Americans with Disabilities Act requires that travel firms serve the needs of all travelers. Some agencies specialize in working with people with disabilities.

➤ TRAVELERS WITH MOBILITY PROBLEMS: **Access Adventures** (✉ 206 Chestnut Ridge Rd., Scottsville, NY 14624, ☎ 716/889–9096, dltravel@ prodigy.net), run by a former physical-rehabilitation counselor. **Accessible Vans of America** (✉ 9 Spielman Rd., Fairfield, NJ 07004, ☎ 877/ 282–8267, FAX 973/808–9713, WEB www.accessiblevans.com). **CareVacations** (✉ 5-5110 50th Ave., Leduc, Alberta T9E 6V4, Canada, ☎ 780/986–6404 or 877/478– 7827, FAX 780/986–8332, WEB www. carevacations.com), for group tours and cruise vacations. **Flying Wheels Travel** (✉ 143 W. Bridge St., Box 382, Owatonna, MN 55060, ☎ 507/ 451–5005, FAX 507/451–1685, WEB www.flyingwheelstravel.com).

DISCOUNTS AND DEALS

Be a smart shopper and **compare all your options** before making decisions. A plane ticket bought with a promotional coupon from travel clubs, coupon books, and direct-mail offers or on the Internet may not be cheaper than the least expensive fare from a discount ticket agency. And always keep in mind that what you get is just as important as what you save.

Paris Tourist Offices, railroad stations, major métro stations, and participating museums sell the *Carte Musées et Monuments* (Museums and Monuments Pass), which offers unlimited access to 74 museums and monuments in Paris—including the Louvre, Musée d'Orsay, Sainte-Chapelle, and Versailles, but not the Eiffel Tower, temporary exhibits, or guided tours—over a one-, three-, or five-consecutive-day period; the cost, respectively, is €13, €26, and €39. From the looks of it, only the most rabid museumgoer will benefit from this pass: you'd have to do three museums in one day, or six in three days, to make any real saving—and it's even less of an attractive proposition now that the museums owned by the City of Paris are free. However, the pass also allows access to museums and monuments without having to wait in line (something to consider if you're going to make the Louvre your home-away-from-home). If you don't plan on seeing that many museums or monuments, you may be better off paying per site.

➤ MUSEUM PASSES: **Association Inter-Musées** (✉ 4 rue Brantôme, 75003 Paris, ☎ 01–44–61–96–60, WEB www. intermusees.com).

DISCOUNT RESERVATIONS

To save money, **look into discount reservations services** with toll-free numbers, which use their buying power to get a better price on hotels, airline tickets, even car rentals. When booking a room, always **call the hotel's local toll-free number** (if one is available) rather than the central reservations number—you'll often get a better price. Always ask about special packages or corporate rates.

When shopping for the best deal on hotels and car rentals, **look for guaranteed exchange rates,** which protect you against a falling dollar. With your rate locked in, you won't pay more, even if the price goes up in the local currency.

➤ AIRLINE TICKETS: ☎ **800/FLY–ASAP.**

➤ HOTEL ROOMS: **Hotel Reservations Network** (☎ 800/964–6835, WEB www. hoteldiscount.com). **International Marketing & Travel Concepts** (☎ 800/790–4682, imtc@mindspring. com). **Players Express Vacations** (☎ 800/458–6161, WEB www. playersexpress.com). **Steigenberger Reservation Service** (☎ 800/223– 5652, WEB www.srs-worldhotels.com). **Travel Interlink** (☎ 800/888–5898, WEB www.travelinterlink.com). **Turbotrip.com** (☎ 800/473–7829, WEB www.turbotrip.com).

PACKAGE DEALS

Don't confuse packages and guided tours. When you buy a package, you travel on your own, just as though you had planned the trip yourself. Fly-drive packages, which combine airfare and car rental, are often a good deal. In cities, ask the local visitors' bureau about hotel packages that include tickets to major museum exhibits or other special events.

ELECTRICITY

To use your U.S.-purchased electric-powered equipment, **bring a converter and adapter.** The electrical current in Paris is 220 volts, 50 cycles alternating current (AC); wall outlets take continental-type plugs, with two round prongs.

If your appliances are dual-voltage, you'll need only an adapter. Don't use 110-volt outlets marked FOR SHAVERS ONLY for high-wattage appliances such as blow-dryers. Most laptops operate equally well on 110 and 220 volts and so require only an adapter.

EMBASSIES

➤ AUSTRALIA: ⊠ 4 rue Jean-Rey, Paris, 15ᵉ, ☎ 01–40–59–33–00, métro Bir-Hakeim, open weekdays 9:15–12:15.

➤ CANADA: ⊠ 35 av. Montaigne, Paris, 8ᵉ, ☎ 01–44–43–29–00, métro Franklin-D.-Roosevelt, open weekdays 8:30–11.

➤ NEW ZEALAND: ⊠ 7 ter rue Léonardo da Vinci, Paris, 16ᵉ, ☎ 01–45–00–24–11, métro Victor-Hugo, open weekdays 9–1.

➤ UNITED KINGDOM: ⊠ 35 rue du Faubourg-St-Honoré, Paris, 8ᵉ, ☎ 01–44–51–31–00, métro Madeleine, open weekdays 9:30–12:30 and 2:30–5.

➤ UNITED STATES: ⊠ 2 rue St-Florentin, Paris, 1ᵉʳ, ☎ 01–43–12–22–22 in English; 01–43–12–23–47 in emergencies, métro Concorde), open weekdays 9–3.

EMERGENCIES

The French National Health Care system has been organized to provide fully equipped, fully staffed hospitals within 30 minutes of every resident in Paris. For signage, hospitals are indicated by a rectangular blue box with a white cross. This guidebook does not list the major Paris hospitals, as the French government prefers an emergency operator to make the judgment call and assign you the best and most convenient option for your emergency. Note that if you are able to walk into a hospital emergency room by yourself, you are often considered "low priority" and the wait can be interminable. So if time is of the essence, the best thing to do is

to call the **fire department** (18); a fully trained team of paramedics will usually arrive within five minutes. You may also dial for a **Samu ambulance** (15); there is usually an English-speaking physician available who will help you assess the situation and either dispatch an ambulance immediately or advise you as to your best course of action.

In a less urgent situation, do what the French do and call **SOS Doctor** or **SOS Dental** services; like magic, a certified, experienced doctor or dentist arrives at the door well within an hour, armed with an old leather doctor case filled with the essentials to diagnose and treat the patient (at an average cost of €53.45). He or she may or may not be bilingual but will, at worst, have a rudimentary understanding of English. This is a very helpful 24-hour service to use for common benign illnesses that need to be treated quickly for comfort, such as high fevers, toothaches, or stomach flus (which seem to have the unfortunate habit of announcing themselves late at night).

The **American Hospital** and the **Hertford British Hospital** both have 24-hour emergency hot lines with bilingual doctors and nurses who can provide advice. For small problems, go to a **pharmacy,** marked by a green neon cross. Pharmacists have the right to administer first aid and recommend over-the-counter drugs, and they can be very helpful in advising you in English or sending you to the nearest English-speaking pharmacist.

Call the **police** (17) if there has been a crime or an act of violence. On the street, some French phrases that may be needed in an emergency are as follows: *Au secours!* (Help!), *urgence* (emergency), *samu* (ambulance), *pompiers* (firemen), *poste de station* (police station), *médicin* (doctor), and *hôpital* (hospital).

➤ DOCTORS AND DENTISTS: **SOS Dentists** (☎ 01–43–37–51–00). **SOS Doctors** (☎ 01–47–07–77–77).

➤ EMERGENCY SERVICES: **Ambulance** (☎ 15). **Fire Department** (☎ 18). **Police** (☎ 17). These numbers are toll-free and can be dialed from any phone.

➤ HOSPITALS: **The American Hospital**
(✉ 63 bd. Victor-Hugo, Neuilly,
☎ 01–46–41–25–25). **The Hertford
British Hospital** (✉ 3 rue Barbès,
Levallois-Perret, ☎ 01–46–39–22–22).

➤ HOT LINES: **FACTS–Line I** ☎ 01–
47–23–80–8), open Monday, Wednesday, and Friday 6–10 PM, offers
HIV/AIDS support in English. **SOS
Help** (☎ 01–47–23–80–80), open
3–11 PM, is an English-language crisis
and information hot line.

➤ LATE-NIGHT AND 24-HOUR PHAR-
MACIES: **Dhéry** (✉ Galerie des
Champs, 84 av. des Champs-Élysées,
8ᵉ, ☎ 01–45–62–02–41) is open 24
hours. **Pharmacie des Arts** (✉ 106 bd.
Montparnasse, 14ᵉ) is open daily until
midnight. **Pharmacie Internationale**
(✉ 5 pl. Pigalle, 9ᵉ, ☎ 01–48–78–38–
12). **Pharmacie Matignon** (✉ rue
Jean-Mermoz, at the Rond-Point de
Champs-Élysées, 8ᵉ) is open daily
until 2 AM.

ENGLISH-LANGUAGE MEDIA

BOOKS

For information about bookstores in
Paris, *see* Specialty Shops *in* Chapter
7. The American Library in Paris is
another resource for English-language
books; it's open Tuesday–Saturday
10–7.

➤ BOOKSTORES: See the listings in
Chapter 7, Shopping.

➤ LIBRARY: **American Library** (✉ 10
rue du Général Ganou, 7ᵉ, ☎ 01–53–
59–12–60). There is a €11 per-day
fee for nonmembers.

NEWSPAPERS AND MAGAZINES

A number of free magazines in English, with all kinds of listings, including events, bars, restaurants, shops,
films, and museums, are available in
Paris. Look for *Time Out Paris,
FUSAC, The Paris Free Voice,* and
Irish Eyes, which are available at
both tourist offices and all Anglo-
American restaurants, bars, and
bookshops. Besides a large selection
of French newspapers and magazines,
all kinds of English-language newspapers and magazines can be found at
newsstands, especially in major
tourist areas, including the *International Herald Tribune, USA Today,*
the *New York Times,* the *European
Financial Times,* the *Times* of London, *Newsweek, The Economist,
Vogue,* and *Elle.*

RADIO AND TELEVISION

Radio in France is an eclectic mix,
with a greater variety of music than
you'd expect. Most stations broadcast
in French. A number of them play
Top 40 music, including Cherie FM
(91.3), Skyrock (96), NRJ (100.3),
Radio Nova (101.5), and Fun Radio
(101.9). A wide range/ of music can
be found on FIP (105.1); classical on
Radio Classique (101.1); '60s–'90s on
Nostalgie (90.4); techno on Radio FG
(98.2); and the news (in French) on
France Info (105.5).

Turn on the television and you'll
notice many American shows dubbed
into French (Canal Jimmy, Channel 8,
shows American shows in their original, undubbed format). France has
both national stations (TF1, France 2,
France 3, La Cinq/Arte, and M6) and
cable stations (most notably Canal-
Plus, France's version of HBO). Every
morning at 7:05 AM, ABC News
(from the night before) is aired. You
can also find CNN, BBC World, and
BBC Prime on cable.

FURTHER READING
AND VIDEOS

BOOKS

For a look at American expatriates in
Paris between the wars, read *Sylvia
Beach and the Lost Generation* by
Noel R. Fitch or *A Moveable Feast* by
Ernest Hemingway. Flaubert's *Senti-
mental Education* includes excellent
descriptions of Paris and its environs,
as do many Zola novels. Other rec-
ommended titles include Charles
Dickens's *A Tale of Two Cities,*
Henry James's *The Ambassadors,*
Colette's *The Complete Claudine,*
Hemingway's *The Sun Also Rises,*
and Gertrude Stein's *Paris, France.*
George Orwell's *Down and Out in
Paris and London* gives an account of
life on a shoestring in these two
European capitals. More essays about
Paris are excerpted in *A Place in the
World Called Paris.* Yet another
anthology of essays on Paris is the
Travelers' Tales Guides: Paris.

Jules Verne's *Paris in the Twentieth Century* provides a view from the past of Paris in the future. A history of Paris from the Revolution to the Belle Epoque is found in Johannes Willms's *Paris: Capital of Europe. A Traveller's History of Paris* by Robert Cole is a good overview. Tyler Stovall's *Paris Noir: African-Americans in the City of Light* is a history of African-Americans in Paris. *Inside Paris* is a photography book of Paris interiors. Two unconventional guides to Paris are Karen Elizabeth Gordon's witty and surreal *Paris Out of Hand* and Lawrence Osborne's *Paris Dreambook.*

Three memoirs by Americans who have lived in Paris are Art Buchwald's *I'll Always Have Paris,* Edmund White's *Our Paris,* and Stanley Karnow's *Paris in the Fifties. Paris Notebooks* by Mavis Gallant is her observations of Paris life. *Between Meals* by A. J. Liebling looks at the art of eating in Paris. *A Corner in the Marais: Memoir of a Paris Neighborhood* is Alex Karmel's history of the neighborhood. More recently, Edmund White and Hubert Sorin weighed in with *Our Paris: Sketches with Memory,* while Adam Gopnik, the distinguished Paris-based correspondent of the *New Yorker* hit the best-seller lists in 2000 with his *Paris to the Moon.*

VIDEOS

For a glimpse of Paris before you go, rent one of the following films: *Gigi* (1958; in English), Hollywood's most opulent valentine to Paris won the Best Picture Oscar, thanks to its memorable Lerner and Loewe musical score and magnificent sets designed by Cecil Beaton; *An American in Paris* (1951; in English), a Hollywood musical with a great Gershwin score stars Gene Kelly and is another Best Picture Oscar winner; *Charade* (1963; in English) is a comic thriller starring Cary Grant and Audrey Hepburn; *How to Steal a Million* (1966; in English) is a chic art-theft caper starring Peter O'Toole, Audrey Hepburn, and many soigné Paris settings; *À Bout de Souffle* (*Breathless,* 1960; in French), by Jean-Luc Godard, is about a car thief who flees with his American girlfriend. Others to try

include *Diva* (1981; in French), about a singer in Paris who becomes involved in murder and drug smuggling; *Funny Face* (1957; in English), a Roger Edens musical with Audrey Hepburn and Fred Astaire immortalizing the high-fashion world of 1950s Paris; *Last Tango in Paris* (1972; in English), a Bertolucci film starring Marlon Brando; *Ready to Wear* (1994; in English), a Robert Altman film about the fashion industry; *Zazie Dans le Métro* (1960; in French), a Louis Malle film about the adventures of a 10-year-old girl in Paris; and *The Red Balloon* (in French), the Oscar-winning short film of 1956, unforgettably filmed in the district of Ménilmontant. Finally, in 2001, the elfin charms of *Amélie* (in French) captured the hearts of moviegoers worldwide.

GAY AND LESBIAN TRAVEL

In Paris, several gay and lesbian organizations provide information on events, medical care, and counseling to one of the largest homosexual communities in the world. A number of informative newspapers and magazines that cover the Parisian gay-lesbian scene are available at stores and kiosks in the city, including *TETU, Gai Guide, Gai Pied Hebdo,* and *Lesbia.*

➤ ORGANIZATIONS: **Association des Médecins Gais** (☎ 01–48–05–81–71) and **Écoute Gaie** (☎ 01–44–93–01–02 after 6 PM) give advice and information over the phone. **Centre Gai et Lesbien** (⊠ 3 rue Keller, 11ᵉ, ☎ 01–43–57–21–47). **Les Mots à la Bouche** (⊠ 6 rue Ste-Croix-de-la-Bretonnerie, 4ᵉ, ☎ 01–42–78–88–30) is Paris's largest gay bookstore and is always a rich resource for current happenings and literature.

➤ GAY- AND LESBIAN-FRIENDLY TRAVEL AGENCIES: **Different Roads Travel** (⊠ 8383 Wilshire Blvd., Suite 902, Beverly Hills, CA 90211, ☎ 323/651–5557 or 800/429–8747, FAX 323/651–3678, lgernert@tzell.com). **Kennedy Travel** (⊠ 314 Jericho Turnpike, Floral Park, NY 11001, ☎ 516/352–4888 or 800/237–7433, FAX 516/354–8849, WEB www.kennedytravel.com). **Now Voyager** (⊠ 4406 18th St., San Francisco, CA 94114,

☎ 415/626–1169 or 800/255–6951, FAX 415/626–8626, WEB www. nowvoyager.com). **Skylink Travel and Tour** (✉ 1006 Mendocino Ave., Santa Rosa, CA 95401, ☎ 707/546–9888 or 800/225–5759, FAX 707/546–9891, WEB www.skylinktravel.com), serving lesbian travelers.

GUIDEBOOKS

Plan well and you won't be sorry. Guidebooks are excellent tools—and you can take them with you. You may want to check out color-photo-illustrated *Fodor's Exploring Paris,* thorough on culture and history, pocket-size *Citypack Paris,* and *Fodor's Around Paris with Kids*—all available at on-line retailers and bookstores everywhere.

HEALTH

For information on doctors and hospitals in Paris, *see* Emergencies, *above.*

HOLIDAYS

With 11 national holidays (*jours feriés*) and five weeks of paid vacation, the French have their share of repose. In May, there is a holiday nearly every week, so be prepared for stores, banks, and museums to shut their doors for days at a time. If a holiday falls on a Tuesday or Thursday, many businesses *font le pont* (make the bridge) and close on that Monday or Friday as well. But some exchange booths in tourist areas, small grocery stores, restaurants, cafés, and bakeries usually remain open. Bastille Day (July 14) is observed in true French form. Celebrations begin on the evening of the 13th, when city firemen open the doors to their stations, often classed as historical monuments, to host their much-acclaimed all-night balls and finish the next day with the annual military parade and air show.

Note that these dates are for the calendar year 2003: January 1 (New Year's Day); April 20–21 (Easter Sunday/Monday); May 1 (Labor Day); May 8 (VE Day); May 29 (Ascension); June 9 –10 (Pentecost Sunday/Monday); July 14 (Bastille Day); August 15 (Assumption); November 1 (All Saints); November 11 (Armistice); December 25 (Christmas).

INSURANCE

The most useful travel-insurance plan is a comprehensive policy that includes coverage for trip cancellation and interruption, default, trip delay, and medical expenses (with a waiver for preexisting conditions).

Without insurance you will lose all or most of your money if you cancel your trip, regardless of the reason. Default insurance covers you if your tour operator, airline, or cruise line goes out of business. Trip-delay covers expenses that arise because of bad weather or mechanical delays. Study the fine print when comparing policies.

If you're traveling internationally, a key component of travel insurance is coverage for medical bills incurred if you get sick on the road. Such expenses are not generally covered by Medicare or private policies. U.K. residents can buy a travel-insurance policy valid for most vacations taken during the year in which it's purchased (but check preexisting-condition coverage). British and Australian citizens need extra medical coverage when traveling overseas.

Always **buy travel policies directly from the insurance company**; if you buy them from a cruise line, airline, or tour operator that goes out of business you probably will not be covered for the agency or operator's default, a major risk. Before making any purchase, **review your existing health and homeowner's policies** to find what they cover away from home.

➤ TRAVEL INSURERS: In the United States: **Access America** (✉ 6600 W. Broad St., Richmond, VA 23230, ☎ 804/285–3300 or 800/284–8300, FAX 804/673–1586, WEB www. accessamerica.com). **Travel Guard International** (✉ 1145 Clark St., Stevens Point, WI 54481, ☎ 715/345–0505 or 800/826–1300, FAX 800/955–8785, WEB www.travelguard. com).

➤ INSURANCE INFORMATION: In Australia: **Insurance Council of Australia** (✉ Level 3, 56 Pitt St., Sydney NSW 2000, ☎ 03/9614–1077, FAX 03/9614–7924). In Canada: **Voyager**

Insurance (✉ 44 Peel Center Dr., Brampton, Ontario L6T 4M8, Canada, ☎ 905/791–8700; 800/668–4342 in Canada). In New Zealand: **Insurance Council of New Zealand** (✉ Box 474, Wellington, New Zealand, ☎ 04/472–5230, 🖷 04/473–3011, ⓦ www.icnz.org.nz). In the United Kingdom: **Association of British Insurers** (✉ 51–55 Gresham St., London EC2V 7HQ, U.K., ☎ 020/7600–3333, 🖷 020/7696–8999, ⓦ www.abi.org.uk).

LANGUAGES FOR TRAVELERS

The French may appear prickly at first to English-speaking visitors. But it usually helps if you **make an effort to speak a little French.** A simple, friendly *bonjour* (hello) will do, as will asking if the person you are greeting speaks English (*Parlez-vous anglais?*). Be patient, and speak English slowly. *See* the French Vocabulary and Menu Guide at the back of the book for more suggestions.

A phrase book and language-tape set can help get you started.

➤ PHRASE BOOKS AND LANGUAGE-TAPE SETS: *Fodor's French for Travelers* (☎ 800/733–3000 in the U.S.; 800/668–4247 in Canada; $7 for phrase book, $16.95 for audio set plus $5.50 for shipping).

LODGING

The lodgings listed are the cream of the crop in each price category. Facilities are always listed—but extra costs for them are not: when pricing accommodations, always ask what's included and what costs extra. Assume that hotels operate on the **European Plan** (with no meals) unless otherwise specified.

APARTMENT RENTALS

If you want a home base that's roomy enough for a family and comes with cooking facilities, **consider a furnished rental.** These can save you money, especially if you're traveling with a group. Home-exchange directories sometimes list rentals as well as exchanges. You might also look in the bimonthly journal *France-USA Contacts* (known as *FUSAC*), which lists rentals as well as apartment exchanges.

➤ INTERNATIONAL AGENTS: **At Home Abroad** (✉ 405 E. 56th St., Suite 6H, New York, NY 10022, ☎ 212/421–9165, 🖷 212/752–1591, ⓦ member.aol.com/athomabrod/index.html). **Drawbridge to Europe** (✉ 102 Granite St., Ashland, OR 97520, ☎ 541/482–7778 or 888/268–1148, 🖷 541/482–7779, ⓦ www.drawbridgetoeurope.com). **Hideaways International** (✉ 767 Islington St., Portsmouth, NH 03801, ☎ 603/430–4433 or 800/843–4433, 🖷 603/430–4444, ⓦ www.hideaways.com; membership $129). **Hometours International** (✉ Box 11503, Knoxville, TN 37939, ☎ 865/690–8484 or 800/367–4668, ⓦ thor.he.net/~hometour). **Interhome** (✉ 1990 N.E. 163rd St., Suite 110, N. Miami Beach, FL 33162, ☎ 305/940–2299 or 800/882–6864, 🖷 305/940–2911, ⓦ www.interhome.com). **Vacation Home Rentals Worldwide** (✉ 235 Kensington Ave., Norwood, NJ 07648, ☎ 201/767–9393 or 800/633–3284, 🖷 201/767–5510, ⓦ www.vhrww.com). **Villanet** (✉ 1251 N.W. 116th St., Seattle, WA 98177, ☎ 206/417–3444 or 800/964–1891, 🖷 206/417–1832, ⓦ www.rentavilla.com). **Villas and Apartments Abroad** (✉ 1270 Ave. of the Americas, 15th floor, New York, NY 10020, ☎ 212/897–5045 or 800/433–3020, 🖷 212/897–5039, ⓦ www.vaanyc.com). **Villas International** (✉ 950 Northgate Dr., Suite 206, San Rafael, CA 94903, ☎ 415/499–9490 or 800/221–2260, 🖷 415/499–9491, ⓦ www.villasintl.com).

➤ LOCAL AGENTS: *See* Chapter 4.

HOME EXCHANGES

If you would like to exchange your home for someone else's, **join a home-exchange organization,** which will send you its updated listings of available exchanges for a year and will include your own listing in at least one of them. It's up to you to make specific arrangements with the party interested in an exchange deal.

➤ EXCHANGE CLUBS: **HomeLink International** (✉ Box 47747, Tampa, FL 33647, ☎ 813/975–9825 or 800/638–3841, 🖷 813/910–8144, ⓦ www.homelink.org; $98 per year). **Intervac U.S.** (✉ 30 Corte San Fernando,

Tiburon, CA 94920, ☎ 800/756–4663, FAX 415/435–7440, WEB www.intervacus.com; $90 yearly fee for a listing, on-line access, and a catalog; $50 without catalog).

HOSTELS

No matter what your age, you can **save on lodging costs by staying at hostels.** In some 5,000 locations in more than 70 countries around the world, Hostelling International (HI), the umbrella group for a number of national youth-hostel associations, offers single-sex, dorm-style beds and, at many hostels, rooms for couples and family accommodations. Membership in any HI national hostel association, open to travelers of all ages, allows you to stay in HI-affiliated hostels at member rates; one-year membership is about $25 for adults (C$35 for a two-year minimum membership in Canada, £13 in the U.K., A$52 in Australia, and NZ$40 in New Zealand); hostels run about $10–$30 per night. Members have priority if the hostel is full; they're also eligible for discounts around the world, even on rail and bus travel in some countries.

Most of Paris's hostels and *foyers* (student hostels) are bargains at €20–€30 a night for a bed with free showers and a baguette-and-coffee wake-up call; some are even set near top city locales. In summer, you should reserve in writing a month in advance (deposits are often taken via credit card, usually MasterCard and Visa, for advance reservations); if you don't have a reservation, it's a good idea to check in as early as 8 AM. Some foyers have age restrictions and tend to house young workers and students in dorm-like accommodations, but other foyers accommodate travelers of all ages. Paris's major public hostels are run by the Féderation Unie des Auberges de Jeunesse (FUAJ)—for about €20, a bed, sheets, shower, and breakfast are provided, with beds usually three to four to a room. Maisons Internationales des Jeunes Étudiants (MIJE) have the plushest hostels, sometimes in historic mansions. Private hostels have accommodations that run from pleasant, if spartan, double rooms to dorm-like arrangements.

➤ BEST OPTIONS: In the Latin Quarter: **Young and Happy Youth Hostel** (⊠ 80 rue Mouffetard, 75005, ☎ 01–45–35–09–53, WEB www.youngand-happy.fr). In the Marais: **Hôtel le Fauconnier MIJE** (⊠ 11 rue de Fauconnier, 75004, ☎ 01–42–74–23–45, FAX 01–42–74–08–93). Near the Eiffel Tower: **Aloha Hostel** (⊠ 1 rue Borromée, 75015, ☎ 01–42–73–03–03, FAX 01–42–73–14–14, WEB www.aloha.fr). Near Montmartre: **Le Village** (⊠ 20 rue d'Orsel, 75018, ☎ 01–42–64–22–02, FAX 01–42–64–22–04, WEB www.villagehostel.fr). Near Père-Lachaise: **Auberge de Jeunesse d'Artagnan FUAJ** (⊠ 80 rue Vitruve, 3ᵉ,. ☎ 01–40–32–34–56, FAX 01–40–32–34–55).

➤ ORGANIZATIONS: **Australian Youth Hostel Association** (⊠ 10 Mallett St., Camperdown, NSW 2050, Australia, ☎ 02/9565–1699, FAX 02/9565–1325, WEB www.yha.com.au). **Féderation Unie des Auberges de Jeunesse** (FUAJ/Hostelling International; ⊠ FUAJ Beaubourg: 9 rue Brantôme, 3ᵉ, Paris, ☎ 01–48–04–70–40, WEB www.fuaj.org; Centre National: ⊠ 27 rue Pajol, 18ᵉ, Paris, ☎ 01–44–89–87–27). **Hostelling International—American Youth Hostels** (⊠ 733 15th St. NW, Suite 840, Washington, DC 20005, ☎ 202/783–6161, FAX 202/783–6171, WEB www.hiayh.org). **Hostelling International—Canada** (⊠ 400–205 Catherine St., Ottawa, Ontario K2P 1C3, Canada, ☎ 613/237–7884, FAX 613/237–7868, WEB www.hostellingintl.ca). **Youth Hostel Association of England and Wales** (⊠ Trevelyan House, Dimple Rd., Matlock, Derbyshire DE4 3YH, U.K., ☎ 0870/870–8808, FAX 0169/592–702, WEB www.yha.org.uk). **Youth Hostels Association of New Zealand** (⊠ P.O.Box 436, Level 3, 193 Cashel St., Christchurch, New Zealand, ☎ 6403/379–9970, FAX 6403/365–4476, WEB www.yha.org.nz).

HOTELS

It's always a good idea to **make hotel reservations in Paris as far in advance as possible,** especially in late spring, summer, and fall. E-mailing is probably the easiest way to contact a hotel if the hotel has Internet connections; faxing is another convenient way to contact the hotel (the staff is probably more likely to read English than to understand it over the phone long distance), though calling also works. In your e-mail or fax (or over the phone), specify the exact dates that you want to stay at the hotel (when you will arrive and when you will check out); the size of the room you want (single or double), and how many people will be sleeping there; what size bed you want (twin beds or double or larger, etc.); and whether you want a bathroom with a shower or bathtub (or both). You might also ask if a deposit (or your credit card number) is required and, if so, what happens if you cancel. Request that the hotel fax you back so that you have a written confirmation of your reservation in hand when you arrive at the hotel.

Here are some French words that can come in handy when booking a room: air-conditioning (*climatisation*); private baths (*salle de bain privée*); bathtub (*baignoire*); shower (*douche*).

If you arrive in Paris without a reservation, one of the two tourist offices may be able to help you. You may be able to get a better rate per night if you are staying a week or longer; ask. Note that the quality of accommodations, particularly older properties and even in luxury hotels, can vary from room to room; **if you don't like the room you're given, ask to see another.** You'll often see a sign outside a hotel with a painted shield bearing one to four stars based on a government rating system. At the bottom end are one-star hotels, where you might have to share a bathroom and do without an elevator. Two- and three-star hotels generally have private bathrooms, elevators, and in-room televisions. The ratings are sometimes misleading, however, since many hotels prefer to be understarred for tax reasons.

In addition to smaller properties and luxury hotels, Paris has—but is not dominated by—big chains. Examples in the upper price bracket are Frantel, Hilton, Hyatt, Marriott, and Novotel. The Best Western, Campanile, Climat de France, Holiday Inn, Ibis, and Timhotel chains are more moderate.

Typically, chains offer a more consistent standard of modern amenities (modern bathrooms, TV, etc.) but tend to lack atmosphere.

All hotels listed have private bath unless otherwise noted.

➤ TOLL-FREE NUMBERS: **Best Western** (☎ 800/528–1234, WEB www. bestwestern.com). **Choice** (☎ 800/ 424–6423, WEB www.hotelchoice. com).**Clarion** (☎ 800/424–6423, WEB www.choicehotels.com). **Comfort** (☎ 800/424–6423,WEB www. choicehotels.com). **Forte** (☎ 800/ 225–5843, WEB www.forte-hotels. com). **Four Seasons** (☎ 800/332– 3442, WEB www.fourseasons.com). **Hilton** (☎ 800/445–8667, WEB www. hilton.com). **Holiday Inn** (☎ 800/ 465–4329, WEB www.basshotels. com). **Hyatt Hotels & Resorts** (☎ 800/233–1234, WEB www.hyatt. com). **Inter-Continental** (☎ 800/ 327–0200, WEB www.intercontinental.com). **Le Meridien** (☎ 800/543– 4300, WEB www.forte-hotels.com). **Logis de France** (☎ 01–45–84–70– 00, FAX 01–44–24–08–74, WEB www. logis-de-france.fr). **Marriott** (☎ 800/ 228–9290, WEB www.marriott.com). **Le Meridien** (☎ 800/543–4300, WEB www.lemeridien-hotels.com). **Nikko Hotels International** (☎ 800/ 645–5687, WEB www.nikkohotels. com). **Quality Inn** (☎ 800/228–5151, WEB www.qualityinn.com). **Radisson** (☎ 800/333–3333, WEB www. radisson.com). **Relais & Châteaux** (☎ 01–45–72–96–50 in France; 212/ 856–0115 or 800/860–4930 in the U.S., FAX 01–45–72–96–69 in France; 212/856–0193 in the U.S., WEB www. relaischateaux.com). **Renaissance Hotels & Resorts** (☎ 800/468–3571, WEB www.renaissancehotels.com). **Sheraton** (☎ 800/325–3535, WEB www. starwood.com). **Small Luxury Hotels of the World** (☎ 713/522–9512; 800/ 525–4800 in the U.S.; 44/01372– 361873 in the U.K., FAX 713/524– 7412 in the U.S.; 44/01372–361874 in the U.K.).

MAIL AND SHIPPING

Post offices, or PTT, are scattered throughout every arrondissement and are recognizable by a yellow LA POSTE sign. They are usually open weekdays 8 AM–7 PM, Saturday 8 AM–noon.

➤ POST OFFICES: **Main office** (✉ 52 rue du Louvre, 1er), open 24 hours seven days a week. **Champs-Élysées office** (✉ 10 rue Balzar, 8e), Monday to Saturday, open until 7 PM.

OVERNIGHT SERVICES

Sending overnight mail from Paris is relatively easy. Besides DHL, Federal Express, and UPS, the French post office has an overnight mail service called Chronopost that has special prepaid boxes for international use (and also boxes specifically made to mail wine). All agencies listed can be used as drop-off points and all have information in English.

➤ MAJOR SERVICES: **DHL** (✉ 6 rue des Colonnes, 7e, ☎ 01–55–35–30–30, WEB www.dhl.com; ✉ 59 rue Iéna, 16e, ☎ 01–45–01–91–00). **Federal Express** (✉ 63 bd. Haussmann, 8e, ☎ 01–40–06–90–16, WEB www.fedex.com/fr; ✉ 2 rue 29 Juillet, 1er, ☎ 01–49–26–04–66; 08–00–12–38–00 information in English about pickups, WEB www.ups.com). **UPS** (✉ 34 bd. Malesherbes, 8e; ✉ 107 rue Réaumur, 2e, ☎ 08–00–87–78–77).

POSTAL RATES

Airmail letters to the United States and Canada cost €.67 for 20 grams, €1.25 for 40 grams, and €1.98 for 60 grams. Letters to the United Kingdom cost €.46 for up to 20 grams, as they do within France. Postcards cost €.46 within France and EU countries and €.67 to the United States and Canada. Stamps can be bought in post offices and cafés sporting a red TABAC sign.

RECEIVING MAIL

If you're uncertain where you'll be staying, have mail sent to American Express (if you're a card member) or to "poste restante" at any post office.

MÉTRO

Métro stations are recognizable either by a large yellow M within a circle or by the distinctive curly green Art Nouveau railings and archway bearing the full title (Métropolitain). Taking **the métro is the most efficient way to get around Paris.** *See* the Métro map, *below.*

Fourteen métro and two RER (Réseau Express Régional, or the Regional Express Network) lines crisscross Paris and the suburbs, and you are seldom more than 500 yards from the nearest station. The métro network connects at several points in Paris with the RER, the commuter trains that go from the city center to the suburbs. RER trains crossing Paris on their way from suburb to suburb can be great time-savers because they only make a few stops in the city (you can use the same tickets for both the métro and the RER within Paris).

It's essential to **know the name of the last station on the line you take,** as this name appears on all signs. A connection (you can make as many as you like on one ticket) is called a *correspondance*. At junction stations, illuminated orange signs bearing the name of the line terminus appear over the correct corridors for each correspondance. Illuminated blue signs marked *sortie* indicate the station exit. Note that tickets are only valid inside the gates, or *limites*.

Métro service starts at 5:30 AM and continues until 1 AM, when the last train on each line reaches its terminus. Some lines and stations in Paris are a bit risky at night, in particular Lines 2 and 13. But in general, the métro is relatively safe throughout, providing you **don't walk around with your wallet hanging out of your back pocket or travel alone late at night.**

FARES AND SCHEDULES

All **métro tickets and passes are valid not only for the métro but also for all RER and bus travel within Paris.** Métro tickets cost €1.30 each; a *carnet* (10 tickets for €9.30) is a better value. The best deal is the weekly (*coupon jaune*) or monthly (*carte orange*) ticket, sold according to zone. Zones 1 and 2 cover the entire métro network; tickets cost €13.25 a week or €44.35 a month. If you plan to take suburban trains to visit places in Ile-de-France, consider a four-zone (Versailles, St-Germain-en-Laye; €21.65 a week) or six-zone (Rambouillet, Fontainebleau; €28.10 a week) ticket. For these weekly/monthly tickets, you need a pass (available from rail and major métro stations) and a passport-size photograph (many stations have photo booths).

A one-day (Mobilis) and the two- to five-day (Paris-Visite) tickets assure unlimited travel on the entire RATP network: métro, RER, bus, tram, funicular (Montmartre) and noctambus (night bus). Unlike the coupon jaune, which is good from Monday morning to Sunday evening, Mobilis and Paris-Visite passes are valid starting any day of the week and give you discounts on a limited number of museums and tourist attractions. The price is €8.38 (one-day), €13.70 (two-day), €18.30 (three-day), and €26.70 (five-day) for Paris only. Rates for children ages 4–11 are approximately half of these prices. Suburbs such as Versailles and St-Germain-en-Laye cost €23.60 (one-day). EuroDisney costs €23.60, €34.30, €42.70, and €53.35 respectively for a one- to four-day pass.

Access to métro and RER platforms is through an automatic ticket barrier. Slide your ticket in and pick it up as it pops out. Be certain to **keep your ticket during your journey;** you'll need it to leave the RER system and in case you run into any green-clad ticket inspectors, who will impose a hefty fine if you can't produce your ticket.

➤ Métro Information: **RATP** (✉ Pl. de la Madeleine, 8ᵉ, ☎ 08–36–68–41–14, ＷＥＢ www.ratp.fr), open daily 9–5.

MONEY MATTERS

Like many capital cities, **Paris is expensive**; the good news is that, as of press time (Spring 2002), it is less expensive than New York City, London, and Tokyo. If you avoid the obvious tourist traps, you can find plenty of affordable places to eat and shop. Prices tend to reflect the standing of an area in the eyes of Parisians; much sought-after residential arrondissements such as the 7ᵉ, 16ᵉ, and 17ᵉ—of limited tourist interest—are far more expensive than the student-oriented, much-visited Latin Quarter. The tourist area where value for money is most difficult to find is the 8ᵉ arrondissement, on and around the Champs-Élysées. Places where you can generally be certain to shop, eat,

and stay without overpaying include the streets surrounding Montmartre (not the Butte, or hilltop, itself); the St-Michel/Sorbonne area on the Left Bank; the mazelike streets around Les Halles and the Marais in central Paris; in Montparnasse, south of the boulevard; and the Bastille, République, and Belleville areas of eastern Paris.

Note that in cafés, bars, and some restaurants, **it's less expensive to eat or drink standing at the counter than it is to sit at a table.** Two prices are listed—*au comptoir* (at the counter) and *à salle* (at a table)—and sometimes a third for the terrace. A cup of coffee, standing at a bar, costs from €1.05; if you sit, it will cost €1.50–€6.10. A glass of beer costs from €1.50 standing and from €2.30 to €6.10 sitting; a soft drink costs between €1.50 and €3.05. A ham sandwich will cost between €2.60 and €4.60.

Expect to pay €6.10–€10.70 for a short taxi ride. Museum entry is €3.05–€6.90, though there are hours or days of the week when admission is reduced or free.

Prices throughout this guide are given for adults. Substantially reduced fees are almost always available for children, students, and senior citizens.

ATMS

ATMs are one of the easiest ways to get euros. Although transaction fees may be higher abroad than at home, banks usually offer excellent, wholesale exchange rates through ATMs. You may, however, have to look around for Cirrus and Plus locations; it's a good idea to get a list of locations from your bank before you go. Note, too, that you may have better luck with ATMs if you're using a credit card or debit card that is also a Visa or MasterCard, rather than just your bank card.

To get cash at ATMs in Paris, **your PIN must be four digits long,** If you are having trouble remembering your pin, do not try more than twice, because at the third attempt, the machine will eat your card and you will have to go back the next morning to retrieve it. Note, too, that you may be charged by your bank for using ATMs overseas; inquire at your bank about charges.

CREDIT CARDS

Throughout this guide, the following abbreviations are used: **AE,** American Express; **DC,** Diners Club; **MC,** MasterCard; and **V,** Visa.

➤ REPORTING LOST CARDS: **American Express** (☎ 336/939–1111 or 336/ 668–5309); call collect. **Diners Club** (☎ 303/799–1504); call collect. **MasterCard** (☎ 0800/90–1387). **Visa** (☎ 0800/90–1179; 410/581–9994 collect).

CURRENCY

On January 1st, 2002, the new single European Union (EU) currency, the euro, became the official currency of the 12 countries participating in the European Monetary Union (with the notable exceptions of Great Britain, Denmark, and Sweden). In France, the long-awaited physical debut of the euro was rather anticlimactic; banks closed their doors for an extra day to prepare for a bustle and confusion that never came. In fact, the transition went quite smoothly (some French equipped themselves with special pocket calculators that automatically calculated euro-franc conversions, out of an unfounded fear that with the change of currency, prices would rise). Actually, the toughest task for Europeans was to familiarize themselves with the newly issued coins and bills so shiny and fresh they had the odd perfection of play money in a new set of Monopoly. But, money is, after all, just money, and with that philosophical nod to reality, the European Monetary Union, over three hundred million strong, was born. The first thing you will notice is that the euro system has quite a lot of coins, eight to be exact: 1 and 2 euros, plus 1, 2, 5, 10, 20, and 50 cents. All coins have one side that has the value of the euro on it, while the opposite side is adorned with each country's own unique national symbol. There are seven colorful notes: 5, 10, 20, 50, 100, 200, and 500 euros. Notes have the principal architectural styles from antiquity onwards on one side and the map and the flag of Europe on the other and are the same for all coun-

tries. The first thing you must do when you change your money is to memorize the coins as soon as you can (notes are much easier to grasp, as they start off at €5) and you'll undoubtedly find yourself quickly weighted down with all those coins. This was the first complaint most Europeans made with this new system and this, in turn, led to the second complaint: Due to their high nickel content, euro coins pose a problem for people with an allergic sensitivity to the mineral (if you're senstive to nickel, try to handle the coins as little as possible, and if you do come in contact with them, rinse your hands as soon as you can).

All that aside, you'll soon realize just how easy the advent of the euro is going to make any whirlwind grand European tour. From France, you'll glide through the borders of Austria, Germany, Italy, Spain, Holland, Ireland, Greece, Belgium, Finland, Luxembourg, and Portugal with no pressing need to run to the local exchange booth to change yet another currency before you even had the time to become familiar with the last. You'll be able to do what drives many tourists crazy—to assess the value of a purchase (for example, to realize that eating a three-course meal in a small restaurant in Lisbon is cheaper than the ham sandwich you bought on the Champs Élysées). Along with the facility of movement from country to country, the euro has another benefit in that it was created as a direct competitor with the U.S. dollar and, therefore, their rates of conversion are quite similar. At press time (spring 2002), one euro equals U.S.$0.97, which means there are only three cents separating them—a definite perk to those who both hated yet felt compelled to convert prices into dollars.

Don't be alarmed if you've forgotten some rumpled francs at home this trip—you have until midnight, February 17, 2005 to change coins and until midnight February 17, 2012 to change notes at the Banque of France (a fixed rate of exchange was established: 1 euro equaling 6.55957 French francs). After these dates, however, you may as well frame those remaining francs and hang them on the wall for posterity, not to say prosperity.

Such are the ground rules when it comes to the euro and the old EU currencies. But **when it comes to the dollar (and all other currencies that are not part of the EU community), you still have to pay close attention to where you change your money**—shop around for the best exchange rates (and also check the rates before leaving home) when it comes to non-EU currencies, such as the U.S. dollar, the Japanese yen, and the British pound. The rates of conversion between the euro and other local currencies have been irrevocably fixed: 1 euro = 1.95 German marks; 0.78 Irish punts; 13.76 Austrian schillings; 1,936.26 Italian lira; 40.33 Belgian francs; 166.38 Spanish pesetas; 2.20 Dutch guilders; 200.48 Portuguese escudos; 40.33 Luxembourg francs; and 5.94 Finnish markkas. Outside the EU, at time of writing, 1 euro = 1.39 Canadian dollars; 1.79 Australian dollars, 2.14 New Zealand dollars; and 0.62 pound sterling.

CURRENCY EXCHANGE

These days, the **easiest way to get euros is through ATMs**; you can find them in airports, train stations, and throughout the city. ATM rates are excellent because they are based on wholesale rates offered only by major banks. It's a good idea, however, to bring some euros with you from home and always to have some cash and traveler's checks as backup. For the best deal when exchanging currencies not within the Monetary Union purview (the U.S. dollar, the yen, and the English pound are examples), compare rates at banks (which usually have the most favorable rates) and booths and look for exchange booths that clearly state "no commission." At exchange booths always confirm the rate with the teller before exchanging money. You won't do as well at exchange booths in airports or rail and bus stations, in hotels, in restaurants, or in stores. Of all the banks in Paris, the Banque de France has the best rates. To avoid lines at airport exchange booths, **get enough euros before you leave home to cover any immediate necessity.**

➤ EXCHANGE SERVICES: **International Currency Express** (☎ 888/278–6628 orders). **Thomas Cook Currency Services** (☎ 800/287–7362 telephone orders and retail locations, WEB www.us.thomascook.com).

TRAVELER'S CHECKS

Will you need traveler's checks? It depends on where you're headed. If you're going to rural areas and small towns, go with cash; traveler's checks are best used in cities. Lost or stolen checks can usually be replaced within 24 hours. To ensure a speedy refund, buy your own traveler's checks—don't let someone else pay for them; such irregularities can cause delays. The person who bought the checks should make the call to request a refund.

PACKING

In your carry-on luggage, **pack an extra pair of eyeglasses or contact lenses** and **enough of any medication you take** to last a few days longer than the entire trip. You may also ask your doctor to write a spare prescription using the drug's generic name, since brand names may vary from country to country. In luggage to be checked, **never pack prescription drugs or valuables.** To avoid customs delays, carry medications in their original packaging. And don't forget to carry with you the addresses of offices that handle refunds of lost traveler's checks. Check *Fodor's How to Pack* (available in bookstores everywhere) for more tips.

CHECKING LUGGAGE

You are allowed one carry-on bag and one personal article, such as a purse or a laptop computer. Make sure that everything you carry aboard will fit under your seat or in the overhead bin. Get to the gate early, so you can board as soon as possible, before the overhead bins fill up.

If you are flying internationally, note that baggage allowances may be determined not by piece but by weight—generally 88 pounds (40 kilograms) in first class, 66 pounds (30 kilograms) in business class, and 44 pounds (20 kilograms) in economy.

Airline liability for baggage is limited to $1,250 per person on flights within the United States. On international flights it amounts to $9.07 per pound or $20 per kilogram for checked baggage (roughly $640 per 70-pound bag) and $400 per passenger for unchecked baggage. You can buy additional coverage at check-in for about $10 per $1,000 of coverage, but it excludes a rather extensive list of items, shown on your airline ticket.

Before departure, **itemize your bags' contents** and their worth, and label the bags with your name, address, and phone number. (If you use your home address, cover it so potential thieves can't see it readily.) Inside each bag, **pack a copy of your itinerary.** At check-in, **make sure that each bag is correctly tagged** with the destination airport's three-letter code. If your bags arrive damaged or fail to arrive at all, file a written report with the airline *before leaving the airport.*

PASSPORTS AND VISAS

When traveling internationally, **carry your passport** even if you don't need one (it's always the best form of I.D.) and **make two photocopies of the data page** (one for someone at home and another for you, carried separately from your passport). If you lose your passport, promptly call the nearest embassy or consulate and the local police.

ENTERING FRANCE

All citizens of Australia, Canada, New Zealand, the United States, and the United Kingdom, even infants, need only a valid passport to enter France for stays of up to 90 days. If you lose your passport, promptly call the nearest embassy or consulate and the local police.

➤ AUSTRALIAN CITIZENS: **Australian Passport Office** (☎ 131–232, WEB www.passports.gov.au).

➤ CANADIAN CITIZENS: **Passport Office** (to mail in applications: ✉ Department of Foreign Affairs and International Trade, Ottawa, Ontario K1A 0G3, ☎ 819/994–3500 or 800/567–6868, WEB www.dfait-maeci.gc.ca/passport).

➤ NEW ZEALAND CITIZENS: **New Zealand Passport Office** (☎ 04/474–8100 or 0800/22–5050, WEB www.passports.govt.nz).

➤ U.K. CITIZENS: **London Passport Office** (☎ 0870/521–0410, WEB www.passport.gov.uk) for fees and documentation requirements and to request an emergency passport.

➤ U.S. CITIZENS: **National Passport Information Center** (☎ 900/225–5674; calls are 35¢ per minute for automated service, $1.05 per minute for operator service; WEB www.travel.state.gov/npicinfo.html).

REST ROOMS

Use of public toilet facilities in cafés and bars is usually reserved for customers. Bathrooms are often located downstairs and are usually unisex, which may mean walking by a men's urinal to reach the cubicle. Turkish-style toilets—holes in the ground surrounded by porcelain pads for your feet—still exist. Stand as far away as possible when you press the flushing mechanism in order to avoid water damage to your shoes. In certain cafés, the lights will not come on in the bathroom until the cubicle door is locked. These lights work on a three-minute timer to save electricity. Simply press the button again if the lights go out. Clean public toilets are available in fast-food chains, department stores, and public parks. You can also find pay-per-use toilet units on the street, which require €.30 (small children, however, should not use these alone, as the self-sanitizing system works with weight-related sensors that might not detect a child's presence). There are bathrooms in the larger métro stations and in all train stations for a cost of €.15–€.30.

SAFETY

Paris is one of the safest big cities in the world, good news for the traveling lone female. Although times are changing, the idea still exists that women traveling alone are fair game for troublesome comments and the like; however, *dragueurs* (men who persistently profess their undying love to hapless female passersby) are a dying breed in this increasingly politically correct world. Certain neighborhoods can still pose problems, thanks to the night trade that goes on around

Les Halles and St-Denis and on boulevard Clichy in Pigalle. Some off-the-beaten-path neighborhoods—particularly the outlying suburban communities around Paris, heavily populated by working-class and immigrant populations—may warrant extra precaution. Note that smiling automatically out of politeness is not part of French culture and can be quickly misinterpreted. If you encounter a problem, don't be afraid to show your irritation. When in doubt, stick to the boulevards, memorize the time of the last métro train to your station, ride in the first car by the conductor, and just use your common sense. Paris is a giant metropolis, so it is always best to be streetwise and alert.

SENIOR-CITIZEN TRAVEL

Travelers 60 years or older to Paris can take advantage of many discounts, such as reduced admissions of 20%–50% to museums and movie theaters. For rail travel outside of Paris, the Carte Senior entitles travelers 60 years and older to discounts.

To qualify for age-related discounts, **mention your senior-citizen status up front** when booking hotel reservations (not when checking out) and before you're seated in restaurants (not when paying the bill). When renting a car, ask about promotional car-rental discounts, which may be cheaper than senior-citizen rates.

➤ EDUCATIONAL PROGRAMS: **Elderhostel** (✉ 11 Ave. de Lafayette, Boston, MA 02111-1746, ☎ 877/426-8056, FAX 877/426-2166, WEB www.elderhostel.org). **Interhostel** (✉ University of New Hampshire, 6 Garrison Ave., Durham, NH 03824, ☎ 603/862-1147 or 800/733-9753, FAX 603/862-1113, WEB www.learn.unh.edu).

SIGHTSEEING TOURS

There are many ways to see Paris on a guided tour.

BIKE TOURS

A number of companies organize bike tours around Paris and its environs (Versailles, Chantilly, and Fontainebleau) for about €23–€30 per person.

➤ INFORMATION: **Butterfield & Robinson** (✉ 70 Bond St., Toronto, M5B 1X3, Canada, ☎ 416/864-1354 or 800/678-1147). **Paris Bike** (✉ 83 rue Daguerre, 14ᵉ, ☎ 01-45-38-58-58). **Paris à Vélo, C'est Sympa** (✉ 37 bd. Bourdon, 4ᵉ, ☎ 01-48-87-60-01).

BOAT TOURS

Boat trips along the Seine run throughout the day and evening for a cost €6.10–€15.25. Many of the tours include lunch or dinner for an average cost of €45.80–€91.60. Reservations for meals are usually essential, and some require jacket and tie.

Bateaux Mouches boats depart from the Pont de l'Alma (Right Bank) 10–noon, 2–7, and 8:30–10:30. Lunch is served at 1 PM and dinner at 8:30 PM. Bateaux Parisiens–Tour Eiffel boats depart from the Pont d'Iéna (Left Bank) every half hour in summer and every hour in winter, starting at 10 AM. The last boat leaves at 9 PM (11 PM in summer). There are lunch and dinner cruises. Bat-O-Bus's trip along the Seine, without commentary, gives the advantage of being able to get on and off at any one of seven stops along the river, including the Eiffel Tower, Musée d'Orsay, St. Germain-des-Prés, the Louvre, Notre-Dame, Hôtel de Ville, and the Champs-Élysées. Get a one day pass for €9.90, or buy a two-consecutive-day pass for €12.10. Note that it operates from May 1 to October 31 and departs every half hour between 10 and 6. Canauxrama organizes leisurely canal tours in flat-bottom barges along the St-Martin and Ourcq canals in East Paris. Departures from the quai de la Loire are at 9:15 and 2:45, and departures from the Bassin de l'Arsenal (opposite 50 boulevard de la Bastille) are at 9:30 and 2:30. The trip lasts about 2½ hours. Reservations should be made. Paris Canal runs three-hour trips with bilingual commentary between the Musée d'Orsay and the Parc de La Villette, between April and mid-November only. Reservations are essential. Vedettes du Pont Neuf boats depart every half hour from square du Vert Galant, 10–noon, 1:30–6:30, and 9–10:30 from March to October. Yachts de Paris organizes 2½-hour "gourmand cruises" (for about €135.90) year-round.

➤ FEES AND SCHEDULES: **Bateaux Mouches** (✉ Pont de l'Alma, 8ᵉ, ☎ 01–42–25–96–10, WEB www.bateauxmouches.com). **Bateaux Parisiens-Tour Eiffel** (✉ Pont d'Iéna, 7ᵉ, ☎ 01–44–11–33–44, WEB www.bateauxparisiens.com). **Bat-O-Bus** (✉ Pont d'Iéna, 7ᵉ, ☎ 01–44–11–33–44 or 01–44–11–33–99, WEB www.ratp.com). **Canauxrama** (✉ 5 bis quai de la Loire, 19ᵉ; Bassin de l'Arsenal, 12ᵉ, ☎ 01–42–39–15–00; WEB www.canauxrama.com). **Paris Canal** (✉ 19 quai de la Loire, 19ᵉ, ☎ 01–42–40–96–97). **Vedettes du Pont Neuf** (✉ Ile de la Cité, 1ᵉʳ, ☎ 01–46–33–98–38). **Yachts de Paris** (✉ Port de Javel, ☎ 01–44–54–14–70, WEB www.yachtsdeparis.com).

BUS TOURS

For a two-hour orientation tour by bus, the standard price is about €23. The two largest bus-tour operators are Cityrama and Paris Vision; for a more intimate—albeit expensive—tour of the city, Cityrama also runs several minibus excursions per day. Paris Bus gives tours in a London-style double-decker bus. You can catch the bus at any of nine pickup points; tickets cost €21 and allow you unlimited use for two days. For €23. the "Paris Open Tour" gives you two (consecutive) days of freedom to visit Paris in a double-decker bus with an open top. The bilingual tour lasts about two hours, but you can get on and off as you please, since the bus stops at more than 20 spots along a circular route. These tours are slow and lose their charm after approximately the first 20 minutes, especially with the long and rather exasperating multilingual commentary. For a more interesting, authentic, and economical trip, why not take a regular Parisian bus for a mere €1.30 per ticket? A copy of the timetables for these tours is available from the main Paris Tourist Office. RATP (Paris Transit Authority) also gives guide-accompanied excursions in and around Paris by bus.

➤ FEES AND SCHEDULES: **Cityrama** (✉ 4 pl. des Pyramides, 1ᵉʳ, ☎ 01–44–55–61–00). **Paris Bus** (☎ 01–42–30–55–50). **Paris Vision** (✉ 214 rue de Rivoli, 1ᵉʳ, ☎ 01–42–60–31–25). **RATP** (✉ Pl. de la Madeleine, 8ᵉ; 53 bis quai des Grands-Augustins, 6ᵉ, ☎ 08–36–68–41–14).

HELICOPTER TOURS

For a spectacular aerial view of Paris, Delta Lima offers a helicopter tour; it takes off from Toussus le Noble (15 minutes from Paris). Tours last 35 minutes and cost €147 per person.

➤ FEES AND SCHEDULES: **Delta Lima** (☎ 01–40–68–01–23).

MINIBUS TOURS

Paris Bus and Paris Major Limousine organize tours of Paris and environs by luxury minibuses (for 4 to 15 passengers) for a minimum of four hours. The price varies from €260 to €397. Reservations are essential.

➤ INFORMATION: **Paris Bus** (✉ 22 rue de la Prévoyance, Vincennes, ☎ 01–43–65–55–55, WEB www.touringfrance.com). **Paris Major Limousine** (✉ 6 pl. de la Madeleine, 8ᵉ, ☎ 01–44–52–50–00, WEB www.parislimousine.fr).

WALKING TOURS

The tourist season after the September 11th terrorist attacks in New York City proved too challenging for most of the small independent companies that ran English-language walking tours in Paris. Luckily the team at Paris Walking Tours have continued to offer a wide selection of tours, from neighborhood visits to museum tours and theme tours such as "Hemingway's Paris," "The Marais," "Montmartre," and "The Latin Quarter." A two-hour tour costs about €10.

Black Paris Tours offers tours exploring the places made famous by African-American musicians, writers, artists, and political exiles. Tours include a four- to five-hour walking-bus-métro tour (€53.45) that offers first-time visitors a city orientation and a primer in the history of African-Americans in Paris. Other options include "Montmartre/Pigalle: The 1920s Harlem of Paris" and tours of top African and soul-food restaurants.

A list of walking tours is also available from the Caisse Nationale des Monuments Historiques, in the weekly magazine *Pariscope,* and in *L'Officiel des Spectacles,* which lists walking tours under the heading *"Conférences"* (most are in French, unless otherwise noted).

➤ FEES AND SCHEDULES: **Black Paris Tours** (☎ 01–46–37–03–96). **Paris Walking Tours** (☎ 01–48–09–21–40, WEB www.paris-walks.com). **Butterfield & Robinson** (✉ 70 Bond St., Toronto, M5B 1X3, Canada, ☎ 416/864–1354 or 800/678–1147). **Caisse Nationale des Monuments Historiques** (✉ Bureau des Visites/Conférences, Hôtel de Sully, 62 rue St-Antoine, 4ᵉ, ☎ 01–44–61–21–70).

STUDENTS IN PARIS

For a detailed listing of deals for students in Paris, ask for the brochure *"Jeunes à Paris"* from the main tourist office. *"France-USA Contacts"* (*"FUSAC"*), a twice-monthly publication available free in restaurants and bookstores, also has useful information.

➤ IDs AND SERVICES: **Council Travel** (✉ 205 E. 42nd St., 15th floor, New York, NY 10017, ☎ 212/822–2700 or 888/226–8624, FAX 212/822–2699, WEB www.councilexchanges.org) for mail orders only, in the United States. **Travel Cuts** (✉ 187 College St., Toronto, Ontario M5T 1P7, Canada, ☎ 416/979–2406 or 888/838–2887 in Canada, FAX 416/979–8167, WEB www.travelcuts.com).

TAXES

All taxes must be included in affixed prices in France. Prices in **restaurants and hotel prices must by law include taxes and service charges:** If these appear as additional items on your bill, you should complain.

VALUE-ADDED TAX

VAT (value-added tax, known in France as TVA), at a standard rate of 19.6% (33% for luxury goods), is included in the price of many goods, but foreigners are often entitled to a refund. To be eligible for the VAT, an item (or items) must be purchased in one day in one place and must equal or exceed €182.20. You cannot combine purchases from different shops to total the required amount, nor combine purchases from various days to total the required amount. The VAT for services (restaurants/theater, etc.) is not refundable for the leisure traveler. To receive the VAT, request a refund form from the business, fill it out on the spot, noting your preferred means of receiving the VAT payment (credit card or a bank check in U.S. dollars). The business must complete the form and stamp it, then mail it in a provided stamped-addressed envelope. Alternatively, you can process your VAT refund at the airport. Go to the airport's VAT or (TVA) counter (at your last point of departure from the European Union) and be ready to show the customs official your goods. The customs official will then (all-importantly) stamp your forms and put the letter into any one of the mailboxes at the airport. Your refund will arrive either as a credit to your credit card or as a check in U.S. dollars. You can also go to the French consulate with your plane tickets, your VAT forms, and the items you purchased to receive the stamp (which costs $21) that will ensure the VAT refund; there is a three-month (after date of purchase) time limit. Finally, there are commercial companies which facilitate this process for you: Global Refund is among the largest.

➤ VAT REFUNDS: **Global Refund** (☎ 800/566–9828, FAX 845/348–1549, WEB www.globalrefund.com).

TAXIS

Taxi rates are based on location and time. Daytime rates, A (7 AM–7 PM), within Paris are €.55 per kilometer (½ mi), and nighttime rates, B, are around €.90 per kilometer. Suburban zones and airports, C, are €1.10 per kilometer. There is a basic hire charge of €2 for all rides, a €.90 supplement per piece of luggage, and a €.75 supplement if you're picked up at an SNCF station. Waiting time is charged at €19.85 per hour. The easiest way to get a taxi is to **ask your hotel or a restaurant to call a taxi for you, or go to the nearest taxi stand** (you can find one every couple of blocks); cabs with their signs lit can be hailed but are annoyingly difficult to spot (and they are not all a single, uniform color). In July 2001, a new law was (finally) implemented requiring chauffeurs to take a fourth passenger for an average supplement of €2.30. It is customary to tip the driver about 10%.

TELEPHONES

AREA AND COUNTRY CODES

The country code for France is 33. The first two digits of French numbers are a prefix determined by zone: Paris and Ile-de-France, 01; the northwest, 02; the northeast, 03; the southeast, 04; and the southwest, 05. Pay close attention to numbers beginning with 08. Calls that begin with 08 followed by 00 are toll-free, but calls that begin with 08 followed by 36—like the information lines for the SNCF for example—cost €.35 per minute, so be careful. Numbers that begin with 06 are reserved for cell phones.

Note that **when dialing France from abroad, drop the initial 0 from the telephone number** (all numbers listed in this book include the initial 0, which is used for calling numbers *from within* France). To call a telephone number in Paris from the United States, dial 011–33 plus the phone number, but minus the initial 0 listed for the specific number in Paris (phone numbers in this book are listed with the full 10 digits, which you use to make local calls). In other words, the local number for the Louvre is 01–40–20–51–51. To call this number from New York City, dial 011–33–1–40–20–51–51. To call this number from within Paris, dial 01–40–20–51–51. To call France from the United Kingdom, dial 00–33, then dial the number in France minus the initial 0 of the specific number.

DIRECTORY AND OPERATOR ASSISTANCE

To find a number in France, **dial 12 for information.** For international inquiries, dial 00–33 plus the country code. These calls have a fixed rate of €.60.

Another source of information is the Minitel, an on-line network similar to the Internet. You can use one—they look like small computer terminals—free in most post offices. To access the on-line phone book, hit the *appel* (call) key, then type the name you are looking for, and hit *envoi* (return). It is also useful for tracking down services: tap in *piscine* (swimming pool) under *activité* (activity), for example, and it will give you a list of all the pools in Paris. Go to other lines or pages by hitting the *suite* (next) key. Newer models will connect automatically when you hit the book-icon key. To disconnect, hit *fin* (end).

INTERNATIONAL CALLS

To make a direct international call out of France, dial 00 and wait for the tone; then dial the country code (1 for the United States and Canada, 44 for the United Kingdom, 61 for Australia, and 64 for New Zealand) and the area code (minus any initial 0) and number.

Good news—telephone rates are actually decreasing in France due to the fact that the France Telecom monopoly now has some stringent competition. As in most countries, the highest rates fall between 8 AM and 7 PM and average out to a hefty €.25 per minute to the United States, Canada, and the closer European countries including Germany and Great Britain. Rates are greatly reduced from 7 PM to 8 AM with an average €.12 per minute.

To call home with the help of an operator, dial 00–33 plus the country code. There is an automatic €6.80 service charge.

Telephone cards are sold that enable you to make long-distance and international calls from any phone. Don't hesitate in investing in one if you plan on making calls from your hotel as hotels often accumulate service charges and also have the most expensive rates.

LOCAL CALLS

Since all local numbers in Paris and the Ile-de-France begin with a 01, **you must dial the full 10-digit number, including the initial 0.** A local call costs €.11 for every three minutes.

LONG-DISTANCE CALLS

To call from region to region within France, **dial the full 10-digit number, including the initial 0.**

LONG-DISTANCE SERVICES

AT&T, MCI, and Sprint access codes make calling long distance relatively convenient, but you may find the local access number blocked in many hotel rooms. First ask the hotel operator to connect you. If the hotel operator balks, ask for an international operator, or dial the international operator yourself. One way to improve your odds of getting connected to your long-distance carrier is to travel with more than one company's calling card (a hotel may block Sprint, for example, but not MCI). If all else fails, call from a pay phone.

➤ ACCESS CODES: **AT&T Direct** (☎ 08–00–99–00–11 or 08–00–99–01–11; 800/222–0300 information). **MCI WorldPhone** (☎ 08–00–99–00–19; 800/444–4444 information). **Sprint International Access** (☎ 08–00–99–00–87; 800/793–1153 information).

PHONE CARDS

Practically all **French pay phones are operated by** *télécartes* (phone cards), which you can buy from post offices, tabacs, magazine kiosks, and any métro station. These phone cards will save you money and hassle, since it is almost impossible to find phones that take change these days. There are as many phone cards these days as bakeries so to be safe, request: the *télécarte international,* which, despite its name, allows you to make either local or international calls and offers greatly reduced rates. Instructions are in English and the cost is €7.65 for 60 units and €15.25 for 120 units. You may also request the simple *télécarte,* which allows you to make calls in France (the cost is €7.50 for 50 units; €14.80 for 120 units). You can also use your credit card in much the same way as a télécarte.

PUBLIC PHONES

Public **telephone booths can almost always be found in post offices, métro stations, bus stops, and in most cafés,** as well as on the street.

TIME

The time difference between New York and Paris is 6 hours (so when it's 1 PM in New York, it's 7 PM in Paris). The time difference between London and Paris is 1 hour; between Sydney and Paris, 8–9 hours; and between Auckland and Paris, 12 hours. All schedules, be it train, plane, or theater, work on a 24-hour or "continual" clock in France, which means that 8 AM is 8h00 but 8 PM is 20h00. Midnight is 24h00.

TIPPING

Bills in bars and restaurants must, by law, include service, but **it is customary to round out your bill with some small change** unless you're dissatisfied. The amount varies—from €.15 for a beer to €1.50–€2.30 after a meal. In expensive restaurants, it's common to leave an additional 5% of the bill on the table.

Tip taxi drivers and hairdressers about 10% of the bill. Give theater and cinema ushers €.25–€.50. In some theaters and hotels, cloakroom attendants may expect nothing (watch for signs that say *pourboire interdit*—tipping forbidden); otherwise, give them €.75. Washroom attendants usually get €.30, though the sum is often posted.

If you stay more than two or three days in a hotel, it is customary to leave something for the chambermaid—about €1.50 per day. Expect to pay about €1.50 (€.75 in a moderately priced hotel) to the person who carries your bags or who hails you a taxi. In hotels providing room service, give €.75 to the waiter (this does not apply if breakfast is routinely served in your room). If the chambermaid does some pressing or laundering for you, give her €.75–€1.50 on top of the bill. If the concierge has been very helpful, it is customary to leave a tip of €8–€16, depending on the type of hotel and the level of service.

Service station attendants get nothing for pumping gas or checking oil but €.75 or €1.50 for checking tires. Train and airport porters get a fixed sum (€.90–€1.50) per bag. Museum guides should get €1.50–€3 after a guided tour. It is standard practice to tip bus drivers about €1.50 after an excursion.

TOURS AND PACKAGES

Because everything is prearranged on a prepackaged tour or independent vacation, you spend less time planning—and often get it all at a good price.

For hundreds of out-of-the-ordinary tour options click on "Adventure Travel" at www.fodors.com.

BOOKING WITH AN AGENT

Travel agents are excellent resources. But it's a good idea to collect brochures from several agencies, as some agents' suggestions may be influenced by relationships with tour and package firms that reward them for volume sales. If you have a special interest, **find an agent with expertise in that area**; ASTA has a database of specialists worldwide.

Make sure your travel agent is familiar with the accommodations and other services of the place they're recommending. Ask about the hotel's location, room size, beds, and whether it has a pool, room service, or programs for children, if you care about these. Has your agent been there in person or sent others whom you can contact?

Do some homework on your own, too: local tourism boards can provide information about lesser-known and small-niche operators, some of which may sell only direct.

BUYER BEWARE

Each year consumers are stranded or lose their money when tour operators—even large ones with excellent reputations—go out of business. So **check out the operator.** Ask several travel agents about its reputation, and try to **book with a company that has a consumer-protection program.** (Look for information in the company's brochure.) In the United States, members of the National Tour Association and the United States Tour Operators Association are required to set aside funds to cover your payments and travel arrangements in the event that the company

defaults. It's also a good idea to choose a company that participates in the American Society of Travel Agents' Tour Operator Program (TOP); ASTA will act as mediator in any disputes between you and your tour operator.

Remember that the more your package or tour includes the better you can predict the ultimate cost of your vacation. Make sure you know exactly what is covered, and **beware of hidden costs.** Are taxes, tips, and transfers included? Entertainment and excursions? These can add up.

➤ TOUR-OPERATOR RECOMMENDATIONS: **American Society of Travel Agents** (☞ Travel Agencies, *below*). **National Tour Association** (NTA; ⊠ 546 E. Main St., Lexington, KY 40508, ☎ 859/226–4444 or 800/682–8886, WEB www.ntaonline.com). **United States Tour Operators Association** (USTOA; ⊠ 342 Madison Ave., Suite 1522, New York, NY 10173, ☎ 212/599–6599 or 800/468–7862, FAX 212/599–6744, WEB www.ustoa. com).

TRAIN TRAVEL
TO AND FROM PARIS

The SNCF, France's rail system, is fast, punctual, comfortable, and comprehensive. There are various options: local trains, overnight trains with sleeping accommodations, and the high-speed TGV, or *Trains à Grande Vitesse* (averaging 255 kph/160 mph on the Lyon/southeast line and 300 kph/190 mph on the Lille and Bordeaux/southwest lines).

The TGVs, the fastest way to get around the country, operate between Paris and Lille/Calais, Paris and Lyon/Switzerland/the Riviera, Paris and Angers/Nantes, Paris and Tours/Poitiers/Bordeaux, Paris and Brussels, and Paris and Amsterdam. As with other main-line trains, a small supplement may be assessed at peak hours.

Paris has six international rail stations: Gare du Nord (northern France, northern Europe, and England via Calais or Boulogne); Gare St-Lazare (Normandy, England via Dieppe); Gare de l'Est (Strasbourg,

Luxembourg, Basel, and central Europe); Gare de Lyon (Lyon, Marseille, the Riviera, Geneva, Italy); and Gare d'Austerlitz (Loire Valley, southwest France, Spain). Note that Gare Montparnasse has taken over as the main terminus for trains bound for southwest France since the introduction of the new TGV-Atlantique service.

CUTTING COSTS

To save money, **look into rail passes.** But be aware that if you don't plan to cover many miles you may come out ahead by buying individual tickets.

RAIL PASSES

If you plan to travel outside of Paris by train, **consider purchasing a France Rail Pass,** which allows three days of unlimited train travel in a one-month period. If you travel solo, first class will run you $240, while second class is $210; you can add up to six days on this pass for $30 a day. For two people traveling together on a Saver Pass, the cost is $196, while in second class, it is $171; additional days (up to 6) cost $25 each. Other options include the France Rail 'n Drive Pass (combining rail and rental car), France Rail 'n Fly Pass (rail travel and one air-travel journey within France), and the France Fly Rail 'n Drive Pass (a rail, air, and rental-car program all in one).

France is one of 17 countries in which **you can use EurailPasses,** which provide unlimited first-class rail travel in all of the participating countries, for the duration of the pass. If you plan to rack up the miles, get a standard pass. These are available for 15 days ($572), 21 days ($740), one month ($918), two months ($1,298), and three months ($1,606). If your plans call for only limited train travel, **look into a Europass,** which costs less money than a EurailPass. Unlike with the EurailPasses, however, you get a limited number of travel days, in a limited number of countries, during a specified time period. For example, a two-month Europass ($360–$710) allows between 5 and 15 days of rail travel but costs around $200 less than the least expensive EurailPass. Keep in mind, however, that the Europass is

good only in France, Germany, Italy, Spain, and Switzerland, and the number of countries you can visit is further limited by the type of pass you buy.

In addition to standard EurailPasses, **ask about special rail-pass plans.** Among these are the Eurail Youthpass (for those under age 26), the Eurail Saver Pass (which gives a discount for two or more people traveling together), a Eurail Flexipass (which allows a certain number of travel days within a set period), the Euraildrive Pass, and the Europass Drive (train and rental car).

Whichever of the above passes you choose, remember that **you must purchase your Eurail and Euro passes at home before leaving for France.**

Another option is to **purchase one of the discount rail passes available only for sale in France** from SNCF.

When traveling together, **two people (who don't have to be a couple) can save money with the Prix Découverte à Deux.** You'll get a 25% discount during "*périodes bleues*" (blue periods: weekdays and not on or near any holidays). Note that you have to be with the person you said you would be traveling with.

You can **get a reduced fare if you're a senior citizen (over 60).** There are two options: for the Prix Découverte Senior, all you have to do is show a valid ID with your age and you're entitled to up to a 25% reduction in fares in first and second class. The second, the Carte Senior, is better if you're planning on spending a lot of time traveling; it costs €44.20, is valid for one year, and entitles you to up to a 50% reduction on most trains with a guaranteed minimum reduction of 25%. It also entitles you to a 30% discount on trips outside of France.

With the Carte Enfant Plus, for €53.35 **children under 12 and up to four accompanying adults can get up to 50% off on most trains for an unlimited number of trips.** This card is perfect if you're planning on spending a lot of time traveling in France with your children, as it's valid for one year. You can also opt for the Prix Découverte Enfant Plus: when you buy your ticket, simply show a valid ID with your child's age and you can get a significant discount for your child and a 25% reduction for up to four accompanying adults.

If you purchase an individual ticket from SNCF in France and you're under 26, you automatically get a 25% reduction (a valid ID, such as an ISIC card or your passport, is necessary). If you're going to be using the train quite a bit during your stay in France and **if you're under 26, consider buying the Carte 12–25** (€41.15), which offers unlimited 50% reductions for one year (provided that there's space available at that price; otherwise you'll just get the standard 25% discount).

If you don't benefit from any of these reductions and **if you plan on traveling at least 200 km (132 mi) round-trip and don't mind staying over a Saturday night, look into the Prix Découverte Séjour.** This ticket gives you a 25% reduction.

Don't assume that your rail pass guarantees you a seat on the train you wish to ride. You need to **book seats ahead even if you're using a rail pass.**

FARES AND SCHEDULES

You can **call for train information or reserve tickets in any Paris station,** irrespective of destination. If you know what station you'll depart from, you can get a free schedule there (while supplies last), or you can access the new, multilingual computerized-schedule information network at any Paris station. You can also make reservations and buy your ticket while at the computer. Go to the Grandes Lignes counter for travel within France and to the Billets Internationaux desk if you're heading out of the country. Note that calling the SNCF's 08 number costs €.35 per minute, which quickly adds up; to save this cost, either go to the nearest station and make the reservations in person or visit the SNCF Web site (www.sncf.fr).

Seat reservations are required on TGVs and are a good idea on trains that may be crowded—particularly in summer and holidays on popular routes. You also need a reservation for sleeping accommodations.

➤ TRAIN INFORMATION: **BritRail Travel** (☎ 800/677–8585 in the U.S.; 020/7834–2345 in the U.K.). **Eurostar** (☎ 08–36–35–35–39 in France; 0345/881881 in the U.K., WEB www.eurostar.com). **InterCity Europe** (✉ Victoria Station, London, ☎ 020/7834–2345 or 020/7828–0892; 0990/848–848 credit-card bookings). **Rail Europe** (☎ 800/942–4866 in the U.S., WEB www.raileurope.com). **SNCF** (✉ 88 rue St-Lazare, 75009 Paris, ☎ 08–36–35–35–35, WEB www.sncf.fr).

BETWEEN THE U.K. AND FRANCE

Short of flying, taking the "Chunnel" is the fastest way to cross the English Channel: 3 hours from London's central Waterloo Station to Paris's central Gare du Nord, 35 minutes from Folkestone to Calais, and 60 minutes from motorway to motorway. There is a vast range of prices for Eurostar—round-trip tickets range from €520 for first class to €105.35 for second class depending on when you travel. It's a good idea to **make a reservation if you're traveling with your car on a Chunnel train;** cars without reservations, if they can get on at all, are charged 20% extra.

British Rail also has four daily departures from London's Victoria Station, all linking with the Dover–Calais/Boulogne ferry services through to Paris. There is also an overnight service on the Newhaven–Dieppe ferry. Journey time is about eight hours. Credit-card bookings are accepted by phone or in person at a British Rail Travel Centre.

➤ CAR TRANSPORT: **Eurotunnel** (☎ 0870/535–3535 in the U.K., 070/223210 in Belgium, 03–21–00–61–00 in France, WEB ww2.eurotunnel.com).

➤ PASSENGER SERVICE: **Eurostar** (☎ 1233/617575 or 0870/518–6186 in the U.K., WEB www.eurostar.co.uk); **Rail Europe** (☎ 800/942–4866 or 800/274–8724; 0870/584–8848 U.K. credit-card bookings; WEB www.raileurope.com).

TRAVEL AGENCIES

A good travel agent puts your needs first. Look for an agency that has been in business at least five years, emphasizes customer service, and has someone on staff who specializes in your destination. In addition, **make sure the agency belongs to a professional trade organization.** The American Society of Travel Agents (ASTA), with 24,000 agents in some 140 countries, is the largest and most influential in the field. Operating under the motto "Integrity in Travel," it maintains and enforces a strict code of ethics and will step in to help mediate any agent-client disputes if necessary. ASTA also maintains a Web site that includes a directory of agents. (If a travel agency is also acting as your tour operator, *see* Buyer Beware *in* Tours & Packages.)

➤ LOCAL AGENT REFERRALS: **American Society of Travel Agents** (ASTA; ☎ 800/965–2782 24-hr hot line, FAX 703/739–3268, WEB www.astanet. com). **Association of British Travel Agents** (✉ 68–71 Newman St., London W1T 3AH, U.K., ☎ 020/7637–2444, FAX 020/7637–0713, WEB www. abtanet.com). **Association of Canadian Travel Agents** (✉ 130 Albert St., Suite 1705, Ottawa, Ontario K1P 5G4, Canada, ☎ 613/237–3657, FAX 613/237–7502, WEB www.acta.ca). **Australian Federation of Travel Agents** (✉ Level 3, 309 Pitt St., Sydney, NSW 2000, Australia, ☎ 02/9264–3299, FAX 02/9264–1085, WEB www.afta.com.au). **Travel Agents' Association of New Zealand** (✉ Box 1888, Wellington 6001, New Zealand, ☎ 04/499–0104, FAX 04/499–0827, WEB www.taanz.org.nz).

➤ PARIS AGENCIES: **American Express** (✉ 11 rue Scribe, 8ᵉ, ☎ 01–47–77–77–07; ✉ 38 av. de Wagram, 8ᵉ, ☎ 01–42–27–58–80). **Nouvelles Frontières** (✉ 5 av. de l'Opéra, 1ᵉʳ, métro Pyramides, ☎ 08–03–33–33–33). **Soltours** (✉ 48 rue de Rivoli, 4ᵉ, métro Hôtel de Ville, ☎ 01–42–71–24–34).

VISITOR INFORMATION

FRANCE TOURIST INFORMATION

France On-Call (☎ 410/286–8310 weekdays 9–7, WEB www.francetourism. com). **Chicago** (✉ 676 N. Michigan Ave., Chicago, IL 60611, fgto@mcs. net). **Los Angeles** (✉ 9454 Wilshire Blvd., Suite 715, Beverly Hills, CA 90212, ☎ 310/271–6665, FAX 310/276–2835, fgto@gte.net). **New York City** (✉ 444 Madison Ave., 16th floor, New York, NY 10022, ☎ 212/838–7800, FAX 212/838–7855, info@ francetourism.com). **Canada** (✉ 1981 av. McGill College, Suite 490, Montréal, Québec H3A 2W9, ☎ 514/288–4264, FAX 514/845–4868, mfrance@ mtl.net). **U.K.** (✉ 178 Piccadilly, London W1V OAL, ☎ 020/76399–3500, FAX 020/76493–6594). **Australia** (✉ 25 Bligh St., Sydney NSW 2000, ☎ 02/9231–5244, FAX 02/9221–8682).

LOCAL TOURISM INFORMATION

Espace du Tourisme d'Ile-de-France (✉ Carrousel du Louvre, 99 rue de Rivoli, 75001 Paris, ☎ 08–03–81–80–00 or 01–44–50–19–98). **Office du Tourisme de la Ville de Paris** (✉ Paris Tourist Office, 127 av. des Champs-Élysées, ☎ 01–49–52–53–54; 01–49–52–53–56 recorded information in English).

➤ U.S. GOVERNMENT ADVISORIES: **U.S. Department of State** (✉ Overseas Citizens Services Office, Room 4811, 2201 C St. NW, Washington, DC 20520, ☎ 202/647–5225 interactive hot line or 888/407–4747, WEB www. travel.state.gov); enclose a business-size SASE.

➤ PARIS/FRANCE WEB SITES: For more specific information on Paris, visit one of the following: **Eurostar** (www. eurostar.com or WEB www.eurail. com). **French Embassy** (WEB www. france.diplomatie.fr). **French Government Tourist Office** (WEB www. francetourism.com). **French Ministry of Culture** (WEB www.culture.fr). **Louvre Museum** (WEB mistral.culture. fr/louvre/louvrea.htm). **Paris Tourist Office** (WEB www.paris.org). **Rail Europe** (WEB www.raileurope.com). **RATP** (WEB www.ratp.fr). **SNCF** (WEB www.sncf.fr).

WEB SITES

Do check out the World Wide Web when planning your trip. You'll find everything from weather forecasts to virtual tours of famous cities. Be sure to **visit Fodors.com** (www.fodors.

com), a complete travel-planning site. You can research prices, check out bargains, read late-breaking travel news, and book plane tickets, hotel rooms, rental cars, vacation packages, and more. In addition, you can post your pressing questions in the Travel Talk section. Other planning tools include a currency converter and weather reports, and there are loads of links to travel resources.

WHEN TO GO

The major tourist season in France stretches from Easter to mid-September, but **Paris has much to offer in every season.** Paris in the early spring can be disappointingly damp, though it's relatively tourist free; May and June are delightful, with good weather and plenty of cultural and other attractions. July and August can be sultry. Moreover, many theaters and some of the smaller restaurants and shops close for the entire month of August. If you're undeterred by the hot weather and the pollution, you'll notice a fairly relaxed atmosphere around the city, as this is the month when most Parisians are on vacation. September is ideal. Cultural life revives after the summer break, and sunny weather often continues through the first half of October. The ballet and theater are in full swing in November, but the weather is part wet and cold, part bright and sunny. December is dominated by the *fêtes de fin d'année* (end-of-year festivities) and a busy theater, ballet, and opera season into January.

CLIMATE

The following are the average daily maximum and minimum temperatures for Paris.

Jan.	43F	6C	May	68F	20C	Sept.	70F	21C
	34	1		49	10		53	12
Feb.	45F	7C	June	73F	23C	Oct.	60F	16C
	34	1		55	13		46	8
Mar.	54F	12C	July	76F	25C	Nov.	50F	10C
	39	4		58	14		40	5
Apr.	60F	16C	Aug.	75F	24C	Dec.	44F	7C
	43	6		58	14		36	2

➤ FORECASTS: **Weather Channel Connection** (☎ 900/932–8437), 95¢ per minute from a Touch-Tone phone.

FESTIVALS AND SEASONAL EVENTS

➤ NOV. 11: **Armistice Day** ceremonies at the Arc de Triomphe include a military parade down the Champs-Élysées.

➤ 3RD THURS. IN NOV.: **Beaujolais Nouveau,** that light, fruity wine from the Beaujolais region of France, is officially released at midnight on Wednesday; its arrival is celebrated on the third Thursday in November in true Dionysian form in cafés and restaurants around the city.

➤ LATE NOV.: **Salon des Caves Particulières** brings French producers to the exhibition center at Porte de Versailles for a wine-tasting jamboree. Galleries and museums also will open their doors for the "Le Mois de la Photo" (Photo Month) event.

➤ LATE NOV.–LATE DEC.: The festive **Christmas Market** (✉ Pl. du 11-Novembre-1918, 10ᵉ, métro Gare de l'Est) features crafts, gifts, and toys from every region of France.

➤ LATE DEC.: **Christmas** is highlighted by illuminations throughout the city, particularly on the Champs-Élysées, avenue Montaigne, and boulevard Haussmann. Many churches open their doors with free Sunday afternoon concerts, the mayor's office sponsors free rides for children on all merry-go-rounds in the city for a period of two weeks, and major department stores and luxury meccas vie for your attention with amazing window displays. In the Jardin des Tuileries there's a fair with a Ferris wheel, and outside the Hôtel de Ville is a giant **crèche plus an ice-skating rink free to the public.**

➤ DEC. 31: On New Year's Eve **L'An 2003**, check out the spectacular fireworks illuminating the Eiffel Tower. On New Year's Day the **Grand Parade de Paris** winds its way from Boulevard Haussement to Madeleine at 2 PM (WEB www. parisparade.com). January 6th is the **Epiphany** and *galettes de rois* ("king's pastries"), deliciously light almond cakes available in all bakeries are traditionally served—whoever gets the porcelain charm embedded in each is king or queen for the day.

➤ FEB.: **Foire à la Feraille de Paris** is an antiques and bric-a-brac fair held in the Bois de Vincennes. **Salon d'Agriculture**, an agricultural smorgesbord and a favorite with some Parisians, is held mid-month at the Porte de Versailles (WEB www.salon-agriculture. com).

➤ MAR.: **Salon du Livre**, an international book exposition, is held annually at the end of the month.

➤ MAR.–APR.: **Foire du Trône**, an amusement park, is set up in the Bois de Vincennes.

➤ MAR.–APR.: The **Prix du Président de la République** takes place at the Auteuil Racecourse. The **Paris Film Festival** is held at the Cinema Gaumont Matignan on the Champs Élysées (WEB www.festival.wannadoo. fr).

➤ LATE APR.: The **International Marathon of Paris** (WEB www. parismarathon.com) runs through the city and large parks on the outskirts.

➤ EARLY MAY: At the **Foire de Paris** (WEB www.comexpo-paris.com), hundreds of booths display everything from crafts to wines. The **Novotel-Perrier French Open** takes place at the national golf course in les Yvelines just outside of Paris.

➤ MAY–LATE SEPT.: **Grandes Eaux Musicales** is a fountain display at the Château de Versailles (Sunday only).

➤ LATE MAY–EARLY JUNE: The **Festival de Jazz de Boulogne-Billancourt** attracts big names and varied styles of jazz in Boulogne-Billancourt, a suburb of Paris.

➤ LATE MAY–EARLY JUNE: The **French Open Tennis Championships** (WEB www.french-open.com) take place at Roland Garros Stadium. The **Grand Steeple Chase** takes place at the Porte D'Auteuil racetrack.

➤ MID-JUNE–MID-JULY: **Festival du Marais** features everything from music to dance to theater in the churches and historic mansions of the Marais (tickets: ✉ 44 rue François-Miron, 4ᵉ, ☎ 01–48–87–60–08, métro St-Paul). A similar celebration takes place at the **Butte Montmartre Festival** (☎ 01–42–62–46–22). Just outside Paris, the **Festival de St-Denis** takes place this year with live music, theatre, and dance.

➤ JUNE: **Paris Air Show** is a display of old and new planes at Le Bourget Airport. The colorful **Gay Pride Parade** takes place mid-month.

➤ LATE JUNE: The **Grand Prix de Paris**, is held on the flat at Longchamp Racecourse. The **45th International Air Show** takes place in Le Bourget.

➤ JULY 13: **Bals des Sapeurs-Pompiers** (Firemen's Balls), held to celebrate the start of Bastille Day the next day, spill into the streets of every arrondissement. Head to any *casern* (fire station) in Paris and dance the night away to live music; spectacular party locations also include historic landmarks in the Marais and a barge on the Seine.

➤ JULY 14: **Bastille Day** celebrates the storming of the Bastille prison in 1789. There's a military parade along the Champs-Élysées in the morning and fireworks at night at Trocadéro.

➤ LATE JULY: The **Tour de France** (WEB www.letour.com), the world's leading bicycle race, speeds to a Sunday finish on the Champs-Élysées.

➤ LATE JULY–END AUG.: The **Fête Musique en l'Ile** (☎ 01–45–23–18–25 for details) is a series of concerts held in the picturesque 17th-century Église St-Louis on Ile St-Louis.

➤ MID–LATE SEPT.: **Biennale des Antiquaires** (even-numbered years only), an antiques fair, takes place at the Carrousel du Louvre.

➤ LATE SEPT.: On the **Journée du Patrimonie**, the third Sunday in September, normally closed historic buildings—such as the state residences of the President and Prime Minister—are open to the public. The world class (second only to Tokyo) **Salon Mondial de l'Automobile** auto show takes place this month. The (very) loud **Techno Parade** winds its way through the streets of Paris to finish at Trocadéro.

➤ EARLY OCT.: The **Montmartre Grape Harvest** (WEB www.montmartrenet. com), held the first Saturday of October, celebrates the grape harvest in the Montmartre vineyard, at the corner of rue des Saules and rue St-Vincent. **FIAC** (International Fair of Contemporary Art) takes place at Porte de Versailles.

Prix de l'Arc de Triomphe, Europe's top flat race, is the first Sunday of the month at Longchamp Racecourse.

➤ MID-OCT.–EARLY NOV.: The **Fête de Jazz de Paris** (☎ 01–47–83–33–58 for information) is a two-week celebration that includes lots of big-name musicians.

➤ OCT.–NOV.: The **Fête d'Art Sacré** (☎ 01–42–77–92–26 for information) is a series concerts and exhibitions held in churches throughout the city.

1 DESTINATION: PARIS

Paris à la Parisienne

What's Where

Pleasures and Pastimes

Fodor's Choice

Great Itineraries

PARIS À LA PARISIENNE

T IS MIDNIGHT at the neighborhood brasserie. Waiters swathed in starchy white glance discreetly at their watches as a family—mother, son, and wife—sip the last of a bottle of Chiroubles and scrape up the remains of their steak tartare on silverware dexterously poised with arched wrists. They are all wearing scarves: the mother's is a classic silk *carré*, tastefully folded at the throat; the wife's is Indian gauze and glitters; the son's is wool and hangs like a prayer shawl over his black turtleneck. Finished, they stir their coffee without looking. They smoke: the mother, Gitanes; the son, Marlboros; the wife rolls her own from a silver case. Alone, they act out their personal theater, uncontrived and unobserved, their Doisneauesque tableau reflected only in the etched-glass mirrors around them, enhanced by the sobriety of their dress and the pallor of their Gallic skin.

Whoever first said that "God found Paris too perfect, so he invented the Parisians" had it wrong. This extraordinary maquette of a city, with its landscape of mansards and chimneys, its low-slung bridges and vast boulevards, is nothing but a rough-sketched stage set that drinks its color from the lifeblood of those infamous Parisians whom everyone claims to hate but whom everyone loves to emulate.

Mythologized for their arrogance, charm, and savoir faire—as well as their disdain for the foreigners they find genetically incapable of sharing these characteristics—the Parisians continue to mesmerize. For the generations of American and English voyeurs who have ventured curiously, enviously into countless mirrored brasseries, downed numerous bottles of *cuvée maison*, fumbled at nautical knots in newly bought scarves, even suffered squashed berets and unfiltered Gauloises, the Parisians remain inimitable—and infinitely fascinating.

Alternately patronizing and self-effacing, they move through their big-city lives with enviable style and urban grit. They are chronically thin, despite the truckloads of beef stew, pâté, and tart Tatin they consume without blushing. They still make the cigarette look glamorous—and a graceful bit of stage business indispensable to good talk—in spite of the gas-mask levels of smoke they generate. They stride over bridges aloof to the monuments framed in every sweeping perspective, yet they discourse—lightly, charmingly—on Racine, NATO, and the latest ruling of the Académie Française. They are proud, practical, often witty, and always chic, from the thrift-shop style of the Sorbonne student to the Chanel suit on the thin shoulders of a well-boned *dame d'un certain âge*.

Ferociously (with some justice) in love with their own culture—theater, literature, film, art, architecture, haute cuisine, and haute couture—Parisians worship France as ardently as New Yorkers dismiss the rest of America. While Manhattanites berate the nonentities west of the Hudson, Parisians romanticize the rest of France, making an art of the weekend foray and the regional vacation: why should we go *à l'étranger* (abroad) when we have the Dordogne, the Auvergne, and Bretagne?

And for all their vulnerability to what they frame as the "American Assault," for every Disney store, action film, and McDonald's in Paris (not to mention Benetton and Laura Ashley, and France's own Celio, Orcade, and Descamps chains), there is a plethora of unique shops selling all-white blouses, African bracelets, dog jackets, and Art Deco jewelry.

And for every commercial bookstore chain there are five tiny *librairies* selling tooled-leather encyclopedias, collections of out-of-print plays, and yellow paperbacks lovingly pressed in waxed paper. The famous *bouquinistes* hover like squatters along the Seine, their folding metal boxes opening to showcase a treasure trove of old magazines, scholarly journals, and hand-colored botanical prints that flap from clothespins in the wind. Yet they are not nomads, these bouquinistes: dormant through winter, their metal stands are fixtures as permanent and respectable as those of the medieval merchants that built shops along the Pont Neuf. They are determinedly Parisian—individual, independent, and one-of-a-kind.

But in spite of their fierce individuality, Parisians also demand that certain conformities be followed. And here the gap between native and visitor widens. If Parisians treat tourists a bit like occupying forces—disdainfully selling them Beaujolais-Nouveau in July, seating them by the kitchen doors, refusing to understand honest attempts at French—they have formed their opinions based on bitter experience. The waiter who scorches tourists with flared nostrils and firmly turned back was trained to respect his métier—meaning not pouring Coke with foie gras or bringing the check with dessert. The meal is a sacred ritual here, and diverging from the norm is tantamount to disgrace.

Doing as the Parisians do, you can go a long way toward closing the gap of disdain. When dining, for example, give yourself over to the meal. Order a kir as an aperitif, instead of a whiskey or beer. Drink wine or mineral water with your meal. Order coffee *after* dessert, not with it. And accept the fact that diet sodas are rarely available in restaurants.

The wine will come chilled, aired, and ready for tasting with the respect usually reserved for a holy relic. Enjoy each course, sipping, discussing, digesting leisurely; the waiter will not be pressed by hurried tourists. When you're done eating, align your silverware on the plate (a sign for the waiter to clear). Cheese can be the climax of the meal, well worth skipping dessert if necessary, and a magnificent way to finish the wine. Have your coffee after dessert and, without exception, black with sugar; a milky froth will not do on a full stomach. The art of stirring *un express* in Paris rivals the art of scarf-tying.

Ask for *l'addition*; the waiter will not commit the gaffe of bringing the check uninvited. And no matter how deeply you enter into your role as Parisian manqué, avoid saying "*Garçon!*" (Say "*S'il vous plaît*" instead.) These are rules that apply at the most unassuming corner bistro and the grandest three-star restaurant; following them can thaw the waiterly chill that can render a meal unforgettable—for all the wrong reasons—and can make for meals that are as memorable as an evening at the Opéra de la Bastille, complete with sets and choreography.

It is this fixed attention to experience and detail that sets the Parisians apart. Desk-eaters they are not: when they work, they work without a coffee break. When they eat, business still grinds to a halt. Weekends are sacred. And oh, do they vacation, all of them at once, all of them abandoning Paris in August with a fierceness of purpose that mirrors their commitment to food—an all-night drive, a rental booked months in advance.

By matching that Parisian passion for the complete, the correct, the *comme il faut*, your own experience will be all the more authentic. Having eaten with proper reverence, keep your sightseeing agenda at the same lofty level. If you go to the Louvre, spend the day; do not lope through the wide corridors in search of *La Joconde* (*Mona Lisa*). You can leave for a three-hour lunch, if you choose, and come back with the same ticket, even avoiding the lines by reentering via the Passage Richelieu. If time won't allow an all-day survey, do as the locals do: choose an era and immerse yourself. Then take a break and plunge into another. Eavesdrop on a guided tour. Go back and look at a painting again. And take the time to stare at the ceilings: the architecture alone of this historic monument merits a day's tour.

As you apply yourself to the Parisian experience in spirit, diverge in fact: walk. The natives may prefer to sit in a café or even hurry straight home by métro ("*métro, boulot, dodo*"—"métro, work, sleep"—as the saying goes). You, as a visitor, are obliged to wander down tortuous medieval streets; up vast boulevards so overscaled you seem to gain no ground; over bridges that open up broad perspectives on illuminated monuments that outnumber even those in Rome.

They are all there, the clichés of Paris romance: the moon over the Seine reflected in the wake of the Bateaux Mouches (river barges); the steps Leslie Caron blushed down in *An American in Paris*; the lovers kissing under the lime tree pollards. But there are surprises, too: a troop of hunting horns striking unearthly sonorities under a resonant bridge; flocks of wild geese flying low over the towers of Notre-Dame; and a ragged expatriate writer leaving a well-scraped plat du jour on the table as he bolts away from the bill. (*C'est dommage*: he would have been well fed by Ragueneau, the baker-writer in *Cyrano de Bergerac* who opened his Paris pastry shop to starving poets.)

The more resourceful you are, the more surprises you will unearth in your Paris wanderings. Follow the strains of Lully into a chamber orchestra rehearsal in St-Julien-le-Pauvre; if you're quiet and still, you may not be asked to leave. Brave the smoking lounge at intermission at the Comédie-Française and you'll find the battered leather chair that the young actor Molière sat in as *L'Invalide Imaginaire*. Take the métro to *L'Armée du Salut* (Salvation Army) in the 13e *arrondissement* (ward), and you'll not only find Art Deco percolators and hand-knit stockings but you'll also be inside the futuristic curves of a 1933 Le Corbusier masterwork.

Tear yourself away from the big-name museums and you'll discover a world of small galleries. Go in: you don't have to press your nose to the glass. The exhibits are constantly changing and you can always find one relevant to Paris—Frank Horvat's photos of Pigalle or a Christo retrospective, including the Pont Neuf wrappings. It is worth buying one of the weekly guides—*Pariscope, L'Officiel des Spectacles, Figaroscope*—and browsing through it over your *café crème* and croissant.

Resourcefulness, after all, is a sign of enthusiasm and appreciation—for when you are well informed and acutely tuned in to the nuances of the city, you can approach it as a connoisseur. Then you can peacefully coexist with Parisians, partaking, in their passion for this marvelous old city, from the same plate of cultural riches. Hemingway, as usual, put it succinctly: "It was always pleasant crossing bridges in Paris." Cultural bridges, too.

Bon séjour à Paris.

— Nancy Coons

WHAT'S WHERE

Proudly bearing the scars of an illustrious 2,000-year history and home to 2 million people, Paris could take multiple lifetimes to explore from top to bottom—and that's not counting the Louvre. From the vast, gilded salons of Proust's world on boulevard Haussmann and the avenue de Messine, to the cramped, gray houses of the Left Bank, from the tortured gargoyles of Notre-Dame to the startling whiteness of the Basilique du Sacré-Coeur (whose stones grow whiter with age), Paris is a city of wonderful contrasts. This bustling metropolis is, in reality, *la cité aux cent villages,* the city of a hundred villages—a constellation of lesser satellites making up one glittering (at least, at night) Milky Way. One way of looking at Paris is as you would a family group: the Faubourg-St-Honoré area is the grande dame matriarch, overdressed and wearing all her finery. The St-Germain district is the beautiful, wealthy daughter, who likes to go shopping for a living but can quote Balzac at the drop of a *chapeau*. The Marais and Bastille neighborhoods are the edgy youngsters, who stay up all night to discuss the meaning of life, death, and the latest fashion over three glasses of *vin rouge*.

The first thing you need do to once you're off the plane is to learn the difference between the Rive Droite (Right Bank) and the Rive Gauche (Left Bank). In the most stereotypical terms, the Rive Droite is traditionally more elegant and commercial, though its less central areas (the Marais, the Bastille, and Belleville, for example) are the hip places of the moment. The Rive Gauche, on the other hand, is the artistic area; the Sorbonne and the Quartier Latin are here, along with the haunts of literary greats, budding artists, and fashion designers. The fancier parts of the Right Bank are home to ritzy shopping districts and many of the big-name sights like the Louvre and the Arc de Triomphe. Between the two banks you have the Ile de la Cité, where you'll find Notre-Dame, and the smaller Ile St-Louis.

Only when you move beyond the classic, core arrondissements does Paris become less a theme park and more a vital urban center in constant evolution. To experience the true Paris, explore the winding side streets of its lesser-known communities—Belleville, Bercy, Parmentier-Charonne, Tolbiac, Gobelins–Butte aux Cailles—which frequently squirm with tiny communities huddling in the shadow of modern high-rises. While some parts of these were razed by modernization projects in the mid-19th century, and again in the latter half of the 20th, new "villages" emerged to take their place, peopled with workers from the provinces and immigrants from the former colonies. Over time, these shifting populations have changed the face and feel of the city as much as Baron

Haussmann's *grands boulevards* and President Mitterand's *grands projets*.

If you have only a few days or weeks in the city, strategy is key. The efficient métro system is the backbone of see-and-flee sightseeing, but moving around by bus—or, better yet, by foot—will give you a much closer feel for Parisian street life: its action, its glamour, its pooper-scoopers. Using foot power, you'll find most of the larger streets—the avenues or boulevards—lead to a pleasingly designed *place*, or square. Likewise many of the smaller streets run adjacent to or parallel and in between these, so that even if you make a wrong turn you eventually spot a recognizable landmark—often that amazing eyeful, the Eiffel Tower. The Parisians really do have a right to boast.

The following overview takes in many of Paris's 20 arrondissements as it spirals outward from the center city to its suburbs. The last two digits of zip codes (e.g., 75015) tells you the arrondissement. Arrondissements are subdivided into *quartiers* (neighborhoods), which are often associated with a specific landmark. Below, each arrondissement is clustered with its adjacent ones to form easily digestible parts of the great Parisian feast.

The Islands (1er and 4e Arrondissements)

The **Ile de la Cité** is where our story starts, some 2,300 years ago, when the island was the strategic stronghold of a Gallic tribe called the Parisii, who held off all comers until 52 BC, the year Julius Caesar's soldiers finally rebuffed the Gauls and established a colony. Today, three buildings here—**Notre-Dame**, erstwhile playground of Quasimodo; the **Conciergerie**, where Marie-Antoinette was sentenced to the guillotine in 1793; and the **Sainte-Chapelle**, "the most beautiful chapel in the world"—still overawe through their sheer scale and unadulterated historical and architectural grandeur. This is as it should be, for you are now in the very heart of the city. Although large tracts of the island were bulldozed by Baron Haussmann in the mid-19th century, there are still enchanting nooks, notably the **Ancient Cloître Quarter,** tucked beneath the shadows of the cathedral, and the pretty garden below Pont Neuf in the **square du Vert-Galant.** If you have time, visit the flower market at Cité, which is especially nice on Sun-

days, when the flowers make way for birds. Just over the little footbridge behind the cathedral is the **Ile St-Louis,** the smaller of the two islands, still home to some of the most charming streets in Paris, and, at Berthillon's, its best ice cream. While strolling the time-stained quais—the views of the Seine and Notre-Dame are unsurpassed from the benches on the quai de Bourbon—keep your eyes open for building plaques, listing the luminaries who lived and worked here: Racine, Molière, Baudelaire, Cézanne, Chopin, Camile Claudel, Ezra Pound; the ballet world's danseur-impresario Barishnikov keeps a pied-à-terre on the island, but so far it's unmarked.

Louvre, Faubourg-St-Honoré, and Opéra (1er, 2e, and 9e Arrondissements)

Yes, it's terribly expensive, snobbish, and packed with crowds. But any neighborhood that for centuries was considered the center of the Western art, theater, and music world can't be dismissed. In the 1er arrondissement, you can see one of the largest collections of art in the world, a theater which has been staging productions for the past 200 years, and a few of the places Louis XIV used to live: not a bad harvest for a single 15-minute walk. While some feel that no trip to Paris is complete without at least one hour spent running frantically through the bowels of the **Louvre** trying to find an exit, for most this remains the greatest museum, period. If the Louvre doesn't satisfy your taste for grandiosity, with its Leonardos, Raphaels, Rubens, and Davids, collect yourself with a stroll to **place de la Concorde** through the majestic **Jardin des Tuileries,** immortalized in many an Impressionist canvas. Braving the traffic tangle of the place—Paris's beating aorta and site of the dreaded guillotine during the French Revolution—head over to the **Pont Alexandre-III,** a bridge that possesses all the elements that characterized the Belle Epoque: style, class, power, exuberance. Double back along the rue de Rivoli to the serene courtyard gardens of the **Palais Royal,** where the Comédie Française is the permanent playground for the ghosts of Great French Theater. After being seduced by the luxe boutiques of the Palais-Royal arcades (Thomas Jefferson was a frequent customer here back when), spend some time window-shopping along rue St-Honoré and

Faubourg St-Honoré, still the world's most exclusive shopping strip. Next, promenade through the **place Vendôme,** the bejeweled mecca of *haute joaillerie* (fancy jewelry), followed by a quick restorative at the Ritz, and then it's on to your private box at the sumptuous, entirely renovated **Palais Garnier,** immortalized by Degas's paintings, Pavlova's dancing, and the Phantom's crashing chandelier. Surrounding the Opéra are some of the great boulevards of Paris where 19th-century Parisians first perfected the art of promenading.

The Marais, Beaubourg, and Les Halles (3e and 4e Arrondissements)

Le Marais translates as "the swamp." Although this appellation refers to the formerly overwhelming presence of the Seine in this area, this lively neighborhood today is anything but stuck in the mud. Three decades ago, some of the chicest people in Paris made the Marais the home of the hip by renovating the multitude of 17th- and 18th-century mansions in the quarter, opening gorgeous shops, and transforming several *hôtels particuliers* (mansions) into museums, including the **Musée Carnavalet** and **Musée Picasso.** At the end of the boutique-busy rue des Francs-Bourgeois is the Marais's showplace, the eternally elegant **place des Vosges.** Built as the place Royale by King Henri II, it was abandoned by the court once Versailles became the hot ticket, but today remains the place to live, just as it was 400 years ago. Today, the lively atmosphere of the Marais makes it one of the city's best areas for eating, drinking, walking, and exploring—its narrow, labyrinthine streets (this was one of the few sectors untouched by Baron Haussmann) still hold all manner of surprises, including the venerable Jewish Quarter, centered around rue des Rosiers, and the rue Ste-Croix-de-la-Bretonnerie and rue Vieille-du-Temple, the lifelines of gay life in Paris. To the west of the Marais lies the Beaubourg quartier, known for eight centuries as the "belly" of Paris, not just for its location but because this was where you went to get grub at any hour of the day or night. Then, in 1969, the iron-and-glass-roofed pavilions of Les Halles were torn down, leaving a large hole in the city's stomach that was filled 10 years later with a hideous but extremely successful shopping mall.

While food still fuels the hip pedestrian area around rue Montorgueil, elsewhere fashion boutiques have taken over where butchers and bakers used to hold sway. The area was given much needed cultural sustenance when the **Centre Georges Pompidou** opened its doors at Beaubourg in 1977. Reputedly the most visited landmark in Paris, its sloping plaza, rooftop restaurant, chaos of a lobby, and adjacent place Igor Stravinsky (landmarked by the wild fountain of Jean Tinguely and Niki de St-Phalle) are among Paris's best people-watching spots.

Quartier Latin (5e Arrondissement)

The backbone of French intellectual life for more than 700 years, the Quartier Latin has been drawing the intellectually restless, the politically discontent, the artistically inspired, and those who like to hang out with them to its universities, cafés, garrets, and alleys. Home to most of the country's major centers of learning (the **Sorbonne,** Ecole Normale Supérieure, Ecole Polytechnique, College de France), the Latin Quarter has also been the site of the city's fiercest street battles: in 1871 against the State; in 1945 against the Germans; and in 1968 against everyone over 30. The medieval labyrinth of streets surrounding rue de la Huchette gives a sense of what the city was like before Haussmann and the automobile transformed everything. Shakespeare and Company, a favorite Anglophile bookstore, faces the bibliophilic **bouquiniste stalls** along the Seine, where you can rummage through rare books, posters, and postcards. A quick hop down the leafy steps to the river's edge and you're Gene Kelly, or Leslie Caron, or both, on the set of *An American in Paris,* singing of love before the rolling floodlights of **Bateaux Mouches** (river barges), to the applause of revelers on the *café-peniches* (restaurant barges) that line the quai. Artistic treasures can be found in the **Musée-National du Moyen-Age** (National Museum of the Middle Ages), housed in the famous Cluny mansion, and the Panthéon church.

St-Germain-des-Prés (6e Arrondissement)

Today one of the chicest (yet most tourist-friendly) neighborhoods in Paris, this quarter is centered around the venerable tower of the **church of St-Germain-des-Prés,** the oldest house of worship in Paris. Aswarm with bookstores and cafés—most notably Café Flore and Les Deux Magots, where Picasso, Camus, Sartre, and de Beauvoir spent their days working and their nights drinking—St-Germain has almost been gentrified into unconsciousness: on some streets, expensive boutiques sit next to expensive galleries which are, more often than not, next to expensive restaurants. But wander off traffic-clogged boulevard St-Germain (a street that fairly cries out for you to shop till you drop), and you'll find winding streets, ancient facades, and hidden courtyards. Particularly pleasing is rue St-André-des-Arts, a pedestrian street lined with sidewalk cafés; near here you'll find what many people consider the most beautiful spot in all Paris—the **Cour de Rohan,** a cul-de-sac off the Cour de Commerce St-André, an alley where time seems frozen in the 18th century. If you love decorative arts, run—do not walk— to the **Carré Rive Gauche** district off the Quai Voltaire (rue de Bac, rue de l'Université, rue de Lille, rue des St-Pères), packed with 120 antiques stores. A cinephile's paradise, the area around Odéon is chock-a-block with first-run and repertory cinema houses. A stroll a little farther south brings you to the sylvan glades of the **Luxembourg Gardens**—Paris's favorite park, where you can catch an afternoon marionette show in the puppet theater or a few rays in one of the green metal armchairs scattered around the elegant fountain. Isadora Duncan used to dance here in the dawn's early light.

Invalides and Eiffel Tower (7ᵉ Arrondissement)

Hidden behind high walls and heavy doors is the staid, serious 7th arrondissement, home of government ministries (including Hôtel Matignon, the Prime Minister's HQ), foreign embassies, and magnificent hôtels particuliers, still occupied by ducs, vicomtes, and princes of France's first families. Blueblood Central, the area attracts tourists for three good reasons: the impressive collections of late 19th-century art at the **Musée d'Orsay** (where the world's most famous Renoirs, Monets, and Gauguins repose), the **Eiffel Tower,** and Napoléon's final resting spot—or spots; his remains are divided into six coffins— at the vast Esplanade des **Invalides.** Yet the district offers much more, including the **Musée Rodin** (in an 18th-century man-

sion within a rose garden), the tea salons and shops along the Rue du Bac, and the fabulous food floor of Au Bon Marché, the city's oldest and poshest department store. Breathtaking vistas abound: at Les Invalides, but also from the Champ de Mars, which has become a popular picnic spot since the city relaxed its lawn-use restrictions a couple of years back. Next to the Eiffel Tower, the single most photographed monument in the neighborhood is the superb Art Nouveau building by Jules Lavirotte on avenue Rapp. And don't forget the odoriferous offerings underfoot in the Paris sewer system; guided tours are offered daily.

Champs-Élysées, Trocadéro, and Monceau-Batignolles (8ᵉ, 16ᵉ, and 17ᵉ Arrondissements)

Majestic with a capital "M," Napoléon's **Arc de Triomphe** crowns the Étoile, a star of the first magnitude with 12 streams of light; by day, you'll see these are avenues, the leading ray of which is the **Champs-Élysées.** From the Arc de Triomphe, follow the avenue Hoche and head northeast to **Parc Monceau,** with its mock ruins and grottoes and surrounding ring of neoclassical mansions, among the most expensive and ostentatious in the city. The Champs, the world's most famous avenue, was once an aristocratic pleasure park, then deteriorated into a garish sprawl of pricey cafés, car showrooms, and bland shopping malls. Today, a restorative facelift has replaced some of its lost grandeur. Adjoining streets like avenue Montaigne, with their palatial hotels, haute-couture shops, and power-lunch bistros, are already posher than ever. Crossing avenue Marceau into the 16ᵉ arrondissement ups the ante even further: This is another stylish pearl-and-cashmere area, rich in Art Nouveau and Art Deco houses and laden with museums (the free Musée de l'Art Moderne and the brand-new, very avant-garde Palais de Tokyo lead the pack).

Bastille, Nation, and Bercy (11ᵉ and 12ᵉ Arrondissements)

The only folks storming the Bastille these days are Opéra-goers lining up for seats at the **Opéra Bastille** and young Parisians and tourists hell-bent on painting the town rouge. The area around the former (now vanished) prison has been gentrified: galleries, shops, theaters, cafés, restaurants, and bars replaced the formerly decrepit buildings and alleys, bringing an artsy crowd to mingle with blue-collar locals—and jacking up the prices. Most of the artists have since defected to cheaper places like Belleville, and some of the atmospheric bars and bistros have been replaced by Tex-Mex joints, but the area still has its charms, especially after dark, when the streets fill and the bars spill out onto the street. To get away from the crowds, avoid rue de Lappe and stick to the parallel streets. Rue Keller and rue des Taillandiers hide cool art galleries and nifty clothing and music stores. Stroll down the redbrick **Viaduc des Arts,** a stylish walkway with flowers and benches above and haute design shops below. Leave the Bastille column and head east along the Faubourg St-Antoine, until recently an area of small tradesmen, now a trendy but still unpretentious extension of the Bastille. Farther on and you are smack in the middle of the bustling Aligre street market, where the best produce and cheapest vintage clothing in the city can be found. Then on to the oft-forgotten neighborhood of Nation, where the Revolution took its heaviest toll. You can view the graves of some 1,300 guillotined nobles at the nearby and little-known St-Picpus cemetery. A jog south towards the Seine brings you to the new **Bercy** district. Once the Paris center of the wine trade, it is now a thriving business and shopping area, best known for the grass-covered Omnisports stadium.

Chinatown, Tolbiac, Buttes-aux-Cailles, and Gobelins (13ᵉ Arrondissement)

Not nearly as concentrated or ornate as its counterpart in San Francisco or New York, Paris's Chinatown is more eclectic than either, offering a wide choice of Asian cuisine—Cambodian, Thai, Laotian, Chinese, Japanese—often in the same restaurant. Tang Frères and Paris-Store on avenue d'Ivry are the biggest, best, and busiest Asian supermarkets in the city. A 20-minute walk from here is the newly revamped Tolbiac district. Once an ugly tangle of rusting factories, the area is now the site of Paris's controversial new national library, the **Bibliothèque François-Mitterand.** The nearby rue Louise Weiss has become Paris's new epicenter of contemporary art. Still in the 13ᵉ arrondissement is the Butte-aux-Cailles (Quail Hill), which offers more of a village atmosphere, especially at the cheap bar, bistro, and apple-tree-lined junction of the rue des Cinq-Diamants and the rue de la Butte-aux-Cailles.

Montparnasse (14ᵉ Arrondissement)

Hemingway, Henry Miller, Picasso, and Sartre all showed up in the cafés, boulevards, and villas of Montparnasse to create or philosophize. Something of them remains in the cemetery, on plaques in front of houses, and chiseled into the tables of bars they frequented, but little elsewhere. The quartet of cafés on the corner of boulevard du Montparnasse and boulevard Raspail—**La Coupole, Le Dôme, Le Sélect, and La Rotonde**—was the center for a "lost generation" of American writers in the years surrounding World War I. Papa Hemingway, Gertrude Stein, Zelda and F. Scott Fitzgerald held court here, rubbing shoulders with the likes of Albert Camus, Anaïs Nin, and Marcel Duchamp, while an exiled Lenin shunned the chitchat and concentrated on his chess game. The four cafés are still here (though only Le Sélect still draws a stylish crowd, while La Coupole remains the American favorite). The rest of the neighborhood looks much as it did in the 1920s, were it not for the oppressive shadow of the Tour Montparnasse, continental Europe's tallest office tower and Paris's biggest eyesore. For cutting-edge contemporary art-lovers, Jean Nouvel's glass-cubed **Fondation Cartier** is hard to top. The Parc Montsouris and Cité Universitaire area is a great place to meet other foreigners in Paris.

Passy, Auteuil, and the Bois de Boulogne (16ᵉ Arrondissement)

Proust's Paris, the Passy and Auteuil neighborhoods on the far west side, form the city's largest and one of its most elegant wards. On one side Passy and Auteuil are bordered by the Seine, on the other by the **Bois de Boulogne,** an extensive wooded park with lakes, flower gardens, the **Bagatelle** mansion (built in just 60 days on a bet with Marie-Antoinette), and the fabled Pré-Catalan restaurant; the park was the opening setting for Vincente Minnelli's incomparable love letter to Paris, the 1958 film of *Gigi*. Benjamin Franklin and Honoré de Balzac once resided in the nearby abodes and the streets of both Passy and Auteuil are still adorned with Paris's choicest selection of Art Nouveau buildings. Along with the **mansions designed by Hector Guimard,** the paintings of Claude Monet will draw you to the 16ᵉ arrondissement since many of his masterpieces are to be found here at the **Musée Marmottan–Claude Monet.**

Montmartre, Pigalle, and Abbesses (18ᵉ Arrondissement)

Rising above the city on the highest hill in Paris is Montmartre, site of the **Basilique du Sacré-Coeur** and once the favorite haunt of the bohemian artist community. Despite the tourist hordes that daily pack the narrow backstreets and steep stairways of the "Butte," Montmartre and neighboring Abbesses (where the film *Amélie* was shot) have retained more of an authentic village flavor than most Paris areas. Strolling here offers glimpses of gardens, small cafés, and wine bars filled with locals, while an essential part of the Montmartre experience is to make your way up the **steep stairways** that grace many a Robert Doisneau photograph and afford great views of Paris. Third-rate artists sell their sidewalk masterpieces on the place du Tertre, but real artists live northwest of the place in million-dollar homes on avenue Junot (the little alley at No. 25 is probably one of the most picturesque in Paris). Montmartre (the name means "hill of martyrs") is also home to a nexus of young designers, attracted by the close proximity to the St-Pierre textile market. Locals will tell you that rue Lépic remains the best street market in the city (halfway down you'll find the Café des Deux Moulins, where Amélie worked and schemed). At the bottom of the hill Lépic spills into the netherworld of **Pigalle,** which still cashes in on its reputation as the sin center of Paris. Steer clear of the portholed "bars américaines" but the Musée de l'Erotisme and the Moulin Rouge remain safe sexy bets. On the other side of the hill, the new Paris looms, especially at La Goutte d'Or, a principally West and North African neighborhood, with pockets of Serb, Pakistani, Portuguese, and Parisian bohemian thrown in to enliven the mix.

North-East Paris (10ᵉ, 11ᵉ, and 20ᵉ Arrondissements)

Princes of the Paris night will tell you that the Bastille's bubble has burst, Pigalle is passé, and the Latin Quarter is for the quaint of heart. The real happening scene has retreated northeast, to the edges of the 11th arrondissement and beyond. **Oberkampf** has been the nocturnal center of things for a few years now, but the areas around are catching up quickly, despite having fallen victim to the city's turn-of-the-millennium urban-renewal frenzy. Particularly thriving is the area around République and the **Canal St-Martin,** whose locks, bridges, and waterside cafés conjure up an unexpected flavor of Amsterdam. Farther north along the canal brings you to **Parc de la Villette,** once Paris's largest complex of slaughterhouses and stockyards, now a giant park with loads of high-tech buildings and toys to run around and play in. Belleville, too, long a center of immigrant, working-class Paris, has become a focal point for artists, musicians, and other like-minded folk who can't afford to live elsewhere. Piaf would barely recognize her childhood home, the neighborhood of **Ménilmontant-Belleville,** thanks to new construction, but the stretch between the original Belleville, centered around rue de Ménilmontant and up to Père-Lachaise cemetery, offers some of the most rewarding rambling anywhere (you'll still see vistas familiar from *The Red Balloon,* the Academy-award winning film shot here in the mid-1950s). Not to be missed is the **Parc des Buttes-Chaumont,** whose simulated natural surroundings make it one of the quirkiest and most comfortable places for a quick collapse in the city. As for the fabled **Père-Lachaise cemetery,** head here if you wish to tell Oscar Wilde, Jim Morrison, Marcel Proust, or Piaf all your problems and have them listen for eternity.

PLEASURES AND PASTIMES

Art: Beyond the Great Museums

Paris's museums range from the ostentatiously grand to the delightfully obscure—the French seem bent on documenting everything any of its citizens have ever done. Not just repositories of masterworks, the city's museums also reveal the endlessly fascinating nuances of French culture. It is fitting that the Musée d'Orsay, a Belle Epoque former train station, houses the city's legacy of art from 1848 to 1914: railroads and other everyday phenomena were—shockingly so at the time—favorite subjects of the period's artists, especially the Impressionists, who enjoy pride of place under the glass-vaulted roof. And it was the French Revolution that opened the Louvre to the masses, so that all can now view the extraordinary collection amassed in good part by seven centuries of monarchs, while imagining the history-shaping intrigues that once fermented in these same salons. A proletarian spirit also holds sway at the Centre Pompidou, where the world's largest collection of modern art is displayed; though opened in 1977, it has been so popular that a recent renovation means it is looking better than ever.

In addition to these big three, other favorites include museums which began life not as museums, but as sumptuous houses. Many of these gilded time-machines are filled with salons aglitter with gilt *boiserie* (carved wood panels), chandeliers, and flocked red velvet walls literally oozing Parisian elegance. For these unique peeps into yesteryear, top bets include the decorative arts treasures found at the Musée Nissim de Camondo, the Musée Jacquemart-André, and the Musée Carnavalet. Skip through the centuries at some modern art museums, as both the Musée Rodin and the Musée Picasso are housed in historic hôtels particuliers—mansions built as private homes for the rich and famous. For a true trip back to the 17th, 18th or 19th centuries, discover overlooked jewels like the Hôtel Lauzun on the Ile St-Louis, the Atelier Delacroix on the Place Furstenberg, and the Musée de la Vie Romantique (where the likes of Chopin and Georges Sand once rendezvoused) at the foot of Montmartre.

Bon Appétit!: The Pleasures of Eating

"Animals feed, men eat, but only wise men know the art of dining," wrote the French gastronome Anthelme Brillat-Savarin. Join them in the pursuit of this art and don't feel guilty if you spend as much time of your stay in Paris in its restaurants as in its museums. Eating is the heart and soul of French culture. Give yourself over to the leisurely meal; two hours for a three-course menu is par, and you may, after relaxing into the routine, begin to feel pressed at less than three. Whether your dream meal is savoring truffle-studded fois gras served on Limoges china or sharing a baguette with *jambon* (ham) and Brie *sur l'herbe* (on the grass), eating in Paris can be a memorable experience. Needless to say, it's well worth splurging on a dinner of outstanding haute cuisine in formal splendor (and many of those restaurants feature historically dazzling interiors, worthy of any museum). But also keep in mind that many famous chefs have opened bistro annexes where you can sample their cooking for less. In addition, younger chefs are setting up shop in more affordable, outlying parts of Paris, where they are serving their own innovative version of bistro classics. Some of these locations can mean a long métro or cab ride, but it will give you the opportunity to discover restaurants in neighborhoods that you might not otherwise see. End any proper meal with a sublime cheese course, then dessert (the more decadent and creamy the better), then an *express* (taken black, with sugar).

Of course, experiencing fine French food consists of much more than selecting a restaurant with "Chez" in the title, forking out a minimum of a three-digit sum in euros, and knowing the best vintages of *vin rouge* (red wine) and *vin blanc* (white wine). The best introductions to French food are the open-air street markets. The biggest is on boulevard de Reuilly between rue de Charenton and place Félix-Eboué (12e, métro Dugommier), open Tuesday and Friday; while others are the south end of rue Mouffetard (5e, métro Monge); rue de Buci (6e, métro Odéon, in the heart of St-Germain-des-Prés); rue Daguerre (14e, métro Denfert-Rochereau) in Montparnasse; and rue Lepic (18e, métro Blanche or Abbesses) in Montmartre. Or head instead to the delightful grocery stores of Paris. Whether you buy the baguettes lined up soldier-style at the *boulangerie* (bakery), where you can also get fine sandwiches, or seductively displayed pastries at the pâtisserie, or *charcuteries*, where butchers sells cold cuts, or *épiceries*—the French equivalent of a deli—or at the *fromagerie* (cheese shop), you'll find it easy to create the fixings for a pique-nique in one of the city's parks. As you'll discover, who needs to pay a fortune to dine amid the Art Nouveau splendors of Maxim's when you can enjoy a peach and Brie on a bench in that even more gorgeous showplace, the 17th-century place des Vosges?

Café Society

Along with air, water, and wine, the café remains one of the basic necessities of life in Paris. You may prefer a posh perch at a renowned spot such as the Deux Magots on boulevard St-Germain or opt for a tiny *café du coin* (corner café) where you can have a quick cup of coffee at the counter. Those on the grands boulevards (such as boulevard St-Michel, boulevard St-Germain, and the Champs-Élysées) and in the big tourist spots (near the Louvre, the Opéra, and the Eiffel Tower, for example) will almost always be the most expensive and the least interesting. The more modest establishments (look for nonchalant locals) are the places to really get a feeling for French café culture. And we do mean culture—Les Deux Magots is still milking its reputation as one of the Left Bank's prime meeting places for intelligentsia as the former hangout of Verlaine, Rimbaud, Gide, Picasso, and Breton. In spite of its heart-stopping prices, the Flore still packs them in—you can't help imagining that something profound is being uttered at the next table, any more than you can resist the ultra-rich onion soup. At La Closerie des Lilas an expensive drink allows you to rest your derrière on the spots once favored by Baudelaire, Apollinaire, and Hemingway. Delightfully, all these cafés are still crammed with locals, so grab a seat, order a Lillet, and settle in for a round of serious people-watching.

Rues with a View: Scenic Strolls and Bus Routes

The French have a word for it: *flâner,* which means to saunter, and this is the way to best appraise Paris. Ignore any urges to speed—just relax and let the *esprit de Paris* take over. It's hard to get lost, thanks to very visible monuments that serve as landmarks. Some favorite walks are from place St-Michel, through the Latin Quarter to the Panthéon, and down rue Mouffetard; along the banks of the Canal St-Martin and Canal de l'Ourcq up to the Parc de la Villette; through the small, winding streets of the Marais from place de la Bastille to the Pompidou Center; along busy rue Faubourg St-Honoré; from the Élysée Palace to the Madeleine; place Vendôme, and the gardens of the Palais-Royal; and along the streets and riverbanks of Ile St-Louis from east to west, ending at Pont St-Louis for a classic view of the Seine and Notre-Dame.

There are also several bus lines that you can take for a good, cheap tour of Paris, sans irritating commentary. Some of these lines are traveled by buses with small balconies in the rear, though the proximity to gusts of carbon monoxide is less than pleasant. No. 29: the interesting section of the 29 stretches from Gare St-Lazaare, past Opéra Garnier and the Pompidou, and through the heart of the Marais, crossing the place des Vosges before ending up at the Bastille. This is one of the few lines that run primarily through the small streets of a neighborhood. No. 69: get on at the Champ de Mars (the park right by the Eiffel Tower) and ride through parts of the Quartier Latin, across the bridge to the Right Bank near the Louvre, by the Hôtel de Ville (City Hall), and on to the Bastille area. No. 72: river-lovers will appreciate this line. It follows the Seine from the Hôtel de Ville west past the Louvre, Trocadéro, and most of the big-name Right Bank sights. You also get good views of the Left Bank, including the Eiffel Tower.

Shopping: Bon Chic, Bon Genre

Quotidian activities are elevated to high art in Paris, and shopping is no exception. Sophisticated city dwellers that they are—many natives live by the motto *bon chic, bon genre* ("well dressed, well bred")—Parisians approach this exercise as a ritual, and an elaborate ritual at that. Picking produce at the open-air markets on rue Mouffetard or rue Montorgueil or at the Marché d'Aligre, or searching for haute couture at Jean-Paul Gaultier, Sonia Rykiel, or Christian Dior, they cast a discerning eye on the smallest detail and demand the highest quality—which may explain why the city's shopkeepers are so famously grouchy. Browsing through old books and maps in the stalls of *bouquinistes* (secondhand booksellers) on quai de l'Hôtel de Ville along the Seine, or prowling through castoffs at the Marché aux Puces St-Ouen, Parisians show their practicality, their sense of economy, and their ability to turn even a piece of junk into an inventively chic treasure. The city's lairs of consumerism are celebrated—the fashion salons, venerable antiques shops around the rue de Beaune and rue Jacob, august fashion showrooms, and *grands magasins* (department stores) such as Au Bon Marché, Au Printemps, and the Galeries Lafayette, which flaunt Belle Epoque extravagance and trendy designers.

Splendid Stones: Churches to Palaces

It may be due to a heightened sense of aesthetics or just typical Gallic disdain, but Parisians always seem to view with skepticism the architectural innovations continually rising in their midst with skepticism—all the while assembling the most beautiful city on earth. "C'est magnifique," say some Parisians of the grandiose glass pyramid by architect I. M. Pei that sprouted in 1989 from the Cour Napoléon at their beloved Louvre. "C'est horrible," say others. The Grand Palais was tolerated only as a frothy oddity when it went up as a temporary pavilion for the World's Fair of 1900, but it's still there, a reassuring glass and iron presence on the banks of the Seine. And some Parisians sniffingly refer to the high-rise complex of La Défense as "Houston on the Seine," though this futuristic area and such other glassy creations as the Institut du Monde Arabe, completed in 1988, continue to provide the visual theatrics with which Paris astonishes. Even the Eiffel Tower wasn't spared Parisian scorn: when the city's graceful icon first appeared above the rooftops in 1889, naysayers quipped that they enjoyed ascending to the top because it was the only place they didn't have to look at the darn thing. Still, the memories you cherish most may be of burnished jewels like the Palais de Chaillot, St-Sulpice, Notre-Dame, or the Sainte-Chapelle. More glass than stone, the latter is one of the supreme achievements of the Middle Ages and its heavenly light has not dimmed over the ages.

FODOR'S CHOICE

Even with so many special places in Paris, Fodor's writers and editors have their favorites. Here are a few that stand out.

Dining

Alain Ducasse. Whether Croesus-rich or sublimely light, Ducasse's culinary triumphs will guarantee you an advanced degree in nouvelle finesse. $$$$

Les Élysées du Vernet. A glass ceiling designed by Gustave Eiffel himself, intoxicating creations by Alain Solivères (try his *Parmentier de sanglier au panais,* or shepherd's pie of roasted boar with garlic parsnips), and alluring touches—women are presented with a rose on their adieu—put this place in the running with better-known spots for your grand Parisian blow-out. $$$$

Le Grand Véfour. Back when Napoléon dined here, this was the most beautiful restaurant in Paris. Guess what? It still is. $$$$

Taillevent. Perhaps the most traditional of all Paris luxury restaurants, this grande dame is suddenly the object of a certain uncharacteristic buzz, since the arrival of new chef Michel Del Burgo. $$$$

La Régalade. Is Yves Camdeborde the chef of the moment? Only time will tell, but as the leading priest who marries bistro and nouvelle cookery—who can resist his soup of lentils and puréed chestnuts poured over a mound of fois gras?—his remains one of the hardest reservations to snag. $$$

L'Astrance. Paris has gone wild over this cool and contemporary spot, thanks to the kitchen's fusion fireworks—anyone for coconut-curry mousseline of scallops studded with tiny green apple ice cubes? $$–$$$

Chez Savy. The Art Deco cream-and-burgundy interior cossets; the rib-sticking specialties from the Auvergne in central France—lentil salad with bacon, beautifully charred lamb with feather-light shoestring *frites,* poached peach with sorbet—delight. $$

Ze Kitchen Galerie. Unbridled creativity and lots of pure fun (check out the windowed kitchen) are the draws here. $$

Les Pipos. With conversation that flows as freely as the wine, this is everything you can ask for in a Latin Quarter bistro. $–$$

Lodging

Costes. Baron de Rothschild hasn't invited you this time? No matter—stay here at Paris's most stylishly sumptuous hotel and you'll hardly know the difference. $$$$

Pavillon de la Reine. Set in one of the 17th-century mansions of the place des Vosges, this has a grand entryway that still brings the age of Henri IV alive. $$$$

L'Hôtel. Superstar decorator Jacques Garcia recently gilded this 19th-century lily with *la touche finale* in Proustian luxe, continuing to make this a favorite for fashionistas and off-duty celebrities. *$$$–$$$$*

Vendôme. The Second Empire–style rooms are simply sumptuous. *$$$–$$$$*

Relais St-Germain. Rooms in this hotel are named for French literary heroes and are at least twice the size of those you'll find elsewhere at this price level. *$$$*

Victoire Opéra. This hotel, with its very Parisian cream-color facade and wrought-iron balconies, has it all—intimacy, comfort, affordability, and a delightful location. *$$$*

Caron de Beaumarchais. As airily elegant as a Beaumarchais comedy (the hotel is named after the 18th-century playwright), this hotel is one of the most popular options in the Marais district. *$$*

Esméralda. Once the ultimate Left Bank *hôtel de charme* and set in a fusty 17th-century building across from Notre-Dame, this has long been cherished for its cozy and eccentric style—who can resist its half-timbered nook of a lobby? *$$*

Familia. The hospitable Gaucheron family bends over backward for you at this pleasant Latin Quarter hotel; more than half the rooms have sepia frescoes of celebrated Paris scenes painted by an artist from the Beaux Arts school. *$*

Grandes Écoles. Like a country cottage dropped smack in the middle of the Latin Quarter, this lovely hotel, set around a leafy garden, comes replete with parquet floors and Louis-Philippe furnishings. *$*

Spectacular Sights

Église du Dôme. Under the dome of this commanding Baroque church, part of Les Invalides, Napoléon rests in imperial splendor.

Louvre. No matter how many times you visit, there will always be something new to see—after all, the *Mona Lisa* is just one of the 800,000 treasures belonging to this fabled museum.

Musée d'Orsay. Pride of place at this spectacularly renovated 19th-century railroad terminal goes to the great Impressionist paintings on view but the lesser-known "academic" works hanging side by side means there is much more here than just Renoir & Co.

Notre-Dame Cathedral. After seeing the spectacular interior, head up to the twin towers—erstwhile playground of Quasimodo—to visit the gargoyles and see the 13-ton bell, which still rings on special occasions (such as when Charles Laughton gets a bit obsessive about Maureen O'Hara).

Sainte-Chapelle. Ascending into this chapel, built by Louis IX to house what he believed to be the Crown of Thorns from Christ's crucifixion and still shimmering with walls of stained glass, is like climbing into a jewel box.

Lesser-Known Jewels

Ancient Cloître Quarter. Hidden beneath the shadows of Notre-Dame, this storybook warren of streets was once called home by Héloïse and Abélard and still bears traces of the Middle Ages.

Cour de Rohan. Immortalized as Gigi's home in the Vincente Minelli Oscar-winner of 1958, this relentlessly picturesque cul-de-sac in the heart of St-Germain-des-Prés wins the beauty contest for pure charm.

Hôtel de Lauzun. The first manifestation in Paris of the floridly magnificent taste for the Baroque, this Ile St-Louis mansion is like Versailles seen through a jeweler's loupe.

Musée de la Vie Romantique. Ingres, Delacroix, Turgenev, Chopin, and Georges Sand all knew and loved this house, now renovated into an enchanting museum.

Musée Nissim de Camondo. Although only constructed in the 19th century by an art-loving millionaire, this mansion showcases the crème de la crème of Rococo and Neoclassical decorative arts and remains the connoisseur's connoisseur's favorite.

GREAT ITINERARIES

Paris in Five Days

As an eager army of bipeds discovers every year, walking is by far the best way to see Paris. Whether you make it a day-long route or cram it all into a few aerobically packed hours, any walk here can turn into an odyssey that allows you to touch the wellsprings of Western civilization. So that you don't show up somewhere and find the doors locked, shuffle the itinerary segments below with closing days in mind. To avoid crowds, go to museums and major sights early in the day. Note, too, that some museums and major sights have reduced entrance fees on Sunday and that many museums are closed early in the week (on Monday your best bet is the Day Two itinerary).

DAY ONE

If you want to be truthful in telling the folks back home that you had "all of Paris at your feet," head first to the Eiffel Tower: morning (or late evening) is the best time to avoid the crowds. The most thrilling approach to this soaring Tinkertoy of an icon is via the Champ de Mars. Afterwards consider visiting the Art Deco Palais de Chaillot, with its numerous museums. Also in the area is the Musée Guimet, with Asian art, and the Musée d'Art Moderne de la Ville de Paris, a superb modern art museum. Or take a tour of the Seine on the Bateaux Mouches; these boats depart regularly from place de l'Alma. From here, walk or take the métro to the Arc de Triomphe; from the top there's a great view of the boulevards emanating from L'Étoile and the noble vistas extending to the Louvre and La Défense. To the northeast is the Parc Monceau, center of one of Paris's ritziest residential areas. Then backtrack to the Champs-Élysées—work your way down this fabled avenue, across place de la Concorde and the Jardin des Tuileries to the Louvre. Don't visit the museum now—wait until the next morning, when it will be less crowded. And don't do this tour on a Monday if you plan to go to the Musée d'Art Moderne because it is closed then.

DAY TWO

Get to the Louvre early to avoid the crowds; in a morning you'll be able to see only part of the museum—it's that big. After lunch, wander along the ritzy rue St-Honoré for some dazzling window-shopping. Near here you'll find that most elegant square, place Vendôme—home to the Ritz—and the neoclassical Église de la Madeleine. For an eye-popping look at Haussmann's 19th-century Paris and the spectacular Opéra Garnier (you can tour

the theater during the day), join up with the Grand Boulevards; nearby are the exquisite house-museums, the Nissim de Camondo and the Jacquemart-André. In the afternoon visit the Centre Pompidou and then explore the winding streets of the picturesque Marais quarter. The Musée Picasso is in one of this old neighborhood's hôtels particuliers. The gorgeously elegant place des Vosges is pleasant for a break. The Marais is overflowing with lovely bistros for your evening repast. This itinerary is fine any day but Tuesday, when the Louvre is closed.

DAY THREE

For a full burst of the glory that was medieval Paris, begin by visiting Notre-Dame Cathedral, its neighboring Ancient Cloître Quarter, and the stained-glass wonder that is the Sainte-Chapelle, all on Ile de la Cité. Then head over to the neighboring Ile St-Louis and wander the narrow streets, still spirit-warm with its former residents, Voltaire, Daumier, Cézanne, Baudelaire, and Chagall. Cross over the Seine to explore the Latin Quarter, using the Panthéon dome as a landmark and set aside more time if you plan to see the magnificent Musée National du Moyen-Age. Then head south to relax in the Jardin du Luxembourg, or sip coffee in a neighborhood café. Double-back to St-Germain-des-Prés, to many minds Paris's chicest and most *charmant* quarter. Travel back in time and visit the neighborhood's Cour de Rohan, the 18th-century alley Cour du Commerce St-André, and the place Furstenberg. Closings make this itinerary a problem on Tuesday (Musée du Moyen-Age, Centre Pompidou, Musée Picasso).

DAY FOUR

Start the morning admiring the Impressionists in the Musée d'Orsay; arrive early to avoid the crowds. Then head west to the Palais Bourbon, home of the Assemblée Nationale (the French parliament), and the Hôtel des Invalides, with its impressive Église du Dôme, where Napoléon is buried. If you're up for another museum, visit the Musée Rodin; if not, see its rose garden, filled with Rodin's sculptures. Continue east toward the enormous church of St-Sulpice. From here jump on the métro to the Pigalle or Blanche stop and spend the afternoon getting a sense of Paris's villagelike character by exploring Montmartre. On boulevard de Clichy you'll find the famous Moulin Rouge.

Continue up into Montmartre, via lovely place des Abbesses. On this square are two Art Nouveau gems: the church of St-Jean de Montmartre, and the Art Nouveau Guimard entrance to the Abbesses métro station. From here walk through the winding, hilly streets to place du Tertre, and then on to Sacré-Coeur, where there's a tremendous view of the city below, and, hopefully, a thunderously beautiful sunset to see it by. This itinerary won't work on Monday, when the Musée d'Orsay and the Musée Rodin are closed.

DAY FIVE

To get a sense of the splendor in which French royalty lived, spend a good part of the day visiting Versailles (fine any day but Monday). If you have more time on your hands, you can return to the Louvre or attack the smaller museums like the Maillol and the Marmottan–Claude Monet and explore the funky Bastille, elegant Passy, and up-and-coming Bercy or Ménilmontant-Belleville neighborhoods. Or take the métro to see attractions on the edge of the city: Père-Lachaise Cemetery, the Parc de La Villette, or the Bois de Boulogne or Bois de Vincennes, Paris's two largest parks.

Paris with Kids

Paris's major museums, like the Louvre and the Musée d'Orsay, can be as engaging as they are educational—as long as you keep your visits short. Many activities and museums are designed especially for children, and some museums even have children's programs. Note that many museums are closed on Monday or Tuesday. You may need to shuffle the itinerary around according to museum closings.

On Day One, give your kids an idea of how Paris was planned by climbing to the top of the Arc de Triomphe. From here work your way down the Champs-Élysées toward place de la Concorde. Stop for a puppet show at the Marionettes des Champs-Élysées, at avenues Matignon and Gabriel, halfway down the Champs. Or head to the Palais de la Découverte, just off the Champs, to catch a planetarium show. Continue walking down the Champs, to the Jardin des Tuileries, where kids can sail boats on a small pond. For an afternoon treat, head for Angélina (on rue de Rivoli), a tearoom famous for its thick hot chocolate. If you want to see the puppet show, do this on a Wednesday, Saturday, or Sunday. Skip this on Monday when the Palais de la Découverte is closed.

On Day Two, head in the morning to the Eiffel Tower for a bird's-eye view of the city. After you descend, either ride on one of the Bateaux Mouches at place de l'Alma, nearby; or brave Les Égouts, the Paris sewers (the tour takes about an hour and departs from place de la Résistance, across the Seine). Next take the métro to the Parc André-Citroën, where there's a computerized "dancing fountain," or to the Bois de Boulogne, where you'll find a zoo (the Jardin d'Acclimatation), rowboats, and plenty of wide-open space. This won't work on Thursday or Friday, when Les Égouts are closed.

On Day Three, introduce your kids to Quasimodo's hangout, Notre-Dame Cathedral; go early so you don't have to wait to get in. Have lunch in the area, and then head to Berthillon on the Ile St-Louis for some of the city's best ice cream. Afterward cross the Seine and walk or take the métro to the Odéon stop. From here walk around the colonnaded Théâtre de l'Odéon to the Jardin du Luxembourg, where there's a playground, a pond where kids can rent miniature boats, a café, and plenty of places to sit. Ready for more? Walk to the Centre de la Mer et des Eaux, an aquarium nearby, then continue on foot or by bus to the Arènes de Lutèce, one of the few vestiges of the former Roman city. Not far on foot or by métro is the Jardin des Plantes, a botanical garden with the state-of-the-art Grande Galerie de l'Évolution, a museum exhibiting a collection of taxidermy of all kinds of animals. Also just a métro ride away in Montparnasse are the Catacombs, Roman quarries that served as headquarters for the French Resistance during World War II. Don't try to see the Catacombs on Monday or the Grande Galerie de l'Évolution on Tuesday, when they're closed.

On Day Four, begin at the Musée Picasso in the Marais to show your kids the paintings and sculptures of one of France's finest artists. Nearby, pick up a sandwich to eat on a bench in the place des Vosges. If your children are up for another museum, one that's more child-oriented, head for the Académie de la Magie and catch a magic show. Or take in the Centre Pompidou; either see an exhibit (often there are special kids' programs related to the shows) or simply ride the escalator to the top for a great view of Paris. Around the corner, on the Square Igor-Stravinsky, watch the imaginative, moving sculptures in the fountain. Behind the Beaubourg is the magical Musée de la Poupée (Doll Museum). Another option is to take the métro from Châtelet–Les-Halles to the Porte de La Villette; in the whimsical park of the same name are an interactive science museum, a museum of musical instruments, an IMAX theater, and various innovative structures to play on and in. Because of closings, do this between Thursday and Sunday: the Parc de La Villette is closed Monday, the Centre Pompidou Tuesday, the Musée Picasso Tuesday, and the Académie de la Magie every day except Wednesday and weekends.

2 EXPLORING PARIS

Reverberating with 2,000 years of history and culture, Paris intrigues, astonishes, provokes, overwhelms . . . and just plain gets under your skin. Its delights combine to form an apex of architectural beauty, artistic expression, and culinary delight, and does it know it! Simultaneously as drop-dead arrogant as the Arc de Triomphe and as disarmingly quaint as a lace-curtained bistro, Paris seduces newcomers with an insistent come-on—then never lets up. Its persuasive charms will soon have you winking back at the Mona Lisa, going head-to-head with the gargoyles at Notre-Dame, then catching your breath over a *café crème* at a sidewalk café.

Revised and
updated by
Simon Hewitt

Introduction by
Nancy Coons

Y**OU'LL ALWAYS HAVE PARIS.** Like the champagne-frosted idyll
Bogie and Bergman reminisced about in *Casablanca*, the time
you spend in this endlessly resonant city will remain a lifelong
reference point. Over and over, as in a reverie, you'll conjure up its sen-
sorial assault—the sting in the nostril of a fresh-lit Gitane cigarette,
the rippling of lights on the misty Seine, the confetti flutter of antique
prints over a *bouquiniste*'s stand, the aromatic bedlam of a street food
market, the waves battering the *Medusa*'s prow in Géricault's epic canvas at the Louvre. And you'll go all mooney again.

Whether weaned on Hemingway or Henry James, Doisneau or Cartier-
Bresson, Brassaï or Cecil Beaton, Westerners share an image of Paris
as the city of lovers, from Rodin's brawny duo to smoldering apache
dancers, from *La Bohème's* Mimi and Rodolfo weeping in a chilly gar-
ret to Anaïs Nin's flappers naked under fur. Sartre and de Beauvoir!
Montand and Signoret! Belmondo and Seberg! The Hollywood pro-
paganda machine melted the hearts of any stubborn holdouts: who could
stand firm in the face of Leslie Caron's blushes as she danced in Gene
Kelly's arms along the Seine in *An American in Paris,* or Audrey Hepburn's fine-boned take on the *Winged Victory* in *Funny Face,* or the
punched-in-the-gut look on Bogie's face when he remembered the German tanks rolling in?

Notice that none of these star-crossed couples was married, and therein
lies part of the yang to Paris's yin. In the past, hazy gaslight enfolded
poignant lovers while rouged demimondaines, petticoats lifted above
a flash of garter, trawled back allées looking for action. Today, gaslight
and garters no longer beckon, but the unsuspecting visitor to Paris must
still be on guard against the recklessness, sophistication, and savoir faire
so deliciously concentrated in this capital city.

The real love affair is with the city of Paris itself, and it can play you
like a violin. Around every corner, down every *ruelle*, or little street, lies
a resonance-in-waiting. You can stand on the rue du Faubourg St-Honoré at the very spot where Edmond Rostand set Ragueneau's pastry shop
in *Cyrano de Bergerac*. You can peruse the letters of Madame de Sévigné in her erstwhile hôtel particulier, now the Musée Carnavalet. You
can hear the words of Racine resound in the hair-ringing diction of the
Comédie Française. You can breathe in the fumes of hubris before the
extravagant porphyry tomb of Napoléon at Les Invalides. You can try
to resist genuflecting in the Panthéon, where religion itself bowed down
before France's great post-Revolution statesmen. You can climb into
César Franck's organ loft at the church of Ste-Clothilde. You can gaze
through the gate at the Ile St-Louis mansion where Voltaire honed his
wit, and then lay a garland on Oscar Wilde's grave.

No matter which way you head, any trip through Paris will be a voyage of discovery. But choosing the Paris of your dreams is a bit like
choosing a perfume or cologne. Do you prefer young and dashing, or
elegant and worldly? Something sporty, or divinely glamorous? No matter—beneath touristy Paris, historic Paris, fashion-conscious Paris,
pretentious-bourgeois Paris, practical working-class Paris, or the legendary bohemian Paris of undying attraction, you will find your own
Paris, and it will be vivid, exciting, unforgettable. Veterans know that
Paris is a city of regal perspectives and ramshackle streets, of formal
espaces vertes, or green open spaces, and quiet squares, and this combination of the pompous and the private is one of the secrets of its peren-
nial lure.

Another draw is its scale: Paris is relatively small as capitals go, with distances between many of its major sights and museums eminently walkable. The city's principal tourist axis is less than 6½ km (4 mi) long, running parallel to the north bank of the Seine, from the Arc de Triomphe to the Bastille. In fact, the best way to get to know Paris is on foot, although public transportation—particularly the métro subway system—is excellent. Serious explorers should buy a *Plan de Paris* booklet: a city map-guide with a street-name index that also shows métro stations (note that all métro stations have a detailed neighborhood map just inside the entrance).

To help you digest Paris in sensible bites, this chapter is divided into 12 neighborhood walks. For the first-timer, there will always be several "musts" at the top of the list—the Louvre, Notre-Dame, and the Eiffel Tower, among them—but a visit to Paris will never be quite as simple as a quick look at à few landmarks. Every *quartier*, or neighborhood, has its own treasures, and you should be ready to explore—a very pleasant prospect in this most elegant of cities. It is no exaggeration to say that the most assiduous explorers of Paris are the Parisians themselves. Each quartier has its own personality and unsuspected charms, which are discovered best by foot power. You can follow our suggested "good walks," but ultimately your route will be marked by your own preferences and your curiosity—as well as your degree of fatigue. You can wander for hours without getting bored—though not, perhaps, without getting lost. By the time you have seen only a few neighborhoods, drinking in the rich variety they have to offer, you should not only be culturally replete but downright exhausted, and hungry, too. Again, take your cue from the Parisians, and plan out your next stop at a sidewalk café. So you've heard stories of a friend of a friend who paid $6 for a coffee at a famous café? So what? What you're paying for is time, and the opportunity to watch the intricate drama of Parisian street life unfold. Hemingway knew the rules: he'd be just another sports writer if the café waiters of Paris had hovered around him impatiently.

After enjoying your ringside seat at the street theater, you're ready to explore the city as a living art gallery. Paris provides, at nearly every turn, a familiar work of art, framed in reality: *promeneurs* in the Bois de Boulogne in perfect pointillist silhouette, broad street perspectives flashing from gold to pink to silver under scudding Impressionist clouds, a woman's abstracted stare over a glass of green liqueur at a Montmartre café, and fine-boned ladies in stylish black and white delicately sniffing at Guerlain's perfume counter.

You'll learn it's all so familiar and all so terribly . . . Parisian. *Rillettes* (preserved goose spread) and *poilâne* (the ubiquitous chewy sourdough bread of baker Lionel Poilâne) and Beaujolais. Ranks of posters, eight at a time, plastered over scaffolding. The discreet hiss of the métro's rubber wheels. The street sweeper guiding rags along the rain gutters with a twig broom. The coins in the saucer by the *pissoir*. The tantalizing hidden carriage courtyards lined with boxwood, gravel, and Peugeots. The shriek of the espresso machine as it steams the milk for your café crème, the flip-lid sugar bowl on the zinc bar. The illuminated monuments looming like Mayan idols. The lovers buried in each others' necks along the banks of the Seine.

Yes, you'll always have Paris. So what are you waiting for?

Paris Exploring

Place de la République to La Villette

From Bastille to Nation

The Marais

The Latin Quarter and the Ile St-Louis

FROM NOTRE-DAME TO THE PLACE DE LA CONCORDE

No matter how one approaches Paris—historically, geographically, emotionally—it is the Seine River that beckons us. The city owes both its development and much of its visual appeal to the Seine, which weaves through its very heart. Each bank of the river has its own personality; the Rive Droite (Right Bank), with its spacious boulevards and formal buildings, generally has a more sober and genteel feel than the more carefree Rive Gauche (Left Bank), to the south. In between, the river harbors two tiny islands that stand at the center of the city— the Ile de la Cité and the Ile St-Louis. Both seem to be gliding downriver, as if the latter were being towed by the former. It is the Ile de la Cité that forms the historic ground zero of Paris.

It was here, for obvious reasons of defense, and in the hope of controlling the trade that passed along the Seine, that the earliest inhabitants of Paris, the Gaulish tribe of the Parisii, settled in about 250 BC. They called their little home Lutetia, meaning "settlement surrounded by water." In the year 53 BC Julius Caesar, in fact, mentioned the settlement of Lutetia, and it was to this island city that he commanded the leaders of the Gaulish tribes to pay him homage, before his general, Labienus, ruthlessly crushed them. Whereas the Ile St-Louis is today largely residential, the Ile de la Cité remains deeply historic and is the site of the first church of Paris—the great, brooding Cathedral of Notre-Dame. Napoléon was crowned here, and kings and queens exchanged marriage vows before its great altar. The cathedral is the symbolic heart of the city, if not the symbolic heart of France itself, as all roads traversing the realm converge here and are marked by a stone in the plaza before the church. Most of the island's other medieval buildings fell victim to town planner Baron Haussmann's ambitious rebuilding program of the 1860s. Among the rare survivors are the jewel-like Sainte-Chapelle, a vision of shimmering stained glass, and the Conciergerie, the former city prison where Marie-Antoinette and other victims of the French Revolution spent their last days.

If Notre-Dame represents Church, another major attraction of this walk—the Louvre—symbolizes State. This royal palace came into existence in the mid-13th century, when Philippe-Auguste built it as a fortress to protect the city's western flank. It was not until pleasure-loving François I began a partial rebuilding of this original rude fortress in the early 16th century that today's Louvre began gradually to take shape. A succession of French rulers were responsible for filling this immense, symmetrical structure, now the largest museum in the world as well as one of the easiest to get lost in, with the world's greatest paintings and works of art. Right in the middle of the Louvre's main courtyard is I. M. Pei's shimmering glass pyramid, reminding all that while Parisians take their role as custodians of a glorious heritage most seriously, they are equally intent on bequeathing something to the future.

Before you leave Notre-Dame, take a cue from Victor Hugo and climb the 387 steps of one of its towers to the former haunts of its legendary resident hunchback, Quasimodo. You'll be rewarded with the ultimate view of Paris—unforgettably framed by the stone gargoyles created by Viollet-le-Duc. From here, one can see how the city—like the trunk of a tree developing new rings—has spread out in circles from the island on which you now stand. To the north is the Butte Montmartre; to the west the Arc de Triomphe at the head of the Champs-Élysées; to the south the towers of St-Sulpice and the domes of the Invalides, the Panthéon, and the Luxembourg palace. Drinking in the view, you can remain here for hours in a pleasant state of medieval suspended animation, but don't delay—you have too much else to see ahead.

Numbers in the text correspond to numbers in the margin and on the From Notre-Dame to the Place de la Concorde map.

A Good Walk

The best approach to the Ile de la Cité is to cross the Pont au Double from quai de Montebello (St-Michel métro stop or RER). This bridge leads to the large, pedestrian place du Parvis and that great landmark, Notre-Dame. Place du Parvis is regarded by the French as *kilomètre zéro,* the spot from which all distances to and from the city are officially measured, and makes a fitting setting for the regal cathedral of **Notre-Dame** ①. Study the magnificent facade, explore the interior, then—you have to head to the special entrance on the left-hand side of the facade—toil up the steps to the towers for a gargoyle-framed view of the heart of Paris. In peak season, there is often a block-long line to do this, so budget your time accordingly.

To escape the crowds, however, relief is just a short—and magical—stroll away. Few people venture to the **Ancient Cloître** ②, a nook of medieval Paris that is tucked behind the northern (or left-hand side as you face the cathedral) buttresses of Notre-Dame. First, history and art buffs will want to visit the **Musée de Notre-Dame** ③ set on rue du Cloître-Notre-Dame. Then enter the quarter—originally the area where seminary students boarded with the church canons—by taking one of the adjoining side streets and head north toward the Seine to reach rue Chanoinesse, once the seminary's cloister walk. Here, at No. 10, is the house that was once paradise to those fabled lovers of the Middle Ages, Héloïse and Abelard. Past some pretty houses (notably No. 24), you'll find rue de Columbe, but make a right at No. 5—a private house which still contains the ruins of the medieval chapel of St-Aignan—to turn onto rue des Ursins. This will take you to a lovely flower garden set by steps leading up to the riverside quai aux Fleurs. While taking a time-out on the steps, feast your eyes (if not your stomach—this could make a cute spot for a picnic) on one of the island's most beautiful medieval mansions. Just a step away is the rue des Chantres, which seems to only exist to strikingly frame Notre-Dame's spire in the distance. Once your Nikon has immortalized this view, head back to the cathedral and take a walk around Notre-Dame's walls, which nicely sets the whole place in proportion, with the gardens between the cathedral and the Seine offering splendid views of the sophisticated medieval masonry. Head through the gardens to **Square Jean-XXIII** ④ and turn right to cross Pont de l'Archevêché for the best view of all, with Notre-Dame's flying buttresses (archlike structural supports enabling the walls to soar heavenward) lending the heavy apse a magical lightness.

Walk (or dance—this is where Leslie Caron and Gene Kelly so memorably pas-de-deuxed in *An American in Paris*) —along quai de la Tournelle until you reach the Petit Pont, then cross back over the Seine and head straight on to rue de Lutèce. Turn left here, pass the flower market, and continue on to the boulevard du Palais and the imposing **Palais de Justice** ⑤, the 19th-century law courts; you can wander around the buildings among the black-robed lawyers or attend a court hearing. But the real interest here is the late Gothic **Sainte-Chapelle** ⑥, which many consider the most beautiful church in the world, tucked away to the left of the main courtyard. Turn left as you leave the Palais de Justice, then left again onto quai de l'Horloge, named for the oldest *horloge* (clock) in Paris, marking time since 1370 from high up on the **Conciergerie** ⑦, the prison where Marie-Antoinette and other aristocratic blue bloods awaited their slice of history at the guillotine. Quai

24

Bibliothèque Nationale

R. des Petits Champs

Av. de l'Opéra

R. St-Anne

R. de Richelieu

R. de la Banque

R. de Cléry

R. d'Aboukir

R. Montmartre

R. Étienne Marcel

R. Réaumur

0

440 yards

0

400 meters

R. Montorgueil

2e

N

Jardin de Palais Royal

Banque de France

R. Tiquetonne

R. de Turbigo

1er

R. du Petits Champs

R. Rambuteau

R. de

Palais Royal

R. Croix des Petits Champs

R. Berger

R. du Louvre

R. St-Honoré

R. Pierre Lescot

R. St-Denis

③

⑫

⑪

Louvre

R. de Rivoli

R. des Halles

Bd de Sébastopol

East Entrance

R. du Pont Neuf

R. St-Martin

Quai du Louvre

Seine

Quai de la Mégisserie

Quai de Gesvres

⑨

⑩

R. Bonaparte

Quai de l'Horloge

ob

R. de Seine

R. Mazarine

Q. des Grands Augustins

R. Dauphine

⑧

⑤ ⑦

⑥

R. de Lutèce

Ile de la Cité

R. du Cloître Notre Dame

r. Chanoinesse

Pl. St-Michel

R. St-André des Arts

Pl. du Parvis

③

②

1

in

Bd. St-Germain

M

Q. de Montebello

Petit Pont

①

du Four

St. Michel

M **Mabillon**

Pont au Double

④

5e

Pont de l'Archevêché

de l'Horloge leads to rue de Harlay and historic **place Dauphine** ⑧. Cross this old-fashioned square to **square du Vert-Galant** ⑨, with its equestrian statue of Henri IV. Steps on the right lead down to the waterside where Vedette motorboats set off for their tours along the Seine.

Cross **Pont Neuf** ⑩—actually the oldest bridge in Paris—to the Rive Droite and turn left along quai du Louvre, past the Art Deco Samaritaine department store, to reach the great **Louvre** ⑪ museum, entering through the frigidly elegant Baroque East Front designed by Claude Perrault in the 1660s. This entry portal leads into Cour Carrée, a grandiose courtyard (which has something of the assured feel of an Oxford or Cambridge quadrangle, though on a much grander scale). Through the massive archway of the domed Pavillon de l'Horloge, straight ahead you can make out the controversial main entrance to the Louvre: I. M. Pei's famous glass pyramid. Settle in for a visit to the home of the *Venus de Milo,* the *Winged Victory of Samothrace,* and the mystifying countenance of the *Mona Lisa.* At the point when one priceless Titian painting begins to look like the next, head back to the main concourse under the pyramid and make for the **Carrousel du Louvre** ⑫, an underground mall with snack bars and designer boutiques fanning out from a smaller, inverted pyramid. If you exit by the **Arc du Carrousel** ⑬—a small relation to the distant Arc de Triomphe—you'll be ideally placed to assess the grand vista (aligned *almost* perfectly) that leads from the Louvre pyramid, through the Arc du Carrousel to the Concorde obelisk, Champs-Élysées, and Arc de Triomphe, with the shadowy towers of La Défense just visible behind.

Continue west, past eccentric diagonal hedges, to the **Jardin des Tuileries** ⑭, or Tuileries Gardens, with its manicured lawns, fountains, rows of trees, and regiments of statues old and new. To the north side is arcaded rue de Rivoli, built for Napoléon to commemorate his Italian conquests. Two smallish buildings stand sentinel by place de la Concorde, at the far end of the Tuileries. Nearest rue de Rivoli is the **Musée du Jeu de Paume** ⑮, host to outstanding exhibits of contemporary art. The almost identical building nearer the Seine is the **Musée de l'Orangerie** ⑯, containing the largest versions of Monet's *Water Lilies* (closed until early 2003 for renovations).

The two museums gaze down on one of the world's most opulent squares, **place de la Concorde** ⑰, centered by its gilt-tipped Egyptian obelisk, with the Seine to the south, the Champs-Élysées and Arc de Triomphe to the west, and rue Royale and the Madeleine church to the north. If you don't have a bad case of gallery feet by now, continue up the Champs-Élysées for 500 yards and turn left onto avenue Winston-Churchill. Looming over the street corner is Jean Cardot's giant bronze statue of General de Gaulle. On the left is the **Petit Palais** ⑱, facing the larger, glass-roofed **Grand Palais** ⑲—two museums built for the Exposition Universelle of 1900 and currently under restoration. The back of the Grand Palais—the entrance is on avenue Franklin-D.-Roosevelt—houses the **Palais de la Découverte** ⑳, a science museum with a planetarium. A 10-ft statue of Churchill gazes toward the Seine and the **Pont Alexandre-III** ㉑. With luck, by the time you reach this exuberant Belle Epoque bridge, you'll be greeted with a memorable sunset to set off the gleaming, gold-leafed Invalides dome that looms up ahead.

TIMING

Allowing for toiling up towers, dancing down quays, and musing at Mona Lisa, this 5½-km (3½-mi) walk will take a full day—enabling you to reach Pont Alexandre-III just before the fabled *l'heure bleue*—the blue hour of dusk.

Heads up: readers have raved about Paris's museum pass, the **Carte Musées et Monuments** (Museums and Monuments Pass), which offers unlimited access to more than 65 museums and monuments over a one-, three-, or five-consecutive-day period; the cost, respectively, is €13, €26, and €39. Considering most Paris museums cost between €4 and €6, you have to be serious about museumgoing to make this pay off, but there is one incredible plus: you get to jump to the head of the line by displaying it—quite a feat when there are 600 people lined up to get into the Musée d'Orsay. Since most museums don't charge for kids under 18, a family of four need only buy 2 passes. The Pass is available at Paris's tourist offices, metro stations, and at all participating museums. Note that many museums are closed on Monday and Tuesday. Information: www.intermusees.com.

Sights to See

★ ❷ **Ancien Cloître Quartier.** Hidden in the shadows of Notre-Dame and just a few steps away from its seething crowds is this magical and often overlooked nook of Paris. Thankfully, when Baron Haussmann knocked down much of the Ile de la Cité in the 19th century, he spared this sector, still set with medieval mansions (lucky folk from the 15th-century composer Pierre du Bellay to Ludwig Bemelmans—creator of the beloved *Madeleine*—and the Aga Khan once called these home) and winding alleys. Back in the Middle Ages, this was the quarter where canons boarded students of the cathedral seminary and one of these was the celebrated Peter Abelard (1079–1142)—questioner of the faith, philosopher, founder of the University of Paris, and scandalizer of the civilized world for his penchant for *les femmes*. Abelard came to this quarter to reside with Canon Fulbert to teach his niece, Héloïse, resulting in a love affair whose denouement—she became pregnant, he was castrated by the law (but survived to become a famous teacher)— is the stuff of legend. Their house, completely redone in the 19th century, stands at No. 10 rue Chanoinesse—a plaque commemorates the lovers on the quayside facade. In the Ancien Cloître, there are no famous sights per se, so just follow your nose and explore its storybook streets. Although defaced by a modern police station and garage, the tiny warren of six streets still casts a spell, particularly at the intersection of rue des Ursins and rue des Chantres, where a lovely medieval palace, tiny flower garden, and quayside steps form a cul-de-sac where time seems to be holding its breath. ⊠ *Rue du Cloître-Notre-Dame north to the quai des Fleurs, Ile de la Cité. Métro: Cité.*

❶❸ **Arc du Carrousel.** Often the place for fashion-magazine photo spreads, this small triumphal arch between the Louvre and the Tuileries was erected by Napoléon from 1806 to 1808. The four bronze horses on top were originally the famous gilded horses that Napoléon looted from Venice; when these were returned in 1815, Bosio designed four new ones harnessed to a chariot, driven by a goddess symbolizing the Restoration (of the monarchy). *Métro: Palais-Royal.*

❶❷ **Carrousel du Louvre.** Part of the early '90s Louvre renovation program, this subterranean shopping complex is centered on an inverted glass pyramid (overlooked by the regional Ile-de-France tourist office) and contains a wide array of stores, spaces for fashion shows (this is Paris, after all), an auditorium, and a huge parking garage. At lunchtime, museum goers rush to the mall-style food court where fast food goes international. Note that you can get into the museum (and avoid some lines) by entering through the mall. ⊠ *Entrance on rue de Rivoli or by the Arc du Carrousel, Louvre/Tuileries. Métro: Palais-Royal.*

❼ **Conciergerie.** Bringing a tear to the eyes of Ancien Régime devotées, this is the famous prison in which dukes and duchesses, lords and ladies, and, most famously, Queen Marie-Antoinette were all imprisoned during the French Revolution and ultimately carted off to the guillotine. By the end of the Reign of Terror (1793–95), countless others fell foul of the revolutionaries, including their own leaders, Danton and Robespierre. Originally part of the royal palace on the Ile de la Cité, the turreted medieval building still holds Marie-Antoinette's cell (with some objects connected with the ill-fated queen); a chapel, embellished with the initials M. A., occupies the true site of her confinement. Out of one of these windows, Toni (the queen's nickname) notoriously saw her best friend, the Comtesse de Lamballe—lover of the arts and daughter of the richest duke in France—torn to pieces by a wild mob, her dismembered limbs then displayed on pikes. Elsewhere are the courtyard and fountain where victims of "The Terror" spent their final days playing piquet, writing letters to their loved ones, and waiting for the dreaded climb up the staircase to the Chamber of the Revolutionary Council to hear their final verdict. You can also visit the guardroom, complete with hefty Gothic vaulting and intricately carved columns, and the monumental Salle des Gens d'Armes, whence a short corridor leads to the kitchen, with its four vast fireplaces. The building's name derives from the governor, or *concierge,* of the palace, whose considerable income was swollen by the privilege he enjoyed of renting out shops and workshops. ⊠ *1 quai de l'Horloge, Louvre/Tuileries,* ☎ *01-53-73-78-50,* WEB *www.monum.fr.* ⊠ *€5.5, joint ticket with Sainte-Chapelle €7.6.* ⊘ *Apr.–Sept., daily 9:30–6:30; Oct.–Mar., daily 10–5. Métro: Cité.*

⑲ Grand Palais. With its curved glass roof and florid Belle Epoque ornament, the Grand Palais is unmistakable when approached from either the Seine or the Champs-Élysées and forms an attractive duo with the Petit Palais on the other side of avenue Winston-Churchill. Both these stone buildings, adorned with mosaics and sculpted friezes, were built for the world's fair of 1900, and, as with the Eiffel Tower, were not intended to remain as permanent additions to the city. But once they were up, no one seemed inclined to take them down. Today, the atmospheric iron-and-glass interior of the Grand Palais plays host to major exhibitions but is closed for renovation until 2004. ⊠ *Av. Winston-Churchill, Champs-Élysées. Métro: Champs-Élysées Clemenceau.*

�803 ⑭ Jardin des Tuileries (Tuileries Gardens). Monet and Renoir captured this impressive garden—really more of a long park—with paint and brush, Left Bank songstresses warble about its beauty, and all Parisians know it as a charming place to stroll and survey the surrounding cityscape. The planting of the Tuileries—the name comes from an ancient clay pit formerly on this spot that supplied material for many of the tile roofs of Paris—is typically French: formal and neatly patterned, with statues, rows of trees, and gravel paths, often adorned with a string quartet or jugglers entertaining large crowds on weekends. No wonder the Impressionists liked this city park—note how the gray, austere light of Paris makes green trees look even greener. ⊠ *Bordered by quai des Tuileries, pl. de la Concorde, rue de Rivoli, and the Louvre, Louvre/Tuileries. Métro: Tuileries.*

NEED A BREAK?	Stop off for a snack or lunch at **Dame Tartine,** one of the two designer brasseries erected in the Tuileries in the late '90s (it's on the left as you arrive from the place de la Concorde, ☎ 01-47-03-94-84). With its glass-paneled walls and roof and light wood and aluminum accents, the restaurant is sober and airy. The cuisine is inventive—try the lamb flan with tomato puree—and a carafe of red Ventoux from the Rhône offers good value. You can also eat outdoors in the leafy shade.

Louvre

2nd floor

1st floor

Ground floor

Richelieu

Entresol (Access to Collections)

Sully

Denon

★ ⑪ **Louvre.** Leonardo da Vinci's *Mona Lisa* and *Virgin and Saint Anne,*
van Eyck's *Madonna of Chancellor Rolin,* Giorgione's *Concert Cham-
pêtre,* and Delacroix's *Liberty Guiding the People* . . . you get the picture. This is the world's greatest art museum—and the largest. In days
of yore, couples would arrive at its front door, race along its miles of
corridors—passing the *Venus de Milo, Winged Victory,* and the *Mona
Lisa*—and 40 minutes later, collapse while exclaiming, "At last, we have
seen the Louvre!" Today, of course, nearly everyone respects the fact
that you don't go to the Louvre to speed past major milestones in civilization. Many thousands of treasures are newly cleaned and lit, so
plan on seeing it all—from the red brocaded Napoléon III salons to
the fabled Egyptian collection, from the 186-carat Regent Diamond
to the rooms crowded with Botticellis, Caravaggios, Poussins, and
Géricaults. After three decades of renovations, the Louvre is now a co-
herent, unified structure and search parties no longer need to be sent
in to find you and bring you out.

To get into the Louvre, you may have to wait in two long lines: one
outside the Pyramide entrance portal and another downstairs at the
ticket booths. You can avoid the first by entering through the Carrousel
du Louvre, but you can't avoid the second. Your ticket will get you
into any and all of the wings as many times as you like during one day.
As enormous as the Louvre is, we've outlined a simple guide in the following pages that is broken up by location (wing, floor, collection, and
room number). If you want a more exhaustively comprehensive guide,
the museum bookstore sells—in addition to the general maps at the
information desk—a plethora of books and leaflets in English.

The Louvre is much more than a museum—it is a saga that began centuries ago. Originally built as a fortress by Philippe-Auguste in the 13th
century, it was not until the reign of pleasure-loving François I, 300
years later, that today's Louvre gradually began to take shape. Through
the years, Henri IV (1589–1610), Louis XIII (1610–43), Louis XIV
(1643–1715), Napoléon I (1804–14), and Napoléon III (1852–70) all
contributed to its construction. Before rampaging revolutionaries
burned part of it down during the bloody Paris Commune of 1871,
the building was even larger. The open section facing the Tuileries Gardens was originally the Palais des Tuileries, the main Paris residence
of the royal family.

The uses to which the building has been put have been almost equally
varied. Though Charles V (1364–80) made the Louvre his residence—
parts of the original medieval fortress have been excavated and can be
seen during your visit—later French kings preferred to live elsewhere,
mainly in the Loire Valley. Even after François I decided to make the
Louvre his permanent home, and accordingly embarked on an ambitious rebuilding program (most of which came to nothing), the Louvre never became more than a secondary palace.

The construction of the stately Cour Carrée (Square Court), mainly
during the reign of Louis XIII, marked the beginning of the Louvre as
you see it today. When a competition for architects to design a suit-
ably imposing east facade was held in 1668, a young draftsman named
Claude Perrault teamed up with the seasoned illustrator and painter
Charles Le Brun to produce the winning proposal. You'd have thought
its muscular rhythms would have wowed the Sun King, but he left the
city for Versailles in 1682. Then, during the remainder of Louis's reign,
the palace underwent a rapid decline. After the revolution, however,
the National Assembly voted in 1783 to turn part of the Louvre into
a public museum. The galleries were stocked with nationalized art taken
from the churches, the king, and other members of the French nobil-

ity, but the greatest boon to the collection came when a Corsican corporal measured his power by how much Great Art he could ransack from the rest of the world. Napoléon Bonaparte moved into the Louvre in 1800 as his armies were marching across Europe. They bravely captured the world's most famous treasures and brought them all back to the Louvre. With Napoléon's fall from grace, the new museum was forced in 1815 to return many of its works to the original owners. Napoléon's stay, however, did not prevent the three remaining French kings—Louis XVIII (1814–24), Charles X (1824–30), and Louis-Philippe (1830–48)—from making the Louvre their home. Fast-forward to the 20th century. During World War II, the invading Germans looted the Louvre and used it as office space; a classical-art buff, Hitler had the *Winged Victory of Samothrace* installed near his desk. Most of the stolen pieces were recovered after the Liberation, but no large-scale changes or innovations were made until François Mitterrand was elected President in 1981.

Reflecting Mitterrand's desire to make his mark on the city, he commissioned the design and construction of I. M. Pei's **Pyramide** (or glass pyramid) surrounded by three smaller pyramids in the Cour Napoléon. Unveiled in March of 1989, it's more than just a grandiloquent gesture. The pyramid provided a new, and much needed, entrance to the Louvre; it also tops a large museum shop, café, and restaurant. Moreover, it acts as the terminal point for the most celebrated city view in Europe, a majestic vista stretching through the Arc du Carrousel, the Tuileries Gardens, across the place de la Concorde, up the Champs-Élysées to the towering Arc de Triomphe, and ending at the giant modern arch at La Défense, 4 km (2½ mi) more to the west.

Among many other improvements, there is now a new entrance, the Porte des Lions, from the quai des Tuileries overlooking the Seine. And thanks to the addition of the underground Carrousel du Louvre—a mall with upscale shops selling clothing, records, and other decidedly non-Louvre-related merchandise—there is even a massive fast-food court. Now you can get a Universal Burger and check out David's *Coronation of Napoléon I* all in the same building. For more soigné dining, be sure to check out the museum's stylish Café Marly.

The Louvre's extraordinary collections encompass paintings, drawings, antiquities, sculpture, furniture, coins, and jewelry—the quality and the sheer variety are overwhelming. The number one attraction is Leonardo da Vinci's enigmatic *Mona Lisa*. While Leonardo's portrait may need some tracking down, this is not a bad thing: along the way, you'll find the Louvre packed with legendary collections, divided into seven areas: Asian antiquities, Egyptian antiquities, Greek and Roman antiquities, sculpture, objets d'art, paintings, and prints and drawings. What follows is no more than a selection of favorites, chosen to act as key points for your exploration.

RICHELIEU WING

Below Ground and Ground Floor: As you enter the Richelieu Wing from the Pyramide, on the left and up a flight of stairs is a gallery that displays temporary exhibits that comprise the Louvre's most recent acquisitions in French sculpture. Straight ahead is **Salle 20** ("salle" is French for room) filled with more French sculpture, including frilly busts of members of the court of Louis XIV, but most people pass through this room to get to the dramatic Cour Marly to the west or Cour Puget to the east. The **Cour Marly** is filled with sculptures, many from the park at Marly commissioned by Louis XIV at the end of the 17th century to provide a lighthearted contrast to the pompous statuary at neighboring Versailles; you can just imagine all these Greco-Roman gods set into the bushes of the Sun King's garden, their clothes falling away from their perfect bodies for all eternity. The Cour Puget is named for the artist who created the sculpture at place des Victoires, now mostly reassembled in the lower court. Back to the southeast corner of Cour Marly, you will find **Salle 1** of French sculpture. In **Salle 2** are fragments of Romanesque chapels from Cluny, the powerful abbey in Burgundy that dominated French Catholicism in the 11th century. In **Salles 4–6** you can see the refinement of sculpture encouraged by the wealthy communities in the Ile-de-France. The funerary art of **Salles 7–10** ranges from spooky to risible. The late 15th-century tomb of Philippe Pot in **Salle 10** is especially eerie: you see Philippe stretched out in eternal prayer, held aloft by eight black-robed pallbearers. Walking through **Salles 11–19,** you can see how the piety and stiffness of medieval French sculpture began to give way to the more natural style of the Italian Renaissance.

To the north of the Cour Puget are **Salles 25–33,** filled with the products of the Académie Royale, the art school of 18th-century France. The smaller works in **Salle 25** are all qualification pieces for the Académie—once admitted into the school based on previous works, the student was asked to produce a sculpture as proof of continuing worth. To the east of the Cour Puget is the start of the Louvre's **Oriental Antiquities** collection. Within the glass case of **Salle 1** are many ancient Mesopotamian carvings, including a 2-inch neolithic figure dating from the 6th millennium BC. Facing the case are the pieced-together fragments of the 3rd millennium BC Stela of the Vultures, containing the oldest written history known to humankind, including images of King Eannatum catching his enemies in a net. Farther along, **Salle 1b** has countless examples of the wide-eyed alabaster statues produced by the Sumerians during the 3rd millennium BC. The centerpiece of **Salle 3** is the "Codex of Hammurabi," an 18th-century BC diorite stela that contains the oldest written laws known to humanity. Near the top of the text you can see Hammurabi, king of the first Babylonian dynasty, meeting a seated Shamash, the god of justice. On the east side of Salle 3 is a lion glazed onto a piece of a terra-cotta-tile wall—just one of hundreds of similar beasts that decorated the multistory 6th-century BC Gates of Babylon.

Salle 4 is the Cour Khorsabad, a re-creation of the temple erected by the Assyrian king Sargon II in the 8th century BC at the palace of Dur-Sharrukin. Walking among the temple's five massive, winged bulls known as *lamassu,* or benign demigods, is one of the most spectacular experiences in the Louvre, even though only three of the bulls and almost none of the reerected reliefs are authentic. The originals were lost on a frigate that sank.

First Floor: The restored rooms from the royal apartments of Napoléon III fill the southwest of the first floor of the Richelieu Wing. Salle 79 is the most spectacular; the corner reception room, decorated for Napoléon III's secretary of state, gives you a good idea of the eye-popping luxury of the Second Empire. These are the sort of rooms that the great 19th-century courtesan Violette—the real-life "Dame aux Camelias," immortalized as the heroine of Verdi's *La Traviata*—would have been familiar with.

Second Floor: Just to the east of the escalators is **Salle 1,** which begins the section devoted to French and Northern School paintings. At the entrance to this room is a single 14th-century gold-backed painting of John the Good—the oldest known individual portrait from north of Italy. In **Salle 4** is *The Madonna of Chancellor Rolin,* by the 15th-century Early Netherlandish master Jan van Eyck. The first artist to extensively use oil paints, van Eyck defined what became known as the "northern style," characterized by a light source illuminating one area on an otherwise dark background. You almost need a microscope to drink in all the detail in this painting, which ranks as one of the top 10 paintings in the Louvre collection. One of the first self-portraits ever painted—a disheveled offering by Albrecht Dürer (1471–1528)—hangs in **Salle 8.** Walking through **Salles 9–17,** you can see how the Dutch developed a fluid and comfortable representation of the body while playing with the shiny, dark palette of oil paints.

The most dramatic gallery in this section is **Salle 18,** where a cycle of giant matching canvases by Peter Paul Rubens (1577–1640) recounts the journey Maria de' Medici made from Florence to Paris—an overbearing immortalization of a relatively cushy trip. The swirling Baroque paintings were commissioned by Maria herself and originally hung in the nearby Palais du Luxembourg). The riveting *Disembarkation of Maria de' Medici at the Port of Marseille* memorably portrays an artificially slimmed-down Maria about to skip over the roly-poly daughters of Poseidon as a personified France beckons her to shore. In **Salle 31** are several paintings by Rembrandt van Rijn (1606–69), including a late self-portrait in which he goes nuts with the chiaroscuro. In his 1648 *Supper at Emmaus,* he challenges many painting conventions, such as centering the subject and delineating objects with bold brush strokes. The masterpiece of the Dutch collection is *The Lacemaker,* by Johannes Vermeer (1632–75), in **Salle 38.** Obsessed with optical accuracy, Vermeer painted the red thread in the foreground as a slightly blurred jumble, just as one would actually see it if focusing on the girl.

SULLY WING

The entrance into the Sully Wing is more impressive than the entrances to the other wings—you get to walk around and through the foundations and moat of the castle built by Philippe-Auguste in the 12th century and expanded by Charles V in the 14th with a series of Cinderella-like towers and moats.

Ground Floor: The northern galleries of the Sully are a continuation of the ancient **Iranian collection** started on the ground floor of the Richelieu Wing. **Salle 12,** housing the Greek, Etruscan, and Roman collections, is also home to the famous 2nd-century BC *Venus de Milo.* The armless statue, one of the most reproduced and recognizable works of art in the world, is actually as beautiful as they say—it is worth your trouble to push past the lecturing curators and tourist groups to get a closer look at the incredible skill with which the Greeks turned cold marble into something vibrant and graceful. Oddly enough, her face is strikingly like the *Mona Lisa*'s, with an additional mystery being the original form of her missing arms—were they holding a mirror or a net? In the 19th century, the Venus was dug up on the Greek island of Milos, then sold for 6,000 francs to the French ambassador in Constantinople, who presented her to King Louis XVIII. **Salles 13–17** are filled with all kinds of statuary: funerary stelae, body fragments, architectural details.

First Floor: The northern galleries of the first floor continue with the **objets d'art collection** started in the Richelieu Wing, picking up at the 17th century and continuing through the Revolution to the Restoration.

Second Floor: Sully picks up French painting where the Richelieu Wing leaves off, somewhere around the 17th century. At this point, a conscious battle was under way in French art between the northern style (epitomized by magical, candlelit canvases of Georges de La Tour and the more stolid Le Nain brothers and centered on the work of the

Dutch) and the southern one (headed by Poussin, and coming from Florence, Venice, and Rome). The result was a blending of northern style and technology (darkly painted interiors and oil paints) with southern subjects and technique (ruined landscapes and one-point perspective). Charles Le Brun (1619–90), Louis XIV's principal adviser on the arts and the man who designed many of the greatest salons at Versailles, painted massive "History Paintings," jam-packed with excruciating details from biblical, historical, or mythological stories. Displayed in **Salle 32** are the four colossal canvases of his late 17th-century *Story of Alexander,* with a powerful view of the trials of the emperor (and no small reference to Louis XIV).

An academic painter of a different genre was Antoine Watteau (1684–1721), long considered the greatest French painter of the 18th century. In scenes such as his 1717 *Pilgrimage to the Island of Cythera* in **Salle 36,** he depicted in wispy pastel brush strokes the bucolic and often frivolous lifestyle of the Baroque-age court set, here depicted arriving (or are they departing?) on Cythera, the mythological isle of love. Here he concentrates on creating an equally poetic mood, but there is an extra layer of emotion: the gallant gentlemen and courtly women seem drugged by the pleasures about to be enjoyed but disturbingly aware of their transitory nature, too. Maurice Quentin de La Tour (1704–88) was another favorite court painter; his 1755 *Marquise de Pompadour* in **Salle 45** captures the leading fashion plate of Louis XV's court. Madame de Pompadour, mistress to the king, is shown with everything a good courtesan should have: books, music manuscripts, engravings, fine clothing, and, of course, pale skin.

One revolution and two republics after the court painters of the 17th and 18th centuries, the Académie continued to define Good Taste. In **Salle 60** you can see the paintings of Jean-Auguste Ingres (1780–1867), which depict the exotic themes popular in the Age of Empires. His 1862 *Turkish Bath* portrays an orgy of steamy women who look anything but Turkish. One of these ladies was the subject of his *La Grande Odalisque*; here, exoticism and the French classical tradition gel to produce a strikingly elegant image.

DENON WING

Below Ground: To the south and east from the Pyramide entrance are galleries displaying Italian sculpture from the early Renaissance, including a 15th-century *Madonna and Child* by the Florentine Donatello (1386–1466).

Ground Level: In the former imperial stables (**Salle 4**) you can see the 1513–15 *Slaves* of Michelangelo. After carefully selecting his slab of marble, Michelangelo (1475–1564) would spend days envisioning the form of the sculpture within the uncut stone. The sculptures that finally emerged openly eroticized the male body. The fact that many were left "unfinished" (i.e., parts of the marble were left rough, making it look as if the sculptures were trying to free themselves from the stone blocks) was controversial at first, but the style was to inspire Rodin and other modern artists.

To the east of the Italian sculpture collection are the galleries containing the sculptures of the **Greek, Etruscan,** and **Roman periods.** In **Salle 18** is the 6th-century BC *Etruscan Sarcophagus* from Cerveteri, showing a married couple pieced together from thousands of clay fragments.

First Floor: Stretching out from a tiny entry next to the Sully Wing is the **Galerie d'Apollon,** a 17th-century hall decorated by the painter Charles Le Brun (who immortalized himself in one of the portraits on the wall) that now holds what remains of France's **Crown Jewels.** Around the corner from the jewels, the sublime *Winged Victory of Samothrace* stands regally, if headless, at the top landing of the grand **Escalier Daru.** The spectacular 3rd-century BC statue was found on a tiny Greek island in the northern Aegean. Depicted in the act of descending from Olympus, the Winged Victory, or *Nike,* to use the ancient Greek name, originally came from the isle of Samothrace and was carved by an unknown master in 305 BC to commemorate the naval victory of Demetrius Poliorcetes over the Turks. She had a more recent moment of glory when she served as a model for Audrey Hepburn and a red Givenchy gown in the movie *Funny Face.* Instinct with motion, "invested with an atmosphere that holds all the significance of fall and destiny," to quote one archaeologist, the Nike is represented alighting on the prow of a ship.

The **Italian painting** collection begins at the western end of the Denon Wing. The paintings in **Salle 6** (also known as the Salle des États) are large-scale canvases from the 16th-century Venetian School. Dominating the room is the massive 1562 *Feast at Cana* by Veronese (1528–88), a sumptuous scene (restored in the 1980s) centered on Jesus turning water into wine. When painted, it was considered scandalous to adorn the holy story with so much contemporary dress and fashionable 16th-century detail, so the painter was obliged to rename the painting *Feast in the House of Levi.*

And now for the Most Famous Painting in the World: the *Mona Lisa* (also known as *La Gioconda,* or *La Joconde* to the French), painted by Leonardo da Vinci (1452–1519) in 1503–06. As the portrait of the wife of one Francesco del Giocondo, a 15th-century Florentine millionaire, Leonardo's masterpiece is now believed by some historians to have been painted as a memorial after the lady's death. To those who recall Théophile Gautier's words "a sphinx of beauty," the portrait is a bit of a disappointment. The picture is smaller than you might expect and kept behind protective glass; it is invariably surrounded by a crowd of worshipers who are intent on studying her enigmatic expression (or is it she who is studying them?). Once you get in front of the videotaping tourists, you, too, may find yourself asking "Is this it?" when you are faced with this 2½- by 1¾-ft painting of an eyebrowless woman with yellowing skin and an annoyingly smug smile. In fact, most art historians award the beauty prize instead to Leonardo's *Virgin and St. Anne,* hanging nearby. Here in this room, you'll find other legendary works of the High Renaissance, including Raphael's *La Belle Jardiniére.*

The 1458 *Calvary* in **Salle 8,** painted by Andrea Mantegna (1431–1506), a follower of the Florentine architect Brunelleschi's treatises on perspective, is one of the first paintings ever with a vanishing point. Although equally renowned during his lifetime as an anatomist and inventor, Leonardo da Vinci was originally trained as a painter. His breathtaking 1483 *Virgin of the Rocks* has an interesting sense of spatial relationships—the four figures create the four corners of a pyramid, while their glances and gestures keep all activity contained within this form.

Behind the *Feast at Cana* are two passages leading to **Salles 75–77,** home of the great epic-scale canvases produced in Paris during the 19th century. When official court painter Louis David (1748–1825) produced the *Coronation of Napoléon* on December 2, 1804, now hanging in Salle 75, he wisely decided not to capture the moment when Napoléon snatched the crown from the hands of Pope Pius VII to place it upon his own head—choosing instead to paint the new emperor turning to crown Josephine.

Also in Salle 75 hang two of the most famous works in the history of French painting: the 1819 *Raft of the Medusa* by Théodore Géricault (1791–1824) and the 1830 *Liberty Leading the People* by Eugène Delacroix (1798–1863). Géricault's epic work conveys a gloomily Romantic view of the human state, nightmarish despite its heroism and grand scale. Painted when Géricault was only 27 years old, it was inspired by the real-life story of the wreck of a French merchant ship: the captain lost control, the ship was without lifeboats or supplies, and ultimately the survivors resorted to cannibalism. The painting caused a stir with the government, which took offense at the stab made at the inefficiency of authority. The Académie was aghast for formal reasons: the painting had no central subject, no hero, no resolution. The survivors are a mess of living and dead bodies jumbled in and out of ominous, sickly green shadows.

Even though Delacroix wasn't directly involved in the "Trois Glorieuses"—a three-day revolution in 1830 that ousted Charles X's autocracy and brought in a parliamentary monarchy with Louis-Philippe as king—he was compelled to paint *Liberty* to commemorate the Parisians who attempted to restore the Republic. Once again, it is an unorthodox subject for a painting: poorly armed bourgeoisie and pugnacious street urchins step over the dead bodies of comrades and slay other French folk in the name of an ultimately short-lived government. The allegorical figure of Liberty is quite a character: She is shown walking barefoot over barricades, her peasant dress falling away from her breasts, the Tricolore (French flag) held aloft with one well-muscled limb while the other grips a rifle.

The above highlights of the Louvre collection are simply the merest tip of the iceberg. You'll also find walls virtually wallpapered with masterpieces by Fra Angelico, Botticelli, Holbein, Hals, Brueghel, El Greco, Murillo, Boucher, Goya, and Caravaggio—whose *Death of the Virgin* towers over La Grande Galerie—just to mention a few of the famous names, along with one-hit wonders like Enguerrand Quarton's magnificent 15th-century *Pietà*. Other collections here will delight connoisseurs, such as the examples of French furniture—the grandiose 17th- and 18th-century productions of Boulle and Riesener, marvels of intricate craftsmanship and elegant luxury, are prized by those with a fondness for opulent decoration.

Admission is often charged for a full calendar of other art-related events at the museum. Lectures take place in the Louvre Auditorium; the films there showcase everything from silent works to the history of art in Paris. A smattering of films, lectures, concerts, and exhibits are included in what's called *Les Midis du Louvre*. For recorded information in five languages (French, English, Spanish, German, and Italian), call 01–40–21–51–51 (press 2 for English). Be sure to pick up the free three-month schedule of events called Louvre at the information desk under the Pyramide, or look at the TV monitors behind the desk.

If you have time for only one visit, these selections give you an idea of the riches of the museum. But try to make repeat visits—the Louvre is one-third cheaper on Sunday (free the first Sunday of each month) and after 3 PM on other days. (Unless you plan to go to a number of museums every day, the one-, three-, and five-day tourist museum passes probably aren't worth your money, since you could easily spend a whole day at the Louvre alone.) Study the plans at the entrance to get your bearings and pick up a map to take with you. ⊠ *Palais du Louvre, Louvre/Tuileries (it's faster to enter through the Carrousel du Louvre mall on rue de Rivoli than through the pyramid),* ☎ *01–40–20–51–51 information,* WEB *www.louvre.fr.* ⌗ *€7.5, €5 after 3 PM and all day*

Sun., free 1st Sun. of month. ⊙ *Thurs.–Sun. 9–6, Mon. and Wed. 9 AM–9:45 PM. Some sections open limited days. Métro: Palais-Royal.*

⑮ **Musée du Jeu de Paume.** Renovations transformed this museum, at the entrance to the Tuileries Gardens, into an ultramodern, white-walled showcase for excellent temporary exhibits of bold contemporary art. The building was once the spot of *jeu de paume* games (literally, "palm game"—a forerunner of tennis). ⊠ *1 pl. de la Concorde, Louvre/Tuileries,* ☎ *01–42–60–69–69.* ☑ *€5.8.* ⊙ *Tues. noon–9:30, Wed.–Fri. noon–7, weekends 10–7. Métro: Concorde.*

⑯ **Musée de l'Orangerie.** Set to open in early 2003 after years of renovation, this museum is most famous as home of several of Claude Monet's largest *Water Lilies* murals. Set in the Tuileries Gardens, the museum also has a noted selection of early 20th-century paintings, with works by Renoir, Cézanne, Matisse, and Marie Laurencin, among other masters. ⊠ *Pl. de la Concorde, Louvre/Tuileries,* ☎ *01–42–97–48–16. Métro: Concorde.*

★ ❶ **Notre-Dame.** Looming above the place du Parvis on the Ile de la Cité is the Cathédrale de Notre-Dame, the most enduring symbol of Paris. Begun in 1163, completed in 1345, badly damaged during the Revolution, and restored by Viollet-le-Duc in the 19th century, Notre-Dame may not be France's oldest or largest cathedral, but in terms of beauty and architectural harmony, it has few peers—as you can see by studying the facade from the open square. The doorways seem like hands joined in prayer and the sculpted kings form a noble procession, while the rose window gleams, to wax poetic, like the eye of divinity. Above, the gallery breaks the guipure of the stone vaults and, between the two high towers, the spire soars from the cross of the transept. Seen from the front, the cathedral gives an impression of strength, dignity, and majestic serenity; seen from the Pont de l'Archevêché, it has all the proud grace of a seagoing vessel, the cross on its steeple borne like the flag on a tall mast.

An army of stonemasons, carpenters, and sculptors arrived in 1163, working on a site that had previously seen a Roman temple, an early Christian basilica, and a Romanesque church. The chancel and altar were consecrated in 1182, but the magnificent sculptures surrounding the main doors were not put into position until 1240. The north tower was finished 10 years later. If both towers seem to some a bit top-heavy, that's because two needlelike spires were originally conceived to top them but were never built. If you look carefully, you will see that the tower on the left is wider than the one on the right.

Despite various changes in the 17th century, the cathedral remained substantially unaltered until the French Revolution, when it was transformed into a Temple of Reason—busts of Voltaire and Rousseau replaced those of saints. The statues of the kings of Israel were hacked down by the mob, chiefly because they were thought to represent the despised royal line of France, and everything inside and out that was deemed "anti-Republican" was stripped away. An interesting postscript to this destruction occurred in 1977, when some of the heads of these statues were discovered salted away in a bank vault on boulevard Haussmann. They'd apparently been hidden there by an ardent royalist who owned the small mansion that now forms part of the bank. (The restored heads are now on display in the Musée National du Moyen-Age.)

By the early 19th century, the excesses of the Revolution were over, and the cathedral went back to fulfilling its religious functions again. Napoléon crowned himself emperor here in May 1804 (David's heroic painting of the lavish ceremony can be seen in the Louvre)—you can stand on the step where he stood when he crowned Josephine. Full-scale restoration started in the middle of the century, the most conspicuous result of which was the reconstruction of the spire. It was then, too, that Haussmann demolished the warren of little buildings in front of the cathedral, creating the place du Parvis.

The facade divides neatly into three levels. At the first-floor level are the three main entrances, or portals: the Portal of the Virgin on the left, the Portal of the Last Judgment in the center, and the Portal of St. Anne on the right. All three are surmounted by magnificent carvings—most of them 19th-century copies of the originals—of figures, foliage, and biblical scenes. Above these are the restored statues of the kings of Israel, the Galerie des Rois. Above the gallery is the great rose window and, above that, the Grand Galerie, at the base of the twin towers. The south tower houses the great bell of Notre-Dame, as tolled by Quasimodo, Victor Hugo's fictional hunchback. The 387-step climb to the top of the towers (use the separate entrance to the left of the facade as you face it is) is worth the effort for a close-up of the famous gargoyles—most of them added in the 19th century—and the expansive view of the city. Unfortunately, some of those views been recently ruined by railings put up because of safety concerns.

As you enter by the Portal of the Virgin, the faith of the early builders permeates all, and the miracle of the quiet, persuasive interior provides an apt contrast to the triumphant glory of the exterior, with the soft glow of the stained-glass windows replacing the statues of saints, virgins, prophets, and apostles. The best time to visit is early in the morning, when the cathedral is at its lightest and least crowded. At the entrance are the massive 12th-century columns supporting the twin towers. Look down the nave to the transepts—the arms of the church—where, at the south (right) entrance to the chancel, you'll glimpse the haunting 12th-century statue of Notre-Dame de Paris, *Our Lady of Paris*. The chancel itself owes parts of its decoration to a vow taken by Louis XIII in 1638. Still without an heir after 23 years of marriage, he promised to dedicate the entire country to the Virgin Mary if his queen produced a son. When this miraculous event came to pass, Louis set about redecorating the chancel and choir. On the south side of the chancel is the **Trésor** (treasury), with a collection of garments, reliquaries, and silver and gold plate.

Under the square in front of the cathedral is the **Crypte Archéologique,** Notre-Dame's archaeological museum. It contains remains of previous churches on the site, scale models charting the district's development, and relics and artifacts dating from the Parisii, who lived here 2,000 years ago, unearthed during excavations here in the 1960s. Slides and models detail the history of the Ile de la Cité. The foundations of the 3rd-century Gallo-Roman rampart and of the 6th-century Merovingian church can also be seen.

❸ If your interest in the cathedral is not yet sated, duck into the **Musée de Notre-Dame** (⊠ 10 rue du Cloître-Notre-Dame, Ile de la Cité), across the street opposite the North Door. The museum's paintings, engravings, medallions, and other objects and documents chart the history of the Cathedral of Notre-Dame. ⊠ *Pl. du Parvis, Ile de la Cité,* ☎ *01–44–32–16–72,* ᵂᴱᴮ *www.monum.fr.* ▦ *Towers €5.4, crypt €3.4, treasury €2.3, museum €2.3.* ☼ *Cathedral daily 8–7. Towers Apr.– Sept., daily 9:30–7:30; Oct.–Mar., daily 10–5. Treasury Mon.–Sat. 9:30–11:30 and 1–5:30. Crypt Tues.–Sun. 10–6. Museum Wed. and weekends 2:30–6. Métro: Cité.*

☾ ❷ **Palais de la Découverte** (Palace of Discovery). A planetarium, work-ing models, and scientific and technological exhibits on such topics as optics, biology, nuclear physics, and electricity make up this science museum behind the Grand Palais. ✉ *Av. Franklin-D.-Roosevelt, Champs-Élysées,* ☏ *01–56–43–20–21,* ⊞ *www.palais-decouverte.fr.* ⌦ *€5.7, €3 extra for planetarium.* ⊘ *Tues.–Sat. 9:30–6, Sun. 10–7. Métro: Champs-Élysées Clemenceau.*

❺ **Palais de Justice** (Law Courts). The city's courts were built by Baron Haussmann in his characteristically weighty neoclassic style in about 1860. You can wander around the buildings, watch the bustle of the lawyers, or attend a court hearing. The solidity of Haussmann's build-ings seems to emphasize the finesse of two important sights enclosed within the complex spared by Haussmann: La Conciergerie and Sainte-Chapelle. ✉ *Bd. du Palais, Ile de la Cité. Métro: Cité.*

⓲ **Petit Palais.** The smaller counterpart to the Grand Palais, just off the Champs-Élysées, presents a permanent collection of French painting and furniture, with splendid canvases by Courbet and Bouguereau, but is closed for restoration until 2004. Outside, take time to admire two fine statues near each corner of the building: French World War I hero Georges Clemenceau, facing the Champs-Élysées; and Jean Cardot's resolute image of Winston Churchill, facing the Seine. ✉ *Av. Winston-Churchill, Champs-Élysées,* ☏ *01–42–65–12–73,* ⊞ *paris-france. org/musees. Métro: Champs-Élysées Clemenceau.*

⓱ **Place de la Concorde.** This majestic square at the foot of the Champs-Élysées is undoubtedly one of the most balanced and harmoniously beau-tiful spaces in the world. Originally consecrated to the glory of Louis XV, it was laid out in the 1770s, but there was nothing in the way of peace or concord about its early years, for it was here that his succes-sor, Louis XVI, and Marie-Antoinette were guillotined, along with more than 2,000 other people between 1793 and 1795. And here it was that Madame Roland cried, "Liberty, what crimes are committed in thy name." When the blood of the victims had been washed away and the yells of the *sans culottes* political extremists had died down, the square was renamed Concorde and, in place of a statue of Louis XV, another monument, freer of political significance, was erected in 1833: a 107-ft obelisk, originally built in the 8th century BC, and a present from the viceroy of Egypt (it received its gilded cap in 1998). Among the handsome, symmetrical 18th-century buildings facing the square is the deluxe Hôtel Crillon, originally built by Gabriel—architect of the Petit Trianon—as an 18th-century home for three of France's wealthiest fam-ilies. At the near end of high-walled rue Royale is the legendary Maxim's restaurant, but unless you choose to eat here, you won't be able to see the riot of crimson velvets and florid Art Nouveau furni-ture inside. *Métro: Concorde.*

❽ **Place Dauphine.** The Surrealists loved place Dauphine, which they called "le sexe de Paris" because of its location—at the western tail end of the Ile de la Cité—and suggestive V shape. Its origins were much more proper: built by Henri IV, the king named the place in homage to his successor, the dauphin, who grew up to become Louis XIII. The triangular place is lined with some 17th-century houses which the writer André Maurois felt represented the very quintessence of Paris and France. Take a seat on the park bench, enjoy a picnic, and see if you agree. *Métro: Cité.*

㉑ **Pont Alexandre-III.** No other bridge over the Seine epitomizes the fin-de-siècle frivolity of the Belle Epoque (or Paris itself) like the exuber-ant, bronze lamp–lined Pont Alexandre-III. A urban masterstroke that seems as much created of cake frosting and sugar sculptures as of stone and iron, it makes an alluring backdrop for fashion shoots and the surrounding Parisian landmarks. The bridge was built, like the Grand and Petit Palais nearby, for the 1900 world's fair; it was inaugurated by the visiting Russian czar, the ill-fated Nicholas II, and ingratiatingly named in honor of his father. *Métro: Invalides.*

⑩ **Pont Neuf** (New Bridge). Crossing the Ile de la Cité, just behind square du Vert-Galant, is the oldest bridge in Paris, confusingly called the New Bridge. It was completed in 1607 and was the first bridge in the city to be built without houses lining either side because, so some historians believe, Henri IV wanted a clear view of Notre-Dame from his windows at the Louvre. *Métro: Pont Neuf.*

★ ⑥ **Sainte-Chapelle** (Holy Chapel). One of the supremely dazzling achievements of the Middle Ages, a Gothic jewel, and home to the most ancient stained-glass windows in Paris, this chapel was built by the pious Louis IX (1226–70), whose good works ensured his subsequent canonization. Constructed in less than three years, it was conceived as an enormous reliquary—as a home for what Louis believed to be the crown of thorns from Christ's crucifixion and fragments of the true cross, acquired from the impoverished Emperor Baldwin of Constantinople at phenomenal expense.

The building is actually two chapels in one. The plainer, first-floor chapel, made gloomy by insensitive mid-19th-century restorations (which could do with restoration themselves), was for servants and lowly members of the court. The infinitely more spectacular upper chapel, up a dark spiral staircase, was reserved for the king and important members of the court. The chapel walls (if you can call them that) consist mainly of stained glass and constitute a technical tour de force. Here, again, some clumsy 19th-century work has added a deadening touch, but the glory of the chapel—the stained glass—is magically intact. The chapel is airy and diaphanous, the walls glowing and sparkling as light plays on the windows. Notice how the walls, in fact, consist of at least twice as much glass as masonry: the entire aim of the architects was to provide the maximum amount of window space.

Architecturally, for all its delicate and ornate exterior decoration—notice the open latticework of the pencil-like *flèche,* or spire, on the roof—the design of the building is simplicity itself. In essence, it's no more than a thin, rectangular box, much taller than it is wide. But think of it first and foremost as an enormous magic lantern, illuminating 1,130 figures from the Bible, to create—as one writer poetically put it—"the most marvelous colored and moving air ever held within four walls." Come early in the day to avoid the dutiful crowds that trudge around it—better still, try to attend one of the regular, candlelit concerts. ⊠ 4 bd. du Palais, Ile de la Cité, ☎ 01–43–54–30–09 concert information, 🖳 www.monum.fr. 💷 €5.5, joint ticket with Conciergerie €7.6. ☉ Apr.–Sept., daily 9:30–6:30; Oct.–Mar., daily 10–5. Métro: Cité.

④ **Square Jean-XXIII.** When it comes to views of Notre-Dame, no visit to the great cathedral is complete without a riverside walk past the cathedral through Square Jean-XXIII. It offers a breathtaking sight of the east end of the cathedral, ringed by flying buttresses and surmounted by the spire. From here, the building seems to float above the Seine like some vast stone ship. *Métro: Cité.*

⑨ **Square du Vert-Galant.** The equine statue of the Vert Galant himself—amorous adventurer Henri IV—surveys this leafy square at the western end of the Ile de la Cité. Henri, king of France from 1589 until his assassination in 1610, was something of a dashing figure, by turns ruthless and charming, a stern upholder of the absolute rights of monarchy, and a notorious womanizer. He is probably best remembered for his cynical remark that *"Paris vaut bien une messe"* ("Paris is worth a mass"), a reference to his readiness to renounce Protestantism to gain the throne of predominantly Catholic France and, indeed, be allowed to enter the city (for a riveting depiction of the king and his role in the St. Bartholomew's Day Massacre, see the French film *Queen Margot,* which stars Isabelle Adjani as his ill-fated consort). To ease his conscience he issued the Edict of Nantes in 1598, according French Protestants (almost) equal rights with their Catholic counterparts. It was Louis XIV's renunciation of the edict nearly 100 years later that led to the massive Huguenot exodus from France—an economic catastrophe for the country. The square itself is a fine spot to linger on a sunny afternoon and is the departure point for the glass-topped Vedette tour boats on the Seine (at the bottom of the steps to the right). *Métro: Pont Neuf.*

FROM THE EIFFEL TOWER TO THE ARC DE TRIOMPHE

The Eiffel Tower lords over southwest Paris, and from nearly wherever you are on this walk, you can see it looming. For years many Parisians felt the Tour Eiffel was an iron eyesore and compared it to a giraffe, a giraffe that weighed 15 million pounds and whose head rose 1,000 ft high. Then, gradually, the tower became part of the Parisian landscape and entered the hearts and souls of Parisians and visitors alike. Thanks to its stunning nighttime illumination, topped by four 6,000-watt projectors creating a lighthouse beacon visible for 80 km (50 mi) around, it continues to make Paris live up to its moniker, *La Ville Lumière*—the City of Light.

Water is the second theme of this walk: fountains playing beneath the place du Trocadéro; tours along the Seine on the Bateaux Mouches; and an underground prowl through the city's sewers, if you can stand it. Museums are the third; the area around Trocadéro is full of them. Military grandeur is the fourth; the Arc de Triomphe is Napoléon's most eye-popping legacy to Paris (the young general often surveyed his troops on the Champ de Mars, near the start of this walk). The arch stands foursquare at the top of the city's most famous avenue: the Champs-Élysées. Site of most French national celebrations, the Champs-Élysées is the last leg of the Tour de France bicycle race on the third or fourth Sunday in July, and the site of vast ceremonies on Bastille Day (July 14) and Armistice Day (November 11). Its trees are often decked with the French tricolor and foreign flags to mark visits from heads of state.

Explore its commercial upper half (its verdant lower section, sloping down gracefully to the place de la Concorde, the Tuileries Gardens, and the Louvre is covered in the first walking tour). Local charm is not a plus of this grand sector of western Paris. The French moan that it is losing its character, and, as you notice the number of fast-food joints along the Champs-Élysées, you'll know what they mean—though renovation has gone some way to restoring the avenue's legendary elegance. For a real dose of high style, head to nearby avenue Montaigne, address to some of the top names in world fashion.

Numbers in the text correspond to numbers in the margin and on the Eiffel Tower to Arc de Triomphe map.

A Good Walk

Graced by the stately facade of the **École Militaire** ①, the verdant expanse of the **Champ de Mars** ②—once used as a parade ground and then as site of the World Exhibitions—provides a thrilling approach to the iron symbol of Paris: the **Tour Eiffel** ③. As you get nearer, the Eiffel Tower's colossal bulk (it's far bigger and sturdier than pictures suggest) becomes spectacularly evident. (If you want to skip this walk through the parade grounds, just take the RER directly to Champ de Mars for the Eiffel Tower.)

Across the Seine from the Eiffel Tower, above stylish gardens and fountains on the heights of the Trocadéro, is the Art Deco **Palais de Chaillot** ④, a cultural center containing three museums. Pause on the piazza, lined by gold statues, to admire the view of the Eiffel Tower. The south wing of the Palais, to your left as you arrive from the Seine, houses the **Musée de l'Homme** ⑤, an anthropology museum, and the **Musée de la Marine** ⑥, a maritime museum. The right wing was badly damaged by fire in 1997, and its **Musée des Monuments Français** ⑦, with copies of statues, columns, and archways from throughout France, is undergoing renovation and was slated at press time to reopen during 2003.

From the Palais head right down the avenue du Président-Wilson, with its street lamps designed by Frank Lloyd Wright. Next block down on your right, surrounded most days by no fewer than nine French tricolors, is another Art Deco building, fronted by a rotunda lined with mosaics and alternating pinkish beige and pebble-dash concrete: the Conseil Economique et Social (Economic and Social Council). Echoing it across the place d'Iéna is another, slightly older rotunda, topped by a pineapple—the **Musée Guimet** ⑧, whose extensive collection of Indo-Chinese and Far Eastern art reopened in 2001 after a major renovation. Farther down the avenue du Président-Wilson, the equally pompous architecture of the **Palais Galliéra** ⑨, an exhibition hall for exhibits on clothing design and fashion, squares up to the cool gray outlines of the 1930s **Musée d'Art Moderne de la Ville de Paris** ⑩, a venue for temporary exhibits as well as the city's high-powered collection of modern art.

Continue down to the place de l'Alma, where a giant golden torch appears to be saluting the memory of Diana, Princess of Wales, who died in a car crash in the tunnel below in 1997. Across the **Pont de l'Alma** ⑪ (to the left) is the entrance to **Les Égouts** ⑫, Paris's sewers. If you prefer a less malodorous tour of the city, stay on the Right Bank and head down the sloping side road to the left of the bridge to the embarkation point of the **Bateaux Mouches** ⑬ (motorboats) and their tours of Paris by water.

From the place de l'Alma head up the grand thoroughfare of avenue Montaigne, one of the leading showcases for the great haute couture houses, such as Dior, Chanel, Nina Ricci, Valentino, Prada, and Dolce & Gabbana. After some world-class window-shopping, continue on to the Rond-Point des Champs-Élysées, the main traffic nexus of Paris's most famous avenue, and turn left up the **Champs-Élysées** ⑭. At 116 bis is the famous **Lido** ⑮ nightclub, opposite the venerable Le Fouquet's restaurant-café, once frequented by Orson Welles and James Joyce. Stop in at the **Office de Tourisme de la Ville de Paris** ⑯ (the main city tourist office) at No. 127, on the left-hand side of the avenue. Continue up to the top of the avenue and place Charles-de-Gaulle, known to Parisians as L'Étoile, or The Star—a reference to the streets that fan out from it—and site of the colossal, 164-ft **Arc de Triomphe** ⑰. L'Étoile is Europe's most chaotic traffic circle: short of attempting a death-

From the Eiffel Tower to the Arc de Triomphe

defying dash, your only way of getting to the Arc de Triomphe in the middle is to take an underground passage from the top right of the avenue des Champs-Élysées. The view from the top of the Arc de Triomphe illustrates the star effect of the 12 radiating avenues and enables you to admire the vista down the Champs-Élysées, toward the place de la Concorde and the distant Louvre. West of the Champs-Élysées, and visible from the Arc de Triomphe, are the verdant Bois de Boulogne; the posh suburb of Neuilly; and the towering office buildings and ultramodern arch of La Défense. (The Charles-de-Gaulle–Étoile métro and RER station, which sprawls underground beneath L'Étoile, provides quick access to the western suburbs, if you want to make the excursion now.)

TIMING

You can probably cover this 5½-km (3½-mi) walk in about four hours, but if you wish to ascend the Eiffel Tower, take a trip along the Seine, or visit any of the plethora of museums along the way, you'd be best off allowing most of the day.

Sights to See

★ ⑰ **Arc de Triomphe.** Inspired by Rome's Arch of Titus, this colossal, 164-ft triumphal arch was planned by Napoléon—who liked to consider himself the heir to the Roman emperors—to celebrate his military successes. Unfortunately, Napoléon's strategic and architectural visions were not entirely on the same plane, and the Arc de Triomphe proved something of an embarrassment. Although the emperor wanted the monument completed in time for an 1810 parade in honor of his new bride, Marie-Louise, the arch was still only a few feet high, and a dummy arch of painted canvas was strung up to save face.

Empires come and go, and Napoléon's had been gone for more than 20 years before the Arc de Triomphe was finally finished, in 1836. It has some magnificent sculpture by François Rude, such as *The Departure of the Volunteers,* better known as *La Marseillaise,* to the right of the arch when viewed from the Champs-Élysées. Names of Napoléon's generals are inscribed on the stone facades—those underlined are the hallowed figures who fell on the fields of battle. After showing alarming signs of decay, the structure received a thorough overhaul in 1989 and is once again neo-Napoleonic in its splendor. There is a small museum halfway up the arch devoted to its history. France's Unknown Soldier is buried beneath the archway; the flame is rekindled every evening at 6:30. ⊠ *Pl. Charles-de-Gaulle, Champs-Élysées,* ☎ *01–55–37–73–77,* WEB *www.monum.fr.* ⊡ *€6.* ☉ *Apr.–Sept., daily 9:30–11; Oct.–Mar., daily 10–10:30. Métro or RER: Étoile.*

👆 ⑬ **Bateaux Mouches.** If you want to view Paris in slow motion, hop on one of these famous motorboats, which set off on their hour-long tours of the city waters regularly (every half hour in summer) from the place de l'Alma. Their route heads east to the Ile St-Louis and then back west, past the Eiffel Tower, as far as the Allée des Cygnes and its miniature version of the Statue of Liberty. Believe it or not, these were once used as regular ferries on a daily basis by Parisians up until the 1930s. As they bounced from bank to bank on the river, they gave rise, some say, to the name *Bateaux Mouches* (which translates as "fly boats"); more sober historians say the name "mouche" actually refers to a district of Lyon, where the boats were originally manufactured. Note that some discerning travelers prefer to take this Seine cruise on the smaller Vedettes du Pont Neuf which depart from the square du Vert-Gallant on the Ile de la Cité. ⊠ *Pl. de l'Alma, Trocadéro/Eiffel Tower,* ☎ *01–40–76–99–99,* WEB *www.bateaux-mouches.fr.* ⊡ *€7. Métro: Alma-Marceau.*

Champ de Mars. This long, formal garden, landscaped at the start of the 20th century, lies between the Eiffel Tower and École Militaire. It was previously used as a parade ground and was the site of the World Exhibitions of 1867, 1889 (date of the construction of the Eiffel Tower), and 1900. *Métro: École Militaire; RER: Champ de Mars.*

Champs-Élysées. Marcel Proust lovingly described the *recherché* elegance of the world's most famous avenue, the Champs-Élysées, during its Belle Epoque heyday, when its cobblestones resounded to the clatter of horse-and-carriage rather than the screech of tires. Although there's still a certain thrill to strutting along Les Champs, the abundance of bland shops and restaurants chains (and the lack of actual Parisians) makes the experience feel suspiciously like a trip to the mall. Originally an expanse of green frequented by cattle, the 2-km (1¼-mi) Champs-Élysées was laid out in the 1660s by the landscape gardener André Le Nôtre as a park sweeping away from the Tuileries. Today, in a losing battle against all those airline offices, car showrooms, and movie theaters, the city has planted extra trees, broadened sidewalks, installed coordinated designer street furnishings (everything from benches and lighting to traffic lights, telephone booths, and trash cans), refurbished (i.e., Disneyfied) Art Nouveau newsstands, built underground parking to alleviate congestion, and clamped down on garish storefronts. To find the beauteous avenue of yore, look for the elegant 19th-century park pavilions along the lower half of the avenue which continue to house the historic restaurants Ledoyen, Laurent, and Le Pavillon Élysées. *Métro: Champs-Élysées Clemenceau, Franklin-D.-Roosevelt, George V, Étoile.*

École Militaire (Military Academy). Napoléon was one of the more famous graduates of this military academy, whose harmonious 18th-century building, facing the Eiffel Tower across the Champ de Mars, is still in use for army training (and, consequently, not open to the public). ⊠ *Pl. du Maréchal-Joffre, Trocadéro/Eiffel Tower. Métro: École Militaire.*

Les Égouts (The Sewers). Everyone visits the Louvre, so surprise your friends back home by telling them you toured the infamous sewers of Paris. Brave their unpleasant—though tolerable—smell to follow an underground city of banks, passages, and footbridges famously immortalized as the escape routes of Jean Valjean in *Les Misérables* and the Phantom of the Opera. Signs indicate the streets above you, and detailed panels and displays illuminate the history of waste disposal in Paris, whose sewer system is the largest in the world after Chicago's. The tour takes about an hour. ⊠ *Opposite 93 quai d'Orsay, Trocadéro/Eiffel Tower,* ☎ *01–53–68–27–81.* ⊡ *€4.* ☉ *Feb.–Dec., Sat.–Wed. 11–5. Métro: Alma-Marceau; RER: Pont de l'Alma.*

OFF THE
BEATEN PATH **AMERICAN CHURCH –** This Left Bank neo-Gothic church, built in 1927–31, offers help and advice to English-speaking foreigners. ⊠ *65 quai d'Orsay, Trocadéro/Eiffel Tower,* ☎ *01–47–05–07–99. Métro: Alma-Marceau; RER: Pont de l'Alma.*

Lido. Free-flowing champagne, foot-stomping melodies in French and English, and topless razzmatazz pack in the crowds (mostly tourists) every night for the show at this famous nightclub, which has been around since 1946. ⊠ *116 av. des Champs-Élysées, Champs-Élysées,* ☎ *01–40–76–56–0,* ᴡᴇʙ *www.lido.fr. Métro: George V.*

Musée d'Art Moderne de la Ville de Paris (Paris Museum of Modern Art). Both temporary exhibits and a permanent collection of top-quality 20th-century art can be found at this modern art museum. It takes over, chronologically speaking, where the Musée d'Orsay leaves off: among the earliest works are Fauve paintings by Vlaminck and Derain, followed by Picasso's early experiments in Cubism. Its vast, unobtrusive, white-walled galleries provide an ideal backdrop for the bold statements of 20th-century art. Loudest and largest are the canvases of Robert Delaunay. Other highlights include works by Braque, Rouault, Gleizes, Da Silva, Gromaire, and Modigliani. There is also a large room devoted to Art Deco furniture and screens, where Jean Dunand's gilt and lacquered panels consume oceans of wall space. There is a pleasant, if expensive, museum café and an excellent bookshop specializing in 19th- and 20th-century art and architecture, with many books in English. ⊠ *11 av. du Président-Wilson, Trocadéro/Eiffel Tower,* ☎ *01–53–67–40–00,* WEB *www.paris-france.org/musees.* ⊠ *Free.* ☉ *Tues.– Fri. 10–5:30, weekends 10–6:45. Métro: Iéna.*

★ ❽ **Musée Guimet.** One of the most refined and cherished of Paris museums, this Belle Epoque treasure was founded by Lyonnais industrialist Émile Guimet, who traveled around the world in the late 19th century amassing priceless Indo-Chinese and Far Eastern objets d'art. A highlight is the largest collection of Cambodian art this side of Cambodia, with celebrated works from the Angkor culture. The museum reopened in 2001 after top-to-toe renovation. ⊠ *6 pl. d'Iéna, Trocadéro/Eiffel Tower,* ☎ *01–56–52–53–00,* WEB *www.museeguimet.fr.* ⊠ *€5.5. Métro: Iéna.*

❺ **Musée de l'Homme** (Museum of Mankind). Picasso, it is said, discovered the bold lines of African masks and sculpture here and promptly went off to paint his *Desmoiselles d'Avignon* and create Cubism. You, too, may be inspired by the impressive artifacts, costumes, and domestic tools from around the world mounted here, the earliest dating from prehistoric times. This earnest anthropological museum is in the south wing of the Palais de Chaillot—to find the entrance, just look for the giant totem pole from British Columbia. ⊠ *17 pl. du Trocadéro, Trocadéro/Eiffel Tower,* ☎ *01–44–05–72–72,* WEB *www.mnhn.fr.* ⊠ *€4.6.* ☉ *Wed.–Mon. 9:45–5:15. Métro: Trocadéro.*

NEED A BREAK? Get a tremendous view of the Eiffel Tower and the Invalides dome with your ice cream, cocktail, or lunch at **Le Totem** (☎ 01–47–27–28–29), an elegant bar and restaurant in the south wing of the Palais de Chaillot.

❻ **Musée de la Marine** (Maritime Museum). In the west wing of the Palais de Chaillot, this museum contains ship models and seafaring paraphernalia illustrating French naval history up to the age of the nuclear submarine. ⊠ *17 pl. du Trocadéro, Trocadéro/Eiffel Tower,* ☎ *01–53–65–69–69.* ⊠ *€6.* ☉ *Wed.–Mon. 10–6. Métro: Trocadéro.*

❼ **Musée des Monuments Français** (French Monuments Museum). One of the most fascinating museums in Paris closed after a fire in 1997 and was slated at press time to reopen during 2003. Founded in 1879 by architect-restorer Viollet-le-Duc (the man mainly responsible for the extensive renovation of Notre-Dame and countless other Gothic cathedrals), it is a vast repository of copies of statues, columns, archways, and frescoes from the Romanesque and Gothic periods (roughly 1000– 1500) and forms an excellent (if somewhat bogus) introduction to French medieval architecture. ⊠ *1 pl. du Trocadéro, Trocadéro/Eiffel Tower,* ☎ *01–44–05–39–10. Métro: Trocadéro.*

⓰ **Office de Tourisme de la Ville de Paris** (Paris Tourist Office). The modern, spacious Paris Tourist Office, near the Arc de Triomphe, is worth a visit at the start of your stay to pick up free maps, leaflets, and information on upcoming events. Most of the staff speak English and can also help book accommodations or tickets for shows. You can also exchange money here and buy métro tickets and souvenirs. ⊠ *127 av. des Champs-Élysées, Champs-Élysées,* ☎ *08–92–68–31–12,* WEB *www. paris-touristoffice.com.* ⊙ *Daily 9–8. Métro: Charles-de-Gaulle–Étoile.*

❹ Palais de Chaillot (Chaillot Palace). This honey-color Art Deco cultural center was built in the 1930s to replace a Moorish-style building constructed for the World Exhibition of 1878. It contains three large museums: the **Musée de l'Homme,** the **Musée de la Marine,** and the **Musée des Monuments Français.** The tumbling gardens leading to the Seine contain sculptures, dramatic fountains, and a large aquarium currently undergoing renovation. The palace terrace, flanked by gilded statuettes (and often invaded by roller skaters and skateboarders), offers a wonderful picture-postcard view of the Eiffel Tower and is a favorite spot for fashion photographers. ⊠ *Pl. du Trocadéro, Trocadéro/Eiffel Tower. Métro: Trocadéro.*

❾ Palais Galliera. This luxurious mansion, built in 1888 for the Duchesse de Galliera, houses rotating exhibits on costumery and clothing design. ⊠ *10 av. Pierre-1ᵉʳ-de-Serbie, Trocadéro/Eiffel Tower,* ☎ *01–56–52–86–00,* WEB *www.paris-france.org/musees.* 🎟 *€7.* ⊙ *Tues.–Sun. 10–6. Métro: Iéna.*

⓫ Pont de l'Alma (Alma Bridge). This bridge is best known for the chunky stone "Zouave" statue carved into one of the pillars. Zouaves were Algerian infantrymen recruited into the French army who were famous for their bravura and colorful uniforms. There is nothing quite so glamorous, or colorful, about the Alma Zouave, however, whose hour of glory comes in times of watery distress: Parisians use him to judge the level of the Seine during heavy rains. *Métro: Alma-Marceau.*

★ ☾ **❸ Tour Eiffel** (Eiffel Tower). If the Statue of Liberty is New York, if Big Ben is London, if the Kremlin is Moscow, then the Eiffel Tower is Paris. For two years French engineer Gustave Eiffel—already famous for building viaducts and bridges—worked to erect this monument, which was designed to exalt the technical era that had begun to shine in the lamp of Edison and to stammer in the first telephone of Bell. It was created for the World Exhibition of 1889, inaugurated by Edward VII, then Prince of Wales, and was still in good shape to celebrate its own 100th birthday. Such was Eiffel's engineering wizardry that even in the strongest winds his tower never sways more than 4½ inches.

Since its colossal bulk exudes a feeling of mighty permanence, you may have trouble believing that it nearly became 7,000 tons of scrap iron when its concession expired in 1909. Many Parisians first hated the structure and agreed with designer William Morris, who arrived at its site one day to exclaim, "Why on earth have I come here? Because it's the only place I can't see it from." Only its potential use as a radio antenna saved the day (it still bristles with a forest of radio and television transmitters). By the days of the German occupation, however, Paris trembled when it was suggested that the 12,000 pieces of metal and its 2,500,000 rivets should be "requisitioned." The nocturnal illumination is breathtaking—every girder highlighted in glorious detail. If you're full of energy, stride up the stairs as far as the third deck. If you want to go to the top, you'll have to take the elevator. The view at 1,000 ft may not beat that from the Tour Montparnasse skyscraper, but the setting makes it considerably more romantic. ⊠ *Quai Branly, Trocadéro/Eiffel Tower,* ☎ *01–44–11–23–23,* WEB *www.tour-eiffel.fr.* 🎟 *By elevator: 2nd floor, €3.7; 3rd floor, €6.9; 4th floor, €9.9. By foot: 2nd and 3rd floors only, €3.* ⊙ *July–Aug., daily 9* AM*–midnight; Sept.–June, daily 9* AM*–11* PM*. Métro: Bir-Hakeim; RER: Champ de Mars.*

THE FAUBOURG ST-HONORÉ

Fashions change, but the Faubourg St-Honoré—the area just north of the Champs-Élysées and the Tuileries—firmly maintains its tradition of high style. As you progress from the President's Palace, past a wealth of art galleries and the neoclassic Madeleine Church to the stately place Vendôme, you will see that all is luxury and refinement here. On the ritzy square, famous boutiques sit side by side with famous banks—after all, elegance and finance has never been an unusual combination. It is not surprising to learn that one of the main arteries of the area, the rue de Castiglione, was named after one of its former residents—the glamorous fashion-plate Countess de Castiglione, sent to plead the cause of Italian unity with Napoléon III. The emperor was persuaded (he was easily susceptible to feminine charms), and the area became a Kingdom of Woman: famous dressmakers, renowned jewelers, exclusive perfume shops, and the most chic hotel in Paris, the Ritz, made this *faubourg* (district) a symbol of luxury throughout the world.

Today, the tradition continues, with leading names in fashion found farther east on the place des Victoires, close to what was, for centuries, the gastronomic heart of Paris: Les Halles (pronounced "lay-*al*"), once the city's main market. These giant glass-and-iron market halls were demolished in 1969 and replaced by a park and a modern shopping mall, the Forum des Halles. The surrounding streets underwent a transformation and are now filled with shops, cafés, restaurants, and chic apartment buildings. The brash modernity of the mall stands in contrast to the august church of St-Eustache nearby. Similarly, the incongruous black-and-white columns in the classical courtyard of Richelieu's neighboring Palais-Royal present a further case of daring modernity—or architectural vandalism, depending on your point of view.

Numbers in the text correspond to numbers in the margin and on the Faubourg St-Honoré map.

A Good Walk

Start your walk in front of the most important home in France: the **Palais de l'Élysée** ①, the Presidential Palace; barriers and gold-braided guards keep the public at bay. There's more to see in the plethora of art galleries and luxury fashion boutiques lining rue du Faubourg St-Honoré, where you will also see Sotheby's auction house and the British embassy. From rue du Faubourg St-Honoré, turn left onto rue Boissy-d'Anglas and cut right through an archway into Cité Berryer, a smart courtyard with several trendy shops. It leads to rue Royale, a classy street lined with jewelry stores. Looming to the left is the sturdy **Église de la Madeleine** ②.

Cross boulevard de la Madeleine and take rue Duphot down to rue St-Honoré, where you'll find **Notre-Dame de l'Assomption** ③, noted for its huge dome and solemn interior. Continue to rue de Castiglione; then head left to one of the world's most opulent squares, the **place Vendôme** ④, ringed with jewelers. That's Napoléon standing at the top of the square's bronze central column—and that's the Ritz, fronted by those Rolls-Royces, halfway down on the left. Return to rue St-Honoré and continue to the mighty church of **St-Roch** ⑤. It's worth having a look inside to see the bombastically Baroque altarpiece in the circular Lady Chapel at the far end.

Take the next right onto rue des Pyramides and cross the place des Pyramides, with its gilded statue of Joan of Arc on horseback, to the northwest wing of the Louvre, home to the **Union Centrale des Arts Décoratifs** ⑥, with three separate museums dedicated to fashion, publicity, and the decorative arts. Stay on arcaded rue de Rivoli to the place du Palais-Royal. On the far side of the square is the **Louvre des Antiquaires** ⑦, a chic shopping mall housing upscale antiques stores. Opposite, beyond the exuberant fountains of the place André-Malraux, Garnier's 19th-century Opéra beckons at the far end of the avenue of the same name.

Just beyond Jean-Michel Othaniel's aluminum and psychedelic glass entrance canopy to the Palais-Royal métro station, erected in 2000, is the **Comédie Française** ⑧, the time-honored setting for performances of classical French drama. To the right of the theater is the unobtrusive entrance to the **Palais-Royal** ⑨; its courtyard is a surprising oasis in the heart of the city and a study in both classical and contemporary French landscape architecture. Walk down to the far end of the garden and peek into the glossy 19th-century interior of Le Grand Véfour, one of the swankiest restaurants in the city.

One block north of here, on rue de Richelieu, stands what used to be France's main national library, the **Bibliothèque Nationale Richelieu** ⑩. Rue des Petits-Champs heads east to the circular **place des Victoires** ⑪: that's Louis XIV astride/ the plunging steed in the center of the square. You'll find some of the city's most upscale fashion shops here and on the surrounding streets, along with the 17th-century church of **Notre-Dame des Victoires** ⑫. Head south down rue Croix-des-Petits-Champs, past the nondescript Banque de France on your right, and take the second street on the left to the circular **Bourse du Commerce** ⑬, the Commercial Exchange. Alongside it is a 100-ft-high fluted column, the **Colonne de Ruggieri.**

Today most of the market area that once sat alongside is occupied by the **Jardin des Halles** ⑭, dominated on the left by the bulky outline of the church of **St-Eustache** ⑮, a curious architectural hybrid of Gothic and classical styles. Take bustling rue de Montorgueil beyond the church, and then turn right on rue Étienne-Marcel to admire the **Tour Jean Sans Peur** ⑯, a tower built into the old city walls in 1409. Backtrack a few yards and turn right onto rue Française, right again along quaint rue Tiquetonne, and then take your first left into rue Dussoubs. Just to your right is the entrance to one of the city's most elegant covered galleries, the **Passage du Grand-Cerf** ⑰. Turn right at the end of the gallery and go down rue St-Denis to the cozy medieval church of **St-Leu–St-Gilles** ⑱.

Stay on rue St-Denis and take a third right, along rue des Prêcheurs, to reach the **Forum des Halles** ⑲, a modern, multilevel shopping mall. Turn left on rue Pierre-Lescot to reach the square des Innocents, with its handsome 16th-century Renaissance fountain. Farther east you can see the futuristic funnels of the Centre Pompidou jutting above the surrounding buildings.

From the far end of the square des Innocents, rue St-Denis leads to place du Châtelet, with its theaters, fountain, and the **Tour St-Jacques** ⑳ looming up to your left—all that remains of a church that once stood here. Turning right on the quai de la Mégisserie, you can divide your attention between the exotic array of caged birds for sale along the sidewalk and the view across the Seine toward the turreted Conciergerie. As you cross rue du Pont Neuf, the birds give way to the Art Deco Samaritaine department store with its panoramic rooftop café. Turn right on rue de l'Arbre-Sec, and then take the first left onto rue des Prêtres to reach **St-Germain l'Auxerrois** ㉑, once the French royal family's parish church. Opposite is the colonnaded eastern facade of the Louvre.

The Faubourg St-Honoré

Bourse M La Bourse

10

R. Vivienne

R. N. D. des Victoires

R. du Mail

R. de Cléry M

Rue d'Aboukir

R. Montmartre

R. de Cléry

R. Montorgueil

R. St-Sauveur

Rue Réaumur

2e

R. Greneta

R. M. Stuart

R. Tiquetonne

R. Etienne Marcel

R. Dussoubs

R. St-Denis

Reaumur Sébastopol M

12

11

Banque de France

R. Coquillère

R. Croix des Petits-Champs

13

1er

15

14

19

R. du Louvre

R. du Faubourg-St.Honoré

R. Berger

Châtelet-Les Halles

Etienne Marcel M

Les Halles M

R. Pierre Lescot

R. St-Denis

R. de Turbigo

17

16

18

Bd. de Sébastopol

3e

R. Rambuteau

Centre Pompidou

7

Louvre M

R. de l'Amiral de Coligny

R. de Prêtres

21

R. de Rivoli

R. de l'Arbre-Sec

R. du Pont Neuf

R. des Halles

R. St-Denis

Sq. des Innocents

Pl.Igor Stravinsky

Châtelet M

Av. Victoria

Pont Neuf M

Quai de la Mégisserie

R. St-Martin

R. du Renard

R. de Rivoli

20

Hôtel de Ville M

4e

Pont Neuf

Conciergerie

Pont au Change

Châtelet M

Pl. du Châtelet

0   220 yards
0   200 meters

TIMING

With brief visits to churches and monuments, this 5½-km (3½-mi) walk should take about three to four hours. On a nice day, linger in the gardens of the Palais-Royal; on a cold day, indulge in an unbelievably thick hot chocolate at the Angélina tearoom on rue de Rivoli.

Sights to See

⑩ Bibliothèque Nationale Richelieu (Richelieu National Library). France's longtime national library used to contain more than 7 million printed volumes; many have been removed to the giant new Bibliothèque Nationale François-Mitterrand, though original manuscripts and prints are still here. You can admire Robert de Cotte's 18th-century courtyard, and peep into the magnificent 19th-century reading room, but you cannot enter (it's only open to researchers). The collections are on exhibit from time to time in the library's galleries. ⊠ *58 rue de Richelieu, Opéra/Grands Boulevards.* ⊙ *Daily 9–8. Métro: Bourse.*

⑬ Bourse du Commerce (Commercial Exchange). The circular, shallow-domed 18th-century Commercial Exchange building near Les Halles began life as the Corn Exchange; Victor Hugo waggishly likened it to a jockey's cap without the peak. ⊠ *Rue de Viarmes, Opéra/Grands Boulevards. Métro or RER: Les Halles.*

Colonne de Ruggieri (Ruggieri's Column). The 100-ft-high fluted column, behind the Bourse du Commerce, is all that remains of a mansion built here in 1572 for Catherine de' Medici. The column is said to have been used as a platform for stargazing by her astrologer, Ruggieri. *Métro: Les Halles.*

⑧ Comédie Française. This theater is one of the most famous venues for performances of classical French drama, with tragedies by Racine and Corneille and comedies by Molière regularly on the bill. The building itself dates from 1790, but the Comédie Française company was created by that most theatrical of French monarchs, Louis XIV, back in 1680. If you understand French and have a taste for the mannered, declamatory style of French acting—it's a far cry from method acting—you'll appreciate an evening here. ⊠ *2 rue de Richelieu, Louvre/Tuileries,* ☎ *01–44–58–15–15. Métro: Palais-Royal.*

② Église de la Madeleine. With its rows of uncompromising columns, this sturdy neoclassical edifice—designed in 1814 but not consecrated until 1842—looks more like a proudly inflated, though unfaithful, version of a Greek temple than a Christian church. The loose interpretation was intentional: The overproportioned porticoes, the interior barrel vaults-cum-domes, and the opulent versions of the Ionic and Corinthian orders were meant to be Parisian one-uppings of anything Athens had to offer. Changing political moods continued to alter the building's purpose—a Greek basilica one day, a temple to Napoléon's glory another, a National Assembly hall the next. At one point, in fact, La Madeleine, as it is known, was nearly selected as Paris's first train station. Inside, the only natural light comes from three shallow domes. The walls are richly and harmoniously decorated; gold glints through the murk. Nowadays the opulent interior is the site of lots of expensive concerts as well as daily masses. And if sitting in the cool interior of a Catholic church is not enough to make you reflect upon your faults, try viewing the huge fresco of the Last Judgment above you. A simpler crypt offers intimate weekday masses. ⊠ *Pl. de la Madeleine, Opéra/Grands Boulevards.* ⊙ *Mon.–Sat. 7:30–7, Sun. 8–7. Métro: Madeleine.*

NEED A
BREAK?   **L'Écluse** (⊠ 15 pl. de la Madeleine, Opéra/Grands Boulevards, ☎ 01–42–65–34–69), a cozy wine bar on the square to the west of the Église

de la Madeleine, serves stylish snacks, such as foie gras and carpaccio, and a range of Bordeaux wines.

⑲ Forum des Halles. Les Halles, the iron-and-glass halls of the central Paris food market, were closed in 1969 and replaced in the late '70s by the Forum des Halles, a characterless, modern shopping mall. Nothing remains of either the market or the rambunctious mise-en-scène that led 19th-century novelist Émile Zola to dub Les Halles *le ventre de Paris* ("the belly of Paris"), although rue de Montorgueil, behind St-Eustache, retains something of its original bustle. Unfortunately, much of the plastic, concrete, glass, and mock-marble facade of the multilevel shopping mall is already showing signs of wear and tear. This state of affairs is not much helped by the hordes of teenagers and down-and-outs who invade it toward dusk. Nonetheless, if you are a serious shopper, you might want to check out the French chain stores, the few small boutiques, and the weekly fashion shows by up-and-coming young designers held here. ⌧ *Main entrance: rue Pierre-Lescot, Beaubourg/Les Halles. Métro: Les Halles; RER: Châtelet Les Halles.*

⑭ Jardin des Halles (Les Halles Garden). This garden, crisscrossed with paths and alleyways flanked by bushes, flower beds, and trim little lawns, takes up much of the site once occupied by Les Halles, the city's central market. Children love the bush shaped like a rhinoceros. *Métro: Les Halles; RER: Châtelet Les Halles.*

❼ Louvre des Antiquaires. This "shopping mall" of super-elegant antiques dealers, off the place du Palais-Royal opposite the Louvre, is a minimuseum in itself. Its stylish, glass-walled corridors—lined with Louis XVI *boiseries* (antique wood paneling), Charles Dix bureaus, and the pretty sort of bibelots that would have gladdened the heart of Marie-Antoinette—deserve a browse whether you intend to buy or not. For more Antiques Heaven, head over to the area around rue Jacob on the Left Bank. ⌧ *Main entrance:Pl. du Palais-Royal, Louvre/Tuileries.* ☉ *Tues.–Sun. 11–7. Métro: Palais-Royal.*

NEED A BREAK?   Once patronized by Proust, founded in 1903, **Angélina** (⌧ 226 rue de Rivoli, Louvre/Tuileries, ☎ 01–42–60–82–00) is a famous *salon de thé* (tearoom), lined with seaside frescoes and huge mirrors, noted for its irresistible €6 *chocolat africain,* a cup of hot, thick chocolate served with whipped cream. The famous writer would probably sniff at the shop-worn air of the place today and reserve his affections for the still-elegant teas served at historic Ladurée, 12 blocks to the east at 16 rue Royale.

❸ Notre-Dame de l'Assomption. This 1670 church, with its huge dome and solemn interior, was the scene of Lafayette's funeral in 1834. It is now a chapel for Paris's Polish community. ⌧ *Rue Cambon, Louvre/Tuileries. Métro: Concorde.*

⑫ Notre-Dame des Victoires. Visit this central Paris church, built from 1666 to 1740, to see the 30,000 ex-voto tablets that adorn its walls. ⌧ *Pl. des Petits-Pères, Beaubourg/Les Halles. Métro: Sentier.*

❶ Palais de l'Élysée. Madame de Pompadour, Napoléon, Joséphine, the Duke of Wellington, and Queen Victoria all stayed at this "palace," today the official home of the French president. Originally constructed as a private mansion in 1718, the Élysée—incidentally, when Parisians talk about "L'Élysée," they mean the president's palace, whereas the Champs-Élysées is known simply as "Les Champs"—has housed presidents only since 1873. President Félix Faure died here in 1899 in the arms, so it is said, of his mistress. Although you can catch a glimpse of the palace forecourt and facade through the Faubourg St-Honoré gateway, it is difficult to get much idea of the building's size, or of the extensive gardens that stretch back to the Champs-Élysées, because it is closed to the public. ✉ *55 rue du Faubourg-St-Honoré, Champs-Élysées. Métro: Miromesnil.*

★ ❾ **Palais-Royal** (Royal Palace). One of the most Parisian sights in all of Paris, the Palais-Royal is especially loved for its gardens, where children play, lovers whisper, and senior citizens crumble bread for the sparrows, oblivious to the ghosts of history that haunt this place. The *palais* dates from the 1630s, and is *royal* only in that all-powerful Cardinal Richelieu (1585–1642) magnanimously bequeathed it to Louis XIII. In his early days as king, Louis XIV preferred the relative intimacy of this place to the intimidating splendor of the nearby Louvre (of course, he soon decided that his own intimidating splendor warranted a more majestic home; hence, Versailles). During the French Revolution, it became Le Palais Egalité (the Palace of Equality) because its owner, Louis-Philippe d'Orléans, the king's cousin, professed revolutionary ideas, one of which was to convert the arcades of the palace into boutiques and cafés (Louis XVI reputedly quipped, "My cousin, now that you are going to keep shop I suppose we shall only see you on Sundays"). Before one of these shops Camille Desmoulins gave the first speech calling for the French Revolution in 1789.

Today the Palais-Royal contains a block of apartments (former residents include André Malraux, Jean Cocteau, and Colette) and the French Ministry of Culture, whose buildings—not open to the public—overlook a colonnaded courtyard with black-and-white-striped half-columns and revolving silver spheres that slither around in two fountains, the controversial work of architect Daniel Buren. The splendid gardens beyond are bordered by arcades harboring discreet boutiques and divided by rows of perfectly trimmed little trees. Back in the early 19th century, this was the haunt of prostitutes and gamblers: a veritable sink of vice. These days it's hard to imagine anywhere more hoity-toity. ✉ *Pl. du Palais-Royal, Louvre-Tuileries. Métro: Palais-Royal.*

⓱ **Passage du Grand-Cerf.** This pretty, glass-roofed *passage* (gallery) is filled with crafts shops offering an innovative selection of jewelry, paintings, and ceramics. ✉ *Entrances on rue Dussoubs, rue St-Denis, Beaubourg/Les Halles. Métro: Étienne Marcel.*

❹ **Place Vendôme.** Snobbish and self-important, this famous square is also gorgeous; property laws have kept away cafés and other such banal establishments, leaving the plaza stately and refined, the perfect home for the rich and famous (Chopin lived and died at No. 12; today's celebs camp out at the Hotel Ritz at No. 15, while a lucky few, including the family of the Sultan of Brunei, actually own houses here). With its granite pavement and Second Empire street lamps, Jules-Hardouin Mansart's rhythmic, perfectly proportioned example of 17th-century urban architecture shines in all its golden-stone splendor. The square is a fitting showcase for the cluster of jewelry display windows found here. Interestingly, when the square was first built, only the facades of the hôtels particuliers were constructed, to maintain a uniform appearance—the lots behind the facades were then sold to buyers who custom-tailored their palaces to individual taste. Napoléon had the square's central column made from the melted bronze of 1,200 cannons captured at the Battle of Austerlitz in 1805, and stands vigilantly on the top. Painter Gustave Courbet headed the Revolutionary hooligans who, in 1871, toppled the column (into a pile of manure, no less) and shattered it into thousands of metallic pieces. The Third Republic stuck them together again and sent him the bill. To raise a glass of champagne to honor the

HEMINGWAY'S PARIS

THERE IS AN OLD FAMILIAR SAYING: "Everyone has two countries, his or her own—and France." For the "Lost Generation" after World War I, these words rang particularly true. Disillusioned by America's Depression and Prohibition, lured by favorable exchange rates and a booming artistic scene, many American writers, composers, and painters moved to Paris in the 1920s and 1930s. F. Scott Fitzgerald, Gertrude Stein, Ezra Pound, e.e. cummings, Janet Flanner, and John dos Passos are just a few of the famous figures, with Ernest Hemingway heading the list. "Papa" found Paris a veritable Land of Cockaigne, where every man does what he pleases, where all could allow their personal idiosyncracies full play and apologize for them with the simple remark, *Je suis comme ça.* "I am like that." It is this freedom that, back then, made Paris the cultural—and hoopla—capital of the world. And the best witnesses to that amazing era were the many expatriates who came to admire, and remained to praise.

Hemingway arrived in Paris with his first wife, Hadley, in December, 1921, and made for the Left Bank—the Hôtel Jacob et d'Angleterre, to be exact (still operating at 44 rue Jacob). To celebrate their arrival, the couple went to the Café de la Paix for a meal they nearly couldn't afford. In 1922 they moved to 74 rue du Cardinal Lemoine (his writing studio was around the corner on the top floor of 39 rue Descartes), then in early 1924 the couple and their baby son settled at 113 rue Notre-Dame des Champs. Nearby, he settled in at La Closerie des Lilas café to write much of *The Sun Also Rises.* It was a time "when we were very young and very happy" as he wrote in *A Moveable Feast.*

Not happy for long. In 1926 Hemingway left Hadley and next year wedded his mistress Pauline Pfeiffer across town at St Honoré-d'Eylau, then moved to 6 rue Férou, near the Musée du Luxembourg, whose collection of Cézanne landscapes (now in the Musée d'Orsay) he revered. Hemingway once declared that "unless you have geography, background, you have nothing." You can follow the steps of Jake and Bill in *The Sun Also Rises* as they "circle" the Ile St-Louis before the "steep walking. . . all the way up to the place de la Contrescarpe," then right along rue du Pot-de-Fer to the "rigid north and south" of rue St-Jacques and on to boulevard du Montparnasse.

For gossip and books, Papa would visit Shakespeare and Company at 12 rue de l'Odéon, owned by Sylvia Beach, an early buddy (the bookstore can now be found at 37 rue de la Bûcherie). For cash and cocktails, Hemingway usually headed to the upscale Right Bank. The first was found at the Guaranty Trust Company, at 1 rue des Italiens. The second, when he was flush, at the bar of the Hôtel Crillon, or, when poor, at the Caves Mura, at 19 rue d'Antin, or Harry's Bar, still in brisk business at 5 rue Daunou, with photos of Papa gazing down from the walls. Hemingway's legendary association with the Hotel Ritz, where he now has his own bar named for him, dates from the Liberation in 1944, when he strode in at the head of his platoon and "liberated" the joint by ordering 73 dry martinis. Here, Hemingway asked Mary Welsh to become his fourth wife, and also righted the world with Jean-Paul Sartre, George Orwell, and Marlene Dietrich. Paris loves naming streets after adopted sons and it is only fitting that Hemingway has a plaque of his own, heralding short Rue Ernest-Hemingway in the 15th arrondissement. This, after all, was the man who wrote: "There is never any ending to Paris."

place's famous ghosts, repair to Hemingway's Bar at the Ritz (☞ Close-Up Box, Hemingway's Paris, *below*). *Métro: Opéra.*

⓫ **Place des Victoires.** This circular square, now home to many of the city's top fashion boutiques, was laid out in 1685 by Jules Hardouin-Mansart in honor of the military victories of Louis XIV, that indefatigable warrior whose nearly continuous battles may have brought much prestige to his country but came perilously close to bringing it to bankruptcy, too. Louis is shown galloping along on a bronze horse in the middle; his statue dates from 1822 and replaced one destroyed during the Revolution. Louis was so taken with this plaza that he commissioned the architect, who also designed much of Versailles, to build another, the place Vendôme, on the other side of the avenue de l'Opéra. *Métro: Sentier.*

⓯ **St-Eustache.** Since the demolition of the 19th-century iron-and-glass market halls at the beginning of the '70s, St-Eustache has reemerged as a dominant element on the central Paris skyline. It is a huge church, the "cathedral" of Les Halles, built as the market people's Right Bank reply to Notre-Dame on the Ile de la Cité. St-Eustache dates from a couple of hundred years later than Notre-Dame. With the exception of the feeble west front, added between 1754 and 1788, construction lasted from 1532 to 1637, spanning the decline of the Gothic style and the emergence of the Renaissance. As a consequence, the church is a curious architectural hybrid. Its exterior flying buttresses are Gothic, but its column orders, rounded arches, and thick, comparatively simple window tracery are unmistakably classical. Few buildings bear such eloquent witness to stylistic transition. St-Eustache also hosts occasional organ concerts. ⊠ *2 rue du Jour, Beaubourg/Les Halles,* ☎ *01–46–27–89–21 concert information.* ⊘ *Daily 8–7. Métro: Les Halles; RER: Châtelet Les Halles.*

㉑ **St-Germain l'Auxerrois.** Until 1789, this church was used by the French royal family as its Paris parish church, in the days when the adjacent Louvre was a palace rather than a museum. The fluid stonework of the facade reveals the influence of 15th-century Flamboyant Gothic style, enjoying its final shrieks before the classical takeover of the Renaissance. Notice the unusually wide windows in the nave and the equally unusual double aisles. The triumph of classicism is evident, however, in the fluted columns around the choir, the area surrounding the altar. These were added in the 18th century and are characteristic of the desire of 18th-century clerics to dress up medieval buildings in the architectural raiment of their own day. ⊠ *Pl. du Louvre, Louvre/Tuileries. Métro: Louvre-Rivoli.*

⓲ **St-Leu–St-Gilles.** Near the Centre Pompidou, this intimate church presents a stylistic contrast between its large-windowed, 14th-century nave and the raised, 17th-century Renaissance choir. ⊠ *Rue St-Denis, Beaubourg/Les Halles. Métro: Étienne Marcel.*

❺ **St-Roch.** Designed by Lemercier in 1653 but completed only in the 1730s, this huge church is almost as long (138 yards) as Notre-Dame, thanks to Hardouin-Mansart's domed Lady Chapel at the far end, with its elaborate Baroque altarpiece. Classical playwright Pierre Corneille (1606–84) is buried here; a commemorative plaque honors him at the left of the entrance. ⊠ *Rue St-Honoré, Louvre/Tuileries. Métro: Tuileries.*

⓰ **Tour Jean Sans Peur.** This sturdy medieval tower was built by Jean Sans Peur (John the Fearless), Duke of Burgundy, in 1409 to defend his long-since-vanished Paris mansion. You can explore the spiral staircase and admire the magnificent vaulting with its intertwined array of sculpted vines, hops, and hawthorn flowers. Ask for an English translation for all the banners detailing Paris's medieval architecture. ✉ *20 rue Éti-enne-Marcel, Beaubourg/Les Halles,* ☎ *01–40–26–20–28.* 🎟 *€4.6.* ☉ *Sept.–June, Wed. and weekends 1:30–6; July–Aug., Tues.–Sun. 1:30–6. Métro: Étienne Marcel.*

㉒ Tour St-Jacques. Now used for meteorological purposes and not open to the public, this ornate 170-ft stump tower belonged to a 16th-century church destroyed in 1797. It sits forlornly, swallowed up by surrounding traffic. ✉ *Pl. du Châtelet, Beaubourg/Les Halles. Métro: Châtelet.*

NEED A BREAK? Twenty different international beers are available on draft, and more than 180 in bottles, at **Le Trappiste** (✉ 4 rue St-Denis, Beaubourg/Les Halles, ☎ 01–42–33–08–50), just north of the place du Châtelet. Mussels and french fries are the traditional accompaniment, although various other snacks (hot dogs, sandwiches) are also available.

★ ❻ Union Centrale des Arts Décoratifs (Decorative Arts Center). A must for lovers of fashion and the decorative arts, this northwestern wing of the Louvre building houses three famously chic museums: the **Musée de la Mode,** devoted to costumes and accessories dating back to the 18th century, usually displayed in temporary exhibitions devoted to a single theme or designer—needless to say, the place is a second home to Paris's enormous fashion community; the **Musée des Arts Décoratifs,** with furniture, tapestries, glassware, paintings and other necessities of life from the Middle Ages through Napoléon's time and beyond—a highlight here are the sumptuous period-style rooms (note the ostentatious number of chairs in the salon); and the **Musée de la Publicité,** opened in 1999, perhaps less of interest for its temporary exhibits of advertisements and posters than for Jean Nouvel's brash decor—described by one Paris critic as "hi-tec miserabalism"—combining metal-plaqued walls with exposed brickwork and faded gilding, as well as black-lacquered parquet floors, leopard-skin pillars, and a battery of TV monitors over the bar. ✉ *107 rue de Rivoli, Louvre/Tuileries,* ☎ *01–44–55–57–50,* 🌐 *www.ucad.fr.* 🎟 *€5.5.* ☉ *Tues.–Sun. 11–6. Métro: Palais-Royal.*

THE GRANDS BOULEVARDS

Famously immortalized in the canvases of Monet, Renoir, and Pissarro, the Grands Boulevards are the long chain of avenues that join the Madeleine to the Opéra, continue via the ancient gates of St-Denis and St-Martin to place de la République, and on to Bastille. Together they constitute the longest, most commercial, most representative artery of Paris, and also the most diverse. Parisians have always loved to promenade down their great avenues to feel the pulse of the city throbbing at its strongest. The focal point of this walk is the avenue that runs west to east from St-Augustin, the city's grandest Second Empire church, to place de la République, whose very name symbolizes the ultimate downfall of the imperial regime. The avenue's name changes six times along the way, which is why Parisians refer to it, in plural, as "Les Grands Boulevards."

This walk starts at the Parc Monceau, heart of one of the most fashionable residential neighborhoods, but the makeup of the neighborhoods along the Grands Boulevards changes steadily as you head from the posh 8ᵉ *arrondissement* (district) toward working-class east Paris. The *Grands Magasins* (department stores) at the start of the walk epitomize upscale Paris shopping. They stand on boulevard Haussmann, named in honor of the regional prefect who oversaw the reconstruction of the city in the 1850s and 1860s. The opulent Opéra Garnier, just past the Grands Magasins, is the architectural showpiece of the period (often termed *Second Empire* and corresponding to the rule of Napoléon III).

Haussmann's concept of urban planning proved grand enough to ward off the postwar skyscrapers and property sharks that bedevil so many other European cities (Paris's urban planners have relegated them to the outskirts). Though lined with the seven-story blocks typical of Haussmann's time, the boulevards date from the 1670s, when they were created on the site of the city's medieval fortifications. These were razed when Louis XIV's military triumphs appeared to render their raison d'être obsolete, and were replaced by leafy promenades known from the outset as "boulevards" (the work has the same origin as bulwark).

This walk takes in some of the older sights on both sides of the boulevard, including the city's traditional auction house, the colonnaded stock exchange, and the Sentier district with its busy fabric traders. It ends on the tranquil banks of the little-known Canal St-Martin.

Numbers in the text correspond to numbers in the margin and on The Grand Boulevards map.

A Good Walk

Take the métro to Monceau in the tony 8e arrondissement and step through gold-topped iron gates to enter the **Parc Monceau** ①—the heart of an elegant residential neighborhood once called home by the likes of Paderewski, Rostand, and Sarah Bernhardt. Once past the sculpted busts of Gounod, Chopin, and Bizet, near the middle of the park, head left to avenue Velasquez, which is ornamented with spectacular gates and mansions, one of which is the **Musée Cernuschi** ②, which has a refined collection of Chinese art from Neolithic pottery to contemporary paintings. Continue on to boulevard Malesherbes and turn right, then right again onto rue de Monceau, to reach the **Musée Nissim de Camondo** ③, whose aristocratic interiors sumptuously bring to life the days of the ancien régime.

More splendor awaits at the **Musée Jacquemart-André** ④. Continue down rue de Monceau and turn left onto rue de Courcelles, then left again onto boulevard Haussmann to find this imposing 19th-century marble palace, filled with lacquered antiques and great old-master paintings amassed by a Parisian millionaire. Continue eastward along the boulevard and cross the square in front of the church of St-Augustin. Stay on boulevard Haussmann then turn right down rue d'Anjou to enter the leafy, intimate square Louis XVI with its **Chapelle Expiatoire** ⑤, dedicated to Louis XVI and Marie-Antoinette. Be sure to take a look at the amusing stone carvings on the gleaming 1930s-style facade of the bank at the corner of rue Pasquier and rue Mathurins. Some 300 yards farther down boulevard Haussmann are the Grands Magasins, Paris's most renowned department stores. First comes **Au Printemps** ⑥, then **Galeries Lafayette** ⑦. Marks & Spencer, across the street, provides an outpost for British goods like ginger biscuits and bacon rashers. Opposite Galeries Lafayette is the massive bulk of the **Opéra Garnier** ⑧. Before venturing around to inspect its extravagant facade, colorfully restored in 2000, you might like to take in a multiscreen overview of Paris and its history at the **Paris Story** ⑨ movie venue at No. 11 bis rue Scribe.

Boulevard des Capucines, lined with cinemas and restaurants, heads left from in front of the Opéra, becoming boulevard des Italiens. Look left up rue Laffitte for a startling view of the Sacré-Coeur, looming above the porticoed church of Notre-Dame-de-Lorette. Just after the intersection of boulevard Haussmann with boulevard des Italiens, turn left

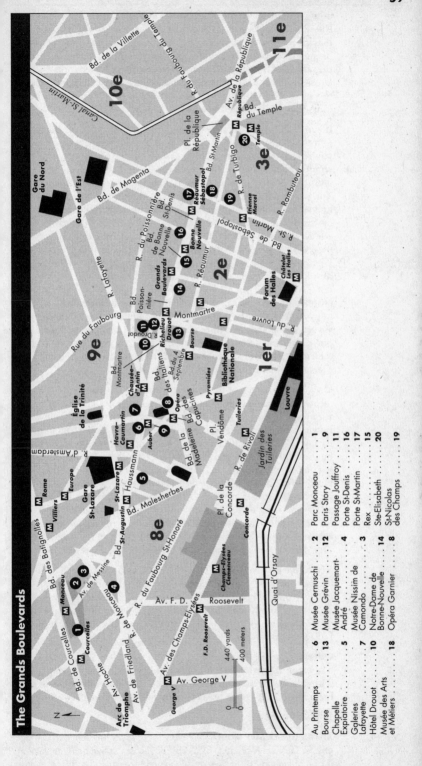

The Grands Boulevards

59

Au Printemps	1	Musée Cernuschi	2	Parc Monceau	1
Bourse	13	Musée Grévin	12	Paris Story	9
Chapelle Expiatoire	5	Musée Jacquemart-André	4	Passage Jouffroy	11
Galeries Lafayette	7	Musée Nissim de Camondo	3	Porte St-Denis	16
Hôtel Drouot	10	Notre-Dame de Bonne-Nouvelle	14	Porte St-Martin	17
Musée des Arts et Métiers	18	Opéra Garnier	8	Rex	15
				Ste-Elisabeth	20
				St-Nicolas des Champs	19

down rue Drouot to the **Hôtel Drouot** ⑩, Paris's central auction house. Rue Rossini leads from Drouot, as it is known, to rue de la Grange-Batelière. Halfway along on the right is the **Passage Jouffroy** ⑪, one of the many covered galleries that honeycomb the center of Paris. At the far end of the passage is the **Musée Grévin** ⑫, a waxworks museum. Cross boulevard Montmartre to the passage des Panoramas, leading to rue St-Marc. Turn right, then left down rue Vivienne, to find the foursquare, colonnaded **Bourse** ⑬, the Paris Stock Exchange.

If you wish, you can continue down rue Vivienne from the Bourse and join the Faubourg St-Honoré walk at the Bibliothèque Nationale. If you're feeling adventurous, head east along rue Réaumur, whose huge-windowed buildings once formed the heart of the French newspaper industry—stationery shops still abound—and cross rue Montmartre. You can catch sight of the St-Eustache church to your right; the distant spires of St-Ambroise emerge on the horizon. Take the second left up rue de Cléry, a narrow street that is the exclusive domain of fabric wholesalers and often crammed with vans, pallets, and delivery people creating colorful chaos. The lopsided building at the corner of rue Poissonnière looks as if it is struggling to stay upright on the district's drunken slopes. Continue up rue de Cléry as far as rue des Degrés—not a street at all but a 14-step stairway—then look for the clock and crooked turnip tower of **Notre-Dame de Bonne-Nouvelle** ⑭, hemmed in by rickety housing that looks straight out of Balzac. You can enter via No. 19 bis and cross through the church to emerge beneath the front portico on rue de la Lune. Head left as far as rue Poissonnière, and then turn right to return to the Grands Boulevards, by now going under the name of boulevard de Bonne-Nouvelle.

On the near corner of the boulevard stands the **Rex** ⑮, an Art Deco movie theater where you can take a backstage tour. Cross the boulevard for a view of its wedding-cake tower; then head up boulevard de Bonne-Nouvelle to the **Porte St-Denis** ⑯, a newly cleaned triumphal arch dating from the reign of Louis XIV. A little farther on is the smaller but similar **Porte St-Martin** ⑰. From here take rue St-Martin south, pausing on leafy square Émile-Chautemps to admire the red marble-pillared facade of the derelict Théâtre de la Gaîté Lyrique, a music hall designed by Jacques Hittorff in 1862; Offenbach conducted here from 1873 to 1875, and Diaghilev's Russian ballets set the stage alight from 1911 to 1913. Then turn left on rue Réaumur to the **Musée des Arts et Métiers** ⑱, an industrial museum, housed partly in the former church of St-Martin, which reopened in 2000 after lengthy restoration.

Across rue Réaumur is the high, narrow, late-Gothic church of **St-Nicolas des Champs** ⑲. Continue past the cloister ruins and Renaissance gateway that embellish the far side of St-Nicolas, and head left on rue Turbigo for 500 yards until you meet the rear end of the Baroque church of **Ste-Elisabeth** ⑳ on your right. Shortly after you will reach place de la République.

TIMING

The distance between Parc Monceau and place de la République is about 7 km (4½ mi), which will probably require at least four hours to walk, including taking coffee breaks and window-shopping.

Sights to See

OFF THE BEATEN PATH

ATELIER DE GUSTAVE MOREAU – A visit to this town house and studio of painter Gustave Moreau (1826–98), doyen of the Symbolist movement, is one of the most distinctive artistic experiences in Paris. The Symbolists strove to convey ideas through images, but many of the ideas Moreau was trying to express were so obscure that the artist had to provide explanatory texts, which rather confuses the point. But it's easy to admire his extravagant colors and flights of fantasy, influenced by Persian and Indian miniatures. From the Trinité church, take rue Blanche to the right, and then turn right on rue de la Tour-des-Dames; the museum is at the far end of rue de la Rochefoucauld. ⊠ *14 rue de la Rochefoucauld, Opéra/Grands Boulevards,* ☎ *01–48–74–38–50.* ☒ *€3.5.* ☉ *Thurs.– Sun. 10–12:45 and 2–5:15, Mon. and Wed. 11–5:15. Métro: Trinité.*

❻ **Au Printemps.** Founded in 1865 by Jules Jaluzot—former employee of Au Bon Marché, which opened 13 years earlier on the Left Bank—Au Printemps swiftly became the mecca of Right Bank shoppers, enabling the current opulent Belle Epoque buildings, with their domes and gold-and-green mosaic signs, to be erected by the turn of the 20th century. The glass cupola in Café Flo dates from 1923; and the rooftop cafeteria has a splendid view of the Paris skyline. ⊠ *64 bd. Haussmann, Opéra/Grands Boulevards. Métro: Havre Caumartin.*

⓭ **Bourse** (Stock Exchange). The Paris Stock Exchange, a serene, colonnaded 19th-century building, is a far cry from Wall Street. Bring your passport if you want to tour it. ⊠ *Rue Vivienne, Opéra/Grands Boulevards.* ☒ *€4.5.* ☉ *Guided tours only (in French), weekdays every ½ hr 1:15–4. Métro: Bourse.*

❺ **Chapelle Expiatoire.** This unkempt mausoleum emerges defiantly from the lush undergrowth of verdant square Louis-XVI off boulevard Haussmann, marking the initial burial site of Louis XVI and Marie-Antoinette after their turns at the guillotine on place de la Concorde. Two stone tablets are inscribed with the last missives of the doomed royals: touching pleas for their revolutionary enemies to be forgiven. When compared to the pomp and glory of Napoléon's memorial at the Invalides, this tribute to royalty (France was ruled by kings until 1792 and again from 1815 to 1848) seems halfhearted and trite. ⊠ *29 rue Pasquier, Opéra/Grands Boulevards,* ☎ *01–44–32–18–00,* ⓌⒺⒷ *www. monum.fr.* ☒ *€2.5.* ☉ *Thurs.–Sat. 1–5. Métro: St-Augustin.*

❼ **Galeries Lafayette.** This turn-of-the-20th-century department store has a vast, shimmering Belle Epoque glass dome that can only be seen if you venture inside. ⊠ *40 bd. Haussmann, Opéra/Grands Boulevards. Métro: Chaussée d'Antin; RER: Auber.*

❿ **Hôtel Drouot.** Hidden away in a grid of narrow streets not far from the Opéra is Paris's central auction house, where everything from stamps and toy soldiers to Renoirs and 18th-century commodes is sold. The 16 salesrooms make for fascinating browsing, and there's no obligation to bid. The mix of ladies in fur coats with money to burn, penniless art lovers desperate to unearth an unidentified masterpiece, and scruffy dealers trying to look anonymous makes up Drouot's unusually rich social fabric. Sales are held most weekdays, with viewings in the morning; anyone can attend. For centuries, the French government refused to allow foreign firms to stage auctions, but that changed in 2001 and Drouot now faces very stiff competition from Sotheby's and Christie's, who instantly set up shop in Paris. ⊠ *9 rue Drouot, Opéra/Grands Boulevards,* ☎ *01–48–00–20–00.* ☉ *Viewings mid-Sept.–mid-July, Mon.–Sat. 11–noon and 2–6, with auctions starting at 2. Métro: Richelieu Drouot.*

⓲ **Musée des Arts et Métiers** (National Technical Museum). The former church and priory of St-Martin des Champs was built between the 11th and 13th centuries. Confiscated during the Revolution, it was used first as an educational institution, then as an arms factory, before becoming, in 1799, the Conservatoire des Arts et Métiers. Today the church and the splendid 13th-century refectory, a large hall supported by central columns, form part of the National Technical Museum, a crafts and industrial museum with a varied collection of models (locomotives, vehicles, and agricultural machinery), astronomical instruments, looms, and glass, together with displays on printing, photography, and the history of television. ✉ *60 rue Réaumur, Opéra/Grands Boulevards,* ☎ *01–53–01–82–00,* WEB *www.cnam.fr/museum.* ☐ *€5.5.* ⊙ *Tues.–Sun. 10–6. Métro: Arts et Métiers.*

❷ Musée Cernuschi. Closed for renovation through 2004, this museum is set within an aristocratic town house. A connoisseur's favorite, the collection includes Chinese art from Neolithic pottery (3rd century BC) to funeral statuary, painted 8th-century silks, and contemporary paintings, as well as ancient Persian bronze objects. ✉ *7 av. Velasquez, Parc Monceau,* ☎ *01–45–63–50–75,* WEB *www.paris-france.org/musees.* ☐ *Free.* ⊙ *Tues.–Sun. 10–5:40. Métro: Monceau.*

☺ ⑫ Musée Grévin. Founded in 1882, and granted a $7-million face-lift in 2001, this waxworks museum, around the corner from the Hôtel Drouot, ranks in scope and ingenuity with Madame Tussaud's in London. Wax renderings of 250 historical and contemporary celebrities are on display; your ticket also allows entry to a 1900 Palace of Illusion. ✉ *10 bd. Montmartre, Opéra/Grands Boulevards,* ☎ *01–47–70– 85–05,* WEB *www.grevin.com.* ☐ *€15.* ⊙ *Daily 10–7. Métro: Grands Boulevards.*

★ ❹ Musée Jacquemart-André. Often compared to New York City's Frick Collection, this was one of the grandest private residences of 19th-century Paris. Built between 1869 and 1875, it found Hollywood fame when used as Gaston Lachaille's mansion in the 1958 musical *Gigi,* as a great stand-in for the floridly opulent home of a sugar millionaire played by Louis Jourdan. Edouard André and his painter-wife, Nélie Jacquemart, the house's actual owners, were rich and cultured, so art from the Italian Renaissance and 18th-century France compete for attention here. Note the freshly restored Tiepolo frescoes in the staircase and on the dining-room ceiling, while salons done in the fashionable "Louis XVI–Empress" style (favored by Empress Eugénie) are hung with great paintings, including Uccello's *Saint George Slaying the Dragon,* Rembrandt's *Pilgrims of Emmaus,* Jean-Marc Nattier's *Mathilde de Canisy,* and Jacques-Louis David's *Comte Antoine-Français de Nantes.* You can tour the house with the free English audio guide. The Tiepolo salon now contains a café, so why not lunch here and enjoy the Fragonard, Mantegna, and Chardin salads, named after great painters. ✉ *158 bd. Haussmann, Parc Monceau,* ☎ *01–42–89–04– 91,* WEB *musee-jacquemart-andre.com.* ☐ *€7.5.* ⊙ *Daily 10–6. Métro: St-Philippe-du-Roule.*

★ ❸ Musée Nissim de Camondo. Molière made fun of the *bourgeois gentilhomme,* the middle-class man who aspired to the class of his royal betters, but the playwright would have been in awe of Comte Moïse de Camondo, whose sense of style, grace, and refinement could have taught the courtiers at Versailles a thing or two. After making a fortune in the late 19th century, the businessman built this grand hôtel particulier in the style of the Petit Trianon and proceeded to furnish it with some of the most exquisite furniture, *boiseries* (carved wood panels), and bibelots of the mid- to late 18th century. His wife and children (the museum is named after his son, who died in combat during World War I) then moved in and lent the house enormous warmth and charm. From ancien régime splendor, however, the family descended to the worst horrors of World War II: after the death of Count Moïse in 1935, the estate left the family's house and treasures to the government while shortly thereafter, family descendants were packed off to Auschwitz by the Nazis, where several of them were murdered. Today, the wealthy matrons of Paris have made this museum their own, and it shines anew with the beauty of the 18th century. If you want to see these enchanting salons in all their candlelit glory, view a video of *Valmont*, Milos Forman's much-overlooked 1989 filmed version of *Les Liaisons Dangereuses*. ⊠ *63 rue de Monceau, Parc Monceau*, ☎ *01–53–89–06–50*, WEB *www.ucad.fr.* 🎫 *€4.6.* 🕐 *Wed.–Sun. 10–5. Métro: Villiers.*

⓮ **Notre-Dame de Bonne-Nouvelle.** This wide, soberly neoclassical church is tucked away off the Grands Boulevards. The previous church (the second) on the spot was ransacked during the Revolution, and the current one, built 1823–29 after the restoration of the French monarchy, was ransacked by Communard hooligans in May 1871. The highlight is the semicircular apse behind the altar, featuring some fine 17th-century paintings beneath a three-dimensional, 19th-century grisaille composition by Abel de Pujol. Note the many pictures, statues, and works of religious art to be found in the side chapels. ⊠ *Rue de la Lune, Opéra/Grands Boulevards. Métro: Bonne Nouvelle.*

★ ⑧ **Opéra Garnier.** Haunt of the "Phantom of the Opera," the real-life setting for some of Degas's famous ballet paintings, and still the most opulent theater in the world, the Paris Opéra was begun in 1862 by Charles Garnier at the behest of Napoléon III. Due to its lavishness, it was not completed until 1875, five years after the emperor's abdication. Awash with Algerian colored marbles and gilded *putti*, it is said to typify Second Empire architecture: a pompous hodgepodge of styles with about as much subtlety as a Wagnerian cymbal crash. The composer Debussy famously compared it to a Turkish bathhouse, but lovers of pomp and splendor will adore it (Hitler called it the most beautiful building in the world)—especially with the façade restored to its original smash-hit glory in 2000.

To see the theater and lobby, you don't actually have to attend a performance: after paying an entry fee, you can stroll around at leisure and view the foyer and have a peek into the auditorium. The monumental Grand Foyer is nearly as big as the auditorium (together they fill 3 acres). After all, this was a theater for Parisians who came to the opera primarily to be seen; on opening nights, you can still see Rothschilds and rock stars preen and prance on the grand staircase. If the lavishly upholstered auditorium seems small, it is only because the stage is the largest in the world—more than 11,000 square yards, with room for up to 450 performers. Marc Chagall painted the ceiling in 1964. The **Opera Museum**, containing a few paintings and theatrical mementos, is unremarkable. If you want a full burst of Parisian grandeur, make sure you catch a performance here—while technically the official home of the Paris Ballet, this auditorium usually mounts one or two full-scale operas a season (most operas are presented at the drearily modern Opéra de la Bastille). ⊠ *Pl. de l'Opéra, Opéra/Grands Boulevards*, ☎ *01–40–01–22–63*, WEB *www.opera-de-paris.fr.* 🎫 *€4.6, guided tours €9.2.* 🕐 *Daily 10–4:30. Guided tours in English at 3 PM. Métro: Opéra.*

NEED A BREAK? — Few cafés are as grand as the Belle Epoque **Café de la Paix** (⊠ 5 pl. de l'Opéra, Opéra/Grands Boulevards, ☎ 01–40–07–30–10). Once described as "the center of the civilized world," it was a regular meeting place for the glitterati of 19th- and 20th-century Paris; the prices are as grand as the setting. Today, probably only the waiters speak French.

👆 ❶ **Parc Monceau.** The most picturesque gardens on the Right Bank were laid out as a private park in 1778 and retain some of the fanciful elements then in vogue, including mock ruins and a faux pyramid. In 1797 André Garnerin, the world's first-recorded parachutist, staged a landing in the park. The rotunda—known as the Chartres Pavilion—is surely the city's grandest public rest room; it started life as a tollhouse. All in all, this remains one of the snobbiest parks in Paris and certainly one of the prettiest—no wonder director Vincente Minnelli used it as a backdrop in his film *Gigi*. ⊠ *Entrances on bd. de Courcelles, av. Velasquez, av. Ruysdaël, av. van Dyck, Parc Monceau. Métro: Monceau.*

⑨ Paris Story. Victor Hugo is your "guide" on this 45-minute split-screen presentation of Paris and its history, with spectacular photography and tasteful musical accompaniment, with St-Saëns's Organ Symphony employed to majestic effect. It's a fun introduction to the city. Be sure to get headphones to hear the English translation. ⊠ *11 bis rue Scribe, Opéra/Grands Boulevards,* ☎ *01–42–66–62–06,* WEB *www. paris-story.com.* ☑ €7.8. ⊙ *Apr.–Oct., daily 9–8; Nov.–Mar., daily 9–6; screenings on the hr. Métro: Opéra.*

⑪ Passage Jouffroy. Built in 1846, as its giant clock will tell you, this shops-filled *passage* (gallery) was one of the first precursors to the modern-day shopping mall. ⊠ *Entrances on bd. Montmartre, rue de la Grange-Batelière, Opéra/Grands Boulevards. Métro: Richelieu Drouot.*

⑯ Porte St-Denis. This 76-ft triumphal arch, which is slightly larger and older than the neighboring Porte St-Martin, was erected by François Blondel in 1672 to celebrate the victories of *Ludovico Magno* (as Louis XIV is here styled) on the Rhine. The bas-reliefs by François Girardon include campaign scenes and military attributes stacked on shallow, slender pyramids. The arch, superbly cleaned in 1998, faces rue St-Denis—formerly the royal processional route into Paris from the north (last so used by Queen Victoria in 1855) but now better known for activity along the sidewalk. ⊠ *Bd. St-Denis, Opéra/Grands Boulevards. Métro: Strasbourg St-Denis.*

⑰ Porte St-Martin. This 56-ft triumphal arch, slightly smaller and younger than the neighboring Porte St-Denis, was designed by Blondel's pupil Pierre Bullet in 1674 and cleaned in 1998. Louis XIV's victories at Limburg (in Flanders) and Besançon in Franche-Comté get bas-relief coverage from Martin Desjardins. ⊠ *Bd. St-Denis, Opéra/Grands Boulevards. Métro: Strasbourg St-Denis.*

☝ ⑮ Rex. If you're a movie buff, you may want to inspect Europe's self-styled "Grandest Cinema," built in 1932—although the 50-minute back-screen tour, full of special effects and loudspeaker commentary (available in English), gives only a tantalizing glimpse of the 2,700-seat auditorium, with its star-spangled roof and onstage fountains. You're surreptitiously filmed as you go around, with an individualized souvenir video (€6) available as you leave. If you still want more, see a movie here. ⊠ *1 bd. Poissonnière, Opéra/Grands Boulevards,* ☎ *08–36–68–70–23.* ☑ €7. ⊙ *Wed.–Sun. 10–7. Métro: Bonne Nouvelle.*

⑳ Ste-Elisabeth. This studied essay in Baroque (built 1628–46) is pleasantly unpretentious; there's no soaring bombast here. The church has brightly restored wall paintings and a wide, semicircular apse around the choir, where biblical scenes are carved into stupendous 17th-century wood paneling transferred from an abbey in Arras in northern France. ⊠ *Rue du Temple, République. Métro: Temple.*

⑲ St-Nicolas des Champs. The rounded-arch, fluted Doric capitals in the chancel of this church date from 1560 to 1587, a full century later than the pointed-arch nave (1420–80). There is a majestic mid-17th-century organ and a fine *Assumption of the Virgin* (1629) by Simon Vouet above the high altar. The south door (1576) on rue au Maire is gloriously carved and surrounded by a small but unexpectedly well-tended lawn complete with rosebushes. ⊠ *Rue St-Martin, Opéra/Grands Boulevards. Métro: Arts et Métiers.*

FROM RÉPUBLIQUE TO LA VILLETTE

Place de la République is the gateway to northeast Paris, a largely residential area that is often underestimated by tourists. But not by the natives: Princes of the Paris night will now tell you that the Bastille bustle has burst, and the eventide pulse has beaten a retreat northeast into the heartland of the 11th arrondissement. For stylemeisters, rue Oberkampf, rue St-Maur, and rue Jean-Pierre-Timbaud is where it's all happening. Another flash-point for trendies is the newly cool area around the Canal St-Martin, which forms the focal point of this walk. Today its barges transport mainly visitors and pleasure boats, but it was once a busy thoroughfare linking the Seine to the city's central slaughterhouse at La Villette. The Mitterrand era saw La Villette landscaped beyond recognition, with science and music museums and a concert hall built amid a wittily designed postmodern park. Nearby, 19th-century city planner Baron Haussmann let his hair down at the tumbling Buttes-Chaumont Park, going to town with a lake, a waterfall, a grotto, and phony cliffs.

Numbers in the text correspond to numbers in the margin and on the place de la République to La Villette map.

A Good Walk

Begin your walk at **place de la République** ①. Cross the square and head up rue du Faubourg-du-Temple to the **Canal St-Martin** ②, whose locks and pale-green footbridges conjure up an unexpected flavor of Amsterdam. At this point, the canal emerges from a 2½-km (1½-mi) tunnel that starts beyond the Bastille. To explore the trendy Oberkampf district, continue along rue du Faubourg-du-Temple until you hit rue St-Maur, then take it south a few blocks to rue Jean-Pierre-Timbaud and rue Oberkampf. Backtrack north to the **Hôpital St-Louis** ③, Paris's oldest hospital, with its serene courtyard and chapel still intact. Leave the hospital on rue de la Grange-aux-Belles, and turn left, then right down rue Bichat, to find the Canal St-Martin bending beneath the unassuming white facade of the **Hôtel du Nord** ④, made famous by the film of the same name. The canal continues north to the circular **Rotonde de La Villette** ⑤. It surveys both the elevated métro line and the unruffled sheen of the Bassin de La Villette, where boats leave on a mile-long trip to the **Parc de La Villette** ⑥, with its postmodern science and music museums. If you prefer to take the 30-minute walk along the canal to the park, keep to the left bank of the quai de la Seine and go past the tiny, 18th-century Portuguese Jewish cemetery at No. 44. Cross over the canal on the Pont de Crimée, near the church of St-Jacques–St-Christophe, before continuing up the quai de la Marne. Yet another option is to follow avenue Secrétan southeast from the Rotonde to the picturesque **Parc des Buttes-Chaumont** ⑦. Wend your way left around this tumbling park—once a quarry—and skirt the lake before climbing to the top of the man-made cliff for a panoramic view of the city.

Leave the park from the eastern corner. Turn left on rue Botzaris, and then right up rue de Crimée. Take the first left up a flight of stairs to the dowdy little street called villa Albert-Robida. You're now on the fringe of the **Quartier d'Amérique** ⑧, so called because the stone quarried in the Buttes-Chaumont is said to have been used to build the White

Place de la République to La Villette

House. The two- and three-story houses around here—originally quar-riers' cottages—are a far cry from the seven-story buildings dominat-ing the rest of Paris. Turn left down rue Arthur-Rozier and continue to rue de Mouzaïa. These days these small houses are very desirable: some of the prettiest are found in the *villas* or mews, leading off of rue de Mouzaïa. Venture up quaint, cobbled villa Émile-Lobet on the right—the five gray skyscrapers looming at the far end are a chilling architectural contrast to the colorful paintwork and ivy-covered rail-ings of the houses. Turn left and left again down flagstone-paved villa de Bellevue and cross to villa du Progrès. Take a left at the bottom of the street and then a right down rue de la Fraternité to reach **place du Rhin-et-Danube** ⑨.

More mewsy alleyways can be found on either side of rue Miguel-Hi-dalgo, with a cute view of the foursquare brick tower of the church of St-Francis d'Assisi at the far end of villa des Boërs. From here, take a right on rue Compans and head up to the **Cimetière de La Villette** ⑩. The entrance is flanked by a grim stone cube that once served as the local morgue. Admire the extrovert windows and roofline of the school opposite; then take allée Darius-Milhaud along the side of the ceme-tery. This promenade curves through the heart of the district, becom-ing allée Arthur-Honegger and ending in a flight of steps topped by the bulky silhouette of the Cité de la Musique, a modern music academy. The entry to the Parc de La Villette is down to the left.

TIMING

If you want to enjoy lunch, dinner, or the sizzling night scene at one of Oberkampf's trendy outposts, begin your exploration at midday. The stretch along the Canal St-Martin from place de la République to the Bassin de La Villette, via the Hôpital St-Louis, is approximately 2 km (1 mi). You may want to allot a whole morning or afternoon to ex-ploring the Parc des Buttes-Chaumont or the Parc de La Villette. Or you may want to return to one of these on another day.

Sights to See

❷ **Canal St-Martin.** The canal was built, at the behest of Napoléon, from 1802 to 1825, with the aim of providing the city with drinking water. It was not assigned to navigable traffic until the 1850s and was partly covered (between Bastille and République) by Haussmann in 1862. With its quiet banks, locks, and footbridges, the canal is much loved by nov-elists and film directors; Simenon's famous inspector, Maigret, solved many a mystery along its deceptively sleepy banks. Major development has transformed the northern end of the canal, around place de Stal-ingrad and its 18th-century rotunda, and there are €1.50 boat trips (⊠ Embarkation at 13 quai de la Loire, La Villette) along the once in-dustrial Bassin de La Villette to the nearby Parc de La Villette. *Métro: Jacques-Bonsergent, Jaurès.*

❿ **Cimetière de La Villette** (La Villette Cemetery). One of Paris's smallest cemeteries, it is reserved for residents of the 19ᵉ arrondissement. ⊠ *En-trance on rue d'Hautpoul, La Villette. Métro: Ourcq.*

❸ **Hôpital St-Louis** (St. Louis Hospital). Though it's not, technically speak-ing, a tourist sight, no one will begrudge you a discreet visit to Paris's first hospital, erected in 1607–10, at the same time as the place des Vosges. The main courtyard, known as the Quadrilatère Historique, with its steep roofs and corner pavilions, has been remarkably preserved. The chapel, tucked away along rue de la Grange-aux-Belles, was the first building in Paris to be lit by gaslight and shelters *Suffer Little Chil-dren to Come unto Me*, a painting by Charles de La Fosse (1636–1716), and a handsome wood balcony carved with trumpeting angels and the

PARIS NOW: TABLE-HOPPING IN TRENDY OBERKAMPF

REMEMBER KIKI DE MONTPAR-NASSE? Once Picasso's playmate, immortalized by Man Ray and other Parisian artists of the 1920s and 1930s, this party-hearty muse often martini-ed the night away at the clubs and ateliers in Montparnasse. Today, that district is more than a bit dim and dull, so if you're looking for today's Kikis (or wannabes), head on over to the Ober-kampf area set to east of the place de la République. Here, the City of Light burns brightest between boulevard Voltaire and boulevard de Ménilmontant, midway between Bastille and Belleville, on rue Oberkampf, rue St-Maur, and rue Jean-Pierre-Timbaud. You've got to take good care to specify the geography because the district didn't really have a name or a strongly defined character—unlike the hilly, neighboring, erstwhile villages of Belleville and Ménilmontant—until very recently, when the *bohos* (Paris slang for arty bohemians) moved in on what had traditionally been proletarian and im-migrant turf.

The mood is the thing here—not just the mood music that plays after sundown but the shabby, down-to-earth feel of nar-row streets, largely unmolested by developers, that exude vague nostalgia for quintessen-tial, lived-in, dyed-in-the-wool Paris. These streets still crackle with energy, none more than rue d'Oberkampf between the Ménilmontant and Parmentier métro stations, whose long stretch of bars and restaurants have taken their cue from Café Charbon (No 109; ☎ 01–43–57–55–13), a converted turn-of-the-20th-cen-tury dance hall ostentatiously proud of its huge mirrors, smoke-stained ceilings, and ultra-trendy dance club, the Nouveau Casino (in the back room). The district plays on its image as a working-class ante to the designer bars of Bastille and Beaubourg: Café Mercerie (No. 98; ☎ 01–43–38–81–30), across from Café Charbon, takes its name—and painted sign—from the draper's shop that used to be here.

Looking back, the first wave of bars and boutiques hereabouts looked like they had been thrown together by impoverished art students during a particularly drunken weekend; many of those, sadly, are long gone, replaced by more conventionally cool joints. Still funky and fun, the street is losing some of its street credo as a better-healed clientele pushes out the pioneering boho crowd that first claimed the district as its own.

But while rue Oberkampf itself looks des-tined to be Bastilled into *bobo* (bour-geois bohemian) complacency, its neighboring streets still have their edges intact, especially rue Jean-Pierre-Timbaud, home to many hot haunts: **L'Auberge** (No 4; ☎ 01–48–06–15–29), **Le Ves-tiaire** (No. 64; ☎ 01–43–55–42–50), **L'Autre Café** (No. 62; ☎ 01–40–21–03–07), and the friendly **Café Cannibale** (No 93; ☎ 01–49–29–95–59), one of the first new-school spots in the area. Rue de la Folie-Méricourt, lined with food shops and restaurants on its way south to the twin-spired neo-Gothic church of St-Ambroise, still epitomizes the area's un-pretentious charm, with discreet, leafy court-yards—passage Beslay, passage Commun, cité Popincourt—sharing sidewalks with upmarket bars and working-class canteens.

A little farther south, near métro Charonne, is one of the city's most famous wine bars, **Jacques Mélac**, at 42 rue Léon Frot (☎ 01–43–70–59–27), where genial Jacques sports the largest mustache in town and grows his own grapes on a vigor-ous vine along the front of the building. The area is changing fast, however. Used to be that the nearest you'd come to a tourist site were the five unphotogenic granite blocks at the angle of rue de la Roquette and rue de la Croix-Faubin, which served as the base for Paris's last public guillotine through 1899. Soon, neck-craners and camera-toters will have investigated every corner of the quartier. So make haste—*faites vite!*

monograms of hospital founders Henri IV and Maria de' Medici. ✉ *Entrances on av. Richerand, rue de la Grange-aux-Belles, av. Claude-Vellefaux, République.* ◷ *Daily 5 AM–9 PM; chapel weekday afternoons.*

❹ Hôtel du Nord (North Hotel). Despite its unassuming white facade, this hotel—restored to its former glory, although now a café-restaurant—is famous in France for its starring role in director Marcel Carné's 1938 movie of the same name. ✉ *102 quai de Jemmappes, République,* ☎ *01–40–40–78–78. Métro: Jacques-Bonsergent.*

⓻ Parc des Buttes-Chaumont. This picturesque, steep-sloped park in northeast Paris has a lake, waterfall, and cliff-top folly. Until Napoléon III's town planner Baron Haussmann got his hands on it in the 1860s, the area was a garbage dump and quarry—legend has it that the local gypsum was used in the foundation of the White House. Children large and small will enjoy the **Guignol de Paris** (an open-air puppet theater) on the northern side of the park; shows start (weather permitting) at 3:30 PM on Wednesday and on weekends (€2.50 charge). ✉ *Rue Botzaris, Buttes-Chaumont. Métro: Buttes-Chaumont, Botzaris.*

⓺ Parc de La Villette. Until the 1970s this 130-acre site, in an unfashionable corner of northeast Paris commonly known as "La Villette," was originally a cattle market and *abattoir* (slaughterhouse). Only the slaughterhouse, known as **La Grande Halle** (Great Hall), remains: a magnificent iron-and-glass structure ingeniously transformed into an exhibition-cum-concert center. But everything else here—from the science museum and spherical cinema to the music academy, each interconnected by designer gardens with canopied walkways and red cubical follies—is futuristic.

Although La Villette breathes the architectural panache of the Mitterrand era, the late president only oversaw one project himself: the **Cité de la Musique,** a giant postmodern music academy designed by architect Christian de Portzamparc, complete with a state-of-the-art concert hall and the spectacular **Musée de la Musique** (Music Museum) (✉ 221 av. Jean-Jaurès, La Villette, ☎ 01–44–84–44–84; ✉ €6; ◷ Tues.–Sat. noon–6). The museum contains a mind-tingling array of 900 instruments; their sounds and story are evoked with wireless headphones (ask for English commentary).

The **park** itself, laid out in the 1980s to the design of Bernard Tschumi—a heavyweight of the cerebral Postmodern movement—links the academy to the science museum half a mile away. Water and the Grande Halle are the park's focal elements. Two bridges cross the Canal de l'Ourcq, which bisects the park; one becomes a covered walkway, running parallel to the Canal St-Denis, and continues up to the science museum—itself surrounded by the unruffled sheen of a broad moat, reflecting the spherical outline of **La Géode.** This looks like a huge silver golf ball but is actually a cinema made of polished steel, with a 100m² hemispherical screen.

The pompously styled **Cité des Sciences et de l'Industrie** (Industry and Science Museum) tries to do for science and industry what the Centre Pompidou does for modern art. Adrien Fainsilber's rectangular building, also conceived in the 1970s, even looks like the Centre Pompidou, minus the gaudy piping. Inside, displays are bright and thought-provoking, though many are in French only. The brave attempt to render technology fun and easy involves 60 do-it-yourself contraptions that make you feel more participant than onlooker. Lines (especially during school holidays) can be intimidating. ✉ *30 av. Corentin-Cariou, La Villette,* ☎ *01–40–05–80–00,* WEB *www.cite-sciences.fr.* ✉ *€7.7 in-*

cludes planetarium. ☉ *Tues.–Sun. 10–6. Métro: Porte de La Villette,*
Porte de Pantin.

❶ **Place de la République.** This large, oblong square, laid out by Haussmann in 1856–65, is dominated by a matronly, Stalin-size statue symbolizing *The Republic* (1883). The square is often used as a rallying
point for demonstrations. République has more métro lines than any
other station in Paris. *Métro: République.*

❾ **Place du Rhin-et-Danube.** Although seven streets intersect at this square
in the Quartier d'Amérique, it retains a rural, unhurried feel. The
small white statue of a young girl clutching a sheaf of wheat recalls
the area's pastoral origins, before it was absorbed into Paris in the 19th
century. The métro station underneath was built in a former quarry.
Métro: Danube.

❽ **Quartier d'Amérique** (America Quarter). This neighborhood is so
named because the gypsum that was once quarried here (mostly on the
site that was transformed into the Parc des Buttes-Chaumont in the
1860s) was shipped to America and used, so the story goes, in building the White House. The quartier is made up of a grid of streets and
narrow mews (known as "villas") lined with modest two- and three-
story houses once inhabited by quarriers—now some of the most
sought-after homes in the city. *Métro: Botzaris.*

❺ **Rotonde de La Villette.** This strange circular building was one of the
tollhouses built around the edge of Paris by Nicolas Ledoux in the 1780s.
Most of these austere, daunting buildings, symbols, to the populace,
of taxes and oppression, were promptly dismantled during the Revolution. Luckily, the Rotunda survived as a relic of Ledoux's thrilling
architecture. Like Mitterrand, Ledoux was fascinated by masonic symbols such as spheres and pyramids. Although the Rotunda is partly ob-
scured by the aboveground métro as you approach from the south, its
clean-cut outlines and honey-color stonework can be admired from the
north, where a paved courtyard overlooks the Bassin de La Villette and
the barges lining up at the lock to reach the Canal St-Martin. ⊠ *Pl.*
de Stalingrad, La Villette. Métro: Stalingrad.

FROM BASTILLE TO NATION

At the center of the Bastille neighborhood is place de la Bastille, site
of the infamous prison attacked by the Parisian people on July 14, 1789—
an event that came to symbolize the beginning of the French Revolution. The only folks likely to storm the Bastille these days are theatergoers
lining up for seats at the modern Opéra Bastille. They are joined by
hipsters, who now flock here as the neighborhood—along with the adjacent sectors of Belleville and Menilmontant (the latter immortalized
in the Oscar-winning 1957 film of Albert Lamorrise, *The Red Balloon*)—
was gentrified, largely in commemoration of the bicentennial of the
Revolution in 1989. Soon, this area became one of the liveliest areas
in Paris and galleries, shops, theaters, cafés, restaurants, and bars still
fill formerly decrepit buildings and alleys. After a decade of the artsy
crowd mingling with the blue-collar natives, many of the latter have
moved on, but the hip spots are holding on and still making fashion
waves. Southeast of the Bastille are the imposing place de la Nation
and the up-and-coming Bercy neighborhood. Other highlights of this
tour include the verdant Bois de Vincennes, the spectacular Bibliothèque
Nationale François-Mitterrand, and the evocative Père-Lachaise cemetery, final resting place of Balzac, Proust, Wilde, and many other famous figures.

Numbers in the text correspond to numbers in the margin and on the
From Bastille to Nation map.

A Good Walk

Start your walk at **place de la Bastille** ①, which is easily accessible by
métro. Today the square is dominated by the Colonne de Juillet and
the curving glass facade of the modern **Opéra de la Bastille** ②. Leading away from the square is rue de la Roquette, a street alive with shops
and cafés, which in turn leads first to vibrant rue de Lappe, lined with
bars, clubs, and restaurants; then to rue des Taillandiers and rue Keller,
with their bookshops and music stores. All these streets are worth exploring—and rue de Lappe is especially hopping at night. Turn right
at the end of rue de Lappe onto rue de Charonne to reach rue du
Faubourg-St-Antoine, famous for its cabinetmakers. You'll see why if
you take the unevenly cobbled passage du Chantier, just opposite. Its
boutiques sell furniture and nothing else. (Peek into other *passages* as
well for more glimpses of the behind-the-scenes life of the Bastille.)

Continue along rue du Faubourg-St-Antoine, and then take a right down
avenue Ledru-Rollin, crossing rue Charenton and passing the modern
church of St-Antoine, to reach avenue Daumesnil. The disused railroad
viaduct has been tastefully transformed into a series of designer boutiques with a walkway on top—restyled the **Viaduc des Arts** ③.

Saunter down as far as rue Hector-Malot; then turn right across avenue Daumesnil and head down boulevard Diderot to Gare de Lyon
métro station. If you'd like to visit the giant national library, the **Bibliothèque Nationale François-Mitterrand** ④, take line 14 from Gare de
Lyon for three stops to the Bibliothèque station. Or get off one stop
earlier at Cour St-Emilion and explore the revamped **Bercy** ⑤ neighborhood, with its restored wine warehouses and innovative park. The
four L-shape towers of the national library loom across the Seine as

you head west toward the grass-covered walls of the Palais Omnisports stadium. Follow rue de Bercy, under the elephantine Ministère des Finances, and then turn right through the tunnel, up to rue de Rambouillet. Here rejoin avenue de Daumesnil and the Viaduc des Arts. Head up the steps to see what's on top of the viaduct: gone are the tracks, ousted by the Promenade Plantée, a walkway lined with trees and flowers. The walkway continues for another 2½ km (1½ mi). But you might just want to stay on it for about 1 km (½ mi) before turning left on rue de Picpus. Some 350 yards up on the right is the entry to the **Cimetière de Picpus** ⑥, where General Lafayette is buried.

Continue on rue de Picpus for about 250 yards, and then cross rue Fabre-d'Eglantine to reach the majestic **place de la Nation** ⑦, flanked to the right by two towering columns that once marked the eastern entry to Paris. From here it's a short métro ride to the city's most famous cemetery, the **Cimetière du Père-Lachaise** ⑧, or to the **Bois de Vincennes** ⑨, a large wooded park with lakes, castle, and a zoo.

TIMING

The walk from place de la Bastille to place de la Nation, including an excursion to the Bercy neighborhood, is about 7 km (4½ mi) long and takes about four hours to complete. Count on more time if you also plan to visit the national library.

Sights to See

❺ **Bercy.** Bercy is a testament to the French genius for urban renewal. Tucked away on the Right Bank of the Seine, south of the Gare de Lyon in the 12ᵉ arrondissement, this colorful district was for decades filled with warehouses storing wine from the provinces. Now sport and finance set the tone. The first thing you'll see as you emerge from the Bercy métro station is the mighty glass wall of the **Ministère des Finances** (Finance Ministry). To the left is the ingeniously sloping, grass-walled **Palais Omnisports,** a weird-looking stadium that hosts sports and music events and seats 17,000, approached on all sides by gleaming white steps. Across the Seine, dominating the city's southeast skyline, are the four glass towers of architect Dominique Perrault's national library, the Bibliothèque Nationale François-Mitterrand. A hundred yards from the Palais Omnisports is a quirky, Cubist building designed by Frank Gehry, who described it as "a dancing figure in the park." It opened as the American Center in 1994 but closed in 1996 due to lack of funds and at press time was slated to reopen as a French movie museum, or **Maison du Cinéma.** The *jardin* (garden) opposite is a witty, state-of-the-art designer park with trim lawns, vines, rose-strewn arbors, and cobbled alleys lined by centurion trees providing a ghostly map of the former wineries. At the **Maison du Jardin** (Garden Center; ✉ rue Paul-Belmondo, Bercy &Tolbiac) you can get gardening advice and see displays of seasonal vegetables. Curved walkways fly over rue de Dijon to land by a Chinese lily pond near the Cour St-Emilion, where two rows of wine warehouses have been preserved, and transformed into boutiques and cafés. *Métro: Bercy, Cour St-Emilion.*

❹ **Bibliothèque Nationale François-Mitterrand** (National Library). As the last of former president François Mitterrand's *grands travaux* (grand building projects) before he left office, the *Très Grande Bibliothèque* (Very Big Library, as some facetiously call it) opened in 1997. The library subsumes the majority of the collections in the old Bibliothèque Nationale and, with some 11 million volumes between its walls, surpasses the Library of Congress as the largest library in the world. Architect Dominique Perrault's controversial design comprises four soaring 24-story towers that house most of the books. The design is thought-provoking—the four towers imitate four open volumes—but criticism was heaped on the project since books are housed in the towers (whose windows need to be covered to protect the stacks), while library goers are relegated to underground reading rooms. A stunning interior court-yard—sunk beneath ground level and invisible as you approach, despite its thicket of full-size evergreens—provides breathing space. You can visit part of the library for free or pay to inspect one of the temporary exhibits or to consult some of the more than 300,000 books (millions more are available to qualified researchers). The library is fronted by a giant flight of wooden steps overlooking the Seine (note the red *Bato-far* lightship, now used for techno concerts), but be warned—the library's two entrances are tucked away almost secretively at either end. ⊠ *11 quai François-Mauriac, Bercy/Tolbiac,* ☎ *01-53-79-59-59,* WEB *www.bnf.fr.* ⌨ *Library €3, exhibitions €5.4.* ☾ *Mid-Sept.–Aug., Tues.– Sat. 10–7, Sun. noon–6. Métro or RER: Bibliothèque.*

👌 ❾ **Bois de Vincennes** (Vincennes Woods). Sandwiched between the un-exciting suburb of Charenton and the working-class district of Fonte-nay-sous-Bois, to the southeast of Paris, the Bois de Vincennes is often considered a poor man's Bois de Boulogne. But the comparison is un-fair: the Bois de Vincennes is no more difficult to get to (⊠ métro to Porte Dorée; Bus 46) and has equally illustrious origins. It, too, was landscaped under Napoléon III, although a park had already been cre-ated here by Louis XV in 1731. The park has several lakes, notably **Lac Daumesnil,** with two islands, and **Lac des Minimes,** with three; rowboats can be hired at both. In addition, the park contains a zoo, a tribal art museum, the **Hippodrome de Vincennes** (a cinder-track race-course), a castle, a flower garden, and several cafés. In the spring there's an amusement park, the **Foire du Trône.** Bikes can be rented from the Château de Vincennes métro station for €4 an hour or €15 a day. Note that the Bois suffered severe damage in the hurricane that lashed Paris in 1999.

Some 600 mammals and 200 species of birds can be seen at the Bois de Vincennes's 33-acre **Parc Zoologique,** the largest zoo in France. The most striking element is the 210-ft steel and concrete Grand Rocher, an artificial rock built in 1934, inhabited by wild mountain sheep and penguins. You can take an elevator (⌨ €3) to the top. ⊠ *53 av. de St-Maurice, Bois de Vincennes,* ☎ *01-44-75-20-10.* ⌨ *€7.6.* ☾ *Apr.– Oct., daily 9–6; Nov.–Mar., daily 9–5. Métro: Porte Dorée.*

The **Musée des Arts d'Afrique et d'Océanie** (Museum of the Arts of Africa and Oceania) is at the Porte Dorée entrance to the Bois de Vin-cennes. It's housed in an Art Deco building, opened for the Colonial Exhibition in 1931, whose awesome facade is covered with a sculpted frieze depicting sites and attractions of France's erstwhile overseas empire. Inside, headdresses, bronzes, jewelry, masks, statues, and pot-tery from former French colonies are spaciously displayed under sub-tle spotlighting. There is also a tropical aquarium (open from 10 AM weekends) in the basement, with rows of tanks filled with colorful trop-ical fish. ⊠ *293 av. Daumesnil, Bois de Vincennes,* ☎ *01-44-74-85-01.* ⌨ *€4.6.* ☾ *Wed.–Mon. 10–5:30. Métro: Porte Dorée.*

The historic **Château de Vincennes** is on the northern edge of the Bois de Vincennes. Built in the 15th century by various French kings, the castle is France's medieval Versailles, an imposing, high-walled castle surrounded by a dry moat and dominated by a 170-ft keep. The sprawling castle grounds also contain a modest replica (built 1379–1552) of the Sainte-Chapelle on the Ile de la Cité and two elegant, clas-sical wings designed by Louis Le Vau in the mid-17th century, that house the archives of the French armed forces and are closed to the public. ⊠ *Av. de Paris, Bois de Vincennes,* ☎ *01-48-08-31-20,* WEB *www.*

monum.fr. ✉ €5.5. ⊙ *Apr.–Sept., daily 10–noon and 1:15–6:30; Oct.–Mar., daily 10–noon and 1:15–5. Métro: Château de Vincennes.*

The **Parc Floral de Paris** (Paris Floral Park) is the Bois de Vincennes's 70-acre flower garden. It includes a lake and water garden and is renowned for its seasonal displays of blooms. It also contains a miniature train, a game area, and an "exotarium" with tropical fish and reptiles. ⊠ *Rte. de la Pyramide, Bois de Vincennes,* ☎ *01–55–94–20–20.* ✉ *€1.5. ⊙ Apr.–Sept., daily 9:30–8; Oct.–Mar., daily 9:30–5. Métro: Château de Vincennes.*

★ ❽ **Cimetière du Père-Lachaise** (Father Lachaise Cemetery). The world's most illustrious necropolis, the 118-acre Père-Lachaise cemetery is the final stop for more illustrious people than you could every meet in a lifetime. Plots are prime real estate and now only the outrageously wealthy can afford to be laid to rest with the famous. Jim Morrison's fans rage on at the eternal party in Division 6, but otherwise a serene Gothic aura persists, as tombs compete in grandiosity, originality, and often, alas, dilapidation. Cobbled avenues, steep slopes, and lush vegetation create a powerful atmosphere. Named after the Jesuit father—Louis XIV's confessor—who led the reconstruction of the Jesuit Rest House completed here in 1682, the cemetery houses the tombs of the famed medieval lovers Héloïse and Abelard; composer Chopin; the playwright Molière; the writers Honoré Balzac, Marcel Proust, Paul Eluard, Oscar Wilde, and Gertrude Stein and Alice B. Toklas (buried in the same grave); the popular French actress Simone Signoret and her husband, singer-actor Yves Montand; and Edith Piaf. Perhaps the most popular shrine is to rock star Morrison, where dozens of Doors fans, following the trail of spray-painted graffiti, come to pay homage to the songwriter. (Now, along with the fans, there's a guard who makes sure you don't stay too long.) Of less dubious taste is the sculpted tomb of Romantic artist Théodore Géricault, shown brush in hand above a bronze relief plaque replicating his *Raft of the Medusa.* The cemetery was the site of the Paris Commune's final battle, on May 28, 1871, when the rebel troops were rounded up, lined against the Mur des Fédérés (Federalists' Wall) in the southeast corner, and shot. Get hold of a map at the entrance—Père-Lachaise is an easy place to get lost in. ⊠ *Entrances on rue des Rondeaux, bd. de Ménilmontant, and rue de la Réunion, Père-Lachaise. ⊙ Easter–Sept., daily 8–6; Oct.–Easter, daily 8 AM–dusk. Métro: Gambetta, Philippe-Auguste, Père-Lachaise.*

❻ **Cimetière de Picpus.** Most of those 1,300 executed at the guillotine on place de la Nation in 1794 were buried in a mass grave at the nearby Picpus Cemetery. Also buried here is General Lafayette, whose grave site can be identified by its U.S. flag. ⊠ *Entrance at 35 rue Picpus (once inside, ring bell of caretaker's home for access to cemetery), Bastille/Nation,* ☎ *01–43–44–18–54.* ✉ *€2.3. ⊙ Oct.–Easter, Tues.–Sat. 2–4; Easter–Sept., Tues.–Sat. 2–6. Guided visits Tues.–Sun. at 2:30 and 4. Métro or RER: Nation.*

❷ **Opéra de la Bastille** (Bastille Opera). Designed by Argentine-born architect Carlos Ott, the state-of-the-art Bastille Opera, on the south side of place de la Bastille, opened July 14, 1989, in commemoration of the bicentennial of the French Revolution and in hope of making Paris once more the center of European opera. The steeply sloping auditorium seats more than 3,000 and has earned more plaudits than the curving glass facade, which strikes Parisians as depressingly like that of yet another modern office building. ⊠ *Pl. de la Bastille, Bastille/Nation,* ☎ *01–40–01–19–70.* ✉ Guided tours €10 (call ahead to book). Métro: Bastille.

❶ Place de la Bastille. Nothing remains of the infamous Bastille prison destroyed at the beginning of the French Revolution. Until 1988, there was little more to see here than a huge traffic circle and the **Colonne de Juillet** (July Column). As part of the countrywide celebrations for July 1989, the bicentennial of the French Revolution, the Opéra de la Bastille was erected, inspiring substantial redevelopment on the surrounding streets, especially along rue de Lappe—once a haunt of Edith Piaf—and rue de la Roquette. What was formerly a humdrum neighborhood rapidly became one of the most sparkling and attractive in the city. Streamlined art galleries, funky jazz clubs, and Spanish-style tapas bars set the tone.

The Bastille, or, more properly, the Bastille St-Antoine, was a massive building, protected by eight immense towers and a wide moat (its ground plan is marked by paving stones set into the modern square). It was built by Charles V in the late 14th century. He intended it not as a prison but as a fortress to guard the eastern entrance to the city. By the reign of Louis XIII (1610–43), however, the Bastille was used almost exclusively to house political prisoners. Voltaire, the Marquis de Sade, and the mysterious Man in the Iron Mask were all incarcerated here, along with many other unfortunates. It was this obviously political role—specifically, the fact that the prisoners were nearly always held by order of the king—that led the "furious mob" (in all probability no more than a largely unarmed rabble) to break into the prison on July 14, 1789, kill the governor, steal what firearms they could find, and free the seven remaining prisoners.

Later in 1789, the prison was knocked down. A number of the original stones were carved into facsimiles of the Bastille and sent to each of the provinces as a memento of royal oppression. The key to the prison was given by Lafayette to George Washington, and it has remained at Mount Vernon ever since. The power of legend being what it is, what soon became known as the Storming of the Bastille was elevated to the status of a pivotal event in the course of the French Revolution, demonstrating the newfound power of a long-suffering population. Thus it was that July 14 became the French national day, an event now celebrated with patriotic fervor throughout the country. *Métro: Bastille.*

❼ Place de la Nation. The towering early 19th-century, statue-topped columns on majestic place de la Nation stand sentinel at the Gates of Paris—the eastern sector's equivalent of the Arc de Triomphe, with the bustling but unpretentious Cours de Vincennes providing a down-to-earth echo of the Champs-Élysées. Place de la Nation (known as place du Trône—Throne Square—until the Revolution) was the scene of 1,300 executions at the guillotine in 1794. Most were buried in a mass grave at the nearby Cimetière de Picpus. *Métro or RER: Nation.*

❸ Viaduc des Arts (Arts Viaduct). With typical panache, Paris planners have converted this redbrick viaduct—originally the last mile of the suburban railroad that led to place de la Bastille (the site of the Bastille Opéra was once a station)—into a stylish promenade. Upscale art, crafts, and furniture shops occupy the archways below, and a walkway, with shrubs, flowers, and benches, has replaced the tracks up above. ⊠ *Av. Daumesnil, Bastille/Nation. Métro: Gare de Lyon, Daumesnil, Bel-Air.*

THE MARAIS

The Marais is one of Paris's oldest, most picturesque, and most sought-after residential districts. Renovation is the keynote; well into the '70s this was one of the poorest areas, filled with dilapidated tenements and squalid courtyards. The area's regeneration was sparked by the build-

R. de Poitou

R. Froissart

R. du
Roi-Dorée

Pl. de
la République

10

R. Chariot

3e

R. des 4 Fils

R. de Turenne

St-Sébastien M

R. St-Claude

R. de Thorigny

15

R. de la Perle

14

R. des Arquebusiers

R. Vieille du Temple

13

R. Villehardouin

R. Etzévir

R. du Parc Royal

R. des Francs - Bourgeois

16

R. Payenne

Sq. George
Cain

R. St-Gilles

des Rosiers

17

R. Sévigné

R. des Minimes

R. du Foin

R. de Béarn

**Chemin
Vert** M

Bd. Beaumarchais

Jouffes

R. F Duval

Pavée

R. Pavée

R. de Sévigné

R. de Pas de la Mule

18

Pl. de
la Bastille

**St-Paul–
Le Marais** M

R. St-Antoine

R. de Turenne

19

25

R. de Fourcy

4e

22

R. de Birague

R. des Tournelles

R. Charlemagne

R. des Jardins

R. Neuve

21

R. de Figuier

24

23

St-Pierre

20

ing of the Centre Pompidou (known to Parisians as Beaubourg), which ranks alongside Frank Gehry's Guggenheim Museum in Bilbao, Spain, as Europe's most architecturally whimsical museum. The gracious architecture of the 17th and early 18th centuries, however, sets the tone for the rest of the Marais. Today, most of the Marais's *hôtels particuliers*—loosely, "mansions," onetime residences of aristocratic families—have been restored by rich, with-it couples, and many of the buildings are now museums, the grandest of them being the Musée Carnavalet and the most visited of them the Musée Picasso. There are trendy boutiques and cafés among the kosher shops of the traditionally Jewish neighborhood around rue des Rosiers.

The history of the Marais—the word, incidentally, means marsh or swamp—goes back to when Charles V, king of France in the 14th century, moved his court here from the Ile de la Cité. However, it wasn't until Henri IV laid out place Royale, today place des Vosges, in the early 17th century, that the Marais became *the* place to live. Aristocratic dwellings began to dot the neighborhood, and their salons filled with the beau monde. But following the French Revolution, the Marais rapidly became one of the most deprived, dissolute areas in Paris.

It was spared the attentions of Baron Haussmann, the man who rebuilt so much of Paris in the mid-19th century—so, though crumbling, the Marais's ancient, golden-hue buildings and squares remained intact. You won't be able to get into many of the historic homes that spangle the neighborhood but this shouldn't stop you from admiring their handsome facades or trying to glimpse through the formal portals (*portes cochères*) to study the discreet courtyards that lurk behind them.

Jewish heritage is also an important part of the Marais's history. Jewish immigrants began settling in this area in the 13th century, though the main wave of immigrants (from Russia and Central Europe) came in the 19th century. Another wave—of Sephardic Jews from North Africa—arrived here in the 1960s following Algerian independence. Today there are still many kosher shops and restaurants among the trendy, newer arrivals.

Numbers in the text correspond to numbers in the margin and on the Marais map.

A Good Walk

Begin this walk in front of the **Hôtel de Ville** ①. You can't inspect the lavish interior, but head left to the traffic-free square, with its fountains and forest of street lamps, to admire the exuberant facade. Turn left along the quai de l'Hôtel de Ville; *bouquinistes* (booksellers) line the Seine, and you may catch a glimpse of the towers of Notre-Dame through the trees. Take the next left up picturesque rue des Barres to the church of **St-Gervais–St-Protais** ②, one of the last Gothic constructions in the country and a newly cleaned riot of Flamboyant decoration. From the church, head up to rue de Rivoli and take a left to get to rue du Temple. On your way, you'll pass one of the city's most popular department stores, the Bazar de l'Hôtel de Ville, or BHV, as it's known. Take rue de la Verrerie, the first street on your left, and pause as you cross rue du Renard to take in an impressive clash of architectural styles: to your left, the medieval silhouette of Notre-Dame; to the right, the gaudy colored pipes of the Centre Pompidou.

Cross rue du Renard and take the second right to the ornate 16th-century church of **St-Merri** ③. Rue St-Martin, full of stores, restaurants, and galleries, leads past the designer Café Beaubourg. Turn right to reach **Square Igor-Stravinsky** ④ with its unusual fountain; on one side of the square is IRCAM, where you can hear performances of contemporary classical music. Up ahead looms the newly renovated **Centre Pompidou** ⑤, overlooking a sloping piazza that is often aswarm with musicians, mimes, dancers, and fire-eaters. On the far side you can visit the **Atelier Brancusi** ⑥ before crossing rue Rambuteau to the Quartier de l'Horloge; take pedestrian rue de Brantôme and turn left onto rue Bernard-de-Clairvaux to admire *Le Défenseur du Temps*, a modern mechanical clock that whirs into action on the hour as St. George defends Time against a dragon, an eagle, or a crab (symbols of fire, air, and water). At noon, 6 PM, and 10 PM he takes on all three at once.

Return to rue Rambuteau, turn left, and cross rue Beaubourg. If you're with children, duck into impasse Berthaud to visit the **Musée de la Poupée** ⑦. Otherwise, stay on rue Rambuteau and turn left onto rue du Temple, where the **Musée d'Art et d'Histoire du Judaïsme** ⑧ is in the stately Hôtel de St-Aignan at No. 71. The **Hôtel de Montmor** ⑨ at No. 79 is another splendid 17th-century mansion. Take a right onto rue des Haudriettes; just off to the left at the next corner is the **Musée de la Chasse et de la Nature** ⑩, the Museum of Hunting and Nature, housed in one of the Marais's grandest mansions. Head right on rue des Archives, crossing rue des Haudriettes, and admire the medieval gateway with two fairy-tale towers, now part of the **Archives Nationales** ⑪, the archives museum entered from rue des Francs-Bourgeois around to the left.

Continue past the Crédit Municipal (the city's grandiose pawnbroking concern), the Dôme du Marais restaurant (housed in a circular 18th-century chamber originally used for auctions), and the church of **Notre-Dame des Blancs-Manteaux** ⑫, with its superb inlaid pulpit. A corner-turret signals rue Vieille-du-Temple; turn left past the palatial Hôtel de Rohan (now part of the Archives Nationales), then right onto rue de la Perle to the **Musée Bricard** ⑬, occupying a mansion as impressive as the assembly of locks and keys within. From here it is a step down rue de Thorigny (opposite) to the palatial 17th-century Hôtel Salé, now the **Musée Picasso** ⑭. Church lovers may wish to detour up rue de Thorigny and along rue du Roi-Doré to admire the severe neoclassic portico of **St-Denis-du-St-Sacrement** ⑮ and the *Deposition* by Delacroix inside.

Backtrack along rue de Thorigny and turn left onto rue du Parc-Royal. Halfway down rue Elzévir is the **Musée Cognacq-Jay** ⑯, a must if you are interested in 18th-century furniture, porcelain, and paintings. If you can't face another museum, take the next right, rue Payenne, instead, and tarry in the sunken garden at square Georges-Cain, opposite the 16th-century Hôtel de Marle, now used as a Swedish culture center. Next door you can enjoy a rear view of the steep-roofed Cognacq-Jay building. Rue Payenne becomes rue Pavée as you pass beneath a lookout turret. Peek into the next courtyard on the left at the cheerfully askew facade of the Bibliothèque Historique de la Ville de Paris. Continuing on rue Pavée takes you to rue des Rosiers, with its excellent Jewish bakeries and falafel shops. Back on rue des Francs-Bourgeois is the **Musée Carnavalet** ⑰, the Paris History Museum, in perhaps the swankiest edifice in the Marais, and famous for its period rooms and collection of the decorative arts. A short walk along rue des Francs-Bourgeois takes you to large, pink-brick **place des Vosges** ⑱, lined with covered arcades, and the most beautiful legacy of the French Renaissance still extant in Paris. At No. 6, you can visit the **Maison de Victor Hugo** ⑲, where the workaholic French author once lived.

Exit the square by rue de Birague to reach rue St-Antoine: to the left is the church of **Ste-Marie** ⑳; to the right is the **Hôtel de Sully** ㉑, which houses the Caisse Nationale des Monuments Historiques (Historic Monuments Trust) at No. 62 and a textbook example of 17th-century architecture. Across rue St-Antoine, pause to admire the mighty Baroque church of **St-Paul–St-Louis** ㉒. Take the left-hand side door out of the church into narrow passage St-Paul, and then turn right onto rue St-Paul, past the grid of courtyards that make up the Village St-Paul antiques-shops complex. Children enjoy the **Académie de la Magie** ㉓ farther down at No. 11. At rue de l'Ave-Maria, turn right to reach the painstakingly restored **Hôtel de Sens** ㉔, a strange mixture of defensive stronghold and fairy-tale château. If you are a photography fan, head up rue Figuier, then down rue de Fourcy to the **Maison Européenne de la Photographie** ㉕. Head left on rue François-Miron past the 17th-century **Hôtel de Beauvais** ㉖. Note the two half-timber houses, among the oldest in Paris, across the street at numbers 11 and 13, and the Belle Epoque bakery, Au Petit Versailles, at the corner of Rue Tiron. The next left, rue Geoffroy-l'Asnier, leads past the stark **Mémorial du Martyr Juif Inconnu** ㉗, a huge bronze memorial to those who died in Nazi concentration camps.

TIMING

At just over 5 km (3 mi) long, this walk will comfortably take a whole morning or afternoon. If you choose to spend an hour or two in any of the museums along the way, allow a full day. Be prepared to wait in line at the Picasso Museum. Note that some of the museums don't open until the afternoon and that many shops in the Marais don't open until late morning.

Sights to See

㉓ **Académie de la Magie** (Academy of Magic). Housed in a 16th-century cellar, this museum contains antique magic paraphernalia, including some from Houdini's bag of tricks. There's a magic show every hour. ⊠ *11 rue St-Paul, Le Marais,* ☎ *01–42–72–13–26.* ⊡ €7. ☉ *Wed. and weekends 2–7. Métro: St-Paul.*

★ ⑪ **Archives Nationales** (National Archives). Palatially housed in a mansion that showcases the earliest flowering of the elegant Rococo style of the Louis XV era—the Hôtel de Soubise—the Archives Nationales will tempt serious history buffs, who will be fascinated by the thousands of intricate historical documents, dating from the Merovingian period to the 20th century. The highlights are the Edict of Nantes (1598), the Treaty of Westphalia (1648), the wills of Louis XIV and Napoléon, and the Declaration of Human Rights (1789). Louis XVI's diary is also in the collection, containing his sadly ignorant entry for July 14, 1789, the day the Bastille was stormed and, for all intents and purposes, the French Revolution began: "*Rien*" ("Nothing").

The buildings housing the Archives have their own attractions, too: the **Hôtel de Soubise** and the **Hôtel de Rohan** (originally built for the archbishop of Strasbourg), across the lawn facing rue Vieille-du-Temple, both display the cool, column-fronted elegance of the mid-18th century; the Porte de Clisson, a turreted gateway on rue des Archives, was erected in 1380 for the Hôtel de Clisson, the Paris base of the Duke of Bedford (regent of France during the English occupation from 1420 to 1435). The Hôtel de Soubise was one of the grandest houses in Paris when built. Connoisseurs of the decorative arts flock to this museum to see the apartments of the prince and princess de Soubise; their rooms were among the first examples of the Rococo—the lighter, more dainty style that followed the heavier Baroque opulence favored by the age of Louis XIV. ⊠ *60 rue des Francs-Bourgeois, Le Marais,* ☎ *01–40–27–60–96.* ⊡ €3. ☉ *Mon. and Wed.–Fri. 10–5:45, weekends 1:45–5:45. Métro: Rambuteau.*

❻ Atelier Brancusi (Brancusi Studio). Romanian-born sculptor Constantin Brancusi settled in Paris in 1898 at age 22. This light, airy museum in front of the Centre Pompidou, designed by Renzo Piano, contains four glass-fronted rooms that reconstitute Brancusi's working studios, crammed with smooth, stylized works from all periods of his career. ⊠ *Place Georges-Pompidou, Beaubourg/Les Halles,* ☎ *01–44–78–12– 33.* 🎫 *€5.5.* ☺ *Weekends 1–7. Métro: Rambuteau.*

❺ Centre Pompidou (Pompidou Center). The Centre National d'Art et de Culture Georges-Pompidou is its full name, although it is known to Parisians simply as Beaubourg (for the neighborhood). Georges Pompidou (1911–74) was the president of France who launched the project. Unveiled in 1977, three years after his death, the Centre Pompidou was soon attracting more than 8 million visitors a year—five times more than intended. Hardly surprising, then, that it was soon showing signs of fatigue: the much-vaunted, gaudily painted service pipes snaking up the exterior (painted the same colors that were used to identify them on the architects' plans) needed continual repainting, while the plastic tubing enclosing the exterior escalators was cracked and grimy. The center was closed for two years of top-to-bottom renovation before reopening on the first day of the new millennium.

Place Georges-Pompidou, a gently sloping piazza with a giant gold flowerpot in one corner and the Atelier Brancusi in the other, leads to the center's sprawling, stationlike, concrete-floored entrance hall, with huge, psychedelically colorful signs, ticket counters on the back left, and an extensive art shop to your right, topped by a café. Head left for the escalator that climbs the length of the building, offering spectacular views of Paris, ranging from the Tour Montparnasse to the left, around to the Sacré-Coeur on its hill to the right. Since the recent renovations, the **Musée National d'Art Moderne** (Modern Art Museum, entrance on Level 4) has doubled in size to occupy most of the center's top two stories: one devoted to modern art, largely French; the other to a more international array of abstract work since the '60s. Also look for rotating exhibits of contemporary art. In addition, there's a public reference library, a language laboratory, an industrial design center, two cinemas, and a rooftop restaurant, Georges, which is noted for its great view of the skyline and Eiffel Tower. ⊠ *Pl. Georges-Pompidou, Beaubourg/Les Halles,* ☎ *01– 44–78–12–33,* [WEB] *www.centrepompidou.fr.* 🎫 *€5.5, including Atelier Brancusi; free 1st Sun. of month.* ☺ *Wed.–Mon. 11–9. Métro: Rambuteau.*

NEED A BREAK?
The view at night of the Eiffel Tower from **Georges** (⊠ Pl. Georges-Pompidou, Beaubourg/Les Halles, ☎ 01–44–78–47–99), the restaurant on the roof of the Centre Pompidou, is a marvel. The food is not up to the decor, but the buzz about this place draws a fun crowd.

㉖ Hôtel de Beauvais. Dating from 1655, this newly renovated mansion is one of the finest in the Marais. It was built for Pierre de Beauvais with surprisingly generous funding from the normally parsimonious Louis XIV. The reason for the Sun King's unwonted largesse: a reward for de Beauvais's willingness to turn a blind eye to the activities of his wife, Catherine-Henriette Bellier, in educating the young monarch in matters sexual. Louis, who came to the throne in 1643 at the age of 4, was 14 when de Beauvais's wife first gave him the benefit of her expertise; she was 40. ⊠ *68 rue François-Miron, Le Marais. Métro: St-Paul.*

❾ Hôtel de Montmor. This 17th-century mansion was built by M. Montmor, Louis XIII's financial adviser. His son ran a salon here frequented by such luminaries as philosopher and mathematician Pierre Gassend, physicist Gilles de Roberval, writer and professor of medicine Gui Patin, and Dutch astronomer Christian Huygens. This informal gathering of the "Boffins" prompted the creation of the Académie des Sciences in 1666. Note the huge windows and intricate ironwork on the second-floor balcony. ⊠ *79 rue de Temple, Le Marais. Métro: Rambuteau.*

㉔ Hôtel de Sens. One of a handful of civil buildings in Paris to have survived from the Middle Ages—witness the pointed corner towers, Gothic porch, and richly carved decorative details—this sumptuous Marais mansion was built in 1474 for the archbishop of Sens. Its best-known occupants were Henri IV and his queen, Marguérite, philanderers both. While Henri dallied with his mistresses—he is said to have had 56—at a series of royal palaces, Marguérite entertained her almost equally large number of lovers here. Today the building houses occasional exhibits and a fine-arts library, the **Bibliothèque Forney.** ⊠ *1 rue du Figuier, Le Marais,* ☎ *01–42–78–14–60.* 🎫 *Exhibitions €3.* 🕓 *Tues.–Sat. 1:30–8. Métro: Pont Marie.*

㉑ Hôtel de Sully. A major monument of the French Renaissance style, this mansion, begun in 1624, has a stately garden and a majestic courtyard with statues, richly carved pediments, and dormer windows. It is the headquarters of the **Caisse Nationale des Monuments Historiques,** responsible for administering France's historic monuments. Guided visits to Paris sites and buildings begin here, though all are conducted in French. The excellent bookshop, just inside the gate, has a plethora of publications on Paris, many of them in English. The bookshop is open daily 10–12:45 and 1:45–6. ⊠ *62 rue St-Antoine, Le Marais,* ☎ *01–44–61–20–00. Métro: St-Paul.*

❶ Hôtel de Ville (City Hall). Overlooking the Seine, the City Hall is the residence of the mayor of Paris. Until 1977, Paris was the only city in France without a mayor; with the creation of the post and the election of Jacques Chirac (elected president of France in 1995), leader of the right-of-center Gaullist party, the position became pivotal in both Parisian and French politics. It comes as no surprise, therefore, that Chirac oversaw a thorough restoration of the Hôtel de Ville, both inside and out.

The square in front of the Hôtel de Ville was relaid in the 1980s and adorned with fancy lamps and fountains; an open-air ice rink is installed from December through February. Back in the Middle Ages this was the site of public executions. Most victims were hanged, drawn, and quartered; the lucky ones were burned at the stake. Following the short-lived restoration of the Bourbon monarchy in 1830, the building became the seat of the French government, a role that came to a sudden end with the uprisings in 1848. During the Commune of 1871, the Hôtel de Ville was burned to the ground. Today's exuberant building, based closely on the 16th-century Renaissance original, went up between 1874 and 1884. In 1944, following the liberation of Paris from Nazi rule, General de Gaulle took over the leadership of France from here. ⊠ *Pl. de l'Hôtel-de-Ville, Le Marais.* 🕓 *For special exhibitions only. Métro: Hôtel de Ville.*

㉕ Maison Européenne de la Photographie (European Photography Center). This museum combines spacious modern galleries with the original stonework of a venerable hôtel particulier. Despite its name, the museum has an impressive collection of both European and American photography and stages up to four different exhibitions every three months. ⊠ *5 rue de Fourcy, Le Marais,* ☎ *01–44–78–75–00,* 🌐 *www.mep-fr.org.* 🎫 *€5, free Wed. after 5 PM.* 🕓 *Wed.–Sun. 11–8. Métro: St-Paul.*

⑲ Maison de Victor Hugo (Victor Hugo's Home). The workaholic French author, famed for *Les Misérables* and the *Hunchback of Notre-Dame*, lived in a corner of beautiful place des Vosges between 1832 and 1848. The memorabilia here include several of his atmospheric, Gothic-horror-movie-like ink sketches, tribute to Hugo's unsuspected talent as an artist, along with illustrations for his writings by other artists, including Bayard's rendition of Cosette (from "Les Miz," which has graced countless T-shirts). The rooms upstairs represent Hugo's living style in several of his many homes; the central room of the floor, for instance, is decorated with Chinese-theme panels and woodworks he created for his mistress's home outside Paris. ⊠ *6 pl. des Vosges, Le Marais,* ☎ *01–42–72–10–16.* ☞ *€3.4.* ☉ *Tues.–Sun. 10–5:45. Métro: St-Paul.*

㉗ Mémorial du Martyr Juif Inconnu (Memorial of the Unknown Jewish Martyr). This memorial was erected at the **Centre de Documentation Juive Contemporaine** (Center for Contemporary Jewish Documentation) to honor the memory of the 6 million Jews who died "without graves" at the hands of the Nazis. The basement crypt has a dramatic black marble Star of David containing the ashes of victims from Nazi death camps in Poland and Austria. The center has archives, a library, and a gallery that hosts temporary exhibitions. ⊠ *17 rue Geoffroy-l'Asnier, Le Marais,* ☎ *01–42–77–44–72.* ☞ *€2.3.* ☉ *Sun.–Fri. 10–1 and 2–5:30. Métro: Pont Marie.*

❽ Musée d'Art et d'Histoire du Judaïsme (Museum of Jewish Art and History). With its clifflike courtyard ringed by giant pilasters, the Hôtel St-Aignan, completed in 1650 to the design of Pierre le Muet, is one of the most awesome sights in the Marais. It opened as the city's Jewish museum in 1998 after a 20-year restoration. The interior has been renovated to the point of blandness, but the exhibits have good explanatory English texts on Jewish history and practice, and you can ask for a free audio guide in English. Highlights include 13th-century tombstones excavated in Paris; wooden models of destroyed East European synagogues; a roomful of early Chagalls; and Christian Boltanski's stark, two-part tribute to Shoah victims, in the form of plaques on an outer wall naming the (mainly-Jewish) inhabitants of the Hôtel St-Aignan in 1939, and canvas hangings with the personal data of the 13 residents who were deported and died in concentration camps. Jewish people settled in France in the Rhône Valley as early as the 1st century BC; a synagogue existed in Paris by 582; an expulsion order was issued by Charles VI in 1394 but fitfully enforced; and 40,000 French Jews were granted full citizenship by the Revolution in 1791. France's Jewish population sank from 300,000 to 180,000 with the deportation and departure during World War II but has since grown to around 700,000. ⊠ *71 rue du Temple, Le Marais,* ☎ *01–53–01–86–60.* ☞ *€6.* ☉ *Sun.–Fri. 11–6. Métro: Rambuteau, Hôtel de Ville.*

⑬ Musée Bricard. Also called the Musée de la Serrure (Lock Museum), this museum is housed in a exquisitely elegant Baroque mansion designed in 1685 by the architect of Les Invalides, Libéral Bruant, for himself. Anyone with a taste for fine craftsmanship will appreciate the intricacy and ingenuity of many of the older locks displayed here. One represents an early security system—it would shoot anyone who tried to open it with the wrong key. Another was made in the 17th century by a master locksmith who was himself held under lock and key while he labored over it—the task took him four years. ⊠ *1 rue de la Perle, Le Marais,* ☎ *01–42–77–79–62.* ☞ *€4.6.* ☉ *Weekdays 2–5. Métro: St-Paul.*

★ ⑰ Musée Carnavalet. To get a picture of the eternal yet ever-changing face of Paris throughout the ages, head to these two adjacent mansions in the heart of the Marais. Devoted to Parisian history, they include many

salons filled with antiques and historic artifacts. Material dating from
the city's origins until 1789 is in the Hôtel Carnavalet, and material
from 1789 to the present is in the Hôtel Peletier St-Fargeau. In the late
17th century, the Hôtel Carnavalet was the setting for the most brilliant salon in Paris, presided over by Madame de Sévigné, best known
for the hundreds of letters she wrote to her daughter; they've become
one of the most enduring chronicles of French high society in the 17th
century. The Hôtel Carnavalet, transformed into a museum in 1880,
is full of maps and plans, furniture, and busts and portraits of Parisian
worthies down the ages. The section on the Revolution includes riveting models of guillotines and objects associated with the royal family's final days, including the king's razor, and the chess set used by
the royal prisoners at the approach of their own endgame. Lovers of
the decorative arts will enjoy the period rooms here, especially those
devoted to that most French of French styles, the 18th-century Rococo.
Most entertaining, however, are the recreations of Marcel Proust's cork-
lined bedroom, the late 19th-century Fouquet jewelry shop, and a
room from that Art Nouveau monument, the Café de Paris. ⊠ *23 rue
de Sévigné, Le Marais,* ☎ *01–44–59–58–58,* WEB *www.paris-france.
org/musees.* ▦ *Free.* ☉ *Tues.–Sun. 10–5:40. Métro: St-Paul.*

NEED A
BREAK?

Marais Plus (⊠ 20 rue des Francs-Bourgeois, Le Marais, ☎ 01–48–87–
01–40), on the corner of rue Elzévir and rue des Francs-Bourgeois, is a
delightful, artsy gift shop with a cozy salon de thé in the back.

---

⑩ **Musée de la Chasse et de la Nature** (Museum of Hunting and Nature).
This museum is housed in the Hôtel de Guénégaud, designed around
1650 by François Mansart and one of the Marais's most stately mansions. There's an extensive collection of hunting paraphernalia, including
a series of immense 17th- and 18th-century still lifes (notably by De-
sportes and Oudry) of dead animals and a wide variety of swords, guns,
muskets, and taxidermy. ⊠ *60 rue des Archives, Le Marais,* ☎ *01–
42–72–86–42.* ▦ *€4.6.* ☉ *Wed.–Mon. 11–6. Métro: Rambuteau.*

⑯ **Musée Cognacq-Jay.** Another rare opportunity to see how cultured and
rich Parisians once lived, this mansion is devoted to the arts of the 18th
century and contains an outstanding collection in boiseried rooms of
furniture, porcelain, and paintings (notably by Watteau, Boucher, and
Tiepolo) amassed by Ernest Cognacq and his wife, Louise Jay, founder
of La Samaritaine, the city's largest department store. ⊠ *8 rue Elzévir,
Le Marais,* ☎ *01–40–27–07–21,* WEB *www.paris-france.org/musees.* ▦
Free. ☉ *Tues.–Sun. 10–5:40. Métro: St-Paul.*

★ ⑭ **Musée Picasso.** The Picasso Museum opened in the fall of 1985 and
shows no signs of losing its immense popularity. The building itself,
put up between 1656 and 1660 for financier Aubert de Fontenay,
quickly became known as the Hôtel Salé—*salé* meaning, literally,
"salted"—as a result of the enormous profits made by de Fontenay as
the sole appointed collector of the salt tax. The mansion was luxuri-
ously restored by the French government as a permanent home for the
pictures, sculptures, drawings, prints, ceramics, and assorted works of
art given to the government by Picasso's heirs after the painter's death
in 1973 in lieu of death duties. Unfortunately, these days the hotel particulier is well showing the wear and tear of being one of the city's most
popular museums; on peak summer afternoons, this place is more
congested than the Gare du Lyon. It's the largest collection of works
by Picasso in the world—no masterpieces, but "Picasso's Picassos," all
works kept and sentimentally valued by Picasso himself. There are pictures from every period of his life: a grand total of 230 paintings, 1,500
drawings, and nearly 1,700 prints, as well as works by Cézanne, Miró,

Renoir, Braque, Degas, and Matisse. The scuffed yet palatial sur-
roundings of the Hôtel Salé add to the pleasures of a visit. ⊠ *5 rue de
Thorigny, Le Marais,* ☎ *01–42–71–25–21.* 🎟 *€5.5, Sun. €4.* ☉
Wed.–Mon. 9:30–5:30. Métro: St-Sébastien.

🖐 **❼ Musée de la Poupée** (Doll Museum). If you love dolls, make a detour
to this quaint, low-ceilinged house in a cul-de-sac behind the Centre
Pompidou to admire the rarefied collection of 300 French dolls dating back to the 1850s—many wearing their original costumes. Bisque-
head dolls with enamel eyes were the Paris specialty, with Steiner, Bru,
and Jumeau among the leading makers represented here. Two of the
museum's six rooms are devoted to temporary exhibits, and there's a
well-stocked gift shop. ⊠ *Impasse Berthaud, Beaubourg/Les Halles,*
☎ *01–42–72–73–11.* 🎟 *€6.* ☉ *Tues.–Sun. 10–6. Métro: Rambuteau.*

⓬ Notre-Dame des Blancs-Manteaux. The Blancs Manteaux were white-
robed 13th-century mendicant monks whose monastery once stood on
this spot. For the last 100 years, this late-17th-century church has had
an imposing 18th-century facade that belonged to a now-destroyed
church on the Ile de la Cité. Unfortunately, the narrow streets of the
Marais leave little room to step back and admire it. The inside has fine
woodwork and a Flemish-style rococo pulpit whose marquetry panels are inlaid with pewter and ivory. ⊠ *Rue des Blancs-Manteaux, Le
Marais. Métro: Rambuteau.*

★ **⓲ Place des Vosges.** The oldest monumental square in Paris—and probably still its most nobly proportioned—the place des Vosges was laid
out by Henri IV at the start of the 17th century. Originally known as
place Royale, it has kept its Renaissance beauty nearly intact, although
its buildings have been softened by time, their pale pink brick crumbling slightly in the harsh Parisian air and the darker stone facings pit-
ted with age. It stands on the site of a former royal palace, the Palais
des Tournelles, which was abandoned by the Italian-born queen of
France, Catherine de' Medici, when her husband, Henri II, was killed
in a tournament here in 1559. It was always a highly desirable address,
reaching a peak of glamour in the early years of Louis XIV's reign, when
the nobility were falling over themselves for the privilege of living here.
The two larger buildings on either side of the square were originally
the king's and queen's pavilions. The statue in the center is of Louis
XIII. It's not the original; that was melted down in the Revolution, the
same period when the square's name was changed in honor of the French
département of the Vosges, the first in the country to pay the new revolutionary taxes. With its arcades, symmetrical pink-brick town houses,
and trim green garden, bisected in the center by gravel paths and edged
with plane trees, the square achieves harmony and balance: it's a pleasant place to tarry on a sultry summer afternoon. Better yet, grab an
arcade table at one of the many cafés lining the square—even a simple cheese crepe becomes a feast in this setting. To actually enter one
of the square's imposing town houses, visit the **Maison de Victor Hugo**
at No. 6. *Métro: Chemin Vert.*

⓯ St-Denis-du-St-Sacrement. This severely neoclassical edifice dates from
the 1830s. It is a formidable example of architectural discipline, oozing restraint and monumental dignity (or banality, according to taste).
The grisaille frieze and gilt fresco above the semicircular apse have clout
if not subtlety; the Delacroix *Deposition* (1844), in the front right-hand
chapel as you enter, has both. ⊠ *Rue de Turenne, Le Marais. Métro:
St-Sébastien.*

❷ St-Gervais–St-Protais. This imposing church near the Hôtel de Ville is
named after two Roman soldiers martyred by the emperor Nero in the

1st century AD. The original church—no trace remains of it now—was built in the 7th century. The present church, a riot of Flamboyant-style decoration, went up between 1494 and 1598, making it one of the last Gothic constructions in the country. Pause to look at the facade, constructed between 1616 and 1621. It's an early example of French architects' use of the classical orders of decoration on the capitals (topmost sections) of the columns. Those on the first floor are plain and sturdy Doric; the more elaborate Ionic is used on the second floor; and the most ornate of all—Corinthian—is used on the third floor. The church hosts occasional organ and choral concerts. ⊠ *Pl. St-Gervais, Le Marais,* ☎ *01–47–26–78–38 concert information.* ☉ *Tues.–Sun. 6:30 AM–8 PM. Métro: Hôtel de Ville.*

⑳ Ste-Marie. Constructed 1632–34 by François Mansart as the chapel of the Convent of the Visitation, this is now a Protestant "reformed" church. The large dome above the distinctive nave rotunda is one of the earliest in Paris. ⊠ *Rue St-Antoine, Le Marais. Métro: Bastille.*

❸ St-Merri. This church near the Centre Pompidou, completed in 1552, has a turret containing the oldest bell in Paris (cast in 1331) and an 18th-century pulpit supported on carved palm trees. ⊠ *Rue de la Verrerie, Beaubourg/Les Halles. Métro: Hôtel de Ville.*

㉒ St-Paul–St-Louis. The leading Baroque church in the Marais, with its elegant dome rising 180 ft above the crossing, was begun in 1627 by the Jesuits and partly modeled on their Gesu church in Rome. Look for Delacroix's dramatic *Christ on the Mount of Olives* high up in the transept, and the two huge shells, used as fonts, presented by Victor Hugo when he lived on nearby place des Vosges. ⊠ *Rue St-Antoine, Le Marais. Métro: St-Paul.*

❹ Square Igor-Stravinsky. The café-lined square, next to the Centre Pompidou and backed by the church of St-Merri, has a fountain animated by the colorful and imaginative sculptures of French artist Niki de St-Phalle, together with the aquatic mechanisms of her Swiss partner, Jean Tinguely. The fountain (sculptures and all) was erected in 1980. It is not part of the Centre Pompidou, but it fits right in. *Métro: Rambuteau.*

THE LATIN QUARTER AND THE ILE ST-LOUIS

South of Ile de la Cité on the Left Bank of the Seine is the bohemian Quartier Latin, with its warren of steep sloping streets, populated largely by Sorbonne students and academics who fill the air of the cafés with their ideas—and tobacco smoke. The name Latin Quarter comes from the university tradition of studying and speaking in Latin, a tradition that disappeared during the Revolution. The university began as a theological school in the Middle Ages and later became the headquarters of the University of Paris; in 1968, the student revolution here had an explosive effect on French politics, resulting in major reforms in the education system.

In fact, since ancient times, this quartier has detested the staid *bourgeoisie,* for here walks the ghost of Villon, that great poet and rapscallion who died sordidly in a tavern brawl. And here Verlaine, among the students and the shopkeepers of the rue Mouffetard, drank his eternal absinthe and wrote his poems. Today, however, the area is becoming increasingly upscale, with dozens of Right Bank luxury boutiques and antiques stores rubbing elbows with the bookstores. A grim modern skyscraper at the Jussieu campus, the science division of the University of Paris, reiterates the area's yen for learning yet fails to outgun the mighty dome of the Panthéon in its challenge for skyline supremacy. Most of the district's appeal is less emphatic: Roman ruins, tumbling street markets, the two oldest trees in Paris, and chance glimpses of Notre-Dame all await your discovery.

As does the Ile St-Louis. Of the two islands in the Seine—the Ile de la Cité is located just to the west—it is the Ile St-Louis that best retains the romance and loveliness of *le Paris traditionnel*. It has remained in the heart of Parisians as it has remained in the heart of every tourist who came upon it by accident, and without warning—a tiny universe unto itself, shaded by trees, bordered by Seine-side quais, and over-hung with ancient stone houses. These have long comprised some of the most prized addresses in Paris—Voltaire, Daumier, Cézanne, Baude-laire, Chagall, Helena Rubenstein, and the Rothschilds are just some of the lucky people who have called the Ile St-Louis home. Up until the 1800s it was reputed that some island residents never crossed the bridges to get to Paris proper—and once you discover the island's quiet charm, you may understand why.

Numbers in the text correspond to numbers in the margin and on the Latin Quarter and the Ile St.-Louis map.

A Good Walk

Start at the Seine along the Pont au Double and head to square René-Viviani, where you'll find a battered acacia—which vies with a speci-men in the Jardin des Plantes for the title of oldest tree in Paris—and a spectacular view of Notre-Dame. Behind the square lies the church of **St-Julien-le-Pauvre** ①, built at the same time as Notre-Dame, and the tiny, elegant streets of the Maubert district. Turn left out of the church and cross rue St-Jacques to the elegantly proportioned church of **St-Séverin** ②. The surrounding streets are for pedestrians only and crammed with cheap restaurants fronted by suave waiters touting cus-tomers at most hours of the day and night. Take rue St-Séverin, a right on rue Xavier-Privas, and a left on rue de la Huchette—where you'll find Paris's smallest theater and oldest jazz club—to reach **place St-Michel** ③. The grandiose fountain, depicting St. Michael slaying the dragon, is a popular meeting spot at the nerve center of the Left Bank.

Turn left up boulevard St-Michel and cross boulevard St-Germain. To your left, behind some forbidding railings, lurks a garden with ruins that date from Roman times. These belong to the Hôtel de Cluny, fa-bled repository of the **Musée National du Moyen-Age** ④, the National Museum of the Middle Ages. The entrance is down rue Sommerard, the next street on the left. Cross place Paul-Painlevé, in front of the museum, up toward the **Sorbonne** ⑤ university, fronted by a small plaza where the Left Bank's student population congregates after classes. Con-tinue uphill until you are confronted, up rue Soufflot on your left, by the menacing domed bulk of the **Panthéon** ⑥, originally built as a church but now a monument to France's most glorious historical figures. On the far left corner of place du Panthéon stands **St-Étienne-du-Mont** ⑦, a church whose facade is a mishmash of architectural styles. Explore the top of quaint rue de la Montagne-Ste-Geneviève alongside; then turn right onto rue Descartes to reach **place de la Contrescarpe** ⑧. This square looks almost provincial during the day as Parisians flock to the daily market on rue Mouffetard.

Duck into the old church of **St-Médard** ⑨ at the foot of rue Mouffe-tard; then head left for 250 yards along rue Censier and turn left again into rue du Gril to discover the beautiful white **Mosquée** ⑩, complete with minaret. Blink twice and you'll be convinced you've left Paris be-hind. On the far side of the mosque extends the **Jardin des Plantes** ⑪,

The Latin Quarter and the Ile St-Louis

spacious botanical gardens; the first building you'll come to is the **Grande Galerie de l'Evolution** ⑫, a museum with a startling collection of taxidermy, many of extinct or endangered animals. The museums of entomology, paleontology, and mineralogy are on the south side of the park along rue Buffon; an old-fashioned zoo is on the other.

Although it's a bit out of the way, **St-Louis de la Salpêtrière** ⑬, the church of the Salpêtrière Hospital, is within walking distance from the Jardin des Plantes: take boulevard de l'Hôpital, at the far end of the park; the church is in the grounds of the hospital beyond Gare d'Austerlitz. Farther upriver, via the quai d'Austerlitz and the quai de la Gare, is the Bibliothèque Nationale François-Mitterrand, the French National Library, with its four huge, shiny glass towers.

If you forgo the distant pleasures of southeast Paris, take the northwest exit from the Jardin des Plantes up rue Lacépède then rue de Navarre to the **Arènes de Lutèce** ⑭, the remains of a Roman amphitheater. Rue des Arènes and rue Limé lead to place Jussieu and its hideous 1960s concrete campus; there's greater refinement around the corner down rue des Fossés-St-Bernard at the glass-facaded **Institut du Monde Arabe** ⑮, a center devoted to Arab culture.

Cross the Seine on Pont de Sully to the **Ile St-Louis** ⑯, the smaller of the city's two islands; it's a time capsule of old Paris and a tranquil place for taking a stroll back to the 17th and 18th centuries. The **Hôtel Lambert** ⑰ and the **Hôtel de Lauzun** ⑱, set near the eastern prow of the island, are two of the most majestic mansions on the island. Rue St-Louis-en-l'Ile runs the length of the island, dividing it in two. Walk down the street and admire the strange, pierced spire of **St-Louis-en-l'Ile** ⑲; stop off for an ice cream at Berthillon at No. 31. Then head down to the Pont St-Louis at the island's western tip to admire the celebrated views of Notre-Dame, and the Hôtel de Ville and St-Gervais church on the Right Bank. Just across the bridge on Ile de la Cité lies the **Mémorial de la Déportation** ⑳, a starkly moving modern crypt dedicated to the French Jews who died in Nazi concentration camps. You may wish to linger in the quiet garden above before savoring the view of Notre-Dame from the **Pont de l'Archevêché** ㉑, which links the island to the Left Bank.

TIMING

At just under 6 km (about 3½ mi), this walk can be done in a morning or afternoon, or serve as the basis for a leisurely day's exploring—given that several sites, notably the Musée de Cluny, deserve a lengthy visit. Note that the Grande Galerie d'Évolution stays open until 10 PM on Thursday. You can easily make a brief excursion to St-Louis de la Salpêtrière as well as the Bibliothèque Nationale François-Mitterrand.

Sights to See

⑭ **Arènes de Lutèce** (Lutetia Amphitheater). This Roman arena was only discovered in 1869 and has since been excavated and landscaped to reveal parts of the original amphitheater. Designed as a theater and circus, the arena was almost totally destroyed by the barbarians in AD 280, though you can still see part of the stage and tiered seating. Along with the remains of the baths at the Cluny, this constitutes rare evidence of the powerful Roman city of Lutetia that flourished on the Left Bank in the 3rd century. ⊠ *Entrance at rue Monge or rue de Navarre, Latin Quarter.* ☞ *Free.* ☉ *Daily 8–sunset. Métro: Monge.*

⑫ **Grande Galerie de l'Évolution** (Great Hall of Evolution). This vast, handsome glass-and-iron structure in the Jardin des Plantes was built, like the Eiffel Tower, in 1889 but abandoned in the 1960s. It reopened amid popular acclaim in 1994 and now contains one of the world's finest collections of taxidermy, including a section devoted to extinct and endangered species. There's a reconstituted dodo—only a foot actually remains of this clumsy, flightless bird from Mauritius—and a miniature South African zebra, the quagga, which disappeared early in the 20th century. Stunning lighting effects include push-button spotlighting and a ceiling that changes color to suggest storms, twilight, or hot savannah sun. ☒ *36 rue Geoffroy-St-Hilaire, Latin Quarter,* ☏ *01–40–79–39–39,* WEB *www.mnhn.fr/evolution.* ☐ *€6.* ☉ *Wed. and Fri.–Mon. 10–6, Thurs. 10–10. Métro: Monge.*

⑰ Hôtel Lambert. Without this house—one of the most famous in Paris—Versailles probably wouldn't exist in all its glory. Sitting on the eastern end of the Ile St-Louis, it was created by the three great "Le"'s of the French Baroque: architect Louis Le Vau (1612–70), decorator Charles Le Brun, and painter Eustache Le Sieur. Built by the banker Lambert "le riche," the mansion was so impressive Nicolas Fouquet ordered the team to build his chateau of Vaux-le-Vicomte, which, in turn, inspired Louis XIV to commission them to create Versailles. Voltaire was the most famous occupant of the Lambert, then owned by his lover, the Marquise du Châtelet. Here, in the Galerie d'Hercule, many of Paris's most famous costume balls were held; guests included everyone from Chopin to Empress Eugénie. Today, as through all of its privileged history, the house is private and has been lovingly restored by the Barons Rothschild. If you go around to the neighboring quay and bridge you can see part of the garden and, just possibly, the Galerie illuminated at night. ☒ *2 rue St-Louis-en-l'Ile, Ile St-Louis. Métro: Pont Marie.*

★ ⑱ Hôtel de Lauzun. Gilded and mirrored to within an inch of their lives, the salons here are some of the most important examples of the Baroque style in Paris and are a must-see for art historians—others will be curious to visit this Ile St-Louis mansion because of the house's fascinating history. It was built by Louis Le Vau in 1657 and decorated in part by Charles Le Brun for Charles Gruyn, a supplier of goods to the French army who accumulated an immense fortune, then landed in jail before the house was even completed. In the 19th century, the revolutionary critic and visionary poet Charles Baudelaire (1821–67) had an apartment here, where he kept a cache of stuffed snakes and crocodiles, and wrote a large chunk of *Les Fleurs du Mal* (The Flowers of Evil), his masterpiece. In 1848, the poet Théophile Gautier (1811–72) moved in, making it the meeting place of the Club des Haschischines (Hashish Eaters' Club); novelist Alexandre Dumas and painter Eugène Delacroix were both members. The club came to represent more than just a den of drug takers and gossips, for these men believed passionately in the purity of art and the crucial role of the artist as sole interpreter of the chaos of life. Art for Art's Sake—the more refined and exotic the better—was their creed. Anything that helped the artist reach heightened states of perception was applauded. Now the building is used for more decorous receptions by the mayor of Paris and is open to the public on weekends from Easter to October. ☒ *17 quai d'Anjou, Ile St-Louis,* ☏ *01–43–54–27–14.* ☐ *€4.* ☉ *Easter–Oct., weekends 10–5:30. Métro: Pont Marie.*

⑯ Ile St-Louis. The smaller of the two Paris islands is linked to the Ile de la Cité by Pont St-Louis. The contrast between the islands is striking: whereas the Ile de la Cité is steeped in history and dotted with dignified public buildings, the Ile St-Louis is a discreet residential district. The island's most striking note is its architectural unity, which stems from the efforts of a group of early 17th-century property speculators. At that time, there were two islands here, the Ile Notre-Dame and Ile aux Vaches—Cow Island, a reference to its use as grazing land. The speculators, led by an energetic engineer named Christophe Marie (after whom the Pont Marie was named), bought the two islands, joined them together, and divided the newly formed Ile St-Louis into building plots. Baroque architect Louis Le Vau was commissioned to erect a series of imposing town houses, and by 1664 the project was largely complete. People still talk about the quaint, village-street feel of rue St-Louis-en-l'Ile, which runs the length of the island, dividing it neatly in two. From the quai de Bourbon at the western end, facing the Ile de la Cité, there are attractive views of Notre-Dame, the Hôtel de Ville, and the church of St-Gervais. In summer, rows of baking bodies attest to the quay's enduring popularity as the city's favorite sunbathing spot, while crowds line up for a scoop from Berthillon's shop, the mecca of Parisian ice cream. You can savor your cone of *glace de Grande Marnier* by strolling along the isle's Seine-side streets—as Brassaï and other photographers proved, they are among Paris's most romantic sights. *Métro: Pont Marie.*

⑮ Institut du Monde Arabe (Institute of the Arab World). Jean Nouvel's striking glass-and-steel edifice adroitly fuses Arabic and European styles and was greeted with enthusiasm when it opened in 1988. Note the 240 shutterlike apertures that open and close to regulate light exposure. Inside, the institute tries to do for Arab culture what the Centre Pompidou does for modern art, with the help of a sound-and-image center; a vast library and documentation center; and an art museum containing Arab-Islamic art, textiles, and ceramics, plus exhibits on Arabic mathematics, astronomy, and medicine. Glass elevators whisk you to the ninth floor, where you can sip mint tea at the rooftop café and enjoy a memorable view of the Seine and Notre-Dame. ⊠ *1 rue des Fossés-St-Bernard, Latin Quarter,* ☎ *01–40–51–38–38.* 🎫 *€6.* ☉ *Tues.–Sun. 10–6. Métro: Cardinal Lemoine.*

⑪ Jardin des Plantes (Botanical Gardens). Bordered by the Seine, the drab Gare d'Austerlitz, and the utilitarian Jussieu campus (a branch of the Paris University system), this enormous swath of greenery contains botanical gardens, the Grande Galerie de l'Evolution, and three other natural history museums, opened in 1898. The **Grande Galerie de l'Evolution** is devoted to taxidermied animals; the **Musée Entomologique** (closed for renovation at press time) to insects; the **Musée Paléontologique** to fossils and skeletons dating back to prehistoric times; and the **Musée Minéralogique** to rocks and minerals. The stock of plants in the botanical gardens, dating from the first collections from the 17th century, has been enhanced by subsequent generations of devoted French botanists. The garden shelters what is claimed to be Paris's oldest tree, an *acacia robinia,* planted in 1636. There is also an alpine garden, an aquarium, a maze, a number of hothouses, and one of the world's oldest zoos, the Ménagerie, started by Napoléon. ⊠ *Entrances on rue Geoffroy-St-Hilaire, rue Civier, and rue Buffon, Latin Quarter* ☎ *01–40–79–30–00,* 🖳 *www.mnhn.fr.* 🎫 *Museums and zoo €4.6, hothouses €2.5.* ☉ *Museums Wed.–Mon. 10–5. Zoo June–Aug., daily 9–6; Sept.–May, daily 9–5. Hothouses Wed.–Mon. 1–5. Garden daily 7:30 AM–sunset. Métro: Monge.*

⑳ Mémorial de la Déportation (Memorial of the Deportation). On the eastern tip of the Ile de la Cité, in what was once the city morgue, lies a starkly moving modern crypt, dedicated to all the French men, women, and children who died in Nazi concentration camps. 🎫 *Free.* ☉ *Apr.–Sept., daily 9–6; Oct.–Mar., daily 9 AM–dusk. Métro: Maubert Mutualité.*

⑩ Mosquée (Mosque). This beautiful white mosque was built from 1922 to 1925, complete with arcades and minaret, and decorated in the style of Moorish Spain. Students from the nearby Jussieu and Censier universities pack themselves into the tea salon, for cups of sweet mint tea at the café and for copious quantities of couscous at the restaurant. The sunken garden and tiled patios are also open to the public (the prayer rooms are not), as are the *hammams*, or Turkish baths. ⊠ *2 pl. du Puits-de-l'Ermite, Latin Quarter*, ☎ *01–45–35–97–33.* ☜ *Guided tour €2.3, Turkish baths €13.* ☼ *Baths daily 10–9 (Tues. and Sun. men only, Mon. and Wed.–Sat. women only). Guided tours of mosque Sat.–Thurs. 9–noon and 2–6. Métro: Monge.*

....

OFF THE
BEATEN PATH
CHINATOWN – If China, rather than Arabia, is your cup of tea, take the métro at nearby Censier Daubenton to Paris's Chinatown. Although not as ornamental as San Francisco's or New York's, Paris's Chinatown nevertheless has myriad electronics and clothing stores and dozens of restaurants with an exciting choice of Chinese *comestibles* (foods). **Tang-Frères Chinese supermarket** (⊠ 48 av. d'Ivry, Chinatown) packs in a serious crowd of shoppers. The **Temple de l'Association des Résidents d'Origine Chinoise** (⊠ 37 rue du Disque, Chinatown) is a small Buddhist temple that looks like a cross between a school cafeteria and an exotic Asian enclave filled with Buddha figures, fruit, and incense. For a more upscale version of Chinese culture, head out to **Chinagora** in the eastern suburbs. *Métro: Tolbiac.*

....

★ ❹ **Musée National du Moyen-Age** (National Museum of the Middle Ages). Devoted to the arts of the Middle Ages, this highly important museum—sometimes referred to as the Musée de Cluny—is housed in that precious relic of the 15th-century, the Hôtel de Cluny. Adorned with purely decorative machicolations and turrets, the mansion was originally built by the Abbot of Jumièges; note the main *coquilles*, or shells, among the carved stone ornaments—the rue St-Jacques (the Pilgrim's Way) is nearby. Gardens (nicely illuminated at night), an intricately vaulted chapel, and a cloistered courtyard with mullioned windows (that originally belonged to monks of the Cluny Abbey in Burgundy) are some pleasing attractions here, but almost immediately upon entering you encounter the stunning array of tapestries which heads the Cluny's vast collection of medieval decorative arts. There are numerous examples of the *mille-fleur* ("thousand-flower") styles yet all eyes are attracted by the world-famous *Dame à la Licorne* (Lady and the Unicorn) series, woven in the 15th or 16th century, probably in Belgium, and depicting the five senses and the legend of the unicorn. Byzantine crosses, Romanesque architectural capitals, and medieval paintings round out the collection, stunningly augumented in 1977 by the spectacular collection of the heads of the *Kings of Israel and Judah* (originally thought Kings of France), unearthed in northern Paris and originally set upon the Gothic figures of the facade of Notre-Dame. Alongside the mansion are a reconstituted medieval garden, with 58 species of flora and fauna depicted in the *Dame à la Licorne* tapestries, and remnants of the city's Roman baths—both hot (*Caldarium*) and cold (*Frigidarium*), the latter containing the *Boatmen's Pillar,* Paris's oldest sculpture. ⊠ *6 pl. Paul-Painlevé, Latin Quarter*, ☎ *01–53–73–78–00,* WEB *www.musee-moyenage.fr.* ☜ *€5.5, Sun. €4.* ☼ *Wed.–Mon. 9:15–5:45. Métro: Cluny La Sorbonne.*

❻ **Panthéon.** Originally commissioned by Louis XV to mark his recovery from illness in 1744, Germain Soufflot's mighty domed church was not begun until 1764, or completed until 1790—whereupon the godless philosophers of the Revolution had its windows blocked and ordered it transformed into a national shrine. Puvis de Chavannes's giant frescoes in the nave, retracing the life of St. Genevieve, warrant appraisal, along with a model of Foucault's pendulum, first hoisted in 1851 to prove the earth's rotation on its axis. Today the Panthéon is a monument to France's most glorious historical figures; the crypt holds the remains of Voltaire, Zola, Rousseau, and dozens of other national heroes. Nobel Prize–winning scientist Marie Curie became the first woman to join their ranks, in 1995. ⊠ *Pl. du Panthéon, Latin Quarter,* ☎ *01–44–32–18–00,* WEB *www.monum.fr.* ⊡ *€6.5.* ⊙ *Apr.–Sept., daily 9:30–6:30; Oct.–Mar., daily 10–6:15. Métro: Cardinal Lemoine; RER: Luxembourg.*

❽ Place de la Contrescarpe. This intimate square behind the Panthéon doesn't start to swing until after dusk, when its cafés and bars fill up. During the day, the square looks almost provincial as Parisians flock to the daily market at the bottom of rue Mouffetard, a steeply sloping street that retains much of its bygone charm. *Métro: Monge.*

❸ Place St-Michel. This square on the Seine was named for Gabriel Davioud's grandiose 1860 fountain, depicting St. Michael slaying the dragon. *Métro, RER: St-Michel.*

㉑ Pont de l'Archevêché (Archbishop's Bridge). This bridge, built in 1828, links Ile St-Louis to the Left Bank. The bridge offers a breathtaking view of the east end of the cathedral, ringed by flying buttresses, floating above the Seine like some vast stone ship. *Métro: Maubert Mutualité.*

❼ St-Étienne-du-Mont. The ornate facade of this mainly 16th-century church combines Gothic, Baroque, and Renaissance elements. Inside, the curly, carved rood screen (1525–35), separating nave and chancel, is the only one of its kind in Paris. Note the uneven-floored chapel behind the choir, which can be reached via a cloister containing exquisite 17th-century stained glass. ⊠ *Pl. de l'Abbé-Basset, Latin Quarter. Métro: Cardinal Lemoine.*

❶ St-Julien-le-Pauvre. This tiny church was built at the same time as Notre-Dame (1165–1220), on a site where a succession of chapels once stood. The church belongs to a Greek Orthodox order today but was originally named for St. Julian, bishop of Le Mans, who was nicknamed Le Pauvre (The Poor) after he gave all his money away. ⊠ *Rue St-Julien-le-Pauvre, Latin Quarter. Métro: St-Michel.*

❸ St-Louis de la Salpêtrière. The church of the Salpêtrière Hospital stands next to the Gare d'Austerlitz, which it dominates with its unmistakable, lantern-topped octagonal dome. The church was built (1670–77) in the shape of a Greek cross from the designs of Libéral Bruant. ⊠ *Bd. de l'Hôpital, Latin Quarter. Métro: Gare d'Austerlitz.*

❿ St-Louis-en-l'Ile. The only church on the Ile St-Louis, built from 1664 to 1726 to the Baroque designs of architect Louis Le Vau, is lavishly furnished and has two unusual exterior features: its original pierced spire, holy in both senses, and an iron clock, added in 1741. ⊠ *Rue St-Louis-en-l'Ile, Ile St-Louis. Métro: Pont Marie.*

NEED A BREAK? Cafés all over sell the haute couture of ice cream, but **Berthillon** (⊠ 31 rue St-Louis-en-l'Ile, Ile St-Louis, ☎ 01–43–54–31–61) itself is the place to come. More than 30 flavors are served; expect to wait in line. The shop is open Wednesday–Sunday.

❾ St-Médard. This church at the bottom of rue Mouffetard contains the painting *St. Joseph with the Christ Child* by Spanish master Zurbarán. The nave and facade, with its large late-Gothic window, date from the late 15th century. The 17th-century choir is in contrasting classical style. ⊠ *Rue Mouffetard, Latin Quarter. Métro: Censier Daubenton.*

MANUFACTURE DES GOBELINS – Tapestries have been woven on this spot in southeastern Paris, on the banks of the long-covered Bièvre River, which once flowed into the Seine, since 1662. Guided tours—in French only—combine historical explanation with the chance to admire both old tapestries and today's weavers at work in their airy workshops. ⊠ *42 av. des Gobelins, Latin Quarter,* ☏ *01–44–08–52–00,* WEB *www. monum.fr.* ⊠ *€8.* ⊗ *Tues.–Thurs., guided tours only at 2 and 2:45. Métro: Gobelins.*

② **St-Séverin.** This unusually wide Flamboyant Gothic church dominates the Left Bank neighborhood filled with squares and pedestrian streets. In the 11th century, the church that stood here was the parish church for the entire Left Bank. Louis XIV's cousin, a capricious woman known simply as the Grande Mademoiselle, adopted St-Séverin when she tired of St-Sulpice; she then spent vast sums getting court decorator Le Brun to modernize the chancel in the 17th century. Note the splendidly deviant spiraling column in the forest of pillars behind the altar. ⊠ *Rue des Prêtres-St-Séverin, Latin Quarter.* ⊗ *Weekdays 11–5:30, Sat. 11–10. Métro: St-Michel.*

❺ **Sorbonne.** Named after Robert de Sorbon, a medieval canon who founded a theological college here in 1253 for 16 students, the Sorbonne is one of the oldest universities in Europe. For centuries it has been one of France's principal institutions of higher learning, as well as the hub of the Latin Quarter and nerve center of Paris's student population. The church and university buildings were restored by Cardinal Richelieu in the 17th century, and the maze of amphitheaters, lecture rooms, and laboratories, and the surrounding courtyards and narrow streets, retains a hallowed air. You can visit the main courtyard on rue de la Sorbonne and peek into the main lecture hall, a major meeting point during the tumultuous student upheavals of 1968, and also of interest for a giant mural by Puvis de Chavannes, the *Sacred Wood* (1880–89). The square is dominated by the university church, the noble **Église de la Sorbonne,** whose outstanding exterior features are its cupola and Corinthian columns. Inside is the white marble tomb of that ultimate crafty cleric, Cardinal Richelieu himself. ⊠ *Rue de la Sorbonne, Latin Quarter. Métro: Cluny La Sorbonne.*

CENTRE DE LA MER ET DES EAUX – A spell of fish-gazing is a soothing, mesmerizing experience for young and old. The Center of Sea and Waters is one of the principal aquariums in Paris. From the Sorbonne, go up rue de la Sorbonne, and then take the first left on rue Cujas, and a right on rue St-Jacques. ⊠ *195 rue St-Jacques, Latin Quarter,* ☏ *01– 44–32–10–90,* WEB *www.oceano.org.* ⊠ *€4.6.* ⊗ *Tues.–Fri. 10–12:30 and 1:15–5:30, weekends 10–5:30. RER: Luxembourg.*

FROM ORSAY TO ST-GERMAIN

This walk covers the western half of the Left Bank, from the Musée d'Orsay in the stately 7e arrondissement, to the Faubourg St-Germain, a lively and colorful area in the 6e arrondissement. In its northern reaches, this district goes under the monniker of St-Germain-des-Prés, now a prized address for the rich and stylish. In the 19th century, Émile Zola depicted these environs as the backdrop for his sordid tale, *Thérèse Raquin,* Claude Monet and Auguste Renoir shared a studio at No. 20 rue Visconti, and the young Picasso managed to eke out an existence in a flat on the rue de Seine. Where artists go, millionaires follow. Today, St-Germain-des-Prés is one of the chicest and most delightful neighborhoods in the city; with numerous hotels, it is also (surprise) one of the most tourist-friendly.

The headliner on this tour is the Musée d'Orsay, which houses a superb collection of Impressionist paintings in a spectacularly converted Belle Epoque rail station on the Seine. Farther along the river, the 18th-century Palais Bourbon, where the National Assembly convenes, sets the tone. Hereabouts is Edith Wharton territory—select, discreet *vieille France,* where all the aristocrats live in gorgeous, sprawling, old-fashioned apartments or *maisons particulières* (town houses). Luxurious ministries and embassies—including the Hôtel Matignon, residence of the French prime minister—line the surrounding streets, their majestic scale completely in keeping with the Hôtel des Invalides, whose gold-leafed dome climbs heavenward above the regal tomb of Napoléon. The splendid Rodin Museum—one of the few houses here where you can explore the grand interior—is only a short walk away.

To the east, boulevard St-Michel slices the Left Bank in two: on one side, the Latin Quarter; on the other, the Faubourg St-Germain, named for St-Germain-des-Prés, the oldest church in Paris. The venerable church tower has long acted as a beacon for intellectuals, most famously during the 1950s, when Albert Camus, Jean-Paul Sartre, and Simone de Beauvoir ate and drank existentialism in the neighborhood cafés. Today most of the philosophizing is done by tourists, yet a wealth of bookshops, art stores, and luscious antiques galleries ensure that St-Germain retains its very highbrow appeal. A highlight of St-Germain is the Jardin du Luxembourg, the city's most famous and colorful park. The 17th-century palace overlooking the gardens houses the French Senate.

Numbers in the text correspond to numbers in the margin and on the Orsay to St-Germain map.

A Good Walk

Arrive at the **Musée d'Orsay** ① early to avoid the crowds that flock to see the museum's outstanding works of art, including many of the most beloved Impressionist paintings in France. A good meeting point is the pedestrian square outside the museum, where huge bronze statues of an elephant and a rhinoceros disprove the notion that the French take their art too seriously. Across the square stands the **Musée de la Légion d'Honneur** ②, where you can find an array of French and foreign decorations. A stylish two-tiered footbridge, opened in 2000, crosses the Seine to the Tuileries, but opt instead to either cut south down rue de Bellechasse (if you're short of time) to the Hôtel Matignon or head west along rue de Lille to the **Palais Bourbon** ③, home of the Assemblée Nationale (the French Parliament). There's a fine view across the Seine to place de la Concorde and the church of the Madeleine.

Rue de l'Université leads from the Assemblée to the grassy Esplanade des Invalides and an encounter with the **Hôtel des Invalides** ④, founded by Louis XIV to house wounded (*invalid*) veterans. The most impressive dome in Paris towers over the church at the back of the Invalides— the Église du Dôme. From the church, turn left, then left again onto boulevard des Invalides, then right on rue de Varenne to reach the elegant Hôtel Biron, better known as the **Musée Rodin** ⑤. Here you can see a fine collection of Auguste Rodin's emotionally charged statues and some wonderful gardens. The quiet, distinguished 18th-century streets between the Rodin Museum and the Parliament are filled with embassies and ministries. The most famous, farther along rue de Varenne, is the **Hôtel Matignon** ⑥, residence of the French prime minister. Just before, at No. 51, is one of Paris's handful of private culs-

Orsay to St-Germain

de-sac. Next door at No. 53 you can pay your respects to American novelist Edith Wharton, who lived and worked here from 1910 to 1920. Take the next left onto rue du Bac, then right onto rue de Grenelle, past the **Musée Maillol** ⑦, dedicated to the work of sculptor Aristide Maillol, and Bouchardon's monumental **Fontaine des Quatre Saisons** ⑧.

Turn left down boulevard Raspail and cross to rue de Luynes. Carry on across boulevard St-Germain to inspect the stately 17th-century church of **St-Thomas d'Aquin** ⑨; then double back and head east along boulevard St-Germain for 400 yards to the **Café de Flore** ⑩, one of the principal haunts of the intelligentsia after World War II. Another popular café, two doors down, is **Les Deux Magots** ⑪; politicians and showbiz types still wine and dine at the pricey Brasserie Lipp across the street. Looming above cobbled place St-Germain-des-Prés stands **St-Germain-des-Prés** ⑫, Paris's oldest church.

Follow rue de l'Abbaye, along the far side of the church, to rue de Furstenberg. The street opens out into place Furstenberg, an adorably picturesque square bedecked with white globe lamps and catalpa trees (one side now defaced by overly renovated town houses, reputedly among the most expensive lodgings on offer in today's Paris), where you'll find Eugène Delacroix's studio, the **Atelier Delacroix** ⑬. Take a left on rue Jacob and turn right down rue Bonaparte to the **École Nationale des Beaux-Arts** ⑭, whose students can often be seen painting and sketching on the nearby quays and bridges. Wander into the courtyard and galleries of the school to see the casts and copies of the statues stored here for safekeeping during the Revolution.

Continue down to the Seine and turn right along the quai, past the **Institut de France** ⑮. With its distinctive dome and commanding position overlooking the **Pont des Arts** ⑯—a footbridge affording delightful views of the Louvre and Ile de la Cité—the institute is one of the city's most impressive waterside sights. Farther along, on the quai de Conti, you pass the **Hôtel des Monnaies** ⑰, the old national mint.

Head up rue Dauphine, the street that singer Juliet Greco put on the map when she opened the erstwhile Tabou jazz club here in the '50s. It's linked 150 yards up by the open-air passage Dauphine to rue Mazarine, which leads left to the **Carrefour de Buci** ⑱, a busy crossroad. Fanning out from the Carrefour are lively rue de Buci, with one of the best food markets in Paris; rue de l'Ancienne-Comédie, so named because it was the first home of the legendary Comédie Française, cutting through to busy place de l'Odéon; and rue St-André des Arts. Head left along the latter to swiftly find the historic **Cour du Commerce St-André** ⑲ (opposite No. 66), a magnificently cobbled pedestrian street where the 18th century seems preserved in amber, lined with cafés, including, halfway down on the left, Paris's oldest, Le Procope. Opposite this landmark stands the **Cour de Rohan** ⑳, which some people believe is the prettiest spot in Paris: one of the hidden treasures of the city, this series of tiny courtyards offers a trip back to storybook Renaissance France.

Head to the end of cour du Commerce St-André, cross boulevard St-Germain, and climb rue de l'Odéon to the colonnaded **Théâtre de l'Odéon** ㉑. Behind the theater, across rue de Vaugirard, lies the spacious **Jardin du Luxembourg** ㉒, one of the most stylish parks in the city. The large pond, usually animated by an armada of toy boats that can be hired alongside, enjoys the scenic backdrop of the rusticated 17th-century **Palais du Luxembourg** ㉓. Today the palace houses the French Senate and is not open to the public, but its adjacent art museum is.

Return to rue de Vaugirard and head west before turning right down pretty rue Férou to place St-Sulpice, a spacious square ringed with cafés; Yves Saint Laurent's famous Rive Gauche store is at No. 6. Looming over the square is the enormous church of **St-Sulpice** ㉔. If you wish to now explore Montparnasse, walk west down rue du Vieux-Colombier and take the métro three stops to Vavin.

TIMING

Depending on how long you spend in the plethora of museums and shops along the way, this 6½-km (4-mi) walk could take anywhere from four hours to several days. Aim for an early start—that way you can hit the Musée d'Orsay early, when crowds are smaller, then get to the rue de Buci street market in full swing, in the late afternoon (the stalls are generally closed for lunch until 3 PM). Note that the Hôtel des Invalides is open daily, but Orsay is closed Monday. You might consider returning to one or more museums on another day or night—Orsay is open late on Thursday evenings.

Sights to See

⑬ Atelier Delacroix. The studio of artist Eugène Delacroix (1798–1863) contains only a small collection of his sketches and drawings, but it's a good place to visit if you want to pay homage to France's foremost Romantic painter. Another reason to pay a call: the atelier is set on place Furstenberg, one of the tiniest, most romantic squares in Paris. ✉ *6 rue Furstenberg, St-Germain-des-Prés,* ☎ *01-44-41-86-50,* ⓦᴇʙ *www.musee.delacroix.fr.* 🎫 *€3.5.* ⊙ *Wed.–Mon. 9:30–5. Métro: St-Germain-des-Prés.*

⑩ Café de Flore. In the postwar years, Jean-Paul Sartre and Simone de Beauvoir would meet their friends and followers at this popular café. These days it's mostly filled with tourists. ✉ *172 bd. St-Germain, St-Germain-des-Prés. Métro: St-Germain-des-Prés.*

⑱ Carrefour de Buci. This crossroads was once a notorious Left Bank landmark: during the 18th century, it contained a gallows, an execution stake, and an iron collar used for punishing troublemakers. In September 1792 the revolutionary army used this daunting site to enroll its first volunteers, and many Royalists and priests lost their heads here during the bloody course of the Revolution. There's nothing sinister, however, about the carrefour today, as brightly colored flowers spill onto the sidewalk at the flower shop on the corner of rue Grégoire-de-Tours. A couple of the small (and highly congested) streets fanning out from the carrefour are of interest. **Rue de Buci** has a good outdoor food market, open Tuesday–Saturday 8–1 and 4–7, Sunday 9–1. **Rue de l'Ancienne-Comédie** got its name because it was the first home of the Comédie Française. *Métro: Mabillon.*

NEED A BREAK?
If you happen to arrive when the market on rue de Buci is closed, **La Vieille France** (✉ 14 rue de Buci, St-Germain-des-Prés, ☎ 01-43-26-55-13) pâtisserie may help fill the gap.

★ **⑲ Cour du Commerce St-André.** Like an 18th-century engraving come to life, this exquisite, cobblestoned street-arcade is one of Paris's loveliest sights. While it has been tatted up with some faux cafés, its shop signs, awnings, and outdoor tables make it a most festive tableau and Napoléon himself still wouldn't look too out of place taking his coffee here (as he did back when). The alleyway might also be called a very romantic sight, but before you abandon yourself to a tryst at a table here remember that at No. 9, Dr. Guillotin conceived the idea for a new, "humane" method of execution; among its many later victims was Charlotte Corday, who stabbed the famous journalist Jean-Paul Marat (who ran his

Revolutionary newspaper, *L'Ami du Peuple*, at No. 8) in his bath in his house just across the boulevard St-Germain; that other great agitator of the French Revolution, Danton, lived at No. 20.

Marat's ashes were actually kept in a memorial at Paris's oldest café, **Le Procope** (☎ 01–40–46–79–00), halfway up the street, opened in 1686 by an Italian named Francesco Procopio. Many of Paris's most famous literary sons and daughters have imbibed here through the centuries, ranging from erudite academics like Denis Diderot to debauchees like Oscar Wilde, as well as Voltaire, Balzac, George Sand, Victor Hugo, and even Benjamin Franklin, who popped in whenever business brought him to Paris and probably rubbed shoulders with the fomenters of the Revolution. The café started out as the Sardi's of its day because the Comédie-Française had opened nearby; Racine and Molière were regulars. The place is still going strong so you, too, can enjoy its period (though now gussied up) trimmings and haute cuisine menu. Just opposite Le Procope is that hidden treasure of the Cour du Commerce: the picturesque courtyard cul-de-sac, the Cour de Rohan. ⊠ *Linking bd. St-Germain and rue St-André-des-Arts, St-Germain-des-Prés. Métro: Odéon.*

★ ⑳ **Cour de Rohan** (Rohan Courtyard). The most magical hideaway in Paris, this series of three cloistered courtyards and passageways found Hollywood immortality when Cecil Beaton picked it as the locale of Gigi's home in the famed Lerner and Loewe 1958 musical film, *Gigi*. Entered from the arcade of the Cour du Commerce St-André, it lies tucked beyond a fragment of medieval city walls and a turret remaining from the days of King Philippe-Auguste. Once part of the home of the archbishops of Rouen (over the years the name was transformed into Rohan), it remains a storybook stage-set. As you enter, the steep staircase directly to your left leads to "chez Mamita" (Gigi's grandmother); beyond are two sloping courtyards, lined with lovely little apartment-ateliers (now the private property of the Foundation Giacometti). Before you leave, lift your eyes and take in the enchanting surrounding roofscape, much of which seems barely changed since the 17th century, including the back of the towering palace once the Paris pied-à-terre of Diane de Poitiers. ⊠ *Entrance on cour du Commerce St-André, St-Germain-des-Prés. Métro: Odéon.*

⑪ **Les Deux Magots.** This old-fashioned St-Germain café, named after the two Chinese figures, or *magots,* inside, still thrives on its post–World War II reputation as one of the Left Bank's prime meeting places for the intelligentsia. It remains crowded day and night, but these days you're more likely to rub shoulders with tourists than with philosophers. Still, if you are in search of the mysterious glamour of the Left Bank, you can do no better than to station yourself at one of the sidewalk tables—or at a window table on a wintry day—to watch the passing parade. ⊠ *6 pl. St-Germain-des-Prés, St-Germain-des-Prés,* ☎ *01–45–48–55–25. Métro: St-Germain-des-Prés.*

⑭ **École Nationale des Beaux-Arts** (National Fine Arts College). Occupying three large mansions near the Seine, this school—today the breeding ground for painters, sculptors, and architects—was once the site of a convent, founded in 1608 by Marguerite de Valois, the first wife of Henri IV. During the Revolution, the convent was turned into a depot for works of art salvaged from the monuments that were under threat of destruction by impassioned mobs. Only the church and cloister remained by the time the Beaux-Arts school was established in 1816. ⊠ *14 rue Bonaparte, St-Germain-des-Prés.* ☉ *Daily 1–7. Métro: St-Germain-des-Prés.*

NEED A
BREAK?

The popular **La Palette** café (☒ 43 rue de Seine, St-Germain-des-Prés, ☎ 01–43–26–68–15), on the corner of rue de Seine and rue Callot, has long been a favorite haunt of Beaux-Arts students. One of them painted the ungainly portrait of the patron François that presides with mock authority.

⑧ Fontaine des Quatre Saisons (Four Seasons Fountain). This allegorical fountain, designed by Edme Bouchardon in 1739 to help boost the district's water supply, has a wealth of sculpted detail. Flanked by a majestic curved screen, the seated figure of Paris, framed by Ionic columns, surveys the rivers Seine and Marne, while bas-reliefs peopled by industrious cupids represent the seasons. ☒ *57–59 rue de Grenelle, St-Germain-des-Prés. Métro: Rue du Bac.*

★ **❹ Hôtel des Invalides.** Les Invalides, as it is widely known, is an outstanding monumental Baroque ensemble designed by architect Libéral Bruant in the 1670s at the behest of Louis XIV, to house wounded (*invalid*) soldiers. Although no more than a handful of old soldiers live at the Invalides today, the military link remains in the form of the **Musée de l'Armée** (Army Museum), one of the world's foremost military museums, with a vast, albeit musty, collection of arms, armor, uniforms, banners, and military pictures down through the ages. Up in the attic in the same space is the **Musée des Plans-Reliefs** (Model Town Museum), with its fascinating collection of old scale models of French towns; the largest and most impressive is Strasbourg, which takes up an entire room. The main, cobbled courtyard is a fitting scene for the parades and ceremonies still occasionally held at the Invalides.

The 17th-century **Église St-Louis des Invalides**, the Invalides's original church, was the site of the first performance of Berlioz's *Requiem*, in 1837. The most impressive dome in Paris towers over Jules Hardouin-Mansart's **Église du Dôme** (Dome Church), built onto the end of Église St-Louis but blocked off from it in 1793—no great pity, perhaps, as the two buildings are vastly different in style and scale. Fittingly, for this military complex, **Napoléon's Tomb** is found here—his remains are kept in a series of no fewer than six coffins, one inside the next, within a bombastic memorial of red porphyry, ringed by low reliefs and a dozen statues symbolizing his campaigns. Among others commemorated in the church are French World War I hero Marshal Foch; Napoléon's brother Joseph, erstwhile king of Spain; and military architect Sébastien de Vauban. ☒ *Pl. des Invalides, Invalides,* ☎ *01–44–42–37–72 Army and Model museums,* WEB *www.invalides.org.* ☒ *€6.* ☉ *Dome Church, Army, and Model museums Apr.–Sept., daily 10–6; Oct.–Mar., daily 10–4:30. Métro: La Tour Maubourg.*

❻ Hôtel Matignon. The most elegant residence of the French prime minister, built in 1721, is the Left Bank counterpart to the president's Élysée Palace. From 1888 to 1914, it was the embassy of the Austro-Hungarian Empire; only since 1958 has it housed heads of government. ☒ *57 rue de Varenne, Invalides. Not open to the public. Métro: Varenne.*

⓱ Hôtel des Monnaies (Royal Mint). Louis XVI transferred the Royal Mint to this imposing mansion in the late 18th century. Although the mint was moved again, to Pessac, near Bordeaux, in 1973, weights and measures, medals, and limited-edition coins are still made here. The **Musée de la Monnaie** (Coin Museum) has an extensive collection of coins, documents, engravings, and paintings. On Tuesday and Friday at 2 PM you can catch the coin metal craftsmen at work in their ateliers overlooking the Seine. ☒ *11 quai de Conti, St-Germain-des-Prés,* ☎ *01–40–46–55–35.* ☒ *€3.* ☉ *Tues.–Fri. 11–5:30, weekends noon–5:30. Métro: Pont Neuf.*

⑮ Institut de France (French Institute). The Institute is one of France's most revered cultural institutions, and its curved, dome-topped facade is one of the Left Bank's most impressive waterside sights. The Tour de Nesle, which formed part of Philippe-Auguste's wall fortifications along the Seine, used to stand here and, in its time, had many royal occupants, including Henry V of England. The French novelist Alexandre Dumas (1824–95) featured the stormy history of the Tour de Nesle—during which the lovers of a number of French queens were tossed from its windows—in a melodrama of the same name. In 1661 the wealthy Cardinal Mazarin left 2 million French *livres* (pounds) in his will for construction of a college that would be dedicated to educating students from Piedmont, Alsace, Artois, and Roussillon, provinces that had been annexed to France during the years of his ministry. Mazarin's coat of arms is sculpted on the dome, and the library in the east wing, which holds more than 350,000 volumes, still bears his name.

At the beginning of the 19th century, Napoléon stipulated that the Institute be transferred here from the Louvre. The Académie Française, the oldest of the five academies that compose the institute, was created by Cardinal Richelieu in 1635. Its first major task was to edit the definitive French dictionary (still unfinished); it is also charged with safeguarding the purity of the French language. Election to its ranks, subject to approval by the French head of state, is the highest literary honor in the land—there can only be 40 "immortal" lifelong members at any one time. ⊠ *Pl. de l'Institut, St-Germain-des-Prés.* ⊙ *Guided visits reserved for cultural associations only. Métro: Pont Neuf.*

⊛ **㉒ Jardin du Luxembourg** (Luxembourg Gardens). Immortalized in countless paintings, the Jardin du Luxembourg possesses all that is unique and befuddling about Parisian parks: swarms of pigeons, cookie-cutter trees, ironed-and-pressed dirt walkways, and immaculate lawns meant for admiring, not touching. The tree- and bench-lined paths offer a reprieve from the incessant bustle of the Quartier Latin, as well as an opportunity to discover the dotty old women and smooching university students who once found their way into Doisneau photographs. Somewhat austere during the colder months, the garden becomes intoxicating as spring fills the flower beds with daffodils, tulips, and hyacinths; the pools teem with boats nudged along by children, and the paths with Parisians thrusting their noses toward the sun. The park's northern boundary is dominated by the Palais du Luxembourg, surrounded by a handful of well-armed guards; they are protecting the senators who have been deliberating in the palace since 1958. Feel free to move the green chairs around to create your own picnic area or people-watching site.

Although the garden may seem purely French, the original 17th-century planning took its inspiration from Italy. When Maria de' Medici acquired the estate of the deceased Duke of Luxembourg in 1612, she decided to turn his mansion into a version of the Florentine Medici home, the Palazzo Pitti. She ended up with something more Franco-Italian than strictly Florentine. The land behind the palace was loosely modeled on the Boboli Gardens. The landscapers, like the architects, didn't design a true version of the Florentine garden, opting for the emerging style of heavy-handed human manipulation of nature—linear vistas, box-trimmed trees, and color-coordinated flower beds—thereby further defining the "French" garden. A tiny corner of the park still possesses that nature-on-the-brink-of-overwhelming-civilization look that was the trademark of the Renaissance Italian garden—namely, the intentionally overgrown cluster of trees and bushes lining the 1624 Fontaine de Médicis. The park captured the hearts of Parisians when it became public after the Revolution; thousands turned out in the mid-1860s to prevent a Haussmann-directed boulevard from being built through its middle.

One of the great attractions of the park is the **Théâtre des Marionnettes,** where on Wednesday, Saturday, and Sunday at 3 and 4:15 PM you can catch one of the classic guignols (marionette shows) for a small admission charge. The wide-mouthed kiddies, though, are the real attraction; their expressions of utter surprise, despair, or glee have fascinated the likes of Henri Cartier-Bresson and François Truffaut. And finally, for those eager to burn off their pastry breakfasts: the Jardin de Luxembourg has a well-maintained trail around the perimeter, and it is one of the few public places the French will be seen in athletic clothes. It takes an average jogger 20 minutes to get all the way around, and water fountains are strategically placed along the way. Men of all ages are also strategically placed; their comments to female runners are irritating, but otherwise this is a great escape. ⊠ *Bordered by bd. St-Michel and rues de Vaugirard, de Médicis, Guynemer, and Auguste-Comte, St-Germain-des-Prés. Métro: Odéon; RER: Luxembourg.*

❷ Musée de la Légion d'Honneur (Legion of Honor Museum). French and foreign decorations are displayed in this mansion by the Seine, linked to the Tuileries by an elegant, two-tiered footbridge. The original building, constructed in 1786, was one of the largest and grandest mansions in town. The Hôtel de Salm—as it is officially known—was burned down during the Commune in 1871, and rebuilt in 1878 in glittering Neoclassical style. It was under renovation at press time and scheduled to reopen during 2003. ⊠ *2 rue de Bellechasse, St-Germain-des-Prés,* ☎ *01–40–62–84–25. Métro: Solférino; RER: Musée d'Orsay.*

❼ Musée Maillol. Bronzes by Art Deco sculptor Aristide Maillol (1861–1944), whose sleek, stylized nudes adorn the Tuileries Gardens, can be admired at this handsome town house lovingly restored by his former muse, Dina Vierny. Maillol's drawings, paintings, and tapestries are also on show. Works by other artists include a roomful of Poliakoff abstractions and two sensuous Zitman nudes in the barrel-vaulted cellar café. ⊠ *61 rue de Grenelle, St-Germain-des-Prés,* ☎ *01–42–22–59–58.* ▨ *€6.* ☉ *Wed.–Mon. 11–6. Métro: Rue du Bac.*

★ **❶ Musée d'Orsay.** Setting out to form a bridge between the classical collections of the Louvre and the modern collections of the Centre Pompidou, the collection of the Musée d'Orsay includes many of the most famous Impressionist and Postimpressionist paintings in the world. On top of that, the building itself—a spectacularly renovated Belle Epoque train station—is a work of art. Beginning in 1900, the building was used as a depot for routes between Paris and the southwest of France. By 1939, the Gare d'Orsay had become too small for mainline travel, and intercity trains were transferred to the Gare d'Austerlitz, with the d'Orsay becoming a suburban terminus, until it closed in the 1960s. The building was temporarily used as a theater, an auction house, and a setting for Orson Welles's movie *The Trial,* based on Kafka's novel, before it was finally slated for demolition. However, the destruction of the 19th-century Les Halles (market halls) across the Seine provoked a furor among conservationists, and in the late 1970s, former president Giscard d'Estaing ordered the d'Orsay to be transformed into a museum. Architects Pierre Colboc, Renaud Bardou, and Jean-Paul Philippon were commissioned to remodel the building; Gae Aulenti, known for her renovation of the Palazzo Grassi in Venice, was hired to reshape the interior. Aulenti's modern design in a building almost a century old provoked much controversy, but the museum's attributes soon outweighed any criticism shortly after its opening in December 1986.

The collection is devoted to the arts (mainly French) spanning the period 1848–1914. Exhibits take up three floors, but the immediate impression is of a single, vast, stationlike hall. While the chief artistic attraction is the Impressionists, whose works are displayed under the roof, the museum also prominently includes lesser-ranked academic and salon painters, many of whose names will be unfamiliar to most. Renoir, Sisley, Pissarro, and Monet do not, in other words, compose the entire history of French 19th-century art. Still, the highlights include Monet's *Les Coquelicots* (*Poppy Fields*) and Renoir's *Le Moulin de la Galette* (*Wafer Windmill*), which differs from many other Impressionist paintings in that Renoir worked from numerous studies and completed it in his studio rather than painting it in the open air. Nonetheless, its focus on the activities of a group of ordinary Parisians amusing themselves in the sun on a Montmartre afternoon is typical of the spontaneity and fleeting sense of moment that are the essence of Impressionism. Whereas Monet, the only one of the group to adhere faithfully to the tenets of Impressionism throughout his career, strove to catch the effects of light—for more of this great master, remember to also visit the Musée Marmottan—Renoir was more interested in the human figure.

The Postimpressionists—Cézanne, van Gogh, Gauguin, and Toulouse-Lautrec—are also represented on the top floor. You may find the intense, almost classical serenity of Cézanne the dominant presence here; witness his magnificent Mont Ste-Victoire series, in which he paints and repaints the same subject, in the process dissolving form until the step to Cubism and abstract painting seems an inevitability. Or you may be drawn by the vivid simplicity and passion of van Gogh or by the psychedelic, pagan rhythms of Gauguin.

On the first floor are the works of Manet and the delicate nuances of Degas. Be sure to see Manet's *Déjeuner sur l'Herbe* (*Lunch on the Grass*), the painting that scandalized Paris in 1863 at the Salon des Refusés, an exhibit organized by artists refused permission to show their work at the academy's official annual salon. The painting shows a nude woman and two clothed men picnicking in a park. In the background, another girl bathes in a stream. Manet took the subject, poses and all, from a little-known Renaissance print in the Louvre but updated the clothing to mid-19th-century France. What would otherwise have been thought a respectable "academic" painting thus became deeply shocking: two clothed men with a naked woman in 19th-century France! The loose, bold brushwork, a far cry from the polished styles of the Renaissance, added insult to artistic injury. Another reworking by Manet of a classical motif is his reclining nude, *Olympia*. Gazing boldly out from the canvas, she was more than respectable 19th-century Parisian proprieties could stand, with her unfinished hands (they were described as monkey paws) and black cat (a symbol of female sexuality). These two Manet works all but ushered in the age of modern painting. American works are also on view, one of which, Whistler's iconic portrait of his mother, *Arrangement in Black and White,* might seem to be merely a dose of American spartan puritanism; its minimalist palette and striking sense of design, however, were almost as revolutionary as Manet's achievements.

If you prefer more academic paintings, look at Puvis de Chavannes's larger-than-life classical canvases. The pale, limpid beauty of his figures is enjoying renewed attention after years of neglect. For sheer spectacle, lose yourself in Thomas Couture's *Romans of the Decadence,* a Cinerama-screen-size depiction of ancient excess. If you are more excited by more modern developments, look for the early 20th-century

Fauves (meaning "wild beasts," the name given them by an outraged critic in 1905)—particularly Matisse, Derain, and Vlaminck. Thought-provoking sculptures also litter the museum at every turn. Two further highlights are the faithfully restored Belle Epoque restaurant and the model of the entire Opéra quarter, displayed beneath a glass floor, along with an extensive display of drawings and models given over to that 19th-century masterwork, the Opéra Garnier. ⊠ *1 rue de la Légion d'Honneur, St-Germain-des-Prés,* ☎ *01–40–49–48–14,* WEB *www. musee-orsay.fr.* ⊡ *€7, Sun. €5.* ⊙ *Tues.–Wed. and Fri.–Sat. 10–6, Thurs. 10–9:45, Sun. 9–6. Métro: Solférino; RER: Musée d'Orsay.*

NEED A BREAK? Find respite from the overwhelming collection of art in the gorgeous **Musée d'Orsay Café**, in the Musée d'Orsay behind one of the giant station clocks, close to the Impressionist galleries on the top floor (☎ 1–45–49–47–03). The interior is a white-on-white Belle Epoque dazzler, the luncheon is buffet, and the late afternoon *le goûter Orsay* offers a sumptuous high tea. From the rooftop terrace alongside there is a panoramic view across the Seine toward Montmartre and the Sacré-Coeur.

★ ❺ **Musée Rodin.** The splendid Hôtel Biron, with its spacious vestibule, broad staircase, and patrician salons lined with boiseries, retains much of its 18th-century ambience and makes a somewhat startling frame for the sculpture of Auguste Rodin (1840–1917). His funeral, at the height of World War I, drew the largest nonmilitary crowd of the time (26,000); while alive, however, Rodin was stalked by controversy. His career took off in 1876 with *L'Age d'Airain* (The Bronze Age), inspired by a pilgrimage to Italy and the sculptures of Michelangelo. Because the work was so realistic, some critics accused Rodin of having stuck a live boy in plaster, while others blasted him for what was seen as a sloppy sculpting and casting technique. His seeming messiness, though, was intentional; Rodin sought to capture the sculpting process through the imprints of fingers, rags used to keep the clay moist, and tools he left on his works.

Four years later, Rodin was commissioned to create the doors for the newly proposed Musée des Arts Décoratifs (Museum of Decorative Arts). He set out to sculpt a pair of monumental bronze doors in the tradition of Italian Renaissance churches, calling his proposal *La Porte de l'Enfer* (The Gate of Hell). The Gate, a visual representation of stories from Dante's Divine Comedy, became his obsession: he spent the last 37 years of his life working on it. Possibly Rodin's most celebrated work is *Le Penseur* (The Thinker, ca. 1880), the muscular man caught in a moment of deep thought and flex. The version here in the garden is the original—the city of Paris, its intended owner, refused to accept it. Before installing the permanent bronze statue on the steps of the Panthéon, Rodin set up a full-scale plaster cast. Its physicality horrified the public; crowds gathered around the statue, debates ensued, and Rodin was ridiculed in the press. A sad footnote in the collection is evidenced by works by Rodin's mistress Camille Claudel (1864–1943), a remarkable sculptor in her own right. Her torturous relationship with Rodin drove her out of his studio—and out of her mind. In 1913 she was packed off to an asylum, where she remained, barred from any artistic activities, until her death in 1943. As much a work of art as the sculptures on view, the gardens of the Musée Rodin are justly famous for their rosebushes (more than 2,000 of them, representing 100 varieties). Here, you'll find some prime Rodin pieces, such as the powerful *Balzac* and the mythic *Burghers of Calais.* ⊠ *77 rue de Varenne, Invalides,* ☎ *01–44–18–61–10,* WEB *www.musee-rodin.fr.* ⊡ *€5, Sun.*

€3, *gardens only* €1. ☉ *Easter–Oct., Tues.–Sun. 9:30–5:45; Nov.–Easter, Tues.–Sun. 9:30–4:45. Métro: Varenne.*

❸ Palais Bourbon. The most prominent feature of the Palais Bourbon—home of the Assemblée Nationale, the French Parliament since 1798—is its colonnaded facade, commissioned by Napoléon to match that of the Madeleine across the Seine. Cortot's sculpted pediment portrays France holding the tablets of law, flanked by Force and Justice. ⊠ *Pl. du Palais-Bourbon, Invalides. ☉ During temporary exhibits only. Métro: Assemblée Nationale.*

OFF THE BEATEN PATH **STE-CLOTILDE** – Once the most fashionable church in 19th-century Paris, this neo-Gothic church (built 1846–58) is notable for its imposing twin spires, visible from across the Seine. French classical composer César Franck was organist here from 1858 to 1890. From the Palais Bourbon, take rue Bourgogne south; then take a left on rue Las-Cases. ⊠ *Rue Las-Cases, Invalides. Métro: Solférino.*

㉒ Palais du Luxembourg (Luxembourg Palace). The gray, imposing, rusticated Luxembourg Palace was built, like the surrounding Luxembourg Gardens, for Maria de' Medici, widow of Henri IV, at the beginning of the 17th century. Maria was born and raised in Florence's Pitti Palace, and, having languished in the Louvre after the death of her husband, she was eager to build herself a new palace, where she could recapture something of the lively, carefree atmosphere of her childhood. In 1612, she bought the Paris mansion of the Duke of Luxembourg, tore it down, and built her palace. It was not completed until 1627, and Maria was to live there for just five years (the grand series of canvases Rubens painted to decorate the palace are now in the Louvre). In 1632, Cardinal Richelieu had her expelled from France, and she saw out her declining years in Cologne, Germany, dying there almost penniless in 1642. The palace remained royal property until the Revolution, when the state took it over and used it as a prison. Danton, the painter David, and Thomas Paine were all detained here. Today the French Senate meets here, so the building is not open to the public. However, adjacent to the palace is the venerable **Musée de Luxembourg.** Once home to many of the masterpieces now on view at the Musée d'Orsay, it is open occasionally for temporary exhibitions—currently on view for a loan of several years is the Rau Collection, amassed by an eccentric millionaire and studded with famous paintings which may be auctioned off for charity in twenty years' time. ⊠ *Musée: 17 rue de Vaugirard, St-Germain-des-Prés,* ☏ *01–42–34–25– 95. Métro: Odéon; RER: Luxembourg.*

⑯ Pont des Arts (Arts Footbridge). Immortalized in paintings by Renoir and Pissarro, this iron-and-wood footbridge linking the Louvre to the Institut de France is a favorite with painters, art students, and misty-eyed romantics moved by the delightful views of the Ile de la Cité. The bridge got its name because the Louvre was once called the Palais des Arts (Palace of Art). *Métro: Pont Neuf.*

⑫ St-Germain-des-Prés. Paris's oldest church was first built to shelter a relic of the true cross, brought back from Spain in AD 542. The chancel was enlarged and the church then consecrated by Pope Alexander III in 1163; the tall, sturdy tower—a Left Bank landmark—dates from this period. The colorful 19th-century frescoes in the nave by Hippolyte Flandrin, a pupil of the classical painter Ingres, depict vivid scenes from the Old Testament. The church stages superb organ concerts and recitals. ⊠ *Pl. St-Germain-des-Prés, St-Germain-des-Prés. ☉ Weekdays 8–7:30, weekends 8 AM–9 PM. Métro: St-Germain-des-Prés.*

㉔ **St-Sulpice.** Dubbed the Cathedral of the Left Bank, this enormous 17th-century church has entertained some unlikely christenings—the Marquis de Sade's and Charles Baudelaire's, for instance—and the nuptials of irreverent wordsmith Victor Hugo. The 18th-century facade was never finished, and its unequal towers add a playful touch to an otherwise sober design. The interior is baldly impersonal, despite the magnificent Delacroix frescoes—notably *Jacob Luttant avec l'Ange* (*Jacob Wrestling with the Angel*)—in the first chapel on your right. ⊠ *Pl. St-Sulpice, St-Germain-des-Prés. Métro: St-Sulpice.*

❾ **St-Thomas d'Aquin.** This elegant, domed church, designed by Pierre Bulet in 1683, was originally dedicated to St. Dominique and flanked by a convent—whose buildings now belong to the army. The east-end chapel was added in 1722 and the two-tiered facade in 1768. Pope Pius VII popped in during his trip to Paris for Napoléon's coronation in December 1804. ⊠ *Pl. St-Thomas-d'Aquin, St-Germain-des-Prés. Métro: Rue du Bac.*

㉑ **Théâtre de l'Odéon.** At the north end of the Luxembourg Gardens, on place de l'Odéon, sits the colonnaded Odéon Theater—a masterpiece of the neoclassical style. It was established in 1792 to house the Comédie Française troupe; the original building was destroyed by fire in 1807. Since World War II it has specialized in 20th-century productions and was the base for Jean-Louis Barrault's and Madeleine Renaud's theater company, the Théâtre de France, until they fell out of favor with the authorities for their alleged role in spurring on student revolutionaries in May 1968. Today, the theater is the French home of the Theater of Europe and stages excellent productions by major foreign companies, sometimes in English. ⊠ *1 pl. de l'Odéon, St-Germain-des-Prés,* ☎ *01-44-41-36-36. Métro: Odéon.*

MONTPARNASSE

About 15 blocks south of the Seine lies the Montparnasse district, named after Mount Parnassus, the Greek mountain associated with the worship of Apollo and the Muses. Montparnasse's cultural heyday came in the first four decades of the 20th century, when it replaced Montmartre as *the* place for painters and poets to live. Pablo Picasso, Amedeo Modigliani, Ernest Hemingway, Jean Cocteau, Man Ray, and Leon Trotsky were among the luminaries who spawned an intellectual café society—later to be found at St-Germain—and prompted the launch of a string of arty brasseries along the district's main thoroughfare, the broad boulevard du Montparnasse.

The boulevard may lack poetic charm these days, but nightlife stays the pace as bars, clubs, restaurants, and cinemas crackle with energy beneath continental Europe's tallest high-rise, the 59-story Tour Montparnasse. Although the tower itself is a typically bland product of the early 1970s, of note only for the view from the top, several more adventurous buildings have risen in its wake. Ricardo Bofill's semicircular Amphithéâtre housing complex, with its whimsical postmodernist quotations of classical detail, is the most famous. The glass-cubed Cartier center for contemporary art and the Montparnasse train station, with its giant glass facade and designer garden above the tracks, are other outstanding examples.

If you have a deeper feel for history, you may prefer the sumptuous Baroque church of Val-de-Grâce or the quiet earth of Montparnasse cemetery, where Baudelaire, Sartre, Bartholdi (who designed the Statue of Liberty), and actress Jean Seberg slumber. The Paris underground had its headquarters nearby—in the Roman catacombs—during the

Nazi occupation. After ignoring Hitler's orders to blow up the city, Governor von Choltitz signed the German surrender in Montparnasse in August 1944.

Numbers in the text correspond to numbers in the margin and on the Montparnasse map.

A Good Walk

Take the métro or walk to the Vavin station (only three stops from St-Sulpice), beneath Rodin's 10-ft statue of Balzac and alongside the café La Rotonde at the corner of boulevards Raspail and Montparnasse. Three other cafés, famous since Montparnasse's interwar heyday, are all within a stone's throw on boulevard du Montparnasse: Le Sélect at No. 99 and, across the street, the Café du Dôme (No. 108) and **La Coupole** ①, with its painted columns and restored Art Deco interior (No. 102). Head west along boulevard du Montparnasse to **place du 18-Juin-1940** ②. Towering above the square is the **Tour Montparnasse** ③. Behind the building is the huge, gleaming glass facade of Gare Montparnasse, the train station that is home to the 200-mph *TGV Atlantique,* serving western France.

Cross place Bienvenüe, to the right of Tour Montparnasse; then take avenue Maine, then your first left onto rue Antoine-Bourdelle. The sharp brick outlines of the **Musée Bourdelle** ④, full of the powerful sculpture of Antoine Bourdelle, loom halfway along. Continue to the end of the street and turn left onto rue Armand-Moissant; note the elegant beige and green brick facade of the École Commerciale on your left before turning right onto boulevard de Vaugirard. There's a fine view from here of Tour Montparnasse away to your left. A short way along the boulevard is the **Musée de la Poste** ⑤, a must if you're a stamp collector. Cross the boulevard and take the elevator by No. 25 to reach the **Jardin Atlantique** ⑥, a modern park laid over the rail tracks of Montparnasse station. Memories of World War II—notably the French Resistance and the Liberation of Paris—are evoked in a modern museum to the left.

Cross the Jardin Atlantique at the far end and turn left down to **place de Catalogne** ⑦, dominated by the monumental curves of the postmodern Amphithéâtre housing complex. Explore its arcades and circular forecourts, and compare its impersonal grandeur with the cozy charm of the small church of Notre-Dame du Travail behind. Rue Jean-Zay leads from place de Catalogne to the corner of the high-walled **Cimetière du Montparnasse** ⑧. Enter the cemetery down rue Froidevaux if you wish to pay homage to local and foreign worthies. Rue Froidevaux continues to place Denfert-Rochereau, where you can admire the huge bronze *Lion of Belfort* by Frédéric-Auguste Bartholdi, the sculptor of the Statue of Liberty (he, too, is buried in Montparnasse cemetery), and visit the extensive underground labyrinth of the **catacombs** ⑨, which tunnel under much of the Left Bank and the suburbs.

Walk up boulevard Raspail, past the eye-catching glass cube that houses the **Fondation Cartier** ⑩. Take the third right onto rue Campagne-Première, a handsome street once inhabited by Picasso, Miró, Kandinsky, and Modigliani. Note the tiled facade on the artists' residence at No. 31. Turn right at the bottom of the street onto boulevard du Montparnasse. At avenue de l'Observatoire stands perhaps the most famous bastion of Left Bank café culture, the **Closerie des Lilas** ⑪. Up avenue de l'Observatoire is the **Observatoire de Paris** ⑫, Louis XIV's astronomical observatory. In the other direction, the tree-lined avenue sweeps past the **Fontaine de l'Observatoire** ⑬. To the right of the fountain, at the bottom of rue du Val-de-Grâce, is the imposing Baroque dome of **Val de Grâce** ⑭. Straight ahead is the Jardin du Luxembourg.

108

TIMING

This walk around Montparnasse is just under 5 km (3 mi) long and should comfortably take a morning or an afternoon if you choose to check out one of the historic cafés, the cemetery, and the catacombs along the way.

Sights to See

⑨ Catacombs. *"Arrête! C'est ici l'Empire de la Mort"* ("Halt! This is the Empire of Death"). This message scrawled at the entrance was enough to convince German troops in World War II to leave promptly before they guessed that Resistance fighters used the tunnels in the catacombs as a base. This dire warning now welcomes you after a winding descent through dark, clammy passages to Paris's principal ossuary and most disturbing collection of human remains. Bones from the notorious Cimetière des Innocents were the first to be transplanted here in 1786, when decomposing bodies started seeping into neighboring cellars, bringing swarms of ravenous rats with them. The legions of bones dumped here are arranged not by owner but by type—witness the rows of skulls, stacks of tibias, and piles of spinal disks. There are also some bizarre attempts at bone art, like skulls arranged in the shape of hearts. It's macabre and makes you feel quite . . . mortal. Among the bones in here are those of Mirabeau (1749–91), the Revolutionary leader; 16th-century satirist and writer Rabelais (1490–1553) was transplanted from the former cemetery at the Église St-Paul–St-Louis; and famous courtesan Madame de Pompadour (1721–64) is mixed in with the rabble after a lifetime spent as the mistress to Louis XV. Be prepared to walk long distances when you come here—the tunnels stretch for miles, and the only light comes from the flashlight that you bring yourself. ⊠ *1 pl. Denfert-Rochereau, Montparnasse,* ☎ *01-43-22-47-63,* WEB *www.paris-france.org/musees.* ⊡ *€5, guided tours €3 extra.* ☉ *Wed.–Sun. 9–4, Tues. 11–4. Guided tours Wed. at 2:45. Métro and RER: Denfert-Rochereau.*

8 **Cimetière du Montparnasse** (Montparnasse Cemetery). High walls encircle this cemetery, a haven of peace in one of Paris's busiest shopping and business areas. It is not picturesque (with the exception of the towered rump of an old windmill that used to be a student tavern) but contains many of the quarter's most illustrious residents, buried only a stone's throw away from where they lived and loved: Charles Baudelaire, Bartholdi (who designed the Statue of Liberty), Alfred Dreyfus, Guy de Maupassant, Camille Saint-Saëns, Jean-Paul Sartre, Tristan Tzara, and, more recently, photographer Man Ray, playwright Samuel Beckett, actress Jean Seberg, and singer-songwriter Serge Gainsbourg. ⊠ *Entrances on rue Froidevaux, bd. Edgar-Quinet, Montparnasse. Métro: Raspail, Gaîté.*

11 **Closerie des Lilas.** Now a pricey bar-restaurant, the Closerie remains a staple of all literary tours of Paris. Commemorative plaques fastened to the bar mark the places where members of the literati, such as Baudelaire, Verlaine, and Hemingway (who wrote pages of *The Sun Also Rises* here; he lived around the corner at 115 rue Notre-Dame-ds-Champs) used to station themselves. Although the lilacs (*lilas*) that graced the garden here, shading habitués such as Ingres, Whistler, and Balzac, have gone from the terrace, it still opens onto a garden wall of luxuriant evergreen foliage and is as crowded in the summer as it ever was in the '30s. ⊠ *171 bd. du Montparnasse, Montparnasse,* ☎ *01–43–26–70–50. Métro: Vavin; RER: Port Royal.*

OFF THE
BEATEN PATH

MUSÉE ZADKINE – Russian-born sculptor Ossip Zadkine (1890–1967) trained in London before setting up in Paris in 1909. The works on exhibit at this museum, in Zadkine's former house and studio, reveal the influences of Rodin, African art, and Cubism. ⊠ *100 bis rue d'Assas, Montparnasse,* ☎ *01-43-26-91-90,* WEB *www.paris-france.org/musees.* ⊠ *Free.* ☺ *Tues.–Sun. 10–5:40. Métro: Vavin.*

1 **La Coupole.** One of Montparnasse's most famous brasseries, La Coupole opened in 1927 as a bar–restaurant–dance hall and soon became a home-away-from-home for Apollinaire, Max Jacob, Cocteau, Satie, Stravinsky, and Hemingway. It may not be quite the same draw these days, but it still pulls in a classy crowd. The columns painted by a host of Parisian artists, including Chagall and Brancusi, which lend La Coupole its Art Deco panache, were restored in the late '80s, along with the mosaic floor and original citronwood furniture. ⊠ *102 bd. du Montparnasse, Montparnasse,* ☎ *01-43-20-14-20.* ☺ *Daily 7:30 AM–2 AM. Métro: Vavin.*

10 **Fondation Cartier** (Cartier Foundation). Architect Jean Nouvel's eye-catching giant glass cube is a suitable setting for the temporary, thought-provoking shows of contemporary art organized here by jewelry giant Cartier. ⊠ *261 bd. Raspail, Montparnasse,* ☎ *01-42-18-56-50.* ⊠ *€4.6.* ☺ *Tues.–Sun. noon–8. Métro: Raspail.*

13 **Fontaine de l'Observatoire** (Observatory Fountain). Gabriel Davioud's fountain, built in 1873, is topped by Jean-Baptiste Carpeaux's four bronze statues of female nudes holding a globe, representing Les Quatre Parties du Monde (The Four Continents). If you get a sense of déjà vu seeing this, it may because you remember this, stunningly illuminated at night, as backdrop to Louis Jourdan's warbling of "Gigi" in the MGM film of 1958. ⊠ *Av. de l'Observatoire, Montparnasse. RER: Port Royal.*

6 **Jardin Atlantique** (Atlantic Garden). Built over the tracks of Gare Montparnasse, this smart designer park, opened in 1994, is noted for its assortment of trees and plants found in coastal regions near the At-

LA VIE BOHEME: ARTISTS, WRITERS, AND EXILES

FOR THREE-QUARTERS of a century—roughly from the 1880s to the 1950s—Paris enjoyed a reputation as Europe's most creative and bohemian capital, acting as a magnet for the international avant-garde.

The decades before World War I saw the slopes of **Montmartre,** in north Paris, alive with the sound of Belle Epoque music. Whirling windmills and swirling petticoats set the tone, no more so than at the Moulin Rouge cabaret, whose dancers doing the cancan were immortalized in posters and paintings by Toulouse-Lautrec. Femmes fatales? Lautrec drank and drugged himself to premature death.

Artists had moved into the district as early as the 1860s, when Monet and Manet pursued their interest in steam and rail at the Gare St-Lazare. New boulevards meant easier access to nearby Montmartre: cheap and pretty, with an abundance of shady nightlife, the area was an artist's dream. Van Gogh, Cézanne, Seurat, Signac, Degas, Vuillard, and Dufy all followed. Renoir painted his *Moulin de la Galette*; Picasso and Braque sighted Cubism in the Bateau-Lavoir on place Émile-Goudeau.

Montmartre lost its luster after World War I; Utrillo remained, his repetitive street scenes a weak postscript to the powerful austerity of his youthful "White Period."

The Roaring '20s saw the Paris art scene shift south to another hill: **Montparnasse.** Picasso and Modigliani decamped to rue Campagne-Première, joined by Miró and Kandinsky; Braque worked nearby in rue du Douanier-Rousseau.

Belle Epoque cabarets lost out to Art Deco bars and brasseries, a whole string of them along boulevard du Montparnasse: the Coupole, Dôme, Select, Rotonde, and the Closerie des Lilas, most of them assiduously frequented by Ernest Hemingway. Gertrude Stein held court for her "Lost Generation" near the Luxembourg Gardens, hosting Picasso and writers like Ezra Pound, Henry Miller, and Zelda and F. Scott Fitzgerald. Redevelopment, epitomized by the Tour Montparnasse, has long since exiled aesthetes.

After World War II the literati went north to **St-Germain-des-Prés,** whose own cluster of cafés—Flore (where Sartre and de Beauvoir preached existentialism), Lipp, Les Deux Magots (once favored by Rimbaud and Gide)—became the beacon for left-wing intellectuals in the 1950s and 1960s.

Picture and antiques dealers crowd the streets of St-Germain, rubbing shoulders with the publishing houses that have been here since before Joyce first published *Ulysses* at Shakespeare & Company on rue de l'Odéon in 1922. Baudelaire, Voltaire, and Oscar Wilde (as well as Delacroix, Sibelius, and Wagner) all lived in the area; Voltaire died there in 1788, and Wilde expired around the corner at **13 rue des Beaux-Arts**—a plaque on the building commemorates the spot and the street is still home to a fine-arts school.

These days, however, once they finish school, few art students stick around: Paris is no longer the thriving center for contemporary art that it once was. But intellectual ghosts still haunt the Left Bank: at the bouquinistes by the Seine, along the creaking floorboards of Shakespeare & Co. on rue de la Bûcherie, or in the tiny Théâtre de la Huchette nearby, where Ionesco's bald soprano sings nightly for her supper to full houses.

lantic Ocean—thus the name. A museum building at the station end of the garden houses souvenirs and video coverage of World War II inside the **Mémorial du Maréchal-Leclerc,** commemorating the liberator of Paris, and the **Musée Jean-Moulin,** devoted to the leader of the French Resistance. In the center of the park, what looks like a quirky piece of metallic sculpture is actually a meteorological center, with a battery of flickering lights reflecting temperature, wind speed, and monthly rainfall. ⊠ *Pont des Cinq-Martyrs-du-Lycée-Buffon, Montparnasse,* ☎ *01–40–64–39–44,* WEB *www.paris-france.org/musees.* 🖃 *Free,* ⊙ *Musée Tues.–Sun. 10–5:40. Métro: Montparnasse Bienvenüe.*

❹ Musée Bourdelle (Bourdelle Museum). Opened in 1949 in the studios and gardens where Rodin's pupil Antoine Bourdelle (1861–1929) lived and worked, and extended by Christian de Portzamparc in 1992, this spacious brick museum houses 500 works in plaster, marble, and bronze, including castings of Bourdelle's landmark works, the bombastic *Heracles the Archer* and the *Dying Centaur.* ⊠ *18 rue Antoine-Bourdelle, Montparnasse,* ☎ *01–49–54–73–73,* WEB *www.paris-france. org/musees.* 🖃 *Free.* ⊙ *Tues.–Sun. 10–5:40. Métro: Falguière.*

❺ Musée de la Poste (Postal Museum). On display at this five-story museum of postal history, renovated in 2000, are international and French stamps (dating as far back as 1849), postal carriers' uniforms and mailboxes, sorting and stamp-printing machines, and one of the balloons used to send mail out of Paris during the Prussian siege of 1870. ⊠ *34 bd. de Vaugirard, Montparnasse,* ☎ *01–42–79–24–24,* WEB *www.laposte. fr/musee.* 🖃 *€4.6.* ⊙ *Mon.–Sat. 10–6. Métro: Montparnasse Bienvenüe.*

⑫ Observatoire de Paris (Paris Observatory). The observatory was constructed in 1667 for Louis XIV by architect Claude Perrault. Its four facades are aligned with the four cardinal points—north, south, east, and west—and its southern wall is the determining point for Paris's official latitude, 48° 50′11″N. French time was based on this Paris meridian until 1911, when the country decided to adopt the international Greenwich Meridian. The interior is not open to the general public. ⊠ *Av. de l'Observatoire, Montparnasse. RER: Port Royal.*

❼ Place de Catalogne (Catalonia Square). This circular square is dominated by the monumental **Amphithéâtre,** a housing complex built in the 1980s by architect Ricardo Bofill. Its chunky reinvention of classical detail may strike you as witty—or as overkill. Behind is the turn-of-the-20th-century **Notre-Dame du Travail** church, which made a powerful statement when it was built: its riveted iron-and-steel framework was meant to symbolize the work ethos enshrined in the church's name. The Sebastopol Bell above the facade is a trophy from the Crimean War. ⊠ *Pl. de Catalogne, Montparnasse. Métro: Gaîté.*

❷ Place du 18-Juin-1940. This square beneath the Tour Montparnasse is named for the date of the radio speech Charles de Gaulle broadcast from London, urging the French to resist the Germans after the Nazi invasion of May 1940. It was here that German military governor Dietrich von Choltitz surrendered to the Allies in August 1944, ignoring Hitler's orders to destroy the city as he withdrew. A plaque on the wall of what is now a shopping center—originally the Montparnasse train station extended this far—commemorates the event. *Métro: Montparnasse Bienvenüe.*

❸ Tour Montparnasse (Montparnasse Tower). Continental Europe's tallest skyscraper, completed in 1973, this 680-ft building offers a stupendous view of Paris from its open-air roof terrace. It attracts 800,000 gawkers each year; on a clear day, you can see for 40 km (25 mi). A glossy brochure, "Paris Vu d'en Haut" ("Paris From On High") explains just what to look for. It also claims to have the fastest elevator in Europe. Fifty-two of the 59 stories are taken up by offices, and a vast commercial complex, including a Galeries Lafayette department store, spreads over the first floor. Banal by day, the tower becomes Montparnasse's neon-lit beacon at night. ⊠ *Rue de l'Arrivée, Montparnasse,* ☎ *01–45–38–52–56,* WEB *www.tourmontparnasse56.com.* ☞ *€7.5.* ⊙ *Daily 9:30 AM–11 PM. Métro: Montparnasse Bienvenüe.*

⑭ Val de Grâce. This imposing 17th-century Left Bank church was commissioned by Anne of Austria and designed by François Mansart. Its powerfully rhythmic two-story facade rivals the Dôme Church at the Invalides as the city's most striking example of Italianate Baroque. Pierre Mignard's 1663 cupola fresco bursts with more than 200 sky-climbing figures. The church's original abbey buildings are now a military army hospital, with a small museum of army medical history. ⊠ *1 pl. Alphonse-Laveran, Latin Quarter,* ☎ *01–40–51–51–94.* ☞ *€4.6.* ⊙ *Museum Tues.–Wed. noon–6, weekends 1:30–5. RER: Port Royal.*

MONTMARTRE

Topped by its "sculpted cloud"—the famous Sacré-Coeur Basilica—and set on a dramatic rise above the city, Montmartre is the picturesque quartier that was once the haunt of Toulouse-Lautrec, Utrillo, and van Gogh. Although the fabled nightlife of old Montmartre has fizzled down to some glitzy nightclubs and porn shows, the neighborhood still exudes a sense of history, a timeless quality infused with that hard-to-define Gallic charm.

Windmills once dotted Montmartre (often referred to by Parisians as *La Butte,* meaning "the mound"). They were set up here not just because the hill was a good place to catch the wind—at more than 300 ft, it's the highest point in the city—but because Montmartre was covered with wheat fields and quarries right up to the end of the 19th century. Today, only two of the original 20 windmills remain.

Visiting Montmartre means negotiating a lot of steep streets and flights of steps. The crown atop this urban peak, Sacré-Coeur, is something of an architectural oddity. It has been called everything from grotesque to sublime; its silhouette, viewed from afar at dusk or sunrise, looks more like a mosque than a cathedral.

There is a disputed story of how Montmartre got its name. Some say the name comes from the Roman temple to Mercury that was once here, called the Mound of Mercury, or *Mons Mercurii.* Others contend that it was an adaptation of *Mons Martyrum,* a name inspired by the burial here of Paris's first bishop, St. Denis. The popular version of his martyrdom is that he was beheaded by the Romans in AD 250 but arose to carry his severed head from rue Yvonne-Le-Tac to a place 6½ km (4 mi) to the north, an area now known as St-Denis. A final twist on the name controversy is that Montmartre briefly came to be known as Mont-Marat during the French Revolution. Marat was a leading Revolutionary figure who was stabbed to death in his bath.

Numbers in the text correspond to numbers in the margin and on the Montmartre map.

A Good Walk

Take the métro to the Blanche stop and start your tour at one of Paris's least-known but most atmospheric cemeteries, the tumbling **Cimetière de Montmartre** ① at the end of avenue Rachel (off boulevard de Clichy). Return to **place Blanche,** where all eyes are drawn to the **Moulin Rouge** ②, the windmill–turned–dance hall immortalized by Toulouse-

Montmartre

Lautrec and, in 2001, the Baz Lurhman/Nicole Kidman film. The Café Cyrano, next door to the Moulin Rouge, was once the haunt of Salvador Dalí and his fellow Surrealists. A few steps along the boulevard is the **Musée de l'Erotisme** ③, whose collection of erotic artifacts from around the world pays fulsome tribute to Montmartre's Sin City image.

Walk up lively rue Lepic from place Blanche. The tiny Lux Bar at No. 12 has a 1910 mosaic showing place Blanche at the beginning of the 20th century. Wind your way up to the **Moulin de la Galette** ④, on your left, atop its leafy hillock opposite rue Tholozé, once a path over the hill. Then turn right down rue Tholozé, past **Studio 28** ⑤, the first cinema built expressly for experimental films.

Continue down rue Tholozé to rue des Abbesses, and turn left toward the triangular **place des Abbesses** ⑥. Note the austere, redbrick facade of **St-Jean l'Evangéliste** ⑦. Tiny rue André-Antoine, to the right of the popular Café St-Jean, leads to what was originally the **Théâtre Libre** ⑧, or Free Theater, at No. 37. Return to the square and take rue Yvonne-Le-Tac, off to the right. Paris's first bishop, St. Denis, is commemorated by the 19th-century **Chapelle du Martyre** ⑨ at No. 9, built on the spot where he is said to have been beheaded.

Return to the square and follow rue Ravignan as it climbs, via place Émile-Goudeau, an enchanting little cobbled square, to the **Bateau-Lavoir** ⑩, or Boat Wash House, at its northern edge. Painters Picasso and Braque had studios in the original building; this drab concrete building was built in its place. Continue up the hill via rue de la Mire to **place Jean-Baptiste-Clément** ⑪, where Modigliani had a studio.

The upper reaches of rue Lepic lead to rue Norvins, formerly rue des Moulins (Windmill Street). At the end of the street, to the left, is stylish avenue Junot, site of the Cité Internationale des Arts (International Residence of the Arts), where the city authorities rent out studios to artists from all over the world. Continue right past the bars and tourist shops until you reach famous **place du Tertre** ⑫. Check out the restaurant **La Mère Catherine** ⑬, a favorite with the Russian Cossacks when they occupied Paris in 1814. Fight your way through to the southern end of the square for a breathtaking view of the city. Around the corner on rue Poulbot, the **Espace Salvador-Dalí** ⑭ houses works by Salvador Dalí, who once had a studio in the area.

Return to place du Tertre. Just off the square is the tiny church of **St-Pierre de Montmartre** ⑮. Looming menacingly behind is the scaly white dome of the **Sacré-Coeur basilica** ⑯. The cavernous interior is worth visiting for its golden mosaics; climb to the top of the dome for the view of Paris, or just settle for the Cinerama-size vista seen from its entrance parterre.

Walk back toward place du Tertre. Turn right onto rue du Mont-Cenis and left onto rue Cortot, site of the **Musée de Montmartre** ⑰, which, like the Bateau-Lavoir, once sheltered an illustrious group of painters, writers, and assorted cabaret artists. One of the best things about the museum, however, is its view of the tiny vineyard on neighboring rue des Saules. Another famous Montmartre landmark is at No. 22: the bar-cabaret **Lapin Agile** ⑱, originally one of the raunchiest haunts in Montmartre and the subject of one of Picasso's most famous paintings. Opposite the Lapin Agile is the tiny **Cimetière St-Vincent** ⑲.

Return to Sacré-Coeur and head down the cascading staircases to place St-Pierre. On the corner to the left is the **Halle St-Pierre** ⑳, site of the Museum of Naive Art. The neighboring streets teem with fabric shops, which are good places to find inexpensive materials. From the top of rue de Steinkerque, one of the busiest shopping streets, you can take in the archetypal view of Sacré-Coeur soaring skyward atop its grassy mound, with the funicular railway to the left. Turn right at the bottom of rue de Steinkerque and head toward place Pigalle, still notorious as a center of sleazy nightlife, despite the classier bars and nightclubs that have been springing up.

If, after you've walked around Montmartre, you still have the energy to see another illustrious church, make the excursion to the Gothic **Basilique de St-Denis** in the nearby suburb of St-Denis. Take the métro at place de Clichy to St-Denis Basilique. Or get on at Anvers (near the Halle St-Pierre) and transfer at place de Clichy.

TIMING

Reserve four to five hours for this 4-km (2½-mi) walk: many of the streets are steep and slow going. Include half an hour each at Sacré-Coeur and the museums (the Dalí museum is open daily, but the Montmartre museum is closed Monday). Leave about two hours for the excursion to St-Denis, including the métro ride there. From Easter through September, Montmartre is besieged by tourists. Two hints to avoid the worst of the rush: Come on a gray day, when Montmartre's sullen-tone facades suffer less than most in the city; or during the afternoon, and return to place du Tertre (maybe via the funicular) by the early evening, once the tourist buses have departed. More festive times of the year are June 24, when fireworks and street concerts are staged around Montmartre, and the first weekend of October, when revelry accompanies the wine harvest at the vineyard on rue des Saules.

Sights to See

⑩ **Bateau-Lavoir** (Boat Wash House). Montmartre poet Max Jacob coined the name for the original building on this site, which burned down in 1970. He said it resembled a boat and that the warren of artists' studios within was perpetually paint-splattered and in need of a good hosing down. It was in the original Bateau-Lavoir that, early in the 20th century, Pablo Picasso and Georges Braque made their first bold stabs at Cubism—a move that paved the way for abstract painting. The poet Guillaume Apollinaire also had a studio here; his book *The Painters of Cubism* (1913) set the seal on the movement's historical acceptance. The replacement building also contains art studios, but, if you didn't know its history, you'd probably walk right past it. ⊠ *13 pl. Émile-Goudeau, Montmartre. Métro: Abbesses.*

⑨ **Chapelle du Martyre** (Martyr's Chapel). It was in the crypt of the original chapel—built over the spot where St. Denis is said to have been martyred around AD 250—that Ignatius of Loyola, Francis Xavier, and five other companions swore an oath of poverty, chastity, and service to the Church in 1534. This led to the founding of the Society of Jesus (the Jesuits) in Rome six years later—a decisive step in the efforts of the Catholic Church to reassert its authority in the face of the Protestant Reformation. ⊠ *9 rue Yvonne-Le-Tac, Montmartre. Métro: Abbesses.*

❶ **Cimetière de Montmartre** (Montmartre Cemetery). Although not as large as the better-known Père-Lachaise, this leafy split-level cemetery is just as moving and evocative. Incumbents include painters Jean-Baptiste Greuze, Jean-Honoré Fragonard, and Edgar Degas; Adolphe Sax, inventor of the saxophone; composers Hector Berlioz and Jacques Offenbach; and La Goulue, the Belle Epoque cabaret dancer who devised the French cancan. The florid Art Nouveau tomb of novelist Émile Zola (1840–1902), who died in nearby rue de Clichy, lords over a lawn near the entrance—though Zola's mortal remains were removed to the Panthéon in 1908. ⊠ *Av. Rachel, Montmartre. Métro: Blanche.*

⑲ Cimetière St-Vincent (St. Vincent Cemetery). It's a small graveyard, but if you're a serious student of Montmartre you may want to visit painter Maurice Utrillo's burial place. ⊠ *Entrance on rue Lucien-Gaulard (via rue St-Vincent), behind the Lapin Agile, Montmartre. Métro: Lamarck Caulaincourt.*

⑭ Espace Salvador-Dalí (Dalí Center). Some of Salvador Dalí's less familiar works are among the 25 sculptures and 300 signed etchings and lithographs housed in this museum. The "ambience" is meant to approximate the surreal experience, with black walls, low lighting, and a New Agey musical score—punctuated by recordings of Dalí's own voice. ⊠ *11 rue Poulbot, Montmartre,* ☏ *01–42–64–40–10.* ☟ *€7.* ☉ *Daily 10–6:30. Métro: Abbesses.*

☙ ⑳ Halle St-Pierre (St. Peter's Market Hall). This elegant iron-and-glass 19th-century market hall, at the foot of Sacré-Coeur, houses a children's play area, a café, and the **Musée de l'Art Naïf Max-Fourny** (Max Fourny Museum of Naive Art), with its psychedelic collection of contemporary international Naive painters. ⊠ *2 rue Ronsard, Montmartre,* ☏ *01–42–58–72–89.* ☟ *Museum €6.* ☉ *Daily 10–6. Métro: Anvers.*

★ ⑱ Lapin Agile. This bar-cabaret is still one of the most picturesque spots in Montmartre. It got its curious name—the Nimble Rabbit—when the owner, André Gill, hung up a sign (now in the Musée du Vieux Montmartre) of a laughing rabbit jumping out of a saucepan clutching a bottle of wine. In those days, the place was still tamely called *La Campagne* (The Countryside). Once the sign went up, locals rechristened it the Lapin à Gill, meaning Gill's Rabbit. When, in 1886, it was sold to cabaret singer Jules Jouy, he called it the *Lapin Agile*, which has the same pronunciation in French as *Lapin à Gill*. In 1903, the premises were bought by the most celebrated cabaret entrepreneur of them all, Aristide Bruand, portrayed by Toulouse-Lautrec in a series of famous posters, and soon thereafter Picasso painted his famous *Au Lapin Agile* (sold at auction in the 1980s for nearly $50 million and on view at New York City's Metropolitan Museum). Today, the Lapin Agile manages to preserve at least something of its earlier flavor, unlike the Moulin Rouge. ⊠ *22 rue des Saules, Montmartre,* ☏ *01–46–06–85–87.* ☟ *€20.* ☉ *Tues.–Sun. 9 PM–2 AM. Métro: Lamarck Caulaincourt.*

⑬ La Mère Catherine. This restaurant was a favorite with the Russian Cossacks who occupied Paris in 1814. Little did they know that when they banged on the tables and shouted *"bistro,"* the Russian word for "quickly," they were inventing a new breed of French restaurant. ⊠ *6 pl. du Tertre, Montmartre. Métro: Abbesses.*

④ Moulin de la Galette (Wafer Windmill). This windmill, on a hillock shrouded by shrubbery, is one of the remaining two in Montmartre. It was once the focal point of an open-air cabaret (made famous in a painting by Renoir, now part of the collection of the Musée d'Orsay), and rumor has it that the miller, Debray, was strung up on its sails and spun to death after striving vainly to defend it against invading Cossacks in 1814. Unfortunately, it is now privately owned and can only be admired from the street below. ⊠ *Rue Tholozé, Montmartre. Métro: Abbesses.*

② Moulin Rouge (Red Windmill). Built originally as a windmill, this world-famous cabaret was transformed into a dance hall in 1889. Those wild, early days were immortalized by Toulouse-Lautrec in his posters and paintings. It still trades shamelessly on the notion of Paris as a city of sin: if you fancy a Vegas-style night out, with computerized light shows and troupes of bare-breasted Doriss Girls sporting feather headdresses, this is the place to go. The cancan, by the way—still a regular sight here—was considerably raunchier when Toulouse-Lautrec was around. ⊠ *82 bd. de Clichy, Montmartre,* ☏ *01–53–09–82–82,* WEB *www.moulin-rouge.com. Métro: Blanche.*

❸ **Musée de l'Erotisme** (Museum of Eroticism). This seven-story museum at the foot of Montmartre claims to provide "a prestigious showcase for every kind of erotic fantasy." Its 2,000 works of art—you may find that this term is used rather loosely—include Peruvian potteries, African carvings, Indian miniatures, Nepalese bronzes, Chinese ivories, and Japanese prints. Three floors are devoted to temporary exhibitions of painting and photography. ⊠ *72 bd. de Clichy, Montmartre,* ☏ *01–42–58–28–73.* 🎫 *€6.* ☉ *Daily 10 AM–2 AM. Métro: Blanche.*

⑰ **Musée de Montmartre** (Montmartre Museum). In its turn-of-the-20th-century heyday, Montmartre's historical museum was home to an illustrious group of painters, writers, and assorted cabaret artists. Foremost among them were Renoir—he painted the *Moulin de la Galette,* an archetypal Parisian scene of sun-drenched revelers, while he lived here—and Maurice Utrillo, Montmartre painter par excellence. Utrillo was encouraged to paint by his mother, Suzanne Valadon, a model of Renoir's and a major painter in her own right. Utrillo's life was anything but happy, despite the considerable success his paintings enjoyed. He was an alcoholic continually in trouble with the police and spent most of his declining years in hospitals. He took the gray, crumbling streets of Montmartre as his subject matter, working more effectively from postcards than from the streets themselves. For all that, almost all his best works—from his "White Period"—were produced before 1916 (he died in 1955). They evoke the *parfum* of old Montmartre hauntingly: To help convey the decaying buildings of the area, he mixed plaster and sand in with his paints. The museum also provides a view of the tiny **vineyard**—the only one in Paris—on neighboring rue des Saules. A token 125 gallons of wine are still produced every year. It's hardly *grand cru* stuff, but there are predictably bacchanalian celebrations during the harvest on the first weekend of October. ⊠ *12 rue Cortot, Montmartre,* ☏ *01–46–06–61–11.* 🎫 *€4.* ☉ *Tues.–Sun. 11–6. Métro: Lamarck Caulaincourt.*

❻ **Place des Abbesses.** This triangular square is typical of the picturesque, slightly countrified style that has made Montmartre famous. The entrance to the Abbesses métro station, designed by the great Hector Guimard as a curving, sensuous mass of delicate iron, is one of the two original Art Nouveau entrance canopies left in Paris. *Métro: Abbesses.*

Place Blanche. The name place Blanche—White Square—comes from the clouds of chalky dust that used to be churned up by the carts that carried wheat and crushed flour from the nearby windmills, including the Moulin Rouge. *Métro: Blanche.*

OFF THE BEATEN PATH

MUSÉE DE LA VIE ROMANTIQUE – This tranquil, countrified town house, set in a little park at the foot of Montmartre (head down rue Blanche from place Blanche; the third left is rue Chaptal), was for years the site of Friday-evening salons hosted by the Dutch-born painter Ary Scheffer and including the likes of Ingres, Delacroix, Turgenev, Chopin, and Sand. The memory of author George Sand (1804–76)—real name Aurore Dudevant—haunts the museum. Portraits, furniture, and household possessions, right down to her cigarette box, have been moved here from her house in Nohant in the Loire Valley. There's also a selection of Scheffer's competent artistic output on the first floor. The salons are newly asparkle, thanks to the eye of Jacques Garcia, France's most fashionable interior decorator. Take a moment to enjoy a cup of tea in the garden café. ⊠ *16 rue Chaptal, Montmartre,* ☎ *01–48–74–95–38,* WEB *paris-france.org/musees.* 🎫 *Free.* ⊙ *Tues.–Sun. 10–5:40. Métro: St-Georges.*

⑪ **Place Jean-Baptiste-Clément.** Painter Amedeo Modigliani (1884–1920) had a studio here at No. 7. Some say he was the greatest Italian artist of the 20th century, fusing the genius of the Renaissance with the modernity of Cézanne and Picasso. He claimed that he would drink himself to death—and he eventually did, and chose the right part of town to do it in. Look for the octagonal tower at the north end of the square; it's all that's left of Montmartre's first water tower, built around 1840 to boost the area's feeble water supply. ⊠ *Pl. Jean-Baptiste-Clément, Montmartre. Métro: Abbesses.*

⑫ **Place du Tertre** (Mound Square). This tumbling square (*tertre* means hillock) regains its village atmosphere only in the winter, when the branches of the plane trees sketch traceries against the sky. At any other time of year you'll be confronted by crowds of tourists and a swarm of artists clamoring to do your portrait. If one produces a picture of you without your permission, you're under no obligation to buy. *Métro: Abbesses.*

NEED A
BREAK?   **Patachou** (⊠ *9 pl. du Tertre, Montmartre,* ☎ *01–42–51–06–06*) sounds the one classy note on place du Tertre, serving exquisite, if expensive, cakes and teas.

★ ⑯ **Sacré-Coeur** (Sacred Heart Basilica). The white domes of this basilica patrol the Paris skyline from the top of Montmartre. The French government decided to erect Sacré-Coeur in 1873, as a sort of national guilt-offering in expiation for the blood shed during the Commune and Franco-Prussian War in 1870–71. It was meant to symbolize the return of self-confidence to late 19th-century Paris. Even so, the building was to some extent a reflection of political divisions within the country: it was largely financed by French Catholics fearful of an anticlerical backlash and determined to make a grandiloquent statement on behalf of the Church. Construction lasted until World War I; the basilica was not consecrated until 1919. Stylistically, the Sacré-Coeur borrows elements from Romanesque and Byzantine models. Built on a grand scale, the church is strangely disjointed and unsettling; architect Paul Abadie (who died in 1884, long-before the church was finished) had made his name by sticking similar scaly, pointed domes onto the medieval cathedrals of Angoulême and Périgueux in southwest France. The gloomy, cavernous interior is worth visiting for its golden mosaics; climb to the top of the dome for the view of Paris. Grand vistas of the city can be seen from the entrance terrace *and* from the steps at the back of the basilica. ⊠ *Pl. du Parvis-du-Sacré-Coeur, Montmartre. Métro: Anvers.*

⑦ **St-Jean l'Evangéliste.** This redbrick church, built in 1904, was one of the first concrete buildings in France; despite its sinuous Art Nouveau curves, the bricks had to be added later to soothe offended locals. ⊠ *Pl. des Abbesses, Montmartre. Métro: Abbesses.*

NEED A
BREAK?   **Le St-Jean** (⊠ *23 rue des Abbesses, Montmartre*) is an intimate, large-windowed café, popular with locals on account of its authentic 1950s decor—neon lighting, vast bar, and mosaic-tile floor. The tables outside offer a good vantage point of busy place des Abbesses.

⑮ **St-Pierre de Montmartre.** Sitting awkwardly beneath the brooding silhouette of Sacré-Coeur, just off place du Tertre, is this church—one of the oldest in Paris. Built in the 12th century as the abbey church of a substantial Benedictine monastery, it has been remodeled on a number of occasions through the years; thus the 18th-century facade, built under Louis XIV, clashes with the mostly medieval interior. ⊠ *Off pl. du Tertre, Montmartre. Métro: Anvers.*

⑤ Studio 28. What looks like no more than a generic little movie theater has a distinguished dramatic history: When it opened in 1928, it was the first one purposely built for *art et essai,* or experimental theater, in the world. Over the years, the movies of directors like Jean Cocteau, François Truffaut, and Orson Welles have been shown here before their official premieres. ⊠ *10 rue Tholozé, Montmartre,* ☎ *01–46–06–36–07. Métro: Abbesses.*

⑧ Théâtre Libre (Free Theater). Founded in 1887 by director André Antoine (1858–1943), this theater was immensely influential in popularizing the work of iconoclastic young playwrights such as Ibsen and Strindberg. Antoine later became the director of the Odéon Theater in 1906. ⊠ *37 rue André-Antoine, Montmartre. Métro: Abbesses.*

PASSY, AUTEUIL, AND THE BOIS DE BOULOGNE

Passy and Auteuil were independent villages until Baron Haussmann soldered them together in 1860 and annexed them to Paris under the mundane title of the 16e arrondissement. Tumbling alleys and countrified cul-de-sacs recall those bygone days, colliding with some of the city's finest 20th-century architecture, by Guimard, Perret, Le Corbusier, and Mallet-Stevens. One of the city's most overlooked museums is here—the Musée Marmottan, with its enormous Monet collection.

Not far away from those Monets is the sprawling Bois de Boulogne—an enormous park that also assumed its present form during the days of Haussmann and Napoléon III, when it became the Parisians' favorite day trip. The 16e is the largest arrondissement in Paris, and Le Bois, as it is known, is of almost equal size. Public transportation to the Bois is poor, and few Parisians ever get to know all its glades and pathways—but all know and love the Bois's Pré Catalan and Bagatelle gardens, two of Paris's prettiest spots. The photogenic Lac Supérieur, however, which anchors the Bois's eastern sector, is easy to reach by foot and métro.

Numbers in the text correspond to numbers in the margin and on the Passy, Auteuil, and the Bois de Boulogne map.

A Good Walk

Start at the **Cimetière de Passy** ①, above place du Trocadéro. A map to the left of the entrance charts the tombs of the famous buried here. Leaving the cemetery, cross avenue Paul-Doumer, and veer left to a small garden (Square Yorktown) where there is a statue of Benjamin Franklin. Turn right down rue Benjamin-Franklin. Verdant gardens flank the curved wing of the Palais de Chaillot to your left. On the right, at No. 25 bis, note the huge-windowed Immeuble Perret—an innovative building for its time (1903), with a reinforced-concrete facade clad in floral-patterned ceramic tiles. Auguste Perret, then just 29, was to become one of the century's leading architects.

Cross place Costa-Rica, with its plummeting view of the aboveground métro as it shoots across the Seine, and take rue Raynouard. Opposite No. 12, turn left down rue des Eaux, a sinister-looking stone staircase flanked by barbed wire: the nearest Paris gets to urban hell,

Passy, Auteuil, and the Bois de Boulogne

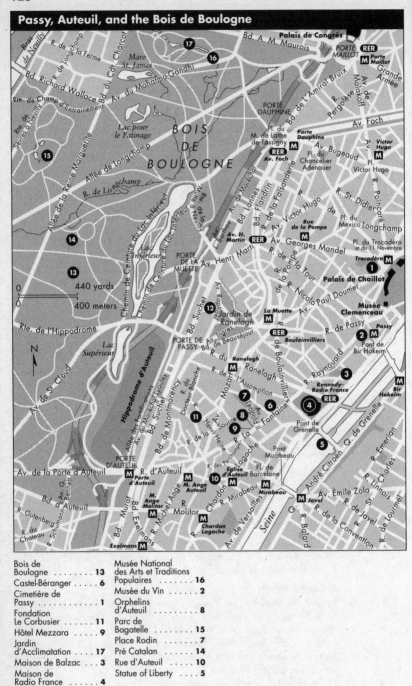

straight out of Dickens, and duly depositing you on rue Charles-Dickens at the bottom. You reemerge into daylight to be confronted by a templelike town house with huge Greek columns and, to your left, the quaint **Musée du Vin** ②, with exhibits on wine in its medieval cellars. After an excursion through pastures bacchanalian, big-city reality hits again as you retrace your steps along rue Charles-Dickens and venture right into avenue Marcel-Proust, in search of the time when the fortresslike walls on the right supported some of the fanciest flats in Paris, and the majestic double-staircase halfway along led down to the grand entrance of the Ministry of Public Works (relocated to La Défense) rather than, as is presently the case, the Parc de Passy housing complex.

A policeman generally lurks a hundred yards on, barring the leafy driveway to the Turkish embassy. You might have to consult him for advice as you search for rue Bertin, a cobbled, ivy-clad alley that sneaks off right, undisturbed by traffic, to a flight of stairs that leads back to rue Raynouard and the **Maison de Balzac** ③, a dachalike bungalow with trim lawns, once home to France's own Dickens. Rue Benjamin-Franklin returns at the corner of rues Raynouard and Singer where— says a tall, tapering plaque—the great man invented the lightning conductor between 1777 and 1785. Rue Raynouard tumbles down past the circular bulk of **Maison de Radio France** ④, the headquarters of state radio and television. If you'd like to see a miniversion of the **Statue of Liberty** ⑤, head left toward the Seine; it's at the end of the Allée des Cygnes, a striplike artificial island backed by the skyscrapers of the 1970s Front de Seine complex that cynical Parisians dub their mini-Manhattan.

Continue on rue Raynouard, which becomes rue La Fontaine, to inspect the **Castel-Béranger** ⑥ at No. 14, one of the city's earliest Art Nouveau buildings. If you're a fan of sculptor Auguste Rodin you may want to make a detour next right up avenue du Recteur-Poincaré to **place Rodin** ⑦ to see a small bronze casting of his male nude, *The Bronze Age*. Otherwise stay on rue La Fontaine, pass the **Orphelins d'Auteuil** ⑧— a still-functioning orphanage. Pause at No. 60, the **Hôtel Mezzara** ⑨, another fine Guimard mansion. Some 150 yards along, turn left onto rue des Perchamps. Note the bay-windowed, striped-tile Studio Building at No. 20—it looks contemporary but was built by Henri Sauvage in 1927. Also note the funky white mansion at the corner of rue Leconte-de-l'Isle, with its heavy, outsized triglyphs. Some beefy Baroque caryatids on loan from Vienna are visible across the street at No. 33, incongruously supporting a row of wafer-thin balconies.

Continue along rue des Perchamps to **rue d'Auteuil** ⑩. To the left is the elongated dome of the Église d'Auteuil, modeled on the papal tiara. Head right along this old, crooked shopping street to sloping place Jean-Lorrain, where you'll find a crowded market on Wednesday and Saturday mornings; then turn right down rue La Fontaine toward the chunky Crédit Lyonnais bank. Veer left up avenue Mozart and pause at No. 122; the elongated doorway and sinuous window frames again pay tribute to Guimard. Around the corner in Villa Flore, a tiny cul-de-sac, you can see the odd-shape site Guimard had to contend with: The building ends in a narrow point, with jagged brickwork vainly beckoning an addition.

Take the next left up rue Henri-Heine, with its row of elegant town houses; then turn left onto rue du Dr-Blanche, and left again to get to square du Dr-Blanche, a leafy cul-de-sac. At the far end is the **Fondation Le Corbusier** ⑪. If you like such spartan interwar architecture and want to see more, backtrack along rue du Dr-Blanche and explore rue Mallet-Stevens, a mews lined with sturdy evergreens and elegant houses from the late 1920s. Turn left at the end of rue du Dr-Blanche onto rue de l'Assomption, then right, and, opposite the end of rue du Ranelagh, cross the disused St-Lazare-Auteuil rail line. Take a right on avenue Raphaël, which overlooks the elegant Jardin du Ranelagh—site of the world's first hot-air balloon launch, in 1783. At the corner of rue Louis-Boilly is the **Musée Marmottan–Claude Monet** ⑫, famed for its collection of Impressionist pictures and illuminated manuscripts.

Continue on avenue Raphaël and cross boulevard Suchet to sprawling place de Colombie. Turn left down avenue de St-Cloud to reach the large **Bois de Boulogne** ⑬. Straight ahead is the bigger of the park's two lakes, the Lac Inférieur; you can cross to the island in the middle on a little ferry for a picnic or café lunch. When you're done, skirt south around the lake to check out the less picturesque Lac Supérieur; then take the chemin de Ceinture, then route de la Grande-Cascade to the **Pré Catalan** ⑭ and its Shakespeare Garden, trim lawns, stately trees, and historic restaurant. Cross the Pré Catalan and exit from its north side. If you're short on time or energy, head right via the Lac Inférieur and return to civilization at Porte Dauphine; otherwise head left along route des Lacs à Bagatelle to the **Parc de Bagatelle** ⑮, with its magnificent flower garden and 18th-century château. A good walk east from here will take you along avenue du Mahatma-Gandhi, past the **Musée National des Arts et Traditions Populaires** ⑯ and the children's amusement park, the **Jardin d'Acclimatation** ⑰, to Porte Maillot, where you can get a métro back to central Paris.

TIMING

This walk, which divides neatly into two—town (Paris) and country (Bois de Boulogne)—will probably take you a full day. (You may want to save the Bois de Boulogne for another day.) The Lac Inférieur is a good midway spot to stop for lunch. By then you'll have covered 5–6 km (3–3½ mi), depending on whether you detour to the Statue of Liberty and place Rodin. The second half of the tour covers just under 4 km (2½ mi) if you return from the Pré Catalan to **Porte Dauphine,** or just under 6 km (3½ mi) if you take in the Parc de Bagatelle and return to Porte Maillot. Sturdy, comfortable footwear is a must to negotiate the slopes and steps of the Paris sector and the gravelly pathways of the Bois de Boulogne.

Sights to See

⊙ ⑬ **Bois de Boulogne.** Class and style have been associated with this 2,200-acre wood—known to Parisians simply as *Le Bois*—ever since it was landscaped into an upper-class playground by Baron Haussmann in the 1850s. Emphasizing that onetime glamour is Haussmann's approach road from the Arc de Triomphe: avenue Foch, Paris's widest boulevard (120 yards across), originally named avenue de l'Impératrice in honor of Empress Eugénie (wife of Napoléon III). The Porte Dauphine métro station at the bottom of avenue Foch retains its original Art Nouveau iron-and-glass entrance canopy, designed by Hector Guimard.

The wood, which lost thousands of trees during 100-mph wind storms in 1999, is crisscrossed by broad, leafy roads, is much favored by rowers, joggers, strollers, riders, *pétanque* (a sort of bowling game) players, picnickers, and lovers. Meetings at **Longchamp** and **Auteuil** racetracks are high up the social calendar and re-create something of its Belle Epoque heyday. The French Open tennis tournament at the beautiful **Roland Garros** stadium in late May is another occasion when Parisian style and elegance are on full display.

The manifold attractions of Le Bois include cafés, restaurants, lakes, waterfalls, gardens, and museums. Rowboats can be rented at both **Lac**

Inférieur and Lac Supérieur. A cheap and frequent ferry crosses to the idyllic island in the middle of Lac Inférieur. The Fête à Neu-Neu, a giant carnival, takes place every September and October around the two lakes. Buses traverse the Bois de Boulogne during the day (take Bus 244 from Porte Maillot), but Le Bois becomes a distinctly adult playground after dark, when prostitutes of various genders come prowling for clients. ⊠ *Main entrance at bottom of av. Foch, Bois de Boulogne. Métro: Porte Maillot, Porte Dauphine, Porte d'Auteuil; Bus 244.*

6 Castel-Béranger. Dreamt up in 1895 by Hector Guimard (of métro fame) when he was 28, this building is considered the city's first Art Nouveau structure. The apartment building once housed Postimpressionist Paul Signac as well as Guimard himself. Today, the place looks a little dowdy and its occupants are less illustrious—though this hasn't stopped them from posting a menacing sign on the asymmetrical iron doorway warning you to keep out. Rust-streaked pale green paintwork, however, fails to detract from the florid appeal of the iron doors and balconies, or from the eccentric use of colored brick. Cross the street to admire the mask-fronted iron balconies and quilt-patterned brown, red, and turquoise brickwork; then venture around the side into Hameau Béranger to see rampant ivy obliterating the original fancy iron fencing, beneath the dismayed gaze of stylized sea horses halfway up the walls. There's a cleaner, subtler display of Art Nouveau at the corner of rue Lafontaine and rue Gros, where a finely carved stone apartment building segues into the dainty rue Agar. Tucked away at the corner of rue Gros is a tiny café-bar with Art Nouveau glass front and furnishings. ⊠ *14 rue la Fontaine, Passy-Auteuil. Métro: Ranelagh; RER: Maison de Radio France.*

NEED A BREAK? It seats just 15, but the **Café-Bar Antoine** (⊠ 17 rue la Fontaine, Passy-Auteuil, ☏ 01–40–50–14–30) warrants a visit for its Art Nouveau facade, floor tiles, and carved wooden bar. Count on €30 for a meal or stick to a snack and coffee.

1 Cimetière de Passy (Passy Cemetery). Perched on a spur above place du Trocadéro in the shadow of the Eiffel Tower and Palais de Chaillot, this cemetery was opened in 1820 when Passy was a country village. Its handsome entrance—two sturdy pavilions linked by a colonnade—is a 1930s Art Deco cousin to the nearby Palais de Chaillot. Precocious painter-poetess Marie Baskirtseff's tomb, with its pinnacles and stone Byzantine dome, dominates the cemetery; a Pietà behind Plexiglas mourns Hungarian peer Pierre Perenyi nearby. Just left of the main crossroads is a weathered bust of Impressionist Edouard Manet, buried with his wife, Berthe Morisot, next to the poignant figure of a girl in a hat—calling to mind Zola's novel *Une Page d'Amour* (Love Episode), which ends with the burial of the young heroine Jeanne in Passy Cemetery, "alone, facing Paris, forever." Claude Debussy is also among the incumbents. ⊠ *Rue du Commandant-Schloesing, Trocadéro/Eiffel Tower.* ☉ *Daily 9–8 or dusk. Métro: Trocadéro.*

11 Fondation Le Corbusier (Le Corbusier Foundation). The Villa Laroche is less of a museum in honor of Swiss architect Charles-Edouard Jeanneret, better known as Le Corbusier (1887–1965), than a well-preserved 1923 example of his innovative construction techniques, based on geometric forms, recherché color schemes, and unblushing recourse to iron and concrete. The sloping ramp that replaces the traditional staircase is one of the most eye-catching features. ⊠ *10 sq. du Dr-Blanche, Passy-Auteuil,* ☏ *01–42–88–41–53.* ⌑ *€1.5.* ☉ *Weekdays 10–12:30 and 1:30–6. Métro: Jasmin.*

⑨ Hôtel Mezzara. With its sumptuous wrought-iron staircase, Art Nouveau windows, and plaster molding, this Hector Guimard mansion, built in 1911 as a workshop for textile designer Paul Mezzara, has one of the finest 20th-century interiors in Paris. Unfortunately, it is only open during exhibitions, though a bit of curiosity and perseverance might get you through the door. ⊠ *60 rue la Fontaine, Passy-Auteuil,* ☎ *01-45-27-02-29. Métro: Jasmin.*

✋ ⑰ Jardin d'Acclimatation (Amusement Park). At this children's zoo and amusement park on the northern edge of the Bois de Boulogne(☞ *above*), you can see a mix of exotic and familiar animals, take a boat trip along an "enchanted river," ride a miniature railway, and enjoy various fairground booths that keep young and old entertained. The zoo and amusement park can be reached via the miniature railway—a surefire hit with children—that runs from Porte Maillot on Wednesday and weekends, beginning at 1:30; tickets cost €1. Many of the attractions have separate entry fees (except the zoo, which is spread throughout the park), notably the child-oriented art museum and workshop center, the **Musée en Herbe** (literally, "museum in the grass"); admission is €3. ⊠ *Bd. des Sablons, Bois de Boulogne,* ☎ *01-40-67-97-66.* ⊠ *€2.5.* ☉ *Daily 10-6. Métro: Les Sablons.*

❸ Maison de Balzac (Balzac's House). The Paris home of the great French 19th-century novelist Honoré de Balzac (1799-1850) contains exhibits charting his tempestuous life. ⊠ *47 rue Raynouard, Passy-Auteuil,* ☎ *01-55-74-41-80,* 🌐 *paris-france.org/musees.* ⊠ *Free.* ☉ *Feb.-Dec., Tues.-Sun. 10-5:40. Métro: Passy.*

❹ Maison de Radio France (Radio France Building). Headquarters to France's state radio, this monstrous circular building, completed in 1962, is more than 500 yards in circumference and said to be the largest in France in terms of floor space; a 200-ft tower overlooks the Seine. You can explore the foyer, obtain tickets to attend recordings, or join a guided tour (in French) of the studios and the museum, with its notable collection of old radios. ⊠ *116 av. du Président-Kennedy, Passy-Auteuil,* ☎ *01-56-40-15-16.* ⊠ *Guided tours (at half past the hour) €4.* ☉ *Mon.-Sat. 10:30-11:30 and 2:30-4:30. Métro: Ranelagh; RER: Maison de Radio France.*

★ ⑫ Musée Marmottan–Claude Monet. One of the most underestimated museums in town, the Marmottan is Paris's "other" Impressionist museum (after the Musée d'Orsay). A few years ago this museum, in an elegant 19th-century mansion, tacked "Claude Monet" onto its official name—and justly so, as this may be the best collection of the artist's works anywhere. Monet occupies a specially built basement gallery, where you'll find such spectacular works as the *Cathédrale de Rouen* (1892-96) series and *Impression: Soleil Levant* (Impression–Sunrise, 1872), the work that helped give the Impressionist movement its name. Other exhibits include letters exchanged by Impressionist painters Berthe Morisot and Mary Cassatt. There's a roomful of priceless illuminated medieval manuscripts on the ground floor, and impressive Empire furniture from Napoléon's time makes you feel as if you're at an actual salon, with comfortable couches and grand windows overlooking the Jardin de Ranelagh on one side and the hotel's private yard on the other. ⊠ *2 rue Louis-Boilly, Passy-Auteuil,* ☎ *01-42-24-07-02,* 🌐 *www.marmottan.com.* ⊠ *€6.* ☉ *Tues.-Sun. 10-6. Métro: La Muette.*

⑯ Musée National des Arts et Traditions Populaires (National Museum of Folk Arts and Traditions). In a nondescript modern building next to the Jardin d'Acclimatation, this museum is an impressive pile of artifacts related principally to preindustrial rural life. Many exhibits have buttons to press and knobs to twirl; however, there are no descriptions in English. The museum is a favorite destination for school field trips, so avoid weekday afternoons. ⊠ *6 av. du Mahatma-Gandhi, Bois de Boulogne,* ☎ *01–44–17–60–00.* ☒ *€3.5.* ⊙ *Wed.–Mon. 9:30–5:15. Métro: Les Sablons.*

② **Musée du Vin** (Wine Museum). In the vaulted 15th-century cellars of a former abbey, this small museum is devoted to traditional wine-making artifacts. The premises double as a wine bar and the visit includes a wine tasting. ⊠ *5 sq. Charles-Dickens, Passy-Auteuil,* ☎ *01–45–25–63–26.* ☒ *€6.* ⊙ *Tues.–Sun. 10–6. Métro: Passy.*

⑧ **Orphelins d'Auteuil** (Auteuil Orphanage). This still-functioning orphanage, founded in 1866 by Abbé Roussel, has pretty sloping gardens, a redbrick cloister, a crafts shop, and a tasteful neo-Gothic chapel (built 1927). ⊠ *40 rue La Fontaine, Passy-Auteuil,* ☎ *01–44–14–75–20. Métro: Jasmin.*

⑮ **Parc de Bagatelle.** This beautiful floral garden counts irises, roses, tulips, and water lilies among its showstoppers; it is at its most colorful between April and June. The velvet green lawns and the bijou château (only open when hosting exhibitions) are fronted by a terrace with attractive views of the Seine. The white-walled château was built by the Comte d'Artois in 1777 on a bet with Marie-Antoinette that it could be finished within two months; 900 construction workers toiled day and, by torchlight, at night, to make it happen. ⊠ *Rte. de Sèvres-à-Neuilly or rte. des Lacs-à-Bagatelle, Bois de Boulogne,* ☎ *01–40–67–97–00.* ☒ *Gardens €1.5, château entrance according to exhibition.* ⊙ *Daily 9–8 or dusk. Métro: Pont de Neuilly.*

⑦ **Place Rodin.** A half-sized bronze casting of Rodin's virile *L'Age d'Airain* (*The Bronze Age*) nude, created in 1874, emerges unblushingly from rosebushes at the heart of this minor roundabout. *Métro: Ranelagh.*

⑭ **Pré Catalan.** This garden in the Bois de Boulogne contains one of Paris's largest trees: a copper beech more than 200 years old. The **Jardin Shakespeare** (Shakespeare Garden) on the west side has a sampling of the flowers, herbs, and trees mentioned in Shakespeare's plays. Nearby still stands the restaurant Le Pré Catalan, where *le tout Paris* in the Belle Epoque era used to dine on its beautiful garden terrace. ⊠ *Rte. de la Grande-Cascade, Bois de Boulogne.* ☒ *Pré Catalan free, Shakespeare Garden €1.* ⊙ *Pré Catalan daily 8–dusk, Shakespeare Garden daily 3–3:30 and 4:30–5. Métro: Porte Dauphine.*

⑩ **Rue d'Auteuil.** This narrow, crooked shopping street escaped the attentions of Baron Haussmann and retains a country feel. Molière once lived on the site of No. 2; Racine was on nearby rue du Buis; the pair met up to clink glasses and exchange drama notes at the Mouton Blanc Inn, now a brasserie at No. 40. Note some genuinely old buildings dating from the 17th and 18th centuries at Nos. 19, 21, 25, and 29; the elegant courtyard of the school at No. 1 bis; and the scaly dome of the **Église d'Auteuil** (built in the 1880s), an unmistakable small-time cousin of the Sacré-Coeur. Rue d'Auteuil is at its liveliest on Wednesday and Saturday mornings, when a much-loved street market crams onto place Jean-Barraud. *Métro: Michel-Ange Auteuil, Église d'Auteuil.*

OFF THE BEATEN PATH

MUSÉE NATIONAL DE LA CÉRAMIQUE – Hundreds of the finest creations of the world-famous Sèvres porcelain works are displayed at the National Ceramics Museum, at the southern end of the tumbling, wooded Parc de St-Cloud, a short métro ride from the Michel-Ange Auteuil stop. ⊠ *Pl. de* *la Manufacture, Sèvres,* ☎ *01–41–14–04–20.* ⚏ *€3.5.* ☉ *Wed.– Mon. 10–5:15. Métro: Pont de Sèvres; Tramway: Musée de Sèvres.*

SERRES D'AUTEUIL – Tropical and exotic plants sweat it out in mighty hothouses just off place de la Porte-d'Auteuil, on the southern fringe of the Bois de Boulogne. A bewildering efflorescence of plants and flowers are grown here for use in Paris's municipal parks and for displays on official occasions. The surrounding gardens' leafy paths and well-tended lawns offer cooler places to admire floral virtuosity. ⊠ *3 av. de la Porte-d'Auteuil, Bois de Boulogne,* ☎ *01–40–71–76–07.* ⚏ *€1.* ☉ *Daily 10–6. Métro: Porte d'Auteuil.*

⑤ **Statue of Liberty.** Just in case you'd forgotten that the enduring symbol of the American dream is actually French, a reduced version of Frédéric-Auguste Bartholdi's matriarch brandishes her torch at the southern tip of the Allée des Cygnes. To Bartholdi's dismay, she originally faced the city and was only turned around to gaze across the waters of the Seine in 1937. The best view of her can be had during a Bateaux-Mouche river tour: boats usually make an obliging U-turn right in front. The original statue—the one in New York City—is known in French as *La Liberté Éclairant le Monde* (Liberty Lighting Up the World); it was made in Paris in 1886 with the help of a giant steel framework designed by Gustave Eiffel. ⊠ *Allée des Cygnes, Passy-Auteuil. Métro: Javel; RER: Maison de Radio France.*

OFF THE BEATEN TRACK

If you're in search of wide-open green spaces, skyscrapers, the church where Gothic architecture made its first appearance, or great Art Deco architecture, make a brief excursion to the city's peripheries.

Sights to See

★ **Basilique de St-Denis.** Built between 1136 and 1286, St. Denis Cathedral is in some ways the most important Gothic church in the Paris region. It was here, under dynamic prelate Abbé Suger, that Gothic architecture (typified by pointed arches and rib vaults) arguably made its first appearance. Suger's writings also show the medieval fascination with the bright, shiny colors that appear in stained glass. The kings of France soon chose St-Denis as their final resting place, and their richly sculpted tombs—along with what remains of Suger's church—can be seen in the choir area at the east end of the church. The vast 13th-century nave is a brilliant example of structural logic; its columns, capitals, and vault are a model of architectural harmony. The facade, retaining the rounded arches of the Romanesque style that preceded the Gothic style, is set off by a small rose window, reputedly the earliest in France. ⊠ *1 rue de la Légion d'Honneur, St-Denis,* ☎ *01–48– 09–83–54.* ⚏ *Choir and tombs €5.5.* ☉ *Easter–Sept., Mon.–Sat. 10– 6:30, Sun. noon–6; Oct.–Easter, Mon.–Sat. 10–4:30, Sun. noon–4:30. Guided tours daily at 11:15 and 3. Métro: St-Denis Basilique.*

La Défense. You may be pleasantly surprised by the absence of high-rise buildings and concrete towers in central Paris; one of the reasons for this is that French planners, with their usual desire to rationalize, ordained that modern high-rise development be restricted to the city's outskirts. Over the last 20 years, La Défense, just west of Paris across the Seine from Neuilly, has been transformed into a futuristic showcase for state-of-the-art engineering and architectural design. A few people actually live amid all this glass and concrete; most just come to work. The soaring high-rises are mainly taken up by offices—often the French headquarters of multinational companies—with no expense spared in the pursuit of visual ingenuity. Crowning the plaza is the **Grande Arche de La Défense,** an enormous open cube aligned with avenue de la Grande-Armée, the Arc de Triomphe, the Champs-Élysées, and the Louvre. Tubular glass elevators whisk you 360 ft to the top. ⊠ *Parvis de La Défense, La Défense,* ☎ *01–49–07–27–57,* WEB *www.grandearche. com.* ⊒ *€7.* ☉ *Daily 10–7. Métro, RER: Grande Arche de La Défense.*

☾ **Parc Andre-Citroën** (Andre-Citroën Park). This innovative and lovely park in southwest Paris was built on the site of the former Citroën automobile factory. Now it has lawns, Japanese rock gardens, rambling wildflowers, and elegant greenhouses full of exotic plants and flowers. There's also a delightful, computer-programmed "dancing fountain" that you can play in. On a sunny day, it's a great place to take a break from sightseeing. ⊠ *Entrances on rue St-Charles and rue de la Montagne de l'Esperou, Passy-Auteuil. Métro, RER: Javel.*

☾ **Parc Montsouris and Cité Universitaire** (Montsouris Park and University City). The picturesque, English-style Montsouris Park and the University "City," or campus, are in the residential 14ᵉ arrondissement, south of Montparnasse. Parc Montsouris has cascades, a lake, and a meteorological observatory disguised as a Tunisian Palace. The Cité Universitaire, opposite Parc Montsouris and next to the futuristic Stade Charléty athletics stadium, houses 5,000 international students in buildings that date mainly from the 1930s and reflect the architecture of different countries. Le Corbusier designed the Swiss and Brazilian houses; John D. Rockefeller funded the Maison Internationale; and the Sacré-Coeur church recalls the simple, muscular confidence of buildings erected in Mussolini's Italy. ⊠ *Parc Montsouris: entrances on av. Reille, bd. Jourdan, and rue Gazan; Cité Universitaire: entrance at 19 bd. Jourdan, Montparnasse,* ☎ *01–44–16–64–00 Cité Universitaire information. RER: Cité Universitaire.*

Parcours des Années Trente and Musée des Années 30 (1930s Trail and 1930s Museum). For a look at outstanding Art Deco buildings by such architects as Le Corbusier, Auguste Perret, Raymond Fisher, and Robert Mallet-Stevens, follow the 1930s Trail in the suburb of **Boulogne-Billancourt.** The route is outlined in an illustrated booklet available at the magnificent Hôtel de Ville (⊠ av. André-Morizet), built by Tony Garnier in 1934. More Art Deco is to be found at the 1930s Museum, next to the Hôtel de Ville. This museum has a wealth of beautifully presented paintings and sculpture produced in France during the interwar period. There's also an intriguing section on "colonial art," which borders between the naive and the patronizing. The collection of furniture and objects is disappointingly sparse. ⊠ *28 av. André-Morizet, Boulogne-Billancourt,* ☎ *01–55–18–46–42.* ⊒ *€4.6.* ☉ *Tues.–Sun. 11–6. Métro: Marcel-Sembat.*

3   DINING

Forget the Louvre, the Tour Eiffel, and the
Bateaux Mouches—the real draws for
visitors to Paris are its famous temples of
gastronomy. Whether you get knee-deep
in white truffles at Taillevent or simply lower
your sights to pistachioed sausage (the
poor man's caviar) at a classic corner
bistro, you'll discover that food here is an
obsession, an art, a subject of endless
debate. And if the lobster soufflé is
delicious, the historic ambience in which
it is often presented may be even more
so; request Empress Josephine's table at
Le Grand Véfour and find out for yourself.

Revised and
updated by
Rosa Jackson

PARIS HAS WORKS OF ART OF VARIED KINDS. Some hang on the walls of the Louvre. Some smile up at you from a plate. Clearly anyone who has ordered a dessert at Le Cinq and received a concoction that looks like a hat styled by Christian Lacroix knows that in Paris food is not merely something to fill up on. To the French, gastronomy is always regarded as the larger part of the art of living, the art of transforming the gross and humdrum aspects of existence into something witty, charming, gracious, and satisfying. Parisians, above all, feel that every meal is—if not a complete way of life—certainly an event that demands undivided attention. Happily, the city's chefs exist principally to please its citizens on that score, so it is no surprise that Paris is also a place where you come to experience full gastronomic rapture.

Even though a dramatic and widely heralded improvement in the restaurants of cities from Boston to Brisbane has narrowed the gap that once made Paris nonpareil, no other metropolis in the world has yet developed a food sensibility as refined, reasoned, and deeply rooted as that clinging to the French capital. From the edible genius of haute cuisine wizards Eric Frechon, Alain Ducasse, and Pierre Gagnaire—whose marriage of heated fois gras, pressed caviar, and Japanese seaweeds will make you purr—to brilliant bistro chef Yves Camdeborde's red mullet with chestnuts and cèpes, dining out in Paris can easily reduce you to a pleasurable stupor. For a change of pace, you can always slip away to a casual little place for an earthy, bubbling cassoulet; make a midnight feast of the world's silkiest oysters; or even opt out of Gaul altogether for superb paella, couscous, or an herb-bright Vietnamese stir-fry. Once you know where to go (and this is crucial), Paris is a city where perfection awaits at all stations of the food chain.

Today, Parisian cooking is perfectly exemplified by the cooking of Pascal Barbot, who worked at the landmark Lapérouse before wowing the critics at his own restaurant, L'Astrance. His overnight success seems to point to a certain restlessness in the Paris restaurant world—now that the modern bistro has made its mark, what's next? With dishes that subtly combine French and Asian flavors, plus a few surprise nibbles in the course of a meal (such as a "toasted-bread" chicken soup), this chef has introduced a style that defies categorization—neither bistro nor haute cuisine, it is simply Barbot.

The traditional bistro, meanwhile, continues to thrive, thanks to two breeds of chef: those who take pride in cultivating the classics (think boeuf bourguignon or sole meunière), and members of a young, energetic set who offer ever-changing seasonal menus, usually influenced by their native regions. If you can't wait three weeks to secure one of the three evening sittings at Yves Camdeborde's La Régalade, try booking, a few days in advance, at Chez Michel, where Thierry Breton works with the finest ingredients to update hearty dishes from his native Brittany—a pumpkin soup served in the squash shell adorned with salted herring eggs and tiny, crunchy croutons is one example. Or head to Chez Savy, a sepia-tone bistro that defies the galloping fashionization of the 8^e arrondissement with such hearty delights as its charred shoulder of lamb and mounds of crisp *frites* (fries). The bistro boom is so big, in fact, that it has now invaded the haunts of haute cuisine. Even the most luxurious kitchens are getting back to the bedrock of French culinary traditions—a.k.a. The Patrimony. Don't, therefore, be surprised to find *grandmère*'s lamb with white beans on the *carte* at the superexpensive Le Bristol. *Cuisine rassurante* ("cookery that reassures") is all the rage in Paris these days.

In addition, the craze for fashionable restaurants around the Champs-Élysées shows no sign of abating. Super-swish Korova with its lobster hot dogs is practically old news since the opening of Nobu nearby in the fall of 2001. The twin Pourcel brothers (of Le Jardin des Sens fame in Montpellier) have also made a splash by taking over La Maison Blanche, where the view across Paris is as splendid as their modern cuisine. Though Alain Ducasse's Spoon, Food and Wine is the granddaddy of fashion restaurants in the area, having arisen on the (then-nonexistent) scene in 1998, it remains as popular today as when it first opened.

Ghislaine Arabian—formerly the two-star chef of Ledoyen—has returned to the haute cuisine scene after a two-year absence. An antidote to olive-oil overdose, her cuisine takes its inspiration from northern France and Belgium—this is the only place in Paris where beer features in many of the desserts. Arabian's new eponymously named spot, with its modern dining room and relaxed staff, offers a breath of fresh air in a world that can sometimes seem stifling (fess up: it can be unnerving to have five waiters jump to attention every time you twitch). But for a meal that delivers on every aspect of the dream haute cuisine experience, from sumptuous decor to precision service, it's hard to go wrong at Taillevent, Les Ambassadeurs at the Hôtel Crillon, or Guy Savoy. Gastronomads—those who travel to eat—won't want to miss the far-flung culinary acrobatics at Pierre Gagnaire. Just don't bat an eyelash when *l'addition,* or bill, is presented. Speaking of budgets, if you're a budget-wise gourmand, the chimes of noon should be music to your ears. Many of Paris's best restaurants have prix-fixe lunch menus that are dramatically more affordable (but much more limited) than ordering from their regular à la carte menus. You'll probably have to ask for the lunch menu, for obvious reasons—most restaurants would prefer that you order à la carte. So watch out for that chilly look if you do pipe up and ask to see the prix-fixe lunch menu.

For those who come to Paris looking for a dose of elegance in an increasingly Gap-dressed world, the revival of the dining rooms in the city's grande dame hotels provides an ideal opportunity to show off new Diors and Balmains in truly gilded surroundings. Decor, of course, is not always the key to great food: some of the best bistros in Paris look downright simple—a kind of reverse *snobbisme.* For regal ambience but no demand to wear jacket and tie, don't forget the restaurants to be found in some of the city museums, notably the Restaurant Musée d'Orsay—a gigantic Second Empire salon swimming in gilt, frescoes, chandeliers, and marble; the café at the Musée Jacquemart-André (where else can you munch on salads beneath a Tiepolo ceiling?); and the Café Marly, set in the main courtyard of the Louvre (in all, meals are more than decent and lovely afternoon teas are also offered).

Included in this listing are a wide range of restaurants and prices. More than half are in the 1er–8e arrondissements, within easy reach of hotels and sights; many others are in the 14^e and 16^e, also popular visitor areas; and some are in the 11^e–20^e, outlying, often residential neighborhoods where cheaper rents allow young chefs to strike out on their own. Recognizing that even in Paris you may not want to eat French food at every meal, ethnic restaurants are also included. (One area worth exploring—especially at lunchtime—is Paris's Chinatown in the 13^e arrondissement; the main streets are avenue d'Ivry and avenue du Choisy.)

Mealtimes

Generally, Paris restaurants are open from noon to about 2 and from 7:30 or 8 to about 11. Brasseries have longer hours and often serve all day and late into the evening; some are open 24 hours. The iconoclastic wine bars pretty much do as they wish, frequently serving hot food only through lunch, then cold assortments of charcuterie and cheese until a late-afternoon or early evening close. Assume a restaurant is open every day unless otherwise indicated. Surprisingly, many restaurants close on Saturday as well as Sunday. July and August are the most common months for annual closings, but Paris in August is no longer the total culinary wasteland it used to be.

Menus

All establishments must post menus outside, so study them carefully before deciding to enter. Most restaurants have two basic types of menu: à la carte and fixed price (prix fixe, *un menu,* or *la formule*). The prix-fixe menu is usually the best value, though choices are more limited. Most menus begin with a first course (*une entrée*), often subdivided into cold and hot starters, followed by fish and poultry, then meat; it's rare today that anyone orders something from all three. However, outside of brasseries, wine bars, and other casual places, it's usually inappropriate to order a single dish, as you'll understand when you see the waiter's expression. If you feel like indulging more than usual, the *menu dégustation* (tasting menu), consisting of numerous small courses, allows for a wide sampling of the chef's offerings. In general, consider the season when ordering; daily specials are usually based on what's freshest in the market that day.

See the Menu Guide at the back of the book for guidance with menu items that appear frequently on French menus and throughout the reviews that follow.

Prices

Although prices can be steep at luxury restaurants, an effort has been made to include a number of lower-priced establishments. By French law, prices must include tax and tip (*service compris* or *prix nets*), but pocket change left on the table in basic places, or an additional 5% in better restaurants, is always appreciated. Beware of bills stamped "Service Not Included" in English or restaurants slyly using American-style credit-card slips, hoping that you'll be confused and add the habitual 15% tip. In neither case should you tip beyond the guidelines suggested above.

CATEGORY	COST*
$$$$	over €38
$$$	€23–€38
$$	€12–€23
$	under €12

* per person for a main course, including tax (19.6%); note that if a restaurant only offers prix-fixe (set-price) meals, it has been given the price category that reflects the full prix-fixe price.

Reservations

In the following reviews, the topic of reservations has been covered by indicating only where they are essential (and when booking weeks or months in advance is necessary), and where they are not accepted. Because restaurants are open for only a few hours for lunch and dinner, and because meals are long affairs here, it's always wisest to make reservations. To help you translate some of the needed phrases—"Hello/Good evening. I'd like to make a reservation for X people for today/tomorrow/day-of-week at X-time. The last name is . . . Thank you"—here are a few sentences to help out if needed: "*Bonjour* (*Bonsoir* after 6 PM). *Je voudrais faire une reservation pour X (1, un/une; 2, deux; 4, quatre; 6, six) personnes pour le diner* (evening); *le déjeuner* (lunch) *aujourd'hui à X heures* (today at X o'clock)/*demain à X heures* (tomorrow at X o'clock); *lundi (Monday), mardi (Tuesday), mercredi*

(Wednesday), jeudi (Thursday), vendredi (Friday), samedi (Saturday), dimanche (Sunday) à X heures. Le nom est (your own name). *Merci bien.*" Note that most wine bars do not take reservations; reservations are also unnecessary for brasserie and café meals at odd hours.

Restaurant Types

What's the difference between a bistro and a brasserie? Can you order food at a café? Can you go to a restaurant just for a snack? The following definitions should help.

A **restaurant** traditionally serves a three-course meal (first, main, and dessert) at both lunch and dinner. Although this category includes the most formal, three-star establishments, it also applies to more casual neighborhood spots—the line can be fuzzy between bistros and restaurants. In general, restaurants are what you choose when you want a complete meal and have the time to linger over it; don't expect to grab a quick snack. Wine is typically ordered with restaurant meals. Hours are fairly consistent.

It has been said that **bistros** served the world's first fast food. After the fall of Napoléon, the Russian soldiers who occupied Paris were known to bang on zinc-topped café bars, crying *bistro*—"quickly" in Russian. In the past, bistros were simple places with minimal fixings and service. Although many nowadays are quite upscale, with beautiful interiors and chic clientele, most remain cozy establishments serving straightforward, frequently gutsy cooking; a wide variety of meats; and long-simmered dishes such as pot-au-feu and veal blanquette.

Brasseries—ideal places for quick, one-dish meals—originated when Alsatians fleeing German occupiers after the Franco-Prussian War came to Paris and opened restaurants serving specialties from home. Pork-based dishes, *choucroute* (sauerkraut), and beer (*brasserie* also means brewery) were—and still are—mainstays here. The typical brasserie is convivial and keeps late hours. Some are open 24 hours a day—a good thing to know, since many restaurants stop serving at 10:30 PM.

Like bistros and brasseries, **cafés** come in a confusing variety. Often informal neighborhood hangouts, cafés may also be veritable showplaces attracting chic, well-heeled crowds. At most cafés, regulars congregate at the bar, where coffee and drinks are cheaper than at tables. At lunch, tables are set and a limited menu is served. Sandwiches, usually with *jambon* (ham), *fromage* (cheese, often Gruyère or Camembert), or *mixte* (ham and cheese), are served throughout the day. Cafés are for lingering, for people-watching, and for daydreaming; they are listed separately below.

Wine bars, or *bistros à vins,* are a newer phenomenon. These informal places often serve very limited menus, perhaps no more than open-face sandwiches (*tartines*) and selections of cheeses and cold cuts (*charcuterie*). Owners concentrate on their wine lists, which often include less well-known, regional selections, many of them available by the glass. Like today's bistros and brasseries, some wine bars are very upscale indeed, with full menus and costly wine lists. Still, most remain friendly and unassuming places for sampling wines you might otherwise never have a chance to try.

Smoking

You can count on it: Parisians smoke before, during, and after meals. Restaurants are supposed to have no-smoking sections—if you want to sit in one, make this clear at the outset—though these areas are often limited to a very few tables where the no-smoking policy is not strictly monitored.

What to Wear

Casual dress is acceptable at all but the fanciest restaurants. Be aware that in Paris, however, casual usually means stylish sportswear, which is often more dressed up than you may be used to. When in doubt, leave the blue jeans and sneakers behind. Most of all, use your judgment. If an establishment requires jacket and tie, it is noted in the reviews below.

Wine

No matter what restaurant you're heading to, try to enjoy a taste of the grape along the way, whether *vin ordinaire* (table wine) or a Romanée-Conti. As the French say, a day without wine is like a day without sunshine. The wine that suits your meal is the wine you like. The traditional rule of white with fish and red with meat no longer applies. If the restaurant has a sommelier, let him (yes, it's usually a man) help you. Most sommeliers are knowledgeable about their lists and will suggest what is appropriate after you've made your tastes and budget known. In addition to the wine list, informal restaurants will have a *vin maison* (house wine) that is less expensive. Simpler spots will have wines *en carafe* (in a carafe) or *en pichet* (in a pitcher). Except for wine bars and brasseries, most restaurants do not sell wine by the glass. If you'd like something before the meal, consider ordering your wine for the meal ahead of time, or sample a typical French *apéritif,* such as a *kir,* chilled white wine with black-currant liqueur.

Restaurants by Arrondissement

1ᵉʳ Arrondissement (Louvre/Les Halles)

See Right Bank Dining map.

CONTEMPORARY

$$$–$$$$ ✕ **Cabaret.** The food—poached egg with sea urchin coral, seared tuna with Thai spices, beef carpaccio—isn't substantial enough to give you indigestion, but you might find other reasons to recline, literally, on a settee-bed at this hyper-trendy new restaurant after your meal. Lunch is served in the cool white dining room but dinner in the funky basement is where it's at—star-decorator Jacques Garcia has gone all-out with phosphorescent floors, silk cushions, an "African bar," and Indian-style beds, surrounded by veils, each with a table built into the center. ✉ *2 pl. du Palais-Royal, Louvre/Tuileries,* ☎ *01–58–62–56–25. AE, DC, MC, V. Closed Sun. Métro: Palais-Royal.*

FRENCH

$$$$ ✕ **Gérard Besson.** With its collection of ceramic and metallic roosters in lit glass cases, pale pink fabrics, and carved wood boiseries, this seems like an old-fashioned but intimate Parisian favorite masterminded by your French maiden aunt (if you had one). Chef Besson has mastered a superb classical repertoire, subtly enlivened by creative touches, such as his terrine of Bresse chicken with foie gras and oyster flan. In winter, his game menu is probably the best in town: try the perfectly executed *lièvre à la royale,* braised hare in a luscious truffled sauce. For dessert, sample the distinctive confit of fennel with vanilla ice cream. Other pluses include an excellent wine cellar and a good-value €46 lunch menu. ✉ *5 rue du Coq-Héron, Louvre/Tuileries,* ☎ *01–42–33–14–74. AE, DC, MC, V. Closed Sun. No lunch Sat. and Mon. Métro: Les Halles.*

$$$$ ✕ **Le Grand Véfour.** Victor Hugo could stride in and still recognize this place—in his day, as now, a contender for the title of most beautiful restaurant in Paris. Originally built in 1784, set in the arcades of the Palais-Royal, it has welcomed everyone from Napoléon to Colette to Jean Cocteau—nearly every seat bears a plaque commemorating a famous patron. The mirrored ceiling and Restauration-era (early 19th-

Right Bank Dining

Left Bank Dining

century) glass paintings of goddesses and muses create a beguiling atmosphere of restrained seduction. Foodies as well as the fashionable gather here to enjoy chef Guy Martin's unique blend of sophistication and rusticity. He hails from Savoie, so you'll find lake fish and mountain cheeses on the menu alongside such luxurious dishes as foie gras–stuffed ravioli. For dessert, try the house specialty, *palet aux noisettes* (meringue cake with milk chocolate mousse, hazelnuts, and caramel ice cream)—or just drink in the glittering salons. If you can't spring for the extravagantly priced plates on the the à la carte menu, try the lunchtime prix fixe for a mere €70. ⊠ *17 rue Beaujolais, Louvre/Tuileries,* ☎ *01–42–96–56–27. Reservations essential at least a wk in advance. Jacket and tie. AE, DC, MC, V. Closed weekends and Aug. No dinner Fri. Métro: Palais-Royal.*

$$$ ✕ **Au Pied de Cochon.** Part of the Frères Blanc chain, this 24-hour classic is famous for its trademark dishes of breaded pig's trotters with béarnaise and cheesy onion soup (the latter said to cancel out the effects of a boisterous night on the town). The setting is Busby Berkleyesque—wall sconces are adorned with giant bunches of frosted-glass grapes. Though tourists make up the bulk of the clientele, Au Pied de Cochon also attracts a frisky crowd of night owls—club kids, off-duty cops, couples coming up for air—and the terrace is a good spot for people-watching. ⊠ *6 rue Coquillière, Beaubourg/Les Halles,* ☎ *01–40–13–77–00. AE, DC, MC, V. Métro: Les Halles.*

$$$ ✕ **Macéo.** If you want to enjoy classic French food with a modern spin, then Macéo delivers in eat-your-*gâteau*-and-still-have-it fashion. Run by the owner of Willi's Wine Bar, the restaurant is bathed in natural light streaming in from both sides; a broad, curved staircase leads to a spacious upstairs room. Bold modern lamps lend a contemporary air to the traditionally designed dining room, painted brick red and cream. With its reasonably priced set menus (€34 at lunch and €38 in the evening), this is an ideal spot for an elegant yet relaxed meal after a day at the Louvre and Palais-Royal gardens. The subtly modernized cooking reflects the decor and might include such dishes as foie gras with chutney, duck breast with spices and chicory, and almond cake on a bed of mango "marmalade." Service can be unnecessarily haughty. ⊠ *15 rue des Petits-Champs, Louvre/Tuileries,* ☎ *01–42–97–53–85. MC, V. Closed Sun. No lunch Sat. Métro: Palais-Royal.*

$$$ ✕ **Restaurant du Palais-Royal.** Tucked away in the northeast corner
★ of the magnificent Palais-Royal garden, this pleasant bistro offers traditional cuisine with a few contemporary touches and—most appropriate for a prime real estate situation—a lovely terrace. Sole and scallops are beautifully prepared, but juicy steak with symmetrically stacked frites is also a favorite of the expense-account lunchers who love this place. Finish up with an airy puff pastry–and–cream *mille-feuille* that changes with the seasons—mango or berries in summer, hazelnut in winter. Be sure to book in advance, especially during the summer, when the terrace tables are hotly sought after. ⊠ *Jardins du Palais-Royal, 110 Galerie Valois, Louvre/Tuileries,* ☎ *01–40–20–00–27. AE, MC, V. Closed weekends. Métro: Palais-Royal.*

$$–$$$ ✕ **Aux Crus de Bourgogne.** This delightfully old-fashioned bistro, with its bright lights and red-check tablecloths, attracts a lively crowd. Open since 1905, it has been run by the same family since 1932. They made it popular by serving two luxury items—foie gras and cold lobster with homemade mayonnaise—at surprisingly low prices, a tradition that happily continues. Among the bistro classics on the seasonal menu are soul-warming winter dishes such as *boeuf au gros sel* (beef and vegetables in bouillon with rock salt) and *confit de canard* (duck confit). ⊠ *3 rue Bachaumont, Beaubourg/Les Halles,* ☎ *01–42–33–48–24. AE, MC, V. Closed weekends. Métro: Sentier.*

$$–$$$ ✕ **Le Poquelin.** The theater-like scenery gives this little restaurant a welcome that's both elegant and relaxed. Owners Maggie and Michel Guillaumin proudly serve classic French cooking with a twist, such as duck breast topped with foie gras. The popular, regularly changing *menu Molière* is excellent value at €30.80, offering a choice of six starters, six mains, and six desserts. Wines are well chosen and fairly priced. ✉ *17 rue Molière, Louvre/Tuileries,* ☎ *01–42–96–22–19. AE, DC, MC, V. Closed Sun. and 3 wks in Aug. No lunch Sat. or Mon. Métro: Palais-Royal.*

$$–$$$ ✕ **Le Safran.** If food scares have made you eye steak-frites with suspicion, this is the place to treat yourself to a reassuringly *biologique* bistro meal. Passionate chef Caroll Sinclair works almost exclusively with organic produce, and her small menu changes according to what she finds in the market—creamy shellfish and spinach soup brightened by fresh coriander, red mullet stuffed with cèpe mushrooms, and *gigot de sept heures* (leg of lamb cooked for seven hours) are some signature dishes. Cool it all off with dessert such as black grapes with caramelized pineapple or a saffron crème brûlée. Brunch is served on Sunday from 10 AM to 5 PM. Though Sinclair herself is charming and the room painted in the seductive color that gives the place its name, the service can be off-puttingly stiff. ✉ *29 rue d'Argenteuil, Louvre/Tuileries,* ☎ *01–42–61–25–30. MC, V. Closed 2 wks in Sept. Métro: Tuileries, Pyramides.*

$$ ✕ **L'Ardoise.** This minuscule storefront, painted white and decorated
★ with enlargements of old sepia postcards of Paris, is the very model of contemporary bistros making waves in Paris. This one's claim to fame is chef Pierre Jay, who trained at La Tour d'Argent. His first-rate three-course menu for €28 (you can also order à la carte at no extra cost) is adorned with such original dishes as crab flan in a creamy parsley emulsion and fresh cod with grilled chorizo chips, served on a tempting bed of mashed potatoes. Just as enticing are the desserts, such as a superb *feuillantine au citron*—caramelized pastry leaves filled with lemon cream and lemon segments. With friendly service and a small but well-chosen wine list, L'Ardoise would be perfect if it weren't often crowded and noisy. ✉ *28 rue du Mont Thabor, Beaubourg/Les Halles,* ☎ *01–42–96–28–18. Reservations essential. MC, V. Closed Mon.–Tues. Métro: Concorde.*

$$ ✕ **La Tour du Montlhéry.** When the centuries-old Les Halles marketplace became a soulless shopping mall, many neighborhood bistros closed or went upscale. The Montlhéry managed to hang on to the old-market feel, with its sagging wood-beam ceilings, red-check tablecloths, and exposed brick walls lined with imaginative portraits. If you don't mind passing under hanging samples of your future meal (sausages, etc.) on your way into the dining room, then you can enjoy the simple grilled food served by jovial waiters. Go for the *côte de boeuf* (prime rib) or grilled lamb and wash it down with a good Beaujolais. ✉ *5 rue des Prouvaires, Beaubourg/Les Halles,* ☎ *01–42–36–21–82. Reservations essential. MC, V. Closed weekends and July 14–Aug. 15. Métro: Les Halles.*

$$ ✕ **Willi's Wine Bar.** Don't be fooled by the name—this English-owned spot is no modest watering hole but a stylish haunt for Parisian and visiting gourmands. The often original menu changes daily to reflect the market's offerings and might include chicken liver terrine, cod with pesto and eggplant, and crème brûlée or a bitter chocolate *terrine* (pudding). Owner Mark Williamson has a passion for Rhône Valley wines, reflected in the extensive list, and for Spanish sherries. Service can be leisurely, so come with time on your hands. ✉ *13 rue des Petits-Champs, Louvre/Tuileries,* ☎ *01–42–61–05–09. MC, V. Closed Sun. Métro: Bourse.*

THAI

$ ✕ **Baan Boran.** Baan Boran steers clear of Thai kitsch with its sunny
★   yellow dining room and contemporary plastic chairs. The home-style
cooking, concocted by two women from central and northern Thai-
land, is just as original. Instead of the Royal cuisine favored at most
Thai restaurants in Paris, here you'll find such regional dishes as *gaeng
mussaman,* beef in a rich, peanuty sauce scented with cinnamon and
cardamom. Dishes with no added fat are listed separately: why not try
the *yam som-o,* tangy chunks of pomelo in a creamy coconut sauce?
⊠ *17 rue Duphot, Louvre/Tuileries,* ☎ *01–40–15–90–45. AE, MC,
V. Closed Sun. Métro: Palais-Royal.*

2ᵉ Arrondissement (La Bourse/Opéra)
See Right Bank Dining map.

FRENCH

$$-$$$ ✕ **Chez Georges.** When you ask sophisticated Parisian bankers, aris-
tocrats, or antiques dealers to name their favorite bistro, many would
choose Georges. The traditional bistro fare is good—herring, sole,
kidneys, steaks, and frites—and the atmosphere is better. A wood-paneled entry leads you to an elegant yet unpretentious dining room where
one long, white-clothed stretch of tables lines the mirrored walls and
attentive waiters sweep efficiently along the entire length. ⊠ *1 rue du
Mail, Louvre/Tuileries,* ☎ *01–42–60–07–11. AE, DC, MC, V. Closed
Sun. and 3 wks in Aug. Métro: Sentier.*

$$ ✕ **Café Runtz.** Next to the noted theater Salle Favart, in a neighbor-
hood once filled with theaters, this friendly bistro is still gleaming from
Jacques Garcia's stage-set makeover a few years ago. Old brass gas lamps
on each table and rich *boiseries* (woodwork) create a cozy and Flauber-
tian mise-en-scène. Tasty, hearty Alsatian dishes include Gruyère salad,
onion tart, choucroute, and fresh fruit tarts. Order a pitcher of Ries-
ling or other Alsatian wine to accompany your meal. The two prix-
fixe menus are a good value; one of them, the "*Salé-Sucré,*" is served
all afternoon. ⊠ *16 rue Favart, Opéra/Grands Boulevards,* ☎ *01–42–
96–69–86. AE, MC, V. Closed Sun. and 1 wk in Aug. No lunch Sat.
Métro: Richelieu Drouot.*

$$ ✕ **Le Grand Colbert.** One of the few independently owned brasseries
remaining in Paris, Le Grand Colbert, with its globe lamps and ceil-
ing moldings, feels grand yet not overpolished—old theater posters still
line the walls. The high-ceilinged dining room attracts a wonderfully
Parisian mix of elderly lone diners, business lunchers, tourists, and couples, who come for hearty nourishment in the form of steak with frites,
robust stews, and well-prepared fish. It's best to stick to classics,
though, as this is what the kitchen does best: finish with profiteroles
or a fluffy chocolate mousse. To aid digestion, stroll through the gorgeous Galerie Vivienne next door, which houses tempting clothing
and gift shops. ⊠ *2–4 rue Vivienne, Louvre/Tuileries,* ☎ *01–42–86–
87–88. AE, DC, MC, V. Métro: Bourse.*

$$ ✕ **Le Souletin.** Sandwiched between the fashion and financial districts
on either side of place des Victoires, this polished bistro attracts a po-
tentially intimidating crowd of designer suits, but the air is jovial and
the food reassuringly rustic. Specializing in the gutsy cuisine of the Basque
country, Le Souletin serves such regional dishes as *axua*—a veal,
tomato, and pepper stew spiced with dried Espelette pepper—and
smooth white bean soup with nibbles of panfried foie gras. Sorbets,
so often an afterthought, are exceptionally fruity here. ⊠ *6 rue La Vril-
lière, Louvre/Tuileries,* ☎ *01–42–61–43–78. MC, V. Closed Sun. No
lunch Sat. Métro: Bourse.*

$$ ✕ **Le Vaudeville.** One of Jean-Paul Bucher's seven Flo brasseries, Le
Vaudeville is filled with journalists, bankers, and locals *d'un certain*

âge who come for its good-value assortment of prix-fixe menus. Shell-fish, house-smoked salmon, and desserts such as profiteroles are particularly enticing. Enjoy the handsome 1930s decor—almost the entire interior of this intimate dining room is done in real or faux marble—and lively dining until 2 AM daily. ⊠ *29 rue Vivienne, Opéra/Grands Boulevards,* ☎ *01–40–20–04–62. AE, DC, MC, V. Métro: Bourse.*

3ᵉ Arrondissement (République/Marais)

See Right Bank Dining map.

FRENCH

$$–$$$ ✕ **Chez Jenny.** Part of the Frères Blanc group, this classic two-story brasserie is famed for its infectious buzz and outstanding choucroute, delivered weekly by a private supplier in Alsace and served with a panoply of charcuterie and an oversize grilled ham knuckle. To finish, the perfectly aged Muenster cheese and homemade blueberry tart are fine choices. Staff in regional dress add a charming Alsatian touch. ⊠ *39 bd. du Temple, République,* ☎ *01–44–54–39–00. AE, DC, MC, V. Métro: République.*

$$–$$$ ✕ **Le Pamphlet.** Chef Alain Carrere's modern and very affordable take
★ on the hearty cooking of the Basque and Béarn regions of southwestern France has made this Marais bistro popular with an artsy crowd. Beyond the delicious, homey food, what many Parisians love is the provincial feel, with a beamed ceiling, old-fashioned lamps, and a selection of faience that seems to have been borrowed from *grandmère*. The market-fresh menu runs from first courses such as sea bream and salmon tartare with oyster sauce to a juicy pork chop with béarnaise sauce and hand-cut frites. Finish up with a slice of sheep's cheese. ⊠ *38 rue Debelleyme, Le Marais,* ☎ *01–42–72–39–24. Reservations essential. MC, V. Closed Sun., first 2 wks of Jan., and Aug. 8–23. No lunch Sat. Métro: St-Sébastien Froissart.*

$$ ✕ **Le Hangar.** For years Le Hangar hasn't changed its winning formula, serving food that's far more refined than its too-bright room (hidden down a gloomy impasse near the doll museum) or the prices might suggest. A meal here begins with a little pot of tapenade and ends with *mignardises* (luscious minipastries), a touch of haute cuisine. Panfried foie gras on a cushion of olive-oil mash is about as good as it gets in Paris, and the chocolate soufflé makes a suitably extravagant ending. Wines are well priced, too. ⊠ *12 impasse Berthaud, Le Marais,* ☎ *01–42–74–55–44. Reservations essential. No credit cards. Closed Sun. No lunch Mon. Métro: Rambuteau.*

NORTH AFRICAN

$–$$ ✕ **Chez Omar.** Popular with a high-voltage fashion crowd—yes, that is Vivienne Westwood having dinner with Alexander McQueen—this is the place to come for couscous with all the trimmings. Order it with grilled skewered lamb, spicy *merguez* sausage, a lamb shank, or chicken—portions are generous—and wash it down with robust Algerian or Moroccan wine. Proprietor Omar Guerida speaks English and is famously friendly. Since he doesn't take reservations, arrive early or be prepared for a mouthwatering wait. ⊠ *47 rue de Bretagne, République,* ☎ *01–42–72–36–26. Reservations not accepted. No credit cards. No lunch Sun. Métro: Filles du Calvaire.*

4ᵉ Arrondissement (Beaubourg/Marais/Ile St-Louis)

See Right Bank Dining map.

CONTEMPORARY

$$–$$$ ✕ **Georges.** One of those roof-top, showstopping venues so popular
★ in Paris, decorated in white and gray, with angular chairs and giant metallic shells, Georges stands in stark contrast to its graceful city view

from the top floor of the Centre Georges Pompidou. Staff are as sleek as the furniture, and at night the terrace has distinct snob appeal: come snappily dressed or suffer the consequences (you may be relegated to something resembling a dentist's waiting room). As an addition to the ever-expanding empire of the Costes brothers, the menu here trots out predictable Costes comfort food such as macaroni with morel mushrooms, steak tartare, and raw tuna with a sesame crust, but, sadly, the food is considerably less dazzling than the view—with the exception of desserts by star pâtissier Stéphane Secco, whose YSL (as in Yves St-Laurent, darling) bitter chocolate cake is an event. ⊠ *Centre Pompidou, 6th floor, rue Rambuteau, Beaubourg/Les Halles,* ☎ *01–44–78–47–99. AE, DC, MC, V. Closed Tues. Métro: Rambuteau.*

FRENCH

$$ ✕ **Au Bourguignon du Marais.** The handsome, contemporary look of this Marais bistro and wine bar is the perfect backdrop for the good traditional fare and excellent Burgundies served by the glass and bottle. Always on the menu are Burgundian classics such as *jambon persillé* (ham in parsleyed aspic jelly), escargots, and *oeufs en meurette* (eggs poached in a red-wine sauce); another favorite is the steak, served grilled or chopped and nicely seasoned in a tartare. ⊠ *19 rue de Jouy, Beaubourg/Les Halles,* ☎ *01–48–87–15–40. AE, MC, V. No dinner Sun. Métro: St-Paul.*

$$ ✕ **Baracane.** Come to this small, plain place for the food, not the atmosphere, which is scant. The menu is robust, with specialties from the owner's native southwestern France—roast lamb with thyme, cassoulet, and madeleine cakes with stewed rhubarb are three delights. The reasonable dinner menu and the even cheaper lunch menu keep Baracane solidly affordable and one of the best values in the Marais. ⊠ *38 rue des Tournelles, Le Marais,* ☎ *01–42–71–43–33. MC, V. Closed Sun. No lunch Sat. Métro: Bastille.*

$$ ✕ **Bofinger.** One of the oldest, most beautiful, and most popular brasseries in Paris has generally improved since brasserie maestro Jean-Paul Bucher (of the Flo group) took over. Settle in to one of the tables dressed in crisp white linen under the gorgeous Art Nouveau glass cupola—this part of the dining room is no-smoking—and enjoy classic brasserie fare, such as oysters, grilled sole, or lamb fillet. The prix fixe includes a decent half bottle of red or white wine (Provençal on our last visit). ⊠ *5–7 rue de la Bastille, Bastille/Nation,* ☎ *01–42–72–87–82. AE, DC, MC, V. Métro: Bastille.*

$$ ✕ **Trumilou.** Crowds of students, artists, and others on a budget come here to eat bistro cuisine, such as leg of lamb and apple tarts. The non-decor is somehow homey, the staff is friendly, and the location facing the Seine and the Ile St-Louis is especially pleasant in nice weather, when you can sit on the narrow though noisy terrace under the trees. ⊠ *84 quai de l'Hôtel de Ville, Le Marais,* ☎ *01–42–77–63–98. MC, V. Closed 1 wk in Aug. Métro: Pont Marie.*

$–$$ ✕ **Brasserie de l'Ile St-Louis.** Set on picturesque Ile St-Louis and opened in 1870—when Germany took over Alsace-Lorraine and its chefs decamped to the capital—this outpost of Alsacian cuisine remains a cozy cocoon filled with stuffed animal heads, antique fixtures fashioned from barrels, and folk-art paintings. The food is gemütlich, too: *coq-au-Riesling,* omelets with Muenster cheese, onion tarts, and *choucroutes garni* (sauerkraut studded with ham, bacon, and pork loin—one variant is made with smoked haddock). Pots of cumin seeds (for sprinkling on Muenster cheese) accompany the salt and pepper shakers on the communal tables and in warm weather, the crowds move out to the terrace overlooking the Seine and Notre-Dame. ⊠ *55 quai de Bourbon, Ile St-Louis,* ☎ *01–43–54–02–59. MC, V. Métro: Pont Marie.*

$–$$ ✕ **Grizzli Café.** The closing of this beloved 19th-century bistro in 2001 for renovations sent shudders down the spines of its many French and foreign devotees. The result is, well, not disastrous—much of the historic main floor dining room has been preserved, while the upstairs has been modernized (though the new owners wisely hung on to the bizarre bear tableau). The chef has fortunately stayed on but some of the hearty classics have vanished to make way for pastas and salads. All-day serving hours are good news—too bad about the thumping music, which sadly makes the place feel like just another trendy Marais bar. ⊠ *7 rue St-Martin, Le Marais,* ☎ *01–48–87–77–56. AE, DC, MC, V. Métro: Châtelet.*

MIDDLE EASTERN

$ ✕ **L'As du Fallafel.** Look no farther than the fantastic falafel stands on rue de Rosiers for some of the cheapest and tastiest meals in Paris, with the laurel crown usually awarded to this place. A falafel costs €3.50, but shell out a little extra money for the "spécial" with grilled eggplant, cabbage, hummus, tahini, and hot sauce. Though takeout is popular, you might find that it's quicker, easier and more entertaining to eat off a plastic plate in the buzzy dining room. ⊠ *34 rue des Rosiers, Le Marais,* ☎ *01–48–87–63–60. MC, V. Closed Fri. dusk–Sat. dusk Métro: St-Paul.*

$ ✕ **Chez Marianne.** You'll know you've found Marianne's place when you see the line of people reading the bits of wisdom and poetry painted across her windows. The restaurant-deli serves excellent Middle Eastern specialties such as hummus, fried eggplant, and soul-warming chopped liver. The sampler platter lets you try four, five, or six items—even the smallest plate makes a filling feast. Falafel is served only on weekdays in the restaurant, though you can get it every day at the take-out window. ⊠ *2 rue des Hospitalières-St-Gervais, Le Marais,* ☎ *01–42–72–18–86. MC, V. Métro: St-Paul.*

5e Arrondissement (Latin Quarter)
See Left Bank Dining map.

CHINESE

$–$$ ✕ **Mirama.** Regulars at this popular and rather chaotic Chinese restaurant order the soup, a rich broth with a nest of thick noodles garnished with dumplings, barbecued pork, or smoked duck. Main courses are generous—the best are made with shellfish; the Peking duck is also excellent. Service is brisk, so plan on coffee in a nearby café. For dining alone, it's quick and easy. ⊠ *17 rue St-Jacques, Latin Quarter,* ☎ *01–43–29–66–58. MC, V. Métro: St-Michel.*

FRENCH

$$$$ ✕ **La Tour d'Argent.** Beyond the pretty wonderful food (the current chef
★ is Jean-François Sicallac), many factors conspire to make a meal at this venerable landmark memorable: the extraordinary wine cellar, considerate service, and, of course, that privileged vista across the Seine and beyond. If the price of dinner makes you pause, you can't go wrong with the €60 lunch—you'll even be entitled to succulent slices of one of the restaurant's numbered ducks (the great duck slaughter began in 1919 and they are well past their millionth mallard, as your numbered certificate will attest). Don't get too daunted by the wine list—more of a Bible, really—for with the help of one of the famous sommeliers, you can splurge a little (about €80) and get to taste a rare vintage Burgundy. The lunch crowd is remarkably casual, while evenings are a more formal affair (jacket and tie required for men), attracting a mix of suited tycoons and smoochy couples. ⊠ *15 quai de la Tournelle, Latin Quarter,* ☎ *01–43–54–23–31. Reservations essential. AE, DC, MC, V. Closed Mon. Métro: Cardinal Lemoine.*

\$\$\$–\$\$\$\$ ✕ **Lapérouse.** Émile Zola, George Sand, and Victor Hugo were regu-
★ lars, and grandes dames are said to have mercilessly tested the authenticity
of their diamonds on the restaurant's mirrors, which still bear the
scratches today. It's hard not to fall in love with this 17th-century Seine-
side town house, whose warren of intimate, boiserie-graced salons
breathes history. The latest chef, Alain Hacquard, has found the right
track with a daring (for Paris) spice-infused menu: his lobster, Dublin
Bay prawns, and crayfish bisque is flavored with Szechuan pepper and
a lemon vinaigrette. Game is prominent in the fall, with a selection of
southwestern wines to accompany dishes such as Scottish grouse. For
the ultimate romantic meal, reserve one of the legendary private salons where anything could happen (and probably has). ⊠ *51 quai des
Grands Augustins, Latin Quarter,* ☎ *01–43–26–68–04. Reservations
essential. AE, DC, MC, V. Closed Sun., 3 wks in July, 1 wk in Aug.
No lunch Sat. Métro: St-Michel.*

\$\$–\$\$\$ ✕ **Bistrot Côte Mer.** Run by celebrated chef Michel Rostang's daugh-
ter, Caroline, this reasonably priced fish house has become a local hit
for the professionalism of its staff, warm decor, and very delicious food.
Best bets include a celery and apple remoulade with fresh scallops,
shrimps cooked *à la plancha,* and grilled sea bass with black-olive po-
lenta. End it all with crepes flamboyantly flamed in Grand Marnier or
the first-rate cocoa soufflé. The dining room can get a bit noisy when
full; the summertime terrace is more peaceful. ⊠ *16 bd. St-Germain,
Latin Quarter,* ☎ *01–43–54–59–10. AE, DC, MC, V. Closed 1 wk in
Aug. Métro: Maubert Mutualité.*

\$\$–\$\$\$ ✕ **Chez René.** Cozy and appealingly shabby, this reliable address at the
★ eastern end of boulevard St-Germain has satisfied three generations of
Parisians, who count on finding dishes from Burgundy here, such as
boeuf bourguignon and coq au vin. As you sit on the red leatherette
banquettes, be sure to enjoy some of the wines of the Mâconnais and
Beaujolais available here. ⊠ *14 bd. St-Germain, Latin Quarter,* ☎ *01–
43–54–30–23. MC, V. Métro: Cardinal Lemoine.*

\$\$ ✕ **Le Buisson Ardent.** Just across the street from the ugly Jussieu cam-
★ pus of the University of Paris, this cozy spot is a good example of how
the modern bistro genre is thriving in Paris. The airy front room is a
pleasant place for a meal, with a solicitous proprietor, good waiters,
and scrumptious food from chef Philippe Duclos. His style shows in
such dishes as the rolled country ham filled with cucumber remoulade,
creamy tomato and eggplant gratin, and pork chop with lentils and
foie gras. ⊠ *25 rue Jussieu, Latin Quarter,* ☎ *01–43–54–93–02. AE,
MC, V. Closed weekends and Aug. Métro: Jussieu.*

\$\$ ✕ **Le Reminet.** Chandeliers and mirrors add an unexpected note of el-
★ egance at this relaxed and unusually good bistro, set in a narrow salon
with stone walls. The menu changes regularly and displays the young
chef's talent with dishes like a salad of scallops, greens, and sesame
seeds, and roasted guinea hen with buttered savoy cabbage. If it's
available, try the luscious caramelized pear with cream. A prix-fixe dinner menu for €17 is served on Monday and Thursday only. ⊠ *3 rue
des Grands-Degrés, Latin Quarter,* ☎ *01–44–07–04–24. MC, V.
Closed Tues.–Wed., 2 wks in Aug., and 3 wks in Feb. Métro: Maubert
Mutualité.*

\$ ✕ **Les Pipos.** The tourist-trap restaurants along romantic rue de la Mon-
tagne Ste-Geneviève are enough to make you despair—and then you
stumble across this corner bistro, bursting with chatter and laughter.
Slang for students of the famous École Polytechnique nearby, Les Pipos
is everything you could ask of a Latin Quarter bistro: the space is
cramped, the food is substantial (the cheese comes from the Lyon market), and conversation flows as freely as the wine. ⊠ *2 rue de L'École*

Polytechnique, Latin Quarter, ☎ *01–43–54–11–40. No credit cards. Closed Sun. Métro: Maubert Mutualité.*

SPANISH

$$ ✕ **Fogon St-Julien.** On one of Paris's oldest streets, this intimate, sunny yellow restaurant serves outstanding Spanish food. Begin, of course, with some tasty tapas selections; then make a beeline for one of the six superb paellas, such as saffron with seafood, inky squid, or Valencia-style with rabbit, chicken, snails, and vegetables. Finish up with the custardy crème Catalan, accompanied by a glass of Muscatel, or splurge on one of the excellent Riojas. ⊠ *10 rue St-Julien-le-Pauvre, Latin Quarter,* ☎ *01–43–54–31–33. Reservations essential. MC, V. Closed 2 wks. in Aug., 2 wks in Jan. No lunch weekdays. Métro: St-Michel.*

6ᵉ Arrondissement (St-Germain-des-Prés/ Montparnasse)

See Left Bank Dining map.

BELGIAN

$–$$ ✕ **Le Bouillon Racine.** Originally a *bouillon*—Parisian soup kitchens
★ popular at the turn of the 20th century—this two-story restaurant is now a lushly renovated Belle Epoque oasis featuring a sophisticated Belgian menu. The leek terrine and the ham mousse are fine starters; *waterzooi* (Belgian stewed chicken and vegetables) and roast cod with white beans are excellent main dishes. For a finale, opt for the mocha-beer mousse with malt sauce. In honor of Belgium's some 400 different brews, the beer selection is vast: 6 on tap and about 50 by the bottle. You can drop into the new annex next door for a quick snack. ⊠ *3 rue Racine, St-Germain-des-Prés,* ☎ *01–44–32–15–60. Reservations essential. AE, MC, V. Métro: Odéon.*

CONTEMPORARY

$$ ✕ **Le Café des Délices.** There is a lot to like about this new bistro, from
★ the Art Nouveau facade and the warm and spacious Asia-meets-Africa decor (lots of dark wood and little pots of spices on each table), to the polished service and lip-smacking food. Drop in for the bargain €13 lunch (the *plat du jour* with a glass of wine and coffee), or indulge in *à la carte* dishes such as sea bream on white beans, cooked with anchovy, lemon, coriander, and chili-pepper. Tongue-in-cheek comfort-food desserts tout such ingredients such as Chupa Chups (lollipops) and sugary cereal. ⊠ *87 rue d'Assas, Montparnasse,* ☎ *01–43–54–70–00. AE, MC, V. Closed weekends. Métro: Vavin.*

$$ ✕ **Ze Kitchen Galerie.** Baby bistros grow up so fast—now they are even
★ spawning their own offshoots. William Ledeuil made his name at the popular Les Bookinistes (a Guy Savoy baby) before opening this pared-down contemporary bistro nearby in late 2001. If the name isn't exactly inspired, the cooking shows unbridled creativity and a sense of fun: from a deliberately deconstructed menu featuring raw fish, soups, pastas, and "à la plancha" plates, expect dishes such as a chicken wing, broccoli, and artichoke soup with lemongrass, or pork ribs with curry jus and white beans. Typical of the outstanding desserts is the macaroon with cinnamon-caramel ice cream and a chestnut "milkshake." ⊠ *4 quai des Grands-Augustins, Latin Quarter,* ☎ *01–44–32–00–32. AE, DC, MC, V. Closed Sun. No lunch Sat. Métro: St-Michel.*

FRENCH

$$$–$$$$ ✕ **Hélène Darroze.** Hélène Darroze has been crowned the newest female culinary star in Paris, thanks to the creative flair she has given the classics of southwestern French cooking, from the lands around Albi and Toulouse. You know it's not going to be *la meme chanson*—the same old song—as soon as you see the contemporary Tse & Tse

tableware, and her intriguingly modern touch comes through in such dishes as a sublime duck foie gras confit served with chutney of exotic fruits, or a blowout of roast wild duck stuffed with foie gras and truffles. Be warned, however, that portions are small and service can be downright unprofessional. Few can resist the *île flottante* meringue in a rose water–flavored crème anglaise. Recently made over, the downstairs bistro offers similar food in smaller, tapas-style portions, but you can still expect to pay €53–€61 per person with wine. ⊠ *4 rue d'Assas, St-Germain-des-Prés,* ☎ *01–42–22–00–11. AE, DC, MC, V. Closed Sun.–Mon. Métro: Sèvres Babylone.*

$$$ ✕ **La Bastide Odéon.** Just a few steps from the Luxembourg Gardens you can find this little corner of Provence in Paris—a bright and cheerful restaurant with old oak tables and chairs, and a fine, loving hand with Mediterranean cuisine in the kitchen. Chef Gilles Ajuelos cooks good fish dishes; wonderful pastas, such as tagliatelle in *pistou* (basil and pine nuts) with wild mushrooms; and heartwarming main courses, like roast suckling pig and cod with capers. ⊠ *7 rue Corneille, St-Germain-des-Prés,* ☎ *01–43–26–03–65. AE, MC, V. Closed Sun.–Mon., 1st wk in Jan., 1 wk in Apr., and 3 wks in Aug. Métro: Odéon; RER: Luxembourg.*

$$–$$$ ✕ **Alcazar.** To take in the scene at Sir Terence Conran's brasserie—and
★ quite a scene it is, as this place seats 300 under a skylight roof—opt for a table on the mezzanine, where a long, brushed-steel bar gives you a bird's-eye view. Recently revamped to satisfy cool Parisians' evolving tastes, the menu now proffers "so British" fish-and-chips and such contemporary dishes as scallops with caramelized Belgian endive, plus a lunch menu for calorie counters. Chef Guillaume Lutard trained at Taillevent and Prunier, which shows in the quality of the predictably pricey food. For €25 in the restaurant at lunch and in the bar in the evening you can snack on a main dish with a glass of wine. ⊠ *62 rue Mazarine, St-Germain-des-Prés,* ☎ *01–53–10–19–99. AE, DC, MC, V. Métro: Odéon.*

$$–$$$ ✕ **Les Bookinistes.** Run by inventive chef William Ledeuil, this is the most popular of Guy Savoy's "baby bistros." You can expect to hear more English than French in the cheery dining room, looking out onto the Seine, but the food—such as mussel and pumpkin soup or baby chicken roasted in a casserole with root vegetables—is as authentic as you could hope for. Only the vegetarian option disappoints: unimaginative steamed vegetables drizzled with olive oil. The rather expensive wine list contrasts with the reasonable food prices. Service is friendly but erratic and occasionally overfamiliar. ⊠ *53 quai des Grands-Augustins, St-Germain-des-Prés,* ☎ *01–43–25–45–94. AE, DC, MC, V. Closed Sun. No lunch Sat. Métro: St-Michel.*

$$–$$$ ✕ **Chez Dumonet–Josephine.** Stylish and convivial, this venerable bistro with amber walls, moleskin banquettes, and frosted glass lamps is popular with theater people and politicians. Generous portions of classic French cuisine are served; typical are the very good boeuf bourguignon and the roasted saddle of lamb with artichokes. The wine list is excellent but expensive. ⊠ *117 rue du Cherche-Midi, St-Germain-des-Prés,* ☎ *01–45–48–52–40. AE, MC, V. Closed weekends, Aug., and 1 wk in Feb. Métro: Duroc.*

$$–$$$ ✕ **L'Épi Dupin.** Other bistros are more welcoming, but L'Épi Dupin's cramped, beamed dining room continues to attract an eager crowd of tourists and Gaultier-clad locals who don't seem to mind waiting in the rain for their reserved tables. The prix-fixe-only menu of updated French classics is revised regularly and might include an upside-down tart of caramelized Belgian endive and goat's cheese, curried saddle of rabbit with sweet-potato chutney, and crisp, pyramid-shape pastry filled with apples and candied fennel for dessert. ⊠ *11 rue Dupin, St-*

Germain-des-Prés, ☎ *01–42–22–64–56. Reservations essential. AE, MC, V. Closed weekends and 3 wks in Aug. No lunch Mon. Métro: Sèvres Babylone.*

$$–$$$ ✕ **Le Montagnard.** This rustic little spot—"The Mountaineer"—has a hip, festive crowd that comes to dine on fondue and *raclette* (cheese melted on potatoes) before hitting the many local bars. Split an *assiette montagnard,* an appetizing assortment of Savoyard cold cuts such as *viande de Grisons* (air-dried beef), and then go for the cheese or beef fondue. And bear in mind a little tip from the mountains: fresh black pepper makes a cheese meal much more digestible. ✉ *24 rue des Canettes, St-Germain-des-Prés,* ☎ *01–43–26–47–15. AE, MC, V. Closed Aug. Métro: Mabillon.*

$$ ✕ **Chez Maître Paul.** This calm, comfortable spot is a great place to discover the little-known cooking of the Jura and Franche-Comté regions of eastern France. Though sturdy, this cuisine appeals to modern palates, too, as you'll discover with the *montbéliard,* a smoked sausage served with potato salad, ample enough for two. Also try one of the succulent free-range chicken dishes, either in a sauce of *vin jaune*—a dry wine from the region that resembles sherry—or baked in cream and cheese. The walnut meringue is sinfully wonderful, and the regional Arbois wines are not the usual selection. ✉ *12 rue Monsieur-le-Prince, St-Germain-des-Prés,* ☎ *01–43–54–74–59. AE, DC, MC, V. Closed Sun. and Mon., July–Aug., Dec. 20–27 Métro: Odéon.*

$$ ✕ **La Table d'Aude.** Rive Gauche students, senators, and book editors
★ who dine here are on to a good thing, since this jolly restaurant serves some of the best *cuisine régionale* in Paris. Owner Bernard Patou and his wife, Véronique, take a contagious pleasure in serving up the best of their home turf—the Aude, a long, narrow region in the Languedoc-Roussillon. Almost everyone orders the cassoulet, bubbling hot in a small, high-sided ceramic dish and filled to the brim with white beans, sausage, and preserved duck. Of the house wines, go with the rich, cherry-color Corbières. Good-value prix-fixe menus are also available for €24 and €29. ✉ *8 rue de Vaugirard, St-Germain-des-Prés,* ☎ *01–43–26–36–36. MC, V. Closed Sun. and Aug. No lunch Sat., no dinner Mon. Métro: Odéon.*

$ ✕ **Claude Sainlouis.** This cheerful spot has served the same dependable food for a very long time: steak with frites, lamb knuckle, pork with lentils, and salad. Most of the locals and tourists who add their own boisterous color to the discreetly lit red dining room come here to refuel on the €23 prix fixe. ✉ *27 rue du Dragon, St-Germain-des-Prés,* ☎ *01–45–48–29–68. MC, V. Closed Sun.–Mon. and Aug. Métro: St-Germain-des-Prés.*

JAPANESE

$$ ✕ **Yen.** If you're having what is known in French as a *crise de foie* (liver
★ crisis)—the result of overindulging in rich food—this Japanese noodle house offers the perfect antidote. The blond-wood walls soothe the senses, the staff are happy to explain the proper slurping technique, and the soba (buckwheat noodles), served in soup or with a restorative broth for dipping, will give you the courage to face another round of caramelized foie gras. ✉ *22 rue St-Benoît, St-Germain-des-Prés,* ☎ *01–45–44–11–18. AE, MC, V. Closed Mon. No lunch Sun. Métro: St-Germain-des-Prés.*

7ᵉ Arrondissement (Invalides)
See Left Bank Dining map.

CONTEMPORARY

$$$–$$$$ ✕ **Petrossian.** If you think even serious food should be playful, you'll
★ be delighted by this deceptively plain-looking restaurant. Left Bank politi-

cos and intellectuals gather here for one of the most entertaining dining experiences in Paris—Philippe Conticini serves many of his dishes in straight-sided glasses, rather than plates, to be scooped out with a small spoon. Since Petrossian is very *à la Russe,* smoked fish and caviar star prominently, but another winning concoction is fried frogs' legs and snails in garlic sauce. Originally a pastry chef, Conticini ends the meal—after a pause for "drinkable perfumes"—with a symphony of flavors, from sweet vanilla to bitter chocolate and caramel. ⊠ *18 bd. de La Tour-Maubourg, Invalides/Eiffel Tower,* ☎ *01–44–11–32– 32. AE, DC, MC, V. Closed Sun. and Mon. Métro: La Tour-Maubourg, Invalides.*

FRENCH

$$$$ ✕ **L'Arpège.** Alain Passard, one of the most respected chefs in Paris, has shocked the French culinary world by eliminating most meat and fish from his menu at L'Arpège. His recent menus have elevated the humblest vegetables to sublime heights: beets are served with aged balsamic vinegar, leeks with black truffles, black radishes and cardoon with *parmigiano reggiano,* while he earned his place in the vegetarian hall of fame with his "twelve-flavor" tomato stuffed with fruits and spices. He offers lobster and sea bass when he is sure of the source, and very occasionally poultry. Fans have come flocking—rich ones: count on spending at least €150 per person, unless you opt for the €90 prix fixe, served at lunch and dinner. ⊠ *84 rue de Varenne, Invalides/Eiffel Tower,* ☎ *01–45–51–47–33. AE, DC, MC, V. Closed weekends. Métro: Varenne.*

$$$$ ✕ **Jules Verne.** Top-flight chef Alain Reix's cuisine, not to mention a
★ location 400 ft high—on the second level of the Eiffel Tower—makes a table at the Jules Verne one of the hardest dinner reservations to get in Paris. Sautéed baby squid with duck foie gras and veal filet mignon cooked with preserved lemon and dried fruits are examples of Reix's cooking. A mere €48 will buy you the Jules Verne experience at lunch, though the food doesn't live up to the *à la carte* offerings. A table is easier to snag at lunch—arrive early for a prime seat near the window, and be prepared for the distinctive all-black decor, a rather strange and tired hybrid of *Star Trek* and '70s disco (where else in Paris can you still find octagonal black plates?). Though service has been variable in the past, on our last visit the waiters showed exceptional good humor and patience. ⊠ *Eiffel Tower, Invalides/Eiffel Tower,* ☎ *01–45–55– 61–44. Reservations essential. Jacket and tie. AE, DC, MC, V. Métro: Bir-Hakeim.*

$$$–$$$$ ✕ **Le Violon d'Ingres.** Christian Constant, former head of the Hôtel
★ Crillon's kitchens and mentor to many a successful bistro chef, runs his own dressed-up bistro in one of the quieter but elegant parts of the city. A suit-clad crowd comes to sample the regularly revised menu, which may include such dishes as cream of pumpkin soup with sheep's cheese, risotto with boned chicken wings, and guinea hen on a bed of diced turnips. Constant recently revamped the sleek decor and his reliable presence in the kitchen ensures a high standard. ⊠ *135 rue St-Dominique, Invalides/Eiffel Tower,* ☎ *01–45–55–15–05. Reservations essential. AE, DC, MC, V. Closed Sun and 2 wks in Aug. No lunch Sat. Métro: École Militaire.*

$$–$$$ ✕ **Au Bon Accueil.** To see what well-heeled Parisians like to eat these days, book a table at this extremely popular bistro as soon as you get to town. The excellent, reasonably priced *cuisine du marché* (a daily, market-inspired menu, €25.15 at lunch and €28.20 at dinner) has made it a hit: typical of the winter fare is roast suckling pig with thyme and endives. Desserts are homemade and delicious, from the fruit tarts to the superb *pistache,* a pastry curl filled with homemade pistachio ice cream. ⊠ *14 rue de Montessuy, Invalides/Eiffel Tower,* ☎ *01–47–05–46–11. Reservations essential. MC, V. Closed weekends and 2 wks in Aug. Métro, RER: Pont de l'Alma.*

$$–$$$ ✗ **Les Olivades.** The staid 7ᵉ arrondissement seemed a little less sunny after Les Olivades closed its doors in early 2002—then the restaurant reopened with a brighter color scheme and a chef as skilled in Provençal cuisine as Flora Mikula, who made her name here. Bruno Deligne relies on top-notch ingredients for dishes such as a snail fricassée with serrano ham, rabbit sauté with fennel and rosemary, and a pissaladière (Provençal pizza) with red mullet. For dessert, try his ice cream made with diamond-shaped almond cakes called calissons d'Aix. ⊠ *41 av. Ségur, Invalides/Eiffel Tower,* ☎ *01–47–83–70–09. Reservations essential. AE, MC, V. Closed Sun. and 2 wks in Aug. No lunch Mon. or Sat. Métro: Ségur, École Militaire.*

$$–$$$ ✗ **Thoumieux.** Delightfully Parisian, this place charms with red velour banquettes, yellow walls, and bustling waiters in white aprons. Budget prices for rillettes, duck confit, and cassoulet make Thoumieux—owned by the same family for three generations—popular. Don't come with lofty expectations but for a solid, gently priced meal. ⊠ *79 rue St-Dominique, Invalides/Eiffel Tower,* ☎ *01–47–05–49–75. AE, MC, V. Métro: Invalides.*

$$ ✗ **Le Petit Troquet.** In the shadow of the Eiffel Tower is this tiny, pleasant bistro filled with homey antiques like old tin signs for clocks and soda siphons. The prix-fixe-only menu changes daily but may include such dishes as goat's cheese mousse with smoked salmon, roast chicken, and fruit crumble for dessert. It's popular with locals, so book ahead. ⊠ *28 rue de l'Exposition, Invalides/Eiffel Tower,* ☎ *01–47–05–80–39. Reservations essential. MC, V. Closed Sun. and 3 wks in Aug. No lunch Mon. and Sat. Métro: École Militaire.*

SEAFOOD

$$$–$$$$ ✗ **Paul Minchelli.** Minchelli is a minimalist who believes that seasonings should not distract from the taste of his impeccably fresh—and very expensive—catch of the day. The baby clams with garlic and fiery Espelette peppers as well as the sea bass drizzled with lemon and olive oil are just two of his wonderful dishes. The dressy dining room with gentle lighting and witty trompe l'oeil "views" out of "portholes" is the backdrop for a very stylish crowd, often sprinkled with celebrities like Catherine Deneuve. ⊠ *54 bd. de La Tour Maubourg, Invalides/Eiffel Tower,* ☎ *01–47–05–89–86. MC, V. Closed Sun.–Mon. and Aug. Métro: École Militaire.*

8ᵉ Arrondissement (Champs-Élysées)
See Right Bank Dining map.

CONTEMPORARY

$$$–$$$$ ✗ **Market.** Following hot on the heels of Nobu, New York chef Jean-
★   Georges Vongerichten (think Vong, Mercer Kitchen, Jean-Georges, and JoJo) set up shop in Paris in late 2001, in partnership with business mogul François Pinault and film director Luc Besson. Put together with deceptively simple raw materials—burnt pine and stone offset with African masks—the dining room makes a stylish and relaxed, if sometimes noisy, arena for well-traveled dishes such as pizza with raw tuna and wasabi cream, Thai-style chicken-coconut soup with galangal, and duck fillet with sesame jus and tamarind confit. Politicians and power shoppers are delighted—the dining room has been packed since it opened. ⊠ *15 av. Matignon, Champs-Élysées,* ☎ *01–56–43–40–90. AE, MC, V. Métro: Franklin-D.-Roosevelt.*

$$$ ✗ **Spoon, Food and Wine.** Star chef Alain Ducasse's bistro may be the granddaddy of style-conscious restaurants around the Champs-Élysées

(it opened five years ago) but its popularity shows no signs of waning. What draws the trendy crowd is the playful, Asian- and American-inspired menu; the *Wallpaper*-y decor (white by day, plum by night); and the fact that it's so hard to get a reservation (you can always drop by for a snack at the bar). For a quick fashion hit, opt for the 40-minute "Speedy Spoon" menu (€37.35, or €46.50 with a glass of wine), which continent-hops every weekday: Africa on Monday, Europa on Tuesday, and so on. High-style vegetarians love this place for its many vegetable, pasta, and grain dishes. Come late for the models and movie stars. ⊠ *14 rue de Marignan, Champs-Élysées,* ☎ *01–40–76–34–44. Reservations essential. AE, MC, V. Closed weekends and 4 wks in July/Aug. Métro: Franklin-D.-Roosevelt.*

$$–$$$ ✕ **Korova.** Named after the Milk Bar in the film *Clockwork Orange* (*korova* is Russian for "cow"), this funky yet high-style "diner" attracts the area's moooovers and shakers. Four curvy rooms are done up in white, pearl gray, and watery green: groovy music and soft lighting complete the space-age picture. The jet-set menu hops from hot dogs (with lobster and mayonnaise) to chicken (with Coca-Cola sauce) to vintage canned sardines. Desserts are by none other than master pâtissier Pierre Hermé. A meal will set you back at least €46 a head, but you could always drop in from 8 AM for breakfast or after 11 PM for a drink in the lounge to watch the city's fashion victims in action. ⊠ *33 rue Marbeuf, Champs-Élysées,* ☎ *01–53–89–93–93. AE, DC, MC, V. No lunch Sat. and Sun. Métro: Franklin-D.-Roosevelt.*

$$–$$$ ✕ **Maison Blanche.** The celebrated twin Pourcel brothers (Laurent and
★ Jacques) of Le Jardin des Sens in Montpellier preside over this "White House," which front-and-centers a show-off view across Paris from the top floor of the Théâtre du Champs- Élysées. The formerly gray decor has gone fashionably white and the food offers a refreshing taste of the south: hot and iced tomatoes on a pumpkin purée with fresh truffles, scallop carpaccio with sea urchin coral, and Swiss chard ravioli with tomato confit. Unfortunately, though, the waiters take themselves just a tad too seriously—this restaurant could do with being more fun. Still, once you soothe frayed urban nerves with comforting desserts such as a caramel popsicle with pecan cake, or crunchy chocolate and banana cake with spice fritters, you'll forgive all. ⊠ *15 av. Montaigne, Champs-Élysées,* ☎ *01–47–23–55–99. AE, DC, MC, V. Closed Sun. No lunch Sat. Métro: Franklin-D.-Roosevelt.*

FRENCH

$$$$ ✕ **Alain Ducasse.** You may need to set a steel trap outside his door ac-
★ tually to catch megastar chef Alain Ducasse in this kitchen—he now has restaurants around the globe (and never cooks on weekends)—but it would probably be worth the wait. The rosy rococo salons in the Hôtel Plaza Athenée were updated by decorator Patrick Jouin, who draped metallic organza over the chandeliers and, in a symbolic move, made time stand still by stopping the clock. Overlooking the prettiest courtyard in Paris, this makes for a setting as delicious as Ducasse's roast lamb garnished with "crumbs" of dried fruit or duckling roasted with fig leaves. When you sample the *bisque de homard* (lobster bisque) or the pork belly, you know you are getting the real thing—each is made from as many elements (shell, skin, juice, pan drippings) as possible and offers the absolute essence of the ingredients. At these prices, the level of presentation—there are few sauce "paintings," orchid blossoms, or other visual adornments on the plate—could be enhanced. To be on the safe side, reserve weeks in advance. ⊠ *Hôtel Plaza Athenée, 27 av. Montaigne, Champs-Élysées,* ☎ *01–53–67–66–65. AE, DC, MC, V. Closed weekends, Christmas wk, 2 wks in July, 3 wks in Aug. No lunch Mon.–Wed. Métro: Alma-Marceau.*

$$$$ ✕ **Les Ambassadeurs.** Looking as if Madame de Pompadour might stroll
★ in the door at any moment, Les Ambassadeurs is Paris in full ancien
régime dress. With its dramatic black-and-white diamond floor and
honey-color marble walls, the place is polished and furnished to such
a degree it would still make Louis XV (who had it built in 1758)
proud. Chef Dominique Bouchet likes to mix luxe with more down-
to-earth flavors: potato pancakes topped with smoked salmon, caviar-
flecked scallops wrapped in bacon with tomato and basil, duck with
rutabaga, turbot with cauliflower. The €62 lunch menu is well worth
the splurge—especially in summer, when you can while away the rest
of the afternoon on the gorgeous terrace. There is even a breakfast—
talk about luxury—served from 7 to 10:30 AM. ✉ *10 pl. de la Concorde, Louvre/Tuileries,* ☎ *01–44–71–16–16. Jacket and tie at dinner.
AE, DC, MC, V. Métro: Concorde.*

$$$$ ✕ **Le Bristol.** After a rapid ascent at his own nouvelle-wave bistro that
led to his renown as one of the more inventive young chefs in Paris,
Eric Frechon has become head chef at the Bristol, that home-away-from-
home of billionaires and power brokers. By choosing him, this elegant
hotel made a savvy choice that underlines the Bristol's importance as
a showcase in the world of Paris haute cuisine. Frechon uses one of
the grandest pantries in Paris to create masterworks—ravioli of foie
gras in mushroom cream with truffles, or scallops on a bed of diced
celery root in truffle juice—that never stray too far away from the com-
fort-food tastes found in bistro cooking: no wonder his tables are so
coveted. Courtly service and two beautiful dining rooms—an oval
oak-paneled one for fall and winter and a marble-floored pavilion overlooking the courtyard garden for spring and summer—make this a top
destination for a memorable meal. ✉ *Hôtel Bristol, 112 rue du
Faubourg-St-Honoré, Champs-Élysées,* ☎ *01–53–43–43–00. Reservations essential. Jacket and tie. AE, DC, MC, V. Métro: Miromesnil.*

$$$$ ✕ **Les Élysées du Vernet.** Often overlooked, this may be the perfect choice
★ for a *classique* blowout in Paris today, thanks to its remarkable har-
monic alignment of staff, decor, and kitchen. Chef Alain Solivères is a
passionate cook and one taste of his *Parmentier de sanglier au panais*
(shepherd's pie of roasted boar with garlic parsnips) will tell you why
he's a hero in food circles. Service is impeccable and the intimate dining room, under a magnificently beautiful turn-of-the-20th-century *verrière* (glass ceiling) designed by Gustave Eiffel himself, is the kind of
place where you want to linger. Solivères's menu changes seasonally,
drawing inspiration from the Basque country, Bordeaux, and Langue-
doc. Other remarkable dishes include a risotto of wheat grains cooked
in squid's ink, and a roasted duck liver served with baby artichokes
and arugula. There's also superb wine service from a rosy-cheeked young
man who was formerly the personal sommelier of President Jacques
Chirac. ✉ *Hôtel Vernet, 25 rue Vernet, Champs-Élysées,* ☎ *01–44–
31–98–98. Reservations essential. AE, DC, MC, V. Closed weekends,
Aug., and 2 wks in Dec. Métro: George V.*

$$$$ ✕ **Maxim's.** Count Danilo sang "I'm going to Maxim's" in Lehar's
The Merry Widow, Leslie Caron was klieg-lit here by Cecil Beaton for
Gigi, and Audrey Hepburn adorned one of its banquettes with Peter
O'Toole in *How to Steal a Million.* In reality, Maxim's has lost some
of its luster—the restaurant had its heyday 100 years ago during La
Belle Epoque, when *le tout Paris* swarmed here—but this exuberant
Art Nouveau sanctuary still offers a taste of the good life under its breathtaking painted ceiling. Opened in 1893 by Maxime Gaillard, Maxim's
has belonged to designer Pierre Cardin since 1981 (who proceeded to
clone Maxim's around the world, greatly tarnishing the allure of this
home base). Happily, current chef Bruno Stril has breathed new life
into the formerly tired food with such dishes as foie gras with mango

(traditionalists can still enjoy the Edward VII lamb fillet and sole with vermouth). It's just a shame that Maxim's is so jaw-droppingly expensive, and that—in a fit of cost-cutting not reflected in the menu prices—a lone pianist has replaced the orchestra. ⊠ *3 rue Royale, Louvre/Tuileries,* ☎ *01–42–65–27–94. Reservations essential. AE, DC, MC, V. Closed Sun.–Mon. and July–Aug. Métro: Concorde.*

$$$$ ✕ **Pierre Gagnaire.** Legendary chef Pierre Gagnaire's cooking is at once
★ intellectual and poetic—in a single dish at least three or four often unexpected tastes and textures come together in a sensational experience—so if you want to venture to the frontier of luxe cooking today, a meal here is a must. Just taking in the menu requires concentration, so complex are descriptions such as "suckling lamb from Aveyron: sweetbreads, saddle and rack; green papaya and turnip velouté thickened with Tarbais beans." The *"Grand Dessert,"* a seven-dessert marathon, is not to be missed. The businesslike gray-and-wood dining room is hardly stylish but feels refreshingly informal. Unfortunately, some misses on the menu, uneven service, and a scanty wine list linger as drawbacks at these prices, but the fact remains: There are few chefs as thrilling as Gagnaire today. ⊠ *6 rue de Balzac, Champs-Élysées,* ☎ *01–58–36–12–50. Reservations essential. AE, DC, MC, V. Closed Sat. and mid-July–mid-Aug. No lunch Sun. Métro: Charles-de-Gaulle–Étoile.*

$$$$ ✕ **Taillevent.** Perhaps the most traditional—for many diners this is only
★ high praise—of all Paris luxury restaurants, this grande dame has been subtly modernized since the arrival of chef Michel Del Burgo. He has judiciously revised the conservative menu here, adding creations that sometimes eerily resemble dishes served in modern bistros. Classics such as the *boudin de homard*—an airy sausage-shape lobster soufflé—offer continuity with the fabled past. Service is flawless, the setting—19th-century paneled salons now accented with abstract paintings—is *luxe,* the well-priced wine list probably one of the top 10 in the world: All in all, a meal here comes as close to the classic haute cuisine experience as you can find in Paris today. Not surprisingly, you must reserve your table for dinner three weeks in advance—lunch is more accessible. ⊠ *15 rue Lamennais, Champs-Élysées,* ☎ *01–44–95–15–01. Reservations essential. Jacket and tie. AE, DC, MC, V. Closed weekends and Aug. Métro: Charles-de-Gaulle–Étoile.*

$$$–$$$$ ✕ **L'Astor.** Chef Eric Lecerf pays homage to his mentor, Joël Robuchon, by offering some classic Robuchon dishes such as cauliflower cream with caviar and spiced roasted lobster. But he also shows his own talent with sophisticated offerings like sole with baby squid and artichokes. The service and wine list are superb. Trendy interior designer Frédérique Méchiche is responsible for the spacious and attractive dining room, which takes a cue from the '30s with star appliqués on the walls and a checkerboard carpet. The €50 prix-fixe lunch menu is great value. ⊠ *Hôtel Astor, 11 rue d'Astorg, Opéra/Grands Boulevards,* ☎ *01–53–05–05–20. AE, DC, MC, V. Closed weekends and Aug. Métro: Madeleine.*

$$$–$$$$ ✕ **Stella Maris.** A pretty Art Deco front window is the calling card for this spot near the Arc de Triomphe. An expense-account crowd mixes with serious French gourmands to dine on the very subtle cuisine of Japanese chef Taderu Yoshino, who trained with Joël Robuchon and rewrites his menu four times a year. You'll find nuances of Japan in delicious dishes—made with organic ingredients—such as eel *blanquette* (stew) with grilled cucumber, and rice pudding with white truffle. ⊠ *4 rue Arsène-Houssaye, Champs-Élysées,* ☎ *01–42–89–16–22. Reservations essential. AE, DC, MC, V. Closed Sun. and 2 wks in Aug. No lunch Sat. or Mon. Métro: Étoile.*

$$$–$$$$ ✕ **Le Cinq.** The massive flower arrangement at the entrance proclaims the no-holds-barred luxury that is on offer here. Painted powder blue, with stuccoed medallions worked into the ceiling trim, this beautiful though staid room overlooks the freshly renovated hotel's atrium and makes a fitting stage-set for chef Philippe Legendre. Formerly a superstar at Taillevent, he is clearly thriving in these kitchens, where he has apparently been given carte blanche. His fricassee of Breton lobster is astounding as is his *amuse-bouche* of a single oyster sublimated by truffle and caviar. Occasionally, the luxe menu is brought back down to earth by such heady selections as lièvre à la royale—hare and mashed potatoes. ⊠ *Hôtel Four Seasons George V, 31 av. George V, Champs-Élysées,* ☎ *01–49–52–70–00. Reservations essential. Jacket and tie. AE, DC, MC, V. Métro: George V.*

$$–$$$ ✕ **La Fermette Marbeuf.** Graced with one of the most magically beautiful Belle Epoque rooms in town—accidentally rediscovered during renovations in the 1970s—this is a favorite haunt of French celebrities who adore the sunflowers, peacocks, and dragonflies of the Art Nouveau mosaic and stained-glass mise-en-scène. The menu rolls out a solid, updated classic cuisine. Try the snails in puff pastry, saddle of lamb with *choron* (a tomato-spiked béarnaise sauce), and bitter-chocolate fondant—but ignore the prix fixe unless you are on a budget, as the chef seems to have cut corners on ingredients. Popular with tourists and businesspeople at lunch, La Fermette becomes truly animated around 9 PM. ⊠ *5 rue Marbeuf, Champs-Élysées,* ☎ *01–53–23–08–00. AE, DC, MC, V. Métro: Franklin-D.-Roosevelt.*

$$–$$$ ✕ **Rue Balzac.** Opened by haute cuisine chef Michel Rostang and flamboyant French rock star Johnny Hallyday, this restaurant attracts an intriguing crowd of leather-clad (and sometimes leathery) wannabes. The menu is original: you can order anything from a truffle sandwich to roast lamb with shallots caramelized in aged vinegar, and the pineapple crème brûlée, served in the fruit's shell, is an improvement on the original. But prices are steep, service is snooty, and some dishes miss the mark, such as a ham-and-cheese French take on risotto. The scene makes entertaining theater, though, and the high-ceilinged room is pleasant with its ceiling moldings, pastel colors, Miro-esque murals, and modern light fixtures. ⊠ *3–5 rue Balzac, Champs-Élysées,* ☎ *01–53–89–90–91. AE, MC, V. No lunch Sat. and Sun. Métro: Franklin-D.-Roosevelt.*

$$–$$$ ✕ **Sebillon.** The original Sebillon has nurtured chic residents of the fashionable suburb of Neuilly for generations; this elegant, polished branch off the Champs-Élysées continues the tradition. The menu includes lobster salad, lots of shellfish, and—the specialty—roast leg of lamb sliced table-side and served until you beg the waiter to stop. Service is notably friendly. ⊠ *66 rue Pierre-Charron, Champs-Élysées,* ☎ *01–43–59–28–15. AE, DC, MC, V. Métro: Franklin-D.-Roosevelt.*

$$ ✕ **Chez Savy.** Just off the glitzy avenue Montaigne, Chez Savy exists
★ in its own circa-1930s dimension, oblivious to the area's galloping fashionization. The Art Deco cream-and-burgundy interior looks blissfully intact (avoid the back room unless you're in a large group) and the waiters show not a trace of attitude, even offering to change a wine bottle that's just a touch too chilled. Fill up on rib-sticking specialties from the Auvergne in central France—lentil salad with bacon, beautifully charred lamb with feather-light shoestring frites, poached peach with sorbet—order a celebratory bottle of Mercurey, and feel smug that you've found this place. ⊠ *23 rue Bayard, Champs-Élysées,* ☎ *01–47–23–46–98. AE, MC, V. Closed weekends and Aug. Métro: Franklin-D.-Roosevelt.*

$$ ✕ **Chez Tante Louise.** Chef Bernard Loiseau's three Paris outposts—his original eponymous restaurant is in Saulieu in Burgundy—are appealing bastions of traditional Burgundian cooking. Here, he has wisely left the vintage '30s decor almost completely untouched. The food is pleasantly old-fashioned and hearty—like *oeufs en meurette à la bour-guignonne* (poached eggs in red wine sauce with bacon) and sole "Tante Louise," in which a fillet is served on a bed of *duxelles* (finely chopped mushrooms). Of course, there's a nice selection of Burgundies, and service is prompt and professional for the well-dressed crowd. ✉ *41 rue Boissy d'Anglas, Opéra/Grands Boulevards,* ☎ *01–42–65–06–85. Reservations essential. AE, DC, MC, V. Closed weekends and Aug. Métro: Madeleine.*

JAPANESE

$$–$$$ ✕ **Nobu.** The Parisian branch of Nobu opened just in time for the fall
★   2001 fashion shows and has been drawing an insouciant crowd ever since (Nobu is pricey for Paris, but cheaper here than in London or New York). Though it's hardly the only super-cool restaurant in the area, this is one place where *branché* Parisians go as much for the cuisine as the scene: bye-bye to boring salmon and tuna, *bienvenue* eel sashimi, soft-crab sushi, beef toban yaki, and Peruvian-inspired sole with black bean sauce. Nobu is definitely the only restaurant in Paris where waiters kneel to take your order—and, even more shockingly, the dining room is no-smoking (you can indulge in the lounge). ✉ *15 rue Marbeuf, Champs-Élysées,* ☎ *01–56–89–53–53. AE, DC, MC, V. Métro: Franklin-D.-Roosevelt.*

PAN-ASIAN

$$$ ✕ **Buddha Bar.** Opened way back in 1996, the cavernous Buddha Bar has spawned many an imitator—and, even if some of the vogueish glamor has faded (celebrities being fickle creatures), it still makes for a big night out. Eye the scene wistfully from the bar upstairs, or splash out and book a table within reach of the giant gilt Buddha that reigns over the dining room. Japanese snacks are served at lunch and there is a separate sushi menu at night—or choose from a range of quite tasty Asian-Pacific dishes that will do more harm to your wallet than your waistline. Frankly, though, the opulent *chinoiserie* setting and sultry music by world-renowned DJs are more of a draw than the food. ✉ *8 rue Boissy d'Anglas, Louvre/Tuileries.,* ☎ *01–53–05–90–00. AE, MC, V. Métro: Concorde.*

9ᵉ Arrondissement (Opéra/Pigalle-Clichy)

See Right Bank Dining map.

FRENCH

$$$ ✕ **Bistrot des Deux Théâtres.** Quality is high and prices are low at this well-run restaurant in the Pigalle-Clichy area. The prix-fixe only menu includes apéritif, first and main dishes, a cheese or dessert course, half a bottle of wine, and coffee. The food—such as foie gras salad, steak with morels, and apple tart flambéed with calvados—is far from banal. ✉ *18 rue Blanche, Montmartre,* ☎ *01–45–26–41–43. AE, DC, MC, V. Métro: Trinité.*

$ ✕ **Chartier.** People come here more for the bonhomie than the food, which is often stunningly ordinary. This cavernous 1896 restaurant enjoys a huge following among budget-minded students, solitary bachelors, and tourists. You may find yourself sharing a table with strangers as you study the long, old-fashioned menu of such favorites as hard-boiled eggs with mayonnaise, steak tartare, and roast chicken with fries. ✉ *7 rue du Faubourg-Montmartre, Opéra/Grands Boulevards,* ☎ *01–47–70–86–29. Reservations not accepted. AE, DC, MC, V. Métro: Montmartre.*

SEAFOOD

$$$ ✕ **Estaminet Gaya.** Come here for affordable seafood in all its guises, from marinated anchovies to Basque tuna to bouillabaisse. The colorful Portuguese tiles on the ground floor are delightful; the upstairs dining room, decorated with photos, seems plain in comparison. Given the often exorbitant prices at fish restaurants in Paris, the prix-fixe menu at €28 is excellent value. Other prices vary with the day's catch. ✉ *17 rue Duphot, Opéra/Grands Boulevards,* ☎ *01–42–60–43–03. AE, MC, V. Closed weekends. Métro: Madeleine.*

10ᵉ Arrondissement (Opéra/République)
See Right Bank Dining map.

FRENCH

$$$ ✕ **Chez Michel.** Effusive chef Thierry Breton pulls in a stylish crowd
★ of Parisians and tourists with his wonderful market-inspired cooking, despite the out-of-the-way location in a pretty neighborhood near Gare du Nord. The prix-fixe-only menu changes constantly, but you'll almost invariably find the Breton specialties *kig ha farz* (a robust pork stew with a bread stuffing) and *kouing aman* (the butteriest cake imaginable). In winter, don't miss Breton's succulent game dishes (for a €10.70 supplement) such as the surprisingly mild-tasting boar chops, served in a cast-iron pot with tiny potatoes and roasted garlic. The cheese course, served on a slate, is outstanding. There is a long, convivial table in the vaulted cellar. ✉ *10 rue Belzunce, Opéra/Grands Boulevards,* ☎ *01–44–53–06–20. Reservations essential. MC, V. Closed Sun.–Mon. and Aug. Métro: Gare du Nord.*

$$–$$$ ✕ **Brasserie Flo.** The first of brasserie king Jean-Paul Bucher's many
★ Paris addresses is hard to find down its passageway near the Gare de l'Est, but it's worth the effort, as much for its Alsatian rich woods and stained glass and conviviality as for its savory brasserie standards (such as shellfish, steak tartare, and choucroute). Order a carafe of Alsatian wine to go with your meal. It's open until 1:30 AM, with a special late-night menu for €21.50 from 10 PM. ✉ *7 cour des Petites-Écuries, Opéra/Grands Boulevards,* ☎ *01–47–70–13–59. AE, DC, MC, V. Métro: Château d'Eau.*

$$–$$$ ✕ **Julien.** Famed for its 1879 decor—think Majorelle bar, Art Nouveau stained glass, *La-Bohème*-ish street lamps hung with vintage hats—this Belle Epoque dazzler certainly lives up to its oft-quoted moniker, "the poor man's Maxim's." Fare includes smoked salmon, foie gras, stuffed roast lamb, cassoulet, and its famous *profiteroles* (choux pastry smothered in chocolate). Diners are ebullient and lots of fun; this place has a strong following with the fashion crowd, so it's mobbed during the biannual fashion and fabric shows. The downside? Letters from readers have complained about some lackluster dishes and even worse service (and the area is frankly not the safest in Paris). There's service until 1 AM, with a special late-night menu for €21.50 from 10 PM. ✉ *16 rue du Faubourg St-Denis, Opéra/Grands Boulevards,* ☎ *01–47–70–12–06. AE, DC, MC, V. Métro: Strasbourg St-Denis.*

$–$$ ✕ **Chez Casimir.** Another project of chef Thierry Breton of Chez Michel, this (too) brightly lit, easygoing bistro is popular with stylish Parisian professionals for whom it serves as a sort of canteen—why cook when you can eat this well for so little money? The menu shows Breton's cooking style with dishes such as lentil soup with fresh croutons, braised endive and *andouille* (tripe sausage) salad, and roast lamb on a bed of Paimpol beans. Good desserts include *pain perdu*, a dessert version of French toast—here it's topped with a roasted pear or whole cherries. ✉ *6 rue de Belzunce, Opéra/Grands Boulevards,* ☎ *01–48–78–28–80. MC, V. Closed weekends and Aug. Métro: Gare du Nord.*

$ ✕ **Au Vieux Bistrot.** If you're staying near the Gare du Nord or looking for a meal in the area before taking the train, this pleasant, old-fashioned neighborhood bistro is a good bet. From the big zinc bar to the steak with mushroom sauce and veal in cream, this place delivers a traditional bistro experience. Finish up with the fruit tart. Service is friendly. ✉ *30 rue Dunkerque, Opéra/Grands Boulevards,* ☎ *01–48–78–48–01. MC, V. Closed Sun. No dinner Sat. Métro: Gare du Nord.*

11ᵉ Arrondissement (Bastille/République)

See Right Bank Dining map.

CHINESE

$$ ✕ **Wok.** Design-it-yourself Asian stir-fry in a slick, minimalist room has made this spot a hit with the penny-wise hipsters around party-hearty Bastille. You select the type of noodle you want and load up at a buffet with bins of chicken, white fish, shrimp, salmon, beef, and vegetables; then join the line to discuss your preferred seasoning with the chefs who man the woks in the open kitchen. The all-you-can-eat single-price tariff lets you walk the wok as many times as you want. Otherwise, there are deep-fried spring rolls as starters and a signature dessert of caramelized fruit salad. Mobbed on weekends but unfortunately closed at lunch, this place is fun, nourishing, and cheap. ✉ *23 rue des Taillandiers, Bastille/Nation,* ☎ *01–55–28–88–77. MC, V. Closed Sun. No lunch Mon.–Sat. Métro: Bréguet Sabin, Bastille, Ledru-Rollin.*

FRENCH

$$–$$$ ✕ **Le Repaire de Cartouche.** Between Bastille and République, this split-level, dark-wood-hued, '50s-style bistro offers excellent food for good-value prices. Young chef Rodolphe Paquin is a creative and impeccably trained cook who does a stylish take on earthy French regional dishes. The menu changes regularly, but typical are a salad of *haricots verts* (string beans) topped with tender slices of squid, scallops on a bed of diced pumpkin, and old-fashioned desserts like custard with tiny madeleine cakes. The wine list is very good, too, with bargains like a Cheverny from the Loire Valley for €17. ✉ *99 rue Amelot, Bastille/Nation,* ☎ *01–47–00–25–86. Reservations essential. MC, V. Closed Sun.–Mon. and Aug. Métro: Filles du Calvaire.*

$$ ✕ **Astier.** The prix-fixe menu (there's no à la carte) at this popular, old-
★ fashioned restaurant must be one of the best values in town. Among the beautifully prepared seasonal dishes are baked eggs topped with truffled foie gras, fricassee of *joue de boeuf* (beef cheeks), rabbit in mustard sauce with fresh tagliatelle, and plum *clafoutis* (a fruit flan). This is a great place to come if you're feeling cheesy, since it's locally famous for having one of the best *plateaux de fromages* (cheese plates) in Paris—a giant wicker tray lands on the table and you help yourself. The lengthy, well-priced wine list is a connoisseur's dream. ✉ *44 rue Jean-Pierre Timbaud, République,* ☎ *01–43–57–16–35. Reservations essential. MC, V. Closed weekends, Aug., Christmas wk, Easter wk. Métro: Parmentier.*

$$ ✕ **Au Camelot.** This minuscule bistro brings in the crowds with its ex-
★ cellent home-style cooking, consistently some of the best in Paris. Chef Didier Varnier trained with guru Christian Constant at the Crillon and it shows in such creative dishes as pumpkin soup with goat's-cheese ravioli, squid-ink risotto with Dublin Bay prawns, sweet-and-sour duck with dried-fruit tabouleh, and spice bread pudding with lemon cream. In keeping with waist-conscious times, Varnier has dropped his five-course menu and now offers three courses for €30—you can also order à la carte. Though the place is noisy and very crowded, service is friendly, and the house Bordeaux is a treat. ✉ *50 rue Amelot, Bastille/Nation,* ☎ *01–43–55–54–04. Reservations essential. AE, MC, V. Closed Sun.–Mon. and 3 wks in Aug. No lunch Sat. Métro: République.*

$$ ✕ **Les Fernandises.** The chef-owner of this neighborhood spot near place de la République is more concerned with his Normandy-inspired cuisine than with his restaurant's inconsequential decor. Fresh foie gras sautéed in cider and scallops in cream sauce are examples of his varied style. Choose from at least six Camemberts at any given time, including one doused in calvados and another coated in hay. ⊠ *17 rue Fontaine-au-Roi, République,* ☎ *01–43–57–46–25. MC, V. Closed Sun.– Mon. and Aug. Métro: République.*

$–$$ ✕ **Le Passage.** Not far from place de la Bastille, in the obscure passage de la Bonne Graine, is this friendly spot with a homey air. Though it bills itself as a wine bar, it has a full menu, including nine kinds of *andouillette* (chitterling sausage). The initials AAAAA, by the way, mean the sausage has the stamp of approval from the French andouillette aficionados' association. Since the andouillette's pungent aroma makes it an acquired taste, other, less fragrant dishes are available. Le Passage is also a delight for wine lovers, with many unusual bottles. ⊠ *18 passage de la Bonne Graine (enter by 108 av. Ledru-Rollin), Bastille/Nation,* ☎ *01–47–00–73–30. AE, MC, V. Closed Sun. Métro: Ledru-Rollin.*

$ ✕ **Le Kitch.** Fighting the good fight against ennui, this whimsically casual place attracts graphic designers, couturiers-in-training, and other denizens of its arty neighborhood. There's more than a touch of Pee-Wee's Playhouse here—faux-stucco walls, plastic children's furniture, naif paintings of cats, and scudding clouds across the ceiling make this a cute boutique restaurant. Happily, once you taste the dishes here, you won't need to call the chef The Mad Batter: the food here is snappy, if not stylish, and tasty enough to give a satisfied buzz to the room. ⊠ *10 rue Oberkampf, Père Lachaise,* ☎ *01–40–21–94–14. No credit cards. No lunch Sat. and Sun. Métro: Oberkampf.*

12ᵉ Arrondissement (Bastille/Gare de Lyon)
See Right Bank Dining map.

FRENCH

$$–$$$ ✕ **Au Trou Gascon.** This highly popular Belle Epoque establishment—
★ winsomely embellished with Art Nouveau moldings—off place Daumesnil is overseen by much-praised chef Alain Dutournier. He does a nicely affordable take on the cuisine of Gascony—a region of outstanding ham, foie gras, lamb, and duck (don't miss out on his classic white chocolate mousse). The lunch menu is excellent value at €36; you can also order à la carte at lunch and dinner. ⊠ *40 rue Taine, Bastille/Nation,* ☎ *01–43–44–34–26. AE, MC, V. Closed Sun. and Aug. No lunch Sat. Métro: Daumesnil.*

$$–$$$ ✕ **Les Grandes Marches.** The Flo group's first modern brasserie (they are responsible for restoring the historic La Coupole, Julien, et al.) has a gray color scheme, a sweeping metallic staircase, and high-back asymmetrical chairs all designed by hotshots Elizabeth and Christian de Portzamparc—frankly, though, its greatest attribute is the location next door to the Opéra Bastille. Service is efficient enough but the food has been disappointing given that none other than former Crillon chef Christian Constant helped write the menu. The €35 prix fixe is the least risky option, featuring dishes such as raw tuna with sesame oil, chicken tagine, and *baba au rhum* or crème brûlée with raspberry sauce. Seafood platters are also available. ⊠ *6 pl. de la Bastille, Bastille/Nation,* ☎ *01–43–42–90–32. AE, DC, MC, V. Métro: Bastille.*

$$ ✕ **L'Oulette.** Chef-owner Marcel Baudis's take on the cuisine of his native southwestern France is original and delicious, and service here is effusive—qualities that will help you overlook the out-of-the-way location and out-of-date design. The menu changes with the seasons, but you'll always find his trademark dishes: marinated squid, braised oxtail with foie gras and a mousseline of Puy lentils, and *pain d'épices* (spice cake). The restaurant, in the rebuilt Bercy district, is a bit hard

to find, so start out with your map. Prix-fixe menus are available at lunch (€27) and dinner (€44). ⊠ *15 pl. Lachambeaudie, Bastille/Nation,* ☎ *01–40–02–02–12. AE, DC, MC, V. Closed weekends. Métro: Dugommier.*

$$ ✕ **Le Square Trousseau.** This beautiful Belle Epoque bistro is a favorite ★ of the fashion set, led by Jean-Paul Gaultier who has his headquarters nearby. You might see a supermodel—Claudia Schiffer often comes in when in town—while dining on the homemade foie gras, slow-cooked lamb, or tender baby chicken with mustard and bread-crumb crust. Some dishes are more successful than others, but the human scenery is never lackluster and staff are cheerful. Wines might seem a little pricey but are lovingly selected from small producers—you can also buy them at the restaurant's boutique next door. ⊠ *1 rue Antoine Vollon, Bastille/Nation,* ☎ *01–43–43–06–00. AE, MC, V. Closed Sun.–Mon., and Christmas wk. Métro: Ledru-Rollin.*

$–$$ ✕ **Barrio Latino.** This megaseater restaurant has a rather speciously New York–goes–Puerto Rican theme, so don't come here expecting *West Side Story*—the place pulls a rather self-consciously trendy crowd to its theater-like atrium (it used to be a furniture showroom). The food is passable—just—but the raison d'être for this place is to make the scene and hang out over rather watery tropical cocktails. Reserve a table to avoid having to wait outside. ⊠ *46–48 rue du Faubourg St-Antoine, Bastille/Nation,* ☎ *01–55–78–84–75. AE, DC, MC, V. Métro: Bastille.*

13ᵉ Arrondissement (Les Gobelins)

See Left Bank Dining map.

CHINESE

$–$$ ✕ **La Chine Massena.** With wonderfully overwrought rooms that seem draped in what looks like a whole restaurant-supply catalog's worth of Asiana (plus four monitors showing the very latest in Hong Kong music videos), this is a fun place to come with friends. Not only is the Chinese-Vietnamese-Thai food good and moderately priced, but the place itself has a lot of entertainment value—wedding parties often provide a free floor show, and, on weekends, variety shows followed by Asian disco come as part of your meal. Steamed dumplings and lacquered duck are specialties, but for the best value come at noon for the bargain lunch menus. ⊠ *Centre Commercial Massena, 13 pl. de Venetie, Chinatown,* ☎ *01–45–83–98–88. MC, V. Métro: Porte de Choisy.*

FRENCH

$$$ ✕ **Le Petit Marguery.** As the diorama of a stuffed ferret amid a fairytale mushroom forest announces, this spot offers some of the earthiest dishes in the French canon. With its historic fin-de-siècle charm, the charming ruby-color bistro offers more than reliable French classics and is the place to head for if you're hunting for game—catch it here in late fall, in such dishes as the deeply flavored *lièvre à la royale* (hare in a carnivorous wine-and-blood sauce). Some dishes are so *authèntique* they are even topped with pine needles. ⊠ *9 bd. de Port Royal, St-Germain-des-Prés,* ☎ *01–43–31–58–59. AE, MC, V. Closed Sun.–Mon., Christmas wk, and Aug. Métro: Les Gobelins.*

$$–$$$ ✕ **Le Terroir.** A jolly crowd of regulars makes this little bistro festive. Based on first-rate ingredients from all over France, the menu is solidly classical—salads with chicken livers or fresh marinated anchovies, calves liver or monkfish with saffron, and pears marinated in wine for dessert, for instance. There's also a well-balanced wine list. ⊠ *11 bd. Arago, St-Germain-des-Prés,* ☎ *01–47–07–36–99. AE, MC, V. Closed weekends, Easter wk, 3 wks in Aug., Christmas wk. Métro: Les Gobelins.*

$$ ✕ **Anacréon.** André le Letty, who polished his cooking technique at La Tour d'Argent, has transformed a neighborhood café into a pleasant new-wave bistro. Inventive dishes such as pressed duck with red peppercorns and fresh cod with spices have been highlights on the regularly changing menu. Desserts are always good, too, and the St-Joseph is a perfect choice from the wine list. The menu is prix-fixe. ✉ *53 bd. St-Marcel, St-Germain-des-Prés,* ☎ *01–43–31–71–18. Reservations essential. AE, DC, MC, V. Closed Sun.–Mon. and Aug. No lunch Wed. Métro: Les Gobelins.*

$$ ✕ **L'Avant-Gout.** For excellent contemporary French cooking at very reasonable prices, it's worth seeking out this tiny, off-the-beaten-path bistro in a residential part of the city. Though "The Foretaste" can get crowded and noisy, you won't be disappointed by young chef Christophe Beaufront's appealing and unusual daily prix-fixe menu, which might include dishes like sea bass with creamy celery root and almonds, and steak with roasted shallots. Delicious homemade desserts and a good-value wine list round off the meal. ✉ *26 rue Bobillot, Bercy/Tolbiac,* ☎ *01–53–80–24–00. Reservations essential. MC, V. Closed Sat.–Mon., 1st wk in Jan., 1st wk in May, 3 wks in Aug. Métro: Place d'Italie.*

14e Arrondissement (Montparnasse)
See Left Bank Dining map.

FRENCH

$$$ ✕ **Contre-Allée.** Left Bank students and professors crowd this large restaurant, stomach-upsettingly decorated with bullfighting posters. The menu has original selections such as squid salad with mussels and roast cod with Parmesan; homemade fresh pasta accompanies many dishes. A sidewalk terrace enlivens shady avenue Denfert-Rochereau in summer. ✉ *83 av. Denfert-Rochereau, Montparnasse,* ☎ *01–43–54–99–86. AE, DC, MC, V. No lunch Sat. and Sun. Métro: Denfert-Rochereau.*

$$$ ✕ **La Régalade.** Some say Yves Camdeborde is the chef of the moment
★ these days in Paris—perhaps because he disdains star ratings and couldn't care less? Nevertheless, as the leading priest who marries bistro and nouvelle cookery—who can resist his soup of lentils and puréed chestnuts poured over a mound of fois gras?—he has had to satisfy the hordes who trek to the edge of town for three dinner sittings (and you still have to book at least two weeks ahead). The crowded, no-frills rooms evokes the boringest provinces, but the food is worthy of a luxury restaurant: paper-thin Dublin Bay prawn carpaccio, juicy roast capon with chestnuts, fresh duck foie gras panfried in spice-bread crumbs, and a bitter, adult dessert of grapefruit in Campari jelly. Portions are small, but the country pâté that begins each meal will take the edge off your appetite. ✉ *49 av. Jean-Moulin, Montparnasse,* ☎ *01–45–45–68–58. Reservations essential 2 wks in advance. MC, V. Closed Sun.–Mon. and Aug. No lunch Sat. Métro: Alésia.*

$$–$$$ ✕ **La Coupole.** This world-renowned, cavernous spot practically defines the term brasserie—and its Art Deco murals are famous, too. La Coupole might have lost its intellectual aura since the Flo group's restoration—that giant rotating sculpture was one of the "improvements"—but it has been popular since the days when Jean-Paul Sartre and Simone de Beauvoir were regulars and is still great fun. Today it attracts a mix of bourgeois families, tourists, and elderly lone diners treating themselves to a dozen oysters. Expect the usual brasserie menu—including perhaps the largest shellfish platter in Paris—choucroute, and some great over-the-top desserts. ✉ *102 bd. du Montparnasse, Montparnasse,* ☎ *01–43–20–14–20. AE, DC, MC, V. Métro: Vavin.*

SEAFOOD

\$\$ ✕ **Vin et Marée.** The third, lower-priced annex of the fancy Right Bank fish house La Luna is a welcome addition to Montparnasse. Begin with a tasty bowl of baby clams in a creamy lemon-butter sauce, offered as an hors d'oeuvre; then have a generous plate of fresh red shrimp sautéed in thyme, followed by white tuna in shallot sauce or sautéed red mullets, if available—the menu changes depending on what's in the market that day. Nicely chosen wines come by the bottle, carafe, or glass. ⊠ *108 av. du Maine, Montparnasse,* ☎ *01–43–20–29–50. AE, MC, V. Métro: Montparnasse, Gaité.*

15ᵉ Arrondissement (Motte-Picquet/Balard)
See Left Bank Dining map.

FRENCH

\$\$\$ ✕ **Bistrot d'Hubert.** In a studied environment that might have sprung from the pages of *Elle Decor,* this popular bistro draws a stylish crowd and serves food that perfectly expresses the countercurrents of the Parisian culinary landscape. The prix-fixe-only menu is split into two: "tradition" and "discovery." You might have the sardines with Jerusalem artichokes and spiced cream, followed by pork with orange and ginger, or go for more classic roast beef with herb butter. For dessert, try the salted caramel cake with apples and angelica. ⊠ *41 bd. Pasteur, Montparnasse,* ☎ *01–47–34–15–50. Reservations essential. AE, DC, MC, V. No lunch Sat. Métro: Pasteur.*

\$\$–\$\$\$ ✕ **L'Os à Moelle.** This small, popular bistro has a good-value six-
★ course dinner menu (there's no à la carte) that changes daily; portions are generous. A sample meal might include white-bean soup, sautéed foie gras, *rouget* (red mullet fish), lamb with potato purée, cheese with a small salad, and a delicious roasted pear with cinnamon ice cream. At lunch, there is a shorter, equally good prix fixe. With an excellent list of fairly priced wines, your bill can stay comfortably low—but, if you're feeling broke, the restaurant's casual wine bar across the street is a tempting option. ⊠ *3 rue Vasco-de-Gama, Invalides/Eiffel Tower,* ☎ *01–45–57–27–27. Reservations essential. MC, V. Closed Sun.– Mon. and Aug. Métro: Balard.*

\$\$–\$\$\$ ✕ **Le Troquet.** Tucked away on a quiet street in a residential neighborhood
★ near the UNESCO headquarters, this contemporary, outstanding-value bistro feeds a crowd of regulars. They come for chef Christian Etchebest's tasty, constantly changing prix-fixe menu of dishes from the Basque and Béarn regions of southwestern France. A typical meal might include vegetable soup with foie gras and cream, hot scallops on a bed of mixed vegetables, pan-roasted dove, sheep's cheese with cherry preserves, and a chocolate macaroon. The Béarn red wine cheerfully accompanies this food. Though the dining room looks a little fusty, the place is relaxed and the staff eager to please. ⊠ *21 rue François-Bonvin, Invalides/Eiffel Tower,* ☎ *01–45–66–89–00. MC, V. Closed Sun.– Mon., Aug., and Christmas wk. Métro: Ségur.*

THAI

\$–\$\$ ✕ **Sawadee.** Once you've tried the delicious Thai food here, you'll understand why this off-the-beaten-path spot is full every night. Statues and wood carvings dress up the warm dining room, while a casual atmosphere and friendly service add to the charm. Start with the unusual fried-rice salad, or the delicate shrimp and pork ravioli, and then try the shrimp sautéed with salt and pepper or the chopped beef with basil. ⊠ *53 av. Émile-Zola, Invalides/Eiffel Tower,* ☎ *01–45–77–68–90. AE, MC, V. Closed Sun. and 10 days in Aug. Métro: Charles Michel.*

16e Arrondissement (Trocadéro/Bois de Boulogne)
See Right Bank Dining map.

FRENCH

$$$$ ✕ Le Pré Catalan. Dining beneath the chestnut trees on the terrace of this landmark fanciful *pavillon* in the Bois de Boulogne is a Belle Epoque fantasy. Among the winning dishes on chef Frédéric Anton's menu are spit-roasted baby pigeon in a caramelized sauce, sweetbreads with morels and asparagus tips, and roast pear on a caramelized waffle with bergamot ice cream. Unfortunately, some dishes are decidedly lackluster. Still, the opulent surroundings help you forget that limp turbot, especially if you order the more reasonably priced lunch menu (€55). ⊠ *Bois de Boulogne, rte. de Surèsnes, Champs-Élysées,* ☎ 01–44–14–41–14. *Reservations essential. Jacket and tie. AE, DC, MC, V. Closed Mon., mid-Feb., and 1 wk in Nov. No dinner Sun. Métro: Porte Dauphine.*

$$$–$$$$ ✕ Ghislaine Arabian. After a 2½-year absence from the Paris restau-
★ rant scene, the former chef of Ledoyen is back with a vengeance. Ghislaine Arabian's small, contemporary dining room reflects her sparkling personality, with gold leaf on the walls and a frieze of women's faces sculpted from Murano glass. If Arabian is clearly shooting for the stars, the dining room feels refreshingly casual, and the waiters don't put on airs. Her cooking, as always, is inspired by her northern French roots: try the classic shrimp croquettes with fried parsley and perhaps roasted pigeon with Flemish-style red cabbage confit (the menu changes seasonally). Whatever you do, save room for her frozen parfait of chicory and spice bread with white beer sabayon—and why not accompany your meal with an unusual beer? ⊠ *16 av. Bugeaud, Trocadéro,* ☎ 01–56–28–16–16. *Reservations essential. MC, V. Closed Sun., 2 wks in Aug. No lunch Mon., Sat. Métro: Victor-Hugo.*

$$$–$$$$ ✕ Jamin. At this intimate if rather frilly restaurant, where Joël Robu-
★ chon made his name, you can find excellent haute cuisine at almost half the price of other restaurants of its kind: there is a lunch prix-fixe at just €47 and a €76 menu at lunch and dinner. Benoît Guichard, Robuchon's second for many years, is a subtle and accomplished chef and a particularly brilliant *saucier* (sauce maker). The menu changes regularly, but Guichard favors such dishes as sea bass with pistachios in fennel sauce and braised beef with cumin-scented carrots. The seasonal gratin of rhubarb with a red-fruit sauce makes an excellent dessert. ⊠ *32 rue de Longchamp, Trocadéro,* ☎ 01–45–53–00–07. *Reservations essential. AE, DC, MC, V. Closed weekends and 3 wks in Aug. Métro: Iéna.*

$$$ ✕ 59 Poincaré. It seemed Alain Ducasse could do no wrong—until he opened this hastily conceived concept restaurant in the splendiferous premises of his former Restaurant Alain Ducasse. Downstairs is a sleek modern brasserie where you can drop in for a quick meal, while the legendarily stylish Belle Epoque dining rooms upstairs have been— sigh—jazzed up with giant color photos of farmers, gadgets (chopsticks, notepads, high-tech ashtrays) on the tables, cream linen-draped chairs, and a hip sound track. But the menu is so confused it needs a shrink— after having dropped beef from the menu in (exaggerated) response to the "mad cow" scare, Ducasse has now declared 59 Poincaré "a New York–style steak house," with sides of beef hanging near the entrance. ⊠ *59 av. Raymond-Poincaré, Trocadéro,* ☎ 01–47–27–59–59. *Reservations essential. AE, DC, MC, V. Closed Sun.–Mon. and July 20–Aug. 20. No lunch Sat. Métro: Victor-Hugo.*

$$–$$$ ✕ L'Astrance. Rarely have critics been so enthralled with a new restau-
★ rant: *Le Point* has called L'Astrance "a miracle" while *Le Figaro*'s respected critic Francois Simon has described it as "perfect." What's all

the fuss about? Well, this split-level gray dining room is probably the best place in Paris to part with your hard-earned euros for a special-occasion meal: you get the quality of haute cuisine without the pomposity or the crushing price tag. The house style extends to Asian accents, such as tropical fruits and lemongrass. For a mere €28.20 at lunch, you might feast on an avocado-and-crab mille-feuille, a ballotine of quail and foie gras, spiced mackerel fillet on Asian-style spinach, and orange soufflé with marjoram ice cream (and that's not to mention the surprise extras). Dinner costs twice as much but is well worth it—just don't forget to reserve weeks in advance. ⊠ *4 rue Beethoven, Trocadéro,* ☎ *01–40–50–84–40. Reservations essential 3 wks in advance. AE, DC, MC, V. Métro: Passy.*

$$ ✕ **La Butte Chaillot.** A dramatic iron staircase connects two levels in turquoise and earth tones at one of the most popular of chef Guy Savoy's fashionable bistros. Dining here is part theater, as the à la mode clientele demonstrate, but it's not all show: the very good food includes tasty ravioli from the town of Royans, roast free-range chicken with mashed potatoes, and stuffed veal breast with rosemary. Recent renovations have expanded the dining room and made it feel more harmonious. A wide sidewalk terrace fronts tree-shaded avenue Kléber. ⊠ *112 av. Kléber, Trocadéro,* ☎ *01–47–27–88–88. AE, DC, MC, V. Closed 2 wks in Aug. No lunch Sat. Métro: Trocadéro.*

$$ ✕ **La Grande Armée.** The Costes brothers, who own the most stylish hotel in Paris (the Costes), are perpetually in the forefront of whatever's trendy in town. Their brasserie near the Arc de Triomphe is a great spot to check out their gig, since it's open daily, serves nonstop, and has knockout Napoléon III bordello decor dreamed up by superstar designer Jacques Garcia—black lacquered tables, leopard upholstery, Bordeaux velvet, and a carefully tousled clientele picking at salads, pastas, and soothing potato purée. ⊠ *3 av. de la Grande Armée, Champs-Élysées,* ☎ *01–45–00–24–77. AE, DC, MC, V. Métro: Charles-de-Gaulle–Étoile.*

$$ ✕ **Le Petit Rétro.** Two different clienteles—men in expensive suits at noon and well-dressed locals in the evening—frequent this little bistro with Art Nouveau tiles and bentwood furniture. You can't go wrong with the daily special, which is written on a chalkboard presented by one of the friendly waitresses. Come in some night when you want a good solid meal, like the perfect *pavé de boeuf* (thick steak) in a ruddy red-wine and stock sauce, accompanied by potatoes au gratin and caramelized braised endive. ⊠ *5 rue Mesnil, Trocadéro,* ☎ *01–44–05–06–05. AE, MC, V. Closed Sun. No lunch Sat. Métro: Victor-Hugo.*

SEAFOOD

$$$–$$$$ ✕ **Prunier.** Founded in 1925, this seafood restaurant is one of the best,
    ★   and surely the prettiest, in Paris—even more so following recent renovations (though the wood-paneled upstairs dining room does look a bit saunalike). Now a New York–style caviar house, Maison Prunier doesn't offer much in the way of cooking—a world-weary set from the blasé 16th comes here to feast on Aquitaine caviar (for a cool €100 a tablespoon), chilled oysters with hot, spiced sausages (a Bordeaux specialty), the so-chic "Christian Dior jellied egg" and French vodka or champagne. ⊠ *16 av. Victor-Hugo, Champs-Élysées,* ☎ *01–44–17–35–85. Jacket and tie. AE, DC, MC, V. Closed Sun. and Aug. Métro: Étoile.*

17e Arrondissement (Monceau/Clichy/ Champs-Élysées)

See Right Bank Dining map.

FRENCH

$$$$ ✕ **Guy Savoy.** Redecorated by Jean-Michel Wilmotte, who dressed up
    ★   the space with dark African wood, rich leather (like the inside of a Rolls-

Royce), and cream-color marble, Guy Savoy's luxury restaurant has stepped gracefully into the 21st century. Come here for a perfectly measured, contemporary haute cuisine experience, since Savoy's several bistros have not lured him away from his kitchen. The artichoke soup with black truffles, sea bass with spices, and veal kidneys in mustard-spiked jus reveal the magnitude of his talent, and his mille-feuille is a contemporary classic. Half-portions allow you to graze your way through the menu, and reasonably priced wines are available. Best of all, the atmosphere is joyful—Savoy senses that having fun is just as important as eating well. ⊠ *18 rue Troyon, Champs-Élysées,* ☎ *01–43–80–40–61. AE, MC, V. Closed Sun.–Mon.; mid-July–mid-Aug.; Christmas wk. No lunch Sat. Métro: Charles-de-Gaulle–Étoile.*

$$$ ✕ **Au Petit Colombier.** This is a perennial favorite among Parisians, who come to eat comforting *cuisine bourgeoise* (traditional cuisine) in the warm dining rooms accented with wood and bright copper. Seasonal specialties include milk-fed lamb chop *en cocotte* (in a small, enameled casserole), game in all its guises, and truffles. Service is friendly and unpretentious. ⊠ *42 rue des Acacias, Champs-Élysées,* ☎ *01–43–80–28–54. AE, MC, V. Closed Sun. and Aug. No lunch Sat. Métro: Charles-de-Gaulle–Étoile.*

$$–$$$ ✕ **La Table de Lucullus.** Working in a spot that could be politely de-★ scribed as modest, Nicolas Vagnon has caused quite a stir in the Paris restaurant world with his iconoclastic, comfort-food-meets-haute-cuisine style. A meal here, though not cheap, is a full-on experience—the chef himself describes each dish (in excellent English, too) and his passion is evident. Try the *délice de Lucullus,* smooth foie gras sandwiched between thin slices of beet and white radish, and—in winter—such dishes as steamed scallops with endive salad or boned, long-cooked hare with mashed beet and crushed potatoes. This is that rarest of things in Paris, a no-smoking restaurant. ⊠ *129 rue Legendre, Montmartre,* ☎ *01–40–25–02–68. MC, V. Closed Sun.–Mon. No lunch Sat. Métro: La Fourche.*

$$ ✕ **Café d'Angel.** A trend-conscious yuppie crowd frequents this relaxed little bistro near the Arc de Triomphe, whose name is echoed in its angel-print tablecloths. The menu changes regularly but offers interesting modern bistro dishes and good value for the money. Try the seasonal fish dishes, rabbit compote with lentils, and intriguing upside-down mille-feuille with apple, quince, and spice bread. ⊠ *16 rue Brey, Champs-Élysées,* ☎ *01–47–54–03–33. MC, V. Closed weekends, 3 wks in Aug., 2 wks at Christmas. Métro: Charles-de-Gaulle–Étoile.*

$$ ✕ **Le Graindorge.** Formerly at the justly popular Au Trou Gascon, chef-owner Bernard Broux has thrived since he opened his own establishment. He prepares an original mix of the cuisines of southwestern France and his native Flanders: experience the succulent eel terrine in a delicious herb aspic (seasonal) and red mullet with endives in beer sauce, followed by a small but judicious selection of potent northern cheeses. Madame Broux oversees the pleasant, provincial-style dining rooms and can help you select one of the many fine beers. ⊠ *15 rue de l'Arc-de-Triomphe, Champs-Élysées,* ☎ *01–47–54–00–28. AE, MC, V. Closed Sun. and 2 wks in Aug. Métro: Charles-de-Gaulle–Étoile.*

ITALIAN

$$–$$$ ✕ **Il Baccello.** Young chef Raphael Bembaron is pulling crowds to this ★ outpost with first-rate contemporary Italian food, inspired by his training at the top-draw vegetarian restaurant Joia in Milan. He works almost entirely with organic ingredients, whose quality shows in dishes such as whole-wheat pappardelle with wild mushrooms, risotto cooked with Barolo wine and garnished with duck breast and aged Mimolette cheese, and almond-flavored panna cotta in prune sauce. This is a good address for vegetarians. The dining room is done in sleek (if noisy) minimalist style. ⊠ *33 rue Cardinet, Parc Monceau,* ☎ *01–43–80–63–60. Reservations essential. AE, DC, MC, V. Closed Sun.–Mon., Christmas wk, and 3 wks in Aug. Métro: Wagram.*

JAPANESE

$$–$$$ ✕ **Kifuné.** Removed from the Japanese hub of rue Ste-Anne near Opéra, Kifuné attracts those with a yen for the real thing. It's rare to see a non-Japanese face in the modest dining room, where you can sit at the bar and admire the sushi chef's lightning-quick skills or opt for a more intimate table. Futo maki (inside-out seaweed rolls) is a popular choice among the Japanese customers; crab and shrimp salad makes a sublime starter and the miso soup with clams is deeply flavored. A meal here will leave a dent in your wallet—consider it a mini-trip to Japan. ⊠ *44 rue St-Ferdinand, Champs-Élysées,* ☎ *01–45–72– 11–19. Reservations essential. MC, V. Closed Sun., 2 wks in Aug. No lunch Mon. Métro: Argentine.*

NORTH AFRICAN

$$$ ✕ **Le Timgad.** For a stylish evening out and a night off from French food, head to this elegant, beautifully decorated North African restaurant. Start with a savory *brick* (crispy parchment pastry filled with meat, eggs, or seafood), followed by tasty couscous or succulent *tagine* (meat or poultry that's slowly braised inside a domed pottery casserole). The lamb tagine with artichokes is especially good. ⊠ *21 rue de Brunel, Champs-Élysées,* ☎ *01–45–74–23–70. AE, DC, MC, V. Métro: Argentine.*

SEAFOOD

$$–$$$ ✕ **L'Huîtrier.** If you have a single-minded craving for oysters, this is the place for you. The friendly owner will describe the different kinds available; you can follow these with any of several daily fish specials. The excellent cheeses are from the outstanding shop of Roger Alléosse. Blond wood and cream tones prevail. Should you have trouble getting a table, L'Huîtrier also runs the Presqu'île next door. ⊠ *16 rue Saussier-Leroy, Parc Monceau,* ☎ *01–40–54–83–44. AE, MC, V. Closed Mon. and Aug. Métro: Ternes.*

18ᵉ Arrondissement (Montmartre)

See Right Bank Dining map.

FRENCH

$$ ✕ **Le Poulbot Gourmand.** Engravings of old Montmartre and discreet lighting create a relaxed, comfortable conviviality at this tiny neighborhood restaurant named after the chef and owner's favorite painter, Francisque Poulbot. Working in a mostly traditional register, Jean-Paul Langevin whips up dishes such as escargots on artichoke hearts and roast duckling with turnips. The *sablé* (a shortbread pastry) with raspberries is a treat. There's a well-chosen wine list and good-buy prix-fixe menus for €18 and €31. ⊠ *39 rue Lamarck, Montmartre,* ☎ *01– 46–06–86–00. MC, V. No dinner Sun. Oct.–May. Métro: Lamarck Caulaincourt.*

$ ✕ **Le Moulin à Vins.** The atmosphere at this popular wine bar–bistro is sepia-toned, since both the place itself and surrounding neighborhood evoke premodern Paris. It's perfect for a lunch of salad or a cold-meat-and-cheese plate while touring Montmartre. In the evening it's much livelier, when devoted regulars—a great mix that runs from bikers to bankers—come for the daily short list of hot dishes. Opt for the delicious rabbit in mustard sauce with tagliatelle if it's available, or one of the southwestern dishes. Standards like the country terrine and quiche Lorraine are excellent, too, and the wine list is outstanding, especially the Côtes du Rhône. ✉ *6 rue Burq, Montmartre,* ☏ *01–45–52–81–27. AE, MC, V. Closed Sun.–Mon. and 3 wks in Aug. No lunch Tues., Fri., or Sat. Métro: Abbesses.*

VIETNAMESE

\$–\$\$ ✗ **Thu Thu.** Just across the street from the town hall of the 18ᵉ arrondissement, this little spot is a great address for thrifty fans of Vietnamese cooking. The engaging owner, Julia Le Phuong, serves up first-rate *pho* (Vietnamese noodle soup); *nems* (deep-fried spring rolls); duck with ginger; and great pork spareribs simply roasted with salt and pepper. There's also a good choice of vegetarian dishes here, and the lunch menu, at €8.35, is a real bargain. ✉ *51 bis rue Hermel, Montmartre,* ☏ *01–42–54–70–30. MC, V. Closed Mon. No lunch Sun. or in Aug. Métro: Simplon.*

19ᵉ Arrondissement (Buttes-Chaumont/La Villette)

See Right Bank Dining map.

FRENCH

\$\$–\$\$\$ ✗ **Le Pavillon Puebla.** A bucolic setting and original, flavorful cuisine, such as squid sautéed in saffron and boned pigeon with chorizo-stuffed cabbage, are the draw at this 1900s building in the spectacular Parc des Buttes-Chaumont. The elegant dining rooms are a romantic cold-weather lure, and the large terrace is extremely popular in summer. The restaurant feels wonderfully removed from the bustle of the city, but it's a bit hard to find. Seduction comes (relatively) cheaply here if you opt for the prix-fixe menus at €29.85 or €40.40. ✉ *In the Parc Buttes-Chaumont (entrance on rue Botzaris), Parc de la Villette,* ☏ *01–42–08–92–62. AE, MC, V. Closed Sun.–Mon., 3 wks in Aug., and Christmas wk. Métro: Buttes-Chaumont.*

20ᵉ Arrondissement (Père Lachaise)

See Right Bank Dining map.

FRENCH

\$\$ ✗ **Le Zéphyr.** Don't let the obscure location put you off—this restau-
★ rant is easy to get to from central Paris and well worth the small effort for its buzzy Art Deco dining room and inventive bistro food. The menu changes often, but you might find such creations as a northern-inspired soup of endives and potent Maroilles cheese, roast duck with lavender honey, spiced polenta and quince, and banana mousse layered with coconut and chocolate. Edith Piaf grew up near here, and you can still feel her spirit in this part of the neighborhood—Le Zéphyr's popular terrace allows you to take in the street theater. ✉ *1 rue du Jourdain, Père Lachaise,* ☏ *01–46–36–65–81. AE, DC, MC, V. Closed Sun., 3 wks in Aug., and Christmas wk. No lunch Sat. Métro: Jourdain.*

\$ ✗ **La Boulangerie.** This friendly, incredibly good-value bistro—three courses cost €18—is a great bet if you're planning on a night out in the increasingly trendy Ménilmontant neighborhood or maybe are hoping to bring yourself back to life after a visit to Père-Lachaise Cemetery. Occupying an old bakery, this place attracts a relaxed, young local crowd, which comes for the sincere and satisfying seasonal dishes. The menu changes daily but runs to dishes like tuna tartare, grilled red mullet on a bed of spinach, pot au feu, and excellent desserts like the rhubarb-filled mille-feuille. ✉ *15 rue des Panoyaux, Père Lachaise,* ☏ *01–43–58–45–45. MC, V. Closed 2 wks in Aug. No lunch Sat. Métro: Père-Lachaise.*

Cafés and Salons de Thé

Along with air, water, and wine (Parisians eat fewer and fewer three-course meals), the café remains one of the basic necessities of life in

Paris. Though they continue to close in the face of changing work and eating habits, cafés can still be found on almost every corner. Many of them look alike—the unfortunate result of '60s and '70s renovations—and only if you stick around long enough and become a regular (or write entire books, as Simone de Beauvoir did) will you discover their true intrigue. The more modest establishments (look for nonchalant locals) will give you a cheaper cup of coffee and a feeling of what real French café life is like. Cafés are required to post a *tarif des consommations*, a list that includes prices for the basics ranging from *café* (espresso) to *vin rouge* (red wine) and list two prices, *au comptoir* (at the counter) and *à terrasse* or *à salle* (seated at a table). If you just need a quick cup of coffee, have it at the counter and save yourself money. If you have a rendezvous, take a table: remember you're paying rent on that little piece of wood, and hang out as long as you like.

1er and 2e Arrondissements (Les Halles/Palais-Royal)

A Priori Thé. Stop in for tea while browsing through the lovely Galerie Vivienne shopping arcade. ⊠ *35–37 Galerie Vivienne, at 66 rue Vivienne, Louvre/Tuileries,* ☎ *01–42–97–48–75. Métro: Bourse.*

Au Père Tranquille. One of the best places in Paris for people-watching, this café also offers free entertainment from street artists and local performers. ⊠ *16 rue Pierre Lescot, Beaubourg/Les Halles,* ☎ *01–45–08–00–34. Métro: Les Halles.*

Bernardaud. Decorated by interior-design star Olivier Gagnère, this quiet spot in a covered atrium serves good snacks on the company's own china. ⊠ *11 rue Royale, Opéra/Grands Boulevards,* ☎ *01–42–66–22–55. Métro: Concorde.*

Café Marly. Run by the Costes brothers, this café overlooking the main courtyard of the Louvre and I. M. Pei's glass pyramid is one of the most chic places in Paris to meet for a drink or a coffee. Note that ordinary café service shuts down during meal hours, when overpriced, mediocre food is served. ⊠ *Cour Napoléon du Louvre (enter from the Louvre courtyard), 93 rue de Rivoli, Louvre/Tuileries,* ☎ *01–49–26–06–60. Métro: Palais-Royal.*

Café Verlet. Many Parisians think this compact spot serves the best coffee in town. You can also get sandwiches and delicious tarts. ⊠ *256 rue St-Honoré, Louvre/Tuileries,* ☎ *01–42–60–67–39. Métro: Tuileries.*

Le Fumoir. From the same team that made the China Club one of the more enduringly hip addresses in Paris, this café-restaurant has passed over the curve of red-hot chic to become permanent and useful. Its location just across from the Louvre helps, but ultimately what makes it work is that the fashionable folks—press attachés with cell phones, sulky tattooed model-artists, and so on—actually like this place, with its salons that seem variously inspired by Vienna, Edward Hopper, and Scandinavia. The most intimate room is the book-lined library, where book exchanges take place. The food's expensive and indifferent, so come play for the price of a coffee or a glass of wine. ⊠ *Pl. du Louvre, 6 rue de l'Amiral-Coligny, Louvre/Tuileries,* ☎ *01–42–92–00–24. Métro: Louvre.*

Le Ruc Univers. Actors from the Comédie Française and young hipsters hang out at this sleekly modern café near the Louvre. ⊠ *1 pl. André-Malraux, Louvre/Tuileries,* ☎ *01–42–60–31–57. Métro: Palais-Royal.*

4e Arrondissement (Marais/Beaubourg/Ile St-Louis)

Café Beaubourg. Near the Centre Pompidou, this slick, modern café, designed by architect Christian de Portzamparc, is one of the trendiest rendezvous spots for fashion and art types. Omelets and decent salads are served if you've missed lunch or want a light dinner. ⊠ *43 rue St-Merri, Beaubourg/Les Halles,* ☎ *01–48–87–63–96. Métro: Hôtel de Ville.*

La Charlotte en l'Ile. The witch who baked gingerbread children in *Hansel and Gretel* might take a fancy to this place—set with fairy lights, carnival masques, and decoupaged detritus, it's a storybook nookery that offers more than 30 varieties of tea along with a sinfully good hot chocolate. ⊠ *24 rue St-Louis-en-l'Ile, Ile St-Louis,* ☎ *01–43–54–25–83. Métro: Pont Marie.*

L'Etoile Manquante. Owned by Xavier Denamur, who runs several stylish cafés in this street, the "Missing Star" is a great spot for people-watching, but the real attraction is the rest rooms: an electric train is just one of the surprises in store. ⊠ *34 rue Vieille-du-Temple, Le Marais,* ☎ *01–42–72–48–34. Métro: Hôtel de Ville, St-Paul.*

Le Flore en l'Ile. At this café on the Ile St-Louis you can find renowned Berthillon ice cream and a magnificent view of the Seine. ⊠ *42 quai d'Orléans, Ile St-Louis,* ☎ *01–43–29–88–27. Métro: Pont Marie.*

Le Loir dans la Théière. This wonderful tea shop in the heart of the Marais has comfortable armchairs and delicious pâtisseries. ⊠ *3 rue des Rosiers, Le Marais,* ☎ *01–42–72–90–61. Métro: St-Paul.*

Ma Bourgogne. On the exquisite place des Vosges, this is a calm oasis for a coffee or a light lunch away from the noisy streets. ⊠ *19 pl. des Vosges, Le Marais,* ☎ *01–42–78–44–64. Métro: St-Paul.*

Mariage Frères. This elegant salon de thé serves 500 kinds of tea, along with delicious tarts. ⊠ *30 rue du Bourg-Tibourg, Le Marais,* ☎ *01–42–72–28–11. Métro: Hôtel de Ville.*

Petit Fer à Cheval. Great coffee is served in the perfect setting for watching the fashionable Marais locals saunter by. ⊠ *30 rue Vieille-du-Temple, Le Marais,* ☎ *01–42–72–47–47. Métro: St-Paul.*

6e Arrondissement (St-Germain/Montparnasse)

Brasserie Lipp. This brasserie, with its turn-of-the-20th-century decor, was a favorite spot of Hemingway's; today television celebrities, journalists, and politicians come here for coffee on the small glassed-in terrace off the main restaurant. ⊠ *151 bd. St-Germain, St-Germain-des-Prés,* ☎ *01–45–48–53–91. Métro: St-Germain-des-Prés.*

Café de Flore. Picasso, Chagall, Sartre, and de Beauvoir, attracted by the luxury of a heated café, worked and wrote here in the early 20th century. Today you'll find more tourists than intellectuals, but its outdoor terrace is still popular. ⊠ *172 bd. St-Germain, St-Germain-des-Prés,* ☎ *01–45–48–55–26. Métro: St-Germain-des-Prés.*

Café de la Mairie. Preferred by Henry Miller and Saul Bellow to those on noisy boulevard St-Germain, this place still retains the quiet and unpretentious air of a local café—although Catherine Deneuve could easily be a passerby here. ⊠ *8 pl. St-Sulpice, St-Germain-des-Prés,* ☎ *01–43–26–67–82. Métro: St-Sulpice.*

Café Orbital. Have a snack while you access your e-mail or the Internet. ⊠ *13 rue de Médicis, Latin Quarter,* ☎ *01–43–25–76–77. RER: Luxembourg.*

Les Deux Magots. Dubbed the second home of the *élite intellectuelle,* this café counted Rimbaud, Verlaine, Mallarmé, Wilde, and the Surrealists among its regulars. These days it's overpriced and mostly filled with tourists. ⊠ *170 bd. St-Germain, St-Germain-des-Prés,* ☎ *01–45–48–55–25. Métro: St-Germain-des-Prés.*

La Palette. In good weather, the terrace is as popular with local art students and gallery owners as it is with tourists. On a rainy afternoon, the interior, too, is cozy—it's decorated with works of art by its habitués. ⊠ *43 rue de Seine, St-Germain-des-Prés,* ☎ *01–43–26–68–15. Métro: Odéon.*

La Rotonde. The café, a second home to foreign artists and political exiles in the '20s and '30s, has a less exotic clientele today. But it's still a pleasant place to have a coffee on the sunny terrace. ⊠ *105 bd.*

Montparnasse, Montparnasse, ☎ *01–43–26–68–84. Métro: Mont-parnasse.*

Le Sélect. Isadora Duncan and Hart Crane used to hang out here; now it's a popular spot for a post-cinema beer. ✉ *99 bd. Montparnasse, Montparnasse,* ☎ *01–45–48–38–24. Métro: Vavin.*

Le Vieux Colombier. Take a seat on the lovely wicker furniture in front of one of the big windows in this café just around the corner from St-Sulpice and the Vieux Colombier theater. ✉ *65 rue de Rennes, St-Germain-des-Prés,* ☎ *01–45–48–53–81. Métro: St-Sulpice.*

8e Arrondissement (Champs-Élysées)

Ladurée. Pretty enough to bring a tear to Proust's eye, this ravishing and famous salon de thé looks barely changed from 1862. Grandmother's grandmother, antiques dealers, and lovers of beauty make up the clientele, which dotes on the lemon and caramel signature macaroons, little tea sandwiches, and a slew of teas that will make you want to stick out your little pinky. A more recent branch, boasting a convincing faux-time-burnished look, is at 75 avenue des Champs-Élysées. ✉ *16 rue Royale, Opéra/Grands Boulevards,* ☎ *01–42–60–21–79. Métro: Madeleine.*

Le Paris. This buzzy little café with a hip crowd and decor is the latest outpost of the Costes brothers, local trendsetters and high-style mavens, and it reflects the fact that the famous avenue is coming back into fashion. Service can be chilly, but it's worth putting up with for the interesting crowd and good, light food. ✉ *93 av. des Champs-Élysées, Champs-Élysées,* ☎ *01–47–23–54–37. Métro: George V.*

11e Arrondissement (Bastille)

Café de l'Industrie. Have a late-afternoon coffee or beer in the warm yellow rooms of this Bastille hangout, where the walls are covered with photos of movie stars. ✉ *16 rue St-Sabin, Bastille/Nation,* ☎ *01–47–00–13–53. Métro: Bastille.*

Pause Cafe. This hip Bastille spot attracts a chic, artsy crowd for coffee, cheap beer, and tasty, inexpensive chili and quiche at its red-and-yellow Formica tables. ✉ *41 rue de Charonne, Bastille/Nation,* ☎ *01–48–06–80–33. Métro: Ledru-Rollin.*

14e Arrondissement (Montparnasse)

Café du Dôme. Now a fancy brasserie—though you can still just have a cup of coffee or a drink here—this place began as a dingy meeting place for exiled artists and intellectuals such as Lenin, Picasso, and Chaim Soutine. ✉ *108 bd. Montparnasse, Montparnasse,* ☎ *01–43–35–25–81. Métro: Vavin.*

Café de la Place. This café is a charming wood-paneled spot that is perfect for watching the activity inside and out. ✉ *23 rue d'Odessa, Montparnasse,* ☎ *01–42–18–01–55. Métro: Montparnasse.*

18e Arrondissement (Montmartre)

La Crémaillère. Alphonse Mucha frescoes decorate the walls at this veritable monument to 19th-century fin-de-siècle art in Montmartre. ✉ *15 pl. du Tertre, Montmartre,* ☎ *01–46–06–58–59. Métro: Anvers.*

Le Sancerre. Sit on the terrace sipping a coffee or a beer and watch the artists, hipsters, and tourists all pass by on their way through Montmartre. ✉ *35 rue des Abbesses, Montmartre,* ☎ *01–45–58–08–20. Métro: Abbesses.*

19e Arrondissement (Buttes-Chaumont/La Villette)

Café de la Musique. This vast, stylishly postmodern café is adjacent to the Cité de la Musique in the Parc de La Villette. In the evenings it's primarily filled with people attending concerts, but the free jazz on Wednesday night and the interesting crowd make it worth the excursion. ✉ *214 av. Jean-Jaurès, Parc de la Villette,* ☎ *01–48–03–15–91. Métro: Porte de Pantin.*

Wine Bars

Paris wine bars are the perfect place to enjoy a glass (or bottle) of wine with a plate of cheese, charcuterie, or a simple but delicious hot meal. Bar owners are often true wine enthusiasts ready to dispense expert advice. Hours vary widely, so it's best to check ahead if your heart is set on a particular place; many, however, close around 10 PM.

Au Sauvignon. A stylish but jolly Left Bank crowd frequents this homey, friendly spot with an ideally placed terrace. Delicious *tartines* (open-face sandwiches) are served. ⊠ *80 rue des Sts-Pères, 7ᵉ, St-Germain-des-Prés,* ☎ *01–45–48–49–02. Métro: Sèvres Babylone.*

Aux Bons Crus. This cramped, narrow venue has an authentic Parisian feel (it dates from 1905). ⊠ *7 rue des Petits-Champs, 1ᵉʳ, Louvre/Tuileries,* ☎ *01–42–60–06–45. Métro: Bourse.*

Le Baron Bouge. Formerly known as Le Baron Rouge, this wine bar near the Place d'Aligre market has changed in name only. In winter months you'll often find an oyster feast in mid-swing outside its door; inside, expect the regulars to welcome you with the same frosty suspicion as cowboys at their local saloon. ⊠ *1 rue Théopile-Roussel, 12ᵉ, Bastille/Nation,* ☎ *01–43–43–14–32. Métro: Ledru-Rollin.*

Le Comptoir. Glasses of Burgundy and Bordeaux, as well as more unusual selections such as wines from Corsica, are served. ⊠ *5 rue Monsieur-Le-Prince, 6ᵉ, St-Germain-des-Prés,* ☎ *01–43–29–12–05. Métro: Odéon.*

Jacques Mélac. This wine bar is named after the jolly owner who harvests grapes from the vine outside and bottles several of his own wines—he even hosts a harvest festival every September. Nonsmokers, make your way through the tiny kitchen to the fume-free back room. ⊠ *42 rue Léon-Frot, 11ᵉ, Bastille/Nation,* ☎ *01–43–70–59–27. Métro: Charonne.*

La Robe et le Palais. Come here for the more than 120 wines from all over France, served *au compteur* (according to the amount consumed), as well as a daily selection of good bistro-style dishes for lunch and dinner. ⊠ *13 rue des Lavandières-Ste-Opportune, 1ᵉʳ, Beaubourg/Les Halles,* ☎ *01–45–08–07–41. Métro: Châtelet Les Halles.*

Le Rouge Gorge. This sophisticated Marais wine bar attracts discriminating locals, who come for unusual wines by the glass and the hearty food. ⊠ *8 rue St-Paul, 4ᵉ, Le Marais,* ☎ *01–48–04–75–89. Métro: Bourse.*

Le Rubis. This resolutely old-time bar specializes in Burgundies. It's most crowded during the day; from 7 to 9:30 PM it's best to be smoke-resistant. ⊠ *10 rue du Marché St-Honoré, 1ᵉʳ, Louvre/Tuileries,* ☎ *01–42–61–03–34. Métro: Tuileries.*

La Tartine. Inexpensive wine and tartines in a tatty, almost seedy, late 19th-century bar have given this place antihero status among the rebel cognoscenti. ⊠ *24 rue de Rivoli, 4ᵉ, Le Marais,* ☎ *01–42–72–76–85. Métro: St-Paul.*

4 LODGING

Hemingway had it right: Paris is indeed
a moveable feast. But even he had to
occasionally push himself away from the
table, lay his head upon a pillow, and call it
a night. But where? For Papa, it was usually
the Ritz, but you might feel just as at home in
a clean, well-lit room off a garden courtyard
in Montmartre, or a Starck-designed suite
near the shops of St-Honoré, or perhaps
you aspire to the Hotel Meurice apartment
once favored by the Duke and Duchess of
Windsor. Whether you're an heiress, a
CEO, or just someone out for a budget lark,
you'll find most of these options deliciously
combine charm and tradition.

Revised and
updated by
Christopher
Mooney

A RIGHT BANK HOTEL SUITE: Late-morning sunshine streams through the drift of tulle curtains on the gilded windows. Outside floats a Monet-worthy view of the nearby Tuileries Gardens, and beyond them, the violet-hue Seine flowing past the quayside dwellings. Still lolling under crisp sheets, down-stuffed duvet, and bed canopy circa 1925, you're two sips of *petit crème* and half a buttery croissant into your first day in Paris. A Belle Epoque silver service sits on the Napoléon III–style bedside table, next to a leather-bound Pléiade edition of Stendhal, borrowed from the hotel's oak-paneled library. You've slept in and missed housekeeping, but they'll be by again—twice— to tidy up, pick up your laundry, lay out fresh towels and robes, and restock the two marble-and-onyx bathrooms with Hermès toiletries. Your eyes lift from the rim of the Limoges cup to the gossamer clouds and azure-blue sky in the painted ceiling above, then wander outside to the needle-thin spire of Sainte-Chapelle. Freeze frame. Slow fade to bliss.

Typical? Well yes, if you're paying €8,000 a night. Drop two zeros and you get "Paris Hotel Room, Take 2": sound up on a dripping faucet as we track along peeling chintz wallpaper to the rusting bed where you lie, U-shaped and shivering, under thin blankets and dun-color sheets. Someone coughs on the other side of the paper-thin wall. A diesel truck rumbles past the mud-streaked window. Freeze frame. Slow fade to bleak.

But, budgeting or not, this doesn't have to be your lot. Scores of lackluster, shabby Paris lodgings have been replaced by good-value establishments in the lower-to-middle price ranges. Whatever price you're looking for, compared to most other cities Paris is a paradise for the weary traveler tired of dreary, cookie-cutter rooms. If you're out for luxury, Paris has places so luxe they make Versailles look like a Zen teahouse—and the bar keeps getting raised higher and higher: recently, the Sultan of Brunei sank a fortune into refurbishing the beloved Meurice, while the grande dame George V underwent a $100 million face-lift. In the middle range are those wonderful *hôtels de charme* operating in slightly over-the-hill 19th-century town houses, usually with large windows to catch the elusive Paris sun. Even if you find yourself in a too-snug room with gurgling water pipes, an iffy heating system, and cooing pigeons parked on the window ledge, just tell yourself that it's decor. After all, you're in Paris.

The leading criteria when selecting the hotels reviewed below were quality, location, and authenticity. Few chain hotels are listed, since most (with some notable exceptions) lack the charm and character found in typical Parisian lodgings. Similarly, fewer hotels are in outlying arrondissements (the 10^e to the 20^e) because these are farther from the major sights. Generally, there are more hotels on the Right Bank offering luxury—at any rate, formality—than on the Left Bank, where the hotels are frequently smaller and richer in old-fashioned charm. The Right Bank's 1er and 8e arrondissements are still the most exclusive, and prices here reflect this. Less-expensive alternatives on the Right Bank may be found in the fashionable Marais quarter (3e and 4e arrondissements) and the 11e and 12e, near the Opéra Bastille.

Despite widespread improvement, many Paris hotels (especially budget-level accommodations) still have idiosyncrasies—some endearing, others less so. Hotel rooms in Paris's oldest quarters are generally much smaller than their American counterparts. The French double bed is slightly smaller than the American standard. Although air-conditioning has become de rigueur in mid- to higher-priced hotels, it is generally not a prerequisite for comfort except during the hottest summer days, nor is it always available (ask, if you want to be absolutely sure). Reviews indicate the number of rooms with private baths (which may include a shower or a tub, but not necessarily both). It's rare to find moderately priced places that expect guests to share toilets or bathrooms, but be sure you know what facilities you are getting when you book a budget hotel.

Always reserve well in advance, especially if you're determined to stay in a specific place. You can do this by telephoning or faxing ahead, and asking for written or faxed confirmation. As you will probably be asked to send a deposit, be sure to discuss refund policies before releasing your credit card number or mailing a check or money order. During peak seasons, some hotels require total prepayment. Always demand written confirmation of your reservation, detailing the duration of your stay, the price, the location and type of room desired (single or double, twin beds or double), and the bathroom: shower (*douche*) or bath (*baignoire*), and whether private or shared.

Almost all Paris hotels charge extra for breakfast, with per-person prices ranging from €4 to more than €30 at the luxury establishments. Though hotels may not automatically add the breakfast charge to your bill, it's prudent to inform the desk staff if you plan to breakfast away from the hotel (you may want to find the nearest café instead). For anything more than the standard Continental breakfast of café au lait and baguette or croissant, the price will be higher. Some hotels have especially pleasant breakfast areas, and we have noted this where appropriate. Luxury hotels often have restaurants, but finding a place to eat in Paris is rarely a problem.

Hotels are listed by price. Over the past few years luxury hotel prices have risen faster than their more moderate counterparts. Often a hotel in a certain price category will have a few less-expensive rooms; it's worth asking about. Rates must be posted in all rooms (usually on the back of the door), with all extra charges clearly shown. There is a nominal *taxe de séjour* of €1 per person, per night.

Unless otherwise stated, hotel rooms have elevators, air-conditioning, TV (many with cable), telephones, and private bath, and English is spoken. Additional facilities, such as restaurants and health clubs, are listed at the end of each review.

CATEGORY	COST*
$$$$	over €270
$$$	€150–€269
$$	€90–€149
$	under €89

All prices are for a standard double room in high season, including tax and service.

1er Arrondissement (Louvre/Tuileries)

See Right Bank Lodging map.

$$$$ ⊞ **Costes.** Six years after opening its doors onto the city's most expensive
★   shopping street, Jean-Louis and Gilbert Costes's eponymous hotel remains the darling of decorating magazines and a magnet for supermodels and off-duty celebrities. Nearly every room is swathed in enough rich garnet, $400-a-yard fabrics, swagging, and *passementerie* (applied trim) to blanket the Champs-Élysées. Naturally, the bathrooms are truly marvelous affairs. A seductive, go-for-baroque bar, with its labyrinth of little rooms and secluded nooks, is *the* place in Paris to be seen try-

ing not to be seen. For taste, in every sense of the word, this is the top Paris hotel. ⊠ *239 rue St-Honoré, Louvre/Tuileries, 75001,* ☏ *01–42– 44–50–50,* FAX *01–42–44–50–01,* WEB *www.hotelcostes.com. 77 rooms, 5 suites, with bath. Restaurant, bar, cable TV, in-room data ports, in-room safes, minibars, room service, indoor pool, sauna, gym, laundry service. AE, DC, MC, V. Métro: Tuileries.*

$$$$ 🏨 **Inter-Continental.** Stravinsky not only stayed here, he gave concerts in several of the hotel's magnificent salons, and famous names from the music world, such as Jessye Norman, continue to stud the guest register. This exquisite, late 19th-century hotel, with period details sumptuously restored, was designed by the architect of the Paris Opéra, Charles Garnier, and three of its gilt-and-stuccoed salons are historic monuments. Guest rooms, more sedate than the public areas, nevertheless have Empire-style furnishings and rich period fabrics. The most coveted and spacious guest rooms overlook quiet inner courtyards. In summer, breakfast on the patio is a delicious experience. ⊠ *3 rue de Castiglione, Louvre/Tuileries, 75001,* ☏ *01–44–77–11–11; 800/327– 0200 in the U.S.,* FAX *01–44–77–14–60,* WEB *www.interconti.com. 375 rooms, 70 suites, with bath. Restaurant, bar, in-room safes, cable TV, minibars, no-smoking floor, room service, baby-sitting, laundry service. AE, DC, MC, V. Métro: Concorde.*

$$$$ 🏨 **Meurice.** One of the finest hotels in the world is now even finer, thanks to the Sultan of Brunei's extravagant largesse. The rooms—furnished with Persian carpets, marble mantelpieces, and ormolu clocks—are now more soigné than ever, if that's possible (book well in advance for one overlooking the Tuileries Gardens). The bathrooms, redone in red and ocher marble from the Pyrénées and white and gray marbles from Italy, are truly elaborate affairs. Suite 628, decorated in the style of a Napoléonic tent, is next to impossible to book, unless your celebrity stardom precedes your arrival. But anyone can book one of the 20 tables at the Restaurant le Meurice, where the decor of chandeliers and gilt-boiserie seems as precious as jewelry (with food appropriately priced, as most entrées hover around €35 to €45): for Paris splendor in excelsis, there are few equals to this famous salon. ⊠ *228 rue de Rivoli, Louvre/Tuileries, 75001,* ☏ *01–44–58–10–10,* FAX *01–44–58– 10–15,* WEB *www.meuricehotel.com. 161 rooms, 35 suites, with bath. 2 restaurants, bar, in-room data ports, in-room safes, cable TV, minibars, no-smoking rooms, room service, sauna, laundry service, business services. AE, DC, MC, V. Métro: Tuileries, Concorde.*

$$$$ 🏨 **Régina.** On handsome place des Pyramides, this 100-year-old Art Nouveau gem oozes old-fashioned grandeur in both its public spaces and guest rooms, where fine antiques abound. There's also a sublime Belle Epoque lounge. Request a room on rue de Rivoli, facing the Louvre and the Tuileries Gardens. ⊠ *2 rue des Pyramides, Louvre/Tuileries, 75001,* ☏ *01–42–60–31–10,* FAX *01–40–15–95–16,* WEB *www.regina-hotel.com. 105 rooms, 15 suites, with bath. Restaurant, bar, cable TV, minibars, in-room safes, no-smoking rooms, room service, laundry service. AE, DC, MC, V. Métro: Tuileries.*

$$$$ ★ 🏨 **Ritz.** Surrounded by the city's finest jewelers, the Ritz is the crowning gem on sparking place Vendôme. Festooned with Napoléonic gilt and ormolu, sparkling with crystal chandeliers, and adorned with *qualité de Louvre* antiques, it was founded in 1896 by Cesar Ritz and has been regilded at a cost of $150 million by owner Mohammed al-Fayed. Be warned, however, that there really are two Ritz spheres. The first is the gilded place Vendôme wing—where Gary Cooper serenaded Audrey Hepburn in *Love in the Afternoon*—which houses suites named after former high-profile residents, such as Marcel Proust and Coco Chanel. The newer wing, off the back of the building, remains surprisingly (disappointingly?) intimate. Still, every room is highly com-

Right Bank Lodging

Left Bank Lodging

fortable and endowed with all the latest gimmickry (many have a control panel hidden in the nightstand). The lack of a bona-fide lobby discourages sightseers, so you'll have to hang out in the wood-paneled bars, including one that Papa Hemingway "liberated" in 1944. The hotel's Espadon restaurant's terrace patio, with tables and chairs covered in elegant fabrics, is swooningly pretty. To work off any extra calories, lucky guests can then repair to the basement health club and pool—a splendid spa that looks like a Louis XIV temple of sweat. ⊠ *15 pl. Vendôme, Louvre/Tuileries, 75001,* ☎ *01–43–16–30–30,* FAX *01–43–16–36–68,* WEB *www.ritz.com. 135 rooms, 40 suites, with bath. 3 restaurants, 2 bars, in-room data ports, in-room safes, room service, minibars, cable TV, indoor pool, hair salon, health club, shops, laundry service, parking (fee). AE, DC, MC, V. Métro: Opéra.*

$$$–$$$$ 🏨 **Vendôme.** This hotel has the highest staff-to-guest ratio in Paris and
★   offers every conceivable luxury. Rooms are handsomely done in Second Empire style, with walls and furnishings in muted earth tones and hand-carved wood detailing throughout. Bathrooms are over the top: brass, marble, and silver bathtubs; waterproof telephones; and toiletries from Guerlain. Best of all, besides a videophone for checking out callers at the door, is the fully automated bedside console that controls the lights, curtains, and electronic do-not-disturb sign. ⊠ *1 pl. Vendôme, Louvre/Tuileries, 75001,* ☎ *01–42–60–32–84,* FAX *01–49–27–97–89. 19 rooms, 10 suites, with bath. Restaurant, bar, cable TV, minibars, in-room data ports, room service, laundry service. AE, DC, MC, V. Métro: Concorde, Opéra.*

$$$ 🏨 **Paris Hôtel des Tuileries.** This remarkably quiet hotel, tucked away in an 18th-century town house on a small side street, is within walking distance of the Louvre, Tuileries Gardens, and place Vendôme. Everything, from the creaky cage elevator and wide French windows to the sturdy wooden armoires and gilt mirrors, is quaintly old-fashioned. A tiny lobby lounge and tapestry-covered breakfast room are the only public areas. ⊠ *10 rue Ste-Hyacinthe, Louvre/Tuileries, 75001,* ☎ *01–42–61–04–17,* FAX *01–49–27–91–56. 21 rooms, 5 suites, with bath. Bar, cable TV, minibars, in-room safes, room service, laundry service. AE, DC, MC, V. Métro: Tuileries, Concorde.*

$$ 🏨 **Britannique.** Open since 1870, and just a stone's throw from the Louvre, the Britannique blends courteous English service with old-fashioned French elegance. It has a handsome winding staircase and soundproof rooms appointed in mahogany and warm-color tones (which the staff likes to compare to the hues of a Turner painting). During World War I, the hotel served as headquarters for a Quaker mission. ⊠ *20 av. Victoria, Beaubourg/Les Halles, 75001,* ☎ *01–42–33–74–59,* FAX *01–42–33–82–65,* WEB *www.hotel-britannic.com. 40 rooms, 31 with bath, 9 with shower. Bar, no air-conditioning, cable TV, minibars, in-room data ports, no-smoking rooms. AE, DC, MC, V. Métro: Châtelet.*

$$ 🏨 **Londres St-Honoré.** An appealing combination of character and comfort distinguishes this small, inexpensive hotel, a five-minute walk from the Louvre. Exposed oak beams, statues in niches, and rustic stone walls give this place old-fashioned charm, while modern pluses include satellite TV. Though rooms have floral bedspreads and standard hotel furniture, they are pleasant and the price is right. Note that the elevator only starts on the second floor. ⊠ *13 rue St-Roch, Louvre/Tuileries, 75001,* ☎ *01–42–60–15–62,* FAX *01–42–60–16–00. 29 rooms with bath. In-room data ports. AE, DC, MC, V. Métro: Pyramides.*

$$ 🏨 **Therese.** This location is almost *too* convenient—right in the heart of Paris and within a stone's throw of the Opéra Garnier, Palais-Royal, the Louvre, and the throbbing Grands Boulevards. Rooms are more spacious than you'd expect for the price, though they are furnished very generically, with pastel hues, floral bedspreads, and standard-issue furnishings. ✉ *5 rue Thérèse, Opéra/Grands Boulevards, 75001,* ☎ *01–42–96–10–01,* FAX *01–42–96–15–22. 43 rooms with bath. Bar, cable TV, minibars, in-room data ports, no-smoking floor, room service, baby-sitting, laundry service. AE, DC, MC, V. Métro: Pyramides.*

$ 🏨 **Henri IV.** The sole hostelry on the Ile de la Cité, this old-fashioned landmark is one of the city's cheapest deals and worst-kept "secrets." The lobby is drab, the narrow staircase (five flights, no elevator) creaks, and the rooms, though spacious enough, are shabby. But the price and the super location—on time-stained place Dauphine and just a short walk from Notre-Dame—have made it one of the toughest reservations to obtain. Bathrooms are in the hallway; pay a little extra and get one of the three rooms with private shower. ✉ *25 pl. Dauphine, Ile de la Cité, 75001,* ☎ *01–43–54–44–53. 21 rooms with shared bath, 3 with shower. No air-conditioning, no room TV. No credit cards. Métro: Cité, St-Michel, Pont Neuf.*

$ 🏨 **Louvre Forum.** This hotel is a find: smack in the center of Paris, it has reasonably priced, clean, comfortable, well-equipped rooms, and a friendly feel. What it lacks in time-burnished appeal it makes up for in location, amenities, and low rates. Breakfast is served in a homey vaulted cellar. ✉ *25 rue du Bouloi, Louvre/Tuileries, 75001,* ☎ *01–42–36–54–19,* FAX *01–42–33–66–31. 27 rooms with bath. Bar, minibars. AE, DC, MC, V. Métro: Louvre.*

$ 🏨 **Tiquetonne.** Just off marché Montorgueil and a short hoof from Les Halles, this is one of the least expensive hotels in the city center. The rooms aren't much to look at but they're always clean and some are downright spacious. Book on one of the top two floors facing the quiet, pedestrian rue Tiquetonne, not the loud, car-strangled rue Turbigo. ✉ *6 rue Tiquetonne, Beaubourg/Les Halles, 75002,* ☎ *01–42–36–94–58,* FAX *01–42–36–02–94. 47 rooms with bath or shower. AE, MC, V. Métro: Étienne Marcel, Châtelet.*

2ᵉ Arrondissement (La Bourse/Opéra)

See Right Bank Lodging map.

$$$$ 🏨 **Westminster.** This former private mansion on an elegant street between the Opéra and place Vendôme was built in the mid-19th century and happily retains the requisite marble fireplaces, crystal chandeliers, and parquet floors. The pleasant piano bar is a popular rendezvous spot, and the hotel's restaurant, Le Céladon, serves outstanding French cuisine. Recently added was a small health club. ✉ *13 rue de la Paix, Opéra/Grands Boulevards, 75002,* ☎ *01–42–61–57–46; 800/203–3232 in the U.S.,* FAX *01–42–60–30–66,* WEB *www.warwickhotels.com. 83 rooms, 18 suites, with bath. Restaurant, bar, in-room data ports, in-room safes, cable TV, minibars, no-smoking rooms, room service, health club, baby-sitting, laundry service, meeting room, parking (fee). AE, DC, MC, V. Métro: Opéra.*

$$$ 🏨 **Victoire Opéra.** This terrific hotel is an oasis of calm amid the colorful bustle of Montorgueil, a very popular pedestrian-only market street near Les Halles, the Centre Pompidou, and the Marais. It was recently renovated and renamed (formerly the Besançon), and the rooms are spacious by central Paris standards and decorated in a tastefully restrained modern style. ✉ *56 rue Montorgueil, Beaubourg/Les Halles, 75002,* ☎ *01–42–36–41–08,* FAX *01–45–08–08–79. 20 rooms with bath. In-room data ports, in-room safes, cable TV, minibars, room service, baby-sitting, laundry service. AE, DC, MC, V. Métro: Étienne Marcel, Les Halles.*

$$ 🏨 **Hôtel de Noailles.** With a nod to the work of postmodern designers like Putman and Starck, this nouveau-wave inn (part of the Tulip Inn group) is near the top of Paris's short list of well-priced, style-driven

boutique hotels. Though not to everyone's taste, rooms are imaginatively decorated with funky furnishings and contemporary details, such as rubbery curtains; when it succeeds, the look is fun and very hip (or, depending on your outlook, extremely dated). A young, cosmopolitan clientele has made this one its own. ⊠ *9 rue de Michodière, Opéra/Grands Boulevards, 75002,* ☎ *01–47–42–92–90,* FAX *01–49–24–92–71. 58 rooms with bath. Bar, cable TV, minibars, sauna, health club, no-smoking rooms, laundry service, meeting room. AE, DC, MC, V. Métro: Opéra.*

3ᵉ Arrondissement (Marais)

See Right Bank Lodging map.

$$$$ 🏨 **Pavillon de la Reine.** There is nothing like the feeling of pulling up
★   in front of this fabled, gorgeous 17th-century mansion on the place des Vosges and knowing that it is your Paris home-away-from-home. Complete with a picture-perfect gatehouse entryway, this magnificent abode has been reconstructed from original plans and is now filled with Louis XIII–style antiques, rich-tone fabrics, and fireplaces. For an absolutely royal feeling, ask for a duplex with French windows overlooking the first of two flower-filled courtyards behind the historic Queen's Pavilion. Breakfast is served in the vaulted cellar, apéritifs in front of the salon's gargantuan fireplace. Most conveniently, some of Paris's finest museums, such as the Picasso, Carnavalet, and Cognacq-Jay, are just blocks away. ⊠ *28 pl. des Vosges, Le Marais, 75003,* ☎ *01–40–29–19–19; 800/447–7462 in the U.S.,* FAX *01–40–29–19–20. 31 rooms, 24 suites, with bath. Bar, cable TV, minibars, in-room data ports, room service, laundry service, free parking. AE, DC, MC, V. Métro: Bastille, St-Paul.*

4ᵉ Arrondissement (Marais/Ile St-Louis)

See Right Bank Lodging map.

$$$ 🏨 **Hôtel du Jeu de Paume.** The showpiece of this lovely 17th-century hotel on the Ile St-Louis is the stone-walled, vaulted lobby-cum-breakfast room. It stands on an erstwhile court where French aristocrats once played *jeu de paume,* an early version of tennis using palm fronds. The bright rooms are nicely done up in butter yellow, with rustic antiques, tasteful objets and bric-a-brac, beamed ceilings, and damask upholstery. The little garden is a haven of sun-drenched tranquility. ⊠ *54 rue St-Louis-en-l'Ile, Ile-St-Louis, 75004,* ☎ *01–43–26–14–18,* FAX *01–40–46–02–76,* WEB *www.jeudepaumehotel.com. 30 rooms, 1 junior suite, with bath. Bar, no air-conditioning, cable TV, minibars, in-room data ports, sauna, health club, baby-sitting, laundry service, meeting room. AE, DC, MC, V. Métro: Pont Marie.*

$$ 🏨 **Axial Beaubourg.** A solid bet in the Marais, this hotel in a 16th-century building has beamed ceilings in the lobby and in the six first-floor rooms. Most have pleasant if functional decor, and all have cable TV. The Centre Pompidou and the Picasso Museum are a five-minute walk away. ⊠ *11 rue du Temple, Le Marais, 75004,* ☎ *01–42–72–72–22,* FAX *01–42–72–03–53. 39 rooms with bath. Cable TV, minibars, in-room data ports, in-room safes, no-smoking rooms. AE, DC, MC, V. Métro: Hôtel de Ville.*

$$ 🏨 **Bretonnerie.** This small hotel is in a 17th-century *hôtel particulier* (town house) on a tiny street in the Marais, a few minutes' walk from the Centre Pompidou. The Louis XIII–style rooms come complete with upholstered walls, antiques, beamed ceilings, four-poster beds, and marble-clad bathrooms, or some combination thereof. Their size varies considerably from spacious to cramped; the larger ones are pricier. Breakfast is served in the vaulted cellar. ⊠ *22 rue Ste-Croix-de-la-Bretonnerie, Le Marais, 75004,* ☎ *01–48–87–77–63,* FAX *01–42–77–26–78,* WEB *www.labretonnerie.com. 22 rooms, 7 suites, with bath. No air-conditioning, in-room data ports, In-room safes, cable TV, parking (fee). MC, V. Métro: Hôtel de Ville.*

$$ ★ ⊞ **Caron de Beaumarchais.** The theme of this intimate hotel is the work of Caron de Beaumarchais, who wrote the play *The Marriage of Figaro* and who lived just next door. First-edition copies of his books adorn the public spaces and the salons faithfully reflect the taste of 18th-century French nobility, right down to the wallpaper and upholstery—one room, famously photographed by *Travel & Leisure,* is headlined by one of the prettiest canopy beds in Paris. Street-side rooms on the second through fifth floors are the largest, while the slightly smaller sixth-floor garrets under the mansard roof have beguiling views across Right Bank rooftops. ⊠ *12 rue Vieille-du-Temple, Le Marais, 75004,* ☎ *01–42–72–34–12,* FAX *01–42–72–34–63. 19 rooms with bath. Cable TV, minibars, in-room data ports, laundry service. AE, DC, MC, V. Métro: Hôtel de Ville.*

$$ ⊞ **Deux-Iles.** This converted 17th-century mansion on the tranquil Ile St-Louis has long won plaudits for charm and comfort. Flowers and plants are scattered throughout the stunning main hall, and tapestries cover the exposed stone walls. The delightfully old-fashioned rooms, blessed with exposed beams, are small but airy and sunny. Ask for one overlooking the little garden courtyard. In winter, a roaring fire warms the lounge. ⊠ *59 rue St-Louis-en-l'Ile, Ile-St-Louis, 75004,* ☎ *01–43–26–13–35,* FAX *01–43–29–60–25. 17 rooms with bath. Cable TV, minibars, in-room data ports, in-room safes, baby-sitting. AE, MC, V. Métro: Pont Marie.*

$$ ⊞ **Hôtel du 7ᵉ Art.** The theme of this hip hotel fits its name ("The 7th Art" is what the French call filmmaking): Hollywood from the '40s to the '60s. Posters of Marilyn Monroe, Charlie Chaplin, and other stars decorate the walls throughout. Rooms are small but clean, quiet, and equipped with cable TV. There is no elevator for the four floors. Breakfast is served in the handsome wood-paneled lounge; there's also an invitingly kitschy bar, and a brand-new gym in the rustic cellar room. The clientele is young, trendy, and *très* American. ⊠ *20 rue St-Paul, Le Marais, 75004,* ☎ *01–44–54–85–00,* FAX *01–42–77–69–10. 23 rooms with bath. Bar, no air-conditioning, cable TV, in-room safes, gym. AE, DC, MC, V. Métro: St-Paul.*

$$ ⊞ **Place des Vosges.** A loyal, eclectic clientele swears by this small, historic Marais hotel on a delightful street just off place des Vosges. The Louis XIII–style reception area and rooms with oak-beamed ceilings, rough-hewn stone, and a mix of rustic finds from secondhand shops evoke the old Marais. Ask for the top-floor room, the hotel's largest, for its view over Right Bank rooftops; others the size of walk-in closets are less expensive. ⊠ *12 rue de Birague, Le Marais, 75004,* ☎ *01–42–72–60–46,* FAX *01–42–72–02–64. 16 rooms with bath. Bar, no air-conditioning, cable TV, minibars, in-room safes, gym. AE, DC, MC, V. Métro: Bastille.*

$$ ⊞ **St-Louis.** Louis XIII–style furniture and oil paintings set the tone in the public areas in this 17th-century town house on the coveted Ile St-Louis. Guest rooms are much simpler and more standard, but exposed beams and stone walls make them appealing. Breakfast is served in the atmospheric cellar. ⊠ *75 rue St-Louis-en-l'Ile, Ile-St-Louis, 75004,* ☎ *01–46–34–04–80,* FAX *01–46–34–02–13. 21 rooms with bath. No air-conditioning, cable TV, in-room data ports, in-room safes. MC, V. Métro: Pont Marie.*

$$ 🏨 **Vieux Marais.** This pleasingly old-fashioned hotel with a turn-of-the-20th-century facade is on a quiet street in the heart of the Marais. Rooms are bright, impeccably clean, and equipped with satellite TV; try to get one overlooking the just-renovated courtyard. Recently, they've made the bathrooms much bigger and brighter. Breakfast is served in a pretty lounge. The staff is exceptionally courteous. ⊠ *8 rue du Plâtre, Le Marais, 75004,* ☎ *01–42–78–47–22,* 🅵🅰🆇 *01–42–78–34–32. 30 rooms with bath. Cable TV, in-room safes. MC, V. Métro: Hôtel de Ville.*

$ 🏨 **Castex.** This Marais hotel in a Revolution-era building is a bargain-hunter's dream. Rooms are low on frills but squeaky clean. The owners are extremely friendly, and the prices are rock-bottom, which ensures that the hotel is often booked months ahead by a largely young, largely American clientele. There is no elevator for the five floors, and only one room has a TV (another one graces the ground-floor salon). ⊠ *5 rue Castex, Le Marais, 75004,* ☎ *01–42–72–31–52,* 🅵🅰🆇 *01–42–72–57–91.* 🆆🅴🅱 *www.castexhotel.com. 29 rooms with bath. No air-conditioning, no room TV, in-room data ports. MC, V. Métro: Bastille.*

$ 🏨 **Grand Hôtel Jeanne-d'Arc.** If you're on a budget, you're sure to get your money's worth at this hotel near place des Vosges in the Marais. Though rooms are on the spartan side, they are clean, well maintained, and fairly spacious (some have a couch). The staff is welcoming and friendly. ⊠ *3 rue de Jarente, Le Marais, 75004,* ☎ *01–48–87–62–11,* 🅵🅰🆇 *01–48–87–37–31. 36 rooms with bath. No air-conditioning. MC, V. Métro: St-Paul.*

5ᵉ Arrondissement (Latin Quarter)

See Left Bank Lodging map.

$$$ 🏨 **Libertel Quartier Latin.** The flagship of the Libertel chain combines sleek design with intellectual rigor. It takes its cues from the nearby Sorbonne university, with an elegant reading room and photos and portraits of celebrated writers on the walls. Rooms, furnished with ebony furniture and quilted bedcovers, emphasize sculpted lines and quiet comfort. Ask for one on the sixth floor, preferably No. 602 or 603, which have beautiful views of Notre-Dame from their balconies. If this doesn't inspire you finally to write that novel, maybe the carpets will: they're inscribed with quotations from Balzac and Baudelaire. ⊠ *9 rue des Écoles, Latin Quarter, 75005,* ☎ *01–44–27–06–45,* 🅵🅰🆇 *01–43–25–36–70. 23 rooms, 6 suites, with bath. Cable TV, in-room safes, minibars, room service. AE, DC, MC, V. Métro: Cardinal Lemoine.*

$$ 🏨 **Esméralda.** Once the best-kept secret of any *Vogue* editor, this place
★ was, in its day, the ultimate *hôtel de charme.* Set in a 17th-century building catty-cornered from Notre-Dame, it is still cherished for its cozy, eccentric charm. Some closet-size rooms are nearly overpowered by gaudy imitation antiques or 1970s fabrics, while others could be cleaner; for the best and largest rooms, book those in *l'annexe* (there are even some triples). On the street side, there are several rooms with fine views of the cathedral. Best of all is the tiny lobby: adorned with silk flowers, wood moldings, and snoozing cats, it's right out of a Flaubert novel and may be the quaintest nook in all Paris. ⊠ *4 rue St-Julien-le-Pauvre, Latin Quarter, 75005,* ☎ *01–43–54–19–20,* 🅵🅰🆇 *01–40–51–00–68. 19 rooms, 15 with bath. No air-conditioning, no room TV. No credit cards. Métro: St-Michel.*

$$ 🏨 **Jardin du Luxembourg.** Blessed with a personable staff and a smart,
★ stylish look, this hotel, on a calm side street just a block from the Luxembourg Gardens, is one of the most sought-after in the Latin Quarter, especially among psychoanalysts—Freud slept here. Rooms are small

but cleverly furnished, to optimize space; the rustic pieces and warm colors give them a Provençal feel. Ask for one with a balcony over-looking the street; the best room, No. 25, has dormer windows revealing a peekaboo view of the Eiffel Tower. ⊠ *5 impasse Royer-Collard, Latin Quarter, 75005,* ☎ *01–40–46–08–88,* FAX *01–40–46–02–28. 27 rooms with bath. In-room safes, no-smoking rooms, sauna. AE, DC, MC, V. Métro: Luxembourg.*

$$ ⊞ **Timhotel Jardin des Plantes.** Across the street from the lovely Jardin des Plantes, this pleasant, modern hotel—part of the Timhotel chain—has very reasonable prices and perfectly suitable rooms with blond-wood furnishings and floral upholsteries. There's a fifth-floor terrace where you can breakfast or sunbathe in summer, and a sauna in the cellar. ⊠ *5 rue Linné, Latin Quarter, 75005,* ☎ *01–47–07–06–20,* FAX *01–47–07–62–74. 33 rooms with bath. No air-conditioning, sauna. AE, DC, MC, V. Métro: Jussieu.*

$–$$ ⊞ **Saint-Jacques.** Want to live Paris à la Audrey Hepburn and/or Cary Grant? Star in your own version of *Charade* in the hotel made famous by the movie (though most of the film's hotel interiors were created on a film set). Impressionist murals brighten the lounge and breakfast room, and an antique staircase leads to small but comfortable rooms decorated in the same romantic mode. No. 25 has a balcony with a view of Notre Dame and the Panthéon. The cheapest rooms are on the top floor; the most spacious and comfortable on the first two. ⊠ *35 rue des Ecoles, Latin Quarter, 75005,* ☎ *01–44–07–45–45,* FAX *01–43–25–65–50. 35 rooms with bath. No air-conditioning, in-room data ports. AE, MC, V. Métro: Maubert Mutualité.*

$ ⊞ **Familia.** It's hard to beat the price or this level of homespun com-
★ fort—the hospitable Gaucheron family, the hotel's owners, bend over backward for you. More than half the rooms have sepia frescoes of celebrated Paris scenes painted by an artist from the Beaux Arts school; some are appointed with exquisite Louis XV–style furnishings, while others have nice mahogany or cherrywood pieces. Those overlooking the animated Latin Quarter street have double-glazed windows, and those on the second and fifth floors have their own walk-out balcony with breakfast table and chairs. Book at least a month in advance. ⊠ *11 rue des Écoles, Latin Quarter, 75005,* ☎ *01–43–54–55–27,* FAX *01–43–29–61–77. 30 rooms with bath. No air-conditioning, cable TV, mini-bars. AE, MC, V. Métro: Cardinal Lemoine.*

$ ⊞ **Grandes Écoles.** This delightfully intimate hotel looks and feels like a country cottage dropped smack in the middle of the Latin Quarter. It is off the street and occupies three buildings on a beautiful, leafy garden, where breakfast is served in summer. Parquet floors, Louis-Philippe furnishings, lace bedspreads, and the absence of TV all add to the rus-tic ambience. ⊠ *75 rue du Cardinal Lemoine, Latin Quarter, 75005,* ☎ *01–43–26–79–23,* FAX *01–43–25–28–15. 51 rooms with bath. No air-conditioning, parking (fee). MC, V. Métro: Cardinal Lemoine.*

$ ⊞ **Minerve.** If you waited too long and can't get a room at the Familia, this Gaucheron-run hotel is the next best thing. Just next door and twice as big, the hotel has been completely refurbished in the inimitable Gaucheron style: flowers and breakfast tables on the balconies; fres-coes in the rooms and in the spacious, well-appointed lobby; tapestries on the walls; and cherrywood furniture throughout. Then, again, you might want to give this place a miss, as readers have complained about an extremely surly staff. ⊠ *13 rue des Écoles, Latin Quarter, 75005,* ☎ *01–43–26–26–04,* FAX *01–44–07–01–96. 54 rooms with bath. No air-conditioning, in-room data ports. AE, MC, V. Métro: Cardinal Lemoine.*

6ᵉ Arrondissement (St-Germain/Montparnasse)

See Left Bank Lodging map.

$$$$ 🏨 **Bel Ami.** "Affordable chic" is the business concept behind this Grace Leo-Andrieu hotel, and it works: situated around the corner from Café Flore and Deux Magots, the Bel Ami attracts a young, fashionable clientele who want a hip address but don't want to dish out $2,000 a night for a suite at the Lancaster. The sleek yet casual look is à la Christian Liagre: a brown, cream, and olive palette; copper and glass-mosaic bar; and a fireplace lounge. Rooms continue in the same hiply elegant aesthetic and are equipped with marble, glass, and chrome bathrooms, and cotton bathrobes of such heft you'll never want to take yours off. ✉ *7–11 rue St-Benoît, St-Germain-des-Prés, 75006,* ☎ *01–42–61–53–53,* FAX *01–49–27–09–33,* WEB *www.hotel-bel-ami.com. 113 rooms, 2 suites with bath. Bar, in-room data ports, cable TV, minibars, room service, baby-sitting, laundry service, concierge. AE, DC, MC, V. Métro: St-Germain-des-Prés.*

$$$$ 🏨 **Relais Christine.** On a quiet street between the Seine and boulevard St-Germain, this luxurious and extremely popular hotel, occupying 16th-century abbey cloisters, oozes romantic ambience. Rooms are spacious (particularly the duplexes on the upper floors) and well appointed in the old Parisian style (rich upholsteries, mahogany pieces); the best have exposed ceiling beams and overlook the garden. The breakfast room is an erstwhile stone chapel. ✉ *3 rue Christine, St-Germain-des-Prés, 75006,* ☎ *01–40–51–60–80; 800/447–7462 in the U.S.,* FAX *01–40–51–60–81. 31 rooms, 18 suites, with bath. Bar, cable TV, minibars, no-smoking rooms, room service, baby-sitting, laundry service, meeting room, free parking. AE, DC, MC, V. Métro: Odéon.*

$$$–$$$$ 🏨 **L'Hôtel.** Rock idols and movie stars adore this eccentric Left Bank
★ hotel. In fact, how can you resist a place with such an intriguing history? Originally an 18th-century *pavilion d'amour* (inn for trysts), it had become a hotel by the time Oscar Wilde checked in, and then died, in Room 16 (for €455, you can spend a night in the bed where he took his last breath). Wilde's last words about his room's wallpaper—"One of us will have to go"—must have come back to haunt today's owners, who spent a fortune to make it into a decorator's dream. One small double is decorated entirely in Louis-Philippe leopard-skin motifs; another handsome suite flaunts the mirrored, Art Deco boudoir furniture of vaudeville star Mistinguett. The downside? Many rooms are snug. Still, you can always hang out in the bar, popular with an international crowd. In 2001, the superstyle decorator Jacques Garcia gilded this lily by refurbishing some of the hotel's special rooms (the Wilde and Roi de Naples), so call even further ahead than usual to book. ✉ *13 rue des Beaux-Arts, St-Germain-des-Prés, 75006,* ☎ *01–44–41–99–00,* FAX *01–43–25–64–81. 25 rooms, 2 suites, with bath. Bar, in-room safes, baby-sitting. AE, DC, MC, V. Métro: St-Germain-des-Prés.*

$$$–$$$$ 🏨 **Hôtel d'Aubusson.** This 17th-century mansion, once setting to
★ Paris's first literary salon, is now one of the finest *petites hôtels de luxe* in the city, with original Aubusson tapestries, Versailles-style parquet floors, a chiseled stone fireplace, and restored antiques. Even the smallest rooms are good-size by Paris standards, and all are decked out in rich burgundies, greens, or blues. The 10 best rooms have canopied beds and ceiling beams. In summer, you can have your breakfast or pre-dinner drink in the paved courtyard. ✉ *33 rue Dauphine, St-Germain-des-Prés, 75006,* ☎ *01–43–29–43–43,* FAX *01–43–29–12–62,* WEB *www.hoteldaubusson.com. 49 rooms with bath. Bar, in-room data ports, in-room safes, cable TV, minibars, room service, baby-sitting, laundry service. AE, MC, V. Métro: Odéon.*

$$$ ⊡ **Buci Latin.** Modern artwork on the walls and zebra-upholstered chairs
★ in the lobby set the tone at this funky, upscale hotel, set on an extremely
congested and unphotogenic street. Each room's door is inspired by
the work of a famous artist—Magritte, Léger, Monet, or Basquiat—
done by local painters. Rooms are small, but their Santa Fe "look"—
ocher walls, exposed beams, and arty contoured tables—give them a
quirky feel. The more spacious duplex suite on the top floor, right under
the roof, has a small bathroom loft with a shower, makeup table, and
freestanding bathtub. ⊠ *34 rue de Buci, St-Germain-des-Prés, 75006,*
☎ *01–43–29–07–20,* FAX *01–43–29–67–44. 25 rooms, 2 suites, with
bath. In-room data ports, cable TV, minibars, room service, laundry
service. AE, DC, MC, V. Métro: Mabillon.*

$$$ ⊡ **Hôtel de l'Abbaye.** Once a convent, this delightful hotel near St-Sulpice
welcomes you with a stone-vaulted entrance and a lovely flower-filled
back garden with a stone fountain. The blend of stylishly rustic antiques and earthy apricot and ocher tones makes for some calm, cozy
cocooning. The first-floor rooms open onto the garden; most of those
on the upper floors have oak beams and sitting alcoves. The four duplexes with private terraces are more expensive. Breakfast is included.
⊠ *10 rue Cassette, St-Germain-des-Prés, 75006,* ☎ *01–45–44–38–11,*
FAX *01–45–48–07–86. 42 rooms, 4 suites, with bath. Bar, cable TV, minibars, room service, baby-sitting, laundry service. AE, MC, V. Métro:
St-Sulpice.*

$$$ ⊡ **Hôtel de Buci.** The eager-to-please staff adds to the luxurious feel-
ing of this small hotel on the lively and crammed rue de Buci market
street. Rooms, which vary in size from cozy to spacious, have ar-
moires and reproductions of 18th-century fabrics in warm, regal pat-
terns; bathrooms are done in marble. Ask for a room overlooking the
rear for a quieter night's sleep, or one in front for a glimpse of Paris.
The lobby, filled with club chairs and fresh flowers, and the cellar break-
fast room are good spots to rendezvous. ⊠ *22 rue de Buci, St-Ger-
main-des-Prés, 75006,* ☎ *01–55–42–74–74,* FAX *01–55–42–74–44,* WEB
*www.hotelbuci.fr. 24 rooms with bath. In-room data ports, cable TV,
minibars, business services, meeting room. AE, DC, MC, V. Métro:
Odéon.*

$$$ ⊡ **Manoir de St-Germain-des-Prés.** This stylish hotel is right next to
the Brasserie Lipp and across from the Café de Flore. Rooms are done
up in traditional 18th-century luxe, with wainscoting and rich upholsteries. Amenities promote genuine R&R, from hot tubs and sound-
proof rooms to thirsty terry robes and well-stocked minibars; and
breakfast is included. ⊠ *153 bd. St-Germain-des-Prés, St-Germain-des-
Prés, 75006,* ☎ *01–42–22–21–65,* FAX *01–45–48–22–25. 32 rooms with
bath. Bar, in-room data ports, in-room safes, cable TV, minibars, hot
tub, laundry service. AE, DC, MC, V. Métro: St-Germain-des-Prés.*

$$$ ⊡ **Relais St-Germain.** The interior-designer owners of this outstand-
ing hotel in the heart of St-Germain-des-Prés have exquisite taste and
a superb respect for tradition and detail. Moreover, rooms are at least
twice the size of what you find at other hotels in the area for the same
price. Much of the furniture was selected with a knowledgeable eye
from the city's *brocantes* (secondhand dealers), and every room has
its own unique treasures. Doubles have separate sitting areas; four have
kitchenettes. Breakfast is included. ⊠ *9 carrefour de l'Odéon, St-Ger-
main-des-Prés, 75006,* ☎ *01–43–29–12–05,* FAX *01–46–33–45–30. 21
rooms, 1 suite, with bath. Bar, in-room data ports, in-room safes,
cable TV, minibars, room service, baby-sitting, laundry service. AE, DC,
MC, V. Métro: Odéon.*

$$–$$$ ⊡ **Le Clos Médicis.** Contemporary style meets Provençal tradition at
this classy little hotel. Warm colors and a mix of modern pieces, painted
country furnishings, and wrought-iron items set the tone. Rooms are

small (except for the duplex) but laden with comforts, such as mini-bars and crisp terry robes. ⊠ 56 rue Monsieur-le-Prince, St-Germain-des-Prés, 75006, ☎ 01–43–29–10–80, FAX 01–43–54–26–90. 38 rooms with bath. Bar, in-room data ports, cable TV, minibars, no-smoking rooms. AE, DC, MC, V. Métro: Luxembourg.

$$–$$$ 🏨 **Fleurie.** On a quiet side street near place de l'Odéon, this spiffy, family-run hotel has pretty, pastel-color rooms and many modern luxury amenities, including beautifully tiled bathrooms with heated towel racks. Antiques, Oriental rugs, and rich upholsteries fill the 18th-century building. The staff is helpful. ⊠ 32–34 rue Grégoire-de-Tours, St-Germain-des-Prés, 75006, ☎ 01–53–73–70–00, FAX 01–53–73–70–20. 29 rooms with bath. Bar, in-room data ports, in-room safes, cable TV, minibars, baby-sitting, laundry service. AE, DC, MC, V. Métro: Odéon.

$$–$$$ 🏨 **Grand Hôtel de l'Univers.** In the very heart of Paris's festive, adorable, vacation-friendly St-Germain-des-Prés quarter, this hotel is on a quiet side street, yet only steps away from numerous restaurants. The house dates back to the 15th century, which explains the dimensions of some rooms; if snug, they are so stylishly and delightfully decorated ("La Bonbonniere" is a toile de Jouy-fabric wonder), you won't notice. For breakfast, you're treated to a medieval, Louis XI–style vaulted cellar which only Walt Disney's Imagineers could top. The staff is lovely. ⊠ 6 rue Gregoire-de-Tours, St-Germain-des-Prés, 75006, ☎ 01–43–29–37–00, FAX 01–40–51–06–45. 34 rooms with bath. Bar, cable TV, minibars. AE, DC, MC, V. Métro: Odéon.

$$–$$$ 🏨 **Relais St-Sulpice.** A savvy clientele with discerning taste frequents this fashionable little hotel. It's a stylish blend of various periods and regions—African artwork lines the hallways; Provençal tiles adorn the bathrooms; Chinese engravings wink to Parisians' penchant for the Orient in the 1930s; heavy fabrics drape the windows; and thick, cotton-piqué downy comforters envelop wrought-iron beds. There's a sauna downstairs, right off the atrium breakfast salon. Room 11 has a terrific view of St-Sulpice. ⊠ 3 rue Garancière, St-Germain-des-Prés, 75006, ☎ 01–46–33–99–00, FAX 01–46–33–00–10. 26 rooms with bath. In-room safes, cable TV, minibars, no-smoking rooms, sauna, baby-sitting, laundry service, meeting room, parking (fee). AE, DC, MC, V. Métro: St-Germain-des-Prés, St-Sulpice.

$$–$$$ 🏨 **St-Grégoire.** On a calm street off bustling rue de Rennes, this dis-
★   creet little hotel offers quiet and comfortable refuge from the hectic pace of Paris. Rooms, done in muted pinks, yellows, and beiges, have simple antique furnishings and bucolic prints on the walls. The sitting room–lobby is especially cozy, with its rustic fireplace and flowery wall-paper. Particularly romantic are Rooms 14 and 16, which have enclosed, ivy-covered terraces. ⊠ 43 rue de l'Abbé-Grégoire, St-Germain-des-Prés, 75006, ☎ 01–45–48–23–23, FAX 01–45–48–33–95. 19 rooms, 1 suite, with bath. Minibars, baby-sitting. AE, DC, MC, V. Métro: St-Placide.

$$ 🏨 **Aramis-St-Germain.** You get great value for your money at this hotel. Part of the Best Western chain, it manages to be understated yet classically French. Rooms have damask bedspreads and sturdy cherrywood armoires. All are soundproof and equipped with cable TV; about half have air-conditioning, and nine have whirlpool baths. Harvey's Piano Bar, on the ground floor, is popular with the smart business set. ⊠ 124 rue de Rennes, St-Germain-des-Prés, 75006, ☎ 01–45–48–03–75; 800/528–1234 in the U.S., FAX 01–45–44–99–29. 42 rooms with bath. Bar, no air-conditioning, cable TV, minibars, laundry service. AE, DC, MC, V. Métro: St-Placide.

$$ 🖭 **Atelier Montparnasse.** This Art Deco–inspired gem was designed with style and comfort in mind. Rooms are tastefully done, and all the bathrooms feature unique mosaic reproductions of famous French paintings. The hotel is across the street from the famous brasseries Le Sélect and La Coupole and within walking distance of the Luxembourg Gardens and St-Germain-des-Prés. Art lovers, take note: the hotel hosts monthly exhibits of the works of local painters. Families will want to book the room with three beds. ⊠ *49 rue Vavin, Montparnasse, 75006,* ☎ *01–46–33–60–00,* FAX *01–40–51–04–21. 17 rooms with bath. Bar, no air-conditioning, room service, baby-sitting, laundry service. AE, DC, MC, V. Métro: Vavin.*

$$ 🖭 **Bonaparte.** The congeniality of the staff only makes a stay in this intimate place more of a treat. Old-fashioned upholsteries, 19th-century furnishings, and paintings create a quaint feel in the relatively spacious rooms. And the location in the heart of St-Germain is nothing short of fabulous. ⊠ *61 rue Bonaparte, St-Germain-des-Prés, 75006,* ☎ *01–43–26–97–37,* FAX *01–46–33–57–67. 29 rooms with bath. In-room safes, cable TV, refrigerator, laundry service. MC, V. Métro: St-Germain-des-Prés.*

7ᵉ Arrondissement (Invalides/Eiffel Tower)

See Left Bank Lodging map.

$$$$ 🖭 **Pont Royal.** Once a favorite watering hole of everyone in the literary world from T. S. Eliot to Gabriel Garcia Marquez, this sump-
★ tuously refurbished hotel now attracts more businessmen than writers: the famous bar in the basement has been converted into a deluxe conference room, and for the time being the only recognizable authors you'll see are the ones whose photographs line the the lobby. You can't find a more comfortable hotel, however, nor a better location—a quiet street just off Rue du Bac and around the corner from boulevard St-Germain. And the views from the top floors are magnificent, especially the Cinerama one from Suite 801. The restaurant, a popular luncheon spot among the well-heeled locals, has become the new favorite of Antoine Gallimard, whose publishing house is just up the street. So perhaps this will soon become, once again, Paris's *hôtel littéraire.* ⊠ *7 rue de Montalembert, St-Germain-des-Prés, 75007,* ☎ *01–42–84–70–00,* FAX *01–42–84–71–00,* WEB *www.hotel-pont-royal. com/hpr. 65 rooms, 10 suites, with bath. Restaurant (lunch only), bar, cable TV, minibars, in-room data ports, in-room safes, concierge, business center, babysitting, room service, health center, parking (fee). AE, DC, MC, V. Métro: Rue de Bac.*

$$–$$$ 🖭 **Le Tourville.** Here is a rare find: a cozy, upscale hotel that doesn't
★ cost a fortune. Each room has crisp, virgin-white damask upholstery set against pastel or ocher walls, a smattering of antique bureaus and lamps, original artwork, and fabulous old mirrors. The hotel attracts a young, fashionable crowd, especially in the dishy Art Deco bar. The junior suites have hot tubs. The staff couldn't be more helpful. ⊠ *16 av. de Tourville, Invalides/Eiffel Tower, 75007,* ☎ *01–47–05–62–62; 800/528–3549 in the U.S.,* FAX *01–47–05–43–90,* WEB *www.hoteltourville. com. 27 rooms, 3 junior suites, with bath. Bar, cable TV, minibars, laundry service. AE, DC, MC, V. Métro: École Militaire.*

$$ 🖭 **Hôtel du Cadran.** Colorful window boxes lend a welcoming touch to this cheerful hotel in a handsome corner building near the market on rue Cler. The charming Madame Chaine and her gracious staff go out of their way to ensure that you enjoy your stay, from recommending a bistro to booking theater tickets. Rooms have coordinating drapes and bedspreads in cheery colors and are very comfortable. Ask about special weekend rates. ⊠ *10 rue du Champ de Mars, In-*

valides/Eiffel Tower, 75007, ☎ *01–40–62–67–00,* FAX *01–40–62–67–13. 42 rooms with bath. Bar, in-room data ports, in-room safes, cable TV, minibars, no-smoking rooms, baby-sitting, laundry service, concierge, meeting room, travel services. AE, DC, MC, V. Métro: École Militaire.*

$$ 🏨 **Hôtel de l'Université.** Staying at this hotel in a 17th-century town house between boulevard St-Germain and the Seine feels like going back in time. Guest rooms have English and French antiques and original fireplaces. Ask for one with a terrace on the fifth floor. Note that the cheapest guest rooms have showers—no tubs—in the bathrooms. ✉ *22 rue de l'Université, St-Germain-des-Prés, 75007,* ☎ *01–42–61–09–39,* FAX *01–42–60–40–84. 27 rooms with bath. In-room data ports, in-room safes, cable TV, minibars, room service. AE, MC, V. Métro: Rue du Bac.*

$$ 🏨 **Latour Maubourg.** In the heart of the elegant 7ᵉ arrondissement, a stone's throw from the Invalides and the prime minister's residence, is this small hotel where personalized service is emphasized. The place is homey and unpretentious, from its very helpful staff to its simply furnished rooms with their mix of appealingly mismatched finds. ✉ *150 rue de Grenelle, Invalides/Eiffel Tower, 75007,* ☎ *01–47–05–16–16,* FAX *01–47–05–16–14,* WEB *www.latour-maubourg.fr. 9 rooms, 1 suite, with bath. Air-conditioning in some rooms, in-room data ports, cable TV, minibars. MC, V. Métro: La Tour Maubourg.*

$$ 🏨 **Orsay.** Across the street from the Musée d'Orsay, the Orsay (formerly the Solférino) is a cheerful little hotel, with spacious, comfortable rooms and attentive service. The look is upbeat, with bright color schemes and flower-filled window boxes; rooms have satellite TV. The skylighted breakfast room is a pleasant place to greet the day. ✉ *93 rue de Lille, St-Germain-des-Prés, 75007,* ☎ *01–47–05–85–54,* FAX *01–45–55–51–16. 41 rooms with bath. No air-conditioning, cable TV, minibars. AE, DC, MC, V. Métro: Solférino.*

$ 🏨 **Champ de Mars.** Françoise and Stéphane Gourdal's comfortable
★ hotel has an appealing blue-and-yellow "Liberty" style. Rooms are equipped with satellite TV and CNN; the two on the ground floor open onto a leafy courtyard. The location—near the Eiffel Tower and Invalides—is difficult to beat. ✉ *7 rue du Champ de Mars, Invalides/Eiffel Tower, 75007,* ☎ *01–45–51–52–30,* FAX *01–45–51–64–36,* WEB *www.hotel-du-champ-de-mars./com. 25 rooms with bath. No air-conditioning, in-room data ports, cable TV. MC, V. Métro: École Militaire.*

$ 🏨 **Eiffel Rive Gauche.** On a quiet side street just a couple of blocks from the Eiffel Tower, this modern hotel with a leafy patio is a great budget find. The look is functional, but rooms are spacious and comfortable. The owner, Monsieur Chicheportiche, is a multilingual, walking encyclopedia of Paris. One caveat: a steep phone surcharge is added if you make a collect call. ✉ *6 rue du Gros Caillou, Invalides/Eiffel Tower, 75007,* ☎ *01–45–51–24–56,* FAX *01–45–51–11–77. 30 rooms with bath. No air-conditioning, cable TV, minibars. AE, MC, V. Métro: École Militaire.*

$ 🏨 **Grand Hôtel Lévêque.** The Eiffel Tower is just around the corner, but the real draw here is the picturesque street market just outside the hotel's front door. Recently renovated, this immaculate hotel has an eager-to-please staff, comfortable rooms, satellite TV, and a bistro-style breakfast room. Make sure to get a room facing the street and reserve early—this is a very popular address among French and American foodies. ✉ *29 rue Cler, Invalides/Eiffel Tower, 75007,* ☎ *01–47–05–49–15,* FAX *01–45–50–49–36. 50 rooms, 45 with bath. No air-conditioning, in-room data ports, cable TV. AE, MC, V. Métro: École Militaire.*

8e Arrondissement (Champs-Élysées)

See Right Bank Lodging map.

$$$$ ⊞ **L'Astor.** Part of the Sofitel hotel group, L'Astor is a bastion of highly stylized, civilized chic. The Art Deco lobby is decked out in boldly patterned armchairs, huge mirrors, and clever ceiling frescoes. There's also a cozy bar; a small, neoclassic-inspired library; and a stunning trompe l'oeil dining room. Guest rooms are testimonials to the sober Regency style, with weighty marble fireplaces and mahogany furnishings. Several suites have walk-out balconies with superb vistas. The hotel's restaurant is supervised by the celebrated chef Joël Robuchon. ⊠ *11 rue d'Astorg, Champs-Élysées, 75008,* ☎ *01–53–05–05–05; 800/763–4385 in the U.S.,* ⅎ *01–53–05–05–30,* ⅦⅢ *www.hotel-astor.net. 129 rooms, 5 suites, with bath. Restaurant, bar, in-room data ports, in-room safes, cable TV, minibars, no-smoking rooms, room service (24-hr), massage, health club, baby-sitting, laundry service. AE, DC, MC, V. Métro: Miromesnil, St-Augustin.*

$$$$ ⊞ **Bristol.** The understated facade on rue du Faubourg St-Honoré
★ might mislead the unknowing, but the Bristol ranks among Paris's most exclusive hotels and has the prices to prove it. Many billionaires and celebrities refuse to stay anywhere else, attracted by the tasteful luxe and the staff's finishing-school discretion. Some of the spaciously elegant rooms have authentic Louis XV and Louis XVI furniture and magnificent marble bathrooms in pure 1920s Art Deco; others have a more relaxed 19th-century style. The public salons are palatially stocked with old master paintings, sculptures, sumptuous carpets, and tapestries. ⊠ *112 rue du Faubourg St-Honoré, Miromesnil, 75008,* ☎ *01–53–43–43–00,* ⅎ *01–53–43–43–01. 154 rooms, 41 suites, with bath. Restaurant, bar, in-room data ports, in-room safes, minibars, cable TV, room service, indoor pool, sauna, health club, laundry service, meeting room, free parking. AE, DC, MC, V. Métro: Miromesnil.*

$$$$ ⊞ **Crillon.** To anyone with a taste for history, the name Crillon pro-
★ duces a whole carillon's worth of chimes. In 1758, Louis XV commissioned the architect Jacques-Ange Gabriel to build two facades of the mansion which sits on the north side of the place de la Concorde. As the Comte de Crillon's palace, it welcomed Marie-Antoinette, who took singing lessons here (one of the original *grands appartements* has been named after her), then lost her life on the guillotine on the square just outside. In 1909 it became a hotel and since then has played host to generations of diplomats, politicians, and refined travelers (movie stars prefer the rooms that face the square, which come with double-glazed windows). Most rooms are lavishly decorated with rococo and Directoire antiques, crystal and gilt wall sconces, and gold-leaf fittings. The sheer quantity of marble in the highly praised Les Ambassadeurs restaurant is staggering. ⊠ *10 pl. de la Concorde, Louvre/Tuileries, 75008,* ☎ *01–44–71–15–00; 800/888–4747 in the U.S,* ⅎ *01–44–71–15–02,* ⅦⅢ *www.crillon-paris.com. 117 rooms, 43 suites, with bath. 2 restaurants, 2 bars, tea shop, in-room data ports, in-room safes, cable TV, minibars, no-smoking rooms, room service, gym, baby-sitting, laundry service, meeting room. AE, DC, MC, V. Métro: Concorde.*

$$$$ ⊞ **George V.** General Eisenhower's headquarters in 1945 is now owned
★ by a Saudi prince (who gets first dibs on the Royal Suite) and managed by the Four Seasons group. Thanks to a recent $125 million renovation, the hotel is as bright and shiny as the day it opened in 1928: the original Art Deco detailing and 17th-century tapestries have been restored; the bas-reliefs re-leafed in gold; the marble-floor mosaics rebuilt tile by tile. The private health-club facilities are an added attraction, as is the gourmand Hédiard boutique next to the lobby, and the restaurant, Le V, has become one of Paris's hottest tables, thanks to

the legendary Philippe Legendre of Taillevent fame. ⊠ *31 av. George V, Champs-Élysées, 75008,* ☎ *01–49–52–70–00,* FAX *01–49–52–70–10,* WEB *www.fourseasons.com. 185 rooms, 60 suites, with bath. Restaurant, bar, in-room data ports, in-room safes, cable TV, minibars, nosmoking rooms, room service, indoor pool, hair salon, sauna, health club, laundry service, business services, meeting room. AE, DC, MC, V. Métro: George V.*

$$$$ ⊞ **Hyatt Regency Paris-Madeleine.** This Haussmannesque building near the Opéra Garnier feels more like a boutique hotel than an international chain, thanks to stylized details like cherry paneling and mismatched bedside tables. You can also expect the usual plush carpeting and luxurious upholsteries. Book a room on the seventh or eighth floor facing boulevard Malesherbes for a view of the Eiffel Tower. ⊠ *24 bd. Malesherbes, Opéra/Grands Boulevards, 75008,* ☎ *01–55–27–12–34; 800/223–1234 in the U.S.,* FAX *01–55–27–12–35. 81 rooms, 5 suites, with bath. Restaurant, bar, in-room data ports, in-room safes, minibars, cable TV, no-smoking floor, room service, sauna, gym, laundry service, business services, meeting room. AE, DC, MC, V. Métro: St-Augustin.*

$$$$ ⊞ **Lancaster.** Another jewel in hotelier Grace Leo-Andrieu's crown, the
★ Lancaster, one of Paris's most venerable institutions, has been transformed by her legion of star designers into a stellar and modish luxury hotel. The overall feel—a seamless blend of traditional with contemporary—is one of timeless elegance. Every detail speaks of quality, from the hotel's own line of bath products to the Porthault linens. Many of the suites pay homage to the hotel's colorful regulars, from Garbo to John Huston to Sir Alec Guinness. Marlene Dietrich's is decorated in lilac (her favorite color) and is adorned with superb Louis XV antiques. ⊠ *7 rue de Berri, Champs-Élysées, 75008,* ☎ *01–40–76–40–76; 877/757–2747 in the U.S.,* FAX *01–40–76–40–00,* WEB *www. hotel-lancaster.com. 50 rooms, 10 suites, with bath. Restaurant, bar, in-room data ports, in-room safes, in-room VCRs, cable TV, minibars, room service, sauna, gym, baby-sitting, laundry service, meeting room, parking (fee). AE, DC, MC, V. Métro: George V.*

$$$$ ⊞ **Paris Marriott Champs-Élysées.** Take a ground-zero locale, a stylish atrium lobby, and a chic, 19th-century style, and you've got the Paris Marriott. Ebony furnishings and antique prints are some of the nice touches that make you forget this is a chain, and state-of-the-art soundproofing shuts out the cacophonous Champs. The hotel restaurant specializes in high-end *cuisine americaine.* ⊠ *70 av. des Champs-Élysées, Champs-Élysées, 75008,* ☎ *01–53–93–55–00; 800/228–9290 in the U.S.,* FAX *01–53–93–55–01. 174 rooms, 18 suites, with bath. Restaurant, 2 bars, in-room data ports, in-room safes, cable TV, minibars, no-smoking floor, room service, sauna, gym, baby-sitting, laundry service, business services, meeting room. AE, DC, MC, V. Métro: George V.*

$$$$ ⊞ **Pershing Hall.** Formerly an American Legion Hall, Pershing Hall is
★ the new must-see, must-stay address in Paris. Designed by Andrée Putman, the grande dame of French interior architecture, this boutique hotel exudes an almost masculine minimalism, with hefty American elm doors, Limoges porcelain pulley-lights, square washbasins in the dark marbled bathrooms, and, in the central courtyard, a spectacular jungle garden carpeting a six-story high felt wall. The stylish lounge bar has become a hot nightspot, serving drinks, dinners and DJ-driven music until 2:00 AM. And the restaurant is not just another pretty-face place; the food, by Alain Ducasse/Marco Pierre White/Daniel Boulud–trained Erwan Louaisil is wonderful. ⊠ *49 rue Pierre Charron, Champs-Élysées, 75008,* ☎ *01–58–36–58–00,* FAX *01–58–36–58–01,* WEB *www. pershinghall.com. 20 rooms, 6 suites, with bath. Restaurant, bar, cable TV, minibars, concierge, health center, business center, babysitting, room*

service, in-room data ports, in-room safes, parking (fee). AE, DC, MC, V. Métro: George V, Franklin Roosevelt.

$$$$ ★ 🏨 **Plaza Athenée.** With Alain Ducasse (or, rather, his hand-picked minions) in the kitchens and a brand-new, very contempo bar off the Louis XVI lobby, the landmark Plaza Athenée has suddenly become hip. The avenue Montaigne palace, entirely refurbished, is once again attracting a Blahnik-heeled crowd, partly because of its glamorous allure—after all, this was the favorite Paris hotel of Grace Kelly and Jackie Kennedy—and partly because it's only a croissant lob from the top couture and luxury shops in the city. Most of the rooms are appointed with Regénce and Louis Seize–style accent pieces, while the top two floors go Art Deco (and are adorned with historic sketches by Dior himself). The geranium-filled, vine-drunk courtyard—with its signature red awnings, one of the most beautiful sights in all Paris—is a sublime spot for a summer cocktail. There are—count them—460 staff members. ⊠ *25 av. Montaigne, Champs-Élysées, 75008,* ☎ *01–53–67–66–65; 866/732–1106 in the U.S.,* FAX *01–53–67–66–66,* WEB *www.plaza-athenee-paris.com. 121 rooms, 66 suites, with bath. 2 restaurants, 2 bars, in-room data ports, in-room safes, cable TV, minibars, no-smoking rooms, room service, massage, health club, baby-sitting, laundry service. AE, DC, MC, V. Métro: Alma-Marceau.*

$$$$ 🏨 **Prince de Galles.** This Art Deco palace is the kinder, gentler brother of its next-door neighbor, the George V. Here, 1920s don't so much roar as purr. Rooms and suites are spacious and bright, with crystal chandeliers in every room—except the marbled bathrooms. The restaurant, with its summer patio of Moorish blue and gold mosaics, is a quiet, sane refuge from the frenzied interplay of boulevards and business just outside. Le Regency, a cigar-friendly, club-style bar boasting a wall of single malts and a special luncheon for those with temporal (rather than financial) restrictions, is the perfect *entent cordial* between English sobriety and French culinary expertise. ⊠ *33 av. George V, Champs-Élysées, 75008,* ☎ *01–53–23–77–77,* FAX *01–53–23–78–78,* WEB *www. luxurycollection.com. 138 rooms, 30 suites, with bath. Restaurant, bar, in-room data ports, in-room safes, minibars, room service, hair salon, health club, baby-sitting, laundry service, concierge, business services, meeting room. AE, DC, MC, V. Métro: George V.*

$$$–$$$$ 🏨 **Franklin D. Roosevelt.** One of the last family-run boutique hotels in the area, this is an intimate alternative to grander establishments in the same price category. The hotel has the look and feel of a London club, with hunting scenes on the walls and a fire crackling in the smoking salon. French fashion magazines have done photo spreads on the cozy bar and the three colonial-style lounges, but it is just as stylish upstairs—rooms and suites have mahogany doors and antiques, Oriental carpets and ceramics, cashmere draperies and printed calico wall coverings. Book a room on the fifth floor if you want to breakfast on a balcony. ⊠ *18 rue Clément Marot, Champs-Élysées, 75008,* ☎ *01–53–57–49–50,* FAX *01–47–20–44–30,* WEB *www.franklin-roosevelt.com. 42 rooms, 3 suites, with bath. In-room data ports, in-room safes, cable TV, minibars, meeting room. AE, DC, MC, V. Métro: Marbeuf.*

$$$ 🏨 **Bradford-Élysées.** This turn-of-the-20th-century hotel conserves its old-fashioned feel while providing modern amenities. An old wooden elevator carries you from the flower-filled lobby to the spacious, luxurious rooms equipped with Louis XVI–style furniture, brass beds, and marble fireplaces. ⊠ *10 rue St-Philippe-du-Roule, Champs-Élysées, 75008,* ☎ *01–45–63–20–20,* FAX *01–45–63–20–07. 50 rooms with bath. In-room data ports, in-room safes, cable TV, minibars, no-smoking rooms, baby-sitting, laundry service. AE, DC, MC, V. Métro: St-Philippe-du-Roule.*

$$ 🏨 **Résidence Monceau.** Within a stone's throw of the elegant Parc Monceau, this friendly and fashionable hotel is an oasis of refined tranquility. Warm tones make rooms cozy; the efficient and professional staff makes your stay easy. The breakfast garden, surrounded by ivy-covered trellises, is a lovely place to start the day. ⊠ *85 rue du Rocher, Parc Monceau, 75008,* ☎ *01–45–22–75–11,* 𝖥𝖠𝖷 *01–45–22–30–88. 50 rooms, 1 suite, with bath. Bar, no air-conditioning, no-smoking rooms. AE, DC, MC, V. Métro: Villiers.*

9ᵉ Arrondissement (Opéra)

See Right Bank Lodging map.

$$$$ 🏨 **Grand Hôtel Inter-Continental.** Opened by Napoléon III and his empress Eugénie in 1862, Paris's biggest luxury hotel has a facade that seems as long as the Louvre's. The hotel got a latter-day Art Deco makeover, and the grand salon's dome and the restaurant's splendidly painted ceilings are registered landmarks. Even the spacious guest rooms are Art Deco. The stunningly lush Second Empire grand ballroom is the scene of many of the city's top fashion shows and charity events. As in the days of the Impressionists, the hotel's famed Café de la Paix is one of the city's great people-watching spots. ⊠ *2 rue Scribe, Opéra/Grands Boulevards, 75009,* ☎ *01–40–07–32–32; 800/327–0200 in the U.S.,* 𝖥𝖠𝖷 *01–42–66–12–51,* 𝖶𝖤𝖡 *www.interconti.com. 492 rooms, 22 suites, with bath. 3 restaurants, 2 bars, in-room data ports, in-room safes, in-room VCRs, cable TV, minibars, no-smoking rooms, room service, sauna, health club, laundry service, business services, meeting room. AE, DC, MC, V. Métro: Opéra.*

$$$$ 🏨 **Millennium Opéra.** The grande dame of boulevard Haussmann is one of the best-equipped luxury hotels in the city, with fiber-optic PC links in the rooms and a regal oyster bar in the bright, shiny brasserie. The glass Belle Epoque elevator still sweeps guests from their floors to the spacious lobby below, but those wanting to cut a rug will have to hoof it elsewhere, as the basement cabaret has been converted into a seven-room conference center. ⊠ *12 bd. Haussmann, Opéra/Grands Boulevards, 75009,* ☎ *01–49–49–16–00,* 𝖥𝖠𝖷 *01–49–49–17–00,* 𝖶𝖤𝖡 *www.mill-cop.com. 152 rooms, 11 suites, with bath. Restaurant, bar, in-room data ports, in-room safes, cable TV, minibars, room service, baby-sitting, laundry service, concierge, meeting room. AE, DC, MC, V. Métro: Le Peletier.*

$ 🏨 **Chopin.** A connoisseur's delight, located at the end of the passage Jouffroy—one of the many glass-roofed shopping arcades built in Paris in the early 19th century—the Chopin's newly renovated, comfortable rooms overlook the arcade's quaint toy shops and bookstores, once favorite haunts of Baudelaire and the Surrealists. The hallways and corridors are charmingly fussy, with lots of lace and comfy Chesterfields. Best rooms are 409, 310, and 412, while the cheapest are the darker, smaller rooms ending with a 7. Blissful silence, however, reigns throughout: the passage gates are closed at dusk, making this the quietest hotel in the city. ⊠ *10 bd. Montmartre (46 passage Jouffroy), Opéra/Grands Boulevards, 75009,* ☎ *01–47–70–58–10,* 𝖥𝖠𝖷 *01–42–47–00–70. 35 rooms with bath. No air-conditioning, minibars. AE, DC, MC, V. Métro: Grands Boulevards.*

$ 🏨 **Hôtel des Croisés (Langlois).** After starring in Jonathan Demme's remake of *Charade,* this darling hotel has hit the big time, with a new name (Hôtel Langlois, from the film), refurbished rooms, and a hip clientele. Thankfully, prices don't reflect its newfound celebrity. An impressive Art Nouveau building with beautiful wood-paneled reception area and vintage wrought-iron elevator, its rooms are fabulously spacious and decked out with elegant period furniture. Most have marble fireplaces. Rooms on the lower floors have the largest bathrooms, but those on the fifth and sixth have more star quality, with Cinemascopic views of Paris rooftops. No. 63 and 64 look out upon the top of Sacré-Coeur. ⊠ *63 rue Saint-Lazare, Opéra/Grands Boulevards, 75009,* ☎ *01–48–74–78–24,* ℻ *01–49–95–04–43. 26 rooms, 1 suite, with bath. No air-conditioning, minibars. AE, DC, MC, V. Métro: Trinité.*

11ᵉ Arrondissement (Bastille)

See Right Bank Lodging map.

$ 🏠 **Garden Hôtel.** This family-run hotel is on a pretty garden just out of earshot of Oberkampf. Rooms are basically functional, but spotless; those in front have lovely views of the verdant square, and all have double-glazed windows to ensure quiet. The staff speaks little English. Bathtubs are half size. Triples (rooms with three beds) go for €70. ⊠ *1 rue du Général-Blaise, Oberkampf, 75011,* ☎ *01–47–00–57–93,* ℻ *01–47–00–45–29. 42 rooms with bath. No air-conditioning. AE, MC, V. Métro: St-Ambroise.*

$ 🏠 **Résidence Alhambra.** The white facade, rear garden, and flower-filled window boxes brighten an otherwise lackluster neighborhood. Inside, the look is more spartan, with smallish, modernly appointed rooms; all have cable TV. The best reason to stay here is that prices are rock-bottom and the hotel is near the Marais and accessible to five métro lines at place de la République. A major renovation is scheduled here sometime in late 2002. ⊠ *13 rue de Malte, République, 75011,* ☎ *01–47–00–35–52,* ℻ *01–43–57–98–75. 58 rooms with bath. No air-conditioning, cable TV. MC, V. Métro: Oberkampf.*

12ᵉ Arrondissement (Bastille/Gare de Lyon)

See Right Bank Lodging map.

$$–$$$ 🏠 **Le Pavillon Bastille.** Here's a smart address (across from the Opéra Bastille) for savvy travelers who appreciate getting perks for less. The transformation of this 19th-century hôtel particulier into a colorful, high-design hotel garnered architectural awards. A fiercely loyal, hip clientele loves its bright blue and yellow interior and whimsical touches. Every detail is pitch-perfect, from the friendly staff right down to the 17th-century fountain in the garden. ⊠ *65 rue de Lyon, Bastille, 75012,* ☎ *01–43–43–65–65; 800/233–2552 in the U.S.,* ℻ *01–43–43–96–52. 24 rooms, 1 suite, with bath. Bar, in-room safes, cable TV, minibars, room service. AE, DC, MC, V. Métro: Bastille.*

$$ 🏠 **Modern Hôtel-Lyon.** Just a block from the Gare de Lyon is this cozy, congenial, family-run hotel, open since 1903. Rooms done up in blues and lavenders give the place a French-country feel. ⊠ *3 rue Parrot, Bastille, 75012,* ☎ *01–43–43–41–52,* ℻ *01–43–43–81–16. 47 rooms, 1 suite, with bath. No air-conditioning, in-room safes. AE, DC, MC, V. Métro: Gare de Lyon.*

13ᵉ Arrondissement (Gobelins)

See Left Bank Lodging map.

$ 🏠 **Résidence les Gobelins.** Wicker furniture and warm colors create a cozy touch at this small, simple hotel on a quiet side street between place d'Italie and the Latin Quarter. Some rooms overlook a small, flower-filled garden, as does the lounge where breakfast is served. ⊠ *9 rue des Gobelins, Gobelins, 75013,* ☎ *01–47–07–26–90,* ℻ *01–43–31–44–05. 32 rooms with bath. No air-conditioning, in-room data ports, cable TV. AE, DC, MC, V. Métro: Gobelins.*

14ᵉ Arrondissement (Montparnasse)

See Left Bank Lodging map.

$$–$$$ ☎ **Raspail-Montparnasse.** Guest rooms here are named after the artists who made Montparnasse the art capital of the world in the '20s and '30s—Picasso, Chagall, and Modigliani, to name a few. Instead of their raw, fauve colors, pastels are the dominant shades here, complemented by contemporary blond-wood furniture and crisp cotton upholsteries. Most rooms are at the low end of this price category; five have spectacular panoramic views of Montparnasse and the Eiffel Tower. All are soundproofed. ✉ *203 bd. Raspail, Montparnasse, 75014,* ☎ *01–43–20–62–86; 800/448–8355 in the U.S.,* FAX *01–43–20–50–79,* WEB *www. globe-market.com./h75014raspail.htm. 38 rooms with bath. Bar, in-room data ports, in-room safes, cable TV, minibars. AE, DC, MC, V. Métro: Vavin.*

$–$$ ☎ **Istria.** This small, family-run hotel on a quiet side street was a Montparnasse artists' hangout in the '20s and '30s. It has a flower-filled courtyard and simple, clean, comfortable rooms with soft, pastel-tone Japanese wallpaper and light-wood furnishings. Breakfast is served in a pretty, vaulted cellar. ✉ *29 rue Campagne-Première, Montparnasse, 75014,* ☎ *01–43–20–91–82,* FAX *01–43–22–48–45. 26 rooms with bath. No air-conditioning, cable TV, minibars, in-room safes. AE, DC, MC, V. Métro: Raspail.*

$–$$ ☎ **Lenox-Montparnasse.** The hotel may be modern, '60s-era, but it's in the heart of Montparnasse, just around the corner from the famous Dôme and Coupole brasseries, and close to the Luxembourg Gardens. The best rooms have fireplaces, old mirrors, and exposed beams; others follow a more functional, contemporary style. ✉ *15 rue Delambre, Montparnasse, 75014,* ☎ *01–43–35–34–50,* FAX *01–43–20–46–64. 52 rooms, 6 suites, with bath. Bar, no air-conditioning, in-room data ports, cable TV, minibars, no-smoking rooms, room service, laundry service, parking (fee). AE, DC, MC, V. Métro: Vavin.*

$ ☎ **Hôtel des Bains.** A charming neighborhood, tastefully decorated rooms, satellite TV, friendly staff: can anyone explain why this hotel has only one government-ranked star? The price can't be beat, especially for the family-friendly two-room suites (€88–€115) in a separate building off the courtyard garden. ✉ *33 rue Delambre, Montparnasse, 75014,* ☎ *01–46–56–26–27,* FAX *01–42–79–82–78. 40 rooms with bath. MC, V. Métro: Vavin or Edgar Quinet.*

$ ☎ **Midi.** Don't be put off by the facade and the reception area, which might make you think you're in a chain hotel. Rooms are French-provincial style—rich colors, stenciled furniture, and lots of wrought iron—and have large floor-to-ceiling windows. Some have air-conditioning, others have whirlpool baths, and those facing the street are quite spacious. ✉ *4 av. Réné-Coty, Montparnasse, 75014,* ☎ *01–43–27–23–25,* FAX *01–43–21–24–58. 46 rooms with bath. Air-conditioning in some rooms, cable TV, minibars, parking (fee). AE, DC, MC, V. Métro and RER: Denfert-Rochereau.*

$ ☎ **Parc Montsouris.** This modest hotel in a 1930s villa is on a quiet residential street next to the city's nicest park, Parc Montsouris. Recently renovated, the small but clean rooms are embellished with attractive oak pieces and high-quality French fabrics; satellite TV is another plus. Those with showers are very inexpensive; suites sleep four. Adjoining double rooms are available. Ask for a room at the front; the views onto the park are lovely. ✉ *4 rue du Parc-Montsouris, Montparnasse, 75014,* ☎ *01–45–89–09–72,* FAX *01–45–80–92–72. 28 rooms, 7 suites, with bath. In-room data ports, no-smoking rooms, cable TV, minibars, laundry service. AE, MC, V. Métro: Montparnasse Bienvenüe.*

15ᵉ Arrondissement (Champ de Mars)

See Left Bank Lodging map.

$ 🖪 **Timhotel Tour Eiffel.** Inside this '70s-era hotel, within walking distance of the Eiffel Tower, are inexpensive, comfortable rooms with modern bathrooms, cable TV, and double-glazed windows that block out street noise. The light-wood furniture and crisp damask give rooms a clean if simple feel; some of them have great views of the Eiffel Tower. The buffet breakfast is one of the city's least expensive. ✉ *11 rue Juge, Invalides/Eiffel Tower, 75015,* ☎ *01–45–78–29–29,* ℻ *01–45–78–60–00. 40 rooms with bath. No air-conditioning, cable TV, minibars, no-smoking floor, laundry service, travel services, parking (fee). AE, DC, MC, V. Métro: Dupleix.*

16ᵉ Arrondissement (Trocadéro/Bois de Boulogne)

See Right Bank Lodging map.

$$$$ 🖪 **Saint James Paris.** Called the "only château-hôtel in Paris," this gracious, late 19th-century (viz., neo-faux-echt Second Empire) mansion is surrounded by a lush private park. Ten rooms—done in the neoclassic mode—on the third floor open onto a winter garden; the poshest option is booking one of the two duplex gatehouses. The magnificent bar-library is lined with floor-to-ceiling oak bookcases. The restaurant is reserved for guests; in warm weather, meals are served in the garden. ✉ *43 av. Bugeaud, Trocadéro, 75116,* ☎ *01–44–05–81–81; 800/447–7462 in the U.S.,* ℻ *01–44–05–81–82. 20 rooms, 28 suites, with bath. Restaurant, bar, in-room data ports, in-room safes, cable TV, minibars, no-smoking rooms, room service, sauna, health club, baby-sitting, laundry service, meeting room, free parking. AE, DC, MC, V. Métro: Porte Dauphine.*

$$$$ 🖪 **Trocadéro's Dokhan's.** Popular among fashionistas, Trocadéro's Dokhan's has an idiosyncratic style all its own. Its attention to detail is what truly sets it apart from other posh flophouses in this very upscale neighborhood: a Louis Vuitton steamer trunk elevator; an elegant bar stocked with 50 varieties of bubbly; a tea salon; and, in every room and suite, overequipped marble bathrooms with Roger et Gallet toiletries. The best rooms are the deluxe doubles; only the suites have views of the Eiffel Tower. ✉ *111 rue Lauriston, Trocadéro, 75116,* ☎ *01–53–65–66–99,* ℻ *01–53–65–66–88. 41 rooms, 4 suites, with bath. Bar, in-room data ports, in-room safes, cable TV, minibars, no-smoking rooms, room service. AE, DC, MC, V. Métro: Porte Dauphine.*

$$$ 🖪 **Alexander.** Everything about this hotel smacks of Old Europe, from the old-fashioned cage elevator to the 20-ft corniced ceilings and period wall sconces (which bathe all in warm, rosy hues). It's also on one of Paris's finest shopping avenues. Note that air-conditioning is available on the sixth floor only. ✉ *102 av. Victor Hugo, Trocadéro, 75116,* ☎ *01–45–53–64–65; 800/843–3311 in the U.S.,* ℻ *01–45–53–12–51. 60 rooms, 2 suites, with bath. Cable TV, minibars, laundry service. AE, DC, MC, V. Métro: Victor-Hugo.*

$$$ 🖪 **Square.** There's little that's "square" about this very hip boutique hotel. Rooms are bright and spacious, decorated in what is best described as extravagant minimalism. Curved doors, walls, and furniture break up a hard-edged design dominated by stripes and squares, while flowers, designer lamps, and enormous beds soften the Zen aesthetic. Large desks, plus three phone lines and a fax-answering machine in each room make it ideal for business travelers. But the reading room, art gallery, and very sleek bar make it a good choice for pleasure seek-

ers as well. ⊠ *3 rue de Boulainvilliers, Trocadéro, 75001,* ☎ *01–44–14–91–90,* 𝖥𝖠𝖷 *01–44–14–91–99,* 𝖶𝖤𝖡 *www.hotelsquare.com. 16 rooms, 6 suites, with bath. Restaurant, bar, in-room data ports, in-room safes, cable TV, minibars, room service, laundry service, parking (fee). AE, DC, MC, V. Métro: Passy.*

$$–$$$ 🏨 **Jardins du Trocadéro.** This good-value hotel near the Trocadéro and the Eiffel Tower seamlessly blends old-style French elegance (period antiques, Napoléon draperies) with modern conveniences (sound-proofing, satellite TV, VCRs, modem lines). Marble bathrooms come complete with terry robes and whirlpool baths. ⊠ *35 rue Benjamin-Franklin, Trocadéro, 75116,* ☎ *01–53–70–17–70; 800/246–0041 in the U.S.,* 𝖥𝖠𝖷 *01–53–70–17–80. 18 rooms, 5 suites, with bath. Bar, in-room data ports, in-room safes, cable TV, minibars, no-smoking rooms, room service, hot tub, laundry service, parking (fee). AE, DC, MC, V. Métro: Trocadéro.*

$ 🏨 **Keppler.** On the border of the 8e and 16e arrondissements, near the Champs-Élysées, is this small hotel in a 19th-century building. The spacious, airy rooms have simple teak furnishings and floral upholsteries and some nice amenities (like cable TV and room service) for the price. ⊠ *12 rue Keppler, Champs-Élysées, 75016,* ☎ *01–47–20–65–05,* 𝖥𝖠𝖷 *01–47–23–02–29. 49 rooms with bath. Bar, no air-conditioning, in-room safes, cable TV, no-smoking rooms, room service. AE, MC, V. Métro: George V.*

$ 🏨 **Queen's Hotel.** One of only a handful of hotels in the tony residen-
★ tial district near the Bois de Boulogne, Queen's is a small, comfortable, old-fashioned hotel with a high standard of service. Each room focuses on a different 20th-century French artist. The newly renovated rooms with baths have hot tubs and brand new beds. ⊠ *4 rue Bastien-Lepage, Bois de Boulogne, 75016,* ☎ *01–42–88–89–85,* 𝖥𝖠𝖷 *01–40–50–67–52,* 𝖶𝖤𝖡 *www.queens-hotel.fr. 22 rooms with bath. In-room safes, cable TV, minibars, no-smoking rooms. AE, DC, MC, V. Métro: Michel-Ange Auteuil.*

17e Arrondissement (Monceau/Clichy)

See Right Bank Lodging map.

$$–$$$ 🏨 **Eber-Monceau.** This small hotel—part of the Relais du Silence group—is just one block from the Parc Monceau. It attracts a stylish media and fashion set, though the engaging owner, Jean-Marc Eber, delights in welcoming all first-time guests. Rooms are tastefully done in bright, cheerful colors; ask for one overlooking the courtyard. ⊠ *18 rue Léon-Jost, Parc Monceau, 75017,* ☎ *01–46–22–60–70,* 𝖥𝖠𝖷 *01–47–63–01–01. 18 rooms, 13 with bath, 5 with shower. Bar, cable TV, minibars, laundry service, parking (fee). AE, DC, MC, V. Métro: Courcelles.*

$$ 🏨 **Étoile-Péreire.** The extremely congenial owner has created a unique,
★ intimate hotel, behind a quiet, leafy courtyard in a chic residential district. It consists of two parts: a fin-de-siècle building on the street and a 1920s annex overlooking an interior courtyard. Rooms and duplexes—in deep shades of rose or blue with crisp, white damask upholstery—have a very tailored, very finished look. Only the duplex suites have air-conditioning. The copious breakfast is legendary, featuring 40 assorted jams and jellies. ⊠ *146 bd. Péreire, Parc Monceau, 75017,* ☎ *01–42–67–60–00,* 𝖥𝖠𝖷 *01–42–67–02–90. 21 rooms, 5 suites, with bath. Bar, no air-conditioning, in-room safes, no-smoking rooms, cable TV, minibars, laundry service. AE, DC, MC, V. Métro: Péreire.*

$$ 🏨 **Excelsior.** Only a five-minute walk from Montmartre and near more than a dozen bus and métro lines is this tiny, endearing place. Rustic antiques and heavy armoires in the small, spotless rooms exude a warm, cozy feel. Request one overlooking the little garden. ⊠ *16 rue Caroline, Montmartre, 75017,* ☎ *01–45–22–50–95,* ℻ *01–45–22–59–88. 22 rooms with bath. No air-conditioning.. AE, DC, MC, V. Métro: Place de Clichy.*

$$ 🏨 **Regent's Garden.** Built in the mid-19th century by Napoléon III for his doctor, this Best Western hotel near the Arc de Triomphe is adorned, as you might imagine, with marble fireplaces, mirrors, gilt furniture, and cornicing. Ask for a room overlooking the gorgeous garden, where breakfast is served in summer. ⊠ *6 rue Pierre-Demours, Champs-Élysées, 75017,* ☎ *01–45–74–07–30,* ℻ *01–40–55–01–42. 39 rooms with bath. Cable TV, minibars, parking (fee). AE, DC, MC, V. Métro: Charles-de-Gaulle–Étoile, Ternes.*

$ 🏨 **Palma.** This modest hotel in a small 19th-century building between the Arc de Triomphe and Porte Maillot is one of the best deals in the city. Cheerful and homey, if not luxurious, rooms have basic wood furnishings and bright floral wallpaper; ask for one on the top floor with a view across Right Bank rooftops. There's air-conditioning on the sixth (top) floor only. ⊠ *46 rue Brunel, Champs-Élysées, 75017,* ☎ *01–45–74–74–51,* ℻ *01–45–74–40–90. 37 rooms with bath. No air-conditioning. AE, MC, V. Métro: Argentine.*

18ᵉ Arrondissement (Montmartre)

See Right Bank Lodging map.

$ 🏨 **Ermitage.** This elfin, family-run hotel dates from Napoléon III's time and is filled with antiques of the period. Rooms have a feeling of old-fashioned elegance. The building is only two stories high, but the hilly Montmartre neighborhood ensures that some rooms have a nice view of Paris. ⊠ *24 rue Lamarck, Montmartre, 75018,* ☎ *01–42–64–79–22,* ℻ *01–42–64–10–33. 12 rooms with bath. No air-conditioning, parking (fee). No credit cards. Métro: Lamarck Caulaincourt.*

$ 🏨 **Regyn's Montmartre.** Despite the small rooms, this owner-run hotel on Montmartre's evocative place des Abbesses provides comfortable accommodations. Rooms are spotless but functional. Ask to stay on one of the two top floors for great views of either the Eiffel Tower or Sacré-Coeur; those on the lower floors are darker and less inviting. Overall, courteous service and a relaxed charm make this an attractive choice. ⊠ *18 pl. des Abbesses, Montmartre, 75018,* ☎ *01–42–54–45–21,* ℻ *01–42–23–76–69. 22 rooms with bath. No air-conditioning. AE, MC, V. Métro: Abbesses.*

$ 🏨 **Utrillo.** This very likable hotel is on a quiet side street at the foot of Montmartre, near colorful rue Lepic. Reproduction prints and marble-top breakfast tables in every room make them feel charmingly old-fashioned, while the white-and-pastel color scheme makes them feel brighter and more spacious than they actually are. Two rooms (Nos. 61 and 63) have views of the Eiffel Tower. ⊠ *7 rue Aristide-Bruant, Montmartre, 75018,* ☎ *01–42–58–13–44,* ℻ *01–42–23–93–88. 30 rooms with bath. No air-conditioning, cable TV, minibars, sauna. AE, DC, MC, V. Métro: Abbesses, Blanche.*

19ᵉ Arrondissement (Buttes-Chaumont)

See Right Bank Lodging map.

$ 🏨 **Le Laumière.** Though it's some distance from the city center, the rock-bottom rates of this family-run hotel near the rambling Buttes-Chaumont park make it hard to resist. The staff, too, is exceptionally helpful. Unfortunately, the modern, modular furniture is less inspiring, though some of the larger rooms overlook a garden. Ask about special rates. ⊠ *4 rue Petit, Père-Lachaise, 75019,* ☎ *01–42–06–10–*

77, FAX *01–42–06–72–50. 54 rooms with bath. No air-conditioning, parking (fee). MC, V. Métro: Laumière.*

Apartment Rentals

f you will be staying longer than a week, want to do your own cooking, or need a base large enough for a family, consider a furnished rental. Policies differ from company to company, but you can generally expect a minimum required stay of one week; a refundable deposit (expect to pay $200–$500), payable on arrival; and weekly or biweekly maid service.

Following is a list of good-value residence hotels, each with multiple properties in Paris. **Citadines Résidences Hôtelières** (⊠ 18 rue Favart, Louvre/Tuileries, 75002, ☎ 01–41–05–79–04, FAX 01–44–50–23–50). **Mercure** (⊠ 20 esplanade Charles-de-Gaulle, La Défense, 92000, Nanterre, ☎ 01–46–69–79–00, FAX 01–47–25–46–48). **Orion** (⊠ 30 pl. d'Italie, Chinatown, 75013, ☎ 01–40–78–54–54; 212/688–9538; 800/546–4777 in the U.S., FAX 01–40–78–54–55; 212/688–9467 in the U.S.). **Paris Appartements Services** (⊠ 69 rue d'Argout, Louvre/Tuileries, 75002, ☎ 01–40–28–01–28, FAX 01–40–28–92–01).

The **Rothray** agency (⊠ 10 rue Nicolas Flamel, Beaubourg/Les Halles, 74004, ☎ 01–48–87–13–37 or 01–40–28–91–84, FAX 01–42–78–17–72 or 01–40–26–34–33) has pretty apartments for short- or long-term rental in stylish neighborhoods like the Marais. U.S.-based agencies also rent apartments in Paris; for information about these, *see* Lodging *in* Smart Travel Tips A to Z.

5 NIGHTLIFE AND THE ARTS

With a heritage that includes the Folies-Bergère, the Moulin Rouge and its cancan dervishes, the music-hall stars Mistinguett and Chevalier, and the headliner Josephine Baker, Paris is a city where no one has ever wondered, "Isn't there anything exciting to do tonight?" Today, the city's nightlife and arts scenes are still filled with pleasures: hear a *chansonnier* belt out Piaf, take in a Victor/Victoria show, catch a Molière play at the Comédie Française, commune with the Phantom's spirit at the Opéra Garnier, or order a Martini Chocolat at the Buddha Bar. And at the stroke of midnight, remember that Paris is one of the greatest jazz cities in the world.

NIGHTLIFE

Revised and
updated by
Christopher
Mooney

THE CITY OF LIGHT truly heats up after dark. So, if you want to paint the town *rouge* after dutifully pounding the parquet in museums all day, there's a dazzling array of options to partake of. Whether you're a jazz fiend or a dance freak, a patron of the arts or a lounge lizard seeking refuge in a bar where the model count is high, Paris provides ample destinations for nocturnal creatures. From opulent opera houses to low-key bars, dance floors in 17th-century cellars, or just the light-splintered Seine, you can find it all in Paris after dark. The hottest nightspots are near Menilmontant and Parmentier, the Bastille, and the Marais. By comparison, the Left Bank is definitely a minor happening scene. The Champs-Élysées is making a comeback, especially with stylish singles bars on its side streets, though the clientele on the main drag itself remains predominantly foreign. Midweek, people are usually home after closing hours, around 2 AM, but weekends mean late-night partying. Take note: the last métro runs between 12:30 and 1 AM (you can take a cab, though they can be hard to find between midnight and 2 AM on weekends); you may just have to stay out until the métro starts running again at 5:30 AM.

Bars

The best of the bars in Paris have character, witty waiters, local color, and inventive cocktails at prices that permit consuming without counting. The variety of bar ambiences is also impressive—there are bars serving light food, moody late-night bars, bars with DJs, and bars with live music. Other options include cafés, many of which become bars at night, and wine bars. If you want to hit bars at a relatively quiet hour, try hitting them during the *apéritif* (around 6 PM). That's when Parisians congregate to decide where they want to meet up later. In many bars, you'll find two different tariffs–*au comptoir* (cheap prices if you stand with your drink at the bar) and *à salle* (more expensive rates if you sit down at at table).

BASTILLE AND THE EASTERN RIGHT BANK

In the early 1990s, the Bastille was the hottest nightlife area in town. Though the scene for those in the know has moved to the adjacent Belleville sector, the Bastille still remains popular. The block-long rue de Lappe has more bars per foot than any other street in Paris; nearby rue de la Roquette and rue de Charonne also have many options.

Barrio Latino (⊠ 46–48 rue du Faubourg St-Antoine, 12ᵉ, Bastille/nation, ☎ 01–55–78–84–75, métro Bastille) is one of the latest additions to the Bastille party district, and it's a better bet for a drink than a meal. The decor is a lush cross of casbah, Old Havana, and SoHo loft that pulls a very mixed crowd of hipsters, including everyone from threadbare art students to ambitious young lawyers. Though pricey, it can be a fun scene, more so if the drinks were better.

Café Charbon (⊠ 109 rue Oberkampf, 11ᵉ, Oberkampf, ☎ 01–43–57–55–13, métro St-Maur, Parmentier) is a beautifully restored 19th-century café whose trendsetting clientele converses to jazz in the background. The atmosphere gets livelier after 10 PM, when a DJ takes over.

Café de la Musique (⊠ 213 av. Jean Jaurès, 19ᵉ, Parc de la Villette, ☎ 01–48–03–15–91, métro Porte de Pantin) has a large and enticing selection of cocktails and limited brasserie offerings in a comfortable setting harking back to the '40s. DJs take to the turntables from Wednesday to Saturday with a hip menu of laid-back, jazzy sounds.

Chez Prune (⊠ 36 rue Beaurepaire, 10ᵉ, République, ☎ 01–42–41–30–47, métro Jacques Bonsergent) is a lively bar with a terrace overlooking one of the footbridges crossing the Canal St-Martin. The area has become one of the hottest in Paris, yet, while you're more than likely to spot some hip fashion designer, celebrity photographer Mario Testino, and lots of beautiful people, the neighborhood ambience is refreshingly more relaxed that poseur-y.

China Club (⊠ 50 rue de Charenton, 12ᵉ, Bastille/Nation, ☎ 01–43–43–82–02, métro Ledru-Rollin) has three floors of bars and a restaurant with lacquered furnishings and a colonial-Asia theme. During happy hour (7–9), all cocktails are €5.3. There are also jazz concerts at 10 PM in the basement club on Friday and Saturday.

La Fabrique (⊠ 53 rue du Faubourg St-Antoine, 11ᵉ, Bastille/Nation, ☎ 01–43–07–67–07, métro Bastille) is a bar and restaurant that brews its own beer (look for the huge copper vats by the entrance). It really gets going every evening after 9 PM, when a DJ hits the turntables.

La Favela Chic (⊠ 18 rue du Faubourg du Temple, 11ᵉ, République, ☎ 01–40–21–38–14, métro République) was originally one of the bars that made Oberkampf into the hippest area in Paris a few years back. A couple of years ago, however, it decamped to this new, large space, hidden in a courtyard behind iron gates. There is an organic juice bar, caipirinhas and mojitos, guest DJs, and an almost nonstop Latino party atmosphere.

La Flèche d'Or (⊠ 102 bis rue de Bagnolet, 20ᵉ, Charonne, ☎ 01–43–72–04–23, métro Alexandre Dumas), housed in a former railway station, is one of the best places in Paris to take in some live music. There are concerts at 9 PM Monday to Saturday and at 5 PM on Sunday. The music runs the gamut from reggae to rock to world music, plus an open stage on Tuesday for any budding stars.

Le Gast (⊠ 5 rue Crespin-du-Gast, 11ᵉ, Oberkampf, ☎ 01–43–55–53–34, métro Ménilmontant) is a rarity—a quiet, friendly neighborhood bar in the bustling Oberkampf district. There is a curvaceous wooden counter, cocktails such as Ti punch and piña colada, and Polaroids of regulars stuck on the walls.

Le Piston Pélican (⊠ 15 rue de Bagnolet, 20ᵉ, Charonne, ☎ 01–43–70–35–00, métro Alexandre Dumas), with its pewter bar and Belle Epoque trimmings, is one of those quintessential Parisian places. Often packed with a vibrant crowd, it plays host to DJs and live music on Friday and Saturday.

Sanz Sans (⊠ 49 rue du Faubourg St-Antoine, 11ᵉ, Bastille/Nation, ☎ 01–44–75–78–78, métro Bastille) has added a new twist to bar life—the "actors" performing on the upstairs lounge's gilt-framed video screen are really the habitués of the downstairs bar.

Wax (⊠ 15 rue Daval, 11ᵉ, Bastille/Nation, ☎ 01–40–21–16–16, métro Bastille) would be worth a visit simply for its psychedelic-moderne decor—check out the orange and pink walls, multicolored squiggles on the columns, and molded plastic banquettes by the window. It is also one of the most happening places in the city music-wise, with DJs spinning techno and house every evening.

CHAMPS-ÉLYSÉES/OPÉRA/LOUVRE

The Champs-Élysées ("Les Champs" to the initiated) and the streets branching off from it have seen many glitzy bars open and quickly gain a reputation by inviting models and stars. After the first few weeks, however, the model count goes down and slicked-back hair, sharp suits, and mobile phones moves in.

Barramundi (⊠ 3 rue Taitbout, 9ᵉ, Opéra/Grands Boulevards, ☎ 01–47–70–21–21, métro Richelieu Drouot) is one of Paris's hubs of nouveau-riche chic. The lighting is dim, the copper bar long, and the walls artfully textured. During the week, chill-out and world music is piped through to the bar. By the weekend, however, things get moving with a program of regular *soirées,* with names like "Super Nature," "Reelax," and "Corpus Noctem."

Buddha Bar (✉ 8 rue Boissy d'Anglas, 8ᵉ, Champs-Élysées, ☎ 01–53–05–90–00, métro Concorde) offers one of the most glittery settings in Paris, with its towering gold-painted Buddha contemplating enough Dragon Empress screens and colorful chinoiserie for five MGM movies. The crowd ranges from camera-friendly faces—*Vogue* did a big fashion spread here—to suburban trendsetters, with groups of office ladies out on the town now making the scene. A spacious mezzanine bar overlooks the dining room, where cuisines East and West meet somewhere between Blandsville and California.

Le Fumoir (✉ 6 rue Amiral-de-Coligny, 1ᵉʳ, Louvre/Tuileries, ☎ 01–42–92–00–24, métro Louvre) is a fashionable spot for a late-afternoon beer or early evening cocktail (dinner is also served). There's a large bar in front, a library with shelves of books in back, and leather couches throughout.

Harry's New York Bar (✉ 5 rue Daunou, 2ᵉ, Opéra/Grands Boulevards, ☎ 01–42–61–71–14, métro Opéra), a cozy, wood-paneled hangout decorated with dusty college pennants and popular with expatriates, is haunted by the ghosts of Ernest Hemingway and F. Scott Fitzgerald. This place claims to have invented the Bloody Mary, and one way or another, the bartenders here do mix a mean one.

Man Ray (✉ 34 rue Marbeuf, 8ᵉ, Champs-Élysées, ☎ 01–56–88–36–36, métro Franklin-D.-Roosevelt) is one of the hottest places in town, which is not surprising given that it is owned by Johnny Depp, Sean Penn, and Simply Red's Mick Hucknall. The ravishing Asian–Art Deco style is reminiscent of a slightly Disneyesque 1930s supper club in Chinatown. The bar is open until 2 AM and serves cocktails, tapas, and sushi.

Polo Room (✉ 3 rue Lord Byron, 8ᵉ, Champs-Élysées, ☎ 01–40–74–07–78, métro George V), situated on the first floor of a building in a sleepy street off the Champs-Élysées, is the very first martini bar in Paris. The American owner's target clientele is the world of business (35- to 45-year-olds), and his aim is to give this space a very New York feel. There are polo photos on the wall, a 36-ft bar, and a selection of 28 different martini cocktails (who can resist the Martini Chocolat?). There are also regular live jazz concerts and DJs every Friday and Saturday night.

LATIN QUARTER/ST-GERMAIN-DES-PRÉS

In the heart of expensive (and touristy) Paris, bars here can't afford to be too cutting-edge. While the price you may pay for your beer can be high, the good news is that you'll probably meet a lot of other English-speaking travelers out on the town.

Alcazar (✉ 62 rue Mazarine, 6ᵉ, St-Germain-des-Prés, ☎ 01–53–10–19–99, métro Odéon), Sir Terence Conran's first makeover of a Parisian landmark, has a stylish bar on the first floor, where you can sip a glass of wine under the huge glass roof. From Wednesday to Saturday, a live DJ spins either lounge or Latin music.

Chez Georges (✉ 11 rue de Canettes, 6ᵉ, St-Germain-des-Prés, ☎ 01–43–26–79–15, métro Mabillon) has been serving glasses of red wine, pastis, and beer for the past 60-odd years. Down in the basement, young folk crowd around tiny tables, but don't be intimidated if the place looks packed—there's always room to squeeze in somewhere, and the regulars are more than willing to make new friends.

Le Comptoir (✉ 5 rue Monsieur-Le-Prince, 6ᵉ, Latin Quarter, ☎ 01–43–29–12–05, métro Odéon) is a wine bar serving Burgundies and Bordeaux by the glass, as well as more unusual wines, such as ones from Corsica.

Les Etages (⊠ 5 rue de Buci, 6ᵉ, St-Germain-des-Prés, ☎ 01–46–34–26–26, métro Odéon) is a laid-back, student-y type of place occupying three floors of a building near St-Germain-des-Prés. The walls are rustic red and ocher, the decor is simple, and the terrace is the perfect place to sit out in the summer.

Oya (⊠ 25 rue de la Reine Blanche, 13ᵉ, Latin Quarter, ☎ 01–47–07–59–59, métro Gobelins) is a haven for fans of board games. The owners have assembled more than 200 from around the world, which you can play for €4.6 a game.

Le Piano Vache (⊠ 8 rue Laplace, 5ᵉ, Latin Quarter, ☎ 01–46–33–75–03, métro Cardinal Lemoine) has music that is sufficiently angst-inspiring and a bar sufficiently dark to keep you from getting too optimistic. The place is wallpapered with '70s posters, super-smoky, and has a Goth party every Wednesday eve.

MARAIS

Creative souls tend to live in Le Marais, so the neighborhood bars are very welcoming and pleasant.

Le Café du Trésor (⊠ 5 rue Trésor, 4ᵉ, Le Marais, ☎ 01–44–78–06–60, métro St-Paul) is a lively, sophisticated bar, where every night except Sunday DJs spin a mixture of house and funk. There's also a restaurant adjacent.

La Chaise au Plafond (⊠ 10 rue du Trésor, 4ᵉ, Le Marais, ☎ 01–42–76–03–22, métro St-Paul) has the feel of a traditional bistro with a few offbeat contemporary touches. Never overcrowded, it's the perfect place for an excellent glass of wine.

La Perla (⊠ 26 rue François Miron, 4ᵉ, Le Marais, ☎ 01–42–77–59–40, métro Hôtel de Ville, St-Paul) is one of the chic-est spots in town for Latin lovers. Sit back, sip a margarita, munch on a few tapas, and take in all the lovely people.

La Tartine (⊠ 24 rue de Rivoli, 4ᵉ, Le Marais, ☎ 01–42–72–76–85, métro St-Paul) serves inexpensive glasses of wine and *tartines* (open-face sandwiches) in a tatty, almost seedy turn-of-the-20th-century bar that has earned antihero status among the cognoscenti.

Le Web Bar (⊠ 32 rue de Picardie, 3ᵉ, Le Marais, ☎ 01–42–72–66–55, métro Temple) is a lively, eclectic place, where you can surf the Net, join in free salsa classes on Monday, or take in a photo exhibition or short film. There are also musical brunches on Sunday and a whole host of soirées. For detailed information of events, check out the Web site (www.webbar.fr).

MONTMARTRE

Amid the tourist tat are some distinctive options for imbibing.

Café Carmen (⊠ 22 rue de Douai, 9ᵉ, Montmartre, ☎ 01–45–26–21–17, métro Pigalle) bears a name that is homage to Georges Bizet, whose opera set Paris ablaze in the early 20th century. The building once belonged to his composer's widow, then became a soup kitchen, then a high-class brothel. Today, it maintains the magnificent Napoléon III-era molded ceilings, chandeliers, and gilt mirrors. In the basement is a cozy bar, where there are regular operetta concerts given by a distant relative of Toulouse-Lautrec and evenings dominated by deep lounge music.

Le Jungle Montmartre (⊠ 32 rue Gabrielle, 18ᵉ, Montmartre, ☎ 01–46–06–75–69, métro Abbesses) is a gem of a place in a very sleepy, off-the-beat street in Montmartre. Upstairs is an African restaurant; downstairs is a small bar with Senegalese sculptures and tiger and leopard designs on the tabletops. There is a DJ every evening from 9 PM (music ranges from reggae and funk to techno and drum and bass), who is often joined by traditional African musicians.

Moloko (✉ 26 rue Fontaine, 9ᵉ, Montmartre, ☎ 01–48–74–50–26, métro Blanche), a smoky late-night bar with several rooms, a mezzanine, a jukebox, and a small dance floor, is a popular spot with a trendy, fun-loving crowd.

Le Sancerre (✉ 35 rue des Abbesses, 18ᵉ, Montmartre, ☎ 01–42–58–08–20, métro Abbesses), a café by day, turns into a lively watering hole for jovial Montmartrois and artist types at night.

MONTPARNASSE

Raise a glass to the resident spirits of long-gone writers, artists, and poets.

American Bar at La Closerie des Lilas (✉ 171 bd. du Montparnasse, 6ᵉ, Montparnasse, ☎ 01–40–51–34–50, métro Montparnasse) lets you drink in the swirling action of the adjacent restaurant and brasserie and do it at a bar hallowed by plaques honoring such former habitués as Man Ray, Jean-Paul Sartre, and Samuel Beckett. Happily, many Parisians still call this watering hole their home-away-from-home.

Hotel Bars

Elegant and upscale, with a classic Parisian feel, the city's hotel bars are quiet spots to meet for a drink. Following are some of the best: **Bristol** (✉ 112 rue du Faubourg St-Honoré, 8ᵉ, Champs-Élysées, ☎ 01–53–43–43–42, métro Miromesnil) attracts the rich and powerful. **Costes** (✉ 239 rue St-Honoré, Louvre/Tuileries, 75001, ☎ 01–42–44–50–50) attracts many many big names in the fashion world during Collections weeks. **Crillon** (✉ 10 pl. de la Concorde, 8ᵉ, Champs-Élysées, ☎ 01–44–71–15–39, métro Concorde) allures with creamy elegance. **Le Dokhan's** (✉ 117 rue Lauriston, 16ᵉ, Trocadéro, ☎ 01–53–65–66–99, métro Trocadéro) has a bar decorated by top Parisian designer Frédéric Méchiche (emerald velvet walls and gilt Empire-style boiserie make for a very soigné setting) which serves nothing but champagne. Every week, there is a different champagne by the glass, as well as special musical evenings once a month. **L'Hôtel** (✉ 10 rue des Beaux-Arts, 6ᵉ, St-Germain-des-Prés, ☎ 01–44–41–99–00, métro St-Germain-des-Prés) had stylemeister Jacques Garcia revamp the historic decor. **Inter-Continental** (✉ 3 rue Castiglione, 1ᵉʳ, Louvre/Tuileries, ☎ 01–44–77–10–47, métro Tuileries) comes replete with 19th-century grandeur. **Lutétia** (✉ 45 bd. Raspail, 6ᵉ, Montparnasse, ☎ 01–49–54–46–09, métro Sèvres Babylone) has three bars, one of which, the Saint Germain, offers a seductive boîte with red table lamps, semi-nude bronze statues, and live jazz four nights a week: no wonder legend Catherine Deneuve like to chill out here. **Le Meurice** (✉ 228 rue de Rivoli, 1ᵉʳ, Louvre/Tuileries, ☎ 01–44–58–10–66, métro Tuileries). **Ritz Hemingway Bar** (✉ 15 pl. Vendôme, 1ᵉʳ, Louvre/Tuileries, ☎ 01–43–16–33–65, métro Opéra) has Colin Field, the best barman in Paris, and Papa memorabilia (this is where the writer drank to the liberation of Paris) but with a dress code and cognac aux truffes on the menu, Hemingway might now stay away; the Ritz's Vendôme bar is far prettier, as it overlooks the Espadon restaurant garden terrace.

Cabarets

Paris's cabarets range from boîtes once haunted by Picasso and Piaf to those sinful showplaces where tableaux vivants offer acres of bare female flesh (so much so that one critic recently exclaimed, "I'm not going to look anymore unless somebody has three of them"). These extravaganzas—sadly more Las Vegas than the petticoat vision recreated by Hollywood in Baz Lurmann's *Moulin Rouge*—are often shunned by Parisians but loved by tourists. You can dine at many of them, but come with tempered expectations, since the food is more about mass-catering than providing gourmand pleasure: prices range from €30 (simple admission plus one drink) to more than €115 (dinner plus show). For €61–€77, you get a seat plus half a bottle of champagne.

L'Âne Rouge (✉ 3 rue Laugier, 17ᵉ, Champs-Élysées, ☏ 01–43–80–79–97, métro Ternes) is a typical French cabaret playing to a mixed Parisian and foreign crowd, where the emphasis is on laughs and entertainment, with a host of singers, magicians, comedians, and ventriloquists.

Au Lapin Agile (✉ 22 rue des Saules, 18ᵉ, Montmartre, ☏ 01–46–06–85–87, métro Lamarck Caulaincourt), in Montmartre, considers itself the doyen of cabarets and is a miraculous survivor from the 19th century. Founded in 1860, it is still housed in a fetchingly picturesque maison-cottage, once a favorite subject of painter Maurice Utrillo. At one point owned by Aristide Bruant (immortalized in many Toulouse-Lautrec posters), it became the home-away-from-home for Braque, Modigliani, Apollinaire, and Vlaminck. The most famous habitué, however, was Picasso, who once paid for a meal with one of his paintings, then promptly went out and painted another, which he named after this place—today, after being purchased for nearly $50 million, it hangs in New York's Metropolitan Museum. Happily, this glamour hasn't entirely affected the Nimble Rabbit—prices are lower than elsewhere, as it is more of a large bar than a full-blown cabaret. If you want to commune with the spirit of the past (and any visiting ghosts), the best time to come is during the early morning hours.

Au Pied de la Butte (✉ 62 bd. Rochechouart, 18ᵉ, Montmartre, ☏ 01–46–06–02–86, métro Anvers) played host in the past to Edith Piaf, Jacques Brel, and Maurice Chevalier. Today, it has three shows per evening with modern-day songsters interpreting the traditional French repertoire and magicians performing tricks.

Le Caveau de la Bolée (✉ 25 rue de l'Hirondelle, 6ᵉ, Latin Quarter, ☏ 01–43–54–62–20, métro St-Michel) was a prison in the 14th century, but these days you are free to sing along to Edith Piaf melodies or be entertained by magicians, comics, and mind readers.

Crazy Horse (✉ 12 av. George V, 8ᵉ, Champs-Élysées, ☏ 01–47–23–32–32, métro Alma-Marceau) is one of the best-known clubs, which celebrated its 50th anniversary two years ago. It is renowned for pretty dancers and raunchy routines characterized by lots of humor and few clothes.

Éléphant Bleu (✉ 49 rue de Ponthieu, 8ᵉ, Champs-Élysées, ☏ 01–42–25–17–61, métro Franklin-D.-Roosevelt) is a cabaret-cum-restaurant with an exotic (often Asian) touch to most of its shows.

Lido (✉ 116 bis av. des Champs-Élysées, 8ᵉ, Champs-Élysées, ☏ 01–40–76–56–10, métro George V) stars the famous Bluebell Girls; the owners claim no show this side of Las Vegas can rival it for special effects. The extravaganza comes with dinner (€120–170) or Champagne only (€70–85).

Le Limonaire (✉ 21 rue Bergère, 9ᵉ, Opéra/Grands Boulevards, ☏ 01–45–23–33–33, métro Grands Boulevards) is a small restaurant that simply oozes with Parisian charm. This is the kind of place where you could imagine Edith Piaf belting out "*Je ne regrette rien,*" and, in fact, imagination is often not required at 10 PM, Tuesday to Sunday, when the service stops and a singer takes to the floor. The house specialty is *la chanson française,* and one of its finest guest artists is the modern-day Little Sparrow, Kalifa. There are also traditional *bals musettes* (pop-

ular dances with accordion music) at 6 PM the first Sunday of every
month and silent-film screening the third Sunday.

Madame Arthur (✉ 75 bis rue des Martyrs, 18ᵉ, Montmartre, ☎ 01–
42–54–40–21, métro Pigalle) stages a wacky burlesque drag show—
men dressed as famous French female vocalists—that's not for the fainthearted. Boys, as they say, will be girls.

Michou (✉ 80 rue des Martyrs, 18ᵉ, Montmartre, ☎ 01–46–06–16–
04, métro Pigalle) is owned by the always blue-clad Michou, famous
in Paris circles. The men on stage wear extravagant drag—high camp
and parody are the order of the day.

Moulin Rouge (✉ 82 bd. de Clichy, 18ᵉ, Montmartre, ☎ 01–53–09–
82–82, métro Blanche), that old favorite at the foot of Montmartre,
mingles the Doriss Girls, the cancan, and a horse in an extravagant
spectacle. Two shows a night are offered, with tickets ranging from
€125 to €155.

Paradis Latin (✉ 28 rue du Cardinal Lemoine, 5ᵉ, Latin Quarter, ☎
01–43–25–28–28, métro Cardinal Lemoine) is perhaps the liveliest, busiest, and trendiest cabaret on the Left Bank. Show and dinner run from
€125 to €200, €75 for show and Champagne.

Clubs

Paris's *boîtes de nuit* (nightclubs) tend to be both expensive and exclusive—if you know someone who is a regular or your face graces the
cover of *Vogue,* you'll have an easier time getting through the door. If
you don't come up to the standards of the "model-friendly" door policy, stay happy: it would be a stretch to call Paris's club scene really
"happening," as it's really just an outlet for a scrambling crowd of rich,
spoiled teens. Many clubs are closed Monday and some on Tuesday.
The best soirées tend to take place on Thursday and are generally more
intimate and elitist than at the weekend. Nowadays, specific soirées
are hosted at many different venues, so the party-hearty crowd is no
longer faithful to just one club; on Monday, they may go to Disco Night
at the Queen, on Friday to "Automatik" at the Rex, on Saturday to
"Scream" at the Elysée Montmartre. Many of these, such as "Scream"
and "TGV," take place either just once or twice a month. For information about dates, look out for flyers in bars.

BASTILLE AND THE EASTERN RIGHT BANK

Les Bains (✉ 7 rue du Bourg-l'Abbé, 3ᵉ, République, ☎ 01–48–87–
01–80, métro Étienne Marcel), opened in 1978 and often (back in the
disco era) featured in the pages of French *Vogue,* is very much a
Parisian institution. The upstairs bar and restaurant is generally packed
wall-to-wall with stars, while downstairs house music rules on the dance
floors. First, however, you have to get past the particularly selective
door policy: if you don't look like Claudia Schiffer or Brad Pitt's double, this could prove more difficult than you might imagine.

Le Balajo (✉ 9 rue de Lappe, 11ᵉ, Bastille/Nation, ☎ 01–47–00–07–
87, métro Bastille), in an old Java ballroom, offers a bit of everything:
salsa, techno, and retro. On Thursdays and Sunday afternoon, there
are even *bals musettes,* which headline the accordion music so evocative of old-time Montmartre street balls.

Batofar (✉ 11 quai François Mauriac, 11ᵉ, Chinatown, ☎ 01–56–29–
10–00, métro Bibliothèque) is an old Port of Paris lighthouse tug, now
refitted to include a bar, a club, and a concert venue that's become one
of the hippest spots in town. Star DJs from other European capitals
often arrive to animate the dance floor.

Les Étoiles (✉ 61 rue Château d'Eau, 10ᵉ, Opéra/Grands Boulevards,
☎ 01–47–70–60–56, métro Château d'Eau), open Thursday–Saturday,

is the place for salsa (with a live band). Dinner, featuring South American specialties, is served 9–11.

Le Gibus (✉ 18 rue du Faubourg-du-Temple, 11ᵉ, République, ☎ 01–47–00–78–88, métro République) is one of Paris's most famous music venues. In more than 30 years, there have been 6,500 concerts and more than 3,000 performers (including The Police, Deep Purple, and Billy Idol). Today, the Gibus's cellars are *the* place for trance, techno, and jungle. There are also regular Latino house parties on Saturday.

La Java (✉ 105 rue du Faubourg du Temple, 10ᵉ, République, ☎ 01–42–02–20–52, métro Belleville), where Edith Piaf and Maurice Chevalier made their names, has live Latin music and Cuban jam sessions on Thursday, Friday, and Saturday night. Before the party proper gets under way, there are also salsa lessons.

CHAMPS-ÉLYSÉES AND GRANDS BOULEVARDS

Le Cabaret (✉ 68 rue Pierre-Charron, 8ᵉ, Champs-Élysées, ☎ 01–42–89–44–14, métro Franklin-D.-Roosevelt), once just that, still delights with its original red velvet and flock wallpaper. Nowadays it's a hip, chic club. Princess Caroline of Monaco, Liza Minnelli, and Naomi Campbell have all been spotted here.

Maxim's (✉ 3 rue Royale, 8ᵉ, Louvre/Tuileries, ☎ 01–42–65–27–94, métro Concorde) used to be the most stylish restaurant in the city. Today, the restaurant may still be legendary, but its worn-out Belle Epoque cake frosting tends to attract only tourists. Or rather, it did until recently. Now, party organizer Leo Chabot has turned it into the hottest spot in the city on Friday evenings. Young designers, models, and lots of beautiful people, dressed head-to-toe in designer frocks, flock here to groove to the trip-hop and trance in the bar or the funk, salsa, and rock in the blue-lit Jardin d'Hiver.

Niel's (✉ 27 av. Ternes, 17ᵉ, Champs-Élysées, ☎ 01–47–66–45–00, métro Ternes) attracts a well-off set of regulars, as well as top models and showbiz glitterati. Music runs the gamut from salsa to house.

Le Rex (✉ 5 blvd. Poissonnière, 2ᵉ, Opéra/ Grands Boulevards, ☎ 01–42–36–10–96, métro Grands Boulevards), open Thursday through Saturday, is the Paris temple of techno and house. On Thursday, you'll often find France's most famous DJ, Laurent Garnier, at the turntables. The techno "Automatik" soirées on Fridays are particularly popular.

Le VIP Room (✉ 76 av. des Champs-Élysées, 8ᵉ, Champs-Élysées, ☎ 01–56–69–16–66, métro Franklin-D.-Roosevelt), located under Planet Hollywood, is owned by Jean Roch, the ringleader of nightlife in St-Tropez. If you like spending your evenings with young women dressed in micro-mini dresses and men sporting shades (even in the dark), then this is the place for you. You may even spot a few stars. Leonardo DiCaprio, George Michael, and French rocker Johnny Hallyday have all put in appearances. Beware: the club is frequently booked for private parties and film premieres (call ahead to check availability).

MONTMARTRE

Bus Palladium (✉ 6 rue Fontaine, 9ᵉ, Montmartre, ☎ 01–53–21–07–33, métro Blanche) invites women free on Tuesday; on other nights it caters to a fashionable but relaxed crowd. Fear no techno; it serves up a mixture of rock, funk, and disco.

L'Élysée Montmartre (✉ 72 bd. de Rochechouart, 18ᵉ, Montmartre, ☎ 01–55–07–06–00, métro Pigalle) holds extremely popular *bals* (balls) every other Saturday, where the music runs the gamut of hits from the '40s to the '80s and the DJ is backed up by a 10-piece orchestra. Its "Scream" parties (with a predominantly gay crowd) are on top of every serious clubber's list.

Les Folies Pigalle (✉ 11 pl. Pigalle, 9ᵉ, Montmartre, ☎ 01–48–78–55–25, métro Pigalle) is a former cabaret decorated like a '30s bordello. The ambience is decadent; the music varies according to the day of the week (hip-hop on Wednesday and Sunday, a mixture of house and techno at other times); and on Saturday from 9 to 11 PM there's a male strip show (for women only).

MONTPARNASSE

Dancing La Coupole (✉ 100 bd. du Montparnasse, 14ᵉ, Montparnasse, ☎ 01–43–27–56–00, métro Vavin) has retro disco on Friday and Saturday night; and on Tuesday, salsa, preceded at 8:30 by an optional refresher course—an idea that seems to have breathed new life into this monument. There are also popular tea dances at 3 PM on Sunday.

L'Enfer (✉ 34 rue du Départ, 14ᵉ, Montparnasse, ☎ 01–42–71–79–19, métro Montparnasse Bienvenüe) has been given a second lease on life in recent years, with the organization of a number of regular, predominantly gay soirées. There is "Scandal" every Thursday, the monthly "House of Legend," as well as the after-party "Discotek" on the same evenings as "Scream" at the Élysée Montmartre.

Gay and Lesbian Bars and Clubs

Gay and lesbian bars and clubs are mostly concentrated in the Marais and include some of the hippest addresses in the city. Keep in mind, however, that clubs fall in and out of favor at lightning speed. The best way to find out what's hot is by picking up a copy of the free weekly *e.m@le* in one of the bars listed below.

For Men and Women

Amnésia Café (✉ 42 rue Vieille-du-Temple, 4ᵉ, Le Marais, ☎ 01–42–72–16–94, métro Rambuteau, St-Paul) has an under-lit bar and Art Deco ceiling paintings that attract a young, professional gay and lesbian crowd.

Banana Café (✉ 13 rue de la Ferronnerie, 1ᵉʳ, Beaubourg/Les Halles, ☎ 01–42–33–35–31, métro Châtelet Les Halles) has a trendy, energetic, and scantily clad mixed crowd; dancing on the tables is the norm.

Le Dépôt (✉ 10 rue aux Ours, 3ᵉ, République, ☎ 01–44–54–96–96, métro Étienne Marcel) is a bar, club, and back room. The ever-popular Gay Tea Dance on Sunday (from 5 PM) is held here.

Queen (✉ 102 av. des Champs-Élysées, 8ᵉ, Champs-Élysées, ☎ 01–53–89–08–90, métro George V) is one of the most talked-about nightclubs in Paris: everyone lines up to get in. Monday is disco night. On Sunday, there is the "Overkitsch" party, with a mix of hits from the '80s. On other days, expect to dance to house and techno; the "Break" evening on Wednesday is particularly popular and quite mixed.

Mostly Men

Bar d'Art/Le Duplex (✉ 25 rue Michel-Le-Comte, 3ᵉ, Beaubourg/Les Halles, ☎ 01–42–72–80–86, métro Rambuteau) is frequented by young, tortured-artist types who enjoy the frequent art exhibitions, alternative music, and dim lighting.

Café Cox (✉ 15 rue des Archives, 4ᵉ, Le Marais, ☎ 01–42–72–08–00, métro Hôtel de Ville) is a prime gay pickup joint. Behind the smoked-glass windows, men line the walls and check out the talent.

L'Open Café (✉ 17 rue des Archives, 4ᵉ, Le Marais, ☎ 01–42–72–26–18, métro Hôtel de Ville) is more convivial than neighboring Café Cox, with sunny yellow walls. In summer, the crowd spills out onto the street.

Le Scorp (✉ 25 bd. Poissonnière, 9ᵉ, Opéra/Grands Boulevards, ☎ 01–40–26–01–50, métro Rue Montmartre) is one of Paris's longest-standing gay nightclubs. Wednesday is disco night, Thursday is devoted to

French pop, Friday to house, Saturday to techno, and Sunday to New Wave.

Mostly Women

Alcantara Café (✉ 30 rue du Roi de Sicile, 4ᵉ, Le Marais, ☎ 01–42–74–45–00, métro St-Paul) is a cool and friendly bar in the heart of the Marais. There is happy hour every evening from 6 to 8 PM, regular events (flamenco, tap, or salsa dancers), and a DJ in the tiny bar in the basement on Friday and Saturday evenings. Men are allowed in small numbers on weekdays.

Champmeslé (✉ 4 rue Chabanais, 2ᵉ, Opéra/Grands Boulevards, ☎ 01–42–96–85–20, métro Bourse) is the hub of lesbian nightlife (open until dawn). Thursday night (starting at 10) is a cabaret of traditional French songs. There are also regular painting exhibitions and a *voyante* (fortune-teller) on hand the last Friday and Saturday of every month.

Le Pulp (✉ 25 bd. Poissonnière, 2ᵉ, Opéra/Grands Boulevards, ☎ 01–40–26–01–93, métro Grands Boulevards), one of the rare lesbian clubs in Paris, is housed in a space which hosts tea dances for retirees in the afternoon. On Thursday, the music is house and guys are admitted in small numbers. On Friday and Saturday, it's strictly women-only.

Les Scandaleuses (✉ 8 rue des Écouffes, 4ᵉ, Le Marais, ☎ 01–48–87–39–26, métro St-Paul) is probably Paris's hippest lesbian hangout. Men are also allowed in (in small numbers), as long as they are accompanied by "scandalous women."

Jazz Clubs

Remember Audrey Hepburn scatting to "Basil Metabolism" in that dark and smoky jazz club in *Funny Face*? Sorry—you won't find many of those cellar places left, but Paris remains the celebrated home of *le jazz hot*, and its performing calendar offers plenty of variety, including some fine, distinctive local talent. Most jazz clubs are in the Latin Quarter or around Les Halles. For nightly schedules, consult the specialty magazines, *Jazz Hot, Jazzman,* or *Jazz Magazine.* Note that nothing gets going until 10 or 11 PM and that entry prices vary widely from about €6 to more than €15. Also look out for the annual **Villette Jazz Festival** (☎ 01–40–03–75–75), held at La Villette at the end of June. The A Fleur de Jazz Festival also offers free concerts at 4:30 PM on Saturday and Sunday at the Parc Floral in the Bois de Vincennes from early March to the end of July.

CHAMPS-ÉLYSÉES

Lionel Hampton Jazz Club (✉ Méridien Hotel, 81 bd. Gouvion–St-Cyr, 17ᵉ, Porte Maillot, ☎ 01–40–68–30–42, métro Porte Maillot), named for the zingy vibraphonist loved by Parisians, hosts a roster of international jazz musicians in a spacious, comfortable set of rooms.

LES HALLES/GARE DU NORD

Au Duc des Lombards (✉ 42 rue des Lombards, 1ᵉʳ, Beaubourg/Les Halles, ☎ 01–42–33–22–88, métro Châtelet Les Halles) has modern contemporary jazz in an ill-lit, romantic bebop venue with decor inspired by the Paris métro.

Le Baiser Salé (✉ 58 rue des Lombards, 1ᵉʳ, Beaubourg/Les Halles, ☎ 01–42–33–37–71, métro Châtelet Les Halles) attracts a younger crowd with salsa, rhythm and blues, fusion, and funk.

New Morning (✉ 7 rue des Petites-Écuries, 10ᵉ, Opéra/Grands Boulevards, ☎ 01–45–23–51–41, métro Château d'Eau) is a premier spot for serious fans of avant-garde jazz, folk, and world music; the look is spartan, the mood reverential.

Le Petit Opportun (⊠ 15 rue des Lavandières–Ste-Opportune, 1ᵉʳ, Beaubourg/Les Halles, ☎ 01–42–36–01–36, métro Châtelet Les Halles), in a converted bistro, always has French artists and sometimes headlines top-flight American soloists with French backup.

Le Sunset (⊠ 60 rue des Lombards, 1ᵉʳ, Beaubourg/Les Halles, ☎ 01–40–26–46–60, métro Châtelet Les Halles) delivers jazz from both French and American musicians, with an accent on jazz fusion and groove. Concerts start at 10 PM.

Le Sunside (⊠ 60 rue des Lombards, 1ᵉʳ, Beaubourg/Les Halles, ☎ 01–40–26–21–25, métro Châtelet Les Halles) is at the same address as Le Sunset. It specializes in more classic, traditional jazz and swing. There is also a featured vocalist on Monday night. Concerts start at 9 PM.

LATIN QUARTER/ST-GERMAIN/MONTPARNASSE

Le Bilboquet (⊠ 13 rue St-Benoît, 6ᵉ, St-Germain-des-Prés, ☎ 01–45–48–81–84, métro St-Germain-des-Prés) is the place to find primarily French musicians playing mainstream jazz in a faded Belle Epoque salon.

Le Petit Journal (⊠ 71 bd. St-Michel, 5ᵉ, Latin Quarter, ☎ 01–43–26–28–59, métro Cluny La Sorbonne; ⊠ 13 rue du Commandant-Mouchotte, 14ᵉ, Montparnasse, ☎ 01–43–21–56–70, métro Montparnasse Bienvenüe), with two locations, has long attracted the greatest names in French and international jazz. It now specializes in Dixieland jazz and also serves dinner 8:30–midnight.

Pubs

Pubs wooing English-speaking clients with a selection of beers are becoming increasingly popular with Parisians. They are also good places to find reasonably priced food at off-hours.

The Auld Alliance (⊠ 80 rue François Miron, 4ᵉ, Le Marais, ☎ 01–48–04–30–40, métro St-Paul) has walls adorned with Scottish shields and a bar staff dressed in kilts. There are more than 120 malt whiskies to choose from, true Scottish beers, darts and pool competitions, and the odd evening of bagpipe music.

Connolly's Corner (⊠ 12 rue Mirbel, 5ᵉ, Latin Quarter, ☎ 01–43–31–94–22, métro Place Monge) is a convivial Irish pub with Guinness on tap and traditional Irish music on Tuesday, Thursday, Saturday, and Sunday. Just make sure you don't wear a tie—it will be snipped off and stuck on the wall (though you'll be compensated with a free pint).

The Cricketer (⊠ 41 rue des Mathurins, 8ᵉ, Opéra/Grands Boulevards, ☎ 01–40–07–01–45, métro St-Augustin) replies to the virtual Irish monopoly on Paris pubs with Newcastle Brown Ale on tap. Cricket memorabilia adorn the walls.

Finnegan's Wake (⊠ 9 rue des Boulangers, 5ᵉ, Latin Quarter, ☎ 01–46–34–23–65, métro Jussieu) is a wonderfully quiet and charming Irish pub situated on a steep cobbled street. There is Guinness, Kilkenny, and Murphys on tap, Breton lessons on Monday at 7 PM, and concerts of Irish music on Friday. Happy Hour runs from 6 to 8 PM every evening.

Frog and Rosbif (⊠ 116 rue St-Denis, 2ᵉ, Beaubourg/Les Halles, ☎ 01–42–36–34–73, métro Étienne Marcel) has everything you could want from an English "local." Beers are brewed on premises, and rugby and football matches are shown on the giant-screen TV.

Rock, Pop, and World Music Venues

Unlike jazz, French rock is generally not considered to be on a par with its American and British cousins. Even so, Paris is a great place to catch some of your favorite groups, because concert halls tend to be smaller and tickets can be less expensive. It's also a good spot to see all kinds of world music. Most places charge about €14–€18 and get going around 11 PM. The best way to find out about upcoming concerts is to consult the bulletin boards in FNAC stores.

Le Bataclan (⊠ 50 bd. Voltaire, 11ᵉ, Oberkampf, ☏ 01–43–14–35–35, métro Oberkampf) is a legendary venue for live rock, rap, and reggae in an intimate setting.

Casino de Paris (⊠ 16 rue de Clichy, 9ᵉ, Opéra/Grands Boulevards, ☏ 01–49–95–99–99, métro Trinité), once a favorite with Serge Gainsbourg, has a horseshoe balcony and a cramped, cozy, music-hall feel.

La Cigale (⊠ 120 bd. Rochechouart, 18ᵉ, Montmartre, ☏ 01–49–25–89–99, métro Pigalle) often plays host to up-and-coming French rock bands.

Divan du Monde (⊠ 75 rue des Martyrs, 18ᵉ, Montmartre, ☏ 01–44–92–77–66, métro Pigalle) attracts a varied crowd, depending on the music of the evening: reggae, soul, funk, or salsa. Most nights after the concert, a DJ takes over.

L'Élysée Montmartre (⊠ 72 bd. Rochechouart, 18ᵉ, Montmartre, ☏ 01–55–07–06–00, métro Anvers) dates from Gustave Eiffel, its builder, who, it is hoped, liked a good concert. It's one of the prime venues for emerging French and international rock groups.

Olympia (⊠ 18 rue Caumartin, 9ᵉ, Opéra/Grands Boulevards, ☏ 01–47–42–25–49, métro Madeleine), a legendary venue once favored by Jacques Brel and Edith Piaf, still hosts leading French singers. Rather strangely, the original hall was demolished a few years ago to make way for an underground carpark and an identical theater constructed in the same building.

L'Opus Café (⊠ 167 quai de Valmy, 10ᵉ, Canal-St-Martin, ☏ 01–40–34–70–00, métro Louis Blanc), on the picturesque Canal St-Martin, has jazz and soul concerts.

Palais Omnisports de Paris-Bercy (⊠ 8 bd. de Bercy, 12ᵉ, Bastille/Nation, ☏ 08–25–03–00–31, métro Bercy) is the largest venue in Paris and is where English and American pop stars perform.

Zenith (⊠ Parc de La Villette, 211 av. Jean-Jaurès, 19ᵉ, Parc de La Villette, ☏ 01–42–08–60–00, métro Porte de Pantin) is a large concert hall that primarily stages rock shows; check posters and listings for details. The neighboring Grande Halle de La Villette organizes lively world music festivals in June.

After-Hours Dining

Chances are that some of your nocturnal forays will have you looking for sustenance at an unlikely hour. If so, you might find it handy to know that there are restaurants open around the clock.

L'Alsace (⊠ 39 av. des Champs-Élysées, 8ᵉ, Champs-Élysées, ☏ 01–53–93–97–00, métro Franklin-D.-Roosevelt) is a smart, if characterless, brasserie-restaurant, serving seafood and sauerkraut around the clock.

Au Chien Qui Fume (⊠ 33 rue du Pont-Neuf, 1ᵉʳ, Louvre/Tuileries, ☏ 01–42–36–07–42, métro Les Halles), open until 2 AM, is filled with witty paintings (in the style of old masters) of smoking dogs. Traditional French cuisine and seafood platters are served.

Au Pied de Cochon (⊠ 6 rue Coquillière, 1ᵉʳ, Beaubourg/les Halles, ☏ 01–40–13–77–00, métro Les Halles), near St-Eustache church, once catered to the all-night workers at the adjacent Paris food market. Its Second Empire carvings and gilt have been restored, and traditional dishes like pig's trotters and chitterling sausage still grace the menu.

Le Bienvenu (⊠ 42 rue d'Argout, 2ᵉ, Louvre/Tuileries, ☏ 01–42–33–31–08, métro Louvre) certainly doesn't look like much (check out the slightly kitsch mural on the back wall), but it serves up a welcome cous-cous in the early hours of the morning. Open until 7 AM, it also offers simple French food, such as pâté and niçoise salad.

La Cloche d'Or (⊠ 3 rue Mansart, 9ᵉ, Montmartre, ☎ 01–48–74–48–88, métro Place de Clichy) is a Paris institution where the likes of the late François Mitterrand, Depêche Mode, and the dancers from the Moulin Rouge have all dined on its traditional French cuisine. It's open until 4 AM every day except Sunday, when it closes at 1 AM.

Les Coulisses (⊠ 5 rue du Mont-Cenis, 18ᵉ, Montmartre, ☎ 01–42–62–89–99, métro Lamarck Caulaincourt), in Montmartre, near pic-turesque place du Tertre, has the most character of all the late-night restaurants: its red banquettes and 18th-century Venetian mirrors make it look like an Italian theater. The food—traditional French—is served until 4 AM. In the basement is a club, open Thursday–Saturday.

Grand Café des Capucines (⊠ 4 bd. des Capucines, 9ᵉ, Montmartre, ☎ 01–43–12–19–00, métro Opéra), whose exuberant pseudo–Belle Epoque dining room matches the mood of the neighboring Opéra, serves excellent oysters, fish, and meat dishes at hefty prices. It's open around the clock.

Le Tambour (⊠ 41 rue Montmartre, 2ᵉ, Montmartre, ☎ 01–42–33–06–90, métro Étienne Marcel, Les Halles) is full of old-fashioned, flea-market charm. The owner has one of those quintessentially profuse Parisian moustaches, there is an old métro map on the wall, and ad-vertising signs from yesteryear catch the eye. Le Tambour calls itself a "*bistrot de l'urbain bucolique*" (a "bistro for the bucolic city dweller") and serves up traditional French fare (onion soup, foie gras, steak tartare, confit de canard—what else?). It's open around the clock.

THE ARTS

Without a doubt, Paris has been one of the 20th century's greatest cap-itals of the arts. In 1909, Sergey Diaghilev arrived in the city with his Ballets Russes. In the '20s, Josephine Baker charmed audiences at the Théâtre des Champs-Élysées. And in the '40s, Jean-Paul Sartre and Si-mone de Beauvoir wrote masterpieces at the Café de Flore. Nowadays, despite lavish government subsidies, the city's artistic life doesn't have the avant-garde edge it once did, but Parisians are still proud of being intellectual and passionate about all things cultural. The city has an impressive number of venues and regularly attracts international the-ater, dance, and opera companies. In addition, the phenomenal num-ber of movie theaters makes Paris a cinephile's heaven.

The music and theater season runs September to June; in summer, most productions are found at festivals elsewhere in France. There is, how-ever, an excellent festival in Paris during July and August called Paris–Quartier d'Eté, which attracts international stars of dance, classical music, and jazz. Detailed entertainment listings can be found in the weekly magazines **Pariscope** (which has an English-language section), *L'Offi-ciel des Spectacles, Zurban,* and **Figaroscope** (a supplement to *Le Fi-garo* newspaper). The **Paris Tourist Office's 24-hour hot line** in English (☎ 08–36–68–31–12) and its Web site (ⓌⒺⒷ www.paris-touristoffice. com) are other good sources of information about activities in the city.

Tickets can be purchased at the theater itself (try to get them in ad-vance, as many of the more popular performances sell out quickly). Your hotel or a travel agency such as **Opéra Théâtre** (⊠ 7 rue de Clichy, 9ᵉ, Opéra/Grands Boulevards, ☎ 01–40–06–01–00, métro Trinité) may also be able to help you. They take a 20% commission on each ticket and also have a Web site (ⓌⒺⒷ www.operatheatre.com). Tickets can also be purchased at **FNAC** stores, especially the one in the

Forum des Halles (✉ 1–5 rue Pierre Lescot, 3rd level down, 1ᵉ, Beaubourg/Les Halles, ☎ 01–49–87–50–50, métro Châtelet Les Halles). **Virgin Megastore** (✉ 52 av. des Champs-Élysées, 8ᵉ, Champs-Élysées, ☎ 08–03–02–30–24, métro Franklin-D.-Roosevelt) also sells theater and concert tickets. Half-price tickets for same-day theater performances are available at the **Kiosques Théâtre** (✉ across from 15 pl. de la Madeleine, Opéra/Grands Boulevards, métro Montparnasse Bienvenüe; outside the Gare Montparnasse, pl. Raoul Dautry, 15ᵉ, Montparnasse, métro Montparnasse Bienvenüe), open Tuesday–Saturday 12:30–8 and Sunday 12:30–4. Expect to pay a €2.44 commission per ticket and stand in line. Half-price tickets are also available in numerous private theaters during the first week of each new show. Check the weekly guides for details.

Circus

You don't need to know French to enjoy the circus. Venues change frequently, so it is best to check one of the weekly guides; tickets range €6–€27. **Cirque Alexandra Bouglione** (✉ Jardin d'Acclimatation, Bois de Boulogne, ☎ 01–44–17–96–22, métro Sablons) has acrobats, jugglers, clowns, contortionists, trapeze artists, snakes, doves, and a show inspired by Greek mythology. **Cirque Alexis Gruss** (✉ Pelouse de Madrid, Allée de la Reine, Bois de Boulogne, ☎ 01–44–17–96–22, métro Porte Maillot, then Bus 244 to the Route des Lacs stop) is in Paris five months of the year and remains an avowedly old-fashioned production with showy horsemen. From tigers to yaks, dogs, and clowns, **Cirque Diana Moreno Bormann** (✉ 9 bd. du Bois Leprêtre, 17ᵉ, Porte de St-Ouen, ☎ 01–64–05–36–25, métro Porte de St-Ouen) is good for all ages; performances are on Saturday, Sunday, and Wednesday at 3 PM. **Cirque d'Hiver** (✉ 110 rue Amelot, 11ᵉ, République, ☎ 01–47–00–12–25, métro Filles du Calvaire), constructed in 1852 as a circus hall, is now only occasionally a venue for the circus; more often fashion shows and parties are held here. **Cirque de Paris** (✉ 115 bd. Charles-de-Gaulle, Villeneuve-la-Garenne, ☎ 01–47–99–40–40, métro Porte de Clignancourt, then Bus 137) offers "A Day at the Circus": a peek behind the scenes in the morning, lunch with the artists, and a performance in the afternoon.

Classical Music

Cité de la Musique (✉ in the Parc de La Villette, 221 av. Jean-Jaurès, 19ᵉ, Parc de La Villette, ☎ 01–44–84–44–84, métro Porte de Pantin) presents a varied program of classical, experimental, and world music concerts in a postmodern setting.

IRCAM (✉ 1 pl. Igor-Stravinsky, 4ᵉ, Beaubourg/Les Halles, ☎ 01–44–78–48–16, métro Châtelet Les Halles, Hôtel de Ville) organizes concerts of contemporary classical music on the premises, at the Centre Pompidou next door, or at the Cité de la Musique.

Maison de Radio France (✉ 116 av. du Président-Kennedy, 16ᵉ, Passy, ☎ 01–56–40–15–16, RER Maison de Radio-France), the base for countless radio and TV stations, also often hosts the Orchestre National de France. The Orchestre Philharmonique de Radio France often performs in the smallish, modern Salle Olivier Messiaen.

L'Opéra Royal (✉ Château de Versailles, Versailles, ☎ 01–30–83–78–88, RER Versailles–Rive Gauche) was built in 20 months for the marriage of the future Louis XVI and Marie-Antoinette. In the 18th century, both *Castor et Pollux* by Rameau and *Iphigénie* by Glück were given there. Today, it plays host to a season of chamber and orchestral concerts, vocal recitals, dance, and theater called "Les Nouveaux Plaisirs" (March–September).

Salle Cortot (✉ 78 rue Cardinet, 17ᵉ, Parc Monceau, ☎ 01–47–63–85–72, métro Malesherbes) is an acoustic gem, built by Auguste Perret in 1918. At the time, he promised to construct a "hall that sounds like a violin." Today, it plays host to jazz and classical concerts. There are also free recitals at 12:30 PM on Tuesday and Thursday by the students of the adjoining École Normale de Musique.

Salle Gaveau (✉ 45 rue de la Boétie, 8ᵉ, Champs-Élysées, ☎ 01–49–53–05–07, métro Miromesnil) is a small hall of only 1,200 seats with a distinctly faded Parisian allure and fantastic acoustics. Its original gold and white decoration was restored during recent renovation work. It plays host to chamber music, piano, and vocal recitals.

Salle Pleyel (✉ 252 rue du Faubourg St-Honoré, 8ᵉ, Champs-Élysées, ☎ 08–25–00–02–52, métro Ternes) is Paris's principal home of classical music. The Orchestre de Paris and other leading international orchestras play here regularly, and there's a fine series of recitals by international stars.

Théâtre des Champs-Élysées (✉ 15 av. Montaigne, 8ᵉ, Champs-Élysées, ☎ 01–49–52–50–50, métro Alma-Marceau) was the scene of the famous Battle of the Rite of Spring in 1913, when police had to be called in after the audience started ripping up the seats in outrage at Stravinsky's *Le Sacre du Printemps* music and Nijinsky's choreography. Today, this elegantly restored, plush Art Deco temple is worthy of a visit based solely on architectural merit. It also hosts top-quality concerts and ballet performances.

Théâtre du Palais-Royal (✉ 38 rue Montpensier, 1ᵉʳ, Louvre/Tuileries, ☎ 01–48–24–16–97, métro Palais-Royal) is a sparkling 750-seat Italian theater bedecked in gold and purple. From January until June, it plays host to "*Les Concerts du Palais-Royal*": a series of performances of Baroque music, vocal recitals, and opera bouffe.

Church and Museum Concerts

Paris has a never-ending stream of free or inexpensive lunchtime and evening church concerts, ranging from organ recitals to choral music and orchestral works. Some are scheduled as part of the **Festival d'Art Sacré** (☎ 01–44–70–64–10 for information) between mid-November and Christmas. Check the weekly listings for information; telephone numbers for most church concerts vary with the organizer.

Here are the main venues for church concerts. **Sainte-Chapelle** (✉ 4 bd. du Palais, 1ᵉʳ, Ile de la Cité, ☎ 01–42–77–65–65, métro Cité) holds memorable candlelit concerts April through mid-October; make reservations well in advance. **Notre-Dame** (✉ Ile de la Cité, 4ᵉ, Ile de la Cité, métro Cité). **St-Eustache** (✉ Rue du Jour, 1ᵉʳ, Beaubourg/Les Halles, métro Les Halles). **St-Germain-des-Prés** (✉ Pl. St-Germain-des-Prés, 6ᵉ, St-Germain-des-Prés, métro St-Germain-des-Prés). **St-Julien-Le-Pauvre** (✉ 23 quai de Montebello, 5ᵉ, Latin Quarter, métro St-Michel). **St-Louis-en-l'Ile** (✉ 19 bis rue St-Louis-en-l'Ile, 4ᵉ, Ile-St-Louis, métro Pont Marie). **St-Roch** (✉ 296 rue St-Honoré, 1ᵉʳ, Louvre/Tuileries, métro Tuileries).

Museums are another good place to find classical concerts. Some of the best are held in the **Auditorium du Louvre** (✉ Palais du Louvre, Louvre/Tuileries, ☎ 01–40–20–84–00, métro Palais-Royal, Musée du Louvre) on Wednesday evening and Thursday lunchtime. The **Musée d'Orsay** (✉ 1 rue de Bellechasse, 7ᵉ, St-Germain-des-Prés, ☎ 01–40–49–47–57, RER Musée d'Orsay) regularly holds small-scale concerts (song cycles, piano recitals, or chamber music) at lunchtime or in the early evening. The **Musée du Moyen Age** (✉ 6 pl. Paul Painlevé, 5ᵉ, Latin Quarter, ☎ 01–53–73–78–16, métro Cluny La Sorbonne) stages early music concerts between March and October.

There is also a fine Chopin Festival at the delightfully picturesque **Orangerie de Bagatelle** (✉ Parc de Bagatelle, av. de Longchamp, Bois de Boulogne, ☎ 01–45–00–22–19, métro Sablons) in late June and early July. In August and September, there are also free classical concerts in the Parc Floral of the Bois de Boulogne on Saturday and Sunday at 4:30 PM.

Dance

As a rule, more avant-garde or up-and-coming choreographers show their works in the smaller performance spaces in the Bastille and the Marais and in theaters in nearby suburbs. Classical ballet is found in places as varied as the opera house and the sports stadium. Check the weekly guides for listings.

Maison des Arts et de la Culture (✉ 1 pl. Salvador Allende, Créteil, 94000, ☎ 01–45–13–19–19, métro Créteil Préfecture), situated just outside Paris, is a fine venue for dance, which often attracts top-flight international and French companies, such as Blanca Li, Mikhail Baryshnikov's White Oak Project, and Philippe Decouflé.

Opéra Garnier (✉ Pl. de l'Opéra, 9ᵉ, Opéra/Grands Boulevards, ☎ 08–36–69–78–68, WEB www.opera-de-paris.fr, métro Opéra) is the sumptuous Napoléon-III home of the well-reputed Ballet de l'Opéra National de Paris and rarely hosts other dance companies. When performing, it offers the same program—a full-length ballet like *Sylvia* or *La Sylphide* or an evening of shorter works—for six or so consecutive performances. Special events (offered in multiple performances), such as evening devoted to works featuring the choreography of Maurice Béjart or the music of Stravinsky—are often interspersed among the regular performances. Seat prices range €4.5–€60; note that many of the cheaper seats have obstructed views, more of an obstacle than in opera performances.

Théâtre de la Bastille (✉ 76 rue de la Roquette, 11ᵉ, Bastille/Nation, ☎ 01–43–57–42–14, métro Bastille) merits mention as an example of the innovative activity in the Bastille area; it has an enviable record as a launching pad for tomorrow's modern-dance stars.

Théâtre de la Cité Internationale (✉ 21 bd. Jourdan, 14ᵉ, Parc Montsouris, ☎ 01–43–13–50–50, métro Cité-Universitaire) is a complex of three theaters at the heart of the international student residence, the Cité Universitaire. It often plays host to young, avant-garde companies and is also the main venue for the Presqu'Iles de Danse festival in February.

Théâtre de la Ville (✉ 2 pl. du Châtelet, 4ᵉ, Beaubourg/Les Halles, métro Châtelet; 31 rue des Abbesses, 18ᵉ, Montmartre, métro Abbesses; ☎ 01–42–74–22–77 for both) is *the* place for contemporary dance. Troupes like La La La Human Steps and Anne-Teresa de Keersmaeker's Rosas company are presented here. The queen of modern European dance, Pina Bausch, also comes every June.

Film

Paris has hundreds of cinemas showing contemporary and classic French and American movies, as well as a tempting menu packed with independent, international, and documentary films. A number of theaters, especially in principal tourist areas such as the Champs-Élysées, boulevard des Italiens near the Opéra, St-Germain-des-Prés, and Les Halles, run English-language films. Check the weekly guides for a movie of your choice. The initials "v.o." mean *version originale*, or not dubbed; films that are dubbed are indicated by the initials "v.f." (*version française*). Cinema admission runs €5–€8; some cinemas have reduced rates on certain days (normally Monday, sometimes Wednesday) or for early shows; others offer reductions with the purchase of a multiple-entry card. Most theaters post two show times: the *séance*, when the commercials, previews, and, sometimes, short films begin; and the feature presentation, which usually starts 10–25 minutes later.

Paris has a number of big-screen cinemas. **Gaumont Grand Écran** (⊠ 30 pl. d'Italie, 13ᵉ, Chinatown, ☎ 01–45–80–77–00, métro Place d'Italie) boasts the biggest screen in Paris. **Grand Rex** (⊠ 1 bd. Poissonnière, 2ᵉ, Opéra/Grands Boulevards, ☎ 01–42–36–83–93, métro Bonne Nouvelle) opened in 1932 with a mammoth house of 2,800 seats. **Kinopanorama** (⊠ 60 av. de la Motte-Piquet, 15ᵉ, Motte-Piquet, ☎ 01–43–06–50–50, métro La Motte–Picquet Grenelle) is a small theater of just 520 seats, so get there early for screenings. **Max Linder Panorama** (⊠ 24 bd. Poissonnière, 9ᵉ, Opéra/Grands Boulevards, ☎ 01–48–24–00–47, métro Grands Boulevards) opened in 1932 and was named after French burlesque actor Max Linder; check out the marble floors and Florentine stucco on the walls. **MK2 Quai de Seine** (⊠ 14 quai de Seine, 19ᵉ, Canal-St-Martin, ☎ 01–53–26–41–77, métro Stalingrad), a restaurant-cinema complex showing major releases, is well worth a visit for its location on the Bassin de la Villette. **UGC Ciné Cité Les Halles** (⊠ Pl. de la Rotonde, Forum des Halles, Level 3, access by the Porte du Jour near St-Eustache church, 1ᵉʳ, Beaubourg/Les Halles, ☎ 01–40–26–40–45, métro Les Halles) is a huge complex of 19 theaters in the underground Les Halles shopping complex.

Unique in all the world is **La Pagode** (⊠ 57 bis rue de Babylone, 7ᵉ, Invalides/Eiffel Tower, ☎ 01–45–55–48–48, métro St-François Xavier)—where else but in Paris would you find movies screened in an antique pagoda? A Chinese fantasy, this structure was built in 1896 for the wife of the owner of the Au Bon Marché department store, whose salon attracted notable writers and painters here. By the 1970s, it had become a cinema slated for demolition (and then was saved by director Louis Malle). Though the fare is standard, the surround is enchanting—who can resist seeing a flick in the silk-and-gilt Salle Japonaise? After the film, repair to the historic little tea salon on site.

For the *cinéaste* (movie lover) brought up on Fellini, Bergman, and Resnais, the main mecca is the famed **Cinémathèque Française** (⊠ 42 bd. de Bonne-Nouvelle, 10ᵉ, Opéra/Grands Boulevards, ☎ 01–56–26–01–01, métro Bonne Nouvelle) and **Palais de Chaillot** (⊠ 7 av. Albert-de-Mun, 16ᵉ, Trocadéro, ☎ 01–56–26–01–01, métro Trocadéro). This venerable institution pioneered the preservation of early films. Today, its schedules often pay homage to major film directors, with the main programs scheduled for the Palais de Chaillot venue Wednesday–Sunday.

Other than the Cinémathèque Française, Paris has many other theaters showing classic and independent films, often found in the Latin Quarter (with some notable exceptions). Showings are often organized around retrospectives (check "Festivals" in weekly guides). Following is a list of some of the noteworthy independent cinemas. **Accatone** (⊠ 20 rue Cujax, 5ᵉ, Latin Quarter, ☎ 01–46–33–86–86, métro Cluny La Sorbonne, Luxembourg) shows mainly European art films. **Action Écoles** (⊠ 23 rue des Écoles, 5ᵉ, Latin Quarter, ☎ 01–43–29–79–89, métro Maubert Mutualité) specializes in old American classics. **Champo** (⊠ 51 rue des Écoles, 5ᵉ, Latin Quarter, ☎ 01–43–54–51–60, métro Cluny La Sorbonne) often programs Hitchcock films. **Grande Action** (⊠ 5 rue des Écoles, 5ᵉ, Latin Quarter, ☎ 01–43–29–44–40, métro Cardinal Lemoine, Jussieu) usually runs American classics. **Quartier Latin**

(⊠ 9 rue Champollion, 5ᵉ, Latin Quarter, ☎ 01–43–26–84–65, métro Cluny La Sorbonne) is one of a number of cinemas near the Sorbonne. **St-André-des-Arts** (⊠ 30 rue St-André-des-Arts, 6ᵉ, Latin Quarter, ☎ 01–43–26–48–18, métro St-Michel) is one of the best cinemas in Paris, and generally has a festival devoted to one director, such as Bergman or Tarkovski.

Several film venues offer special events and attractions. **Balzac** (⊠ 1 rue Balzac, 8ᵉ, Champs-Élysées, ☎ 01–45–61–10–60, métro George V) often holds talks by directors before screenings. **Centre Pompidou** (⊠ Pl. Georges-Pompidou, Beaubourg/Les Halles, ☎ 01–44–78–12–33) hosts regular themed film festivals. **Cinéma des Cinéastes** (⊠ 7 av. de Clichy, 17ᵉ, Montmartre, ☎ 01–53–42–40–20, métro Place de Clichy) shows previews of feature films, as well as documentaries, short subjects, and rarely shown movies; it's in an old cabaret transformed into a movie theater and wine bar. **Dôme Imax** (⊠ La Défense, La Défense, ☎ 08–36–67–06–06, RER La Défense) shows 3-D flicks. **L'Entrepôt** (⊠ 7 rue Francis-de-Pressensé, 14ᵉ, Montparnasse, ☎ 01–45–40–78–38, métro Pernety) screens films and has a café, bar, restaurant, and bookstore. **Le Forum des Images** (⊠ Forum des Halles, Porte St-Eustache entrance, 1ᵉʳ, Beaubourg/Les Halles, ☎ 01–44–76–62–00, métro Les Halles) organizes thematic viewings of its archives of films and videos on the city of Paris. For €5 you can watch up to four films, two hours of video, and surf the Web for 30 minutes. **La Géode** (⊠ At the Cité des Sciences et de l'Industrie, Parc de La Villette, 26 av. Corentin-Cariou, 19ᵉ, Parc de La Villette, ☎ 01–40–05–12–12, métro Porte de La Villette) screens wide-angle Omnimax films—usually documentaries—on a gigantic spherical surface. In summer at the **Parc de La Villette** (métro Porte de Pantin, Porte de La Villette) movies are shown outdoors on a large screen. Most people take along a picnic. You can also rent deck chairs by the entrance; check the weekly guides for film listings.

Galleries

Art galleries are scattered throughout the city, but those focusing on the same aesthetic period are often clustered in one neighborhood. There are many contemporary art galleries, for instance, near the Centre Pompidou, the Picasso Museum, and the Bastille Opéra. More recently, several avant-garde galleries have moved to rue Louise Weiss near the Bibliothèque François-Mitterrand in the 13ᵉ. (Note that it's not uncommon for galleries to be hidden away in courtyards, with the only sign of their presence a small plaque on the front of the buildings; take these as invitations to push through the doors.) Around St-Germain, the galleries are generally more traditional, and works by old masters and established modern artists dominate the galleries around rue du Faubourg St-Honoré and avenue Matignon. To help you plot your gallery course, get a free copy of the map published by the Association des Galeries; it's available at many of the galleries listed below. For listings of antiques galleries, *see* the Shopping chapter.

These days the Parisian art world is abuzz because, after many years' delay, the main French auctioneers, most based at the **Hôtel Drouot** (⊠ 9 rue Drouot, 9ᵉ, Opéra/Grands Boulevards, ☎ 01–48–00–20–00, métro Richelieu Drouot), have lost their monopoly on art auctions in Paris. **Christie's** (⊠ 9 av. Matignon, 8ᵉ, Champs-Élysées, ☎ 01–40–76–85–85) opened shop in 2001 with lavish new showrooms and a calendar of auctions. **Sotheby's** (⊠ 76 rue du Faubourg St-Honoré, 8ᵉ, Champs-Élysées, ☎ 01–53–05–53–05, métro St-Philippe-du-Roule), Christie's archrival, has an ambitious calendar of sales scheduled..

Agathe Gaillard (✉ 3 rue Pont Louis-Philippe, 4ᵉ, Le Marais, ☎ 01–42–77–38–24, métro Hôtel de Ville) was the first person to open a photo gallery in Paris way back in 1975. Since then, she has exhibited many of the great names of the genre, from Kertesz and Cartier-Bresson to Edouard Boubat. Today, she also represents a stable of up-and-coming stars.

Artcurial (✉ 61 av. Montaigne, 8ᵉ, Champs-Élysées, ☎ 01–42–99–16–16, métro Franklin-D.-Roosevelt) has the feel of a museum shop. It sells artist-designed decorative objects and exhibits works by such artists as Bram van Velde and Zao Wou-Ki.

Carré Rive Gauche (métro St-Germain-des-Prés, Rue du Bac) is an area sheltering dozens of art and antiques galleries on its narrow lanes.

Galerie Arnoux (✉ 27 rue Guénégaud, 6ᵉ, St-Germain-des-Prés, ☎ 01–46–33–04–66, métro Odéon), one of many galleries on this street, specializes in abstract painting of the '50s, as well as in the works of young painters and sculptors.

Galerie Camera Obscura (✉ 12 rue Ernest Cresson, 14ᵉ, Montparnasse, ☎ 01–45–45–67–08, métro Mouton Duvernet) is a small photography gallery with a very Zen-like atmosphere. The work on show is top quality, and the photographers represented include Lucien Hervé, Willy Ronis, and Yasuhiro Ishimoto.

Galerie Claude Bernard (✉ 5 rue des Beaux-Arts, 6ᵉ, St-Germain-des-Prés, ☎ 01–43–26–97–07, métro St-Germain-des-Prés) is very well established in the domain of traditional figurative work.

Galerie Dina Vierny (✉ 36 rue Jacob, 6ᵉ, St-Germain-des-Prés, ☎ 01–42–60–23–18, métro St-Germain-des-Prés) was set up after the war by the former muse of sculptor Aristide Maillol. Since, she has discovered artists such as Serge Poliakoff, Vladimir Yankelevsky, and Ilya Kabakov.

Galerie Laage-Salomon (✉ 57 rue du Temple, 4ᵉ, Le Marais, ☎ 01–42–78–11–71, métro Hôtel de Ville) shows a well-known, very international group of artists, such as Per Kirkeby, Georg Baselitz, and Candida Höfer.

Galerie Lelong (✉ 13 rue de Téhéran, 8ᵉ, Miromesnil, ☎ 01–45–63–13–19, métro Miromesnil), which also has galleries in New York and Zurich, represents a mix of contemporary artists.

Galerie Louis Carré (✉ 10 av. de Messine, 8ᵉ, Miromesnil, ☎ 01–45–62–57–07, métro Miromesnil) has a long history of promoting French artists, including Bazaine, but it is not lost in the past.

Galerie Maeght (✉ 42 rue du Bac, 7ᵉ, St-Germain-des-Prés, ☎ 01–45–48–45–15, métro Rue du Bac) is the Paris branch of the Fondation Maeght in St-Paul-de-Vence. You can find paintings as well as books, prints, and reasonably priced posters.

Galerie Templon (✉ in courtyard of 30 rue Beaubourg, 3ᵉ, Beaubourg/Les Halles, ☎ 01–42–72–14–10, métro Rambuteau) was the first to bring American artists to Paris in the '60s; now it represents many artists, including French star Jean-Pierre Raynaud.

Galerie 213 (✉ 213 bd. Raspail, 14ᵉ, Montparnasse, ☎ 01–43–22–83–23, métro Raspail) is owned by Marion de Beaupré, former agent of top photographers like Peter Lindbergh and Paolo Roversi. Today, she runs this gallery, which has a bookstore on the ground floor, in a magnificent early Art Nouveau space. On the first floor is a white gallery salon, where she exhibits work by the likes of Elger Esser, Gueorgui Pinkhassov, and Guido Mocafico.

Galerie Yvon Lambert (✉ 108 rue Vieille-du-Temple, 3ᵉ, Le Marais, ☎ 01–42–71–09–33, métro St-Sébastien Froissart) is run by the man known to the French as "the discoverer of minimalism and Conceptual Art"—indeed, one of his more famous exploits was his sale of a painting to a blind man. Over the years, he has exhibited everyone from Daniel Buren and Christo to Sol Lewitt and Julian Schnabel. Today, he exhibits artists like Jenny Holzer, Douglas Gordon, and Christian Boltanski.

Joyce (✉ Palais-Royal, 9 rue de Valois, 1ᵉʳ, Louvre/Tuileries, ☎ 01–40–15–03–72, métro Palais-Royal) is a gallery and boutique set up by successful Asian retailer Joyce Ma, who regularly invites Asian artists to show their work.

Louvre des Antiquaires (✉ 2 pl. du Palais-Royal, 1ᵉʳ, Louvre/Tuileries, ☎ 01–42–97–27–00, métro Palais-Royal) is an elegant multifloor complex where 250 of Paris's leading dealers showcase their rarest objects, including Louis XV furniture, tapestries, and antique jewelry. The center is open Tuesday–Sunday 11 AM–7 PM; it is closed Sunday in July and August.

Opera

Paris offers some of the best opera in the world—and thousands know it. Consequently, getting tickets to the two main venues, the **Opéra de la Bastille** and the **Opéra Garnier,** can be difficult on short notice, so it is a good idea to plan ahead. Review a list of performances by getting a copy of the Paris Tourist Office's *"Saison de Paris"* booklet or by writing to the **Opéra de la Bastille** (✉ 120 rue de Lyon, Bastille, 75576 Paris, Cedex 12) well in advance. Make your selection and send back the booking form, giving several choices of nights and performances. If the response is affirmative, just pick up and pay for your tickets before the performance (you can also pay for them by credit card in advance). A word of caution: buying from a scalper is not recommended, as there have been reports of people selling counterfeit tickets.

Opéra de la Bastille (✉ Pl. de la Bastille, 12ᵉ, Bastille, ☎ 08–36–69–78–68, WEB www.opera-de-paris.fr, métro Bastille), the ultramodern facility built in 1989 and designed by architect Carlos Ott, has taken over the role as Paris's main opera house from the Opéra Garnier; tickets for the Opéra de Paris productions range €7–€103 and go on sale at the box office two weeks before any given show or a month ahead by phone. The opera season usually runs September through July and the box office is open Monday to Saturday 11–6:30 (the Web site is very informative and complete and allows you to order tickets).

Opéra Comique (✉ 5 rue Favart, 2ᵉ, Opéra/Grands Boulevards, ☎ 01–42–44–45–46, métro Richelieu Drouot) is a lofty old hall that has been given a new lease on life ever since Jérôme Savary—one of France's *enfants terribles* of theater—took over as director in 1999. As well as staging operettas, the hall also plays host to modern dance, classical concerts, and vocal recitals.

Opéra Garnier (✉ Pl. de l'Opéra, 9ᵉ, Opéra/Grands Boulevards, ☎ 08–36–69–78–68, WEB www.opera-de-paris.fr, métro Opéra), the magnificent and magical former haunt of the Phantom, the painter Edgar Degas, and any number of legendary opera stars, still hosts occasional performances of the Opéra de Paris, along with a fuller calendar of dance performances, as the auditorium is the official home of the Ballet de l'Opéra National de Paris. The grandest opera productions are usually mounted at the Opéra de la Bastille, while the Garnier now presents smaller-scale opera, such as Mozart's *La Clemenza di Tito* and *Cosi fan Tutte.* Gorgeous though the Garnier is, its tiara-shape theater means that many seats have limited sight lines, so it's best to ask specifically what the sight lines are when booking (partial-view in French is *visibilité partielle*). Needless to say, the cheaper seats are often those with partial views—of course, views of Garnier's house could easily wind up being much more spectacular than any sets on stage, so it's not really a loss. Budget-minded American and British opera-goers will be shocked to learn there is no standing room at either opera house. Ticket prices for opera range €4.60–€103. Seats go on sale at the box office two weeks before any given show or a month ahead by phone; you must go in person to buy the €4.60 and €9.20 tickets. Sometimes rush tickets, if available, are offered 15 minutes before a performance. The box office is open 11 to 6:30 daily.

Théâtre Musical de Paris (✉ Pl. du Châtelet, 1er, Beaubourg/Les Halles, ☎ 01–40–28–28–40, métro Châtelet), better known as the Théâtre du Châtelet, puts on some of the finest opera productions in the city and regularly attracts international divas like Cecilia Bartoli and Anne-Sofie von Otter. It also plays host to classical concerts, dance performances, and the occasional play.

Puppet Shows

On most Wednesday, Saturday, and Sunday afternoons, the Guignol—the French equivalent of Punch and Judy—can be seen going through their ritualistic battles in a number of Paris's parks, including the **Champ de Mars** (☎ 01–48–56–01–44, métro École Militaire) and the **Jardins du Ranelagh** (☎ 01–45–83–51–75, métro La Muette). The **Jardin d'Acclimatation** (✉ Bois de Boulogne, ☎ 01–45–01–53–52, métro Sablons) and the **Jardin du Luxembourg** (☎ 01–43–26–46–47, métro Vavin) both have year-round, weatherproof performance spaces.

Theater

A number of theaters line the Grands Boulevards between the Opéra and République, but there is no Paris equivalent to Broadway or the West End. Shows are mostly in French, with a few notable exceptions. Information about performances can be obtained on a Web site (www.theatreonline.fr), which lists 170 different theaters, offers critiques, and provides an on-line reservation service. A genre that has become particularly popular in France is the "Broadway musical." Up until very recently, Parisians had shunned most all-singing-and-dancing shows, but then came the smash hit *Notre-Dame-de-Paris*, which launched the fashion for Broadway-style musicals (and went on to be produced in Las Vegas and London's West End); for years, the French weren't into musicals at all, but they have now become crazy about them. Numerous other Gallic musicals have since debuted; most are staged at either the Palais des Sports or the Palais des Congrès.

Bouffes du Nord (✉ 37 bis bd. de la Chapelle, 10e, Stalingrad/La Chapelle, ☎ 01–46–07–34–50, métro La Chapelle) is the wonderfully atmospheric, slightly decrepit home of English director Peter Brook, who regularly delights with his wonderful experimental productions. **Café de la Gare** (✉ 41 rue du Temple, 4e, Le Marais, ☎ 01–42–78–52–51, métro Hôtel de Ville) is a fun spot to experience a particularly Parisian form of theater, the *café-théâtre*—a mixture of satirical sketches and variety show riddled with slapstick humor, performed in a café salon. You need a good grasp of French. **La Cartoucherie** (✉ In the Bois de Vincennes, Bois de Vincennes, ☎ 01–43–74–24–08 or 01–43–28–36–36, métro Château de Vincennes, then shuttle bus), a complex of five theaters in a former munitions factory, turns cast and spectators into an intimate theatrical world. The resident director is the revered Ariane Mnouchkine. Go early for a simple meal; the cast often helps serve "in character." **Comédie des Champs-Élysées** (✉ 23 rue de la Huchette, 5e, Champs-Élysées, ☎ 01–43–26–38–99, métro St-Michel) offers fine productions in a theater neighboring the larger Théâtre des Champs-Élysées.

This is where Yasmina Reza's international hit *Art* first came to the public's attention.

Comédie Française (✉ Pl. Colette, 1ᵉʳ, Louvre/Tuileries, ☎ 01–44–58–15–15, ᴡᴇʙ www.comedie-francaise.fr, métro Palais-Royal) dates back to 1680 and is the most hallowed institution in French theater. It specializes in classical French plays by the likes of Racine, Molière, and Marivaux. Reserve seats in person about two weeks in advance, or turn up an hour beforehand and wait in line for cancellations.

MC93 Bobigny (✉ 1 bd. Lenine, Bobigny, Bobigny, ☎ 01–41–60–72–72, métro Bobigny–Pablo-Picasso), in a suburb northeast of Paris, often stages top-flight English and American productions.

Théâtre Gérard Philippe (✉ 59 bd. Jules-Guesdes, St-Denis, ☎ 01–48–13–17–00, métro St-Denis–Basilique) is run by one of France's most talented young directors, Stanislas Nardey. For only €7.6, you can see high-caliber, innovative theater and the occasional contemporary dance performance.

Théâtre de la Huchette (✉ 23 rue de la Huchette, 5ᵉ, Latin Quarter, ☎ 01–43–26–38–99, métro St-Michel) is a highlight for Ionesco admirers; this tiny Left Bank theater has been staging *The Bald Soprano* every night since 1950! (Note that the box office is only open Monday–Saturday 5 PM–9 PM.)

Théâtre de Marigny (✉ Carré Marigny, 8ᵉ, Champs-Élysées, ☎ 01–53–96–70–00, métro Champs-Élysées Clemenceau) is a private theater, where you're likely to find a big French star topping the bill.

Théâtre Mogador (✉ 25 rue de Mogador, 9ᵉ, Opéra/Grands Boulevards, ☎ 01–53–32–32–00, métro Trinité), one of Paris's most sumptuous theaters, is the place for musicals and other productions with popular appeal.

Théâtre National de Chaillot (✉ 1 pl. du Trocadéro, 16ᵉ, Trocadéro, ☎ 01–53–65–30–00, métro Trocadéro) is a cavernous place with two theaters dedicated to drama and dance. The program ranges from Shakespeare to cabaret shows and tango festivals. Top-flight dance companies like the Ballet Royal de Suède and William Forsythe's Ballet Frankfurt are also regular visitors.

Théâtre de l'Odéon (✉ Pl. de l'Odéon, 6ᵉ, St-Germain-des-Prés, ☎ 01–44–41–36–36, métro Odéon) has made pan-European theater its primary focus and offers some of the finest productions in Paris.

Théâtre de la Renaissance (✉ 20 bd. St-Martin, 10ᵉ, Opéra/Grands Boulevards, ☎ 01–42–08–18–50, métro Strasbourg St-Denis) was put on the map by Belle Epoque star Sarah Bernhardt (she was manager from 1893 to 1899). Big French stars often perform in plays here.

6 OUTDOOR ACTIVITIES AND SPORTS

Parisians are often envied, mistakenly for their ability to stay thin despite a love of buttery foods and chocolate treats and their seeming disdain for exercise. The truth is they do actually like to be *sportif*. Nowadays, if they're not walking or bicycling, many Parisians are swimming, playing soccer, or working out at health clubs. Although facilities in the heart of the city are limited, you can nevertheless find places to exercise and be in the outdoors. There are also a number of large stadiums in and around the city where you can see soccer, rugby, and tennis matches.

PARISIANS MAY NOT BE AS FANATICAL about exercising as people elsewhere, but in the past few years their interest in sports has been growing. A new network of bike lanes has seen the number of cyclists boom, there has been a citywide fad for in-line skating, and the number of gyms has been steadily rising. The fact remains that most of them tend to be on the outskirts of the city—space for athletic activities in the heart of it remains somewhat limited. In fact, it was only in 1997 that laws were passed allowing people to sit, walk, or even play sports on the grass in parks (once strictly forbidden); these days you can enjoy (some) lawns without being reprimanded. One of the best spots for sports in Paris is the Buttes-Chaumont, a park with enough space for soccer and other games. Also good are Paris's two large parks—the Bois de Boulogne, on the western fringe of the city, and the Bois de Vincennes, on the eastern side—where wide-open spaces allow for an array of activities.

Revised and updated by Nicola Keegan

The best starting point for finding out about athletic activities in Paris is the booklet *Le Guide du Sport à Paris,* available from the Paris Tourist Office. In French, it lists sports facilities in each arrondissement, has a map of bike lanes throughout the city, and contains a calendar of major sporting events. Further information can be obtained by calling the **Allô-Sports Service** (☏ 01–42–76–54–54), Monday–Thursday 10:30–5 and Friday 10:30–4:30; it's in French only.

PARTICIPANT SPORTS

Aerobics

From 9 to noon on Sunday, the Paris town authorities organize free aerobics and stretch classes in 11 venues dotted throughout the city. Left Bank devotees head to the Pavillon des Gardes in the **Jardin du Luxembourg** (RER Luxembourg). For the Montparnasse area, classes are offered at the Mire de l'Observatoire in the **Parc Montsouris** (✉ Bd. Jourdan, 14ᵉ, Montparnasse, RER Cité-Universitaire). At the **Parc des Buttes-Chaumont,** the meeting place is the music kiosk on place Armand Carrel in front of the town hall of the 19ᵉ arrondissement. Note that there are no classes at any of these venues during July and August.

Bicycling

Maps of Paris's main cycle paths can be found in *Le Guide du Sport à Paris.* Paris's two large parks are the best places for biking. Bike enthusiasts on the western side of Paris tend to flock to the **Bois de Boulogne** (métro Porte Maillot, Porte Dauphine, Porte d'Auteuil; Bus 244). On the east side of Paris, the largest number of bike trails can be found in the vast **Bois de Vincennes** (métro Château de Vincennes, Porte Dorée).

The city also has more than 167 km (94 mi) of **bike lanes,** and there are plans to develop even more. Unfortunately, most bike routes are along the main axes of the city, which means that you may find yourself riding in traffic. Cars, however, have been banned altogether on Sunday from certain scenic routes, including the banks of the Seine from 9 to 5, mid-March through late autumn, and the picturesque **Canal St-Martin** from noon to 6 year-round.

The following places rent bikes, and many of these establishments also organize guided excursions. **Bike 'n Roller** (✉ 6 rue St-Julien-le-Pauvre, 5ᵉ, Latin Quarter, ☏ 01–44–07–35–89, métro Cité, St-Michel) hires bikes for €12 for three hours and €17 for the day. **Escapade Nature** (✉ 69 bd. Diderot, 12ᵉ, Bastille/Nation, ☎ 01–53–17–03–18, métro Reuilly Diderot) organizes daily bike tours of Paris. Their *Ballades Détentes* (leisure rides) begin at 11 AM and last for about two hours and cost €15.50 (including bike rental). The more comprehensive three-hour *Ballades Découvertes* at 3 PM cost €25 (including bike rental). There are also regular tours on Sunday of the greater Paris region (€38, including the price of the train and bike hire), which last the whole day. **Pariscyclo** (✉ Rond Point de Jardin d'Acclimatation, in the Bois de Boulogne, Bois de Boulogne, ☎ 01–47–47–76–50, métro Les Sablons) is the perfect place for bike rentals if you want to explore the Bois de Boulogne. **Paris à Vélo, C'est Sympa** (✉ 37 bd. Bourdon, 4ᵉ, Bastille/Nation, ☎ 01–48–87–60–01, métro Bastille) rents bikes for €9.50 for half day and €12.50 for full day and also organizes three-hour excursions of both the heart of Paris and lesser-known sites. Times vary according to season, so either call ahead for information or consult the organization's Web site (WEB www.parisvelosympa.com). Tours cost €28.50 (€24.50 for under-26s). A security deposit of €307 is also required, so do take along a credit card. **Paris Vélo Rent a Bike** (✉ 2 rue Fer à Moulin, 5ᵉ, Latin Quarter, ☎ 01–43–37–59–22, métro Censier Daubenton) charges €11.50 for half-day and €14 for full-day bike rental (with an additional security deposit of €300).

Health Clubs

Short-term passes are available from the following health clubs.

Club Jean de Beauvais (✉ 5 rue Jean-de-Beauvais, 5ᵉ, Latin Quarter, ☎ 01–46–33–16–80, métro Maubert Mutualité) has an entire floor of exercise equipment and classes, as well as a sauna. A one-day pass costs €38; a week is €95. There is also the possibility of balneotherapy treatments at an additional cost. It's open Monday, Tuesday, and Thursday 7 AM–10:30 PM; Wednesday and Friday 7 AM–10 PM; Saturday 8:30–7; and Sunday 9:30–6. For more information, consult the Web site (WEB www.clubjeandebeauvais.com).

Club Quartier Latin (✉ 19 rue de Pontoise, 5ᵉ, Latin Quarter, ☎ 01–55–42–77–88, métro Maubert Mutualité) has a skylighted pool, squash courts, and exercise equipment. For €13 per day you can use the gym and pool (the pool only is €4); add another €11.5 per 40 minutes for squash (€2.30 racket rental). It's open weekdays 9 AM–midnight, weekends 9:30–7.

Espace Vit'Halles (✉ Pl. Beaubourg, 48 rue Rambuteau, 3ᵉ, Beaubourg/Les Halles, ☎ 01–42–77–21–71, métro Rambuteau) has a broad array of aerobics classes (€15.30 per class, €138 for 10), exercise machines, sauna, and steam room (€15.30 a day). It's open Monday, Wednesday, and Friday 8 AM–10 PM; Tuesday and Thursday 8 AM–11 PM; Saturday 10–7; and Sunday 10–6.

Pilates Studio (✉ 39 rue du Temple, 4ᵉ, Le Marais, ☎ 01–42–72–91–74, métro Hôtel de Ville) is run by Philippe Taupier, who studied in New York with one of the pupils of the technique's founder, Joseph Pilates. It may be based in just a three-room apartment but it attracts numerous celebrities, such as actress Kristin Scott Thomas and former French *Vogue* editor Joan Juliet Buck. One-hour solo classes cost €58. Duo classes are €46 per person and group classes €23.

Hotel Health Clubs

The hotels with the best fitness facilities are generally the newer ones situated along the perimeter of the city center.

Ritz Health Club (⊠ Pl. Vendôme, 1ᵉʳ, Louvre/Tuileries, ☎ 01–43–16–30–60, métro Opéra), as fancy as the hotel, has a swimming pool, sauna, steam room, hot tub, exercise machines, and aerobics classes (all for €92.30 on weekdays, €107 on weekends). It's open daily 7 AM–10 PM.

Sofitel Paris Vitatop Club (⊠ 8 rue Louis-Armand, 15ᵉ, Montparnasse, ☎ 01–45–54–79–00, métro Balard) has a 15-m pool, a sauna, a steam room, and a hot tub, plus a stunning view of the Paris skyline (€30.70 per day, free to hotel guests). It's open Monday and Wednesday–Friday 8 AM–10 PM, Tuesday 8 AM–midnight, Saturday 9–7, and Sunday 9–5.

Ice-Skating

From mid-December through the end of February, weather permitting, a small skating rink is erected on **place de l'Hôtel de Ville** (the square in front of the Hôtel de Ville); hours are 9 AM–10 PM daily. In the suburb of St-Ouen is the **Patinoire de St-Ouen** (⊠ 4 rue Dr-Bauer, St-Ouen, ☎ 01–40–11–43–38, métro Mairie de St-Ouen), an indoor rink, open year-round. Admission ranges from €2 to €7, with skate rental, depending on when you go. It's open Tuesday 11:30–1 and 8:30–11; Wednesday 10–noon and 2:30–6; Thursday 11:30–1 and 6–8; Friday 11:30–1 and 8:30–11; Saturday 2:30–6 and 8:30–11; and Sunday 10–12:30 and 2:30–6.

In-line Skating

A craze for in-line skating has swept over Paris in the last five years. Where once it was rare to see people with a pair of skates on their feet, now it seems like almost every other Parisian is an adept of *le roller*. To avoid pedestrians and road crossings, they often use the city's cycle paths. You'll also see them doing their tricks on **place du Palais-Royal** and the esplanade at the **Musée d'Art Moderne de la Ville de Paris** on avenue du Président-Wilson. On Sunday, when cars are banned, **quai de la Tournelle**, along the Seine (9–5), and the **Canal St-Martin** (noon–6) are also ideal in-line skating spots.

Every Friday night starting at 10, thousands of in-line skaters gather at **place de l'Italie** to take a different weekly three-hour route through Paris (roads are blocked off). The pace is pretty hairy, so novices are discouraged. For details, check the Web site (WEB www.pari-roller.com). A more leisurely three-hour route is organized on Sunday at 2:30 PM and leaves from **Roller Location Nomades** near place de la Bastille. For those who want to practice their acrobatics, there are two ramps in the **Stade Boutroux** (⊠ 1 av. Boutroux, 13ᵉ, Chinatown, ☎ 01–45–84–08–46, métro Porte d'Ivry).

In-line skates can be rented from **Bike 'n Roller** (⊠ 6 rue St-Julien-le-Pauvre, 5ᵉ, Latin Quarter, ☎ 01–44–07–35–89, métro St-Michel; ⊠ 137 St-Dominique, 7ᵉ, Invalides/Eiffel Tower, ☎ 01–44–18–30–39, métro École Militaire; and ⊠ 38 rue Fabert, 7ᵉ, Invalides/Eiffel Tower, ☎ 01–45–50–38–27, métro La Tour Maubourg) for €9.20 for three hours and €12.30 per day. **Rollerland** (⊠ 3 bd. Bourdon, 4ᵉ, Bastille/Nation, ☎ 01–40–27–96–97, métro Bastille, Quai de la Rapée; ⊠ 34 rue Bayen, 17ᵉ, Parc Monceau, ☎ 01–45–72–39–59, métro Ternes) offers individual and group lessons and rents out skates. **Roller Location Nomades** (⊠ 37 bd. Bourdon, 4ᵉ, Bastille/Nation, ☎ 01–44–54–07–44, métro Bastille) rents skates for about €9.50. **Vertical Line** (⊠ 60 av. Raymond Poincaré, 16ᵉ, Trocadéro, ☎ 01–47–27–21–21, Métro: Victor Hugo) rents skates for 30–60 minutes for €4.60–€9.20.

The rink **La Main Jaune** (⊠ Rue du Caporal-Peugeot, 17ᵉ, Parc Monceau, ☎ 01–47–63–26–47, métro Porte de Champerret) is the spot for old-fashioned roller-skating. It's open Wednesday, Saturday, and Sunday 2:30–7 and Friday and Saturday from 10 PM on for roller discos; admission is €8 with skate rental.

Jogging

Running through the streets of Paris may sound romantic, but it can be quite unpleasant if you don't go early in the day: there's just too much traffic on the narrow streets. Exceptions are quai de la Tournelle, along the Seine, and along the Canal St-Martin. The city's parks are better places to run. The **Champ de Mars** (métro École Militaire), next to the Eiffel Tower, measures 2½ km (1½ mi) around the perimeter. Many jogging fans prefer the pleasant route—though shorter and more crowded that the Champ de Mars—that is the 1½-km (1-mi) loop just inside the fence around the **Jardin du Luxembourg** (métro Odéon, RER Luxembourg). The **Jardin des Tuileries** (métro Concorde, Tuileries) measures about 1½ km (1 mi) around. The **Bois de Boulogne** has miles of trails through woods, around lakes, and across grassy meadows. There are 1,800-m and 2,500-m loops. The especially bucolic **Bois de Vincennes** has a 14½-km (9-mi) circuit or a 1½-km (1-mi) loop around the Château de Vincennes itself. Maps of routes in both bois can be found in *Le Guide du Sport à Paris*. Those who prefer track running can have access to Paris's athletics facilities during times when they have not been booked by schools or clubs. Try any of the following, but make sure to call ahead to check availability. In the 12ᵉ district, head to the **Centre Sportif Léo-Lagrange** (⊠ 68 bd. Poniatowski, Bastille/Nation, ☎ 01–46–28–31–57, métro Porte de Charenton). In the 15ᵉ district, try the **Centre Sportif Suzanne-Lenglen** (⊠ 2 rue Louis-Armand, Montparnasse, ☎ 01–45–54–72–85, métro Balard). In the 16ᵉ district, check out **Stade Porte-de-la-Muette** (⊠ 60 bd. Lannes, Trocadéro, ☎ 01–45–04–54–85, RER Av. Henri-Martin).

There are a number of annual running races that are open to the public. The **Paris Marathon** takes place in April (subscription details from Athlétisme Organisation; ☎ 01–41–33–15–94). A lesser-known event is the **20km de Paris,** held in October (⊠ Atalante, 9–11 rue Letellier, 15ᵉ, Montparnasse, ☎ 01–45–75–67–12). **Le Cross du Figaro** is a cross-country race organized each December by the French national daily, *Le Figaro* (for information, contact the paper's Service Événements; ☎ 01–42–21–60–00).

Swimming

Every arrondissement has its own public *piscine* (pool); the Paris Tourist Office's *Le Guide du Sport à Paris* lists addresses. One of the biggest and best is the **Piscine des Halles** (⊠ Pl. de la Rotonde, Forum des Halles, 1ᵉʳ, Beaubourg/Les Halles, ☎ 01–42–36–98–44, métro Châtelet Les Halles), a 50-m pool inside the shopping mall in the center of Paris. It's open Monday 11:30–8; Wednesday 10–7; Tuesday, Thursday, and Friday 11:30–10; and weekends 9–5. Admission is €4 and you can stay as long as you like. The **Piscine St-Germain** (⊠ 12 rue de Lobineau, 6ᵉ, St-Germain-des-Prés, ☎ 01–43–29–08–15, métro Mabillon), one of the nicest pools in Paris, is open Tuesday 7 AM–8 AM, 11:30 AM–1 PM, and 5 PM–7:30 PM; Wednesday 7 AM–8 AM and 11:30 AM–5:30 PM; Thursday and Friday 7 AM–8 AM and 11:30 AM–1 PM; Saturday 7 AM–5:30 PM; and Sunday 8 AM–5:30 PM. Admission is €2.5. Those who fancy taking in a bit of architectural heritage while they swim should try the **Piscine Butte-aux-Cailles** (⊠ 5 pl. Paul-Verlaine, 13ᵉ, Buttes-aux-Cailles, ☎ 01–45–89–60–05, métro Place d'Italie). Classed as a historic monument, the **Piscine des Amiraux** (✉ 6 rue Hermann-Lachapelle, 18ᵉ, Mont-martre, ☎ 01–46–06–46–47, métro Simplon, Marcadet-Poissonniers) is also a picturesque venue. In summer, many Parisians head off to the open-air **Piscine de la Grenouillère** (✉ Parc d'Antony, 146 bis av. du Général-de-Gaulle, Antony, ☎ 01–46–60–75–30, RER Croix-de-Berny), which is open daily 9–7 from mid-May to mid-September.

Aquaboulevard (✉ 4 rue Louis-Armand, 15ᵉ, Montparnasse, ☎ 01–40–60–10–00, métro Balard), the best place to take kids, has an enor-mous indoor wave pool with water slides and in summer, a simulated outdoor beach. It's open Monday–Thursday 9 AM–11 PM, Friday 7 AM–8 AM, Saturday 7 AM–8 AM, and Sunday 7 AM–8 AM. Last admission each day is at 9 PM. Adults can stay for six hours for €18.5. The **Club Quartier Latin** (✉ 19 rue de Pontoise, 5ᵉ, Latin Quarter, ☎ 01–55–42–77–88, métro Maubert Mutualité) has a very nice, skylighted, 33-m pool that you can use for €4.

Tennis

Paris has a number of municipal courts, but getting to play on them is not so easy. Normally, you must apply for a special card from the local *mairie* (town hall; each arrondissement has one), which takes one month to process, and then reserve a court in advance. You can, how-ever, take a chance, turn up at the public courts, and, if there is one available, play (the best time to go is the middle of the day during the week); the cost is €5.80 an hour per court, which you pay there. The most central, and most crowded, courts are in the **Jardin du Luxem-bourg.**

SPECTATOR SPORTS

The French passion for sport is amazing—the daily sports paper *L'Equipe* is actually the country's best-selling national newspaper. Paris often hosts major international sporting events; in 1998 it was the site of the Soccer World Cup and is the location for the French Open every May. Information on upcoming events can be found on posters around the city or in the weekly guide *Pariscope.* You can also call the ticket agency of **FNAC** (☎ 08–03–80–88–03). **Virgin Megastore** (☎ 08–03–02–30–24) runs a popular agency with tickets for sporting events of all kinds.

A far-ranging calendar of sporting events, including indoor athletics, ice-skating, horse shows, gymnastics, and stock-car racing, take place at the **Palais Omnisports de Paris-Bercy** (✉ 8 bd. de Bercy, 12ᵉ, Bastille/Nation, ☎ 08–03–03–00–31, métro Bercy, Gare de Lyon). Details of events are also on their Web site (WEB www.bercy.com). **Parc des Princes** (✉ 24 rue du Cdt. Guilbaud, 16ᵉ, Auteuil, ☎ 01–42–88–02–76, métro Porte d'Auteuil) is where the city's soccer team, Paris St-Germain, plays its home matches. **Roland-Garros** (✉ 2 av. Gordon Ben-nett, 16ᵉ, Bois-de-Boulogne, ☎ 01–47–43–48–00, métro Porte d'Auteuil) is the venue for the French Open tennis tournament. The **Stade de France** (✉ St-Denis, ☎ 01–55–93–00–00, RER La Plaine–Stade de France) was built for the World Cup in 1998 and is now home to the French national soccer and rugby teams.

Athletics

The annual **Paris Marathon** (Athlétisme Organization, ☎ 01–41–33–15–94) takes place in early April and attracts more than 20,000 par-ticipants. It sets off from the Champs-Élysées and finishes at the top of avenue Foch, near the Arc de Triomphe. Along the route, in spots like place de la Concorde and place de la République, there are groups who play live music to create a more festive ambience. The Paris track-and-field **Grand Prix** meeting is held at the Stade de France in June and generally attracts a host of top international stars.

Horse Racing

Paris and its suburbs are remarkably well endowed with *hippodromes* (racetracks). Admission is between €2.30 and €7.63. Details of meetings can be found in the daily newspaper *Le Parisien* or the specialist racing paper *Paris Turf.* The easiest racetrack to get to is the **Hippodrome d'Auteuil** (⊠ Bois de Boulogne, 16ᵉ, Bois de Boulogne, ☎ 01–40–71–47–47, métro Porte d'Auteuil) in the Bois de Boulogne. Also in the Bois de Boulogne is the city's most beautiful track, the **Hippodrome de Longchamp** (⊠ Rte. des Tribunes, Bois de Boulogne, 16ᵉ, Bois de Boulogne, ☎ 01–44–30–75–00, métro Porte d'Auteuil, then free shuttle), stage for the prestigious (and glamorous) Prix de l'Arc de Triomphe in October. The **Hippodrome de Vincennes** (⊠ Rte. Ferme, Bois de Vincennes, Bois de Vincennes, ☎ 01–49–77–17–17, RER Joinville-Le-Pont) is a cinder track used for trotting races. The French Derby (Prix du Jockey-Club) and the very chic French Oaks (Prix de Diane-Hermès) are held at the beginning of June at **Chantilly,** north of Paris; direct trains from the Gare du Nord take about 40 minutes. Other racetracks near Paris are in **Enghien-les-Bains, Évry,** and **St-Cloud.**

Soccer

As in most other European cities, *football* (soccer) is the sport that pulls in the biggest crowds. Paris St-Germain, the city's main club, was founded in 1970 and has won various titles, including the European Cup in 1996. It plays at the **Parc des Princes** stadium in southwest Paris. Most matches are on Saturday evening at 8 PM, although times do vary. It is best to check ahead on the club's official Web site (⬚WEB www.psg.fr). Admission is €16–€55; your best bet is to get tickets from FNAC in advance.

Tennis

The highlight of the tennis season—in fact the second most important European tennis tournament after Wimbledon—is the **French Open,** held during the last week of May and the first in June at the Roland-Garros Stadium. Center-court tickets are difficult to obtain; try your hotel or turn up early in the morning (matches start at 11 AM) and buy a general ground ticket. Tickets range from €13 to €55. The **Bercy Indoor Tournament** in November at the Palais Omnisports de Paris-Bercy awards one of the largest prizes in the world and attracts most of the top players. The **Open Gaz de France** at the Stade Pierre de Coubertin (⊠ 82 av. Georges-Lafont, 16ᵉ, St-Cloud, ☎ 01–45–27–79–12, métro Porte de St-Cloud) every February is one of the official tournaments on the women's tour. Tickets for both events can be purchased at FNAC or Virgin Megastore, or at the stadium.

7 SHOPPING

In the most beautiful city in the world, it's no surprise to discover that the local greengrocer displays his tomatoes as artistically as Cartier does its rubies. The capital of style, Paris has endless delights to tempt shop-til-you-droppers, from grand couturiers to the funkiest flea markets. Glamour is everywhere—even the Champs-Élysées stamp market was immortalized in the Audrey Hepburn–Cary Grant thriller, *Charade*. Happily, Paris chic is often about pairing a vintage Dior jacket with a casual crewneck T-shirt, so whether you're *fauché*—broke—or want to buy up a storm, this city can be the most rewarding of hunting grounds.

Revised and
updated by
Nicola Keegan

DON'T BE SURPRISED TO SEE SPEEDWALKING PARISIANS slow to a crawl as their eyes lock on an attractive store window. Window shopping is one of this city's greatest spectator sports, and the French have come up with a wonderful expression for this highly cultivated art. They call it *lèche-vitrine*—literally, "licking the windows"—which is quite fitting because many of the displays are good enough to eat. Sonia Rykiel always fills her windows with the latest literary releases, Dior has commissioned artwork for its windows, and a coffee-table book has even been dedicated to those at Hermès, whose *vitrines,* or shop windows, are sometimes like diminutive theaters, small masterpieces of fantasy whose presentation is almost as worthy a sight as the Eiffel Tower. Yet, even the sight of the local *traiteur,* or delicatessen, is sure to set you drooling quite uncontrollably.

Truth is, shopping here can be contagious, and if you don't buy something—bottles of fruit-flavored *eaux-de-vie* that Hemingway and Fitzgerald loved so much, antique brooches from the 1930s, modern vases crafted from Parisian rooftop-tile zinc, rare artwork, or lacy lingerie (this *is* Paris)—you're missing out on a truly Parisian experience, a chance to mix with the natives and feel the heartbeat of the city. Who can understand the magic of French cuisine until he or she has explored a Paris open-air produce market on a weekend morning? Or resist the thrill of seeing a Chanel evening gown displayed in a boutique where even the doorknobs are shaped like Chanel crystal perfume-bottle stoppers?

Happily, the shopping options in Paris are endless and geared to every taste. You can price emerald earrings at Cartier, spend an afternoon browsing through bookstalls along the Seine, tour the high-gloss department stores, or haggle over the price for one of those flea-market "Souvenir de Paris" bracelets, which clank with tin Arc de Triomphes and poodles. But no matter where you head, you'll find scores of unique boutiques that sell Parisian staple: chic. Style, after all, is one of the things the French do best. No matter if a waitress or a countess, all *Parisiennes* seem to share a common denominator: that elusive chic that depends less on the way she chooses her clothes than on her manner of wearing them. It is this unique sense of style that inspires all those foreign-born couturiers and tastemakers to this day—if you get your inspiration from the catwalk, the couturiers often get their ideas from the streets. Today, every neighborhood seems to reflect a unique attitude and style: designer extravagance and haute couture characterize avenue Montaigne and rue Faubourg St-Honoré; classic sophistication pervades St-Germain; avant-garde style dresses up the Marais; while a hip feel suffuses the area around the place des Victoires.

In addition, there are the delightful flea markets and *brocantes* (secondhand shops) where you'll always have the chance of finding a stray bit of Quimper faience, Art Deco brooches, or evocative old copies of *Paris-Match.* At such markets, or in antiques stores, bargaining is accepted. So if you're thinking of buying several items, you've nothing to lose by cheerfully suggesting to the proprietor, *"Vous me faites un prix?"* ("How about a discount?"). Other bits of lingo to keep in mind: *braderie* or *fin de série* (clearance); *occasions* or *brocante* (secondhand); and *nouveautés* (new arrivals). Finally, most stores in Paris—excepting department stores and flea markets—stay open until 6 or 7 PM, but many take a lunch break sometime between noon and 2 PM. Although shops traditionally close on Sunday, regulations have been greatly relaxed in the past decade, and you'll find a number of stores open on that day, most especially in the Marais.

Credit Cards

Credit cards are widely used in France. Even the flea market is likely to honor plastic for purchases of more than €15. Visa is the most common and preferred card, followed closely by MasterCard/EuroCard. American Express, Diners Club, and Access are also accepted in the larger international stores.

Duty-Free Shopping

A value-added tax of 19.6%, known in France as the TVA is imposed on most consumer goods. Non–European Union residents, ages 15 and over, who stay in France and/or the EU for less than six months can reclaim the part of this tax known as the *détaxe*. To qualify, your purchases in a single shop in a single day need to total €185 or more. The refund ranges between 13% and 16%—some wish to be reimbursed by check, but a refund credited directly to your credit card is the fastest way to receive the money. Department stores offer special détaxe desks where the *bordereaux* (export sales invoices) help streamline the process, while high-profile shops often offer détaxe forms, but are not required to do paperwork. If the discount will be a sizeable one, ask if the détaxe is available before purchasing. Note there is no refund for food, wine, and tobacco. Invoices and bordereaux forms are to be shown to French customs upon leaving the country, with items in question available for inspection.

Sales

There are a number of boutiques that specialize in bargains and are every savvy Parisian's secret for maintaining incredible style without breaking the bank. *Soldéries* offer stacks of low-priced designer labels permanently on sale, while *stocks* are stores that specialize in one label and sell last season's leftovers with prices slashed at least in half. *Dépôts-Vente* are consignment shops that carry barely worn designer outfits in great condition at killer prices. Fashionable *friperies* stock clothes and accessories from the '50s to the '80s and are a constant inspiration to the international design teams that come to Paris during the collections. *Surplus* sell army surplus jackets, pants, and great lace-up boots for nearly nothing. When out and about watch for the word *soldes* (sales). By law, the two main sale seasons are January and July, when the average discount is 30%–50% off regular prices. Sales last six weeks. Also look for goods marked *dégriffé*—designer labels, often from last year's collection, for sale at a deep discount.

Shopping by Neighborhood

Avenue Montaigne and Surroundings

Shopping really doesn't come much more chic than on avenue Montaigne. This exclusive, elegant boulevard and the area around are a showcase of international haute couture houses: **Chanel, Dior, Nina Ricci, Céline, Valentino, Max Mara, Genny, Krizia, Escada, Thierry Mugler, Hanae Mori, Emanuel Ungaro, Prada,** and **Dolce & Gabbana.** You'll also find accessories by **S. T. Dupont, Loewe,** and **Louis Vuitton.** Many of the boutiques are housed in exquisite mansions with wrought-iron gates in front. On the sidewalks, you'll spy effortlessly elegant "ladies who lunch"—brandishing tiny, manicured dogs and more than a dash of true Parisian attitude. Neighboring rue François 1er and avenue George V are also lined with many designer boutiques: **Versace, Givenchy** and **Balenciaga.**

Champs-Élysées

Cafés and movie theaters keep the once-chic Champs-Élysées active 24 hours a day, but the invasion of exchange banks, car showrooms, and fast-food chains has certainly lowered the tone. Nowadays, shops like the **Virgin Megastore, Gap,** and the **Disney Store** capture most of the

Champs-Élysées and Avenue Montaigne Area

retail action. Meriting a stop is the cosmetic wonderstore **Sephora,** as well as the quintessentially fashionable **Louis Vuitton** boutique, whose partnership with American designer Marc Jacobs has turned this bourgeois institution into the epitome of cool.

The Faubourg St-Honoré and Place Vendôme

Prime shopping ground for the rich and beautiful, this residential and political hub—you'll find the the Élysée Palace here, as well as the official residences of the American and British ambassadors—contains some of the most famous shops in the world. Renowned antiques galleries such as **Didier Aaron** add artistic flavor. Boutiques include **Hermès, Lanvin, Gucci, Chloé,** and **Christian Lacroix.** Head a bit north to find the place Vendôme, home to many of the world's most elegant jewelers, such as **Cartier, Boucheron, Chaumet,** and **Jar's.**

Left Bank

After decades of clustering on the Right Bank's venerable shopping avenues, the high-fashion houses have stormed the Rive Gauche. The first to arrive were **Sonia Rykiel** and **Yves Saint Laurent** in the late '60s. Forty years later **Christian Dior, Louis Vuitton, Emporio Armani,** and **Cartier** have also set up shop in this dynamic area. Rue des St-Pères and rue de Grenelle are lined with designer names; the latter is especially known for its top-quality shoe shops, such as **Christian Louboutin, Sergio Rossi, Patrick Cox,** and **Stéphane Kélian.**

Louvre–Palais-Royal

The elegant and eclectic shops clustered in the 18th-century arcades of the Palais-Royal sell such items as antiques, toy soldiers, cosmetics, jewelry, and vintage designer dresses. The glossy, marble **Carrousel du Louvre** mall, beneath the Louvre Museum, is lit by an immense inverted glass pyramid. Shops, along with a lively international food court, are open on Sunday—still a rare convenience in Paris.

Le Marais

Between the pre-Revolution mansions and tiny kosher food shops that characterize this area are seemingly hundreds of trendy gift and clothing stores, as well as some of the best furniture and home-wares boutiques in Paris. Avant-garde designers **Azzedine Alaïa** and **Tsumori Chistato,** have boutiques within a few blocks of stately place des Vosges and the Picasso and Carnavalet museums. The Marais is one of the few neighborhoods where nearly all shops are open on Sunday.

Opéra to Madeleine

Two major department stores—**Printemps** and **Galeries Lafayette** — dominate boulevard Haussmann, behind Paris's ornate 19th-century Opéra Garnier. Place de la Madeleine is home to two luxurious food stores, **Fauchon** and **Hédiard. Lalique** and **Baccarat Crystal** also have opulent showrooms near the Église de la Madeleine.

Place des Victoires and Rue Étienne Marcel

The graceful, circular place des Victoires, near the Palais-Royal, is the playground of cutting-edge fashion icons such as **Kenzo** and **Victoire.** Seriously avant-garde designers like **Comme des Garçons** and **Yohji Yamamoto** line rue Étienne Marcel. In the nearby oh-so-charming **Galerie Vivienne** shopping arcade, **Jean-Paul Gaultier** has a shop. And at 3 rue d'Argout, the hottest club-wear emporium in Paris, **Le Shop,** rents retail space to hip, up-and-coming designers.

Rue St-Honoré

A fashionable set makes its way to rue St-Honoré to shop at Paris's most trendy boutique, **Colette.** The street is lined with numerous designer names, as well as the delightful vintage jewelry store **Dary's.** On

236

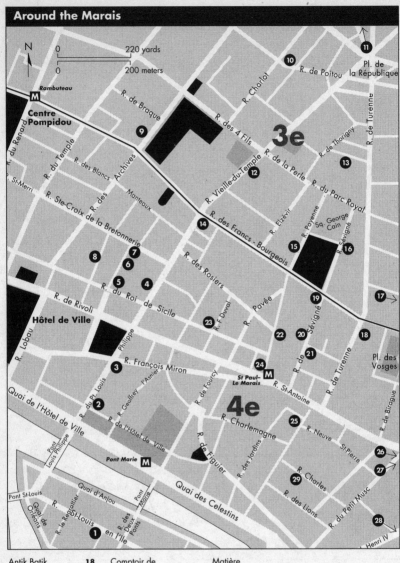

Around the Marais

237

nearby rue Cambon, you'll find the wonderfully elegant **Maria Luisa** and the main **Chanel** boutique. A number of hip designers, such as **Jean-Charles de Castelbajac** and **Comme des Garçons,** have also opened stores on place du Marché St-Honoré.

Department Stores

For an overview of Paris *mode,* visit *les grands magasins,* Paris's monolithic department stores. Visit to gawk at the sometimes ornate architecture, scoff at prices, and marvel at the historical value of it all, as some of these stores have been around since 1860. Most are open Monday through Saturday from about 9:30 AM to 7 PM, and some are open until 10 PM one weekday evening. All five major stores listed below have multilingual guides, international welcome desks, détaxe offices, and restaurants. Most are on the Right Bank, near the Opéra and the Hôtel de Ville; the notable exception is Au Bon Marché, on the Left Bank.

Au Bon Marché (⊠ 24 rue de Sèvres, 7ᵉ, St-Germain-des-Prés, ☎ 01-44-39-80-00, métro Sèvres Babylone), founded in 1852, is an excellent hunting ground on the Left Bank for linens, table settings, and high-quality furniture. In the last few years, it has undergone a complete face-lift and is now incontestably Paris's most chic department store. You often spot public figures, such as French prime minister Lionel Jospin, doing their shopping here. La Grande Épicerie is one of the largest groceries in Paris and a gourmand's home-away-from-home, and the basement is a great place for books, records, classy stationery, and arty gifts.

Au Printemps (⊠ 64 bd. Haussmann, 9ᵉ, Opéra/Grands Boulevards, ☎ 01-42-82-50-00, métro Havre Caumartin, Opéra, Auber) spent a whopping €30 million in revamping its three major stores; Printemps de la Maison (home furnishings), Printemps de l'Homme (menswear—six floors no less), and the brilliant Printemps de la Mode (fashion, fashion, fashion), which is cool, happening, and has everything from cutting-edge Helmut Lang to glitzy-gold Jeremy Scott, from the midrange Zara line to the teenage Free. Fashion shows are held on Tuesday (all year) and Friday (April–October) at 10 AM under the cupola on the seventh floor of La Mode and are free. (**Reservations** can be made in advance by calling ☎ 01-42-82-63-17; tickets can also be obtained on the day of show at the service desk on the first floor.)

Bazar de l'Hôtel de Ville (⊠ 52–64 rue de Rivoli, 4ᵉ, Beaubourg/Les Halles, ☎ 01-42-74-90-00, métro Hôtel de Ville), better known as BHV, houses an enormous basement hardware store that sells everything from doorknobs to cement mixers that has to be seen to be believed. The fashion offerings are minimal, but BHV is noteworthy for quality household goods, home-decor materials, and office supplies.

Galeries Lafayette (⊠ 40 bd. Haussmann, 9ᵉ, Opéra/Grands Boulevards, ☎ 01-42-82-34-56, métro Chaussée d'Antin, Opéra, Havre-Caumartin) is one of those places that you wander into unawares, leaving hours later a poorer and more humble person. It has everything (over 75,000 brand names). Along with the world's largest perfumery, the main store has the "Espace Lafayette Maison," a huge Yves Taralon–designed emporium dedicated to the art of living *à la française.* There is fashion for every style and then some. Free **fashion shows** are held Wednesday at 11:30 AM and Friday (April–October) at 2:30 PM (☎ 01-48-74-02-30 reservations). Don't miss the delectable comestibles department, stocked with the best of everything from herbed goat cheese to Iranian caviar. There is also a branch in Montparnasse (⊠ Centre Commercial Montparnasse, 14ᵉ, Montparnasse, ☎ 01-45-38-52-87, métro Montparnasse Bienvenüe) but this is a pale shadow of its sister store.

La Samaritaine (⊠ 19 rue de la Monnaie, 1ᵉʳ, Louvre/Tuileries, ☎ 01–40–41–20–20, métro Pont Neuf, Châtelet), a sprawling five-store complex, has everything from designer fashions to a free climbing wall but is especially known for kitchen supplies, housewares, and furniture. Its most famous asset is the Toupary restaurant in Building 2, from which there's a marvelous view of Notre-Dame and the Left Bank.

Budget

Monoprix is *the* French dime store par excellence (with branches throughout the city) that stock everyday items like toothpaste, groceries, toys, typing paper, and bath mats—a little of everything. It also has a line of relatively inexpensive basic wearables for the whole family and is, on the whole, not a bad place to stock up on good wines and fine French liqueurs at a reasonable price.

Tati (⊠ 2–28 bd. Rochechouart, 18ᵉ, Montmartre, ☎ 01–55–29–50–00, métro Barbès Rochechouart) is one of Paris's most iconic stores. The ultimate haven for bargain-basement prices, it is certainly not for the fainthearted or claustrophobic. On an average day, it is jam-packed with people of all colors, classes, and sizes, rifling through the jumbled trays in search of a great buy, which they always succeed in doing, since the key word here is cheap, utterly unabashedly cheap. One of its most famous scoops was to offer underwear for just €.15 a pair (they sell 5 million pairs a year). You can also get panty hose for €1 or a cotton T-shirt for €2. It is also well known for its pink and white Vichy shopping bags, ridiculously inexpensive bridal store, and chain of cheap jewelry shops, **Tati Or.**

Markets

Flea Markets

Le Marché aux Puces St-Ouen (métro Porte de Clignancourt), on Paris's northern boundary, still attracts the crowds when it opens on weekends and Monday, but its once-unbeatable prices are now a feature of the past. This century-old labyrinth of alleyways packed with antiques dealers' booths and junk stalls spreads for more than a square mile. Arrive early to pick up the most worthwhile loot (like old prints). But be warned—if there's one place in Paris where you need to know how to bargain, this is it! For lunch, stop for mussels and fries in one of the rough-and-ready cafés.

On the southern and eastern sides of the city—at **Porte de Vanves** (métro Porte de Vanves) and **Porte de Montreuil** —are other, smaller flea markets. Vanves is a hit with the fashion set and specializes in smaller objects—mirrors, textiles, handbags, clothing, and glass. Arrive early if you want to find a bargain, the good stuff goes fast and stalls are liable to be packed up before noon.

Flower and Bird Markets

Paris's main flower market is in the heart of the city on the Ile de la Cité (métro Cité), between Notre-Dame and the Palais de Justice. It's open every day. On Sunday, it also plays host to a bird market. Other colorful flower markets are held beside the Madeleine church (métro Madeleine, open Monday–Saturday 9 AM–9 PM and alternate Sundays 9:30 AM–8:30 PM) and on place des Ternes (métro Ternes, open Tuesday–Sunday).

Food Markets

Many of the better-known markets are in areas you'd visit for sightseeing; here is a list of the top bets. **Rue de Buci** (⊠ 6ᵉ, St.-Germain-des-Prés, métro Odéon), in the chic and lively St-Germain-des-Prés quarter, is closed Sunday PM and Monday. **Rue Mouffetard** (⊠ 5ᵉ, Latin Quarter, métro Place Monge), near the Jardin des Plantes, is best on weekends. **Rue Montorgueuil** (⊠ 1ᵉʳ, Beaubourg/Les Halles, métro Châtelet Les Halles) is closed Monday. **Rue Lepic** in Montmartre (⊠ 18ᵉ, Montmartre, métro Blanche or Abbesses) is best on weekends. **Rue Lévis** (⊠ 17ᵉ, Parc Monceau, métro Villiers), near Parc Monceau, is closed Sunday PM and Monday. **Boulevard Richard Lenoir** (⊠ 11ᵉ, Bastille/Nation, métro Bastille). **Bir-Hakeim** (⊠ 15ᵉ, Invalides/Eiffel Tower, métro Bir-Hakeim). The **Marché d'Aligre** (⊠ Rue d'Aligre, 12ᵉ, Bastille/Nation, métro Ledru-Rollin), open until 1 PM every day except Monday, is a bit farther out but is the cheapest market in Paris; on weekends a small flea market is also held here.

Stamp Market

Philatelists (and fans of the Audrey Hepburn–Cary Grant 1963 thriller, *Charade*) will want to head for Paris's unique **stamp market** at the intersection of avenue Marigny and avenue Gabriel (métro Champs-Élysées Clemenceau) overlooking the gardens at the bottom of the Champs-Élysées. On sale are vintage postcards and stamps from all over the world. It is open Thursday, weekends, and public holidays.

Shopping Arcades

Paris's 19th-century commercial arcades, called *passages*, are the forerunners of the modern shopping mall. Glass roofs, decorative pillars, and inlaid mosaic floors make these spaces real architectural gems. In 1828, they numbered 137, of which only 24 are left. The major arcades are in the 1ᵉʳ and 2ᵉ arrondissements on the Right Bank.

Galerie Véro-Dodat (⊠ 19 rue Jean-Jacques Rousseau, 1ᵉʳ, Louvre/Tuileries, métro Louvre) was built in 1826. At what is now the Café de l'Epoque, the French writer Gérard de Nerval took his last drink before heading to Châtelet to hang himself. The gallery has painted ceilings and slender copper pillars, and shops selling old-fashioned toys, contemporary art, stringed instruments, and leather goods. It is best known, however, for its antiques stores.

Galerie Vivienne (⊠ 4 rue des Petits-Champs, 2ᵉ, Opéra/Grands Boulevards, métro Bourse), between the Stock Exchange (Bourse) and the Palais-Royal, is home-base for a range of interesting and luxurious shops; a quite delicious tearoom, A Priori Thé; and Cave Legrand, a quality wine shop.

Passage du Grand-Cerf (⊠ 145 rue St-Denis, 2ᵉ, Beaubourg/Les Halles, métro Étienne Marcel) is now certainly the hippest of all of Paris's shopping arcades. Take a look at the design showroom, Haute Definition, at No. 4, check out the African objects and furniture at As'Art and the Zen-like furnishings at PM Style, or pop into the boutiques of milliner Jean-Louis Pinabel and jewelers Marie-Lise Goëlo, Eric & Lydie, and Didier Guillemin.

Passage Jouffroy (⊠ 12 bd. Montmartre, 9ᵉ, Montmartre, métro Montmartre) is full of shops selling toys, antique canes, Oriental furnishings, and cinema books and posters. Try Pain d'Épices at No. 29 and Au Bonheur des Dames at No. 39.

Passage des Panoramas (⊠ 11 bd. Montmartre, 2ᵉ, Montmartre, Opéra/Grands Boulevards), opened in 1800, is the oldest arcade; it's especially known for its stamp shops.

Passage Verdeau (⊠ 4–6 rue de la Grange Batelière, 9ᵉ, Opéa/Grands Boulevards, métro Montmartre) is across the street from passage Jouffroy and has shops carrying antique cameras, comic books, and engravings.

Specialty Shops

Arts and Antiques

Antiques dealers proliferate in the **Carré Rive Gauche** (⊠ Between St-Germain-des-Prés and the Musée d'Orsay, 6ᵉ, St-Germain-des Prés, métro St-Germain-des-Prés, Rue du Bac)—head to the area around the rue de Bac, rue de l'Université, rue de Lille, and rue des St-Pères to find a cluster of more than 120 stylish shops. Several antiques dealers are around the **Drouot** auction house (⊠ Corner of rue Rossini and rue Drouot, 9ᵉ, Opéra/Grands Boulevards, métro Richelieu Drouot) near the Opéra. The **Louvre des Antiquaires** (⊠ Pl. du Palais-Royal, 1ᵉʳ, Louvre/Tuileries, métro Palais-Royal) is a stylish mall devoted primarily to antiques. Many big-name dealers—price tags often *start* in the five figures at these places—such as **Didier Aaron, Ariane Dandois,** and **Jacques Perrin** are on rue du Faubourg St-Honoré, place Beauvau, and place Bourbon. The **Viaduc des Arts** (⊠ 9–147 av. Daumesnil, 12ᵉ, Bastille/Nation, métro Ledru-Rollin) houses dozens of art galleries, artisans' boutiques, and upscale shops under the arches of a stone viaduct that once supported train tracks. **Village St-Paul** (⊠ Enter from rue St-Paul, 4ᵉ, Le Marais, métro St-Paul) is a clutch of streets with many antiques shops.

Bags, Scarves, and Accessories

Le Cachemirien (⊠ 13 rue de Tournon, 6ᵉ, St-Germain-des-Prés, ☎ 01–43–29–93–82, métro Odéon) is exclusively dedicated to the fabrics of the Kashmir region of India. Decorated with silk rugs and Anglo-Indian armchairs, the store is also flocked with exquisitely embroidered shawls, pashminas, scarves, and elegantly pared-down clothing made from materials like pashmina and silk.

E. Goyard (⊠ 233 rue St-Honoré, 1ᵉʳ, Louvre/Tuileries, ☎ 01–42–60–57–04, métro Tuileries) has been making the finest luggage since 1853. Clients in the past included Arthur Conan Doyle, Gregory Peck, and the Duke and Duchess of Windsor. Today, Karl Lagerfeld and Madonna are both Goyard fans. Check out the house's signature chevron monogram, which can be found on everything from polo chests and hatboxes to suitcases and wallets.

Hermès (⊠ 24 rue du Faubourg St-Honoré, 8ᵉ, Louvre/Tuileries, ☎ 01–40–17–47–17, métro Concorde) was established as a saddlery in 1837 and went on to create the famous, eternally chic Kelly bag, for Grace Kelly. The magnificent silk scarves—truly fashion icons—are legendary for their rich colors and intricate designs, which change yearly (and men, don't overlook the sumptuous ties). The pared-down women's wear collection is created by avant-garde Belgian designer Martin Margiela. Bags start at a mere €2,300. During semiannual sales, in January and July, prices are slashed by up to 50% and the crowds line up for blocks.

Jamin Puech (⊠ 61 rue d'Hauteville, 10ᵉ, Opéra/Grands Boulevards, ☎ 01–40–22–08–32, métro Poissonière) is where you'll find the entire collection of bags from this happening duo. What makes the bags of Benoit Jamin and Isabelle Puech so unique and desirable is the soft classic shapes with the witty details. They do beaded bags in every shade of the rainbow with thin link chains, dark embossed leather bags with fringe, small evening bags in shell, or hand-dyed crochet numbers—all whimsical, unique, and fun.

Losco (⊠ 20 rue de Sévigné, 4ᵉ, Le Marais, ☎ 01–48–04–39–93, métro St-Paul; ⊠ 5 rue de Sèvres, 6ᵉ, Latin Quarter, ☎ 01–42–22–77–47, métro Sèvres Babylone) allows customers to design their own high-quality, reasonably priced belts by mixing and matching buckles and straps.

Madeleine Gely (⊠ 218 bd. St-Germain, 7ᵉ, St-Germain-des-Prés, ☎

01–42–22–63–35, métro Rue du Bac) is the queen of walking sticks. Late president François Mitterrand used to buy his at this tiny shop also filled with an amazing range of umbrellas.

Miguel Lobato (⊠ 6 rue Malher, 4e, Le Marais, ☎ 01–48–87–68–14, métro St-Paul) is a sweet little boutique filled with stylish accessories for the girl who wants it all: beautiful avant-garde shoes by Rodolphe Menudier, Bruno Frisoni, and Alain Tondowski; bags and nifty little coin purses by Jamin Puech; mod belts by Paris 75000; and beaded bracelets by Azuni. Most thankfully, the charming Miquel is on hand to help you sort it all out.

Peggy Huynh Kinh (⊠ 11 rue Coëtlogon, 6e, Latin Quarter, ☎ 01–42–84–83–82, métro St-Sulpice), a former architect who made her name designing accessories for the prestigious Parisian houses of Balmain and Céline, is now behind the structural line of bags at Cartier. In this boutique, she diffuses her own line of accessories; chicly pared-down totes, shoulder bags, wallets, and belts in quality leather, as well as a line of office accessories.

Renaud Pellegrino (⊠ 78 rue de Seine, 6e, Latin Quarter, ☎ 01–43–54–62–25, métro Odéon) sells his creations under his own name in this discreet boutique at the back of a courtyard. Inspiration for his shoulder bags and totes comes from artists like Matisse and Braque; fans include Catherine Deneuve and model Laetitia Casta. Recently, Pellegrino has also successfully turned his hand to shoes.

DISCOUNT

Accessoires à Soie (⊠ 21 rue des Acacias, 17e, Champs-Élysées, ☎ 01–42–27–78–77, métro Argentine) is where savvy Parisians buy superb silk scarves and ties in all shapes and sizes. The wide selection includes many big-name designers, and everything costs about half of what you'd pay elsewhere.

Books (English-Language)

The scenic open-air bookstall *bouquinistes* along the Seine sell secondhand books (mostly in French), prints, and souvenirs. Numerous French-language bookshops—specializing in a wide range of topics including art, film, literature, and philosophy—are found in the scholarly Latin Quarter and the publishing district, St-Germain-des-Prés. For English-language books and magazines, try the following.

The Abbey Bookstore (⊠ 29 rue Parcheminerie, 5e, Latin Quarter, ☎ 01–46–33–16–24, métro Cluny La Sorbonne) is Paris's Canadian bookstore. It sells Canadian newspapers (*La Presse* and the *Toronto Globe & Mail*), books on Canadian history, as well as new and secondhand Québecois and English-language novels. The Canadian Club of Paris also organizes regular poetry readings and literary conferences here.

Brentano's (⊠ 37 av. de l'Opéra, 2e, Opéra/Grands Boulevards, ☎ 01–42–61–52–50, métro Opéra) is stocked with everything from classics to children's titles. It also has a slightly haphazardly arranged international magazine section.

La Chambre Claire (⊠ 14 rue St-Sulpice, 6e, Latin Quarter, ☎ 01–46–34–04–31, métro Odéon) is chock-a-block with photography books by everyone from Edward Weston to William Wegman. It even stocks instruction manuals and is a favorite with fashion folk, including designer Martine Sitbon.

Comptoir de l'Image (⊠ 44 rue de Sévigné, 3e, Le Marais, ☎ 01–42–72–03–92, métro St-Paul) is where designers John Galliano, Marc Jacobs, and Emanuel Ungaro stock up on old copies of *Vogue*, *Harper's Bazaar*, and *The Face*. It also sells trendy magazines like *Dutch*, *Purple*, and *Spoon*, designer catalogs from the past, and rare photo books.

Galignani (⊠ 224 rue de Rivoli, 1ᵉʳ, Louvre/Tuileries, ☎ 01–42–60–76–07, métro Tuileries) stocks both French- and English-language books and is especially known for its extensive shelves filled with art books and coffee-table tomes.

La Hune (⊠ 170 bd. St-Germain, 6ᵉ, St-Germain-des-Prés, ☎ 01–45–48–35–85, métro St-Germain-des-Prés), sandwiched between the Café de Flore and Les Deux Magots, is a landmark for intellectuals. French literature is downstairs, but the main attraction is the comprehensive collection of international books on art and architecture upstairs. Stay here until midnight with all the other genius-insomniacs.

Ofr (⊠ 78 rue de Seine, 6ᵉ, Latin Quarter, ☎ 01–43–54–62–25, métro Odéon) provides magazines to hip stores from London to San Francisco. In this messy store, you can rub shoulders with photo and press agents and check out the latest in underground, artistic, and alternative monthlies.

The Red Wheelbarrow (⊠ 13 rue Charles, 4ᵉ, Le Marais, ☎ 01–42–77–42–17, métro St-Paul) is *the* anglophone bookstore—if it was written in English, they can get it. It also has a complete academic section and every literary review you can think of. They have readings at least once a month.

7L (⊠ 7 rue de Lille, 7ᵉ, St-Germain-des-Prés, ☎ 01–42–92–03–58, métro St-Germain-des-Prés) is a rather minimalistic space, owned by the book-addicted Karl Lagerfeld. The fashion designer has a personal library of more than 240,000 different volumes, and in this store, he chooses to display and sell a selection of his favorite new releases, as well as the books he edits himself.

Shakespeare and Company (⊠ 37 rue de la Bûcherie, 5ᵉ, Latin Quarter, ☎ 01–43–26–96–50, métro St-Michel), the sentimental Left Bank favorite, is named after the publishing house that first edited James Joyce's *Ulysses*. Nowadays, it specializes in expatriate literature. The staff tends to be rather pretentious, but the shelves of secondhand books hold real bargains. Poets give readings upstairs on Monday at 8 PM; there are also tea-party talks on Sunday at 4 PM.

Tea & Tattered Pages (⊠ 24 rue Mayet, 6ᵉ, St-Germain-des-Prés, ☎ 01–40–65–94–35, métro Duroc) sells cheap secondhand paperbacks, plus new books (publishers' overstock) at low prices. Tea and brownies are served, and browsing is encouraged.

Village Voice (⊠ 6 rue Princesse, 6ᵉ, St-Germain-des-Prés, ☎ 01–46–33–36–47, métro Mabillon), known for its selection of contemporary authors, hosts regular literary readings.

W. H. Smith (⊠ 248 rue de Rivoli, 1ᵉʳ, Louvre/Tuileries, ☎ 01–44–77–88–99, métro Concorde) carries a multitude of travel and language books, cookbooks, and fiction for adults and children. It also has the best selection of foreign magazines and newspapers in Paris (which you are allowed peruse without interruption—many magazine dealers in France aren't so kind).

Clothing (Children's)

Almost all the top designers make minicouture, but you can expect to pay unearthly prices for each wee outfit. Following is where mere mortal Parisian parents shop to keep their kids looking chic.

L'Angelot par Gilles Neveu (⊠ 28 rue Bonaparte, 6ᵉ, St-Germain-des-Prés, ☎ 01–56–24–21–22, métro St-Germain-des-Prés) has everything the newborn to one-year-old baby could desire: clothes in white and beige, bed linen, cuddly teddy bears and rabbits, and jewelry in solid gold. Personalized embroideries and engravings are available upon request, as are deliveries to foreign destinations.

Du Pareil Au Même (⊠ 15 and 23 rue des Mathurins, 8ᵉ, Opéra/Grands Boulevards, ☎ 01–42–66–93–80, métro Havre Caumartin; ⊠ 14 rue

St-Placide, 6e, St-Germain-des-Prés, ☎ 01–45–44–04–40, métro St-Placide) is *the* address for French children from toddlers to preteens. Clothes have a decided French twist with strict attention to details; Peter Pan collars, wool coats with velvet insets, and white shirts embroidered with sweet things.

Pom d'Api (⊠ 28 rue du Four, 6e, St-Germain-des-Prés, ☎ 01–45–48–39–31, métro St-Germain-des-Prés) stocks medium to pricey footwear for babies and preteens in quality leathers and wonderfully vivid colors. Expect well-made, eye-catching fashion—bright gold sneakers, sandals with feathers and beads, and fringed suede boots as well as the classic Mary Janes in shades of silver, pink, and gold. There is also standard utility boots for boys and sturdy rain gear.

Wowo (⊠ 4 rue Hérold, 1er, Beaubourg/Les Halles, ☎ 01–53–40–84–80, métro Châtelet Les Halles) is an original line of well-made clothes for children (from three months) to the preteen. Designer Elizabeth Relin blends her fashion sensibility and love of color with her respect for the world of childhood—no baby Spice Girls here. The clothes are high-quality, wearable, and fun.

Clothing (Discount)

L'Habilleur (⊠ 44 rue Poitou, 3e, Le Marais, ☎ 01–48–87–77–12, métro Sébastien Froissart) is a favorite with the fashion press and anyone else looking for a great deal. For women there's a great selection from designers like Prada, Barbara Bui, and Martine Sitbon. Men can find suits from Mugler, Strelli, and Paul Smith at slashed prices.

Rue d'Alésia (métro Alésia), in the 14e arrondissement, is the main place to find shops selling last season's items at a discount. Mendès, in the 2e, is a notable exception. Be forewarned: most of these shops are much more downscale than their elegant sister shops, and dressing rooms are not always provided.

Clothing (Men's)

Charvet (⊠ 28 pl. Vendôme, 1er, Opéra/Grands Boulevards, ☎ 01–42–60–30–70, métro Opéra) is the Parisian equivalent of a Savile Row tailor: a conservative, aristocratic institution famed for made-to-measure shirts, exquisite ties and accessories, for garbing John F. Kennedy, Charles de Gaulle, and the Duke of Windsor, and its regal address.

L'Eclaireur (⊠ 12 rue Mahler, 4e, Le Marais, ☎ 01–44–54–22–11, métro St-Paul) has opened this loft-style menswear store, just a stone's throw from its flagship store on rue des Rosiers. At the front of the boutique is a counter selling Diptyque candles and scents; at the back, fashions by designers like Jil Sander, Helmut Lang, and Dirk Schönberger.

Le Printemps de L'Homme (⊠ Au Printemps department store, 61 rue Caumartin, 9e, Opéra/Grands Boulevards, ☎ 01–42–82–50–00, métro Havre Caumartin, Opéra) is Paris's menswear fashion leader: six floors of suits, sportswear, coats, ties, and accessories in all price ranges. The funkiest designers, such as Paul Smith, Comme des Garçons, and Martin Margiela, can be found on the third floor, more classic labels like Christian Dior and Burberry on the sixth floor. Make sure you check out the megacool Helmut Lang corner, as well as the rocking World Bar, whose walls are covered with newspapers from around the globe.

Clothing (Resale)

Anouschka (⊠ 6 av. Coq, 9e, Opéra/Grands Boulevards, ☎ 01–48–74–37–00, métro St-Lazare, Trinité) has set up shop in her apartment (open Monday, noon–7; Saturday by appointment) and has rack upon rack of vintage clothing, dating from the '30s to the '70s. It is the perfect place to find a '50s cocktail dress in perfect condition or a mod jacket for him. A former model herself, she calls it a "designer laboratory" and teams from top fashion houses often pop by looking for inspiration.

Catherine Baril (⊠ 14 rue de la Tour, 16ᵉ, Trocadéro, ☎ 01–45–20–95–21, métro Passy) specializes in barely worn designer ready-to-wear from all the big names including Chanel, Saint Laurent, Lacroix, Ungaro, and Rykiel. Few shoppers can pass up one of last season's outfits at one third the price, nor forget to linger over the vast selection of accessories; bags, belts, scarves, shoes, and costume jewelry.

Didier Ludot (⊠ Jardins du Palais-Royal, 20/24 Galerie Montpensier/125 galérie de Valois, 1ᵉʳ, Louvre/Tuileries, ☎ 01–42–96–06–56, métro Palais-Royal) is one of the world's most famous vintage clothing dealers and an incredibly charming man to boot. His clientele ranges from model Stephanie Seymour to fashion designer Azzedine Alaïa. Check out the French couture from the '20s to the '70s on the racks: wonderful old Chanel suits, Balenciaga dresses, and Hermès scarves. He has three boutiques: No. 20 houses his amazing collection of vintage couture, No. 24, his collection of ready-to-wear, and across the way at No. 125, you'll find his collection of vintage black dresses and his coffee-table book aptly titled *The Little Black Dress*.

Guerrisold (⊠ 17 bis bd. Rochechouart, 9ᵉ, Montmartre, ☎ 01–42–80–66–18, métro Barbès Rochechouart) is for that sturdy race of shopper willing to sift through rack upon rack of cheap (often musty) clothing from the 1970s and 1980s to find that heart-stopping treasure, made even more precious by the fact that it will probably cost a mere €10.

Kiliwatch (⊠ 64 rue Tiquetonne, 2ᵉ, Beaubourg/Les Halles, ☎ 01–42–21–17–37, métro Étienne Marcel) is a large concrete cavern that houses one of Paris's hottest places to shop. Everyone comes here; designers, models, journalists, musicians, funky Parisians, and anyone else who loves to shop for stylish vintage pieces, here renovated, dry-cleaned, and slapped with a fairly high price tag. More affordable and fun are the racks upon racks of secondhand finds called "fripes" that are organized according to color and style to ease the immensity of the task of sifting through each and every item (as most of the shop's fans do).

Réciproque (⊠ 88, 89, 92, 95, 101, and 123 rue de la Pompe, 16ᵉ, Trocadéro, ☎ 01–47–04–30–28, métro Rue de la Pompe) Paris's largest and most exclusive swap shop. Savings on designer wear—Hermès, Dior, Chanel, and Louis Vuitton—are significant, but prices are not as cheap as you might expect, and there's not much in the way of service or space. The shop at No. 89 specializes in leather goods. The store is closed Sunday and Monday.

Scarlett (⊠ 10 rue Clément-Marot, 8ᵉ, Invalides/Eiffel Tower, ☎ 01–56–89–03–00, métro Alma-Marceau) offers exceptional vintage couture by the likes of Givenchy, Poiret, Schiaparelli, and Vionnet.

Clothing (Women's)

CHIC AND CASUAL

Celine (⊠ 36 av. Montaigne, 8ᵉ, Champs-Élysées, ☎ 01–56–89–07–91, métro Franklin D. Roosevelt) was venerable and dusty before designer Michael Kors showed up with his version of Jackie Oh—"the Greek magnate years." Slim-fitting white jeans, wide ribbed cashmere sweaters, skin tight T-shirts in Saint-Tropez stripes, and other Park Avenue must-haves have put this king of casual elegance on the map.

Et Vous (⊠ 6 rue des Francs-Bourgeois, 3ᵉ, Le Marais, ☎ 01–42–71–75–11, métro St-Paul) takes its cue from the catwalk; turning out affordable, extremely well-cut clothing: pants (low waist/slim hip), knee-skimming skirts, chunky sweaters, and classic work wear with individual details.

Tara Jarmon (⊠ 18 rue du Four, 6ᵉ, St-Germain-des-Prés, ☎ 01–46–33–26–60, métro Mabillon) is the story of a Canadian who came to Paris to study politics and ended up designing a best-selling line. She is a fave with working Parisians because she emphasizes cut, quality, and style over trends. Best-sellers include transparent feminine blouses worn under light tweed jackets; evening dresses cut on the bias with strategically placed sheer panels, and her wonderfully retro coats cut to last many seasons.

Ventilo (⊠ 27 bis rue du Louvre, 2ᵉ, Louvre/Tuileries, ☎ 01–44–76–83–00, métro Louvre) brings cool ethnic style to the classy city girl. Who else would need a bright orange silk shantung ball skirt with mirror appliqué or a modern Mongol leather coat lined in fur? There is also room for classics to mix and match, such as handmade wool turtlenecks and zippered riding pants that fit perfectly.

Zara (⊠ 44 av. des Champs-Élysées, 8ᵉ, Champs-Élysées, ☎ 01–45–61–52–80, métro Franklin-D.-Roosevelt; ⊠ 109 rue St-Lazare, 9ᵉ, Opéra/Grands Boulevards, ☎ 01–53–32–82–95, métro St-Lazare) is hyped as the most reasonable place to go for the latest trends. While they do have everything copied and on the racks in record time, the prices aren't as low as one would expect for this type of quality. Choose wisely; check the seams, feel the fabric, and whatever you do, try it on before deciding if it's worth the investment. Oh, and don't worry—it's *not* you; the tops are cut small, the pants smaller.

CLASSIC CHIC

No matter, say the French, that fewer and fewer of their top couture houses are still headed by compatriots. It's the chic elegance, the classic ambience, the *je ne sais quoi,* that remains undeniably Gallic. Most of the high-fashion shops are on avenue Montaigne, avenue George-V, and rue du Faubourg St-Honoré on the Right Bank, though St-Germain-des-Prés has also become a stomping ground for renowned designers. Following are just a few of Paris's haute couture highlights.

Chanel (⊠ 42 av. Montaigne, 8ᵉ, Champs-Élysées, ☎ 01–47–23–74–12, métro Franklin-D.-Roosevelt; ⊠ 31 rue Cambon, 1ᵉʳ, Louvre/Tuileries, ☎ 01–42–86–28–00, métro Tuileries) is helmed by the newly svelte Karl Lagerfeld who knows exactly what to do and how to do it. For Chanel, he has modernized the best looks without really changing what could not get better. The navy blue quilted handbag, the black-and-white braided tweed suits, and the two-tone pumps are still the standards. The historical center is at the rue Cambon and is the best place to visit to get that full Chanel effect. Touch the frothy flesh-colored knee-length cocktail dresses or the perfect sequinned jackets, or indulge in one small guiltless pleasure—the always fashionable camellia brooch in your favorite color.

Christian Dior (⊠ 30 av. Montaigne, 8ᵉ, Champs-Élysées, ☎ 01–40–73–54–44, métro Franklin-D.-Roosevelt) installed flamboyant John Galliano as head designer after his triumphant run at Givenchy and, since then, nothing but nothing has been the same. His catwalks are always the most talked-about *evenements* (events) of the fashion season; opulent, crazy events with sheer evening gowns grazing the floor outfitted on a new species of amazonian nomad, hundreds of floating butterflies, bottles of iced champagne, and some of the most beautiful women in the world in attendance (not to mention the men). Despite the theatrical staging and surreal hijinks, his full-length body-skimming evening dresses cut on the bias are brilliantly beautiful in whatever fabric he chooses . . . so what if he pairs them with high tops and a Davy Crockett raccoon hat? It's just fashion, darling.

Jean-Paul Gaultier (✉ 30 rue du Faubourg St-Antoine, 12ᵉ, Bastille/Nation, ☎ 01–44–68–84–84, métro Bastille) first made headlines with his celebrated corset with the ironic i-conic breasts for Madonna, but now sends fashion editors into ecstasy with his supersumptuous Haute Couture creations. Five floors of fashion here include his JPG jeans, accessories, and ready-to-wear. There is a sister store at 6 rue Vivienne in the Beaubourg quartier.

Sonia Rykiel (✉ 175 bd. St-Germain, 6ᵉ, St-Germain-des-Prés, ☎ 01–49–54–60–60, métro St-Germain-des-Prés; ✉ 70 rue du Faubourg St-Honoré, 8ᵉ, Louvre/Tuileries, ☎ 01–42–65–20–81, métro Concorde) has been designing fabulous knitwear since the '60s and is a French icon in her own right. Although the label has lost some of its freshness, her little knit sweaters in lime green and fuchsia are still classics and she has not lost her eye for that perfect accessory.

Ungaro (✉ 2 av. Montaigne, 8ᵉ, Champs-Élysées, ☎ 01–53–57–00–00, métro Alma-Marceau) is the master of the sexy diva look with his floor-length fluid dresses in sheer florals and his famed draped mousseline cocktail dresses that skim the knee in shades of butterfly. His dresses grace the most beautiful women in the world (Sharen Stone, Jennifer Lopez, Sophie Marceau). Check out his line of boho-chic accessories.

TRENDSETTERS

Antik Batik (✉ 18 rue de Turenne, 4ᵉ, Le Marais, ☎ 01–48–87–95–95, métro St-Paul; ✉ 8, rue de Foin, 4ᵉ, Le Marais, ☎ 01–40–29–49–93, métro St-Paul) has a wonderful line of ethnically inspired clothes popular with models and other hip Parisians. There are row upon row of embroidered velvet dress coats, Chinese silk tunics, short fur jackets, fringed printed shawls, and some of Paris's most popular handbags. Children have their own boutique around the corner on the rue de Foin.

Antoine & Lili (✉ 95 quai de Valmy, 10ᵉ, République, ☎ 01–40–37–41–55, métro Jacques-Bonsergent) is a bright fuchsia store packed with eclectic objects from the East and its own line of clothing. The fantasy seems to work for the French because these boutiques are always hopping. There is an ethnic rummage-sale feel, with old Asian posters, small lanterns, and basket upon basket of cheap little doodads, baubles, and trinkets for sale. Oddly, the clothing is on the austere side.

A-POC (✉ 47 rue des Francs-Bourgeois, 4ᵉ, Le Marais, ☎ 01–44–54–07–05, métro St-Paul), stands for "A Piece of Cloth" (also a play on the word "epoch") and is Japanese designer Issey Miyake's latest adventure. The concept is the intellectual side of avant garde; a fabrication technique that allows for hundreds of clothes to be cut from one piece of tubular cloth, resulting in an incredibly interesting line of clothing that one can customize at will. Miyake has an almost religious following and, contrary to first impressions, his clothes are eminently stylish and wearable. There are even adorable styles for children.

Azzedine Alaïa (✉ 7 rue de Moussy, 4ᵉ, Le Marais, ☎ 01–42–72–19–19, métro Hôtel de Ville) is one of the darlings of the fashion set with his perfectly proportioned "king of cling" elasthane dresses. Thanks to his celebrated Tunisian charm, it's no wonder Naomi calls him "Daddy." You don't have to be under 20 to look good in one of his dresses; Tina Turner wears his clothes well as does every other beautiful woman with the courage and the curves. His boutique/workshop/apartment is covered with artwork by Julian Schnabel and is not the kind of place one casually wanders into out of curiosity; the sales staff immediately makes you feel awkward in that distinctive Parisian way.

Beauty by Et Vous (✉ 25 rue Royale, 8ᵉ, Louvre/Tuileries, ☎ 01–55–25–30–30, métro Madeleine) is a concept store filled with exclusive unique creations from the best of the newest young designers, a beauty counter for both men and women with helpful friendly service, the ubiquitous video installation no one pays attention to, wonderful clothes from Et Vous' less expensive diffusion line *EV*, and a whole floor devoted to menswear featuring Mandarina Duck and Trace.

Colette (✉ 213 rue St-Honoré, 1ᵉʳ, Louvre/Tuileries, ☎ 01–55–35–33–90, métro Tuileries) is the address for fashion par excellence and because it is the address for fashion par excellence, it's also the least consumer-friendly. But who cares! There are ultramodern trinkets and trifles of all kinds; perfumes, world-famous cosmetics, creams, and potions of all sorts, including Aesop, Kiehls, and François Nars; plus a jewelry "bar" of Marie-Hélène de Taillac . . . and that's just the ground floor. The first floor has beautiful clothing from every internationally known and unknown designer (clothes, shoes, and accessories) which oozes trendiness and street cred, and a small library for the ultramod hipster in the know. The basement has a water bar (because that's what the models eat) and a small restaurant that's actually quite good for a quick bite.

E2 (✉ 2 rue de Provence, 9ᵉ, Opéra/Grands Boulevards, ☎ 01–47–70–15–14, métro Grands Boulevards) houses, by appointment only, three lines created by designers Michèle and Olivier Chatenet: their own label of ethnic-influenced fashion inspired by the '30s to the '70s; impeccable vintage couture finds like Pucci, Lanvin, and Hermès; plus clothing created with their own unique method of customizing fashion (they take tired fashion and cut it up or sew it into a whole new outfit; for example, sewing emerald-green sequins into the pleats of an ordinary gray kilt). With one of these creations in tow, you will be dressed like no one else, as fashion friends Madonna and Gwyneth would tell you (if you were their fashion friend).

L'Éclaireur (✉ 3 rue des Rosiers, 4ᵉ, Le Marais, ☎ 01–48–87–10–22, métro St-Paul) has been on the cutting edge of fashion for years and stocks avant-garde favorites such as Martin Margiela, Anne Demeulemeester, and Carpe Diem plus a taste of most other ready-to-wear icons like Prada and Dolce & Gabbana.

Eric Bergère (✉ 16 rue de la Sourdière, 1ᵉʳ, Louvre/Tuileries, ☎ 01–47–03–33–19, métro Tuileries) is a rare species in Paris these days: a *French* designer. Not only that, he's one of the best. His clothes are timeless not trendy—witness his take on the perfect trench. Contemporary basics that flatter with interesting details often borrowed from folklore, sheer black flouncy saloon skirts, and Anna Karenina flowing cowl capes are just some of the delights here.

Isabel Marant (✉ 16 rue de Charonne, 11ᵉ, Bastille, ☎ 01–49–29–71–55, métro Ledru-Rollin; ✉ 1 rue Jacob, 6ᵉ, St-Germain-des-Prés, ☎ 01–43–26–04–12, métro St-Germain-des-Prés) is a young designer who wowed the fashion world with her bohemian rock-star line for women. This is sexy and fun fashion that skims the body without constricting it: great wide-legged pants in tweed, long corduroy skirts cut on the bias, tight little knitwear sets in cool colors (prune, green, and taupe). Night is devoted to the diva.

Jean-Charles de Castelbajac Concept Store (✉ 26 rue Madame, 6ᵉ, St-Germain-des-Prés, ☎ 01–45–48–40–55, métro St-Sulpice; ✉ 31 pl. du Marché St-Honoré, 1ᵉʳ, Louvre/Tuileries, ☎ 01–42–60–41–55, métro Tuileries) carries the quirkly cerebral yet memorably elegant designs of the designer's own clothing collection, along with furniture, candles, blankets, and luggage. There is also jewelry by different young designers each season; cool books and magazines like *Dutch*, *Crash*, and *Very*; and Keith Haring–designed dominoes.

Kokon To Zaï (⊠ 48 rue Tiquetonne, 2ᵉ, Beaubourg/Les Halles, ☎ 01–42–36–92–41, métro Étienne Marcel) is a Japanese expression to sum up the concept of opposing extremes (such as hot and cold, young and old). It is also a hip boutique, selling the creation of more than 40 young designers, including Jeremy Scott, Bernard Wilhelm, and Viktor & Rolf.

Lagerfeld Gallery (⊠ 40 rue de Seine, 6ᵉ, St-Germain-des-Prés, ☎ 01–55–42–75–51, métro Mabillon) sells Karl's own signature Lagerfeld line, as well as the collection he designs for Italian fur house Fendi. On the first floor are accessories, perfumes, magazines, and exhibitions of Lagerfeld's own photography.

Maria Luisa (⊠ 38 rue du Mont-Thabor, 1ᵉʳ, Louvre/Tuileries, ☎ 01–42–96–47–81, métro Concorde) is one of the most important names in town for cutting-edge fashion. The store at No. 38 is considered a "style laboratory" for young designers for both him and her; No. 2 is the woman's shop stocked by an army of established designers (like Lang and Demeulemeester); No. 4 houses one of the few places in Paris to get übercool shoes by Manolo Blahnik and chichi bags by Lulu Guinness; No. 19 bis is the address for *monsieur*.

NIM (⊠ 16 rue du Bourg-Tibourg, 4ᵉ, Le Marais, ☎ 01–42–77–19–79, métro Hôtel de Ville) is the name of Levi's Parisian concept store. The simple concrete boutique has 501s and customized vintage jeans hanging on hooks on the walls, as well as limited-edition accessories and an exhibition space for avant-garde art installations.

Onward (⊠ 147 bd. St-Germain, 6ᵉ, St-Germain-des-Prés, ☎ 01–55–42–77–55, métro St-Germain-des-Prés), formerly known as Kashiyama, stocks fashion-forward clothes and accessories by the likes of Ann Demeulemeester, Martin Margiela, Martine Sitbon, Véronique Branquinho, and A. F. Vandevorst. It also gives over a space each season to up-and-coming labels, like Luella, Viktor & Rolf, and Alexandre Mathieu.

Paul & Joe (⊠ 46 rueEtienne Marcel, 2ᵉ, Beaubourg/Les Halles, ☎ 01–40–28–03–34, métro Etienne Marcel) is designer Sophie Albou's eclectic mix of modern trends for the fashionable girl who hasn't yet decided where she fits in. There is a decidedly retro feeling to the crisp poplin shirts, A-line skirts with matching fitted jackets, and wonderfully swingy felt coats. In summer she likes to mix in a little hippie chic.

Raw Essentials (⊠ 46 rue Étienne-Marcel, 2ᵉ, Beaubourg/Les Halles, ☎ 01–42–21–44–33, métro Etienne Marcel) is a haven for fans of raw denim. It uniquely stocks the designs of the Dutch-based label G-Star, whose highly desirable jeans have replaced those of Levi's as the ones to be seen in. There is also military-inspired clothing, bags, and T-shirts.

Shine (⊠ 30 rue de Charonne, 11ᵉ, Bastille, ☎ 01–48–05–80–10, métro Ledru-Rollin) travels the world to find clothes and accessories that embody the store's spirit: chic, glamorous, and rock and roll. As well as taking in the fashions, also check out the fabulous floral wallpaper and sparkly, gold wall displays.

Le Shop (⊠ 3 rue d'Argout, 2ᵉ, Louvre/Tuileries, ☎ 01–40–28–95–94, métro Louvre) is the Parisian address for fans of street wear and techno. The industrial-style shop rocks to the beat of resident DJs and carries numerous hip designers as well as skateboards, sports shoes, and flyers for raves and parties. The whole experience is rather like shopping in a nightclub.

Le Webstore (⊠ 29 rue du Louvre, 2ᵉ, Louvre/Tuileries, ☎ 01–40–26–92–77, métro Louvre) is the showcase for the Web site (WEB www.le-webstore.com). Created by brothers Jean-Yves and Hubert Lanvin (great-nephews of the famed couturière Jeanne), it sells everything from funky T-shirts and scented bracelets to designer radiators and miniature cameras.

Cosmetics

When it comes to *maquillage* (makeup), many Parisian women head directly to **Monoprix,** an urban supermarket/dime store and a gold mine for inexpensive, good-quality cosmetics. Brand names to look for are Bourjois, whose products are made in the Chanel factories, and Arcancil.

Anne Sémonin (⊠ 2 rue des Petits-Champs, 2ᵉ, Beaubourg/Les Halles, ☎ 01–42–60–94–66, métro Palais-Royal; ⊠ 108 rue du Faubourg St-Honoré, 8ᵉ, Champs-Élysées, ☎ 01–42–66–24–22, métro Champs-Élysées Clemenceau) sells exceptional skin-care products made out of seaweed and trace elements, as well as essential oils that are popular with fashion models.

By Terry (⊠ 21 Galerie Véro-Dodat, 1ᵉʳ, Louvre/Tuileries, ☎ 01–44–76–00–76, métro Louvre, Palais-Royal; ⊠ 1 rue Jacob, 6ᵉ, St-Germain-des-Prés, ☎ 01–46–34–00–36, métro St-Germain-des-Prés) is the brainchild of Yves Saint Laurent's former director of makeup, Terry de Gunzberg. This small and refined jewel of a store offers her own brand of "ready-to-wear" makeup that is a favorite of French actresses and socialites. Upstairs there is a team of specialists that creates what de Gunzberg calls *haute couleur,* an exclusive made-to-measure makeup line created specifically for each client (very expensive and to be booked way in advance.

Make Up for Ever (⊠ 5 rue de la Boétie, 8ᵉ, Champs-Élysées, ☎ 01–42–66–01–60, métro St-Augustin), at the back of a courtyard, is a must-stop for makeup artists, models (Kate Moss is a regular), and actresses (Madonna has dropped in, too). The ultrahip selection spans 100 shades of foundation, 100 different lipsticks, 125 eye shadows, 24 glittering powders, and scores of fake eyelashes.

Sephora (⊠ 70 av. des Champs-Élysées, 8ᵉ, Champs-Élysées, ☎ 01–53–93–22–50, métro Franklin-D.-Roosevelt; ⊠ 1 rue Pierre Lescot, in the Forum des Halles, 1ᵉʳ, Beaubourg/Les Halles, ☎ 01–40–13–72–25, métro Châtelet Les Halles), the leading chain of perfume and cosmetics megastores in France, sells its own makeup as well as all the big brands. Choose from 365 colors of lipstick, browse through the "Cultural Gallery" at the Champs-Élysées store, and even send e-mails for free from the in-store computers.

Flowers and Gardening Outfitters

Au Nom de la Rose (⊠ 46 rue du Bac, 7ᵉ, St-Germain-des-Prés, ☎ 01–42–22–08–09, métro Rue du Bac; ⊠ 87 rue St-Antoine, 4ᵉ, Le Marais, ☎ 01–42–71–34–24, métro St-Paul), as its name suggests, specializes in roses of all different kinds.

Christian Tortu (⊠ 6 carrefour de l'Odéon, 6ᵉ, Latin Quarter, ☎ 01–43–26–02–56, métro Odéon), Paris's most fashionable florist, has made a name for himself with his very natural-looking bouquets. His annex boutique around the corner sells his popular glassware, tableware, candles, and must-have zinc vases.

Le Prince Jardinier (⊠ 37 rue de Valois (117 Araade Valois, 1ᵉʳ, Louvre/Tuileries, ☎ 01–42–60–37–13, métro Palais-Royal) comes by its name honestly, thanks to owner Prince Louis-Albert de Broglie, whose gardening tools, frocks, and accessories are as soigné and charming as he is.

Food and Wine

À la Mère de Famille (⊠ 35 rue du Faubourg-Montmartre, 9ᵉ, Opéra/Grands Boulevards, ☎ 01–47–70–83–69, métro Cadet) is an enchanting shop well versed in French regional specialties and old-fashioned bonbons, sugar candy, and more.

Les Caves Augé (✉ 116 bd. Haussmann, 8ᵉ, Opéra/Grands Boulevards, ☎ 01–45–22–16–97, métro St-Augustin), one of the best wine shops in Paris since 1850, is just the ticket whether you're looking for a rare vintage for an oenophile friend or a seductive Bordeaux for a tête-à-tête. English-speaking Marc Sibard is a knowledgeable and affable adviser.

Debauve & Gallais (✉ 30 rue des Sts-Pères, 7ᵉ, St-Germain-des-Prés, ☎ 01–45–48–54–67, métro St-Germain-des-Prés) was founded in 1800 by two former chemists to Louis XVI who decided to start making chocolates. Today, their delectable recipes can still be found here.

L'Épicerie (✉ 51 rue St-Louis-en-L'Ile, 4ᵉ, Ile St-Louis, ☎ 01–43–25–20–14, métro Pont Marie) sells 90 types of jam (such as figs with almonds and cinnamon), 70 kinds of mustard (including one with chocolate and honey), numerous olive oils, and flavored sugars.

Fauchon (✉ 26 pl. de la Madeleine, 8ᵉ, Opéra/Grands Boulevards, ☎ 01–47–42–60–11, métro Madeleine) is the most famous and iconic of all Parisian food stores. Established in 1886, it sells renowned pâté, honey, jelly, and private-label champagne. Hard-to-find foreign foods (U.S. pancake mix, British lemon curd) are also stocked, and delectable pastries and chocolates are served in the café. Prices can be eye-popping—chocolates for €70 a pound, marzipan fruits for €95 a pound—but who can nay-say that soigné, top-of-the-line Fauchon chocolate box, whose cover bears an antique engraving of place de la Madeleine.

La Grande Épicerie (✉ 38 rue de Sèvres, 7ᵉ, St-Germain-des-Prés, ☎ 01–44–39–81–00, métro Sèvres Babylone), on the ground floor of Au Bon Marché, stocks a veritable cornucopia of fine French foodstuffs.

Hédiard (✉ 21 pl. de la Madeleine, 8ᵉ, Opéra/Grands Boulevards, ☎ 01–43–12–88–88, métro Madeleine), established in 1854, was famous in the 19th century for its high-quality imported spices. These—along with rare teas and beautifully packaged house brands of jam, mustard, and cookies—are still sold.

La Maison du Chocolat (✉ 56 rue Pierre Charron, 8ᵉ, Champs-Élysées, ☎ 01–47–23–38–25, métro Franklin-D.-Roosevelt; ✉ 8 bd. de la Madeleine, 9ᵉ, Louvre/Tuileries, ☎ 01–47–42–86–52, métro Madeleine; ✉ 225 rue du Faubourg St-Honoré, 8ᵉ, Louvre/Tuileries, ☎ 01–42–27–39–44, métro Ternes) is heaven if you love chocolate: take some home or have a treat in the tearooms at the store on rue Pierre Charron or Madeleine.

La Maison du Miel (✉ 24 rue Vignon, 9ᵉ, Louvre/Tuileries, ☎ 01–47–42–26–70, métro Madeleine) takes *miel* (honey) seriously—more than 30 varieties are in stock, many sweetly packaged for delicious gift-giving.

Mariage Frères (✉ 30 rue du Bourg-Tibourg, 4ᵉ, Le Marais, ☎ 01–42–72–28–11, métro Hôtel de Ville), with its colonial *charme* and wooden counters, is the place to get tea in Paris. You can choose from more than 450 blends from 32 different countries and purchase teapots, teacups, books about tea, and tea-flavor biscuits and candies. There is also an on-site tearoom that serves high tea or a light lunch.

Verlet (✉ 256 rue St-Honoré, 1ᵉʳ, Louvre/Tuileries, ☎ 01–42–60–67–39, métro Palais-Royal) is *the* place in Paris to buy coffee. There are more than 20 varieties, from places as far flung as Hawaii and Papua New Guinea (you can also sample the brews on the premises). Also on sale are teas, jams from the Savoie region, and (during winter months) a stunning assortment of candied fruits.

Hats

Marie Mercié (✉ 23 rue St-Sulpice, 6ᵉ, St-Germain-des-Prés, ☎ 01–43–26–45–83, métro Mabillon, St-Sulpice) is one of Paris's most fashionable hatmakers. Her husband, Anthony Peto, makes men's hats and has a store at 58 rue Tiquetonne.

Philippe Model (✉ 33 pl. du Marché St-Honoré, 1ᵉʳ, Louvre/Tuileries, ☎ 01–42–96–89–02, métro Tuileries) has been confecting amazing hats for *haute société* for many years and has more recently expanded his creative energy to a successful line of shoes and unique objects for the home.

Housewares

Agatha Ruiz de la Prada (✉ 9 rue Guénégaud, 6ᵉ, Latin Quarter, ☎ 01–43–25–86–88, métro Odéon) is nothing if not prolific. She designs clothing and accessories for the Spanish department store El Corte Inglès, watches for Swatch, and furniture for Amat. In this small store, she also sells her own creations, from bags and children's fashions to yo-yos and notebooks. All are typified by naive motifs in primary colors.

Alexandre Biaggi (✉ 14 rue de Seine, 6ᵉ, St-Germain-des-Prés, ☎ 01–44–07–34–73, métro St-Germain-des-Prés) is one of the best addresses for 20th-century furniture. He specializes in the period 1910–50 and also commissions the occasional design from talented contemporary designers, such as Nicolas Aubagnac and Hervé van der Straeten.

A. Simon (✉ 48 rue Montmartre, 2ᵉ, Beaubourg/Les Halles, ☎ 01–42–33–71–65, métro Étienne Marcel) is one of the places where all those wonderful Parisian chefs come to acquire everything they need in the kitchen—from plates and glasses to pans, dishes, and wooden spoons. The quality is excellent and the prices pleasantly reasonable.

Avant-Scène (✉ 4 pl. de l'Odéon, 6ᵉ, Latin Quarter, ☎ 01–46–33–12–40, métro Odéon) has been editing original, poetic furniture for the past 15 years. Owner Elisabeth Delacarte commissions limited-edition pieces from artists like Mark Brazier-Jones, Franck Evennou, and Hubert Le Gall.

Catherine Memmi (✉ 32–34 rue St-Sulpice, 6ᵉ, St-Germain-des-Prés, ☎ 01–44–07–22–28, métro Mabillon, St-Sulpice; ✉ 43 rue Madame, 6ᵉ, St-Germain-des-Prés, ☎ 01–45–48–18–34, métro St-Sulpice) sells wonderfully chic bed linens, bath products, lamps, table settings, furniture, and cashmere sweaters—all in elegantly neutral colors and minimalist designs. Cheaper items in cotton are sold at the rue Madame address.

Christian Liaigre (✉ 42 rue du Bac, 7ᵉ, St-Germain-des-Prés, ☎ 01–53–63–33–66, métro Rue du Bac) is one of the most fashionable interior decorators at the moment. He designed the Mercer Hotel in New York and the homes of designer Kenzo and French actress Carole Bouquet. His fashionably simple furniture is sold in this flagship boutique.

Christofle (✉ 24 rue de la Paix, 2ᵉ, Opéra/Grands Boulevards, ☎ 01–42–65–62–43, métro Opéra; ✉ 9 rue Royale, 8ᵉ, Louvre/Tuileries, ☎ 01–55–27–99–00, métro Concorde, Madeleine), founded in 1830, is *the* name to know in French silver. Come here for perfectly elegant table settings, vases, cigarette holders, jewelry boxes, and more.

Christophe Delcourt (✉ 125 rue Vieille-du-Temple, 3ᵉ, Le Marais, ☎ 01–42–78–44–97, métro Rambuteau, St-Paul) is one of France's most sought-after interior designers. Fashion designers and film stars flock to this store to snap up his lamps based on old-fashioned drawing tools, waxed-steel furniture, and sleek, wooden tables.

Compagnie Française de l'Orient et de la Chine (✉ 163 bd. St-Germain, 6ᵉ, St-Germain-des-Prés, ☎ 01–45–48–00–18, métro St-Germain-des-Prés) imports ceramics and furniture from China and Mongolia. On the first floor are vases, teapots, and table settings; in the basement are straw hats, raffia baskets, and bamboo footstools.

Conran Shop (✉ 117 rue du Bac, 7ᵉ, St-Germain-des-Prés, ☎ 01–42–84–10–01, métro Sèvres Babylone; ✉ 30 bd. des Capucines, 9ᵉ,

Opéra/Grands Boulevards, ☎ 01–53–43–29–00, métro Madeleine) is the brainchild of British entrepreneur Terence Conran. Here you can find expensive contemporary furniture, beautiful bed linens, glassware, kitchen utensils, vases, lamp shades, and bathroom accessories.

Diptyque (✉ 34 bd. St-Germain, 5ᵉ, St-Germain-des-Prés, ☎ 01–43–26–45–27, métro Maubert Mutualité) sells scented candles (fashion designer Karl Lagerfeld is a fan) in natural fragrances such as rose, tea, and honeysuckle. It also has lamp oils and perfumes.

Gien (✉ 18 rue de l'Arcade, 8ᵉ, Louvre/Tuileries, ☎ 01–42–66–52–32, métro Madeleine) has been making fine china since 1821. As well as traditional designs, you'll also find place settings especially designed by contemporary artists.

Laguiole (✉ 1 pl. Ste-Opportune, 1ᵉʳ, Beaubourg/Les Halles, ☎ 01–40–28–09–42, métro Châtelet) is the name of the country's most famous knife. Today, designers like Philippe Starck and Sonia Rykiel have created special models for the company. Starck also designed this striking boutique (note the animal horn sticking out of the wall).

R & Y Augousti (✉ 103 rue du Bac, 7ᵉ, St-Germain-des-Prés, ☎ 01–42–22–22–21, métro Sèvres Babylone) are two Paris-based designers who make furniture and objects for the home in materials like coconut, bamboo, fish skin, palm wood, and parchment. Also on sale is their line of textiles, inspired by peacock feathers. Treat yourself to one of their cushions in pashmina, raffia, leather, or printed cotton.

Sentou Galerie (✉ 24 rue du Pont Louis-Philippe, 4ᵉ, Le Marais, ☎ 01–42–71–00–01, métro St-Paul) specializes in contemporary design objects—lamps designed by artists, furniture by up-and-coming designers, and re-editions of seminal chairs and stools. At No. 18 is a store devoted to tableware.

Van Der Straeten (✉ 11 rue Ferdinand Duval, 4ᵉ, Le Marais, ☎ 01–42–78–99–99, métro St-Paul) is the lofty gallery-cum-showroom of Paris designer Hervé van der Straeten. He started out creating jewelry for Saint Laurent and Lacroix, designed a perfume bottle for Christian Dior, and also moved into making rather baroque and often wacky furniture. On show are necklaces, rugs, chairs, and startling mirrors.

Jewelry

Most of the big names are on or near place Vendôme. Designer semiprecious and costume jewelry can generally be found in boutiques on avenue Montaigne and rue du Faubourg St-Honoré.

Alexandre Reza (✉ 23 pl. Vendôme, 1ᵉʳ, Opéra/Grands Boulevards, ☎ 01–42–96–64–00, métro Opéra), one of Paris's most exclusive jewelers, is first and foremost a gemologist. He travels the world looking for the finest stones and then works them into stunning pieces, many of which are replicas of jewels of historical importance.

Arthus-Bertrand (✉ 6 pl. St-Germain-des-Prés, 6ᵉ, St-Germain-des-Prés, ☎ 01–49–54–72–10, métro St-Germain-des-Prés) dates back to 1803 and is the official purveyor of medals and decorations to the States. It also carries vitrines full of designer jewelry and numerous objects to celebrate births.

Au Vase de Delft (✉ 19 rue Cambon, 1ᵉʳ, Louvre/Tuileries, ☎ 01–42–60–92–49, métro Concorde) specializes in fine vintage jewelry, ivory sculptures from China and Japan, gold boxes, watches, and Russian-made silverware (some by Fabergé).

Chanel (✉ 18 pl. Vendôme, 1ᵉʳ, Opéra/Grands Boulevards, ☎ 01–55–35–50–00, métro Tuileries, Opéra) spent a year renovating the building that houses its jewelry boutique. The interior is extremely refined, with beige sofas, animal sculptures, and Coromandel screens like the famous ones the designer used to have in her apartment. On sale are a selection of Chanel watches, rings, earrings, and bracelets with semi-precious stones, and some extra-special pieces with diamonds, sapphires, and pearls. Prices range from €770 to €2,307,690.

Dary's (⊠ 362 rue St-Honoré, 1ᵉʳ, Louvre/Tuileries, ☎ 01–42–60–95–23, métro Tuileries) is what shopping in Paris is all about—a wonderful cavern of Ali Baba popular with artists, actors, models, and jewelry lovers. It's run by the Dary family, with Katherine—a gemologist and author of a book on collecting jewelry—on hand to help. You'll need to take your time though because the walls are filled with row upon row of antique jewels from every era, more modern secondhand jewelry, and drawer upon drawer of antique one-of-a-kinds.

Christian Dior (⊠ 28 av. Montaigne, 8ᵉ, Champs-Élysées, ☎ 01–47–23–52–39, métro Franklin-D.-Roosevelt; ⊠ 8 pl. Vendôme, 1ᵉʳ, Opéra/Grands Boulevards, ☎ 01–42–96–30–84, métro Opéra) got a big dollop of wit and panache when they signed on young designer Victoire de Castellane to create Dior's first line of fine jewelry. She has taken much inspiration from the life of Christian Dior himself and has come up with lucky charms as a nodding reference to the designer's great superstition and earrings in the form of his favorite flowers—roses and lilies of the valley. All the stones used are the real McCoy, so don't expect to get anything for cheap. Indeed, prices go up to €462,500 for a necklace.

Jewels & Pashminas (⊠ 12 rue Jacob, 6ᵉ, St-Germain-des-Prés, ☎ 01–43–25–84–85, métro St-Germain-des-Prés) is composed of two stores, discreetly situated in a leafy courtyard. The jewelry store is the only outlet in Europe for the sublime creations made in the legendary Gem Palace in Jaipur. In the neighboring pashmina boutique, you'll find Nepalese clothing and hand-embroidered shawls.

Matière Première (⊠ 12 rue de Sévigné, 4ᵉ, Le Marais, ☎ 01–42–78–40–87, métro St-Paul) sells everything you need to make your own necklaces and bracelets—thousands of beads, pendants, and wire. If you prefer to buy ready-made items, there's a delightful in-house jewelry collection.

Lingerie

Alice Cadolle (⊠ 14 rue Cambon, 1ᵉʳ, Louvre/Tuileries, ☎ 01–42–60–94–94, métro Concorde) has been selling the finest lingerie to Parisians since 1889. In the first-floor boutique are ready-to-wear bras, corsets, and sleepwear. Upstairs, Madame Cadolle offers a made-to-measure service, popular with couture clients from nearby Chanel.

Capucine Puerari (⊠ 63 rue des Sts-Pères, 6ᵉ, St-Germain-des-Prés, ☎ 01–42–22–14–09, métro St-Germain-des-Prés) is one of those discreet addresses loved by Parisian women; it's well stocked with lingerie, swimwear, and a stylish collection of clothing.

Les Folies d'Elodie (⊠ 56 av. Paul Doumer, 16ᵉ, Trocadéro, ☎ 01–45–04–93–57, métro Trocadéro) is the address in Paris for elegant, feminine lingerie. In this large, lush boutique you can find anything from a 1950s-style cotton bra and panties in pale pink vichy *à la Bardot* to a risqué sheer silk nightgown with Calais lace insets. Famous lovers seem to feel at home here too—Warren Beatty stops by when he's in town and this year Bill popped in to pick out a champagne-color confection for Senator Clinton.

Sabbia Rosa (⊠ 73 rue des Sts-Pères, 6ᵉ, St-Germain-des-Prés, ☎ 01–45–48–88–37, métro St-Germain-des-Prés) is a discreet, boudoirlike boutique you could easily walk straight past. It is, however, probably the finest lingerie store in the world and the place where actresses Sharon Stone, Catherine Deneuve, and Isabelle Adjani buy their underwear in the finest French silk.

Miscellaneous

Kirk & Richie Rich (⊠ 9 rue de La Trémoille, 8ᵉ, Champs-Élysées, ☎ 01–47–23–81–00, métro Alma-Marceau) has an abundance of objects that owner Gisela Trigano brings back from her travels. Among her *coups de coeur* are shoes and Murano glass from Italy, pashminas from India, blankets from England, wooden sculptures from Nepal, and ancestor paintings from China.

Nature et Découvertes (⊠ In the Carrousel du Louvre, 99 rue de Rivoli, 1ᵉʳ, Louvre/Tuileries, ☎ 01–47–03–47–43, métro Palais-Royal) has a large selection of children's toys as well as objects linked to nature—telescopes, birdseed, gardening equipment, hiking gear, crystals, aromatherapy diffusers, and little Zen gardens.

Music

FNAC (⊠ Forum des Halles, 1ᵉʳ, Beaubourg/Les Halles, ☎ 01–40–41–40–00, métro Les Halles; ⊠ 74 av. des Champs-Élysées, 8ᵉ, Champs-Élysées, ☎ 01–53–53–64–64, métro Franklin-D.-Roosevelt; ⊠ 136 rue de Rennes, 6ᵉ, Montparnasse, ☎ 01–49–54–30–00, métro St-Placide) is a high-profile French chain selling music and books, and photo, TV, and audio equipment at good prices, by French standards.

Fréderic Sanchez (⊠ 5 rue St-Anastase, 3ᵉ, Le Marais, ☎ 01–44–54–89–54, métro St-Paul) is the French fashion world's favorite DJ. He often mixes the music for top catwalk shows and has now opened this small space, which offers everything he considers swank listening.

Virgin Megastore (⊠ 52 av. des Champs-Élysées, 8ᵉ, Champs-Élysées, ☎ 01–49–53–50–00, métro Franklin-D.-Roosevelt; ⊠ In the Carrousel du Louvre, 99 rue de Rivoli, 1ᵉʳ, Louvre/Tuileries, ☎ 01–49–53–52–90, métro Palais-Royal) has acres of CDs and tapes; the Champs-Élysées store has a large book section and a trendy café upstairs.

Perfumes

Annick Goutal (⊠ 14 rue de Castiglione, 1ᵉʳ, Louvre/Tuileries, ☎ 01–42–60–52–82, métro Concorde) sells its own exclusive line of 18 signature scents, which come packaged in gilded gauze purses.

L'Artisanat Parfumeur (⊠ 32 rue du Bourg Tibourg, 4ᵉ, Le Marais, ☎ 01–48–04–72–75, métro Hôtel de Ville) sells its own brand of scents for the home and perfumes with names like Méchant Loup (Big Bad Wolf) and Riviera Palace.

L'Atelier du Savon (⊠ 29 rue Vieille-du-Temple, 4ᵉ, Le Marais, ☎ 01–44–54–06–10, métro St-Paul) is a soap addict's delight. There are blocks of chocolate and lime soap, mint and lemon soap, and others that look strangely like brownies. Fizzy balls for the bath have rose petals and sequins inside of them, and shampoos come in solid blocks.

Comme des Garçons (⊠ 23 pl. du Marché St-Honoré, 1ᵉʳ, Louvre/Tuileries, ☎ 01–47–03–60–72, métro Tuileries) is the very first boutique in the world devoted to the trendy Japanese label's perfumes, scented candles, and body creams. The shop is worth a visit simply to admire the whiter-than-white store design with pink tinted lighting.

Creed (⊠ 38 av. Pierre 1ᵉʳ de Serbie, 8ᵉ, Champs-Élysées, ☎ 01–47–20–58–02, métro George V) was founded in 1760 and was the official perfume supplier to Queen Victoria and numerous European courts. Today, it sells a selection of its own scents and makes personalized perfumes.

Guerlain (⊠ 68 av. des Champs-Élysées, 8ᵉ, Champs-Élysées, ☎ 01–45–62–52–57, métro Franklin-D.-Roosevelt; ⊠ 47 rue Bonaparte, 6ᵉ, St-Germain-des-Prés, ☎ 01–43–26–71–19, métro Mabillon) boutiques are the only authorized Paris outlets for legendary perfumes like Shalimar, Jicky, Vol de Nuit, Mitsouko, Chamade, Champs-Élysées, and their new collection of light toilet waters. They also have an extremely popular makeup and skin care line and "Terra Cotta," their bronzing powder, has been an eternal French favorite.

Parfums de Nicolaï (✉ 69 av. Raymond Poincaré, 16ᵉ, Trocadéro, ☎ 01–47–55–90–44, métro Victor-Hugo) is run by a member of the Guerlain family, Patricia de Nicolaï. Children's, women's, and men's perfumes are on offer, as well as sprays for the home and scented candles. Celebrity clients include Isabelle Adjani and Elton John.

Les Salons du Palais-Royal Shiseido (✉ Jardins du Palais-Royal, 142 Galerie de Valois, 25 rue de Valois, 1ᵉʳ, Louvre/Tuileries, ☎ 01–49–27–09–09, métro Palais-Royal) is a magical boutique with marble floors and lilac walls that open to contain the entire Shiseido cosmetic and skin-care line. But that's not why people flock here. They come because every year Shiseido's creative genius Serge Lutens, dreams up two new scents, which are then sold exclusively in this boutique. There are now 18 parfums and each is wonderfully distinctive from the over-marketed scents out there. Sample the latest, Chergui, named after a desert wind in Tunisia, the sweet almond and vanilla scent of Ralat Loukoum, or the classic Rose de Nuit. "Only in Paris."

DISCOUNT

The airport duty-free shops are your best bet for minor purchases. But if you're going to spend more than €185, it's worthwhile to seek out the top discounters. Don't forget to claim your *détaxe*!

Les Halles Montmartre (✉ 85 rue Montmartre, 2ᵉ, Opéra/Grands Boulevards, ☎ 01–42–33–11–13, métro Bourse) routinely discounts its great selection of perfumes and cosmetics by up to 20%.

Michel Swiss (✉ 16 rue de la Paix, 2nd floor, 2ᵉ, Opéra/Grands Boulevards, ☎ 01–42–61–61–11, métro Opéra; ✉ 24 av. de l'Opéra, 1ᵉʳ, Louvre/Tuileries, ☎ 01–47–03–49–11, métro Pyramides) offers savings of up to 25% on perfumes, designer jewelry, and fashion accessories.

Shoes

Berluti (✉ 26 rue Marbeuf, 8ᵉ, Champs-Élysées, ☎ 01–53–93–97–97, métro Franklin-D.-Roosevelt) has been making fantastically exquisite and expensive men's shoes for more than a century. "Nothing is too beautiful for feet" is Olga Berluti's motto. She even exposes her creations to the moonlight to give them an extra-special patina! One model is named after Andy Warhol, and other famous clients of the past have included the Duke of Windsor, Fred Astaire, and James Joyce.

Christian Louboutin (✉ 19 rue Jean-Jacques Rousseau, 1ᵉʳ, Beaubourg/Les Halles, ☎ 01–42–36–05–31, métro Palais-Royal; ✉ 38 rue de Grenelle, 7ᵉ, St-Germain-des-Prés, ☎ 01–42–22–33–07, métro Sèvres Babylone) is famous for his wacky but elegant creations and his trademark blood-red soles; Caroline of Monaco, Catherine Deneuve, and Elizabeth Taylor are some of his clients.

Mare (✉ 23 rue des Francs-Bourgeois, 4ᵉ, Le Marais, ☎ 01–48–04–74–63, métro St-Paul; ✉ 4 rue du Cherche-Midi, 6ᵉ, St-Germain-des-Prés, ☎ 01–45–44–55–33, métro St-Sulpice) has stylish, trendy shoes made from fine Italian leather.

Michel Perry (✉ 4 rue des Petits-Pères, 2ᵉ, Louvre/Tuileries, ☎ 01–42–44–10–07, métro Palais-Royal) is famous for his elegant, slender, high-heeled shoes. The rose-color boudoir-style store also stocks many hip labels, including Chloé, Colette Dinnigan, and Guy Laroche.

Rodolphe Menudier (✉ 14 rue de Castiglione, 1ᵉʳ, Louvre/Tuileries, ☎ 01–42–60–86–27, métro Tuileries) is a gem of a boutique, which sells some of the most beautiful shoes in the world. As well as creating his own mules and stilettos, he also creates the footwear for Christian Dior. The interior design—think sleek black windows, metal cupboards, and a wall covered in white crocodile leather—is the creation of hip interiors star Christophe Pillet.

Shoe Bizz (✉ 42 rue Dragon, 6ᵉ, St-Germain-des-Prés, ☎ 01–45–44–91–70, métro St-Germain-des-Prés; ✉ 48 rue Beaubourg, 3ᵉ, Beaubourg/Les Halles, ☎ 01–48–87–12–73, métro Rambuteau) zeroes in on the season's hottest shoe styles and replicates them at prices 30% cheaper than you'll find elsewhere in the city.

DISCOUNT

Parisians *in the know* flock to the République *quartier* to check out the boutiques for the luxury-shoe-lover-on-a-slender-budget on the **rue Meslay.** The eight discount boutiques are often jam-packed and the service rather dodgy, but for over 50% off on last season's collections from the biggest names, it's well worth the visit.

Dina Brice (✉ 13 rue Meslay, 3ᵉ, République, ☎ 01–48–87–57–78, métro République) has been selling last season's Jourdan and Clergerie for men and women at half the price for over 25 years.

Mi-Prix (✉ 27 bd. Victor-Hugo, 15ᵉ, Montparnasse, ☎ 01–48–28–42–48, métro Porte de Versailles) is an unruly jumble of end-of-series designer shoes and accessories from the likes of Gucci, Philippe Model, Walter Steiger, Prada, Michel Perry, and Azzedine Alaïa, priced at up to 70% below retail.

Patashoes (✉ 25 rue de Meslay, 3ᵉ, République, ☎ 01–48–04–30–04, métro République) is not the most beautiful boutique in the world but they do have good shoes. They carry a great line of evening shoes from Lolita Lempika and handmade Italian moccasins for men for little or nearly nothing.

Stationery

Calligrane (✉ 4-6 rue Pont Louis Philippe, 4ᵉ, Le Marais, ☎ 01–48–04–31–89, métro St-Paul; ✉ 68 rue de Grenelle, 7ᵉ, St-Germain-des-Prés, ☎ 01–45–49–96–02, métro Sèvres Babylone) has three adjacent stores in the 4ᵉ arrondissement. One uniquely sells an Italian paper called Fabriano, another designer office equipment (pens, staplers, and unique notebooks covered in ostrich skin), and the third accents its different types of paper from India, Japan, and Mexico.

Cassegrain (✉ 422 rue St-Honoré, 8ᵉ, Louvre/Tuileries, ☎ 01–42–60–20–08, métro Concorde; ✉ 81 rue des Sts-Pères, 6ᵉ, St-Germain-des-Prés, ☎ 01–42–22–04–76, métro Sèvres Babylone) is the last word on beautifully engraved cards and elegant French stationery. The desk accessories and inexpensive glass-nib writing pens make great gifts.

Marie Papier (✉ 26 rue Vavin, 6ᵉ, Montparnasse, ☎ 01–43–26–46–44, métro Vavin) sells extraordinary colored, marbled, and Japanese writing paper and notebooks, plus every kind of stylish writing accessory. One fan is fashion designer Donna Karan, who stocks part of the range in her Madison Avenue store.

Toys

L'Arbre de Vie (✉ 21 rue de Sevigne, 3ᵉ, Le Marais, ☎ 01–48–87–05–43, métro St-Paul) is one of those boutiques that's been around for over 30 years and hasn't changed one bit. The window is packed with everything from metal windup toys (some are collector's items) to wooden puppets to snow globes from all over the world. Inside, there is a collection of hand-knit clothes for children and every kind of toy you could possibly imagine except for those of the modern or plastic variety.

Au Nain Bleu (⊠ 408 rue St-Honoré, 8ᵉ, Louvre/Tuileries, ☎ 01–42–60–39–01, métro Concorde) is a high-priced wonderland of elaborate dollhouses, miniature sports cars, and enchanting hand-carved rocking horses.

C'est Ma Chambre (⊠ 45 rue des Archives, 3ᵉ, Le Marais, ☎ 01–48–87–26–67, métro Rambuteau) is the place to spoil your kids; it sells beautiful wooden toys and gorgeous furniture for kids' rooms.

8 SIDE TRIPS FROM PARIS

Parisians are lucky: with just a quick trip to the countryside, they can explore some of the most fabled sights of France's regal past. Versailles—less a monument to Louis XIV than an entire world unto itself—remains the world's most glittering palace. Nearby, *la vie du château* can be yours by calling on Fontainebleau and Vaux-le-Vicomte. Just beyond, Gothic architecture reaches its pinnacle in the soaring spires of Chartres, while Claude Monet's gardens at Giverny offer a sublime day in the country. Last but not least, a newer fairy-tale city beckons to all—Disneyland Paris.

E VEN THOUGH PARIS ITSELF HAS SO MUCH TO SEE, you should plan on taking a short trip outside the city, for just beyond its gates lies the fabled region known as Ile-de-France, the ancient heartland of France—the core from which the French kings gradually extended their power over the rest of a rebellious, individualistic nation. Though Ile-de-France is not really an island (*île*), it is figuratively isolated from the rest of France by three rivers—the Seine, the Marne, and the Oise—that weave majestic, meandering circles around its periphery. Remarkably, this fairly confined region contains 10 million people—one-sixth of France's population. This type of statistic conjures up visions of a never-ending suburban sprawl, but nothing could be further from the truth. There are lovely villages here—notably Auvers-sur-Oise, immortalized by Vincent van Gogh, and Giverny, site of Monet's home and garden.

Revised and
updated by
Simon Hewitt

Grand cathedrals and stately châteaux dot the lush, gently rolling landscape: The kings and clerics who ruled France liked to escape from the capital now and then. The region never lost favor with the powerful, partly because its many forests—large chunks of which still stand—harbored sufficient game to ensure even the most indolent monarch an easy kill. First Fontainebleau, in humane Renaissance proportions, then Versailles, on a minion-crushing, Baroque scale, reflected the royal desire to transform hunting lodges into palatial residences.

In 1992 Disney wrought its own kind of kingdom here: Disneyland Paris. Since then, the park has emerged as France's leading tourist attraction, with 11 million tickets sold a year. Getting from the capital to the sights in this region is easy: almost all are within an hour of central Paris, and most are easily accessible by train.

Contact the Espace du Tourisme d'Ile-de-France (open Wednesday–Monday 10–7, www.pidf.com), under the inverted pyramid in the Carrousel du Louvre, in the center of Paris, for general information on the area.

AUVERS-SUR-OISE

Cézanne, Pissarro, Corot, Daubigny, and Berthe Morisot all painted in Auvers in the second half of the 19th century. But it is Vincent van Gogh whose memory haunts every nook and cranny of this pretty riverside village. Van Gogh moved here from Arles in 1890 to be with his brother, Theo. Little has changed since the summer of 1890, which coincided with the last 10 weeks of van Gogh's life, when he painted no fewer than 70 pictures, then shot himself behind the village château. He is buried in the village cemetery next to his brother in a simple, ivy-covered grave. The whole village is peppered with plaques marking the spots that inspired van Gogh's art; the plaques bear reproductions of his paintings, enabling you to compare his final works with the scenes as they are today. After years of indifference and neglect, van Gogh's last abode has been turned into a shrine. The château is now home to a stunning high-tech exhibit on the Impressionist era. You can also visit the medieval village church, subject of one of van Gogh's most famous paintings, *L'Église d'Auvers*, and admire Ossip Zadkine's powerful modern statue of van Gogh in the village park.

The Auberge Ravoux, the inn where van Gogh stayed, is now the **Maison de van Gogh** (van Gogh House). A dingy staircase leads up to the tiny, spartan wood-floor attic where van Gogh stored some of modern art's most famous pictures under his bed. A short film retraces van Gogh's time at Auvers, and there is a well-stocked souvenir shop. Stop for a drink or for lunch in the ground-floor restaurant. ⊠ *8 rue de la Sansonne,* ☎ *01–30–36–60–60.* ⌑ *€4.60.* ⊙ *Daily 10–6.*

★ ☙ The elegant 17th-century village château, set above split-level gardens, now houses the **Voyage au Temps des Impressionistes** (Journey Through the Impressionist Era). You'll receive a set of infrared headphones (English available), with commentary that guides you past various tableaux illustrating life during the Impressionist years. Although there are no Impressionist originals—500 reproductions pop up on screens interspersed between the tableaux—this is one of France's most imaginative, enjoyable, and innovative museums. Some of the special effects—talking mirrors, computerized cabaret dancing girls, and a simulated train ride past Impressionist landscapes—are worthy of Disney at its best. ⊠ *Rue de Léry,* ☎ *01–34–48–48–40,* 𝕎𝔼𝔹 *www.chateau-auvers.fr.* ⌑ *€10.* ⊙ *May–Oct., Tues.–Sun. 10–8; Nov.–Apr., Tues.–Sun. 11–4:30.*

The landscape artist Charles-François Daubigny, a precursor of the Impressionists, lived in Auvers from 1861 until his death in 1878. You can visit his studio, the **Maison-Atelier de Daubigny,** and admire the remarkable mural and roof paintings by Daubigny and fellow artists Camille Corot and Honoré Daumier. ⊠ *61 rue Daubigny,* ☎ *01–34–48–03–03.* ⌑ *€4.30.* ⊙ *Thur.–Sun. 2–6:30.*

Dining

$$ ✕ **Auberge Ravoux.** For total van Gogh immersion, have lunch in the
★ restaurant he patronized regularly more than 100 years ago and where, in fact, he finally expired. The €30, three-course menu changes regu-

larly, but it's the genius loci that makes eating here special, with glass-work, lace curtains, and wall blandishments carefully modeled on the original designs. A magnificently illustrated book, *Van Gogh's Table* (published by Artisan), by culinary historian Alexandra Leaf and Fred Leeman, recalls Vincent's stay at the Auberge and describes in loving detail the dishes served there at the time. ☒ *52 rue Général-de-Gaulle,* ☎ *01–30–36–60–60. Reservations essential. AE, DC, MC, V. No dinner Sun.–Mon. Closed Jan. and Tues. Oct.–Mar.*

Auvers-sur-Oise A to Z

CAR TRAVEL
Auvers is 38 km (24 mi) northwest of Paris. Take highway A1, then A15 toward Pontoise; then head east along N184 to Méry-sur-Oise and pick up the N328, which crosses the river to Auvers.

TRAIN TRAVEL
Two trains depart every hour for Auvers from Paris's Gare du Nord; a change is necessary, usually at St-Ouen-l'Aumône, and the journey time varies from 60 to 90 minutes. A quicker (53 minutes) but more infrequent train leaves from Paris's Gare St-Lazare and involves a change at Pontoise.

VISITOR INFORMATION
➤ CONTACTS: **Auvers-sur-Oise Office de Tourisme** (☒ Rue de la Sansonne, opposite the Maison de van Gogh, 95430, Auvers-sur-Oise, ☎ 01–30–36–10–06).

CHANTILLY

Celebrated for lace, cream, and the most beautiful medieval manuscript in the world—*Les Très Riches Heures du Duc de Berry*—romantic Chantilly has a host of other attractions: a faux Renaissance château with an eye-popping art collection, splendid Baroque stables, a classy racecourse, and a 16,000-acre forest.

Although its lavish exterior may be 19th-century Renaissance pastiche, ★ the **Château de Chantilly,** sitting snugly behind an artificial lake, houses the outstanding **Musée Condé,** with illuminated medieval manuscripts, tapestries, furniture, and paintings. The most famous room, the **Santuario** (sanctuary), contains two celebrated works by Italian painter Raphael (1483–1520)—the *Three Graces* and the *Orleans Virgin*—plus an exquisite ensemble of 15th-century miniatures by the most illustrious French painter of his time, Jean Fouquet (1420–81). Farther on, in the *Cabinet des Livres* (library), is the world-famous book of hours whose title translates as *The Very Rich Hours of the Duc de Berry,* which was illuminated by the Brothers Limbourg with magical pictures of early 15th-century life as lived by one of Burgundy's richest lords (unfortunately, due to their fragility, painted fascimiles of the celebrated calendar illuminations are on display, not the actual pages of the book). Other highlights of this unusual museum are the **Galerie de Psyché** (Psyche Gallery), with 16th-century stained glass and portrait drawings by Flemish artist Jean Clouet II; the **Chapelle,** with sculptures by Jean Goujon and Jacques Sarrazin; and the extensive collection of paintings by 19th-century French artists, headed by Jean-Auguste-Dominique Ingres. In addition, there are grand and petit salons, all stuffed with palace furniture, family portraits, and Sèvres porcelains, making this an absolute must for lovers of the decorative and applied arts. ☎ *03–44–62–62–62,* WEB *www.chateaudechantilly.com.* ☒ *€6.40 (including* *park).* ☉ *Mar.–Oct., daily 10–6; Nov.–Feb., Wed.–Mon. 10:30–12:45 and 2–5.*

Le Nôtre's **park** is based on that familiar French royal combination of formality (neatly planned parterres and a mighty, straight-banked canal) and romantic eccentricity (the waterfall and the Hameau, a mock-Norman village that inspired Marie-Antoinette's version at Versailles). The **Aérophile**, the world's largest tethered balloon, floats you 450 ft up for a bird's-eye view; the **Hydrophile**, an electric-powered boat, glides you for 30 mins down the Grand Canal. ☎ *03–44–57–35–35.* ⊠ *Park only €2.60, with Hydrophile €8, with Aérophile €10, with both €11 (€16.50 joint ticket including château).* ☉ *Mar.–Oct., daily 10–6; Nov.–Feb., daily 10:30–12:45 and 2–5.*

★ ☾ The palatial 18th-century **Grandes Écuries** by the racetrack, built by Jean Aubert in 1719 to accommodate 240 horses and 500 hounds for stag and boar hunts in the forests nearby, are the grandest stables in France. They're still in use, as the home of the **Musée Vivant du Cheval** (Living Horse Museum), with 30 breeds of horses and ponies housed in straw-lined comfort—in between dressage performances in the courtyard or beneath the awe-inspiring central dome. The 31-room museum has a comprehensive collection of equine paraphernalia: everything from saddles, bridles, and stirrups to rocking horses, anatomy displays, and old postcards. There are explanations in English throughout. ⊠ *7 rue du Connétable,* ☎ *03–44–57–40–40,* ⓦⓔⓑ *www.musee-vivant-du-cheval.fr.* ⊠ *€8.* ☉ *Easter–Sept., Wed.–Mon. 10:30–6:30; Oct.–Easter, Wed.–Fri. and Mon. 2–5, weekends 10:30–5:30.*

Dining

$ ✕ **Capitainerie.** This self-service restaurant is in the château's vaulted medieval basement, adorned with old kitchen utensils. The buffet is available nonstop from 10:30 through 6:30; you'll find salads, cheeses, and desserts, along with a few hot dishes. ⊠ *In Château de Chantilly,* ☎ *03–44–67–40–00. MC, V. Closed Tues.*

Chantilly A to Z

CAR TRAVEL
Take highway A1 from Paris (Porte de la Chapelle) to Senlis, 50 km (31 mi) away; Chantilly is 10 km (6 mi) west along pretty D924.

TRAIN TRAVEL
Chantilly is about 30 minutes from Paris's Gare du Nord; at least one train departs every hour.

VISITOR INFORMATION
➤ CONTACTS: **Chantilly Office de Tourisme** (⊠ 60 av. du Maréchal-Joffre, ☎ 03–44–57–08–58, ⓦⓔⓑ www.ville-de-chantilly.fr).

CHARTRES

The noble, soaring spires of Chartres are one of the most famous sights in Europe. Try to catch a glimpse of them surging out of the vast, golden grain fields of the Beauce as you approach from the northeast. Although you're probably visiting Chartres chiefly for its magnificent Gothic cathedral and its world-famous stained-glass windows, the whole town is also worth leisurely exploration. Ancient streets tumble down from the cathedral to the Eure River; the view of the rooftops beneath the cathedral from rue du Pont-St-Hilaire is particularly appealing. Like the cathedral, the old part of town, studded with picturesque houses and streets, has been preserved in its cloak of mellowing old stone; other sectors have been slapped with modern apartment buildings and whizzing traffic.

The **Cathédrale de Chartres** is the sixth church to occupy the same spot. It dates mainly from the 12th and 13th centuries; the previous, 11th-century building burned down in 1194. A well-chronicled outburst of religious fervor followed the discovery that the relic kept in the church, the Virgin Mary's tunic, had miraculously survived unsinged. Reconstruction went ahead at a breathtaking pace. In only 25 years Chartres Cathedral rose again, and it has remained substantially unchanged ever since.

Worship on the site of the cathedral goes back to before the Gallo-Roman period; the crypt contains a well that was the focus of Druid ceremonies. With the arrival of Christianity, the original cult of the fertility goddess merged into that of the Virgin Mary. In the late 9th century, King Charles the Bold presented Chartres with what was believed to be the tunic of the Virgin Mary. This precious relic attracted hordes of pilgrims, and Chartres swiftly became—and has remained—a prime destination for the faithful. To this day, pilgrims trek to Chartres from Paris on foot.

The lower half of the facade is all that survives from the 11th-century Romanesque church. (The Romanesque style is evident in the use of round, rather than pointed, arches.) The main door—the **Portail Royal** (Royal Portal)—is richly sculpted with scenes from the life of Christ. The flanking towers are also Romanesque, though the upper part of the taller of the two **spires** (380 ft versus 350 ft) dates from the start of the 16th century, and its fanciful flamboyance contrasts with the stumpy solemnity of its Romanesque counterpart. The **rose window** above the main portal dates from the 13th century. The three windows below it contain some of the finest examples of 12th-century stained glass in France.

The interior is somber, so you'll need time to adjust to the dark. Your reward will be a view of the gemlike richness of the stained glass, dominated by the famous deep "Chartres blue." The oldest window, and perhaps the most stunning, is **Notre-Dame de la Belle Verrière** (Our Lady of the Lovely Window), in the south choir. It is well worth taking binoculars, if you have a pair, to pick out the details. If you wish to know more about stained-glass techniques and the motifs used, visit the small exhibit in the gallery opposite the north porch. The vast black-and-white medieval pattern on the floor of the nave is one of the few to have survived from the Middle Ages. The faithful were expected to crawl along its entire length (some 300 yards) on their knees. A long-time Chartres aficionado, Malcolm Miller knows more than most art historians and gives fabulous tours in English daily at noon and 2:45 PM, providing information on the narrative stained glass for a fee. Otherwise, you can head out the cathedral's south door to the crypt across the street and rent a Walkman and a (vastly inferior) tape-recorded tour in English.

Guided tours of the crypt start from the **Maison de la Crypte** (Crypt House) opposite the south porch. You'll see the Romanesque and Gothic chapels that run around the crypt, along with a 4th-century Gallo-Roman wall and some 12th-century wall paintings. ⊠ *16 cloître Notre-Dame,* ☎ *02-37-21-56-33,* WEB *www.ville-chartres.fr.* 🎟 *Towers €1.5, English guided tour €4.6.* ☉ *Guided tours of crypt Easter–Oct., daily at 11, 2:15, 3:30, 4:30, and 5:15; Nov.–Easter, daily at 11 and 4.*

Chartres

Ambulatory

Choir

Transept

Nave

The **Musée des Beaux-Arts** (Fine Arts Museum) is a handsome 18th-century building just behind the cathedral—it used to serve as the bishop's palace. Its varied collection includes Renaissance enamels, a portrait of Erasmus by Holbein, tapestries, armor, and some fine, mainly French paintings of the 17th, 18th, and 19th centuries. There is also a room devoted to the forceful 20th-century works of painter Maurice de Vlaminck, who lived in the region. ⊠ *29 cloître Notre-Dame,* ☎ *02–37–36– 41–39.* ☞ *€2.5.* ☉ *Apr.–Oct., Wed.–Mon. 10–6; Nov.–Mar., Wed.–Mon. 10–noon and 2–5.*

The Gothic **Église St-Pierre** (⊠ Rue St-Pierre) near the Eure River has magnificent medieval windows from a period (circa 1300) not represented at the cathedral. The oldest stained glass here, portraying Old Testament worthies, is to the right of the choir and dates from the late 13th century. There is more fine stained glass (17th century) to admire at the **Église St-Aignan** (⊠ Rue des Grenets), around the corner from St-Pierre.

Dining

$$$–$$$$ ✗ **Château d'Esclimont.** One of the most photogenic of all châteaux-hotels in France, this magnificently restored Renaissance estate—part of the Relais & Châteaux group—is frequented by high-profile Parisian businesspeople. Lamb with asparagus, hare fricassee (in season), and lobster top the menu. After dining on the rich cuisine, take a stroll through the luxuriant grounds, embellished with regal lawns and lake. ⊠ *2 rue du Château-d'Esclimont, St-Symphorien-le-Château, (6 km/4 mi west of Ablis exit on A11 and about 24 km/15 mi from Chartres and Rambouillet)* ☎ *02–37–31–15–15.* ⓌⒺⒷ *www.grandes-etapes-francaises.com/esclimont.htm. Reservations essential. Jacket and tie. AE, DC, MC, V.*

$$ ✗ **La Vieille Maison.** Close to Chartres Cathedral, in the same narrow street as Le Buisson Ardent, this intimate spot with a flower-filled patio has a regularly changing menu. Invariably, however, it includes regional specialties such as truffles and asparagus with chicken. Prices, though justified, can be steep; the €26 prix-fixe lunch menu is a good bet. ⊠ *5 rue au Lait,* ☎ *02–37–34–10–67. AE, MC, V. Closed Mon. No dinner Sun.*

$–$$ ✗ **Le Buisson Ardent.** This wood-beamed restaurant on a quaint old street near Chartres Cathedral has two prix-fixe menus, imaginative food, and attentive service. Some of the excellent dishes include chicken ravioli with leeks and rolled beef with spinach. ⊠ *10 rue au Lait,* ☎ *02–37–34–04–66. AE, DC, MC, V. No dinner Sun.*

Chartres A to Z

To research prices, get advice from other travelers, and book travel arrangements, visit www.fodors.com.

CAR TRAVEL

The A10/A11 expressways link Paris to Chartres, 88 km (55 mi) away.

GUIDED TOURS

Cityrama organizes half-day trips to Chartres (€47) and combined excursions to Chartres and Versailles (€85).

➤ CONTACT: **Cityrama** (⊠ 4 pl. des Pyramides, Paris, ☎ 01–44–55–61–00).

TRAIN TRAVEL

Trains depart hourly from Paris's Gare Montparnasse to Chartres (travel time is 50–70 minutes, depending on service).

VISITOR INFORMATION

➤ CONTACT: **Chartres** (⊠ Pl. de la Cathédrale, 28000 Chartres, ☎ 02–37–18–26–26).

DISNEYLAND PARIS

⌖   In April 1992 American pop culture secured a mammoth outpost just 32 km (20 mi) east of Paris in the form of Disneyland Paris. On 1,500 acres in Marne-la-Vallée, Disneyland Paris has a convention center, sports facilities, an entertainment and shopping complex, restaurants, thousands of hotel rooms, and, of course, the theme park itself. The theme park is made up of five "lands": Main Street U.S.A., Frontierland, Adventureland, Fantasyland, and Discoveryland. The central theme of each land is relentlessly echoed in every detail, from attractions to restaurant menus to souvenirs.

Main Street U.S.A. is the scene of the Disney Parades held every afternoon and—during holiday periods—every evening, too. Top attractions at **Frontierland** are the chilling Phantom Manor, haunted by holographic spooks, and the thrilling runaway mine train of Big Thunder Mountain, a roller coaster that plunges wildly through floods and avalanches in a setting meant to evoke Monument Valley. Whiffs of Arabia, Africa, and the West Indies give **Adventureland** its exotic cachet; the spicy meals and snacks served here rank among the best food in the theme park. Don't miss the Pirates of the Caribbean, an exciting mise-en-scène populated by eerily human computer-driven figures, or Indiana Jones and the Temple of Doom, a breathtaking ride that relives some of our luckless hero's most exciting moments.

Fantasyland charms the youngest parkgoers with familiar cartoon characters from such Disney classics as *Snow White, Pinocchio, Dumbo,* and *Peter Pan.* The focal point of Fantasyland, and indeed Disneyland Paris, is Le Château de la Belle au Bois Dormant (Sleeping Beauty's Castle), a 140-ft, bubble gum–pink structure topped with 16 blue- and gold-tipped turrets. The castle design was allegedly inspired by illustrations from a medieval Book of Hours. In the dungeon is a scaly, green 2-ton dragon who rumbles and grumbles in his sleep and occasionally rouses to roar—an impressive feat of engineering that terrifies every tot in the crowd! **Discoveryland** is a futuristic spin for high-tech Disney entertainment. Robots on roller skates welcome you to Star Tours, a pitching, plunging, sense-confounding ride through intergalactic space. Space Mountain's star-bejewelled roller coaster ride catapults you through the Milky Way.

For entertainment outside the theme park, check out the **Walt Disney Studios,** opened in early 2002, and **Disney Village,** a vast pleasure mall designed by celebrated American architect Frank Gehry. Featured are American-style restaurants (crab shack, diner, deli, steak house), a disco, and a dinner theater where Buffalo Bill stages his Wild West Show twice nightly. An 18-hole golf course is open to the public (☎ 01–60–45–68–04 information). ⊠ *Marne-la-Vallée,* ☎ *01–60–30–60–30,* 🖳 *www.disneylandparis.com.* 🖙 *Disneyland Paris (prices vary according to season)* €27–€36. ☯ *Mid-June–mid-Sept., daily 9 AM–10 PM; mid-Sept.–mid-June, daily 10–8.*

Dining and Lodging

$–$$$ ✕ **Disneyland Restaurants.** Disneyland Paris is peppered with places to eat, ranging from snack bars and fast-food joints to five full-service restaurants—all with a distinguishing theme. In addition, Disney Village and Disney Hotels have restaurants open to the public. But since these are outside the park, it is not recommended that you waste time traveling to them for lunch. Disneyland Paris has relaxed its no-alcohol policy and now serves wine and beer in the park's sit-down restaurants, as well as in the hotels and restaurants outside the park. ☎ *01–60–45–65–40. AE, DC, MC, V accepted at sit-down restaurants.*

$$–$$$$ 🏨 **Disneyland Hotels.** The resort has 5,000 rooms in six hotels, all a short distance from the park, ranging from the luxurious Disneyland Hotel to the not-so-rustic Camp Davy Crockett. Free transportation to the park is available at every hotel. Packages including Disneyland lodging, entertainment, and admission are available through travel agents in Europe. ⊠ *Centre de Réservations, B.P. 100, 77777 Marne-la-Vallée cedex 4,* ☎ *01–60–30–60–30; 407/934–7639 in U.S.,* 🖷 *01–49–30–71–00. All hotels have at least 1 restaurant, bar, café, internet access, indoor pool, sauna, exercise facilities, and free parking. AE, DC, MC, V.*

Disneyland Paris A to Z

To research prices, get advice from other travelers, and book travel arrangements, visit www.fodors.com.

BUS TRAVEL

Shuttle buses link Disneyland Paris to Roissy (56 km/35 mi) and Orly (50 km/31 mi) airports. The trip lasts around 45 minutes and the fare is €13 one-way.

CAR TRAVEL

The Strasbourg-bound A4 expressway leads from Paris to Disneyland Paris, at Marne-la-Vallée, a journey of 32 km (20 mi) that in normal traffic takes about 30 minutes. The 4-km (2½-mi) route from the expressway to the entrance of the theme park is clearly marked. Day visitors must head for the *Parking Visiteurs*, which costs €6 per car and is 600 yards from the theme-park entrance.

TRAIN TRAVEL

Disneyland Paris's suburban train station (Marne-la-Vallée–Chessy) is just 100 yards from the entrance to both the theme park and Festival Disney. Trains run every 10 to 20 minutes from RER-A stations in central Paris: Charles-de-Gaulle–Étoile, Auber, Châtelet Les Halles, Gare de Lyon, and Nation. The trip takes about 40 minutes and costs €12.5 round-trip (including the métro to the RER). A TGV station next to the RER station at Disneyland Paris offers direct train service to and from Lille, Lyon, and Marseille.

VISITOR INFORMATION

➤ CONTACTS: **Disneyland Paris S.C.A.** (✉ Central Reservations Office, BP 104, 77777 Marne-la-Vallée, Cedex 4, France, ☎ 01–60–30–60–30, FAX 01–49–30–71–00). **Walt Disney World Central Reservations** (✉ Box 10, 100 Lake Buena Vista, FL 32830–0100, ☎ 407/934–7639).

FONTAINEBLEAU AND VAUX-LE-VICOMTE

Fontainebleau, with its historic château—favored retreat of King François I and Napoléon—is a favorite place for excursions, especially since the superb Baroque château of Vaux-le-Vicomte is close by.

Fontainebleau

Like Chambord in the Loire Valley and Compiègne to the north of Paris, Fontainebleau earned royal esteem as a hunting base. As at Versailles, a hunting lodge once stood on the site of the current château, along with a chapel built in 1169 and consecrated by exiled (later murdered and canonized) English priest Thomas à Becket.

The **Château de Fontainebleau** you see today dates from the 16th century, although additions were made by various royal incumbents over the next 300 years. The palace was begun under flamboyant Renaissance King François I, the French contemporary of England's Henry VIII.

The king hired Italian artists Il Rosso (a pupil of Michelangelo) and Primaticcio to embellish his château. In fact, they did much more: by introducing the pagan allegories and elegant lines of Mannerism to France, they revolutionized the realm of French decorative art. Their extraordinary frescoes and stuccowork can be admired in the **Galerie François-I** (Francis I Gallery) and the crown jewel of the interior, the

Fontainebleau

Salle de Bal. Here in the ceremonial ballroom, which is nearly 100 ft long, you can admire the dazzling 16th-century frescoes and gilding. Completed under Henri II, François's successor, it is luxuriantly wood paneled, with a parquet floor whose gleaming finish reflects the patterns on the ceiling above. Like the château as a whole, the room exudes a sense of elegance and style—but on a more intimate, human scale than at Versailles: this is Renaissance, not Baroque.

Napoléon's apartments occupied the first floor. You can see a lock of his hair, his Légion d'Honneur medal, his imperial uniform, the hat he wore on his return from Elba in 1815, and one bed in which he definitely did spend a night (almost every town in France boasts a bed in which the emperor supposedly snoozed). There is also a throne room—Napoléon spurned the one at Versailles, a palace he disliked—and the Queen's Boudoir, known as the Room of the Six Maries (occupants included ill-fated Marie-Antoinette and Napoléon's second wife, Marie-Louise). Highlights of other salons include 17th-century tapestries, marble reliefs by Jacquet de Grenoble, and paintings and frescoes by the versatile Primaticcio.

Although Louis XIV's architectural fancy was concentrated on Versailles, he commissioned Mansart to design new pavilions and had André Le Nôtre replant the gardens at Fontainebleau, to which the king and his court returned every fall for the hunting season. But it was Napoléon who made a Versailles out of Fontainebleau, as it were, by spending lavishly to restore it to its former glory. He held Pope Pius VII prisoner here in 1812, signed the second Church-State concordat here in 1813, and, in the cobbled **Cour des Adieux** (Farewell Courtyard), said good-bye to his Old Guard in 1814 as he began his brief exile on the Mediterranean island of Elba. The famous Horseshoe Staircase that dominates the Cour des Adieux, once the Cour du Cheval Blanc (White

Horse Courtyard), was built by Androuet du Cerceau for Louis XIII (1610–43).

Another courtyard—the **Cour de la Fontaine** (Fountain Courtyard)—was commissioned by Napoléon in 1812 and adjoins the Étang des Carpes (Carp Pond). Ancient carp are alleged to swim here, although Allied soldiers drained the pond in 1915 and ate all the fish, and, in the event they missed some, Hitler's hordes did likewise in 1940.

The **Porte Dauphine** is the most beautiful of the various gateways that connect the complex of buildings; its name commemorates the fact that the Dauphin—the heir to the throne, later Louis XIII—was christened under its archway in 1606. ⊠ *Pl. du Général-de-Gaulle,* ☎ *01–60–71–50–70.* ⌦ *Château €5.5, gardens free.* ☉ *Château Wed.–Mon. 9:30–12:30 and 2–5, gardens daily 9 AM–dusk.*

Dining

$$–$$$ ✕ **Le Beauharnais.** Opposite the château, in the Aigle Noir hotel, this restaurant serves classic French fare in a grand salon; especially good is the lamb with thyme and gentian. Prix-fixe menus are €30 and €70. There's a tranquil garden for alfresco dining in summer. ⊠ *27 pl. Napoléon-Bonaparte,* ☎ *01–60–74–60–00. Jacket and tie. AE, DC, MC, V. Closed last week of Dec.*

Vaux-le-Vicomte

The majestic **Château de Vaux-le-Vicomte,** started in 1656 by court finance wizard Nicolas Fouquet, is one of the most impressive buildings in Ile-de-France. The construction process was monstrous: villages were razed, and then 18,000 workmen were called in to execute the plans of architect Louis Le Vau, decorator Charles Le Brun, and landscape gardener André Le Nôtre. The housewarming party was so lavish that star guest Louis XIV, tetchy at the best of times, threw a jealous fit, hurled Fouquet into the slammer, and promptly began building Versailles to prove just who was boss.

Decoration of the château's landmark feature, the **cupola,** was halted at Fouquet's arrest, and the ceiling of the oval **Grand Salon** beneath remains depressingly blank. Le Brun's major achievement is the ceiling of the **Chambre du Roi** (King's Bedchamber) depicting *Time Bearing Truth Heavenward.* The word "squirrel" in French is *écureuil,* but in local dialect they were known as *fouquets;* they appear here (along the frieze) and throughout the château, a sly visual tribute to the château's hapless founder. Le Brun's other masterwork is the ceiling in the **Salon des Muses** (Salon of the Muses), a brilliant allegorical composition painted in glowing, sensuous colors surpassing anything he achieved at Versailles. A clever **exhibit,** complete with life-size wax figures, explains the rise and fall of Nicolas Fouquet. Although accused by Louis XIV and subsequent historians of megalomania and shady financial dealings, he was apparently condemned on little evidence by a court eager to please the jealous, irascible monarch.

Le Nôtre's stupendous, studiously restored **gardens** contain statues, waterfalls, and fountains, which play afternoons on the second and fourth Saturdays of each month. There is also a **Musée des Équipages** (Carriage Museum)—stocked with carriages, saddles, and a smithy—near the entrance. Check with the château office or Web site to see if there are any special events scheduled around the time of your visit—candlelight tours, concerts, and other delights sometimes adorn the Vaux-le-Vicomte schedule. There is a cafeteria on site. ⊠ *Domaine de Vaux-le-Vicomte, 77950 Maincy,* ☎ *01–64–14–41–90,* ⓌⒺⒷ *www.vaux-le-vicomte.com.*

⊠ €10. ⊙ *Château Easter–Nov. 11, daily 10–6. Candlelight visits May–*
Oct., Sat. 8–midnight €13).

Dining

$ ✕ **L'Écureuil.** An imposing barn to the right of the château entrance
has been transformed into this self-service cafeteria, where you can enjoy
fine steaks (insist yours is cooked enough), coffee, or a snack beneath
the ancient rafters of a wood-beam roof. The restaurant is open daily
for lunch and tea, and for dinner during candlelight visits. ⊠ *Château*
de Vaux-le-Vicomte. ☎ 01–60–66–95–66. MC, V.

Fontainebleau and Vaux-le-Vicomte A to Z

To research prices, get advice from other travelers, and book travel ar-
rangements, visit www.fodors.com.

CAR TRAVEL

From Paris's Porte d'Orléans or Porte d'Italie, take A6, then N7 to
Fontainebleau (total distance 72 km/45 mi). Vaux-le-Vicomte is 21 km
(13 mi) north of Fontainebleau. Take N6 to Melun, then N36 northeast (direction Meaux), turning right after 1½ km (1 mi) or so along
D215.

GUIDED TOURS

Cityrama runs half-day trips to Fontainebleau (including a visit to the
nearby painters' village of Barbizon). The cost is €53 and the tours
depart Monday, Wednesday, and Saturday at 1:45. Paris Vision offers
€83 full-day trips to Fontainebleau, Vaux-le-Vicomte, and Barbizon
on Monday and Wednesday, departing at 8:30.
➤ CONTACTS: **Cityrama** (⊠ 4 pl. des Pyramides, Paris, ☎ 01–44–55–
61–00). **Paris Vision** (⊠ 214 rue de Rivoli, Paris, ☎ 01–42–60–30–
01).

TRAIN TRAVEL

Fontainebleau is about 50 minutes from Paris's Gare de Lyon; take a
bus to complete the 3-km (2-mi) trip from the station (Fontainebleau-
Avon) to the château. You can buy a *forfait,* including train and bus
tickets plus château admission, for €20 at Gare de Lyon. Vaux-le-Vicomte is a 7-km (4-mi) taxi ride from the nearest station at Melun,
served by regular trains from Paris and Fontainebleau. The taxi ride
costs about €15.

VISITOR INFORMATION

➤ CONTACT: **Fontainebleau** (⊠ 4 rue Royale, 77300 Fontainebleau,
☎ 01–60–74–99–99).

GIVERNY

The village of Giverny has become a place of pilgrimage for art lovers.
It was here that Claude Monet lived, for 43 years, until his death in
1926 at the age of 86, adorning his house with a water-lily garden that
was, in essence, a three-dimensional Impressionist painting. After
decades of neglect, his pretty pink house with green shutters, the **Maison et Jardin de Claude Monet** (Claude Monet House and Garden),
his studios, and his garden with its famous lily pond were lovingly restored thanks to gifts from around the world and, in particular, from
the United States. Late spring is perhaps the best time to visit, when
the apple trees are in blossom and the garden is a riot of color. Try to
avoid summer weekends and afternoons in July and August, when the
limited capacity of Monet's home and gardens is pushed to the limit
by busloads of tourists.

Monet was brought up in Normandy and, like many of the other Impressionists, was attracted by the soft light of the Seine Valley. After several years at Argenteuil, just north of Paris, he moved downriver to Giverny in 1883 along with his two sons, his mistress Alice Hoschedé (whom he later married), and her six children. By 1890, a prospering Monet was able to buy the house outright. Three years later, he purchased another plot of land across the lane to continue his gardening experiments, diverting the Epte River to make a pond.

Monet's house has a warm family feeling that may come as a welcome break after visiting stately French châteaux. The rooms have been restored to Monet's original designs: the kitchen with blue tiles, the buttercup-yellow dining room, and Monet's bedroom on the second floor. Reproductions of his own works, as well as some of the Japanese prints Monet avidly collected, are displayed around the house. The garden, with flowers spilling out across the paths, is as cheerful and natural as the house—quite unlike formal French gardens. The enchanting water garden, with its water lilies, bridges, and rhododendrons, is across the lane that runs to the side of the house and can be reached through a tunnel. The lilies and Japanese bridges became signature touches of his garden and now help to conjure up an image of a grizzle-bearded Monet dabbing cheerfully at his canvases—capturing changes in light and weather in a way that was to have a major influence on 20th-century art. ⊠ *84 rue Claude-Monet,* ☎ *02–32–51–28–21,* WEB *www.giverny.org.* ◰ *€5.50, gardens only €4.* ☉ *Apr.–Oct., Tues.–Sun. 10–6.*

The spacious, airy **Musée d'Art Américain** (American Art Museum), endowed by Chicago art patrons Daniel and Judith Terra, displays works by American Impressionists who were influenced by—and often studied with—Claude Monet. ⊠ *99 rue Claude-Monet,* ☎ *02–32–51–94–65.* ◰ *€5.* ☉ *Apr.–Oct., Tues.–Sun. 10–6.*

Dining and Lodging

$$　✕ **Baudy.** Back in Monet's day, this pretty-in-pink villa was the hotel of the American painters colony. Today, the dining room and terrace are more modern than historic, but parts of this old *épicerie-buvette* are still so enchanting (notably, the luscious rose gardens and the studio hut where Cézanne once took up residence) that a recent art book was devoted to La Maison Baudy. All this mise-en-scène is quite special, making it easier to forgive the very simple cuisine and busloads of tour groups. ⊠ *81 rue Claude-Monet,* ☎ *02–32–21–10–03. MC, V. No dinner Sun. Closed Mon. and Nov.–Mar.*

$$　✕ **Les Jardins de Giverny.** This restaurant, with a tile-floor dining room overlooking a rose garden, is a few minutes' walk from Monet's house. Enjoy the €20 menu or choose from a repertoire of inventive dishes such as foie gras spiked with calvados, duck in cider, or scallops with wild mushrooms. ⊠ *Rue du Roy,* ☎ *02–32–21–60–80. AE, MC, V. Closed Mon., Feb., and 1st ½ Nov. No dinner Sun.–Fri.*

$–$$$　🏠 **Giverny B&Bs.** Giverny's dire shortage of hotels is made up by a
★　plethora of enticing, stylish, and affordable bed-and-breakfasts set up in many of the town's homes. Particularly notable are **Le Clos Fleuri**, a Norman manor house set in a lovely garden and run by the Fouche family (⊠ 5 rue de la Dime, ☎ FAX 02–32–21–36–51); **La Réserve,** about a mile outside town, an expansive residence surrounded by orchards and with gorgeous, antiques-adorned, and wood-beamed guest apartments, some of which have fireplaces and canopy beds (⊠ Rue Blanche-Hoschedé, ☎ FAX 02–32–21–99–09); and the residence of **Marie-Claire Boscher**, which used to be a hotel-restaurant that Monet frequented (⊠ 1 rue du Colombier, ☎ FAX 02–32–51–39–70). Log onto the Web site WEB www.giverny.org/hotels for all the details.

$–$$ ⊞ **La Musardière.** Just a short stroll from chez Monet, this manor house has a cozy lobby, guest rooms with views overlooking a park, and its own restaurant-crêperie. ⊠ *Rue Claude-Monet, 27620 Giverny,* ☎ *02–32–21–03–18,* ⅨⅩ *02–32–21–60–00. 25 rooms, 5 suites. Restaurant, tennis court, pool; no air-conditioning, no pets. AE, DC, MC, V.*

Giverny A to Z

To research prices, get advice from other travelers, and book travel arrangements, visit www.fodors.com.

CAR TRAVEL
Take expressway A13 from Paris to the Vernon exit (D181). Cross the Seine in Vernon and follow D5 to Giverny (total distance just over 80 km/50 mi).

GUIDED TOURS
Guided excursions are organized by American Express on either a half-day or full-day basis, combined with trips to Rouen. Cityrama run afternoon tours to Giverny, lasting about five hours, Tuesday–Saturday; cost is €58.
➤ CONTACTS: **American Express** (⊠ 11 rue Scribe, Paris, ☎ 01–47–77–77–07). **Cityrama** (⊠ 4 pl. des Pyramides, Paris, ☎ 01–44–55–61–00).

TRAIN TRAVEL
Take the train from Paris's Gare St-Lazare to Vernon (50 minutes). Giverny is 5½ km (3½ mi) away by bus or taxi, which you can get at the train station. Call the Vernon Tourist Office for information.
➤ CONTACT: **Vernon Tourist Office** (☎ 02–32–51–39–60).

VERSAILLES

Numbers in the text correspond to numbers on the Versailles map.

Paris in the 17th century was a rowdy, rabble-ridden city. Louis XIV hated it and set about in search of an alternative power base. He settled on Versailles, 20 km (12 mi) west of Paris, where his father had a small château–hunting lodge.

❶ Today the **Château de Versailles** seems monstrously big, but it wasn't large enough for the army of 20,000 noblemen, servants, and hangers-on who moved in with Louis. A new city—a new capital, in fact—had to be constructed from scratch to accommodate them. Tough-thinking town planners promptly dreamt up vast mansions and avenues broader than the Champs-Élysées—all in bicep-flexing Baroque.

It was hardly surprising that Louis XIV's successors rapidly felt out of sync with their architectural inheritance. The Sun King's successors, Louis XV and Louis XVI, preferred to cower in small retreats in the gardens, well out of the mighty château's shadow. The two most famous of these structures are the Petit Trianon, a model of classical harmony and proportion built by Louis XV; and the Hameau, where Marie-Antoinette could play at being a shepherdess amid the ersatz rusticity of her Potemkin hamlet. The contrast between the majestic and the domesticated is an important part of Versailles's appeal. But pomp and bombast dominate the mood here, and you won't need reminding that you're in the world's grandest palace—or one of France's most popular tourist attractions. The park outside is the ideal place to get your breath back. Le Nôtre's gardens represent formal landscaping at its most rigid and sophisticated.

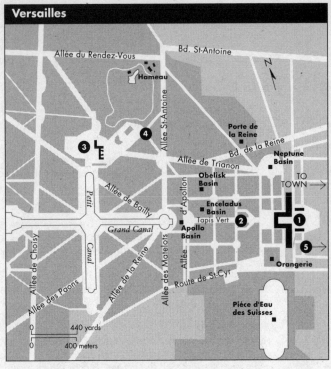

Versailles

*Map labels:* Allée du Rendez-Vous · Bd. St-Antoine · Hameau · Allée St-Antoine · Porte de la Reine · Bd. de la Reine · Neptune Basin · Allée de Trianon · TO TOWN → · Obelisk Basin · d'Apollon · Enceladus Basin · Tapis Vert · Petit Canal · Allée de Bailly · Apollo Basin · Grand Canal · Orangerie · Allée de Choisy · Allée des Matelots · Allée · Route de St-Cyr · Allée des Paons · Allée de la Reine · Pièce d'Eau des Suisses · 440 yards · 400 meters

The château was built under court architects Le Vau and Mansart between 1662 and 1690; the entrance is through the gilt-and-iron gates from huge place d'Armes. In the center of the building, across the sprawling cobbled forecourt, are the rooms that belonged to the king and queen. The two wings were occupied by the royal children and princes; attendants were up in the attics.

One of the highlights of the tour is the **Galerie des Glaces** (Hall of Mirrors), fully restored to its original dazzle. It was here that Bismarck proclaimed the unified German Empire in 1871, and the controversial Treaty of Versailles, asserting Germany's responsibility for World War I, was signed in 1919. The **Grands Appartements** (State Apartments) are formal; the **Petits Appartements** (Private Apartments), where royal family and friends lived, are on a more human scale. The intimate **Opéra Royal**, the first oval hall in France, was designed for Louis XV. Touch the "marble" loges—they're actually painted wood. The chapel, built by Mansart, is a study in white-and-gold solemnity. The former state rooms and the sumptuous debate chamber of the **Aile du Midi** (South Wing) are also open to the public, with infrared headphone commentary (available in English) explaining Versailles's parliamentary history. ☎ *01–30–83–77–88*, WEB *www.chateauversailles.fr.* 🎟 *Château €7.5, parliament exhibition €4 extra.* ☉ *May–Sept., Tues.–Sun. 9–6:30; Oct.–Apr., Tues.–Sun. 9–5:30. Opéra Royal 9:45–3:30 (tours every 15 mins).*

➋ After the awesome feast of interior pomp, the **Parc de Versailles** (Versailles Park) is an ideal place to catch your breath. The gardens were designed by André Le Nôtre, whose work here represents classical French landscaping at its most formal and sophisticated. The 250-acre grounds include woods, lawns, flower beds, statues, artificial lakes, and fountains galore (for a guided tour of the groves, call ☎ 01–30–83–77–

88). An extensive tree-replacement scheme—necessary once a century—was launched in 1998 to recapture the full impact of Le Nôtre's artful vistas; replantings became all the more necessary after 10,000 trees were uprooted by a hurricane in 1999. The cost of that damage came to some $35 million, and American donors contributed 40% of that amount. The distances are vast—the Trianons themselves are more than a mile from the château—so you might want to climb aboard a horse-drawn carriage (return trip from the château to Trianon, €6.40, WEB www.calechesversailles.com), or rent a bike from the **Grille de la Reine** near the Trianon Palace Hotel (€4 per hour) or from the **Petite-Venise** building at the top of the Grand Canal (€5 per hour, or €25 for six hours, ☎ 01–39–66–97–66). You can also drive to the Trianons and Canal through the Grille de la Reine (€4.50 per car). The park is at its golden-leafed best in the fall but is also enticing in summer—especially on Sunday afternoons from mid-April through mid-October, when the fountains are in full flow. Note there is a popular restaurant midway along the Grand Canal. ⊠ *Park free (€5 for Sun. fountain displays).* ⊘ *Daily 7 AM–8 PM or dusk.*

❸ At one end of the Petit Canal, about 1½ km (1 mi) from the château, stands the **Grand Trianon,** a pink-marble pleasure palace built by Jules Hardouin-Mansart in the late 1680s. ⊠ *€5 (joint ticket with Petit Trianon).* ⊘ *May–Sept., Tues.–Sun. noon–6:30; Oct.–Apr., Tues.–Sun. noon–5:30.*

❹ The **Petit Trianon,** close to the Grand Trianon, is a sumptuously furnished neoclassical mansion erected in the 1760s by architect Jacques Gabriel. Louis XV had a superb botanical garden planted here; some of the trees from that era survive today. Louis XVI presented the Petit Trianon to Marie-Antoinette, who spent lavish sums creating an idealized world nearby, the charming **Hameau,** a hamlet of thatched-roof cottages, complete with water mill, lake, and pigeon loft. Here, the tragic queen played out her happiest days pretending to be a shepherdess tending a flock of perfumed sheep, and here, today, her spirit is stronger than anywhere else in France, making this a must-do for fans of the hapless Toinette. ⊠ *€5 (joint ticket with Grand Trianon).* ⊘ *May–Sept., Tues.–Sun. noon–6:30; Oct.–Apr., Tues.–Sun. noon–5:30.*

❺ Facing the château are the Trojan-size royal stables, the **Grandes Écuries** (Great Stables). Nowadays the **Musée des Carosses** (Carriage Museum) is housed here, with its distinguished panoply of royal and imperial carriages. ⊠ *1 av. de Paris,* ☎ *01–30–21–54–82.* ⊠ *€3.* ⊘ *Weekends 2–6.*

The **town of Versailles** is often overlooked. Although you may be tired from exploring the palace and park, it's worth strolling along the town's broad, leafy boulevards. The majestic scale of many buildings is a reminder that this was, after all, the capital of France from 1682 to 1789 (and again from 1871 to 1879). Visible farther to the right, as you look toward the town from the palace, is the dome of the austere **Cathédrale St-Louis** (⊠ Pl. St-Louis), built from 1743 to 1754; it has a fine organ loft and two-tiered facade.

To the left of place d'Armes, beyond elegant, octagonal place Hoche, is the sturdy Baroque church of **Notre-Dame** (⊠ At rue Hoche and rue de la Paroisse), built from 1684 to 1686 by Jules Hardouin-Mansart as the parish church for Louis XIV's brand-new town. The street in front of Notre-Dame, rue de la Paroisse, leads up to **place du Marché**, site of a magnificent morning market every Tuesday, Friday, and Sunday. The **Musée Lambinet,** behind Notre-Dame church, is an imposing 18th-century mansion with a maze of cozy rooms furnished with

MARIE-ANTOINETTE: QUEEN OF TRIANON

WAS MARIE-ANTOINETTE A luxury-mad butterfly flitting from ball to costume ball? Or was she a misunderstood queen who suffered a loveless marriage and became a prisoner of court etiquette at Versailles? Historians now believe the answer was the latter and point to her private retreats at Versailles as proof. Here, in the northwest part of the royal park, far from the main palace, Marie-Antoinette created a tiny universe of her own: her comparatively dainty mansion called the Petit Trianon and its adjacent "farm," the still extant, still magnificently lovely Hameau ("hamlet"). In a life that took her from royal cradle to throne of France to guillotine, her happiest days were spent at Trianon. For here she could live a life in the "simplest" possible way; here the queen could enter a salon and the game of cards would not stop; here women wore simple gowns of muslin without a single jewel; here she could be called "Toni." In the end, this fairytale realm was so alluring it caused the queen to forget about reality and the monstrous injustices then afflicting France. Toinette only wanted to be "Queen of Trianon," not queen of France. And considering the horrible, chamberpot-pungent, gossipinfested corridors of Versailles, you can almost understand why.

From the first, Maria-Antonia (her actual name), was ostracized as an outsider, "l'Autrichienne," an Austrian. Married to Louis XVI—a kind but witless boob—and shamed by her failure to deliver a royal heir, she grew to hate overcrowded Versailles and soon escaped to the Trianon, built in 1768 in the English "Adamesque" style by Gabriel for Madame de Pompadour. Starting in 1774, Toinette refashioned its interior to make it "modern." The gilt trip of the Rococo was banished. Instead, sober neoclassical *boiseries* (carved wall panels), distinguished Riesener and Carlin bureaus, and walls painted in that most dramatic of new shades—off-white—revealed a sea change in taste. The "return to Nature" was *à la mode,* so flowers were carved into wainscoting to mirror real ones outside (unfortunately, the queen's apple-green taffeta curtains have been replaced by loud crimson silk). Today, her spirit is still present, thanks in part to her bibelots—including the ivory clock fashioned for her by Louis XVI himself—and furniture; her initials still can be seen on the wrought-iron railings of the staircase.

Beyond the Petit Trianon lay the queen's storybook Hameau, a mock-Norman village inspired by the peasant-luxe daydreams caught by Boucher on canvas and by Rousseau in literature. Here Marie-Antoinette lived out her romanticized idyll of "the simple life." With its water mill, genuine lake (Grand Lac), thatched-roof houses built in daub-and-wattle style (a since-destroyed "barn" functioned as a ballroom), pigeon loft, and vegetable plots, this make-believe village was run by Monsieur Valy-Busard, a farmer, and his wife, who often helped the queen—outfitted as a Dresden shepherdess with a Sevres porcelain crook—tend her flock of perfumed sheep. As if to destroy any last link with reality, the queen built nearby a jewel-box theater (also surviving but not open to the public). Here she acted in little plays, sometimes essaying the role of a servant girl. Only the immediate royal family, about seven or so titled friends, and her personal servants were permitted entry; disastrously, the Princes of the Blood, ladiesin-waiting, and the entire officialdom of Versailles society were shut out—a move that only served to infuriate courtiers. This is how fate and destiny closed the circle. It was at Trianon that a page sent by Monsieur de Saint-Priest found Marie-Antoinette on October 5th, 1789, to tell her that Paris was marching on Versailles.

paintings, weapons, fans, and porcelain. ⊠ *54 bd. de la Reine,* ☎ *01–39–50–30–32.* 🎫 *€4.6.* ⊙ *Tues.–Sun. 2–5.*

Dining

$$$–$$$$ ✕ **Les Trois Marches.** One of the best-known restaurants in the Paris area, in the Hotel Trianon Palace near an entrance to the château park, serves chef Gérard Vié's creative dishes such as duckling roasted with vinegar and honey. The prix-fixe (€49) weekday lunch is the most affordable option. ⊠ *1 bd. de la Reine,* ☎ *01–39–50–13–21. Reservations essential. Jacket and tie. AE, DC, MC, V. Closed Aug.*

$$ ✕ **Quai No. 1.** Barometers, sails, and model boats fill this small seafood restaurant. In summer you can enjoy your meal outside on the terrace. Fish with sauerkraut and home-smoked salmon are specialties; any dish on the two prix-fixe menus is a good value. ⊠ *1 av. de St-Cloud,* ☎ *01–39–50–42–26. MC, V. Closed Mon. No dinner Sun.*

Versailles A to Z

To research prices, get advice from other travelers, and book travel arrangements, visit www.fodors.com.

CAR TRAVEL
From Paris, head west on highway A13 from Porte d'Auteuil (a total distance of 20 km/12 mi). Allow 15–30 minutes, depending on traffic.

GUIDED TOURS
Many guided-tour companies offer excursions to Versailles. Paris Vision arranges a variety of half- and full-day guided tours of Versailles costing between €32 and €90). Cityrama is another popular Versailles tour-company option.
➤ CONTACTS: **Cityrama** (⊠ 4 pl. des Pyramides, Paris, ☎ 01–44–55–61–00). **Paris Vision** (⊠ 214 rue de Rivoli, Paris, ☎ 01–42–60–30–01).

TRAIN TRAVEL
Three train routes travel between Paris and Versailles (20–30 minutes away). The RER-C to Versailles Rive-Gauche takes you closest to the château (600 yards away via avenue de Sceaux). An all-inclusive *forfait* (fixed price) including return train fare plus château admission costs €14. The other trains run from Paris's Gare St-Lazare to Versailles Rive-Droite (closer to the Trianons and town market but 1 km/½ mi from the château via rue du Maréchal-Foch and avenue de St-Cloud) and from Paris's Gare Montparnasse to Versailles-Chantiers (1 km/½ mi to the château via rue des États-Généraux and avenue de Paris). From Versailles-Chantiers, some trains continue on to Chartres.

VISITOR INFORMATION
➤ CONTACT: **Versailles Office du Tourisme** (⊠ 2 bis av. de Paris, 78000 Versailles, ☎ 01–39–24–88–88).

PARIS AT A GLANCE

ca. 200 BC The Parisii—Celtic fishermen—live on the Ile de la Cité.

52 Romans establish a colony, Lutetia, on the Ile de la Cité, which soon spreads to both Seine banks. Under the Romans, Paris becomes a major administrative and commercial center, its situation on a low, defensible crossing point on the Seine making it a natural communications nexus.

ca. AD 250 St. Denis, the first bishop of Paris and France's patron saint, is martyred in Christian persecutions.

451 The hordes of Attila the Hun are said to be halted before reaching Paris by the prayers of St. Geneviève (died 512); in fact they are halted by an army of Romans and mercenaries. Few traces of the Roman era in Paris remain. Most of those that do are from the late empire, including the catacombs of Montparnasse and the baths that form part of the National Museum of the Middle Ages.

The Merovingian Dynasty (486–751)

507 Clovis, king of the Franks and founder of the Merovingian dynasty, makes Paris his capital. Many churches are built, including the abbey that will become St-Germain-des-Prés. Commerce is active; Jewish and Asian communities are founded along the Seine.

The Carolingian Dynasty (751–987)

Under the Carolingians, Paris ceases to be the capital of France and sinks into political insignificance, but it remains a major administrative, commercial, and ecclesiastical center—and, as a result of the last, one of the foremost centers of culture and learning west of Constantinople.

845–87 Parisians restore the fortifications of the city, which are repeatedly sacked by the Vikings (up to 877).

The Capetian Dynasty (987–1328)

987 Hugh Capet, Count of Paris, becomes king. Paris, once more the capital, grows in importance. The Ile de la Cité is the seat of government, commerce makes its place on the Right Bank, and a university develops on the Left Bank.

1140–63 The Gothic style of architecture appears at St-Denis: Notre-Dame, begun in 1163, sees the style come to maturity. In the late 12th century streets are paved.

1200 Philippe-Auguste charters a university, builds walls around Paris, and constructs a fortress, the first Louvre.

1243–46 The Sainte-Chapelle is built to house the reputed crown of thorns brought by Louis IX (St. Louis) from Constantinople.

1253   The Sorbonne is founded, to become a major theological center.

The Valois Dynasty (1328–1589)

1348–49   The Black Death and the beginning of the Hundred Years' War bring misery and strife to Paris.

1364–80   Charles V works to restore prosperity to Paris. The Bastille is built to defend new city walls. The Louvre is converted into a royal palace.

1420–37   After the battle of Agincourt, Henry V of England enters Paris. Joan of Arc leads an attempt to recapture the city (1429). Charles VII of France drives out the English (1437).

1469   The first printing house in France is established at the Sorbonne.

1515–47   François I imports Italian artists, including Leonardo da Vinci, to work on his new palace at Fontainebleau, bringing the Renaissance to France. François resumes work on the Louvre and builds the Hôtel de Ville in the new style. The Tour St-Jacques (bell tower) is completed (all that now remains of the church of St-Jacques-de-la-Boucherie).

1562–98   In the Wars of Religion, Paris remains a Catholic stronghold. On August 24, 1572, Protestant leaders are killed in the St. Bartholomew's Day Massacre.

The Bourbon Dynasty (1589–1789)

1598–1610   Henri IV begins his reign after converting to Catholicism, declaring "Paris is worth a mass." He embellishes Paris, laying out the Renaissance place des Vosges, first in a new Parisian style of town planning that will last until the 19th century. In 1610, Henri is assassinated. His widow, Maria de' Medici, begins the Luxembourg Palace and Gardens.

1624   Cardinal Richelieu is appointed minister to Louis XIII and concludes the ongoing religious persecution by strictly imposing Catholicism on the country. In 1629 he begins construction of the Palais-Royal.

1635   The Académie Française is founded.

1643–1715   Reign of Louis XIV, the Sun King. Paris rebels against him in the Fronde uprisings (1648–52). Early in his reign, he creates a new palace at Versailles, away from the Paris mobs. It becomes the largest royal complex in Europe, the symbolic center of a centralized French state. His minister of finance, Colbert, establishes the Gobelins factory-school for tapestries and furniture (1667). André Le Nôtre transforms the Jardin de Tuileries (Tuileries Gardens) and lays out the Champs-Élysées (1660s). Louis founds the Hôtel des Invalides (1670).

1715–89   During the reigns of Louis XV and Louis XVI, Paris becomes the European center of culture and style.

1783   New outer walls of Paris are begun, incorporating customs gatehouses to control the flow of commerce into the city. The walls, which include new parks, triple the area of Paris.

The Revolution, Empire and Restoration (1789–1814)

1789–99   The French Revolution begins as the Bastille is stormed on July 14, 1789. The First Republic is established. Louis XVI and his queen, Marie-Antoinette, are guillotined in place de la Concorde. Almost 2,600 others perish in the same way during the Terror (1793–94).

1799–1814   Napoléon begins to convert Paris into a neoclassical city—the Empire style. The Arc de Triomphe and the first iron bridges across the Seine are built. In 1805 he orders the completion of the Louvre Museum.

1815   The Congress of Vienna ensures the restoration of the Bourbon dynasty following the fall of Napoléon.

1828–42   Urban and political discontent causes riots and demonstrations in the streets. Yet another uprising replaces Charles X with Louis-Philippe's liberal monarchy in 1830. Napoléon's remains are returned to Paris in 1840.

The Second Republic and the Second Empire (1848–70)

1852   In 1852 further additions to the Louvre are made. Under Napoléon III, the Alsatian town planner Baron Haussmann guts large areas of medieval Paris to lay out broad boulevards linking important squares. Railroad stations and the vast covered markets at Les Halles are built.

1862   Victor Hugo's *Les Misérables* is published in Paris while the liberal author remains in exile by order of Napoléon III.

1870–71   Franco-Prussian War; Paris is besieged by Prussian troops; starvation is rampant—each week during the winter, 5,000 people die. The Paris Commune, an attempt by the citizens to take power in 1871, results in bloody suppression and much property damage (the Tuileries Palace is razed). Hugo returns to Paris.

The Third Republic (1871–1944)

1875   The Paris Opéra is inaugurated after 14 years of construction.

1889   The Eiffel Tower is built for the Paris World Exhibition.

1900   The International Exhibition in Paris popularizes the curving forms of Art Nouveau with the entrance for the newly opened Paris métro.

1914–18   World War I. The Germans come within 15 km (9 mi) of Paris (so close that Paris taxis are used to carry troops to the front).

1919   The Treaty of Versailles is signed, formally ending World War I.

1925   International Decorative Art exhibition consecrates the restrained, sophisticated design style now known as Art Deco.

1918–39   Between the wars, Paris attracts artists and writers, including Americans Ernest Hemingway and Gertrude Stein. Paris nourishes Existentialism, a philosophical movement, and major modern art movements—Constructivism, Dadaism, Surrealism.

1939–45 World War II. Paris falls to the Germans in 1940. The French government moves to Vichy and collaborates with the Nazis. The Resistance movement uses Paris as a base. The Free French Army, under Charles de Gaulle, joins with the Allies to liberate Paris after D Day, August 1944.

The Fourth and Fifth Republics (1944–present)

1944–46 De Gaulle moves the provisional government to Paris.

1958–69 De Gaulle is president of the Fifth Republic.

1960s–70s Paris undergoes physical changes: Dirty buildings are cleaned, beltways are built around the city, and expressways are driven through the heart of it. Major new building projects (especially La Défense) are banished to the outskirts.

1962 De Gaulle grants Algeria independence; growing tensions with immigrant workers in Paris and other cities.

1968 Parisian students declare the Sorbonne a commune in riots that lead to de Gaulle's resignation.

1969 Les Halles market is moved and its buildings demolished.

1977 The Centre Pompidou opens to controversy, marking a high point in modern political intervention in the arts and public architecture.

1981 François Mitterrand (1916–96) is elected president. Embarks on a major building program throughout the city.

1986 Musée d'Orsay opens in the former Gare d'Orsay train station.

1989 Paris celebrates the bicentennial of the French Revolution. The Louvre's glass pyramid, the Grande Arche of La Défense, and the Opéra Bastille are completed.

1992 Disneyland Paris opens at Marne-la-Vallée east of Paris.

1994 Paris–London rail link via Channel Tunnel becomes operational.

1995 Paris Mayor Jacques Chirac replaces François Mitterrand as the president of France.

1998 Amid scenes of popular fervor in Paris not seen since the Liberation in 1944, France hosts and wins the Soccer World Cup.

1999 Hurricane on December 26 devastates Bois de Boulogne, Bois de Vincennes, and park of Versailles. New Métro Line (No. 14) links Madeleine to new national library in Tolbiac, southeast Paris.

2000 Paris marks the new millennium with a scintillating new lighting scheme for the Eiffel Tower, a giant wheel on Place de la Concorde, and a huge statue of Charles de Gaulle on the Champs-Élysées. The facade of the Opéra is cleaned and the Centre Pompidou reopens after major renovation. A new pedestrian bridge links the Musée d'Orsay to the Tuileries.

2001 The world-ranking Musée Guimet collection of Asian art reopens after many years. Musée Grevin waxworks museum undergoes $7 million face-lift

WORDS AND PHRASES

One of the trickiest French sounds to pronounce is the nasal final *n* sound (whether or not the *n* is actually the last letter of the word). You should try to pronounce it as a sort of nasal grunt—as in "huh." The vowel that precedes the *n* will govern the vowel sound of the word, and in this list we precede the final *n* with an *h* to remind you to be nasal.

Another problem sound is the ubiquitous but untransliterable *eu*, as in *bleu* (blue) or *deux* (two), and the very similar sound in *je* (I), *ce* (this), and *de* (of). The closest equivalent might be the vowel sound in "put," but rounded.

Words and Phrases

	English	French	Pronunciation
Basics			
	Yes/no	Oui/non	wee/nohn
	Please	S'il vous plaît	seel voo play
	Thank you	Merci	mair-**see**
	You're welcome	De rien	deh ree-**ehn**
	That's all right	Il n'y a pas de quoi	eel nee ah pah de kwah
	Excuse me, sorry	Pardon	pahr-**dohn**
	Sorry!	Désolé(e)	day-zoh-**lay**
	Good morning/ afternoon	Bonjour	bohn-**zhoor**
	Good evening	Bonsoir	bohn-**swahr**
	Goodbye	Au revoir	o ruh-**vwahr**
	Mr. (Sir)	Monsieur	muh-**syuh**
	Mrs. (Ma'am)	Madame	ma-**dam**
	Miss	Mademoiselle	mad-mwa-**zel**
	Pleased to meet you	Enchanté(e)	ohn-shahn-**tay**
	How are you?	Comment allez-vous?	kuh-mahn-tahl-ay **voo**
	Very well, thanks	Très bien, merci	tray bee-ehn, mair-**see**
	And you?	Et vous?	ay voo?
Numbers			
	one	un	uhn
	two	deux	deuh
	three	trois	twah
	four	quatre	**kaht**-ruh

five	cinq	sank
six	six	seess
seven	sept	set
eight	huit	wheat
nine	neuf	nuf
ten	dix	deess
eleven	onze	ohnz
twelve	douze	dooz
thirteen	treize	trehz
fourteen	quatorze	kah-torz
fifteen	quinze	kanz
sixteen	seize	sez
seventeen	dix-sept	deez-**set**
eighteen	dix-huit	deez-**wheat**
nineteen	dix-neuf	deez-**nuf**
twenty	vingt	vehn
twenty-one	vingt-et-un	vehnt-ay-**uhn**
thirty	trente	trahnt
forty	quarante	ka-**rahnt**
fifty	cinquante	sang-**kahnt**
sixty	soixante	swa-**sahnt**
seventy	soixante-dix	swa-sahnt-**deess**
eighty	quatre-vingts	kaht-ruh-**vehn**
ninety	quatre-vingt-dix	kaht-ruh-vehn-**deess**
one hundred	cent	sahn
one thousand	mille	meel

Colors

black	noir	nwahr
blue	bleu	bleuh
brown	brun/marron	bruhn/mar-**rohn**
green	vert	vair
orange	orange	o-**rahnj**
pink	rose	rose
red	rouge	rouge
violet	violette	vee-o-**let**
white	blanc	blahnk
yellow	jaune	zhone

Days of the Week

Sunday	dimanche	dee-**mahnsh**
Monday	lundi	luhn-**dee**
Tuesday	mardi	mahr-**dee**
Wednesday	mercredi	mair-kruh-**dee**
Thursday	jeudi	zhuh-**dee**
Friday	vendredi	vawn-druh-**dee**
Saturday	samedi	sahm-**dee**

Months

January	janvier	zhahn-vee-**ay**
February	février	feh-vree-**ay**
March	mars	marce
April	avril	a-**vreel**
May	mai	meh
June	juin	zhwehn
July	juillet	zhwee-**ay**
August	août	ah-**oo**
September	septembre	sep-**tahm**-bruh
October	octobre	awk-**to**-bruh
November	novembre	no-**vahm**-bruh
December	décembre	day-**sahm**-bruh

Useful Phrases

Do you speak English?	Parlez-vous anglais?	par-lay **voo ahn**-glay
I don't speak . . . French	Je ne parle pas . . . français	zhuh nuh parl pah frahn-**say**
I don't understand	Je ne comprends pas	zhuh nuh kohm-**prahn** pah
I understand	Je comprends	zhuh kohm-**prahn**
I don't know	Je ne sais pas	zhuh nuh say **pah**
I'm American/British	Je suis américain/anglais	zhuh sweez a-may-ree-**kehn**/ahn-**glay**
What's your name?	Comment vous appelez-vous?	ko-mahn voo za-pell-ay-**voo**
My name is . . .	Je m'appelle . . .	zhuh ma-**pell** . . .
What time is it?	Quelle heure est-il?	kel air eh-**teel**
How?	Comment?	ko-**mahn**
When?	Quand?	kahn
Yesterday	Hier	yair
Today	Aujourd'hui	o-zhoor-**dwee**
Tomorrow	Demain	duh-**mehn**
This morning/afternoon	Ce matin/cet après-midi	suh ma-**tehn**/set ah-pray-mee-**dee**
Tonight	Ce soir	suh **swahr**
What?	Quoi?	kwah
What is it?	Qu'est-ce que c'est?	kess-kuh-**say**

Why?	Pourquoi?	**poor**-kwa
Who?	Qui?	kee
Where is . . .	Où est . . .	oo ay
the train station?	la gare?	la gar
the subway station?	la station de métro?	la sta-**syon** duh may-**tro**
the bus stop?	l'arrêt de bus?	la-**ray** duh **booss**
the terminal (airport)?	l'aérogare?	lay-ro-**gar**
the post office?	la poste?	la post
the bank?	la banque?	la bahnk
the . . . hotel?	l'hôtel . . .?	lo-**tel**
the store?	le magasin?	luh ma-ga-**zehn**
the cashier?	la caisse?	la **kess**
the . . . museum?	le musée . . .?	luh mew-**zay**
the hospital?	l'hôpital?	lo-pee-**tahl**
the elevator?	l'ascenseur?	la-sahn-**seuhr**
the telephone?	le téléphone?	luh tay-lay-**phone**
Where are the restrooms?	Où sont les toilettes?	oo sohn lay twah-**let**
Here/there	Ici/là	ee-**see**/la
Left/right	A gauche/à droite	a goash/a draht
Straight ahead	Tout droit	too drwah
Is it near/far?	C'est près/loin?	say pray/lwehn
I'd like . . .	Je voudrais . . .	zhuh voo-**dray**
a room	une chambre	ewn **shahm**-bruh
the key	la clé	la clay
a newspaper	un journal	uhn zhoor-**nahl**
a stamp	un timbre	uhn **tam**-bruh
I'd like to buy . . .	Je voudrais acheter . . .	zhuh voo-**dray ahsh**-tay
a cigar	un cigare	uhn see-**gar**
cigarettes	des cigarettes	day see-ga-**ret**
matches	des allumettes	days a-loo-**met**
dictionary	un dictionnaire	uhn deek-see-oh-**nare**
soap	du savon	dew sah-**vohn**
city map	un plan de ville	uhn plahn de **veel**
road map	une carte routière	ewn cart roo-tee-**air**
magazine	une revue	ewn reh-**vu**
envelopes	des enveloppes	dayz ahn-veh-**lope**
writing paper	du papier à lettres	dew pa-pee-ay a **let**-ruh

postcard	une carte postale	ewn cart pos-**tal**
How much is it?	C'est combien?	say comb-bee-**ehn**
It's expensive/cheap	C'est cher/pas cher	say share/pa share
A little/a lot	Un peu/beaucoup	uhn peuh/bo-**koo**
More/less	Plus/moins	plu/mwehn
Enough/too (much)	Assez/trop	a-say/tro
I am ill/sick	Je suis malade	zhuh swee ma-**lahd**
Call a . . . doctor	Appelez un . . . docteur	a-play uhn dohk-**tehr**
Help!	Au secours!	o suh-**koor**
Stop!	Arrêtez!	a-reh-**tay**
Fire!	Au feu!	o fuh
Caution!/Look out!	Attention!	a-tahn-see-**ohn**

Dining Out

A bottle of . . .	une bouteille de . . .	ewn boo-**tay** duh
A cup of . . .	une tasse de . . .	ewn tass duh
A glass of . . .	un verre de . . .	uhn vair duh
Ashtray	un cendrier	uhn sahn-dree-**ay**
Bill/check	l'addition	la-dee-see-**ohn**
Bread	du pain	dew pan
Breakfast	le petit-déjeuner	luh puh-**tee** day-zhuh-**nay**
Butter	du beurre	dew burr
Cheers!	A votre santé!	ah vo-truh sahn-**tay**
Cocktail/aperitif	un apéritif	uhn ah-pay-ree-**teef**
Dinner	le dîner	luh dee-**nay**
Dish of the day	le plat du jour	luh plah dew **zhoor**
Enjoy!	Bon appétit!	bohn a-pay-**tee**
Fixed-price menu	le menu	luh may-**new**
Fork	une fourchette	ewn four-**shet**
I am diabetic	Je suis diabétique	zhuh swee dee-ah-bay-**teek**
I am on a diet	Je suis au régime	zhuh sweez oray-**jeem**

I am vegetarian	Je suis végé-tarien(ne)	zhuh swee vay-zhay-ta-ree-**en**
I cannot eat . . .	Je ne peux pas manger de . . .	zhuh nuh **puh** pah mahn-**jay** deh
I'd like to order	Je voudrais commander	zhuh voo-**dray** ko-mahn-**day**
I'm hungry/thirsty	J'ai faim/soif	zhay fahm/swahf
Is service/the tip included?	Est-ce que le service est compris?	ess kuh luh sair-**veess** ay comb-**pree**
It's good/bad	C'est bon/mauvais	say bohn/mo-**vay**
It's hot/cold	C'est chaud/froid	say sho/frwah
Knife	un couteau	uhn koo-**toe**
Lunch	le déjeuner	luh day-zhuh-**nay**
Menu	la carte	la cart
Napkin	une serviette	ewn sair-vee-**et**
Pepper	du poivre	dew **pwah**-vruh
Plate	une assiette	ewn a-see-**et**
Please give me . . .	Donnez-moi . . .	doe-nay-**mwah**
Salt	du sel	dew sell
Spoon	une cuillère	ewn kwee-**air**
Sugar	du sucre	dew **sook**-ruh
Waiter!/Waitress!	Monsieur!/Mademoiselle!	muh-**syuh**/mad-mwa-**zel**
Wine list	la carte des vins	la cart day an

KEY WORDS
ON THE MENU

French	English
General Dining	
Entrée	Appetizer/Starter
Garniture au choix	Choice of vegetable side
Plat du jour	Dish of the day
Selon arrivage	When available
Supplément/En sus	Extra charge
Sur commande	Made to order
Petit Déjeuner (Breakfast)	
Confiture	Jam
Miel	Honey
Oeuf à la coque	Boiled egg
Oeufs sur le plat	Fried eggs
Oeufs brouillés	Scrambled eggs
Tartine	Bread with butter
Poissons/Fruits de Mer (Fish/Seafood)	
Anchois	Anchovies
Bar	Bass
Brandade de morue	Creamed salt cod
Brochet	Pike
Cabillaud/Morue	Fresh cod
Calmar	Squid
Coquilles St-Jacques	Scallops
Crevettes	Shrimp
Cuisses de grenouilles	Frogs' legs
Daurade	Sea bream
Ecrevisses	Prawns/Crayfish
Harengs	Herring
Homard	Lobster
Huîtres	Oysters
Langoustine	Prawn/Lobster
Lotte	Monkfish
Maquereau	Mackerel
Moules	Mussels
Palourdes	Clams
Saumon	Salmon
Thon	Tuna
Truite	Trout
Viande (Meat)	
Agneau	Lamb
Boeuf	Beef
Boudin	Sausage
Boulettes de viande	Meatballs
Brochettes	Kabobs

Cassoulet	Casserole of white beans, meat
Cervelle	Brains
Chateaubriand	Double fillet steak
Choucroute garnie	Sausages with sauerkraut
Côtelettes	Chops
Côte/Côte de boeuf	Rib/T-bone steak
Cuisses de grenouilles	Frogs' legs
Entrecôte	Rib or rib-eye steak
Épaule	Shoulder
Escalope	Cutlet
Foie	Liver
Gigot	Leg
Porc	Pork
Ris de veau	Veal sweetbreads
Rognons	Kidneys
Saucisses	Sausages
Selle	Saddle
Tournedos	Tenderloin of T-bone steak
Veau	Veal

Methods of Preparation

A point	Medium
A l'étouffée	Stewed
Au four	Baked
Ballotine	Boned, stuffed, and rolled
Bien cuit	Well-done
Bleu	Very rare
Frit	Fried
Grillé	Grilled
Rôti	Roast
Saignant	Rare
Sauté/Poêlée	Sautéed

Volailles/Gibier (Poultry/Game)

Blanc de volaille	Chicken breast
Canard/Caneton	Duck/Duckling
Cerf/Chevreuil	Venison (red/roe)
Coq au vin	Chicken stewed in red wine
Dinde/Dindonneau	Turkey/Young turkey
Faisan	Pheasant
Lapin/Lièvre	Rabbit/Wild hare
Oie	Goose
Pintade/Pintadeau	Guinea fowl/Young guinea fowl
Poulet/Poussin	Chicken/Spring chicken

Légumes (Vegetables)

Artichaut	Artichoke
Asperge	Asparagus
Aubergine	Eggplant
Carottes	Carrots
Champignons	Mushrooms

Chou-fleur	Cauliflower
Chou (rouge)	Cabbage (red)
Laitue	Lettuce
Oignons	Onions
Petits pois	Peas
Pomme de terre	Potato
Tomates	Tomatoes

Fruits/Noix (Fruits/Nuts)

Abricot	Apricot
Amandes	Almonds
Ananas	Pineapple
Cassis	Blackcurrants
Cerises	Cherries
Citron/Citron vert	Lemon/Lime
Fraises	Strawberries
Framboises	Raspberries
Pamplemousse	Grapefruit
Pêche	Peach
Poire	Pear
Pomme	Apple
Prunes/Pruneaux	Plums/Prunes
Raisins/Raisins secs	Grapes/Raisins

Desserts

Coupe (glacée)	Sundae
Crème Chantilly	Whipped cream
Gâteau au chocolat	Chocolate cake
Glace	Ice cream
Tarte tatin	Caramelized apple tart
Tourte	Layer cake

Drinks

A l'eau	With water
Avec des glaçons	On the rocks
Bière	Beer
Blonde/brune	Light/dark
Café noir/crème	Black coffee/with steamed milk
Chocolat chaud	Hot chocolate
Eau-de-vie	Brandy
Eau minérale	Mineral water
gazeuse/non gazeuse	*carbonated/still*
Jus de . . .	. . . juice
Lait	Milk
Sec	Straight or dry
Thé	Tea
au lait/au citron	*with milk/lemon*
Vin	Wine
blanc	*white*
doux	*sweet*
léger	*light*
brut	*very dry*
rouge	*red*

INDEX

NOTES

NOTES

NOTES

NOTES

NOTES

Fodor's Key to the Guides

America's guidebook leader publishes guides for every kind of traveler.
Check out our many series and find your perfect match.

Fodor's Gold Guides
America's favorite travel-guide series
offers the most detailed insider reviews
of hotels, restaurants, and attractions in
all price ranges, plus great background information, smart tips, and
useful maps.

Fodor's Road Guide USA
Big guides for a big country—the
most comprehensive guides to America's roads, packed with places to
stay, eat, and play across the U.S.A.
Just right for road warriors, family va-
cationers, and cross-country trekkers.

COMPASS AMERICAN GUIDES
Stunning guides from top local writers
and photographers, with gorgeous
photos, literary excerpts, and colorful
anecdotes. A must-have for culture
mavens, history buffs, and new residents.

Fodor's CITYPACKS
Concise city coverage with a foldout
map. The right choice for urban travelers
who want everything under one cover.

Fodor's EXPLORING GUIDES
Hundreds of color photos bring your
destination to life. Lively stories lend in-
sight into the culture, history, and people.

Fodor's POCKET GUIDES
For travelers who need only the essentials. The best of Fodor's in pocket-size
packages for just $9.95.

Fodor's To Go
Credit-card–size, magnetized color mi-
croguides that fit in the palm
of your hand—perfect for "stealth"
travelers or as gifts.

Fodor's FLASHMAPS
Every resident's map guide. 60 easy-
to-follow maps of public transit, parks,
museums, zip codes, and more.

Fodor's CITYGUIDES
Sourcebooks for living in the city: Thousands of in-the-know listings for restaurants, shops, sports, nightlife, and other
city resources.

**Fodor's AROUND THE CITY
WITH KIDS**
68 great ideas for family days,
recommended by resident parents. Perfect for exploring in your own
backyard or on the road.

Fodor's ESCAPES
Fill your trip with once-in-a-lifetime
experiences, from ballooning in
Chianti to overnighting in the Moroccan
desert. These full-color dream books
point the way.

Fodor's FYI
Get tips from the pros on planning
the perfect trip. Learn how to pack,
fly hassle-free, plan a honeymoon
or cruise, stay healthy on the road, and
travel with your baby.

Fodor's Languages for Travelers
Practice the local language before hitting the road. Available in phrase
books, cassette sets, and CD sets.

Karen Brown's Guides
Engaging guides to the most charming
inns and B&Bs in the U.S.A. and Europe,
with easy-to-follow inn-to-inn itineraries.

Baedeker's Guides
Comprehensive guides, trusted since
1829, packed with A–Z reviews and
star ratings.
